Ireland

timeout.com

Time Out Guides Ltd
Universal House
251 Tottenham Court Road
London W1T 7AB
United Kingdom
Tel: +44 (0)20 7813 3000
Fax: +44 (0)20 7813 6001
Email: guides@timeout.com
www.timeout.com

Published by Time Out Guides Ltd, a wholly owned subsidiary of Time Out Group Ltd.
Time Out and the Time Out logo are trademarks of Time Out Group Ltd.

© **Time Out Group Ltd 2011**

10 9 8 7 6 5 4 3 2

This edition first published in Great Britain in 2011 by Ebury Publishing.
A Random House Group Company
20 Vauxhall Bridge Road, London SW1V 2SA

Random House Australia Pty Ltd 20 Alfred Street, Milsons Point, Sydney, New South Wales 2061, Australia

Random House New Zealand Ltd 18 Poland Road, Glenfield, Auckland 10, New Zealand

Random House South Africa (Pty) Ltd Isle of Houghton, Corner Boundary Road & Carse O'Gowrie, Houghton 2198, South Africa

Random House UK Limited Reg. No. 954009

Distributed in USA by Publishers Group West
1700 Fourth Street, Berkeley, California 94710

Distributed in Canada by Publishers Group Canada
250A Carlton Street, Toronto, Ontario M5A 2L1

For further distribution details, see www.timeout.com.

ISBN: 978-1-84670-240-2

A CIP catalogue record for this book is available from the British Library.

Printed and bound by Firmengruppe APPL, aprinta druck, Wemding, Germany.

MIX
Paper from
responsible sources
FSC® C004592

PUBLISHED BY
Time Out Guides Limited
Universal House
251 Tottenham Court Road
London W1T 7AB
Tel +44 (0)20 7813 3000
Fax +44 (0)20 7813 6001
email guides@timeout.com
www.timeout.com

ADVERTISING
New Business & Commercial Director Mark Phillips
International Advertising Manager Kasimir Berger
International Sales Executive Charlie Sokol
Advertising Sales (Ireland) Geraldine Brady, Laura Butler,
    Richard Delooze (Media Sales Network)

EDITORIAL
Author Julianne Mooney
Editor Cath Phillips
Researchers William Crow, Jamie Warburton
Proofreader Ismay Atkins
Indexer Jackie Brind

Managing Director Peter Fiennes
Editorial Director Sarah Guy
Series Editor Cath Phillips
Business Manager Daniel Allen
Editorial Manager Holly Pick
Management Accountants Margaret Wright, Clare Turner

MARKETING
Senior Publishing Brand Manager Luthfa Begum
Guides Marketing Manager Colette Whitehouse
Group Commercial Art Director Anthony Huggins

PRODUCTION
Group Production Manager Brendan McKeown
Production Controller Katie Mulhern

TIME OUT GROUP
Chairman & Founder Tony Elliott
Chief Executive Officer David King
Chief Operating Officer Aksel Van der Wal
Group Financial Director Paul Rakkar
Group General Manager/Director Nichola Coulthard
Time Out Communications Ltd MD David Pepper
Time Out International Ltd MD Cathy Runciman
Time Out Magazine Ltd Publisher/MD Mark Elliott
Group Commercial Director Graeme Tottle
Group IT Director Simon Chappell
Group Marketing Director Andrew Booth

DESIGN
Art Director Scott Moore
Art Editor Pinelope Kourmouzoglou
Senior Designer Kei Ishimaru
Group Commercial Designer Jodi Sher

PICTURE DESK
Picture Editor Jael Marschner
Acting Deputy Picture Editor Liz Leahy
Picture Desk Assistant/Researcher Ben Rowe

Contributors Jamie Warburton; and the writers of Time Out Dublin Shortlist.
Thanks to Fáilte Ireland, especially Lorna Demmel, Elaine Dunphy, Grainne Kilcoyne and Louise Tolerton; the Northern Ireland Tourist Board, especially Gabrielle O'Gara; and also Dan Siron, Clare Conway and Sinead McKenna.

Maps © Collins Bartholomew Ltd 2011, except Ireland overview map on pages 22-23.

Back cover photography walshphotos, Ros Kavanagh, Wicker Imaging.

Photography pages 3, 54/55, 75, 81, 174/175, 207, 281 Alamy; page 13 Daniel Kowalczyk; page 15 (top) Anna van Kooij; page 15 (bottom) Valerie Simmons; page 16 Jason McGarrigle/featured establishment; page 20 Dylan Vaughan; page 21 (top) David Clynch; page 21 (bottom) HR Photo 2009; page 30 Sander van der Werf; page 34 (bottom right) Wil Tilroe-Otte; page 35 Robert Zahler; pages 38/39, 66, 89, 254/255 photolibrary.com; pages 42, 117 (bottom), 282 (right), 284, 299 Richard Semik; pages 24/25, 59, 62, 88, 117 (top), 151, 232, 239, 294 walshphotos; page 76 Pierre-Jean Durieu; page 82 Michael Steden; page 84 Patryck Kosmider; page 91 Tony Brindley; page 98 upthebanner; pages 99, 118 (top), 128 (top) Insuratelu Gabriela Gianina; page 101 Ambient Ideas; page 114 David Robbins; page 118 (bottom) Odin M Eidskrem; pages 120 (top and bottom left), 185 M Reel; page 120 (top right) Des Lavelle; page 120 (bottom right) Andreas Juergensmeier; page 122 Michael Herrmann; page 123 Agnieszka Guzowska; page 127 (top and bottom right) Park Hotel Kenmare; page 127 (bottom left) Barry Murphy Photography; page 130 studioworx; pages 138, 150 Andrei Nekrassov; page 140 (left) Miki Barlok; page 140 (right) Daragh Mac Sweeney/Provision; page 144 Rory Cobbe; page 145 John Herriott; page 149 (middle and bottom) Keewi Photography; pages 154, 164/165 Artur Bogacki; page 157 Fáilte Ireland/Jonathan Hes; pages 163, 196 Fáilte Ireland; page 171 Marc C Johnson; page 166 Brendan Davis/ Old Convent; page 179 Shane O'Neill/Tannery; page 183 Panaspics; page 190 Gerry Browne; page 194 Paul Murtagh; page 205 David Cannon/ Getty Images; page 209 Luke Schmidt; page 211 Jean Morrison; page 212 (top) Stephen Kiernan; page 212 (bottom) Eireann; pages 213, 216, 219, 223 Alys Tomlinson; page 235 UnaPhoto; page 215 Losevsky Pavel; page 222 Rob Wilson; page 240 Pato Cassinoni; page 240 Pyma; page 250 Ambient Ideas; pages 257, 264, 272, 282 (left) Northern Ireland Tourist Board; page 261 Josemaria Toscano; pages 263, 266 John Sones; page 283 Andy Poole; page 285 Ciaran McGuckin; pages 288, 289 Charles Forde; page 295 Shane Smith; page 297 (top) Paul McCambridge.

The following images were provided by the featured establishments/artists: pages 11, 12, 17, 19, 27, 33, 34, 37, 41, 44, 45, 46, 49, 53, 57, 58, 61, 63, 65, 67, 69, 74, 77, 78, 92, 104, 107, 115, 125, 131, 139, 141, 143, 146, 147, 149 (top), 176, 186, 188, 189, 197, 200, 202, 208 (top & bottom left), 221, 228, 229, 231, 242, 243, 250, 252, 260, 262, 265, 270, 280, 286, 287, 296, 297 (bottom), 298, 300.

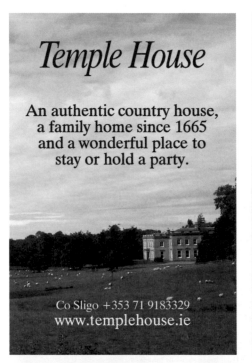

About the Guide

Ireland is the latest in a new Time Out series of guides covering Britain. We've used our local knowledge to reveal the best of both the Republic of Ireland and Northern Ireland, and while we've included all the big attractions, we've gone beneath the surface to uncover small and hidden treasures too.

This little island, sitting on the edge of Europe, has captured the hearts of numerous visitors over the centuries. The diversity of its landscape is astonishing, and its wild, almost mystical, natural beauty has long been immortalised in poetry, painting and song. The west coast battles the elements of the often ferocious Atlantic Ocean, giving rise to towering cliffs such as Slieve League and the Cliffs of Moher, as well as long sandy beaches and weathered mountain ranges. The seaside villages of Donegal, Sligo, Clare and Antrim vie for the title of best surfing spot, while the lively cities of Dublin, Belfast, Cork and Galway brim with history, culture and excitement. Then there is Country Kerry, home to the beautiful Lakes of Killarney and the windswept Iveragh and Dingle peninsulas; the seafood restaurants of Kinsale in Country Cork; and the otherworldly limestone pavement of the Burren in County Clare. Northern Ireland has ruined castles, expansive loughs and the world-famous Giant's Causeway.

Ancient features (prehistoric stone circles and early monasteries) mix with modern attractions (world-class golf courses and luxurious spas), while the country's vibrant traditional culture thrives through numerous festivals. And wherever you travel, north or south, you'll find a cosy pub waiting to welome you with a turf fire, a pint of Guinness and probably a local band playing traditional Irish music.

TELEPHONE NUMBERS

Phone numbers listed in this guide assume that you're calling from within the region in question, either Northern Ireland or the Republic of Ireland. If you're phoning Northern Ireland from mainland Britain, you need to dial the area code 028 first. If you're phoning from the Republic, however, the area code is 048.

And if you're calling the Republic from either Northern Ireland or mainland Britain, you need to dial 00 353 followed by the area code (dropping the initial 0) and the local number.

KEEPING IT LOCAL

We have used the measurement system in place in the respective region, which means metric (metres, kilometres) in the Republic of Ireland, and imperial (yards, miles) in Northern Ireland.

In the Gaeltacht regions of the Republic (which are concentrated in the rural west, in Counties Donegal, Mayo, Galway and Kerry, plus parts of Cork, Meath and Waterford), Irish is the primary language. Expect Irish to be commonly spoken, and road signs to be written only in Irish, rather than both Irish and English. Note that we have used English spellings for place names throughout this guide.

OPENING TIMES

Part of the charm of the countryside is that it's not like the city. But this means beware opening times: places shut up shop for the winter months, or only open at weekends, and some shops still close for lunch. If you're eating out, many places still stop serving at 2pm sharp for lunch and at 9pm for dinner. If you're making a journey, always phone to check. This goes for attractions too, especially outside the summer holiday season. While every effort has been made to ensure the accuracy of the information contained in this guide, the publisher cannot accept any responsibility for errors it may contain.

ADVERTISERS

The recommendations in Time Out Ireland are based on the experiences of Time Out's reviewers. No payment or PR invitation has secured inclusion or influenced content. The author chooses which places to include. Advertisers have no influence over content; an advertiser may receive a bad review or no review at all.

FEEDBACK

We hope you enjoy the guide. We always welcome suggestions for places to include in future editions and take note of your criticism of our choices. You can email us at guides@timeout.com.

Contents

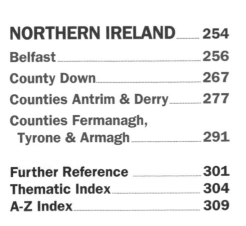

The ultimate guide to London – **it's official**

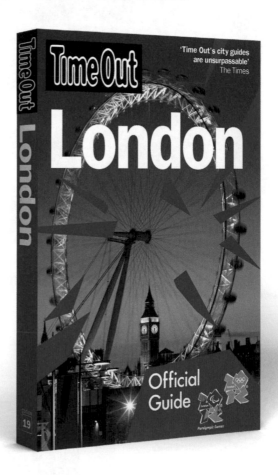

Festivals & Events

Even the smallest village in Ireland holds some kind of annual shindig, usually involving traditional Irish music and much jollity. We've listed the main annual celebrations here, but plenty of other events are mentioned in the main chapters of this book. For the best horse racing events, see p210.

JANUARY

RNLI New Year's Day Swim
www.achilltourism.com. Venue Silver Strand, Dugort, Achill Island, Co Mayo. Date 1 Jan.
This cold introduction to the New Year raises necessary funds for the local branch of the RNLI. The intrepid swimmers brave the water from 1pm onwards.

Winter Music Weekend
086 846 4509, www.wmw.ie. Venue Sixmilebridge, Co Clare. Date Mid Jan.
Irish, bluegrass, blues, country, gypsy and classical music are all represented at this special festival. It takes place in Sixmilebridge, halfway between Ennis and Limerick city, with almost 40 gigs and concerts, most of them free.

Glen of Aherlow Winter Walking Festival
062 56331, www.aherlow.com. Venue Glen of Aherlow, Co Tipperary. Date Late Jan.
A weekend of walking, music and singing in the lovely Glen of Aherlow. There are graded guided walks on the Galtees and Slievenamuck Hills, catering for all levels of expertise. A similar event is held in June.

Temple Bar TradFest
01 703 0700, www.templebartrad.com. Venue Dublin. Date Late Jan.
First held in 2006, Dublin's TradFest grows from strength to strength. Churches, pubs, hotels and other venues around Temple Bar come alive with the sounds of traditional music, played by Irish and international performers.

FEBRUARY

Féile an Earraigh
028 9031 3440, www.feilebelfast.com. Venue West Belfast. Date Early Feb.
Taking place in various venues across West Belfast, this festival of culture, arts and music is the sibling of the popular Féile an Phobail (see p19) in July.

Belfast Nashville Songwriters' Festival
028 9024 6609, www.belfastnashville.com. Venue Belfast. Date Late Feb.
Celebrating Belfast's links with its twin city of Nashville, Tennessee, this five-day festival offers the very best in performances and songwriting from the spiritual home of country music.

Jameson Dublin International Film Festival
01 662 4260, www.jdiff.com. Venue Dublin. Date Mid-late Feb.
Established in 2003, JDIFF brings more than 100 film-related events, including premieres, interviews and discussions, to Dublin over the course of 11 days.

Tedfest
www.tedfest.org. Venue The Aran Islands, Galway & Galway City, Co Galway. Date Late Feb.
Fans of cult C4 sitcom *Father Ted* gather on Inis Mór (the largest of the Aran Islands) to celebrate and recreate the world of Craggy Island. Laughs aplenty are guaranteed, thanks to events such as Ted's Got Talent, the Craggy Cup and stand-up comedians battling it out for the Toilet Duck Award.

MARCH

Belfast Film Festival
028 9032 5913, www.belfastfilmfestival.org. Venue Belfast. Date Mar-Apr.
The fortnight-long Belfast Film Festival showcases local talent as well as the best in international cinema. There are screenings, talks and workshops, and an emphasis on education and practical filmmaking skills.

RNLI New Year's Day Swim

St Patrick's Day

Ballymoney Drama Festival

028 2766 0230, www.ballymoneydramafestival.com. Venue Ballymoney, Co Antrim. Date Early Mar.
Every year since 1934, apart from a break during World War II, Ireland's oldest drama festival has featured the best in amateur dramatic companies from Northern Ireland.

Dublin Book Festival

01 415 1210, www.dublinbookfestival.com. Venue Dublin. Date Early Mar.
A variety of venues around Dublin play host to the best in contemporary Irish publishing and writing. There are talks, readings and book launches, across a wide range of genres and topics.

St Patrick's Day

www.discovernorthernireland.com/stpatrick; www.stpatricksfestival.ie. Date 17 Mar.
Celebrations for St Patrick's Day go on all over the Republic of Ireland and Northern Ireland. In Dublin, expect the famous parade, music, dancing and various cultural happenings. Events in Northern Ireland include celebrations in key towns associated with the life of St Patrick, such as Armagh and Downpatrick, as well as a carnival and a free concert in Belfast.

Só Sligo – Food & Culture Festival

086 109 0675, www.sosligo.com. Venue Sligo, Co Sligo. Date Mid Mar.
Só Sligo involves a multitude of food-related activities over five days, including cooking demonstrations, talks, tastings, farm walks, a food village and Irish stew competitions. Kids' events, street entertainment and music sessions in local pubs and restaurants complete the picture.

Dingle Film Festival

www.dinglefilmfestival.com. Venue Dingle, Co Kerry. Date Mid Mar.
A four-day celebration of Irish filmmaking, held in the picturesque fishing town on Kerry's beautiful Dingle peninsula. Screenings, talks and the awarding of the Gregory Peck Award (past winners include Gabriel Byrne and Stephen Frears).

Carlingford National Leprechaun Hunt

042 937 3033, www.carlingfordleprechaun.ie. Venue Carlingford, Co Louth. Date Late Mar.
Since a local publican found a mysterious set of leprechaun clothes near the local wishing well in 1989, an annual national hunt for the mischievous fairies and their gold has taken place in the area surrounding Carlingford. There's an entrance fee, with all proceeds going to charity.

APRIL

Connemara International Marathon

www.connemarathon.com. Venue Maam Cross, Connemara, Co Galway. Date Mid Apr.
Described as one of the most scenic races in the world, this involves a half marathon, a full marathon and an ultra marathon (39.9 miles). Both runners and walkers can participate in all three distances.

Cúirt International Festival of Literature

091 565886, www.cuirt.ie. Venue Galway, Co Galway. Date Mid Apr.
This literary festival allows writers and audience to interact and create together. Talks and workshops take place in various locations around Galway city.

City of Derry Jazz Festival

028 7137 6545, www.cityofderryjazzfestival.com. Venue Derry, Co Londonderry. Date Late Apr-early May.
Launched in 2002, this is now one of Northern Ireland's biggest music festivals, with thousands coming to hear upcoming and established acts, from Ireland and elsewhere, play in venues all over Derry.

Cork International Choral Festival

021 421 5125, www.corkchoral.ie. Venue Cork, Co Cork. Date Late Apr-early May.
During this week-long festival, over 5,000 singers from all over the world come together to perform in more than 100 concerts and recitals. The action centres around Cork's City Hall, but other venues are used too.

Festival of Fools

028 9023 6007, www.foolsfestival.com. Venue Belfast. Date Late Apr-early May.
Street performers, magicians and comedians take over Belfast to bemuse, delight and entertain in this free family festival.

Heineken Kinsale Sevens

mobile 086 811 2620, www.kinsalesevens.com. Venue Kinsale, Co Cork. Date Late Apr-early May.
Up to 95 teams from all over Europe compete in one of the premier events on the rugby sevens calendar. Entertainment also includes music sessions.

Smithwick's Kilkenny Rhythm & Roots Festival

www.kilkennyroots.com. Venue Kilkenny, Co Kilkenny. Date Late Apr-early May.
Some of the finest names in American roots music take to the stage for more than 80 shows in 30 venues in and around the medieval streets of Kilkenny.

Connemara International Marathon

MAY

Cathedral Quarter Arts Festival
028 9023 2403, www.cqaf.com. Venue Belfast.
Date Early May.
Starting around the May Day bank holiday weekend
and continuing for a week, the well-established
Cathedral Quarter Arts Festival brings the streets
of Belfast to life. Events include exhibitions,
music sessions, talks, dance performances and
children's activities.

Drogheda Arts Festival
www.droghedaartsfestival.ie. Venue Drogheda,
Co Leath. Date May Day bank holiday weekend.
The Drogheda Arts Festival takes place on the banks
of the River Boyne over the May Day bank holiday
weekend, with music, theatre, art and poetry events.

Belfast City Marathon
028 9024 6609, www.belfastcitymarathon.com.
Venue Belfast. Date May Day bank holiday weekend.
More than 20,000 runners take part in this annual
race, which starts at City Hall and finishes in
Ormeau Park. There's also a team event and
a wheelchair race.

Baltimore Fiddle Fair
www.fiddlefair.com. Venue Baltimore, Co Cork.
Date Early May.
The seaside village of Baltimore becomes the stage
for a weekend of concerts and workshops by the
best in national and international fiddle talent.

Great Limerick Run
www.greatlimerickrun.com. Venue Limerick,
Co Limerick. Date Early May.
The three races making up the Great Limerick Run –
a 10km run, half marathon and marathon – are open
to all skill levels and ages. Past events have seen
more than 6,000 participants.

Blues on the Bay Festival
028 4175 2256, www.bluesonthebay.com.
Venue Warrenpoint, Co Down. Date Late May.
Carlingford Lough becomes the backdrop for five days
of blues. More than 90 gigs and workshops showcase
the best in homegrown and overseas music.

Dublin City Soul Festival
www.soul.ie. Venue Dublin. Date Late May.
Dublin's cafés and bars resonate to soul music
performances by musicians from home and abroad.
The Soul Picnic sees families congregating in Merrion
Square Park for an afternoon of music, while the
Soul Jam features international artists in more
intimate settings.

Dublin Dance Festival
01 679 0524, www.dublindancefestival.ie.
Venue Dublin. Date Mid-late May.
The only contemporary dance festival in Ireland
attracts some leading names for a varied programme
that includes performances, children's events, artists'
talks, workshops and masterclasses.

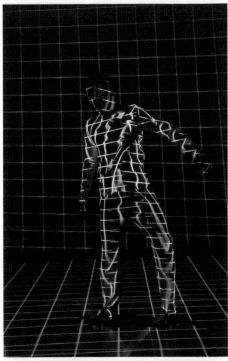

Dublin Dance Festival

Sea Session Surf & Music Festival

Fleadh Nua
www.fleadhnua.com. Venue Ennis, Co Clare.
Date Late May.
See p193.

Limerick International Music Festival
061 331549, www.mbnaicofestival.com.
Venue Limerick, Co Limerick. Date Late May.
Orchestras and choirs perform famous and lesser-
known compositions in a range of venues, including
St Mary's Cathedral, across five days.

JUNE

Bloom
01 295 8185, www.bloominthepark.com.
Venue Phoenix Park, Dublin. Date Early June.
Bloom is Ireland's biggest gardening and food event,
encompassing show gardens, floral displays and
farmers' markets. There are cookery demonstrations
and workshops with industry professionals too.

Belfast City Carnival
028 9024 6609, www.belfastcity.gov.uk.
Venue Belfast. Date Mid June.
The end of the Lord Mayor's term in office is celebrated
with a colourful carnival through the city centre. Floats,
bands, puppets and hundreds of performers keep the
crowds entertained, and it all culminates in a big party.

Cork Midsummer Festival
www.corkmidsummer.com. Venue Cork, Co Cork.
Date Mid June.
This 16-day summer extravaganza focuses on
contemporary art and culture from home and abroad.
There's lots to see, with theatre, dance, visual art,
open-air concerts, circus shows and much more.

Street Performance World Championships
www.spwc.ie. Venue varies. Date Mid June.
Portlaoise, Cork and Dublin host stages of this
competition. Magicians, comedians, breakdancers
and contortionists battle it out to take home the title
of World Street Performance Champion.

Hell of the West
www.limericktriathlon.com. Venue Kilcree, Co Clare.
Date Late June.
Ireland's oldest triathlon event tests around 700
athletes to the limits of their endurance. A 1,500m
swim is followed by a 45km cycle, then a 10km run
up and down the cliffs around Kilcree.

Sea Session Surf & Music Festival
www.seasessions.com. Venue Bundoran, Co Donegal.
Date Late June.
Surfing and music combine in this relatively new
addition to the Irish festival calendar, held in the
seaside town of Bundoran. Enjoy music by established
and new acts, as well as outdoor activities such as tag
rugby, beach soccer and, of course, plenty of surfing.

Celtronic Festival
mobile 07814 918 452, www.celtronicfestival.com.
Venue Derry, Co Londonderry. Date Late June-early July.

The best in local and international electronic DJs
and performers take part in this five-day festival.

Tall Ships Race
023 9258 6367, www.sailtraininginternational.org.
Venue Waterford, Co Waterford. Date Late June-
early July.
More than 70 ships and 250,000 people will converge
on Waterford in 2011 for the beginning of the Tall Ships
Race. Fireworks, food, music and parades all figure in
the celebrations. The 2012 race is set to finish in Dublin.

JULY

Clonmel Junction
www.junctionfestival.com. Venue Clonmel,
Co Tipperary. Date Early July.
Ten days of music, theatre, dance and comedy,
both performances and workshops. The action takes
place in cafés and other venues (including disused
shops) around Clonmel.

Galway Film Fleadh
091 562200, www.galwayfilmfleadh.com.
Venue Galway, Co Galway. Date Early July.
Aiming to bring filmmakers and audiences together in
an intimate environment, the Galway Film Fleadh attracts
film buffs, students, the general public and industry
professionals for six days of screenings and debates.

West Cork Literary Festival
027 52789, www.westcorkliteraryfestival.ie.
Venue Bantry, Co Cork. Date Early July.
The mix on offer includes night-time story sessions,
bookshop readings, seminars and workshops. Leading
poets, journalists, novelists and playwrights interact
with an appreciative audience.

Spraoi. See p19.

Oxegen
www.oxegen.ie. Venue Punchestown Racecourse, Naas, Co Kildare. Date Mid July.
See p193.

Galway Arts Festival
www.galwayartsfestival.com. Venue Galway, Co Galway. Date Mid-late July.
Big-name acts from across the world appear at this fortnight-long arts extravaganza, the biggest of its kind in Ireland. Visual art, theatre, music, theatre, literature, comedy, street shows, talks – all art forms are covered.

Ballyshannon Folk & Traditional Music Festival
mobile 086 252 7400, www.ballyshannon folkfestival.com. Venue Ballyshannon, Co Donegal. Date Late July.
See p192.

Belfast Pride
028 9089 0207, www.belfastpride.com. Venue Belfast. Date Late July.
Over 15,000 people each summer congregate in Belfast's Custom House Square and other venues to celebrate Ireland's LGBT community. First held in 1991, and culminating in a flamboyant parade through the city centre, this is the largest gathering of its kind in Ireland.

Castle Palooza
www.castlepalooza.com. Venue Tullamore, Co Offaly. Date Late July.
See p192.

Fiddler's Green International Festival
028 4173 9819, www.fiddlersgreenfestival.com. Venue Rostrevor, Co Down. Date Late July.
More than 200 events showcase Irish and international music, arts and culture. Families are catered for, with plenty of the events being child-focused.

Killarney Summerfest
064 667 1560, www.killarneysummerfest.com. Venue Killarney, Co Kerry. Date Late July.
Nine days of family-friendly art exhibitions and workshops in various venues around Killarney, plus lots of outdoor activities, from walking and kayaking to horse riding and rock climbing.

Northern Ireland Bog Snorkelling Championships
028 3885 1102. Venue Peatlands Park, Dungannon, Co Tyrone. Date Late July.
Competitors have to complete two lengths of a 55m course. Anybody over the age of 12 can have a go at this mudfest, as long as they come equipped with a snorkel, mask and flippers.

Spraoi
051 841808, www.spraoi.com. Venue Waterford, Co Waterford. Date Late July.
The centre of Waterford city is transformed into a stage for street performers from all over the world. The costumed parade is a highlight; other happenings over the three days include children's activities, music sessions and fireworks.

Oyster season in Galway. See p20.

Féile an Phobail
028 9031 3440, www.feilebelfast.com. Venue Belfast. Date Late July-early Aug.
Ireland's largest community festival, the Féile an Phobail was launched in 1988 as a direct response to the conflict in Northern Ireland. A huge parade attracts 50,000-plus participants, and there are concerts, talks, exhibitions, musicians and street theatre over the festival's ten days.

AUGUST

Dublin Horse Show
01 485 8010, www.dublinhorseshow.com. Venue Royal Dublin Society, Dublin. Date Early Aug.
Now well over a century old, the five-day Dublin Horse Show celebrates Ireland's love of all things equestrian. Numerous events and competitions feature all kinds of horses, from Connemara Ponies to international showjumpers, with Ladies' Day a highlight.

Kilkenny Arts Festival
056 775 2175, www.kilkennyarts.ie. Venue Kilkenny, Co Kilkenny. Date Early-mid Aug.
Now well into its fourth decade, the Kilkenny Arts Festival brings a full programme of music (Irish, jazz, indie, world), theatre, dance, literature, visual arts and crafts to venues around the city, including Kilkenny Castle and St Canice's Cathedral.

Puck Fair
066 976 2366, www.puckfair.ie. Venue Killorglin, Co Kerry. Date Mid Aug.
Thought to date from pre-Christian times, but given an official charter in 1610, the Puck Fair is one of Ireland's oldest festivals. Legend has it that a mountain goat

Tall Ships Race. See p17.

warned the people of Killorglin of the approach of Oliver Cromwell's troops. Since then, a goat is crowned as King Puck every year, and there are three days of entertainment and celebration.

Tullamore Show & AIB National Livestock Show
057 935 2141, www.tullamoreshow.com.
Venue Tullamore, Co Offaly. Date Mid Aug.
Around 50,000 people come to this country-living showcase. Expect to see the finest sheep, horses and cattle in the country, as well as more than 500 trade stands, food, music and children's entertainment.

National Heritage Week
056 777 0777, www.heritageweek.ie. Date Mid-late Aug.
National Heritage Week celebrates the Republic of Ireland's natural, built and cultural heritage. Thousands of events take place all over the country, from walks and tours of historical sites, to dance and music shows and storytelling events.Northern Ireland holds a similar event in early September, when many important and intriguing historical buildings and monuments, usually closed to the public, fling open their doors.

Fleadh Cheoil
087 986 5704, www.fleadh2011.ie. Date Mid Aug.
See p193.

SEPTEMBER

Oyster season in Galway
www.galwayoysterfest.com; www.clarenbridge.com.
Venue Co Galway. Date Sept.
Throughout September, the native oyster is celebrated all over County Galway. Events include the Clarenbridge Oyster Festival, at the beginning of the month, and the Galway International Oyster Festival, with its World Oyster Opening Championships, towards the end.

Electric Picnic
www.electricpicnic.ie. Venue Stradbally Estate,
Co Laois. Date Early Sept.
See p193.

Hillsborough International Oyster Festival
mobile 07802 311388, www.hillsboroughoyster festival.com. Venue Hillsborough, Co Down.
Date Early Sept.
The Georgian village of Hillsborough, near Belfast, welcomes oyster lovers (and others) to the World Oyster Eating finals, a soap box derby, a beauty contest and a market.

NI International Airshow
028 7034 4723, www.niinternationalairshow.co.uk;
www.portrushairshow.com. Venue Portrush, Co Antrim.
Date Early Sept.
The seaside town of Portrush is the setting for Ireland's biggest airshow, held over two days. There are 20 jaw-dropping air displays by vintage planes, military fighter jets and the Red Arrows, as well as sea displays, helicopter flights and a multitude of other aviation-based events.

Waterford Harvest Food Festival
www.waterfordfestivaloffood.com. Venue Waterford,
Co Waterford. Date Early Sept.
Waterford's culinary heritage is celebrated during this ten-day festival, with cookery demonstrations, tastings, picnics and barbecues, plus free music and other entertainment. Most events take place in the central open spaces of Waterford city.

Cois Fharraige Surf & Music Festival
www.coisfharraige.com. Venue Kilkee, Co Clare.
Date Mid Sept.
See p192.

National & European Ploughing Championships
www.npa.ie. Date Late Sept.
The art of ploughing (by tractor and horse) is celebrated at this three-day rural show, alongside displays of livestock and agricultural equipment, sheep shearing and cookery demonstrations, and a fashion show. Venues change each year; past events have been held in Counties Offaly, Kildare and Kilkenny.

OCTOBER

Ballinasloe Horse Fair & Festival
090 964 4793, www.ballinasloeoctoberfair.com.
Venue Ballinasloe, Co Galway. Date Early Oct.
Orginally an agricultural fair and cattle market, this
Galway festival is now a key date for any equine
enthusiast. It's a nine-day knees-up that includes
showjumping, street performances, music sessions,
a tug of war and a beauty pageant.

Open House
www.architecturefoundation.ie/openhouse.
Venue Dublin. Date Early Oct.
Buildings of historical and architectural interest open
to the public for a few days in early October. There
are also free tours and walks.

Cork Jazz Festival
www.guinnessjazzfestival.com. Venue Cork,
Co Cork. Date Late Oct.
See p192.

Dublin Marathon
01 623 2250, www.dublinmarathon.ie.
Venue Dublin. Date Late Oct.
The Dublin Marathon has been a fixture for more
than 30 years. Upwards of 10,000 racers take
part, following a fairly flat, single-lap course around
the city centre.

Sligo Live
www.sligolive.ie. Venue Sligo, Co Sligo.
Date Late Oct.
See p193.

Wexford Festival Opera
053 912 2400, www.wexfordopera.com. Venue
Wexford, Co Wexford. Date Late Oct-early Nov.
Wexford Opera House hosts the best in rarely
programmed and neglected opera with a series
of lectures, recitals and concerts.

Waterford Harvest Food Festival

NOVEMBER

Waterford International Music Festival
051 87 3192. Venue Waterford, Co Waterford.
Date Early Nov.
The 12 days of the Waterford International Music
Festival encompasses all kinds of music: traditional
Irish, gospel, light opera and stage musicals to more
alternative sounds.

Cork Film Festival
021 427 5945, www.corkfilmfest.org. Venue Cork,
Co Cork. Date Mid Nov.
Apart from the short film programmes for which it
has gained an international reputation, the Cork
Film Festival also showcases documentaries and
new Irish cinema, as well as holding exhibitions
and retrospectives, in an electic programme of
movie-related events over ten days.

Tullamore Show & AIB National Livestock Show

Ireland

ATLANTIC OCEAN

NORTHERN IRELAND
pp291-300

BELFAST pp256-266

ANTRIM

LONDONDERRY
pp277-290

Ballycastle

Derry

TYRONE

Omagh

FERMANAGH

Enniskillen

DOWN
pp267-276

Downpatrick

Carlingford

Dundalk Bay

ARMAGH

Armagh

MONAGHAN

Newry

Dundalk

LOUTH
pp234-244

Drogheda

DONEGAL
pp26-47

Dunfanaghy

Letterkenny

Donegal

Killybegs

Glencolumbcille

Donegal Bay

CAVAN

Cavan

LEITRIM
pp59-70

LONGFORD

Longford

Navan

MEATH
pp234-244

Trim

Mullingar

WESTMEATH

SLIGO
pp48-58

Sligo

ROSCOMMON

Roscommon

MAYO

Ballina

Westport

GALWAY
pp71-92

Oughterard

Clifden

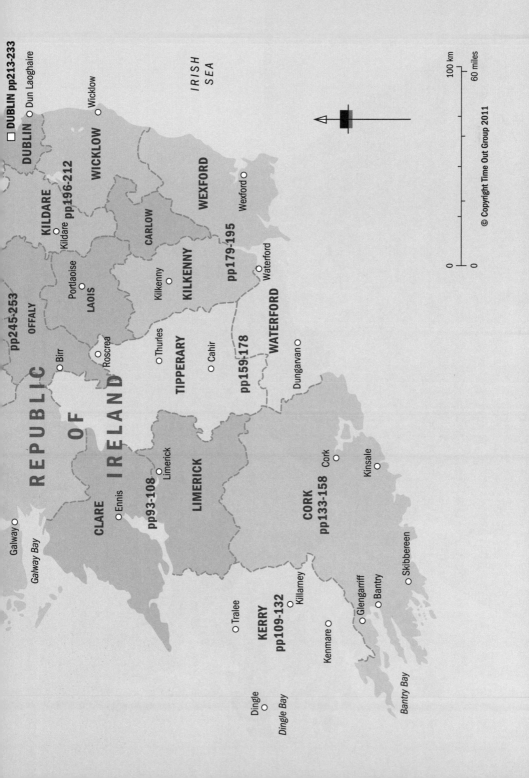

□ **DUBLIN pp213-233**

DUBLIN
○ Dun Laoghaire

WICKLOW
○ Wicklow

*IRISH
SEA*

KILDARE pp196-212

KILDARE
Kildare ○

WEXFORD

CARLOW

Portlaoise ○
LAOIS

Kilkenny ○
KILKENNY
pp179-195

Wexford ○

OFFALY
pp245-253

Birr ○

Roscrea ○

○ Thurles
TIPPERARY

Cahir ○

Waterford ○
WATERFORD
pp159-178

Dungarvan ○

REPUBLIC

OF

IRELAND

Galway ○

Galway Bay

CLARE

Ennis ○

Limerick ○
LIMERICK
pp93-108

CORK
pp133-158
Cork ○

Kinsale ○

Tralee ○

KERRY
pp109-132

Killarney ○
Glengarriff ○
Bantry ○

Skibbereen ○

Dingle
Dingle Bay

Kenmare ○

Bantry Bay

100 km

60 miles

0

0

© Copyright Time Out Group 2011

Republic of Ireland

Gap of Dunloe from Augur Lake, County Kerry. See p114.

County Donegal

Tucked into the north-west corner and one of the largest counties in Ireland, Donegal is not the most accessible place, but its isolation is what makes it so appealing. The tempestuous Atlantic ocean has sculpted the coastline into one of the most beautiful in the country. Long stretches of white sand, occupied by squawling seabirds and lashed by waves, adorn the weathered coast and are ideal if you're seeking remote, unspoilt picnic spots. Inland, the county's majestic mountains entice walkers, cyclists, birdwatchers and landscape enthusiasts. The famous Errigal Mountain challenges hikers to climb its peak, while the Blue Stack Mountains offer less arduous treks. Glenveagh National Park and Ards Forest Park provide more leisurely strolls around the loughs that define the inland landscape. World-class golf courses sprinkled around the county are another attraction. With all this on offer you would expect to meet hordes of holidaymakers, but Donegal manages to retain a sense of peace and quiet.

DONEGAL TOWN & AROUND

Heading north along the N15 from Sligo, the first town you stumble upon is Bundoran. The Irish National Surfing Championships are held here each spring and its reputation for 'awesome' waves makes it popular with surfers and beach-loving youngsters. Compared to the quaint surfing villages of Sligo, Bundoran may be a bit of a let-down, its streets lined with amusement arcades, cheap eateries and noisy bars. Nevertheless, there's no doubt it's well equipped for every type of visitor. Bundoran Surf Co (Main Street, 071 984 1968, www.bundoransurfco.com) offers surf lessons and equipment hire. For children, a safer option than navigating the reef breaks is Waterworld (Sea Front, 071 984 1172, www. waterworldbundoran.com), a complex of indoor pools with slides and wave machines.

A few kilometres further north is lively and attractive Ballyshannon, Ireland's oldest town. The hilly streets overlook the River Erne, which is lined with well-maintained Georgian houses. Inis Saimer, the tiny island rising out of the river, is said to be where Ireland's first inhabitants landed in 2700 BC. If you're visiting in the first week of August, check out the Ballyshannon Folk Festival (www.ballyshannonfolkfestival.com), which attracts some of the best traditional musicians in Ireland.

For those in search of quieter beaches, Rossnowlagh, just north of Ballyshannon, consists of a cluster of houses, a caravan park and the hard-to-miss, salmon-pink Sandhouse Hotel, facing the five-kilometre Blue Flag beach. Fin McCool Surf School (071 985 9020, www.finmccool surfschool.com, closed Jan, Feb), located in front of the hotel, runs classes for novice wave-riders throughout the summer. If you simply want to enjoy the scenery, drive five minutes south to the Smuggler's Creek Inn. Along the way, amid the trees, you will pass the Franciscan Friary (071 985 1342), worth a visit for a meander

around the well-kept gardens and across the hilltop for more superb views.

North of Rossnowlagh, the pretty town of Donegal sits at the mouth of Donegal Bay. Its position by the sea is what attracted invading Vikings in the tenth century, who named their fort Dún na nGall, meaning 'the fort of the foreigners'. Shops, bars, hotels and restaurants cluster around the diamond-shaped centre, the former marketplace. The main point of interest is Donegal Castle (*see p34*), a 15th-century fort on Tirconnell Street, just off the Diamond. The Donegal Railway Heritage Centre (074 972 2655, www.cdrrl.com), based in the Old Station House, tells the history of the train line that ran from Derry to Ballyshannon until its closure in 1959.

Donegal Craft Village (074 972 2225, www. donegalcraftvillage.com), a few minutes out of town on the Sligo road, merits attention. Set around a courtyard is a series of attractive workshops, where you can buy a range of contemporary art and crafts, including jewellery, hand-woven textiles and stone carvings. There's also a pleasant café.

While not the liveliest of towns, Donegal does spring into action in late September/early October, when the Donegal Bay & Blue Stacks Festival brings a wide range of music, theatre and artistic events and exhibitions to the region.

South-east of the town is a series of little lakes, including Lough Derg (071 986 1518, www.lough derg.org), where a rocky island contains the Sanctuary of St Patrick, a place of pilgrimage for more than 1,000 years. Traditionally, pilgrims visit between June and August for a three-day retreat during which they fast and go barefoot; if starving yourself doesn't appeal, there are less austere retreats for those seeking peace and rest.

North of town is another lake, Lough Eske. Beautifully situated at the foot of the Blue Stack Mountains, it's the ideal place for solitary walks. You can also fish, from March to September, for

Harvey's Point Hotel. See p32.

sea trout, spring salmon and char. The more adventurous can walk along the west bank of the lake, following a path that will eventually lead, off to the left, to a trail into the mountains. Don't venture too far unless equipped with maps and proper walking gear.

Where to eat & drink

The smarter hotels in and around Donegal also have excellent restaurants. Harvey's Point Hotel (*see p32*) with its fine-dining restaurant and Wednesday cabaret nights, and Castle Murray House Hotel (*see p31*) with its gourmet French cooking, are both very popular with locals and other non-residents.

Ard na Bréatha
Drumrooske Middle, Donegal (074 972 2288, www.ardnabreatha.com). Dinner served Easter-Sept 7-9pm daily. Oct-Easter 7-9pm Sat, Sun.
Situated slightly out of Donegal town, award-winning Ard na Bréatha is both a guesthouse and a restaurant. It's

situated on a working farm, so much of the kitchen's produce is home-grown. Pinewood furnishings and a relaxed ambience complement the delicious, seasonal fare. Well worth the trip out of town.

Aroma Coffee Shop & Mini Bakery
Donegal Craft Village, nr Donegal (074 972 3222). Open 9am-5pm Mon-Sat.
Located at Donegal Craft Village, the simple decor of Aroma may deceive you into thinking it's just another café serving bought-in sandwiches and lukewarm coffee. Not at all. The menu varies with the seasons, offering hearty dishes from soup with freshly baked bread (which you can buy to take away) to inventive salads, pasta and own-made cakes. All dishes are created with care and a certain flair, offering much more than your average coffee shop.

Blueberry Tea Room
Castle Street, The Diamond, Donegal (074 972 2933). Open 9am-7pm Mon-Sat.
This bustling café next to the Olde Castle Bar (*see p31*) turns out the best cakes in town. The enticing lunch menu of

Things to do

Slieve League

DONEGAL TOWN & AROUND

Blue Stack Way
The rugged Blue Stack Mountains ascend to 600m. You can explore them and the surrounding countryside via the 65km Blue Stack Way. Starting in Donegal town, the route heads past Lough Eske, through the Glenties, and ends in Ardara. You could do just a section or tackle the whole thing over a couple of days – there are plenty of places to stay en route. Check www.walkingireland.ie for information on trekking in Donegal, including guides.

Donegal Adventure Centre
Bay View Avenue, Bundoran (071 984 2418, www. donegaladventurecentre.net). Open by appointment. Rates single surfing lesson €35; €25 reductions.
Bundoran-based Donegal Adventure Centre arranges all sorts of watersports, including surf lessons on one of Donegal's most famous surfing beaches, as well as skateboarding and climbing. Camps for kids and teens are run throughout the summer.

WEST OF DONEGAL TOWN

Slieve League ★
Despite being Ireland's highest and most dramatic marine cliffs, Slieve League remains relatively unscathed by tourism and the uninterrupted views from the top are stunning. At the first (lower) car park, you can open the gate and drive about 2km along a winding and very narrow road – take care – to the small upper car park. But it's probably better to leave the car and walk instead. On a clear day you can see the Sligo mountains to the south and the Blue Stacks and Derryveagh Mountains to the north. The cliff drops sharply towards the sea and the path can get swampy in parts. There's also a narrow arête with alarming drop-offs (aptly named One Man's Path) that leads to the summit, but it's not for the faint-hearted – and don't attempt it in bad or windy weather.

To view Slieve League from a different perspective, take a boat trip on the *Nuala Star*, based in Teelin (074 973 9365, www.sliabhleagueboattrips.com, Mar-Oct) and marvel at the enormity of the magnificent cliffs from below.

DUNFANAGHY & AROUND

Narosa
Dunfanaghy (074 910 0682, www.narosalife.com). Open Shop 9am-5pm Mon-Sat; 10am-5pm Sun. Surf lessons by appointment June-Sept. Rates from €30; €25 reductions.
If it's an action break you're after, contact Lee Wood and Duncan Halliday, owners of Narosa. They run surf lessons throughout the year, mainly at Marble Hill Strand, as well as seasonal beach-based fitness classes, kids' camps and a sporadic walking festival. Their local knowledge is supreme; contact them in advance to arrange activities and accommodation.

THE NORTHERN PENINSULAS

Inishowen Quad Safari
Drumfad, nr Buncrana (mobile 087 664 6346, www.inishowenquadsafari.com). Open phone for details. Rates €40/hr. No credit cards.
If you're keen for speed and don't mind getting down and dirty, then riding a quad bike (90cc and 250cc versions) though a mucky obstacle course is ideal. A fun day out for groups and families.

Mevagh Dive Centre
Milford Road, Carrigart (074 915 4708, www. mevaghdiving.com). Rates €100 for 2 dives incl equipment hire.
Mevagh Dive Centre has a purpose-built pool and offers a range of courses for beginners to experts. You can also join sea dives to shipwrecks in the Loughs, and off Tory Island and the coast of Rosguill. Wetsuits are provided – it's the Atlantic, remember.

freshly made soups and sandwiches means the closely packed tables are often full, but it's worth the short wait.

Olde Castle Bar & Red Hugh Restaurant

Castle Street, The Diamond, Donegal (074 972 1262, www.oldecastlebar.com). Open noon-11.30pm Mon-Thur, Sun; noon-12.30am Fri, Sat. Food served Bar noon-9pm daily. Restaurant Dinner served Summer 6-9.30pm daily. Winter 6-9.30pm Fri, Sat.

As the name suggests, this place is located just across from the Castle. The cosy, traditional bar serves good pub food throughout the day, including sandwiches, seafood platters and typical Irish dishes such as lamb stew. The Red Hugh Restaurant upstairs is open in the evenings and specialises in fish, including mussels and oysters from Donegal Bay.

Reel Inn

Bridge Street, Donegal (086 251 2005 mobile). Open 10.30am-11.30pm Mon-Thur; 10.30am-12.30am Fri, Sat; noon-10.30pm Sun. No credit cards.

The Reel Inn may not be the most beautiful of pubs, but it's got character in spades, drawing a lively mix of locals and visitors looking for a good night out. Trad Irish music is played most nights of the week.

Smugglers Creek Inn ★

Cliff Road, Rossnowlagh (071 985 2367, www. smugglerscreekinn.com). Open Summer noon-midnight Mon-Thur, Sun; noon-12.30am Fri, Sat. Winter noon-midnight Thur, Sun; noon-12.30am Fri, Sat. Food served Summer noon-9pm daily. Winter noon-9pm Thur-Sun.

Smugglers Creek is one of the best bars in south Donegal. The setting is supreme – atop a cliff with resplendent views stretching across Rossnowlagh beach to the Blue Stack Mountains – and the extensive menu offers dishes to suit all tastes, including daily specials of local fish. No matter what time of day, the atmosphere is friendly, laid-back and homely. Live music is played most weekends. The Inn has five B&B rooms; although very compact and a bit dated, they have retained the character of the old inn.

Where to stay

B&Bs and small local hotels are plentiful. The more luxurious accommodation tends to be in the more secluded spots, such as Lough Eske and Dunkineely. In the heart of Donegal town, try the Abbey Hotel (074 972 1014, www.abbeyhotel donegal.com) or the Central Hotel (074 972 1027, www.centralhoteldonegal.com) – both three-star operations, similar in style, located on the Diamond – or the Atlantic Guesthouse (074 972 1187, www.atlanticguesthouse.ie). If you're after a more 'country' experience, consider lovely Coxtown Manor (074 973 4575, www.coxtownmanor.com) in Laghey, just south of Donegal town. Restaurant Ard na Bréatha (*see p27*) also has six bedrooms (€80-€98 double incl breakfast).

Castle Murray House Hotel

St Johns Point, Dunkineely (074 973 7022, www.castlemurray.com). Rates €80-€110 double.

Situated just off the N56 on the way to Killybegs, Castle Murray has panoramic views over a ruined castle towards

BEST SURFING BEACHES

Bundoran

Bundoran in Donegal has long been one of Ireland's top surf spots. While it's best suited to intermediate and advanced surfers, there are also plenty of schools running classes for novices. *See p26.*

Easkey

Experienced surfers head to the small village of Easkey in Sligo, congregating in the car park beside the ruins of Easkey Castle. Although there are few facilities in the village, it's close to Sligo town and Enniscrone for those needing to arrange board hire and accommodation. *See p48.*

Lahinch

The waters off this 3km-long beach in County Clare are dotted with little black figures throughout the day – Lahinch is the best surf spot in south-west Ireland, some say the best on the whole west coast. It's suitable for surfers of all levels, and there are plenty of places offering tuition. Spanish Point, further south, is also a popular surfing spot. *See p105.*

Portrush

In summer, the beaches near Portrush on the north Antrim coast are crowded with families enjoying the sunshine and messing about in the water. Come September, the crowds disperse and the larger waves roll in, drawing plenty of surfers. *See p284.*

Rossnowlagh

While Bundoran has the better waves for more experienced surfers, Rossnowlagh, slightly further north along the Donegal coast, is ideal for beginners – and relatively quiet. The local surf shop runs classes throughout the summer. *See p26.*

Strandhill

Popular year-round, the long curved beach at Strandhill in County Sligo has some of the best surf in Ireland for all abilities, from novices to experienced surfers. There's a buzzing surf culture, with classes and board hire available, as well as relaxing seaweed baths and a lively bar scene. *See p49.*

Tramore

On the Waterford coast, Tramore isn't the prettiest of towns, but it's got an appealing beach, decent waves and surf shops galore. Boarders heading for their favourite break may even be lucky enough to spot a passing whale. *See p172.*

the ocean. Visitors can sit back, relax and watch the world – well, seagulls – go by. The ten guesthouse-style rooms, while compact, are tastefully decorated in a contemporary style. Staff are relaxed and friendly, and the restaurant specialises in local produce with a French twist (fish and seafood in summer, game and meat in winter).

Harvey's Point Hotel ★
Lough Eske (074 972 2208, www.harveyspoint.com). Rates €158-€640 double incl breakfast.
Perched by the waters of Lough Eske with a view of the Blue Stack Mountains, four-star Harvey's is an oasis of calm. It's a grand affair, with ultra-spacious rooms (think ornate beds, oriental rugs and gilt-framed pictures) in the main wing and slightly smaller, cosier rooms in the older courtyard area – there are 70 rooms in total. The dining room overlooks the lake and manages to combine elegance and top-notch cuisine with a relaxed, easy-going atmosphere. Staff are incredibly friendly, and it's no wonder people return year after year. Call ahead to organise walking tours, artistic weekends or various activity breaks.

Lough Eske Castle
Lough Eske (074 972 5100, www.solislougheske castle.com). Rates €175-€400 double incl breakfast.
It may lack a lake view, but Lough Eske Castle is surrounded by beautiful woodland. The main building is a 20th-century re-creation of the original 15th-century castle, complete with tower and crenellations. Bright, airy passageways and elegant yet homely drawing rooms combine with spacious bedrooms (96 in all) that mix old-world and contemporary design. Local and organic produce is the focus in the restaurant, Cedars, where you can dine in intimate, velvet-lined snugs or on the outdoor terrace. There's also a spa in the garden, with a glass-enclosed pool, steam room and assorted treatments.

Sandhouse Hotel
Rossnowlagh (071 985 1777, www.sandhouse-hotel.ie). Rates €160-€240 double incl breakfast. Closed Jan, Dec; weekdays Feb-Easter.
The imposing Sandhouse Hotel has been around for more than half a century. Key to its appeal is its superb location right on the beach. The 50 bedrooms are comfortable, if rather old-fashioned, and the spacious public areas include two bars, two restaurants and an outdoor verandah. There's also a small spa. It was here that Tony Blair spent his summers learning to swim and, according to his autobiography, 'chasing the local talent'. While the grandeur of the hotel has faded somewhat, the views over the beach and out to the Atlantic remain as breathtaking as ever.

WEST OF DONEGAL TOWN

Killybegs & Slieve League
The smell of fish and the cries of seagulls will assail you before you've even rounded the corner into Killybegs. Once one of the most important fishing ports in Ireland, it's still a working port, but many of the buildings now stand empty and run-down. The narrow, twisting streets that heaved with commerce today have a certain air of desolation. The tourist information centre (074 973 2346, www.killybegs.ie, closed Sat & Sun winter) is in the middle of town, on Shore Road. The road west out of Killybegs climbs up, offering panoramic ocean views. It is from here you will begin to sense the wildness that is synonymous with the Donegal coastline. If you're driving in this direction you will no doubt be heading to Slieve League, Donegal's answer to the Cliffs of Moher. Kilcar, home of the Donegal tweed industry, is the next village. It has a number of small factories where you can pick up a tweed item or two. The adjacent village, Carrick, is quainter and more sedate, with the Sliab Liag pub being one of the best options for drinks and music at the weekend.

Well-signposted Slieve League (*see p30*) is further on, past the Ti Linn craft and tea shop (*see right*). The viewpoint (accessible by car or on foot) overlooks Ireland's most spectacular sea cliffs, 600 metres above the ocean – in fact, they're the highest marine cliffs in Europe. Slieve League means 'Grey Mountain', a name that seems singularly inappropriate when you clap eyes on the multicoloured cliffs (mineral deposits have painted them red, white and amber). Majestic, rugged or spectacular would be more fitting descriptions.

Glencolumbcille & Ardara
An 1860s guidebook declared Glencolumbcille (also Glencolmcille or Gleann Cholm Cille, meaning the 'Glen of St Columba's Church') the most isolated place in Europe. Although easier to reach today, the villages of the glen remain tucked away at the end of a peninsula, at what feels like the edge of the world. One of the few remaining Gaeltacht areas, it's been inhabited for more than 5,000 years and prehistoric remains are scattered along the roadsides and within the towns. Malinmore contains a series of dolmens from 1500 BC and also a court cairn (burial chamber), An Clochán Mór. Dating from 3000 BC, it was preserved in a local bog for over 2,000 years. Dotted around the area are 15 early Christian standing stones, collectively known as Turas Colmcille and the basis for a centuries-old pilgrimage route.

The small village of Glencolumbcille consists of several bars, an Irish language and cultural centre, and a Folk Village with attached museum (*see p34*). It is thanks to the vision and hard work of a local priest, Fr James McDyer (1910-87), that the area has become internationally known for its rich music and language culture. To deter young people from emigrating, he set up numerous creative and community initiatives in the 1960s that are still in place today, and also managed to bring electricity and a water supply to the glen. Visitors interested in traditional cultural experiences will not be disappointed. Highlights of the village's many events are the Ceol sa Ghleann Festival (www. ceolsaghleann.com) of traditional music, song and dance, running over the Easter holidays, and the Glencolumbcille Fiddle Festival in August.

On the north side of the peninsula, Maghera has a popular sandy beach and a series of sea caves set beneath a rocky headland. It's said that the villagers of Maghera hid from Cromwell's troops in the caves – all but one were discovered and massacred. A couple of kilometres away, on the coast road to Ardara, is Assarancagh Waterfall, a beautiful spot for a picnic. It's also worth driving along the Glengesh Pass further inland, where the narrow twisting road plunges into a deep valley with lush mountains rearing on either side.

Ardara is an attractive town, known for its hand-woven tweed and knitwear. You can learn about the industry's history in the Ardara Heritage Centre (074 953 7905) or pop into Kennedy's on the main street, where they have made woollen sweaters for a century. While there's not much to see in the town itself, it's a good base for exploring south-west Donegal. Visitors flock to the Cup of Tae Festival (www.cupoftaefestival.com), a traditional music festival held on the early May bank holiday weekend, and there's also an International Walking Festival in March. If you want to explore the area by bike, or cycle the Glengesh Pass, you can rent a mount from Don Byrne's Bikes (West End, 074 954 1658, closed Sun, and weekdays in winter), located on the right as you leave the town towards Glenties.

If you bypass the peninsula, and take the main N56 from Donegal to Ardara and on to the small settlement of Glenties, you'll be rewarded with a beautiful drive through the mountains. Aptly named – it sits at the base of two glens – Glenties has assorted pubs and, surprisingly, one of Donegal's largest nightclubs, Limelight. The mother of famous Irish dramatist Brian Friel lived here, and St Conall's Museum & Heritage Centre, opposite the church, has an entire room devoted to the playwright.

Where to eat & drink

Kitty Kelly's
Kilcar Road, Killybegs (074 973 1925, www.kitty kellys.com). Open phone for details.
An old, red-painted farmhouse a couple of kilometres outside Killybegs on the Kilcar road, Kitty Kelly's specialises in fish and seafood. The unfussy dishes (seafood chowder, lobster or scallops, perhaps) depend on the day's catch, and the atmosphere is friendly and cosy. Note that it's open only in high season and for dinner. Booking advised.

Nancy's Bar
Front Street, Ardara (074 954 1187). Open noon-midnight daily. Food served noon-9pm daily. No credit cards.
Step into the tiny front bar and be transported back to the days when local pubs were nothing more than a cosy space at the front of someone's house, where people gathered for a pint and a chat. Nancy's (still family-owned) has areas out the back and in a loft in which to drink the excellent Guinness, try the home cooking (the fish chowder is recommended) and enjoy the homely atmosphere.

Ti Linn Centre
Teelin, Carrick (074 973 9077, www.sliabhleague.com). Open Easter-Sept 10.30am-5.30pm daily. Mid Feb-Easter, Oct-mid Nov times vary; phone for details.
En route to Slieve League, Ti Linn is a great pitstop for a cup of tea and a freshly made cake or snack. It's also a cultural centre where you can arrange hill walks or archaeological tours, or just pick up information on the nearby cliffs. A shop sells local arts and crafts.

Green Gate. See p37.

Places to visit

Glenveagh Castle

DONEGAL TOWN & AROUND

Donegal Castle
Donegal (074 972 2405, www.heritageireland.ie). Open Apr-mid Sept 10am-6pm daily. Mar, mid Sept-Dec 9.30am-4.30pm Mon, Thur-Sun. Tours by appointment. Admission €4; €2-€3 reductions; €10 family. Tours free. No credit cards.
This is quite an unassuming building, more a stately home than a castle. All that remains of the original 15th-century castle, once the abode of the O'Donnells of Tir Connell, is the rectangular keep. In the early 17th century, in an attempt to prevent the castle falling into the hands of the English, 'Red' Hugh O'Donnell burned it to the ground. An Irish poem suggests he did not want it to live up to its name 'the fort of the foreigners'. Of course, the English did arrive, with new owner Captain Basil Brooke adding a Jacobean-style wing. Much of the building lay in ruins in the 18th and 19th centuries, but after a restoration in the late 1990s, it's open to the public again.

WEST OF DONEGAL TOWN

Glencolumbcille Folk Village Museum
Glencolumbcille (074 973 0017, www.glenfolk village.com). Open Easter-Sept 10am-6pm Mon-Sat; noon-6pm Sun. Admission €3.50; €2-€3 reductions; €11 family.
Founded by enterprising local clergyman Fr James McDyer in 1967, this 'living history' village consists of six traditional cottages overlooking Glenbay beach.

Each building is equipped with furniture, household goods, pictures and clothing from a different period of Irish history, from the 17th, 18th and 19th centuries. Opening in 2011 are two new buildings: a thatched shop/pub and a fisherman's cottage. Refreshments are available in the tearoom, and you can buy local crafts from the shop. Craft workshops and trad music sessions take place in summer.

DUNGLOE TO GLENVEAGH

Arranmore Island
www.arainnmhor.com.
It's a short ferry ride from Burtonport, just west of Dungloe, to rocky Arranmore. Measuring just 9km by 5km, the island has 600 residents, most living on its east and south coasts. Visiting is like stepping back in time, to what the Gaeltacht once was. There's good fishing and a walking route, the Arranmore Way, that provides spectacular views over to the Rosses on the mainland. Green Island, off the south-western tip, draws a variety of seabirds, including some rare species. The website has details of the year-round ferries and the island's accommodation (including a self-catering cottage next to the lighthouse).

Glebe House & Gallery
Churchhill, nr Glenveagh National Park (074 913 7071, www.heritageireland.ie). Open July, Aug 11am-6.30pm daily. June, Sept 11am-6.30pm Mon-Thur, Sat, Sun. Admission Gallery free. House tour €3; €1-€2 reductions; €8 family. No credit cards.

This stunning Regency house, built in 1828 and once owned by English artist Derek Hill, is decorated with William Morris wallpapers and textiles, Japanese and Islamic pieces, and Donegal folk art. You can visit the house by guided tour only, but the art gallery, set in the former stables, is freely open. It displays work by Picasso, Renoir, Kokoshka, Yeats and other leading 20th-century artists. And outside are some lovely woodland gardens.

Glenveagh National Park ★
Churchill, Letterkenny (074 913 7090, www.glenveaghnationalpark.ie). Open Mar-Oct 9.30am-6pm daily. Nov-Feb 9am-5pm daily. Admission free. Castle tour €5; €3 reductions; €7 family. No credit cards.

Glenveagh National Park encompasses 16,000 hectares of heather-covered mountains, lush peat bogland, stunning lakes and woodland. The visitor centre is at its northern end, on the R251; from here, you can catch a shuttle bus or walk 4km to Glenveagh Castle on the edge of expansive Lough Veagh. The castle was built in the 1860s by controversial landowner John George Adair (infamous for ruthlessly evicting 244 tenants); when he died, his wife went about blending the castle into the landscape, developing the now stunning walled gardens and softening the structure with the addition of new wings. Mrs Adair was a popular hostess, with a reputation for being kind, generous and providing much employment in the area. Today, visitors can tour the castle, walk through the immaculate gardens and climb up to the

lookout for panoramic views across Glenveagh Valley. There are organised hikes (€5, booking essential) as well as self-guided walks including a new tree trail along the lakeshore. There's also a café and shop.

Gola Island
The sea cliffs on this uninhabited island a kilometre off Donegal's Gweedore coast are extremely popular with rock climbers. If a gentle stroll is more your thing, you can walk around Gola in a few hours enjoying its undisturbed beauty and tranquility. The island's residents left in the 1960s; ruined houses remain, though some are now being restored. There's a regular ferry service from Bunbeg. For more information, visit www.donegalislands.com/gola.

Tory Island
www.oileanthorai.com,
Diminutive Tory Island – just 4km long and 1km wide – continues to thrive despite its position 15km off the coast; it was nearly evacuated in 1974 after vicious storms that lasted for almost two months. The barren landscape and ragged, weather-worn coastline hold a raw beauty, and the islanders are extremely proud of their rich artistic and musical culture. It's also a great spot for birdwatchers, with a huge range of species, including puffins, gannets and corncrakes. There's a hotel with a bar and restaurant (Tory Hotel, 074 913 5920, www.hoteltory.com), a hostel and a couple of B&Bs, several bars and an art gallery. The island's artists have long been admired; Derek Hill (of Glebe House, *see left*) came here frequently and helped set up the 'Tory School' of painters.

A year-round ferry service runs from Bunbeg and Magheroarty; details on www.toryislandferry.com.

THE NORTHERN PENINSULAS

Doagh Famine Village
Doagh Island, Inishowen (074 937 8078, www.doaghfaminevillage.com). Open Mar-Sept 10am-5pm daily. Admission €7. No credit cards.
An unusual and informative 'outdoor museum' that depicts life in Ireland from the 1840s to the present, through exhibitions in a variety of buildings from traditional whitewashed cottages to a Republican safe house. The complicated role of religion in Irish society is explored via an Orange Order hall, a Presbyterian Meeting Hall and a Mass Rock (where Catholics worshipped outdoors). In December, the village is turned into 'Santa's Island', with visitors flocking to meet Santa and his deer.

Grianán Ailigh
A few kms south-west of Bridgend.
Perched on the top of Greenan Hill, with sweeping views over Loughs Foyle and Swilly, is the impressive Iron Age ring fortress of Grianán Ailigh. It is said that in the year 450, St Patrick baptised Eoghán O'Neill, the founder of the clan that ruled the Kingdom of Ailigh for more than 500 years. The kingdom, and the fort, retained a mythological importance for centuries. During the 12th century, the fort was attacked and many of the original stones were removed; it was restored in the late 19th century and again in the past few years.

Bags packed, milk cancelled, house raised on stilts.

You've packed the suntan lotion, the snorkel set, the stay-pressed shirts. Just one more thing left to do — your bit for climate change. In some of the world's poorest countries, changing weather patterns are destroying lives.

You can help people to deal with the extreme effects of climate change. Raising houses in flood-prone regions is just one life-saving solution.

**Climate change costs lives.
Give £5 and let's sort it *Here & Now***

www.oxfam.org.uk/climate-change

Be Humankind Oxfam

Where to stay

Most visitors choose to base themselves around Donegal town and Lough Eske. However, there are a few options in Killybegs, such as the Bayview Hotel (074 973 1950, www.bayviewhotel.ie), with its small leisure centre and swimming pool, or the newer Tara Hotel (Main Street, 074 974 1700, www.tarahotel.ie). Both overlook the harbour and offer good B&B rates. Glencolumbcille has a range of accommodation, with some places offering additional services, such as the Ionad Siúl hill walking centre (mobile 087 970 9247, www.ionadsiul.ie).

Bruckless House

Bruckless (074 973 7071, www.bruckless.com). Rates €120 double incl breakfast.
On the edge of Bruckless Bay, 7km east of Killybegs, sits this handsome 18th-century house with four B&B rooms (twin, double and two singles). It's a secluded spot, set in 18 acres of land with exquisite gardens that stretch down to the shoreline. Owners Clive and Joan Evans also breed Connemara ponies.

Green Gate

Ardvally, Ardara (074 954 1546, www.thegreengate.eu). Rates €90 double incl breakfast. No credit cards.
Owned and run by charming Frenchman Paul Chatenoud, this traditional thatched B&B cottage may be too spartan and casual for some (there's no shower or TV), but the stunning location and sense of peace and quiet will appeal to visitors looking for something out of the ordinary. There are four bedrooms, delicious breakfasts and even a pet robin, Christopher. Quirky and unique.

Woodhill House

Woodhill, Ardara (074 954 1112, www.woodhill house.com). Rates €88-€110 double incl breakfast.
This country manor dates from the 17th century and was once the home of the Nesbitts, Ireland's last commercial whaling family. There are 13 rooms, some in the main house and others in outbuildings. In recent years, the owners have put time into the gardens, creating a beautiful and tranquil space with superb views over the countryside. The popular restaurant offers French-based dishes using local produce, including succulent Donegal lamb and fish from Killybegs.

DUNGLOE TO GLENVEAGH

Less than half an hour north of Glenties via the N56, Dungloe (the road signs also read An Clochán Liath) is the largest town in the Rosses, a desolate region characterised by its rocky terrain and myriad tiny lakes. A rather uninspiring town, it's most fun during the Mary from Dungloe Festival, which is a beauty pageant of sorts. Held during the last week of July, it offers various events for all ages including a carnival parade, wine tasting, golf competitions and music sessions. And, of course, one local girl is crowned 'Mary from Dungloe'.

In nearby Annagry, a dot of a town, you can take to the coastal waters courtesy of Rapid Kayaking, (mobile 086 151 0979). Further north again, little Bunbeg has a pretty harbour from where there is a regular ferry service to both Tory and Gola islands.

An Chúirt Gweedore. See p39.

But the main attraction in the area is Glenveagh National Park (*see p35*), for which Gweedore (Gaoth Dobhair in Irish), five kilometres east of Bunbeg, is the best base. There's enough in the surrounding area to keep you busy for a couple of days – make sure to bring walking shoes and a camera.

The drive on the R251 towards Glenveagh National Park is incredibly scenic, with viewpoints over eight-kilometre-long Lough Nacung. The most striking vista is that of Mount Errigal, Donegal's highest peak, which towers proudly above the valley. The scree covering its top could easily be mistaken for a sprinkling of snow. Those brave and fit enough to climb the 752-metre summit will be rewarded with unsurpassable views over the entire county. The road winds around the mountain ranges, through the valley (primarily shallow peat bog) and passes numerous loughs. It's a complete contrast to both the rugged coastline and the rolling hills of the Glenties and Glengesh Pass.

At the eastern tip of Lough Nacung is the small community of Dunlewey, from where it's a two- to three-hour walk to the remarkable ice-carved rockface of Poisoned Glen. The Dunlewey Centre (074 953 1699, www.dunleweycentre.com) is jam-packed with local information and staff can also arrange boat trips on the lake, fishing expeditions and walks. It has a good restaurant, a well-stocked craft shop, play areas and farmyard animals. The centre is one of the venues for the Frankie Kennedy Winter School (www.frankiekennedy.com) a week-long festival of Irish music, with classes and performances, held at the end of December. It's named after one of Ireland's best-known traditional flute players, who died aged 38 in 1994.

Tory Island. See p35.

The entrance to Glenveagh National Park, off the R251, leads to a large car park and excellent visitor centre at the tip of Lough Veagh. The area is steeped in beauty and history and you'll need at least half a day to soak it up.

Just outside the eastern edge of the park, in Churchhill, Glebe House & Gallery (*see p34*) is a must for art lovers.

Where to eat & drink

Most local pubs and hotels serve decent pub grub. Two bars hold regular traditional music sessions: Teach Húdaí Beag (074 953 1016, www.trad centre.com/hiudaibeag) in Bunbeg on Monday and Friday, and Sean Ógs (074 953 2999) in Gweedore on Wednesday.

Danny Minnies

Annagry, The Rosses (074 954 8201, www.danny minnies.com). Bar times vary; phone for details. Food served Summer 6.30-9.30pm Mon-Sat. Winter 6.30-9.30pm Thur-Sat.

If you feel like a treat and some excellent food, make your way to family-run, award-winning Danny Minnies. Turf fires, paintings, oak panelling and brightly coloured walls create a smart but intimate feel. The lobster and crab is caught locally by family members, and the small garden provides herbs, while the lamb is reared in the nearby

mountains. Music sessions take place in the bar, with singsongs into the early hours of the morning. Handily, there are also five B&B guest rooms.

Leo's Bar

Meenaleck, nr Crolly (074 954 8143, www.leostavern. com). Open 4pm-midnight Mon-Fri; noon-1am Sat; noon-midnight Sun. Summer Food served 1-8.30pm daily. Winter Dinner served 5-8.30pm Fri. Food served 1-8.30pm Sat, Sun.

Leo's was once simply a local bar in the small village of Meenaleck. Now, coaches filled with American tourists pull up to get a look at where Enya, the famous Irish singer and daughter of owner Leo Brennan, grew up. Other of the nine Brennan offspring formed Irish musical group Clannad. The family still own the place, now extended to include a dining room. Despite its popularity and regular gigs, it remains an unassuming establishment, with locals speaking Irish at the bar, no doubt wondering what all the fuss is about.

Where to stay

For such a small town, Bunbeg and the surrounding area has a surplus of accommodation. In Bunbeg itself are two hotels owned by the same family: Óstán Radharc na Mara (074 953 1159, www. seaviewhotel.ie) and Óstán Gweedore (074 953 1177, www.ostangweedore.com), the latter with a prime location on the beach. Both offer a similar

standard of accommodation. Set in a former cornmill on the edge of the harbour, Bunbeg House (074 953 1305, www.bunbeghouse.com) is a comfortable but budget-priced B&B. There are also a number of B&Bs on the road towards Glenveagh National Park.

An Chúirt Gweedore

Gweedore (074 953 2900, www.gweedorecourt hotel.com). Rates €99-€150 double incl breakfast.
The closest hotel to Glenveagh National Park, Gweedore Court Hotel is a bit corporate in style, but is blessed with 66 smart, comfortable rooms, a bar and restaurant, and friendly staff who are happy to advise on walks and things to do. It's set on the edge of the Clady River with views towards looming Mount Errigal. The attached health club, with swimming pool, steam room, sauna and weights room, is open to the public, so can get quite busy.

Errigal Hostel

Dunlewey (074 953 1180, www.errigalhostel.com). Rates €21-€25 for 2 people incl breakfast.
A purpose-built youth hostel (completed in 2007) at the foot of Mount Errigal, with picture windows providing spectacular views over the lough. The extensive facilities include a common room with TV and DVD player, internet services, laundry, drying room and a well-equipped self-catering kitchen. It sleeps a total of 60 in a mix of two-, four- and six-bed rooms.

DUNFANAGHY & AROUND

From Gweedore it's a 30-minute drive north on the N56 to Dunfanaghy, but the fastest route isn't always the best option. Instead, follow the winding coast road, to take in the grim but impressive Bloody Foreland. From the village of Derrybeg the road is narrow and twisty in parts, but the views south are spectacular. Unfortunately, the headland itself is over-developed, with groups of mismatched houses competing for the view. However, as you continue the buildings disappear and the only inhabitants are the sheep and goats that roam the barren mountainside. The heather covering the mountain turns red under the setting sun, hence the ominous name. Before the road rejoins the N56 you will pass through Magheroarty, a popular windsurfing spot. It's also where ferries leave for Tory Island (*see p35*).

A couple of kilometres before Dunfanaghy is the Workhouse Heritage Centre (074 913 6540, www.dunfanaghyworkhouse.ie), which has an informative exhibition on the building's former life as a workhouse during the 1847 Great Famine – not a happy story – and tourist information for the Sheephaven Bay area. The café serves light snacks and has a room in which to sit back, read a book and relax. The attractive two-storey stone building next door, once the fever hospital for the workhouse, is now the Gallery (074 913 6224), presenting exhibitions of oil paintings and watercolours by local artists along with crafts, antiques and art supplies.

Situated on the waterfront with holiday homes sprinkled here and there, Dunfanaghy has a lot going on for such a small town. One of the more popular spots in north Donegal, it's especially busy in summer but is also one of the few communities that continues business-as-usual throughout the year. A key factor is the proximity of a number of stunning beaches (including Tramore and Falcarragh, a Blue Flag beach with lifeguards in summer) and great surf spots such as Marble Hill. Waterside Dunfanaghy Golf Club (074 913 6335, www.dunfanaghygolfclub.com) offers day or weekend green fees.

Among the many local attractions is the loop drive around Horn Head ★. It's a bit hairy at times, with nothing but a steel barrier keeping you from tumbling off the mountainside, but the views east to Fanad peninsula and west to the Bloody Foreland are incredible. The more energetic can walk to the headland from Dunfanaghy town (take care on the narrow roads). Another picturesque, and isolated, walk leads across the grassy dunes to pristine, secluded Tramore beach: follow the road towards Horn Head, cross the bridge, climb over a stile and walk through the field towards the coast. It takes about 30 minutes.

The citizens of Dunfanaghy are dedicated to making the town a 'destination' – and are succeeding. There are plenty of celebrations throughout the year, including the Dunfanaghy Seafood Festival in May and the Jazz & Blues Festival in September. For walking weekends, contact the guys at Narosa (*see p30*).

Whatever your carbon footprint, we can reduce it

For over a decade we've been leading the way in carbon offsetting and carbon management.

In that time we've purchased carbon credits from over 200 projects spread across 6 continents. We work with over 300 major commercial clients and thousands of small and medium sized businesses, which rely upon our market-leading quality assurance programme, our experience and absolute commitment to deliver the right solution for each client.

Why not give us a call?

T: London (020) 7833 6000

www.CarbonNeutral.com

Wilderness lovers should head to Ards Forest Park, a couple of kilometres outside Port-na-blagh. Here, 480 hectares of deciduous and coniferous woodland, encompassing a diverse range of flora and fauna, is open to the public for a small fee. A series of signposted walks cater for all levels, ranging from a one-hour stroll around Lake Lilly to a four-hour walk through the forest. There's a small coffee shop (open weekends only, noon-5pm) in the car park.

A kilometre from the forest, Ards Friary has a prime location on the inlet; while the friary itself (a retreat and conference centre) is no architectural wonder, the undulating wooded gardens and sweeping views across to Rosguill peninsula are lovely. Walk through the white gates and follow the tree-lined pathway, which leads past deserted coves, eventually opening on to a headland. It's the perfect picnic spot.

Visible from the friary, and tucked into a nook of Sheephaven Bay, are the partially restored ruins of 15th-century Doe Castle. Access is free – take the turning off the main road just before Creeslough.

Where to eat & drink

You'll never go hungry in Dunfanaghy. Options run from casual eateries such as the Green Man (Main Street, 074 910 0800, www.greenman dunfanaghy.com), which also sells wholefoods, gluten-free goodies and wines, to traditional pub grub at Arnold's Hotel (*see right*).

Cove
Port-na-blagh (074 913 6300). Open times vary; phone for details.
Looking down on to Port-na-blagh harbour, this intimate restaurant is very popular, thanks to its combination of smiling service, beautiful views and fresh, imaginative dishes. Chowder, garden salad, slow-cooked pork belly and succulent lamb shank are all house specialities. Fish and seafood feature heavily too. Head upstairs to the lounge for a pre- or post-prandial drink.

Mill Restaurant ★
Figart, Dunfanaghy (074 913 6985, www.themill restaurant.com). Dinner served May-Oct 7-9pm Tue-Sat. Nov-Apr 7-9pm Sat, Sun.
This charming restaurant-cum-guesthouse occupies a former flax mill in an enviable setting on the shores of New Lake. The split-level restaurant offers fantastic views over the water, and there is also a conservatory for drinks before and after dinner. The seasonal menu, designed by owner Derek Alcorn, majors on locally caught fish and shellfish. Equally pleasing are the six very comfortable bedrooms (€100 double incl breakfast), simply but stylishly decorated with antique furnishings and polished floorboards. As the family are all painters, there are beautiful watercolours throughout the building. Booking essential.

Muck'n'Muffins
The Square, Dunfanaghy (074 913 6780, www.muckn muffins.com). Open Summer 9.30am-6pm Mon-Sat; 10am-6pm Sun. Winter 9.30am-5pm Mon-Sat; 10.30am-5pm Sun.

Once a grain store, this ancient stone building on the town square houses a craft and pottery studio on the ground floor, and a small, bustling café upstairs. Visit for lunch – toasties, wraps and light dishes such as quiche or salads – or just pop in for a muffin or a glass of wine.

Starfish Café
Main Street, Dunfanaghy (074 910 0676). Open Summer 9am-6pm daily. Winter 9.30am-5pm daily. No credit cards.
Located on Dunfanaghy's main drag, the Starfish has a beach-chic feel with its bright white walls and soft blue tones. It's a relaxing spot for freshly made cakes, salads and sandwiches. The outside terrace is a boon in summer.

Where to stay
There's no shortage of accommodation in and around Dunfanaghy, including affordable rented options. The Mill Restaurant (*see left*) is also a guesthouse and makes for a very pleasant stay.

Arnolds Hotel & Riding Stables
Main Street, Dunfanaghy (074 913 6208, www.arnoldshotel.com). Rates €99-€119 double incl breakfast.
Set on Dunfanaghy's main street, this cosy, traditional hotel has been in the hands of the Arnold family since the 1920s. The 30 rooms are old-fashioned but comfortable, and there's also a bar (snacks available) and a restaurant if you don't want to venture out. The hotel's stables offers equestrian packages for experienced riders, as well as one-hour beach treks for beginners.

Mill Restaurant

Fanad Head Lighthouse

Corcreggan Mill

Dunfanaghy (074 913 6409, www.corcreggan.com).
Rates B&B €47-€57 double incl breakfast. Hostel
€34 for 2 people. Camping €16 for 2 people.
A useful place to stay for groups, surfers and the more cost-conscious traveller, this converted mill has a range of accommodation from en-suite B&B rooms to hostel dorms and camping. It's in a lovely location a few kilometres outside Dunfanaghy, and has a welcoming, fun atmosphere.

Shandon Hotel

Marble Hill Strand, Sheephaven Bay, Dunfanaghy
(074 913 6137, www.shandonhotel.com). Rates €130-
€160 double incl breakfast.
In a peaceful location in Sheephaven Bay overlooking the beach at Marble Hill, this relatively large, four-star hotel is ideal for families, thanks to its purpose-built play centre, child-centred activities, pitch and putt course and tennis courts. The spa and pool – offering plenty of indulgent massages and treatments – are more recent additions, and there's also a bar and restaurant. All the 83 rooms have sea views. It's been under new managment since April 2011.

THE NORTHERN PENINSULAS

Rosguill

The Atlantic Drive is a 15-kilometre loop around tiny Rosguill peninsula, starting and finishing on the west coast at Downings. A small town with several pubs, two hotels, an amusement arcade and a camping and mobile home site, Downings is a magnet for families and holidaymakers as a result of its long sandy beach. This means the verdant hills are now dotted with a mish-mash of holiday homes, and the magical ruggedness Rosguill was once famed for has lessened somewhat. However, continue around the headland, down the east coast, and the clutter of buildings diminishes. The views across to the Fanad peninsula and even as far as Malin on the Inishowen peninsula are breathtaking.

Rosapenna Golf Course is a major tourist draw; the attached Rosapenna Hotel (074 915 5301, www.rosapenna.ie) is a large, purpose-built hotel for those seeking a comfortable golfing break. It's particularly popular with older guests and families.

Fanad

It's now easy to reach the Fanad peninsula from Carrigart, thanks to the newly built Harry Blaney Bridge. The drive from the bridge, through hills and around numerous inlets, to Fanad Head at the tip of the peninsula is far more scenic than the longer route around the west coast. A startlingly white lighthouse sits perched on the cliff at the Head. It's still in operation, so you can't visit it, but there's a short trail out to the jutting headland, with the Lighthouse Tavern (074 915 9212) conveniently placed for refreshments.

From Fanad Head, take the first left on to the L1072 – a continuation of the 72-kilometre Fanad Drive, another scenic signposted route. A kilometre on is the Tea Stop, where the friendly owner Caruth Logan will provide a refreshing pot of leaf tea and own-made scones on the patio in front of his house or in a tiny room filled with postcards from all over the world. The narrow road, lined with fuchsias, leads to Portsalon, where a crop of hillside holiday homes overlook one of Donegal's most striking bays. Capture the glorious views of Warden Beach from the Stores Bar (074 915 9135) at the tiny harbour. The Portsalon Golf Club has superlative views too.

The Fanad Drive then climbs up, hugging the coastline, with magnificent views across Lough Swilly to the famous fort at Dunree. Tucked beneath the cliffs, but visible from the road, is another, smaller fort. It's a 20-minute drive from Portsalon to Rathmullan, a picturesque town next to the lough that offers the best accommodation on the peninsula. Rathmullan is also famed for being the departure point for the Flight of the Earls in 1607, which marked the end of the Gaelic nation; the Rathmullan Heritage Centre (074 915 8178, open Mon-Sat July, Aug), housed in a gun battery built in 1810 to repel the French, tells the story of the Flight and displays the works of local artists. The beach is perfect for a stroll or a swim. Horse treks can be arranged with Golden Sands Equestrian Centre (074 915 8124), and cruises and fishing trips on Lough Swilly with Rathmullan Charters (www.rathmullancharters.com).

Annual events include the Angling Festival in June and the Rathmullan Shark Festival in September, both fishing competitions with associated celebrations.

Ten or so kilometres further south, sleepy Ramelton, sitting at the mouth of the River Lennon, is another pleasant place to stay with some fine Georgian buildings. The old steamboat store on the Quay has been renovated and now houses the Ramelton Story Exhibition and the Donegal Ancestry Centre (074 915 1266, www.donegalancestry.com, open Mon-Fri June; Mon-Sat July-Sept). The Bridge Bar (074 915 1119, www.bridge-bar.com) has an animated atmosphere, a restaurant upstairs and live music at the weekend.

It's another 12 kilometres to Letterkenny. Once a small fishing village, nowadays, thanks to its hospital and university, it's the largest and most densely populated town in the county. The excellent An Grianán Theatre (Port Road, 074 912 0777, www.angrianan.com) presents a varied programme of drama, music and comedy. Next door, the recently opened Regional Cultural Centre (074 912 9186, www.donegalculture.com) – a striking angular structure in aluminium and glass – covers film, concerts and art. If you're in town on the first or third Saturday of the month, don't miss the Letterkenny Farmers Market in McGinley's car park on Pearse Road.

The student population means that Letterkenny is also the best town for nightlife. The main street is packed with bars, and any night of the week you'll find live music and people to enjoy a drink with. Favoured bars include the Brewery and the Cavern; if you fancy carrying on into the wee hours, head for Pulse nightclub or the new and fashionable Voodoo Lounge.

Inishowen

Not many travellers venture north-east of Letterkenny to Inishowen – the largest of the three northern peninsulas. Which is a shame, since they miss out on some spectacular sea views and beautiful beaches, an undulating interior landscape and Ireland's most northerly point, Malin Head. The Inishowen 100 is the scenic coastal route – about 160 kilometres long – around the peninsula, passing through some quaint villages such as Malin and Culdaff, and looping around majestic Malin Head. August is probably the busiest month and a great time to visit as it's the main season for festivals and regattas.

In summer, there's a regular car ferry (every 80mins) from Rathmullan pier to Buncrana, the peninsula's largest town and main resort, especially for holidaymakers from Derry. Well equipped with shops, pubs, restaurants, hotels and B&Bs, the town has a busy main street lined with multicoloured buildings and a definite buzz. A few kilometres north, in a stirring location overlooking Lough Swilly, is Fort Dunree (074 936 1817, www.dunree.pro.ie), where a small museum in the old fort tells the story of those who once inhabited the now dilapitated outhouses and buildings.

From here, the Inishowen 100 climbs steeply north and inland past thatched cottages into the barren, rock- and heather-covered Urris and Mamore Hills (which are reminiscent of the mountains of Glenveagh). Cutting though Mamore Gap, you'll pass a roadside shrine at Glencolmcille's Well, a place of pilgrimage for centuries. The sea views on the winding descent are spectacular, taking in the white sands of Lennane Strand. To reach the beach, take the sharp left turn at the base of the mountain and follow the tree-covered lane to a small parking area. You can return to the Inishowen 100 the way you came or continue along the road. At the end, turning left leads to Lennane Pier with beautiful views over Mamore Gap and the Strand; turning right connects with the Inishowen 100.

Clonmany and Ballyliffin are the next settlements of note. The former hosts the long-running, family-oriented Clonmany Festival (www.clonmany festival.com) during the first week of August, while the latter is a popular base for exploring the peninsula, with plenty of hotels and B&Bs along its high street. Below is stunning Pollan Bay beach, with the remains of 16th-century Carrickabraghy Castle at one end. The town also boasts two renowned championship links courses at Ballyliffin Golf Club. A few kilometres north is Doagh Famine Village (*see p35*), a must-visit for those interested in the often troubled history of the area.

If you're after a quieter place from which to explore the far north, consider the charming village of Malin on the other side of Trawbreaga Bay. Consisting of a handful of shops, houses and bars around a green, it's also the gateway to Malin Head.

The loop road to the Head takes you through the least populated part of the peninsula. It's a dramatic, isolated place, where the land lies open to the elements. En route you pass the long sandy stretch of Five Fingers Strand, where there's a tiny church and beach parking. The crashing waves have

McGrory's. See p47.

deposited stones along the foreshore and attacked the high sand dunes. The Head's most northerly point is Bamba's Crown, marked by the desolate remains of a 19th-century signal tower. Looking north, there's nothing between you and Iceland and nothing to see but the wild Atlantic Ocean. The wind blows most days – often severely, as fans of the BBC's Shipping Forecast will know – giving the landscape a raw, natural beauty. There are several walks around the Head, the most beautiful leading to Hell's Hole, a deep chasm in the cliffs that thunders with the incoming tide. The area is also a birdwatcher's dream: more than 200 species, some of them exceedingly rare, have been spotted here.

There's a fine youth hostel at Malin Head and – if you need an excuse to stop for a pint – Ireland's most northerly pub, the Seaview Tavern (074 937 0117, www.seaviewtavern.biz), which also has a restaurant and nine guestrooms.

The Inishowen 100 returns via the interior of the peninsula, an area of undulating farmland. Culdaff is a cute village seven kilometres east of Malin, with a good swimming beach, a small craft shop and – most importantly, and the heart and soul of the community – McGrory's bar and restaurant.

Although the east coast of Inishowen lacks the incredible beauty of the west, there are several pretty beaches and towns. The fishing port of Greencastle has some fine seafood restaurants, a good bathing beach and a very popular links course at Greencastle Golf Club. Located in the old coastguard station at the habour, Inishowen Martime Museum & Planetarium (074 938 1363, www.inishowenmaritime.com, closed Sat, Sun winter) is packed with historical nautical memorabilia. Next door is the pier from where ferries run to Magilligan Strand in Northern Ireland, on the opposite side of Lough Foyle. Just outside town (and the reason for its name), the forlorn ruins of a 14th-century castle perch on a rocky mound beside the lough. It's claimed that Edward Bruce of Scotland, who crowned himself King of Ireland in 1316, lived here. It then passed through the hands of various Irish clans before falling into decay in 1700.

North of Greencastle, there are stunning walks from the village of Stroove along the coast to Inishowen Head. You can also walk to isolated and lovely Kinnagoe Bay, where the wreck of *La Trinidad Valencera*, from the Spanish Armada, was discovered in 1971.

South of Greencastle is the holiday resort of Moville, a good place to pick up supplies.

Where to eat & drink

On the Fanad peninsula, Letterkenny is well endowed with restaurants. The light, bright Lemon Tree (Lower Main Street, 074 912 5788) is much liked for its warm welcome and excellent home-style cooking.

There are plenty of established bars and eateries on the Inishowen peninsula, with new places appearing each season. One such newcomer is the Red Door (074 936 0289, www.thereddoor.ie),

Frewin House. See p47.

Rathmullan House

located a short distance south of Buncrana, with stunning views over Lough Swilly. It's fast building a reputation thanks to its excellent contemporary cooking and friendly vibe, and has recently added four smart bedrooms. In Greencastle, low-key Kealys Seafood Bar (074 938 1010, closed Mon-Thur Sept-Mar, Mon-Wed Apr, May) serves delicious classic fish dishes including a renowned seafood chowder with own-baked brown bread. Looking for a lively traditional bar? Then try Rosato's (074 938 2247) in Moville, with its distinctive red and green exterior – it's won countless awards as a pub and also for its food.

Beach House

The Pier, Swilly Road, Buncrana (074 936 1050, www.thebeachhouse.ie). Open Summer noon-midnight daily. Winter 5-11pm Wed-Fri; noon-midnight Sat, Sun. Summer Lunch served noon-4pm, dinner served 5-9.30pm daily. Winter Lunch served noon-4pm Sat, Sun. Dinner served 5-9.30pm Wed-Sun.

Follow the signs for the pier and you'll find the aptly named Beach House. The bright and airy interior – all natural tones and stylish contemporary decor – does indeed exude beach-house chic. A picture window on the mezzanine looks out across Lough Swilly to the Fanad peninsula. The impeccably prepared food (dry-aged Donegal beef, local seafood, organic vegetables) reflects the uncontrived naturalness of the restaurant. One of the best places to eat in the northern peninsulas.

McGrory's ★

Culdaff (074 937 9104, www.mcgrorys.ie). Open Mar-Oct noon-midnight daily. Jan, Feb, Nov, Dec noon-midnight Wed-Sun. Food served Mar-Oct 12.30-9pm daily. Jan, Feb, Nov, Dec 12.30-9pm Wed-Sun.

Run by the McGrory family since 1924, this place is a local institution. Musicians from all over Ireland and beyond flock to the Backroom to play and sing, while the intimate Front Bar, with its rough stone walls and flagstone floor, is the place for traditional music sessions (on Tuesday and Friday). The casual dining room, with local artwork for sale on the walls, serves fresh, uncomplicated fish and meat dishes – and puts great emphasis on local suppliers. There are also 17 comfortable bedrooms, all en suite (€69-€99 double incl breakfast).

Where to stay

Rosguill peninsula gets packed out with tourists in high season. Fanad is also popular, but feels less overrun and also contains one of Donegal's loveliest country house hotels, Rathmullan House (*see right*). Options in Ramelton include Ardeen House (074 915 1243, www.ardeenhouse.com, closed Oct-Easter), a charming 19th-century home on the edge of town with five B&B rooms. On the outskirts of Letterkenny are the large, newly built Clanree Hotel (Derry Road, 074 912 4369, www.clanreehotel.com) with its own leisure centre; a more luxurious option would be Castle Grove (Ramelton Road, 074 915 1118, www. castlegrove.com), a beautiful and spacious Georgian mansion set in peaceful gardens designed by Capability Brown.

Inishowen, although the least visited peninsula, has plenty of hotels and B&Bs catering for all types and wallets. Positioned above the small fishing pier of Port Ronan on remote Malin Head is the Sandrock Holiday Hostel (074 937 0289, www.sandrockhostel.com) – expect dramatic Atlantic views. McGrory's (*see left*) in Culdaff also has accommodation. A few kilometres south of Moville, the Carlton Redcastle Hotel (074 938 5555, www.carltonredcastle.ie) is a modern spa hotel with a restaurant overlooking Lough Foyle and a sizeable bar.

Ballyliffin Lodge

Ballyliffin (074 937 8200, www.ballyliffinlodge.com). Rates €90-€180 double incl breakfast.

Set in the heart of the village overlooking Pollan Bay, this four-star hotel is well equipped, with a bar and an award-winning restaurant. Rooms (40 in total), decorated in a smart, modern style, are a good size. The spa and treatment rooms can provide all the relaxation and pampering you might require.

Fort Royal Hotel

Rathmullan (074 915 8100, www.fortroyalhotel.com). Rates €140-€160 double incl breakfast. Closed Oct-mid Apr.

This three-star hotel, owned and run by the Fletcher family since 1948, occupies an expanded Victorian house set in stunning gardens at the edge of Lough Swilly. Antique furnishings and patterned carpets provide old-fashioned comfort, while most of the 11 cosy bedrooms come with a view of the sea. There's also a small bar and restaurant. Three self-catering cottages in the old stable block make it a useful choice for families. The expansive grounds include a pitch and putt course, croquet lawn, tennis courts and a charming kitchen garden.

Frewin House

Ramelton (074 915 1246, www.frewinhouse.com). Rates €120-€160 double incl breakfast.

Five minutes' walk from the centre of Ramelton, this handsome Victorian rectory set in two acres of mature woodland feels more like a family home than an impersonal hotel. The lovely antique furniture, well-stocked bookshelves and the four spacious, high-ceilinged bedrooms and drawing room set the tone. Pluses are excellent breakfasts, dinner (on request) and lots of helpful tips from the owners, Regina and Thomas Coyle. There's also a self-catering cottage ideal for a couple.

Rathmullan House ★

Rathmullan (074 915 8188, www.rathmullanhouse.com). Rates from €160 double incl breakfast.

Rathmullan House, built in 1820, retains the charm, but not the formality, of an upmarket country retreat from years past. Guests are encouraged to lounge in one of the elegant, yet comfortable drawing rooms, walk the beautiful gardens or take a stroll along the nearby beach. The 34 bedrooms are decorated in traditional country house style, most offering views over the lough. The Weeping Willow restaurant majors on locally sourced produce, some grown in the hotel's walled garden. Friendly staff, delicious food and a relaxing atmosphere – plus a pool, steam room and holistic treatments – make it an oasis of calm.

County Sligo

Known as 'Yeats County', Sligo has been made famous by the poetry of William Butler Yeats and the paintings of his brother Jack, who spent their childhood summers here. The accolades are well deserved, such is the beauty of this small county, with its long, immaculate beaches, verdant rolling hills intercut by century-old stone walls, myriad lakes and romantic forests – all against the dramatic backdrop of Benbulben Mountain. Literary lovers come in search of Yeats' grave and the Isle of Innisfree, while adrenalin junkies ride some of Europe's best waves at Strandhill, and historians visit megalithic tombs and seek out Sligo's many myths and legends.

ENNISCRONE & SLIGO TOWN

Enniscrone to Aughris Head

Enniscrone is a hive of activity in summer, with sunseekers heading straight for the eight-kilometre stretch of white sand. It's a popular surfing beach; lessons are available from the North West Surf School (mobile 087 959 5556, www.nwsurfschool.com, closed Dec-mid Mar) and Seventh Wave Surf School (mobile 087 971 6389, www.seventhwavesurfschool.com, closed Oct-Feb). It's also good for swimming, drawing plenty of bathers with parasols, towels, and buckets and spades. In the colder months, you can strike out for a bracing walk. The town has just one main street, set back from the beach, with a varied collection of pubs that fill up when the sun goes down. After a day on the beach, head to Kilcullen's Bath House (Cliff Road, 096 36238, www.kilcullen seaweedbaths.com) for a soak in a warm bath of seaweed. Early August brings the five-day Black Pig Festival, which includes a parade, gigs and, most importantly, a pig roast.

North of Enniscrone is the small, almost deserted village of Easkey, famed for its two reef breaks. Surfers pull up in campervans, ride the waves all day and then either head to Enniscrone overnight or sleep in their vans. For tips, visit the Easkey Surf & Information Centre (096 49428, www.isasurf.ie), home of the Irish Surfing Association, on the main street. Just down the road is Rosie's Pottery and studio, handy for ceramics and other craft items.

Continue east along the coast road and follow the signs for the Beach Bar, Aughris Head. Aughris itself no longer exists, having, like many places, lost its population to emigration at the end of the 19th century. Once a town of 400, little remains except rubble, a few houses by the harbour and this 17th-century thatched shebeen, now a thriving pub (see p51). From the pier there's an easy, five-kilometre walk along the cliffs, with stunning views across the sea to the Strandhill peninsula.

Sligo town & Strandhill

Sligo town, although the county seat, is representative of Sligo in general in being compact and easy to get around – you can see the sights in a morning before heading out to the surrounding countryside. Wiggling through the centre of town, the Garavogue River is lined with modern glass buildings housing restaurants, apartments and the new, ultra-swish Glasshouse hotel. In complete contrast, the Yeats Memorial Building (Douglas Hyde Ridge, 071 914 2693, www.yeats-sligo.com) is a handsome 19th-century red-brick affair, where you will find a small exhibition on the Yeats family, including photos of WB and drafts of his work. It's also home to the Yeats Society, which has run the Yeats International Summer School, dedicated to the study of WB's work, for more than 50 years. Just across the river is the Sligo County Museum (Stephen Street, 071 911 1679, closed Mon, Sun) and local library, whose diverse holdings include more Yeats memorabilia, including paintings by Jack, and a century-old firkin of 'bog butter'. The flagship contemporary arts centre is undoubtedly the Model (see p58), which reopened in 2010 after major renovations.

A Dominican friary was established in Sligo in 1252; known locally as the Abbey (071 914 6406, www.heritageireland.ie, closed Nov-Mar), it sits in the middle of town and, although ruined, is well preserved, with decorative carvings, tomb sculptures and a 15th-century high altar. But the town's landmark building is the Lyons department store on Quay Street. Operating since 1878, the building has retained its original façade and is still a family-run shop, one of few remaining in Ireland. Also worth a visit, for local fruit and veg, cheeses and bakery goods, is the Saturday morning farmers' market in the car park of the Institute of Technology.

Another Sligo institution is Michael Quirke's shop on Wine Street. Once a butcher, Michael now carves intricate wooden figures from Irish myth and legend; he's a colourful and entertaining character, as skilled in banter as he is in woodwork. The Cat & the Moon on Castle Street sells jewellery designed and made in-house, as well as Irish-crafted textiles, ceramics and furniture.

Sligo is a lively place year round, but really gets going at the beginning of October during Sligo Live (www.sligolive.ie), when a range of traditional and contemporary musicians perform in various

Conrad's Kitchen. See p51.

venues. The town also supports two theatres: Hawk's Well (Temple Street, 071 916 1518, www.hawkswell.com), which mixes dramas, musicals and pantos, and the Factory Theatre, home of the Blue Raincoat company (Lower Quay Street, 071 917 0431, www.blueraincoat.com), which specialises in modern European classics, including works by WB Yeats and Flann O'Brien.

A short drive west of town is the Strandhill peninsula. The landscape is dominated by Knocknarea, a flat-topped mountain with a small tomb-shaped mound, Medb's Cairn, at its summit. This mysterious hill appears in many legends and myths, and the mound is believed to be the burial tomb of mythical Queen Medb. It's a moderate 45-minute hike to the top, though 700 intrepid souls prefer to run it in August, in what's known as the Warriors Run (www.warriorsfestival.com). Near the base of the Knocknarea is Europe's biggest prehistoric graveyard, Carrowmore Megalithic Cemetery (see p58).

Strandhill is a bustling seaside town, with reliable surfing conditions throughout the year. There's a vibrant young feel to the place in high summer, when the pubs heave with locals and visitors. Even on a bitter winter's day you'll see surfers pulling on their wetsuits and braving the icy Atlantic – afterwards heading to Voya Seaweed Baths (see p58) to seep the cold out of their bones. Surf lessons can be arranged through Perfect Day

Surf School (see below), situated on the seafront in a bright yellow bungalow beside Shells Café (see p52). The water is not safe for swimming, but the long beach backed by grass-covered dunes is ideal for walking, whatever the weather.

On the way out of town, pop into Dolly's Cottage (Strandhill, 071 916 8079, open Sat, Sun June; daily July, Aug). This 200-year-old thatched stone cottage still has all its original features, including the walls, roof beams, turf fire and even a bed. It also sells a few local crafts and homemade jams.

Where to eat & drink

The Pilot Bar (096 36131, closed Mon, Tue winter) on Enniscrone's Main Street is ideal for a quiet drink and a bowl of chowder. Gilroy's Bar (096 37222, www.gilroysbar.com) is livelier and has a great restaurant, Áit Eile, serving everything from fish dishes to oven-baked pizzas. Roper's Pub (096 36400), opposite the church, is the place for live music.

You won't go thirsty or hungry in Sligo town. There are plenty of pubs offering *ceoil agus craic* (music and fun), and locals are proud of the high-quality restaurants. The Só Sligo festival (www.sosligo.com) in March celebrates the county's many artisan food producers, restaurant owners and chefs, with a street carnival, food markets and even the World Irish Stew Championships.

Most bars have live music at the weekend. More traditional establishments include the Fiddler's Creek (071 914 1866, www.fiddlers creek.ie) on Rockwood Parade and McHugh's (071 914 2030) on Grattan Street.

Lyons Cafe (Quay Street, 071 914 2969, closed Sun), on the first floor of the Lyons department store, is an old-fashioned gem serving wholesome dishes and great scones. Osta Café & Wine Bar (071 914 4639, www.osta.ie), on Stephen Street overlooking the river, has a lovely ambience and superior pastries, while sister restaurant Tobergal Lane Café (071 914 6599, www.osta.ie) offers bistro fare from breakfast to late, with bands playing upstairs. Clubbers will appreciate the four bars, two dancefloors and varied music at

Things to do

ENNISCRONE & SLIGO TOWN

Perfect Day Surf School

Strandhill (087 202 9399, www.perfectday surfing.com). Classes Summer daily. Winter by appointment only. Fees Group €30 per person. Individual €50 per person. No credit cards.
Strandhill offers the best surfing in Sligo, and is a great place to learn the sport. One of the best-established surf schools in the area, Perfect Day is a family affair; it was set up by Tom Hickey, and is now run by his daughter Elisha (although Tom still pitches in). Experienced and attentive instructors teach throughout the summer; the small class sizes are a bonus. Women-only instruction is available too.

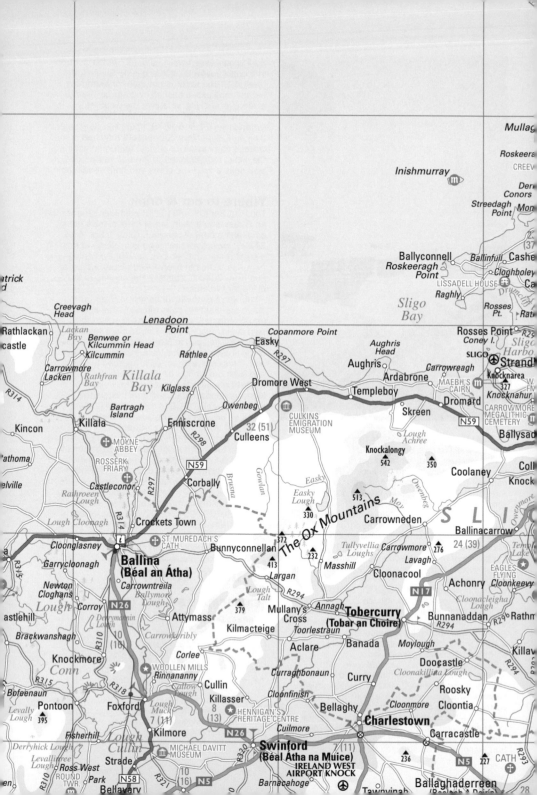

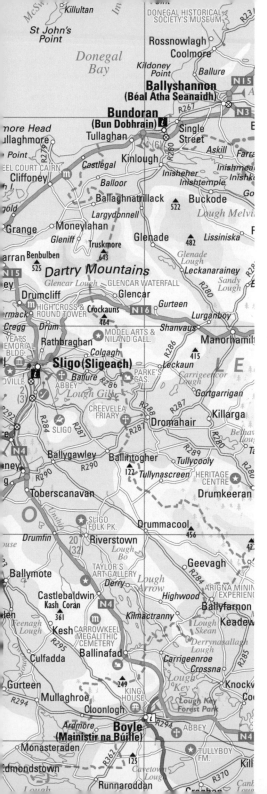

the Velvet Room (Kempten Promenade, 071 914 4721, www.velvetroom.ie, open Sat).

In Strandhill, the Strand Bar (071 916 8140, www.thestrandbar.ie) is the closest pub to the beach, offering pub grub (Irish stew and the like), and traditional music sessions. Above it is Trá Bán restaurant (071 912 8402, www.traban sligo.ie, closed Mon), known for its fish and seafood dishes. Also popular is the Dunes Tavern (Top Road, 071 916 8131, www.accommodation strandhill.com), a bar with rooms that is located at the top of the town.

Beach Bar ★
Aughris Head (071 917 6465, http://thebeachbar sligo.com). Open noon-11.30pm Mon-Thur, Sun; noon-12.30am Fri, Sat. Food served Summer 1-8pm daily. Winter 1-8pm Sat, Sun.
In a former life, 300 years ago, this white cottage was a tiny shebeen called Maggie Mayes. It's been in the hands of the McDermott family since the 1970s, and remains uncontrived and true to tradition, with flagstone floors, wooden beams, open turf fires and small, interconnecting rooms. The walls are lined with photos depicting the history of the bar and those who made it what it is, including the famous fiddler Joe O'Dowd, who used to play here every Saturday night. You'll find homely cooking, and live music at the weekend. B&B accommodation is also available in seven rooms behind the pub (€60 double incl breakfast).

Blue Water Café
Main Street, Enniscrone (087 978 1334). Open Summer 9.30am-7pm daily. Winter 9.30am-5pm Fri-Sun.
This small, unassuming café serves delicious cakes, breads and chutneys, all made on site, as well as open sandwiches, pasta dishes and daily specials. Some dishes cater for coeliacs, while breakfast includes gluten-free pancakes.

Conrad's Kitchen
The Model, The Mall, Sligo (071 911 9400, www.conradskitchen.com). Lunch served 12.30-2.30pm Tue-Sat; 1-4pm Sun. Dinner served 5-11pm Tue-Sat.
Overseen by leading Irish chef Conrad Gallagher, this new venture is on the top floor of the Model arts centre. The menu caters for all tastes and most wallets; you can have posh fish and chips on the set-price lunch/pre-theatre menu, treat yourself at dinner to Galway Bay oysters and an Irish fillet steak with truffle sauce, or really splash some cash on the six-course tasting menu.

Hargadon's
4 O'Connell Street, Sligo (071 915 3709, www.hargadons.com). Open 11am-11.30pm Mon-Thur, Sun; 11am-12.30am Fri, Sat. Lunch served noon-3.30pm daily. Dinner served 4-9pm Mon-Sat.
At first glance, Hargadon's appears to be a small, typically Irish pub with its dark floorboards, original 19th-century fittings and locals perched on bar stools. However, the bar extends back, though the booths and snugs maintain the cosiness and old-world feel. There's also a restaurant and wine shop.

Montmartre ★
1 Market Yard, Sligo (071 916 9901). Dinner served 5-11pm Tue-Sat.

As the name suggests, this is a French restaurant – and possibly the best restaurant in Sligo. French staff, fine wine and classic Gallic cooking create an authentic and very enjoyable dining experience. It's more expensive than other venues, but there is a reasonably priced early bird menu.

Shells Café
Seafront, Strandhill (071 912 2938, www.shells cafe.com). Open Summer 9.30am-7pm Mon-Fri; 9.30am-8pm Sat, Sun. Winter 9.30am-5pm Mon-Fri; 9.30am-6pm Sat, Sun.
This is the perfect beach café: bright and airy, with wooden floors and fabulous (organic, Fairtrade) coffee. Breakfast is served into the afternoon and includes french toast, eggs benedict and freshly baked bread. At lunch, there are warming dishes such as fish and chips and burgers, as well as freshly made salads and sandwiches. In fact, it's a great little spot throughout the day, bustling with surfers and visitors exploring the seafront.

Silver Apple
Lord Edward Street (071 914 6770, www.silverapple.ie). Lunch served 1-4pm Sun. Dinner served 5-10pm Wed-Sun.
Without any bling or fuss, this bistro on the outskirts of Sligo town has managed to create delicious, wholesome food (lamb shank, bangers and mash, prawn linguine) at a very reasonable price. The look is casual (stone walls, wooden floors, stained glass, banquette seating), and staff are attentive and welcoming.

Where to stay
Sligo has no shortage of B&Bs – you'll find at least one or two in even the smallest towns, and Enniscrone and Strandhill have plenty of choices for those wanting to stay by the sea. Check out www.sligo-bnb.com for recommendations.

The Ocean Sands Hotel (096 26700, www.theoceansandshotel.ie) on the main street in Enniscrone is a modern family-run hotel with 50 rooms and 12 self-catering apartments, a bar and restaurant, and views over the Atlantic. The sprawling, four-star Diamond Coast Hotel (Bartragh, 096 26000, www.diamondcoast.ie) on the outskirts is a good choice for families, and also golfers, thanks to the championship course next door at Enniscrone Golf Club. The 92 rooms are sleek and spacious and most have wonderful views over the beach.

At Aughris Head, the Beach Bar (*see p51*) offers B&B rooms in Aughris House, just behind the pub, and basic camping.

Sligo town has a number of smart modern hotels, including Sligo City Hotel (Quay Street; 071 914 4000, www.sligocityhotel.com) and the very pleasant Clarion Hotel (Clarion Road, 071 911 9000, www.clarionhotelsligo.com). The Glasshouse (Swan Point, 071 919 4300, www.theglasshouse.ie) is increasingly popular.

In Strandhill, the Ocean Wave Lodge (071 916 8115, www.oceanwavelodge.com) is a simply decorated, three-star operation. The Strandhill Caravan & Camping Park (071 916 8111, closed Oct-mid Apr) appeals to surfers.

Castle Dargan Hotel
Ballygawley (071 911 8080, www.castledargan.com). Rates €99-€150 double incl breakfast.
A ten-minute drive from Sligo town, this is a four-star operation (with 46 rooms), surrounded by a golf course. Most of the hotel is contemporary in design, with wide marble floors and plenty of glass, but there are also charming rooms in the original 18th-century house. Accommodating staff, a bar, a restaurant and a very comfortable lounge in a converted barn make it hard to leave. Non-golfers can take it easy in the luxurious spa.

Sligo Park Hotel
Pearse Road, Sligo (071 919 0400, www.sligopark hotel.com). Rates from €85 double incl breakfast.
Situated a kilometre outside Sligo town, the four-star Sligo Park is popular with families and groups. Rooms (137 in all, from singles to interconnecting family set-ups) are modern and well equipped, and there's a gym and leisure centre on the premises. Package deals offer surfing, horse riding, golfing and other activity breaks, teaming up with local schools and clubs. They're usually very good value and should be booked well ahead.

LOUGH GILL & NORTH SLIGO

The Yeats Trail
Driving around Sligo, you'll soon spot brown signs adorned with a quill – these mark the Yeats Trail, which follows quiet country roads to the sights that inspired William's poetry and Jack's paintings.

There are four stages of the drive, the first being the Strandhill peninsula. The second is the fabulous circuit of Lough Gill ★, a short drive south-east of Sligo town. The large lake (about eight kilometres long and two wide) is surrounded by forest and the drive is truly stunning in autumn, especially on a still day when the coloured foliage is mirrored in the water. The narrow winding road hugs the shoreline. Parke's Castle (*see p59*) sits serenely next to the lough's eastern edge, with views across to the isle of Innisfree. Seasonal boat tours (071 916 4266, www.roseofinnisfree.com, closed Nov-Easter) depart from the castle. This part of the lake is actually in County Leitrim, as is Dromahair, a picturesque small town a few kilometres further south.

The third stage of the Yeats Trail is Glencar (also in Leitrim, *see p59*), a 20-minute drive north-east of Sligo town. The Trail's fourth and final stage takes in Rosses Point, an incredibly pretty promontory, with a village of the same name, eight kilometres north of Sligo town. At weekends it's often busy with families, thanks to the safe swimming beach and good walks. There are two islands offshore: Oyster Island and larger Coney Island (which gave its name to the resort in New York); you can walk to the latter when the tide is out.

Just north of Rosses Point, on the Donegal road (N15), is the village of Drumcliffe, now famed as the final resting place of WB Yeats. The Yeats brothers' great-grandfather was the rector at Drumcliffe Church and Yeats asked that he be

Davis's Restaurant @ Yeats Tavern. See p55.

Lough Gill. See p52.

buried there. The plain grey headstone contains the simply carved epitaph 'Cast a cold eye/On life, on death/Horseman, pass by', taken from one of his final poems. It was also here that St Columba established a monastery in 574. A beautiful old round tower and an ornate 11th-century high cross remain today – although most visitors speed straight to Yeats' grave. There is a good tearoom and craft shop beside the church.

The Yeats brothers also visited grand Lissadell House in nearly Ballinful, once the childhood home of Constance Markievicz (née Gore-Booth), famed for being one of the leaders in the 1916 Rising and the first woman to be elected to the House of Commons, in 1918. She also painted, wrote poetry and was a leading suffragist. The house was sold by the Gore-Booth family in 2003 and the current owners have done much to restore the Greek Revival mansion, grounds and gardens, but a protracted legal dispute means that, sadly, it's currently not open to the public. However, there is hope that it may reopen in the future.

Benbulben & Mullaghmore

Above Drumcliffe and visible from almost every part of the county is Benbulben Mountain – known as Sligo's Table Mountain thanks to its distinctive shape with steep sides and a flat top. It's possible to walk around the base of the mountain, but reaching the summit (525 metres) can be tricky – the south side is easiest and safest. Local walking clubs frequently take people up the impressive slopes.

In the shadows of the mountain, off the N15 near Cliffoney, is Creevykeel Court Tomb, dating from the Neolithic period. Upon arrival it seems a strange and eerie site, with roughly edged stones and boulders positioned closely together. Excavated in the 1930s and reconstructed, it's the best example of a court cairn in Ireland.

Ten minutes away is the small fishing village of Mullaghmore, blessed with a three-kilometre Blue Flag beach of white sand. The swimming is good, and it's safe for sailing and other watersports (lessons are available). There are two hotels and various B&Bs. You can also take a boat to deserted and atmospheric Inishmurray Island (*see p58*).

Where to eat & drink

The Waterfront (071 917 7122, www.waterfront restaurant.ie) in Rosses Point serves good fish dishes and also has a small art gallery.

Davis's Restaurant @ Yeats Tavern

Drumcliffe (071 916 3117, www.yeatstavern restaurant.com). Open 10.30am-11pm daily. Food served 10.30am-9.30pm daily.
After a recent renovation, this is a striking and thoroughly modern affair, bright and airy. The long and varied menu, ranging from sandwiches and salads to full-blown meals, makes the most of local produce. The attached WB Yeats bar remains traditional and cosy.

Laura's

Main Street, Carney (071 916 3056). Open noon-11.30pm daily. Dinner served 5-9pm Sat, Sun.
A bustling spot, packed with locals at the weekend, Laura's has a front bar (with a bar menu) and assorted restaurant areas: a cosy intimate room directly beside the bar, an airy conservatory, and a terrace for fine weather. The menu suits all tastes, but the fish dishes are recommended.

Where to stay

In Drumcliffe, Yeats Lodge (071 917 3787) is a large modern stone house with five spacious B&B rooms and striking views of Benbulben Mountain.

The Radisson Blu Hotel & Spa (071 914 0008, www.radissonblu.ie/hotel-sligo) at Ballincar on Rosses Point is comfortable and modern, with 132 rooms and a bar and restaurant. Best of all is the spa – it's easy to pass an afternoon clad in your dressing gown, sipping on the complimentary herbal teas. You'll also find a spa, and plenty of child-friendly activities, at the slightly smaller Yeats Country Hotel (071 917 7211, www.yeatscountry hotel.com), tucked off the road in Rosses Point village. Next door is County Sligo Golf Club.

LOUGH ARROW & AROUND

Twenty kilometres south-east of Sligo, just off the N4, is the peaceful village of Riverstown. It's also where the Sligo Folk Park is located (071 916 5001, www.sligofolkpark.com, closed Jan). A series of traditional buildings house a museum and an exhibition of rural history and agricultural artefacts, including a re-created village streetscape. There's also a working blacksmith's, a shop selling traditional Irish crafts and a café. Craft demonstrations include thatching, lime plastering and butter-making.

From Riverstown, follow the narrow backroads south for a few kilometres through the green hills to reach beautiful Lough Arrow ★, one of Ireland's great trout fishing lakes. It's a stunning body of water, about seven kilometres long and four kilometres at its widest point. Fishing (Apr-Sept) is free and boats can be hired from John Hargadon (071 966 6666) or Louis Carthy (071 966 6001). A number of circular walks around the lough leave from Castlebaldwin (at the north end of the lake) and Ballinafad (at the south) – a great way to enjoy the local flora and fauna. Alternatively, the North West Adventure Centre (071 966 7055, www.cootehalladventure.com) can arrange guided walks, as well as kayaking and canoeing on the lough.

Where to eat & drink

The area around Lough Arrow is rural and the villages small, though they usually have a pub or two serving food. For restaurants, you'll have to head to the larger towns to the south, Boyle and Carrick-on-Shannon. The upside is that the country hotels, such as Cromleach Lodge (*see right*), provide excellent food in their restaurants.

Clevery Mill

Castlebaldwin (071 912 7424). Lunch served noon-3.30pm Sun. Dinner served 6.30-11pm Fri, Sat. Rates €70-€96 double incl breakfast.
This old stone building, once a mill, is now a charming restaurant and B&B (with five rooms). There's an open turf fire in the welcoming bar and snug areas. The old water wheel is a feature in the restaurant, where white-covered tables, soft lighting and more open fires create a inviting atmosphere. The excellent food makes the most of local and organic produce, including succulent local lamb and beef and daily specials.

Where to stay

You'll find standard B&Bs and small country houses such as Coopershill (see below), but there's not an abundance of options – book in advance. Well-equipped Lough Arrow Touring & Caravan Park (Ballynarry, 071 966 6018, www.lougharrow caravanpark.com, closed Nov-mid Mar) overlooks the lake at Ballynarry for those wanting to be close to nature.

Coopershill ★

Riverstown (071 916 5108, www.coopershill.com). Rates €198-€244 double incl breakfast.
A luxurious retreat in a handsome 1774 mansion that has belonged to the same family for seven generations. The eight guest rooms are resplendent in glowing colours and original Georgian furniture, and there are gilt-framed mirrors and family portraits everywhere. You can also play croquet, tennis and snooker. Meals (breakfast, afternoon tea and dinner) are a highlight of any visit, and make much of the 500-acre estate's own vegetables and venison – you'll no doubt see some of the 250 fallow deer roaming the fields. The O'Haras provide true Irish hospitality, and their eco-conscious approach has won awards.

Cromleach Lodge ★

Lough Arrow, nr Castlebaldwin (071 916 5155, www.cromleach.com). Rates €90-€150 double incl breakfast.
With breathtaking views over Lough Arrow and to the Bricklieve Mountains, Christy and Moira Tighe's hotel provides the perfect getaway. The four-star hotel first became known for its food – Moira's responsibility – and the intimate restaurant is still a winner, with exquisite cooking and excellent service. The 57 bedrooms (some with private balconies) are smart and stylish, and the Ciúnas Spa includes a sauna and steam room, and a hot tub out in the garden from where you can watch the sunset over the lake. Treatments include candlelit seaweed baths for couples. The hotel's attention to detail, in all areas, is admirable.

Temple House

Ballinacarrow (071 918 3329, www.templehouse.ie). Open Apr-Nov. Rates €170 double incl breakfast.
B&B accommodation doesn't get much grander than at this Georgian mansion set in 1,000 acres of parkland that features a ruined 13th-century castle. There are only six rooms (with a mix of twin or double beds), all individually decorated with antique furnishings. The Temple House festival (www.templehousefestival.com) in September is a new addition to Sligo's arts scene.

Coopershill

Places to visit

ENNISCRONE & SLIGO TOWN

Carrowmore Megalithic Cemetery
*Off the N4, 4km west of Sligo (071 916 1534,
www.heritageireland.ie). Open Apr-mid Oct 10am-6pm
daily. Admission €3; €1 reductions; €8 family.*
One of the oldest and largest Stone Age monuments
in western Europe, Carrowmore Cemetery is firmly
on the tourist trail. The site contains more than
30 visible tombs (and a similar number that are
still buried), some believed to be over 6,000 years
old – that's older than the Pyramids – and varying
in size, from basic stone structures to a large

The Model

tomb surrounded by a rounded cairn. A restored
cottage houses an explanatory exhibition.

The Model
*The Mall, Sligo (071 914 1405, www.themodel.ie).
Open 11am-5.30pm Wed-Sat; noon-5pm Sun.
Admission free.*
With a new extension that has increased its size by
a third, the Model is now the largest arts centre in the
region. It's a fantastic place, offering exhibitions by
contemporary artists from home and abroad, a concert
venue, a cinema, and studios for artists. There's
also a café and bookshop and, on the top floor, a new
fine-dining restaurant, Conrad's Kitchen (*see p51*).
The Sligo New Music Festival is held here in April.

Voya Seaweed Baths
*Seafront, Strandhill (071 916 8686, http://voya
seaweedbaths.com). Open 10am-8pm daily.
Treatments from €25.*
Seaweed has been cultivated for hundreds of years
on the west coast of Ireland. When steamed, it
releases oils that are readily absorbed into the skin,
so seaweed baths have long been a traditional
therapy – used for relaxation, to soften skin and hair,
and to counter skin problems. The Voya experience
is surprisingly spa-like, with natural tones and dark
wood, and smiling staff. The sensation of sinking into
a old-fashioned bath full of (unsmelly) seaweed and
oily water is disconcerting at first, but your skin and
hair will be silky-smooth for days to come. You can
buy products to take home too. The perfect way to
spend an hour on a blustery, or indeed any – day.

LOUGH GILL & NORTH SLIGO

Inishmurray Island
Situated 7km off the Sligo coast, Inishmurray contains
a sixth-century Christian settlement founded by St
Molaise. The site is extremely well preserved, with
an outer wall, the shells of two churches, a beehive-
shaped hut and other structures. The tiny, rugged
island was inhabited until the 1940s, and remnants
of later buildings remain, giving the place a neglected
and mysterious air. The island is also an important
haven for breeding and migrating seabirds, and seals
can often be seen resting on the shore. Boat trips
can by arranged with Ewing's (mobile 086 891 3618,
www.sligoboatcharters.com, Mar-Oct) or Keith Clarke
and his boat *Fiona Tee* (mobile 087 2540 190,
www.inishmurrayislandtrips.com, mid Apr-Oct).

LOUGH ARROW & AROUND

Carrowkeel Cemetery
Just south of Castlebaldwin, signposted from the N4.
On the other side of the N4 from Lough Arrow,
little-visited Carrowkeel Cemetery consists of 14
passage tombs on the top of Bricklieve Mountains,
built around 3,200-2,800 BC. They're not fenced
off and anyone can explore them: from the parking
area, walk a mile or so up the mountain until you
reach the first tomb. They're an incredible sight,
and the views over Lough Arrow and the countryside
are spectacular – and perhaps were the reason for
the positioning of these ancient tombs.

Counties Leitrim
& Roscommon

Often referred to as 'Lovely Leitrim', County Leitrim has a natural, untouched beauty, with rolling green hills and a lot of water: the Shannon-Erne Waterway and lakes including Lough Gill, Lough Allen and Glencar Lough. Most of the county is inland, so it tends to be overlooked by tourists sticking to the well-travelled coastal route, but those that do visit, perhaps to sail a houseboat down the River Shannon, benefit from the tranquil scenery. There's also a thriving artistic community, Leitrim long having been a haven for artists, musicians and filmmakers, and more recently, the county has become one of Ireland's more interesting eco-destinations.

County Roscommon has a number of wonderful attractions, mainly located in the green and pastoral north. At the very north of the county, bordering Leitrim, are the Arigna Mountains; most famous for the iron and coal mining that took place here until the 1990s, and now home to the Miners Way and the Arigna Mining Experience. Just south from here is delightful Lough Key Forest Park, followed by a collection of some of Ireland's best preserved archaeological sites, Rathcroghan/Cruachan.

NORTH LEITRIM

The north of the county is dominated by mountain ranges, while the border between Sligo and Leitrim runs through Lough Gill and Glencar Lough. Here are two of Leitrim's must-sees: Parke's Castle (*see p62*), on the eastern edge of beautiful Lough Gill, and the island of Innisfree, which can be seen from the castle. You can take a boat (071 916 4266, www.roseofinnisfree.com, closed Nov-Easter) from the castle around the lake, and over to the tiny isle of Innisfree, made famous by Yeats' poem: 'I will arise and go now, and go to Innisfree,/And a small cabin build there, of clay and wattles made'. The skipper recites Yeats' poetry as he guides you around the lake.

East of Parke's Castle, the road stays close to the lake and the views are worth stopping for. Slightly away from the lapping waters is the small town of Dromahair. A happy hour can be spent here wandering around Creevelea Abbey: the path to it starts from behind the Abbey Manor Hotel, crosses a small bridge and then runs beside the surging River Bonet. It is only five minutes to Creevelea Abbey, the last Franciscan friary to be established in the 16th century, and a peaceful and beautiful spot.

Dromahair is also one of the sites of a summer film festival: a mobile cinema, with room for 100 guests, pulls up in the main square. The festival is organised by Cinema North West (mobile 086 604 9365, www.cinemanorthwest.com) and takes place around Sligo and Leitrim.

A short drive north of Dromahair, on the other side of the N16, is pristine Glencar Lough, at the foot of the Dartry Mountains. Sharp limestone ridges tower

Glencar Waterfall. See p61.

above, while the sound of running water is never far away, as water cascades down the side of the mountain – spectacularly so in the case of 15-metre-high Glencar Waterfall. The waterfall is north of the lake, and is well signposted, with a car park at the lake's edge and a paved path through a small but pretty wooded area. Glencar is much visited by Yeats lovers wishing to see the inspiration for another of his poems, *The Stolen Child*: 'Where the wandering water gushes/From the hills above Glencar,/In pools above the rushes/ That scarce could bathe a star.'

From here, Manorhamilton, north Leitrim's largest town, lies about 15 kilometres east on the N16. The town is situated at the convergence of four mountain valleys, creating a dramatic setting. The steep limestone hillsides and narrow ravines provide superb mountain walking, yet, as with much of Leitrim, the area is relatively unexplored by visitors, its stark beauty and tranquillity remaining something of a secret. Manorhamilton itself is an artistic hub, with places such as the Leitrim Sculpture Centre (*see p62*), and the Glens Centre (New Line, 071 985 5833, www.theglens centre.com), which is housed in a converted church and runs an eclectic programme of music, theatre and films, plus workshops.

Presiding over the town are the ruins of the 17th-century Manorhamilton Castle (mobile 086 250 2593, www.manorhamiltoncastle.ie, open by appointment). It has recently been renovated and guided tours give an insight into the colourful history of this once-important stronghold.

Some 20 kilometres north of Manorhamilton along the R282 is Rossinver, a village known for the Organic Centre (071 985 4338, www.the organiccentre.ie, closed Sat, Sun Jan, Dec) – one of Ireland's finest. Roam the gardens, take part in a gardening class, sign up for a weekend workshop, browse the eco-shop (filled with seeds for planting and produce from the garden), or simply sit back and enjoy a coffee in the Grass Roof Café.

Just to the north is Lough Melvin ★, which straddles the border with Northern Ireland. One of Ireland's best spots for angling (notably early-run salmon and trout fishing), it is a Site of Special Scientific Interest (Northern Ireland) and an Area of Outstanding Natural Beauty (the Republic). To the south of the lake, the Dartry Mountains run parallel, forming a foreboding backdrop. Other than anglers and locals, and cyclists doing a circuit of the lake, Lough Melvin is undisturbed. Good starting points for walks include the villages of Garrison (across the border) and Kinlough on the western shore. There are stunning views along the R281 from Rossinver to Kinlough before the road climbs into the mountains, descending again towards the village. Along the way a sign for Rosclogher Castle lures you to the ruins of a 15th-century castle, situated on a small island just offshore. You can view the castle from an elevated field, from where the ruins of a small church and a ring fort are also visible.

Kinlough is a pretty village, with an attractive harbour that's popular with anglers looking for a day's fishing. Boats and boatmen can be arranged (071 984 1451, Mon-Fri only).

Ard Nahoo. See p65.

Places to visit

Parke's Castle

St George's Heritage & Visitor Centre
St Mary's Close, Carrick-on-Shannon (071 962 1757).
Open Summer 10.30am-4.30pm Wed-Sat. Winter
10.30am-4.30pm Wed-Fri. Tours €7; €3 reductions;
€10 family. No credit cards.
The visitor centre is adjacent to a restored church, in
which there is a display chronicling Leitrim's history.
The tour takes in the Workhouse Attic: a restored
boys' dormitory from the old workhouse, in which it
is reported that 1,896 died during the Great Famine.

ROSCOMMON

Arigna Mining Experience ★
Arigna (071 964 6466, www.arignamining
experience.ie). Open 10am-6pm daily. Admission
€10; free-€8 reductions; €20-€44 family.
This fascinating museum, crowning the hill overlooking
Lough Allen, is located in what was one of the area's
last working mines. The Experience gives a detailed
history of the industry and the area, and incorporates
a 45-minute tour into the pits. Equipped with a hard
hat, you trek through the dark, dank tunnels, led by
ex-miners. The tour is eerie and frightening, but also
educational and intriguing.

Cruachan Aí Heritage Centre
Tulsk (071 963 9268, www.rathcroghan.ie).
Open 9am-5pm Mon-Sat; by appointment Sun.
Admission €5.
Cruachan Aí Heritage Centre interprets the
Rathcroghan Complex, once the seat of the Kings
of Connacht and, according to legend, where Medb,
the warrior queen, had her palace, Cruachan. Ring
forts, standing stones and ruins of an ancient castle
have been excavated and studied over the years,
and while specific details are vague there is enough
to confirm the importance of Tulsk in both medieval
and legendary Ireland. The centre provides all the
information you need on the background and location
of the sites at Rathcroghan. Informative guided tours
are available with Mike Croghan (094 987 0580,
www.rathcroghantours.com), or from the centre itself.

Strokestown Park House & Famine Museum ★
Strokestown (071 963 3013, www.strokestownpark.
ie). Open Mid Mar-Oct 11am-6pm daily. Nov-mid Mar
11am-5pm daily. Tours Mid Mar-Oct noon, 2.30pm,
4pm daily. Nov-mid Mar 2.30pm daily. Admission (incl
tour) €12; €5-€11 reductions; €25 family.
This 18th-century Palladian mansion is surrounded
by stunning parkland. The admission price includes
a tour of the house (restored to its former glory) and
the splendid walled gardens (six acres, including the
longest herbaceous border in Ireland and the UK), as
well as entry to the Famine Museum, housed in the
old stables. Here, tenants' letters, photos and other
documents are used to portray the events of the Great
Famine not only in Strokestown, but also around
Ireland. Two million people (almost a quarter of the
country's population) died or emigrated between 1845
and 1850, when blight devastated the potato crop.
The Mahon family once owned the estate, and Major
Denis Mahon was murdered by locals enraged by his
cruelty to tenants during the famine.

NORTH LEITRIM

Leitrim Sculpture Centre
New Line, Manorhamilton (071 985 5098,
www.leitrimsculpturecentre.ie). Open 9am-5pm
Mon-Fri. Admission free.
This fine sculpture centre holds exhibitions of local,
national and international artists, while also running
workshops in almost every artistic area possible, from
glass-blowing, bronze-casting and ceramics to film,
photography and digital design.

Parke's Castle ★
Fivemile Bourne (071 916 4149, www.heritageireland.
ie). Open Mid Apr-Sept 10am-6pm daily. Admission
€3; €1-€2 reductions; €8 family. No credit cards.
On the eastern edge of Lough Gill, with views across
to the island of Innisfree, Parke's is a plantation
castle built in the early 17th century, though remnants
of an older moated tower house are still visible. The
castle has been nicely restored, using Irish timber
and period building techniques.

SOUTH LEITRIM

The Dock
St George's Terrace, Carrick-on-Shannon (071 965
0828, www.thedock.ie). Open Exhibitions 10am-6pm
Mon-Sat. Admission free.
Set within a 19th-century building that was once the
courthouse, the Dock is an exhibition and performance
space. See the website for details of forthcoming
music and comedy shows.

Arigna Mining Experience

Discover the best of Britain...

Where to eat & drink

North Leitrim does not have many great eating spots, but in every town and village there's a local pub serving the usual fare. The Grass Roof Café in Rossinver's Organic Centre (*see p61*) serves tasty snacks as well as tea and coffee.

Courthouse

Main Street, Kinlough (071 984 2391, www.the courthouserest.com). Lunch served 12.30-2.30pm Sun. Dinner served 6.30-9.30pm daily.
The Mediterranean menu and modern decor are a surprise in the tiny village of Kinlough. For starters , there's spicy king prawn bruschetta and goat's cheese tartlets; and pasta dishes include a delicious linguine di mare with clams and crab meat in a garlic, tomato and chilli sauce. There's also a paella, as well as pan-fried quail in a balsamic reduction and a choice of steak dishes. The Courthouse has four comfortable rooms (€74 double incl breakfast).

Lough Rynn. See p69.

Where to stay

Leitrim's best accommodation is generally in the south, but there are a number of options in the north. Self-catering accommodation can be found near Manorhamilton at the Mill (071 985 5566, www.themillglenboy.com), while, at Lough Melvin, there are hostel and campsite facilities at the Melvin Holiday Centre (048 6865 8142, www.melvinholidaycentre.com), just over the border in Fermanagh. At Tawley, west of Kinlough, Teapot Lane Luxury Camp (mobile 087 934 0341, www.teapotlaneluxurycamp.com) is an upmarket campsite offering a campfire and yurts with proper beds, as well as two self-catering cottages and a choice of holistic treaments that includes massages and reflexology. Treatments and massages are also available, alongside yoga retreats and workshops, at Ard Nahoo (071 913 4939, www.ardnahoo.com) near Dromahair, where accommodation is in well-equipped eco cabins.

SOUTH LEITRIM

In the heart of Leitrim, cradled between the peaks of the Arigna Mountains and Slieve Anierin, is Lough Allen ★. Dividing the county in two, Allen is the first of the three great lakes along the River Shannon's journey towards the sea. Unlike the north, south of Lough Allen the countryside is green and sprinkled with lakes and waterways. The Lough Allen Adventure Centre (*see p66*) is a great place for both water- and land-based activities.

The main town by the lake is Drumshanbo, at its southern tip. The town's vibrant artistic and musical community organises festivals such as the Written Word Weekend (http://writtenwordweekend. wordpress.com) and the wonderful Joe Mooney Summer School (www.joemooneysummerschool. com) – a festival of traditional music, dance and song, during the third week of July.

Information on walks (including the Miners Way, *see p66*) and other activities can be found at the Sliabh an Iarainn Visitor Centre, together with an exhibition on the history of the area. Drumshanbo

Things to do

Shannon-Erne Waterway

NORTH LEITRIM

Leitrim Way
This 48km route starts on the eastern shore of
Lough Allen and continues north, crossing mountains,
countryside and towns all the way to Manorhamilton.
It takes in some of the beautiful sights of Leitrim and
follows both old and new paths. Note that at the time
of going to press, the Leitrim Way was undergoing
renovation. You can download a brochure from
www.walkingwildireland.com, which has information on
this and other walks in Leitrim and north Roscommon.

SOUTH LEITRIM

Lough Allen Adventure Centre
*Cleighran Beg (071 964 3292, www.loughallen
adventure.com).*
An outdoor activities centre based on the eastern
shore of Lough Allen. Kayaking, canoeing, windsurfing
(it's pretty breezy on the lake – the surrounding
mountains create a tunnel effect and the winds
sweep through), hill walking and wilderness trails
are some of the possibilities.

Shannon-Erne Waterway ★
No trip to Leitrim is complete without a boat excursion
along Europe's longest navigable waterway. The
various pick-up and drop-off points run through
several counties, but Leitrim is one of the most
popular starting points. Trips can range from a day to
a couple of weeks, and you can stop off at riverside
towns along the way. Visit the website of the Inland
Waterways Association of Ireland (www.iwai.ie) for
information about boat hire and excursions.

ROSCOMMON

Miners Way & Historical Trail
071 966 3033, www.unabhan.net.
The Miners Way and Historical Trail are long-distance
waymarked walking trails passing through Leitrim,
Roscommon and Sligo. The two routes are 118km
long in total and can be completed over the course
of a week, though you can also split the walk into
stages, many of which can be done in a day. The walk
is being developed and upgraded, so paper maps
are currently out of print, but you can download maps
from the website, which also provides useful tourist
and accommodation information.

Lough Key Forest Park
*Nr Boyle (071 967 3122, www.loughkey.ie).
Open Apr-Aug 10am-6pm daily. Sept-Nov 10am-4pm
Sat, Sun. Admission €4 per car.*
Lough Key is 4.5km in length and 4km at its widest
point; to the south of the lake is this Forest Park. It's
popular with not only boaters and anglers, but also
walkers, families and nature lovers. The park was
once part of the Rockingham estate, owned by the
MacDermot clan. The family mansion was destroyed
by fire in 1957 – all that remains are the underground
tunnels once used by servants for entering the house.
There's a viewing platform, Moylurg Tower, on the site
of the house. The visitor centre provides headsets
for self-guided tours, which give the history of the
estate as well as the mythology of the area. You could
easily spend a day here, as there's so much to do,
including boat trips around the lough, fishing, forest
walking trails, tree canopy walks, and a café and shop.

is a popular starting point for cyclists circling the lake – much of the road stays close to the shore and, despite the surrounding mountainous terrain, is generally flat. Bikes can be hired at Moran's (Convent Avenue, 071 964 1974, www.morans motorcycles.com, closed Wed, Sun).

East of Drumshanbo the R208 heads through land studded with a series of small lakes and rolling hills to the quiet town of Ballinamore, five kilometres away. Work by local artists is on show at the Solas Gallery (Main Street, 071 964 4210, www.solasart.ie, closed Sun). Drumcoura Lake Resort & Equestrian Centre (Carrigallen Road, 071 964 5781, www.drumcoura.ie) offers plenty of activities – not only fishing, tennis, archery and boating, but also Western-style horse riding. A championship golf course – Slieve Russell Golf Club (049 952 5090, www.slieverussell.ie) in Cavan – is only a short drive east from here.

Carrick-on-Shannon, directly south of Lough Allen, is Leitrim's largest town. It bustles at weekends, when people descend to pick up a houseboat and head down the waterway for a few days. This is the main embarkation point for visitors, with plenty of boat companies to choose from, including Emerald Star (071 962 7633, www.emeraldstar.ie, closed Nov-Mar) and Carrick Craft (048 3834 4993, www.cruise-ireland.com, closed Nov-mid Mar). In summer, it's advisable to book in advance. The Tourist Information Centre (Old Barrel Store, 071 962 0170, www.carrickonshannon.ie, closed Oct-late May) by the bridge is the best place to get information and recommendations on the many options for boat trips and hire.

Attractions are few: the Dock performance space (*see p62*), St George's Heritage & Visitor Centre (*see p62*) and the quaint Costello Chapel on Bridge Street, built by Edward Costello in the 19th century. This is Europe's smallest chapel, and the second smallest in the world. Nevertheless, Carrick-on-Shannon is a lively spot, especially in summer when festivals include the Water Music Festival (www.carrickonshannonwatermusic.com) and the Regatta (www.carrickrowingclub.com), both in August, and the Carrick-on-Shannon Coarse Fishing Festival (071 962 0313) in September.

Where to eat & drink

There are plenty of cafés in the area and, of course, endless secluded spots where you can take a picnic. In Drumshanbo, Henry's Haven (Convent Avenue, 071 964 1805) serves wholesome meals.

Carrick-on-Shannon has a number of good restaurants, including the modern Italian restaurant and wine bar Vittos (Bridge Street, 071 962 7000, www.vittosrestaurant.com, closed Mon) and Victoria Hall (Quay Road, 071 962 0320, www.victoriahall.ie), a restaurant serving both Irish and Thai dishes, set in an old parochial hall. Carrick's bars are buzzing at weekends; Cryan's Bar (Bridge Street, 071 962 0409, www.cryanshotel.ie) is great for traditional music sessions and serves food all day. Fine dining can be found at the Lough Rynn hotel (*see p69*).

Oarsman Bar & Café

Bridge Street, Carrick-on-Shannon (071 962 1733, www.theoarsman.com). Open noon-11.30pm Tue-Thur; noon-12.30am Fri, Sat. Bar Food served noon-9.30pm Tue-Sat. Restaurant Dinner served 6.45-9.30pm Fri, Sat.
The bar at the Oarsman is a traditional one, with cosy seating and open fires, and an enticing bar menu listing the likes of seafood chowder and Irish beef burger. The upstairs

Oarsman Bar & Café

Colloney, Ballygawley, Ballintogher, Tullycooly, Tawnylea, Dowra, Slievenakilla, Glengavlen, Swa

Knockbeg, Toberscanavan, Tullynascreen, HERITAGE CENTRE, Drumkeeran, Corry, Bellavally Gap, Derrynac

Drummacool, Sligo Folk Pk., Corglass, Altagowlan, Drumnafinnila, Iron Mountains

Drumfin, Riverstown, Geevagh, Arigna Mining Experience, Arigna, Mountallen, Aghacashel, Aughnasheelan, Corraleehan

Ballymote, Cloonkeevy, Derry, Highwood, Ballyfarnon, Keadew, Drumshanbo, Drumcong, Keshcarrigan, Fenagh, Ballina

Castlebaldwin, Kash Corán, Kilmactranny, Leitrim, Glenview Folk Mus., Heritage Centre

Rathmullen, Kesh, Carrowkeel Megalithic Cemetery, Ballinafad, Carrigeenroe, Crossna, Knockvicar, Cootehall, Kilnagross, Garvagh

Killavil, Culfadda, King House, Lough Key Forest Park, Costello Chapel, Lisduff, Cloone

Gurteen, Mullaghroe, Cloonlogh, Boyle (Mainistir na Búille), Abbey, Carrick-on-Shannon (Cora Droma Rúisc), Mohill

Monasteraden, Ardmore, Caretown, Tullyboy Fm., Killukin, Jamestown, Drumsna, Cavan & Leitrim Railway

Edmondstown, Runnaroddan, Croghan, Canbo Lough, Clogher, Aghamore, Anna

Carrownurlar, Lurgan, Ballinameen, Hillstreet, Rodeen, Lough Boderg, Drumlish

Tibohine, Frenchpark, Elphin Windmill, Elphin, Drummullin, Dromod, Clooneagh

Moyne, Fairymount, Ballyroddy, Cruachan Aí Heritage Centre, Mantua, Cloonyquin, Strokestown Park House & Famine Museum, Roosky, Pipers Town, Leitrim

Loughglinn, Bellanagare, Gortnasillagh, Tulsk, Strokestown, Roscommon Heritage & Genealogy Centre, Whitehall, Newtown

Railway Museum, Clonalis House, Castlerea (An Caisleán Riabhach), Lissalway, Scramoge, Termonbarry, Cloondara, Longford (An Longfort)

Creggaslin, Castleplunket, Ballintober Castle, Tully, Lackan, Curraghroe, Stonepark

Ballinlough, Trien, Ballintober, Four Mile House, Ballymacurley, Aghamuck, Ballagh, Ballyleague, Lanesborough, Killashee

Ballymoe, Williamstown, Pollshask, Oran, Glinsk, Ballagh, Moneen, Corlea

Kilsallagh, Keeloges, Gortnadeeve, Creggs, Roscommon, Dunamon, Emmoo, Roscommon (Ros Comáin), Turreen, Otter & Wildlife Sanctuary

Cashel, Linbawn Lough, Castlecoote House, Fuerty, Passage, Ballymurry, Portrunny, Corlea Trackway Visitor Centre, Newtowncashel

Kilkerrin, Slievemurry, Toomard, Athleague, Suck Valley Visitor Centre, Scardaun, Clay Pipe Visitor Centre, Knockcroghery, Forthill, Foygh

Milltown, Ballygar, Mount Talbot, Rahara, Lismoyle, Ballagh, Lecarrow, Lough Ree, The Pigeo

Newbridge, Four Roads, Ballyforan, Curraghboy, Kiltoom, Yew Point, Hare Island, Ballynakill, Kilkenny West, Keenag

Ballynamore Bridge, Mountbellew, Ballyvoneen, Dysert, Derryglad Folk Museum, Glasson, Ballykeeran

restaurant has more of a contemporary feel, and a more complex menu, with dishes such as roast loin of Coopershill venison, served with shoulder sausage roll, parsnip purée, red onion marmalade and colcannon croquette.

Where to stay

If you want to stay close to Lough Allen, there's the contemporary Ramada Lough Allen Hotel & Spa (071 964 0100, www.ramadahotelleitrim.com) in Drumshanbo, or Riversdale Farm Guesthouse (071 964 4122, www.riversdale.biz) near Ballinamore, which has ten rooms and a heated pool.

South of here, it's mainly B&Bs, such as Coolabawnhouse (071 963 1033, www.coolabawn house.com) in Mohill; larger hotels can be found in Carrick-on-Shannon, which has some of the better options in the county. The imposing Landmark Hotel (Bridge Street, 071 962 2222, www.thelandmark hotel.com) is a popular choice, while Bush Hotel (Main Street, 071 967 1000, www.bushhotel.com) is a modest but comfortable abode. On the outskirts of town, lovely Hollywell Country House (Liberty Hill, 071 962 1124, closed Nov-Feb) has just four beautifully decorated bedrooms in an ivy-covered manor. The Mahers ensure a friendly welcome and serve delicious breakfasts.

For more B&Bs, try www.leitrimtourism.com.

Lough Rynn

Mohill (071 963 2700, www.loughrynn.ie).
Rates €129-€175 double incl breakfast.
A castle hotel set in 300 acres on the banks of Lough Rynn that seamlessly combines the traditional and the modern. On arrival there's the enticing smell of a turf fire; the palatial drawing room to the left of the entrance is a wonderful place to retreat with a book and drink – one of many lovely hideaways in the castle. There are 43 bedrooms in a more recent part of the building, all decorated in classic style with a modern twist. A glass walkway links to a contemporary function room where many a wedding takes place. Afternoon tea is served in the baronial hall; more serious meals in the Sandstone restaurant. The walled gardens and lake shore make for a glorious and peaceful stroll.

ROSCOMMON

The Arigna Mountains, lying west of Lough Allen, have been mined since the 15th century, when iron ore was extracted. In the 19th century, the focus turned to coal, which continued to be mined until the 1990s. The Miners Way & Historical Trail (*see p66*) is a great way to see the area, offering stunning views over the lake and the surrounding counties. The town of Arigna is not an attraction in itself, but it's worth visiting the Arigna Mining Experience (*see p62*), just to the north.

The scenic drive out of the mountains is on quiet, winding roads. Keadue is a pretty, traditional village with small, well-kept cottages, hanging flower baskets and a rich musical heritage. Every August, the ten-day O'Carolan International Harp Festival (www.ocarolanharpfestival.ie) celebrates Irish music and culture with performances and events, including workshops on how to play all manner of traditional instruments. The festival is named after the harpist Turlough O'Carolan; he's buried in the cemetery just outside the town, and a park in the centre of the village commemorates him.

Driving south for ten kilometres, you pass Lough Key Forest Park (*see p66* to arrive at Boyle, Roscommon's largest and liveliest town. Historical sites of note include King House (Main Street, 071 966 3242, www.kinghouse.ie, open Tue-Sat Apr-Sept), an 18th-century mansion that was once a military barracks and is now beautifully restored. It contains the Boyle Civic Collection of contemporary Irish painting and sculpture and, on the upper floors, an exhibition on the history of the building and its original owners, the Kingstons. It's also home to the Tourist Information Centre (071 966 2145, open Mon-Sat May-Aug).

Also worth seeing are the ruins of Boyle Abbey (071 966 2604, www.heritageireland.ie, closed Oct-Easter), a Cistercian abbey founded in 1161 next to the River Boyle. The restored 15th-century gatehouse has information on the site's history.

The Boyle Arts Festival (www.boylearts.com) runs for ten days in July and includes music, drama, theatre, poetry and children's events.

Burial mound at Rathcrogan. See p70.

FIVE LAKES

Lakes of Killarney
Killarney, Co Kerry.
Muckross, Upper Lake and Lough Leane
are three of Ireland's most romantic
and scenic lakes, drawing visitors to
the south-west of Ireland since Victorian
times. Set within Killarney National Park,
at the foot of the MacGillycuddy's Reeks
mountains, they're surrounded by lush
woodland – the area has a notably mild
climate. Boat trips are available to some
of the islands on the lakes. *See p109.*

Lough Corrib
Connemara, Co Galway.
Ireland's largest lake, covering 178sq km,
Lough Corrib sits mainly in Galway, but
also touches County Mayo. The clear
waters provide superb fishing, for salmon,
pike and especially brown trout. Cruising
around the lake – it's peppered with
hundreds of small islands – and to the
pretty shoreside village of Cong is a
wonderful way to spend an afternoon.
See p82.

Lough Gill
Border of Co Sligo & Co Leitrim.
Benbulben and Keelogyboy mountains
glower in the distance, while verdant
forest skirts the shores of Lough Gill.
The glistening waters captured the
heart of WB Yeats, who wrote *The Lake
Isle of Innisfree,* declaring his desire
to live on one of the tiny tree-covered
islands, where he believed 'I shall have
some peace there, for peace comes
dropping slow'. *See p52 and p59.*

Lough Melvin
Border of Co Leitrim & Northern Ireland.
This enchanting lake remains something
of a secret to those outside Leitrim.
The Dartry Mountains rise dramatically
to the south, and the still waters are
barely touched, except by a few lone
fishermen. The quiet lakeside road is
ideal for walking and cycling. *See p61.*

Lough Neagh
Northern Ireland.
The largest lake in Britain, measuring
over 300sq km, Lough Neagh laps
on to the shores of five of Northern
Ireland's six counties. It's home to
the largest commercial eel fishery in
Europe. Birdwatchers flock to watch
the 100,000 wildfowl that overwinter
here, anglers come for the plentiful fish
supply, and leisure boats take to the
waters in summer. Follow the lakeside
paths to enjoy spectacular views across
what looks like an ocean. There's plenty
of information on www.discoverlough
neagh.com. *See p289.*

Venturing south of Boyle along the N61, a short
detour to Frenchpark village leads you to the
Douglas Hyde Interpretative Centre (mobile
087 782 3751, open May-Sept by appointment).
The centre is dedicated to the academic who
devoted his life to the revival and protection of
Irish language and culture, and who became
Ireland's first president in 1938.

Continue along the N61 for another 15 kilometres
to reach the village of Tulsk, on the outskirts of
which are some of Ireland's most important
archeological sites. Visit the Cruachan Aí Heritage
Centre (*see p62*) in the village to glean essential
background information before exploring the
Rathcroghan Complex.

Eleven kilometres east of Tulsk, along the N5,
is Strokestown, notable for the Strokestown Park
House & Famine Museum (*see p62*) and for having
the second widest road in Ireland. The latter was
built by Strokestown Park's owners, the Mahon
family, in the 19th century, as a display of their
wealth and prestige; the wide, tree-lined avenue
linked the town to their estate. The Roscommon
County Heritage Centre (Church Street, 071 963
3380, www.roscommonroots.com, open Mon-Fri
Apr-Oct) provides a research service for those
investigating Roscommon roots.

Where to eat & drink
The coffee shop at the Arigna Mining Experience
(*see p62*) has spectacular views.

In Boyle, the Royal Hotel (Bridge Street, 071 966
2016, www.royalhotelboyle.com) has a traditional
restaurant with views over the river; a bar menu
is also served. For music and drinks, Clarke's
(St Patrick Street, 071 966 2064) is a good bet.

In addition, there are pleasant cafés at the
Cruachan Aí Heritage Centre (*see p62*) and
Strokestown Park House (*see p62*).

Where to stay
Boyle contains several B&Bs and the old-fashioned
but comfortable Royal Hotel (*see above*).

Lough Key Forest Park, a few kilometres east of
Boyle, has a caravan park and campsite (071 966
2212, www.loughkey.ie, closed Sept-Mar). For
something a little more luxurious, right next to the
entrance of the park is Lough Key House (071 966
2161, www.loughkeyhouse.com), a well-appointed
guesthouse with six charming rooms, generous
breakfasts and an open fire.

Kilronan Castle
Ballyfarnon (071 961 8000, www.kilronancastle.ie).
Rates €99-€185 double incl breakfast.
This restored 19th-century castle, set within 40 acres of
woodland near pretty Keadue, is sister hotel to Lough Rynn
(*see p69*) in south Leitrim. The public spaces, including a
lovely drawing room and restaurant, have been designed to
retain an old-world charm, while the spa is very modern.
There are 84 tastefully decorated bedrooms. The formal
restaurant provides an excellent breakfast – useful for those
heading for a day in the Arigna Mountains.

Counties Galway & Mayo

The west of Ireland is one of the country's most popular tourist destinations. These isolated and windswept lands have long attracted writers and artists seeking solitude and inspiration: JM Synge, Patrick Pearse and Heinrich Böll immersed themselves in the rural communities, beguiled by the way of life and the land's stark beauty. It comes, therefore, as no surprise that Galway City is now a hub for creative and artistic types, a city of art and festivals. Further west lies Connemara, Ireland's largest Gaeltacht region, where countless lakes, large and small, are set against the mountain ranges of Maam Turks and the Twelve Bens. The rugged coastline shelters a number of pretty seaside towns – it is here that visitors flock, not to the fertile, grassy flatlands of east Galway. Roundstone, Clifden and the Aran Islands are the summer playground for Dubliners in search of a rural retreat, and for tourists in search of the 'real Ireland'. While not as wild as it once was, Galway holds fast to its raw beauty and traditional ways.

North of Galway, lightly populated County Mayo combines rolling, green hills and attractive lakeside villages in the east with more barren, mountainous land in the west and north. The craggy coastline is dotted with countless islands, including Achill, Ireland's largest. Most visitors will not realise the immensity of the county until they drive from the harbour town of Westport to Achill Island and up to the prehistoric Céide Fields on the north coast. This is the main tourist trail, though Ballycroy National Park is also worth a stop. The towns in Mayo are rather functional, with the exception of picturesque Cong, next to Lough Corrib.

GALWAY CITY & AROUND

Galway City

Galway City has always had a bohemian reputation and an artistic and dynamic population, but in recent years it has taken on a more cosmopolitan edge. The presence of two major educational institutions give it a young, upbeat energy. Key attractions include music, art, theatre, a great nightlife scene and festivals too numerous to list. Highlights include the huge and internationally renowned extravaganza that is the Galway Arts Festival (www.galwayartsfestival.com), held over two weeks in July, and the Galway Jazz Festival (http://galwayjazzfest.com) and Tulca Festival of Visual Art (www.tulca.ie), both in November.

Sitting near the railway station and at the edge of the old city, expansive Eyre Square (also known as JF Kennedy Memorial Park) had a facelift a few years ago, resulting in manicured grass verges and a number of memorials, making it an attractive place to linger on a sunny day. The centrepiece is a striking fountain built in 1984 to celebrate the city's 500th anniversary. The fountain's copper-coloured sails represent a Galway Hooker – the old fishing boat synonymous with Galway Bay. Also standing here is the imposing Browne Doorway, which was removed from an old mansion in Abbeygate Street and bears the arms of the Browne and Lynch families from 1627.

On the south-east side is Eyre Square Shopping Centre, housing all the usual high-street shops.

Galway Tourist Office (091 537700, www.discover ireland.ie, closed Sun winter) is off the east side of the square, on Forster Street. In December, the square hosts a Christmas Market, selling food, drinks and gifts. The smell of cloves and cooking, twinkling fairy lights and seasonal songs will get you in a festive mood in no time.

The old part of the city, known as the Latin Quarter, consists of a maze of winding cobblestone streets and narrow passageways. It's here that you'll find the restaurants, bars and shops for which Galway is renowned. Shop Street, leading down to High Street and Quay Street, is the main thoroughfare.

Lynch's Castle on Shop Street isn't a castle, but an impressive 16th-century limestone mansion in Irish Gothic style. Once home to the Lynch family, the most prominent family in Galway for more than 200 years, it's now a bank. A display inside tells the history of the family and the house. Around the corner on Market Street is St Nicholas's Church. Built in 1320, it underwent further development in the 15th and 16th centuries; inside are a number of ornate tombs belonging to the Lynch family. Every Saturday morning the bustling Galway Farmers' Market, selling local crafts and food, is held outside the church. To the north, nestled up a small lane called Bowling Green, is Nora Barnacle House Museum (*see p76*), the childhood home of James Joyce's wife.

The remnants of a medieval building, believed to be the Red Earl's Hall, were discovered during

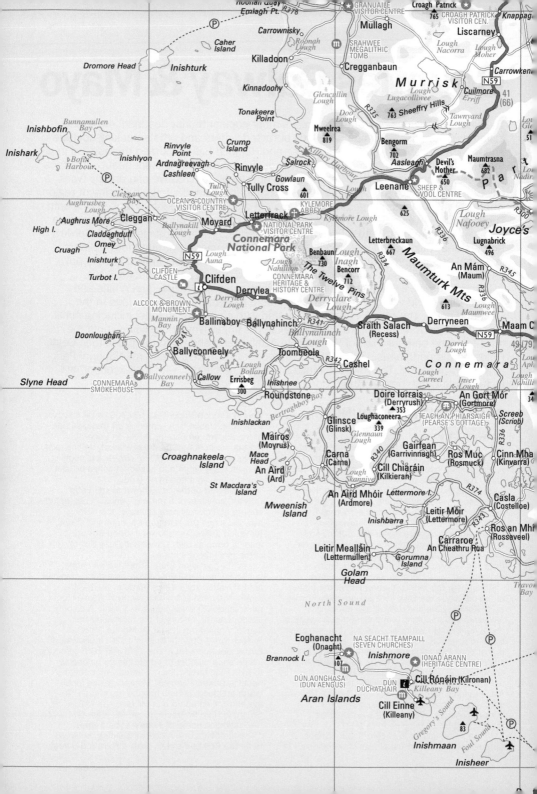

BEST GALWAY CITY NIGHTLIFE

Website www.galwaycitypubguide.com is a useful, up-to-date source of information on Galway City's huge array of pubs, bars and clubs.

Busker Brownes

Cross Street (091 563377, www. buskerbrownes.com). Open 10am-midnight daily.
A great pub containing three separate bars, all tastefully designed with bare stone walls, open fires and fashionable furnishings. The fairly priced food (sandwiches, sausages, steaks and seafood) is good quality, and the Sunday jazz brunch is always fun. Musicians or DJs play most nights.

Front Door

Cross Street (091 563757, www.front doorpub.com). Open 11am-2am daily.
A modern bar with a traditional feel, the Front Door is big, covering two floors and five bars, with Sonny's pizza restaurant next door. DJs play Wed-Sun, and the place is heaving at weekends.

Halo Nightcub

36 Upper Abbeygate Street (091 565976, www.halonightclub.com). Open 11pm-2am Fri, Sat. Admission €10.
One of Galway's best clubs, with four bars over two floors – though the dancefloor is on the small side. Extravagantly decked out, it's often busy with hen parties and large groups. Over-23s only.

Kelly's Bar

Bridge Street (091 563804, www.kellys bar.ie). Open 10.30am-11.30pm Mon-Thur; 10.30am-2.30am Fri, Sat; noon-11.30pm Sun.
Recently renovated Kelly's is an intimate spot, with snugs, booths and small seating areas downstairs, and great food (vegetarians do well here). The upstairs room hosts an eclectic mix of club nights, music and comedy.

Kings Head

15 High Street (091 566630, www. thekingshead.ie). Open 10.30am-11.30pm Mon-Thur; 10.30am-2am Thur-Sat; 11.30am-11pm Sun.
The rough stone walls, flagstone floor and fireplace dating from 1612 are evidence of this building's long life. It gets exceedingly busy, with music seven nights a week (plus comedy and theatre), and good-value food.

an excavation on Druid Lane, off Quay Street. The remains are protected behind glass and open to view. At the bottom of Quay Street is jeweller Thomas Dillon (091 566365, www.claddaghring.ie), established in 1750 and maker of the famous Claddagh ring, with its distinctive design of two hands holding a crown-topped heart. The ring originated in the ancient Claddagh fishing community that once lived along the nearby shore. Across the road to the left, beside the River Corrib, is the much-photographed Spanish Arch, dating from 1584 and originally an extension of the old city walls (it has nothing to do with Spain). Beyond it is the glass-fronted Galway City Museum (see p76), devoted to the history and heritage of the city.

The Latin Quarter is the best area for independent shops. There are plenty of designer-label fashion boutiques, such as Demora and the larger Brown Thomas, both on Cross Street. Twice as Nice, on Quay Street, sells a quirky mix of new, second-hand and vintage jewellery and clothing. Cobwebs on

Ard Bia at Nimmos. See p78.

Quay Lane specialises in (expensive) antique and modern jewellery, while Tempo Antiques on Cross Street has jewellery, porcelain and collectables. For more modern artefacts, try Judy Greene Pottery on Kirwan's Lane. Spread over three floors, it sells ceramic jewellery, pottery, clothing, sculptures and furniture, with a workshop on the top level.

Galway's theatres cater for most tastes. The Town Hall Theatre (091 569777, www.tht.ie) on Courthouse Square and the associated Black Box on Dyke Road present an eclectic mix of dance, musicals, films, plays and comedy throughout the year. The smaller Druid Lane Theatre is home to the long-running Druid theatre company (091 568660, www.druid.ie), which specialises in Irish classics and new writing. Information and tickets are available from the tourist office.

Galway Arts Centre (47 Dominick Street, 091 565886, www.galwayartscentre.ie) – located across the river in the West End district – presents monthly-changing exhibitions of contemporary art, from home and abroad. The centre also runs the

Galway City

Monroe's Tavern
Dominick Street (091 583397). Open 10am-11.30pm Mon-Thur; 10am-1am Fri, Sat; 10am-11pm Sun.
Bustling Monroe's Tavern has free gigs at 9pm most nights, offering a vast array of sounds, from blues to folk to rock to Irish dancing. Above is new Monroe's Live, where popular Irish bands and DJs attract the crowds after the pubs have closed.

Quays
11 Quay Street (091 568347, www.louisfitzgerald.com/quaysgalway). Open 10.30am-2am daily.
Behind a brightly coloured façade is an atmospheric labyrinth of rooms and booths, with floorboards, exposed beams and carved wooden archways. Traditional music sessions take place most nights in the ground-floor Old Bar; upstairs is the larger Music Hall, at its busiest in summer.

Roísín Dubh
Dominick Street (091 586540. www.roisindubh.net). Open varies; check website for details.
Galway's most renowned music venue. With three levels and an extensive, covered, rooftop smoking area, the bar gets packed with students and locals during the week and just about everybody at weekends. Live music – from electro to acoustic to DJs – is played nightly, and it's open until 2am.

Tigh Neachtain
17 Cross Street (091 568820, www.tighneachtain.com). Open 10.30am-11.30pm Mon-Thur, Sun; 10.30am-12.30am Fri, Sat.
One of Galway's oldest and most celebrated pubs, run by the Neachtain family since 1894. It's a charming, authentic spot, with friendly service, open turf fires and great live music sessions, especially on Sundays.

Places to visit

Kylemore Abbey

GALWAY CITY & AROUND

Galway City Museum

Behind the Spanish Arch, Galway City (091 532460, www.galwaycitymuseum.ie). Open Summer 10am-5pm Mon-Sat. Winter 10am-5pm Tue-Sat. Admission free.
The city museum moved to its modern new home in 2007. A variety of displays explore Galway's past, covering such subjects as the Claddagh fishing community, the medieval city and the traditional Galway Hooker sailing boat – a lovely example hangs in the atrium. The statue of a humble-looking fellow (which used to stand in Eyre Square) is of Padraic O'Conaire, a famous early 20th-century storyteller, who played an important role in the Irish-speaking community.

Nora Barnacle House Museum

Bowling Green, Galway City (091 564743) Open End May-mid Sept 10am-1pm; 2-5pm Tue-Sat. Admission €2.50; free-€2 reductions. No credit cards.
This tiny house was the Barnacle family home from 1894 to 1940; Nora Barnacle lived here until she left for Dublin in 1904, where she met and later married James Joyce. The two-room dwelling contains a collection of photographs, letters and other artefacts belonging to the couple. One can't help wonder how a family of seven managed to live in such a small space.

Portumna Castle & Gardens

Portumna (090 9741658, www.heritageireland.ie). Open Mid April-Sept 9.30am-6pm daily. Oct 9.30am-5pm Sat, Sun. Admission €3; €1-€2 reductions; €8 family. No credit cards.
An hour's drive east of Galway City, sitting pretty on the shore of Lough Derg, this impressive semi-fortified house was was the main seat of the de Burgo family for over 200 years. Built in the early 17th century, it

was destroyed by fire in the 1820s, then restored. You can visit the house and stroll the formal gardens and the walled kitchen garden, which has been planted with fruit trees, herbs and vegetables following the original 17th-century plan.

ARAN ISLANDS

Dun Aengus

Halfway along west coast of Inis Mór, Aran Islands.
The most famous of the Aran Islands' prehistoric forts, Dun Aengus is a magnificent sight, perched at the edge of a seacliff at the highest point on Inis Mór. It's semi-circular, with three concentric, terraced, drystone walls surrounding an inner enclosure. It's believed that people lived on the site from 1500 BC, though the fort was built circa 1100 BC. It was protected by *chevaux de frise* – razor-sharp stones dug into the ground, rising up almost 2m. The small visitor centre is a kilometre from the site, and is the only intrusion upon the landscape that has been made.

CONNEMARA

Connemara National Park

(095 41006, www.connemaranationalpark.ie). Open Visitor centre Mar-Oct 9am-5.30pm daily. Admission free.
Stretching from Letterfrack to the Twelve Ben mountains, Connemara National Park contains a diverse range of habitats including low-lying blanket bog, heaths covered in purple moor grass, and woodland. There's a loop of short, well-maintained walking trails, with the steep climb up Diamond Hill offering unforgettable views. Man-made remains include old turf banks, ruined houses, a 19th-century graveyard and, oldest of all, prehistoric court tombs. Look out for the resident herd of Connemara ponies.

Kylemore Abbey ★

Kylemore (www.kylemoreabbeytourism.ie). Open July, Aug 9am-7pm daily. Sept, Oct 9.30am-5.30pm daily. June 9am-6pm daily. Mar, Apr, Nov 10am-5pm daily. Dec 10am-4.30pm daily. Jan, Feb 11am-4.30pm daily. Admission Summer €12; free-€9 reductions; €32.50 family. Winter €9; free-€7 reductions; €25 family.

Nestled at the base of a wooded hill at the edge of a lake, stunningly located Kylemore Abbey is one of Connemara's most popular attractions. Built by Mitchell Henry for his new bride Margaret in the 1860s, the castle has a colourful and varied history. It was converted into an abbey by a community of Benedictine nuns in 1920, who restored the building and set up a girls' boarding school. That closed in 2010, though the nuns remain. The abbey, separate Gothic church, beautiful walled garden and grounds are open to the public. There's an intriguing display about the house's history and owners, as well as a craft shop and restaurant.

COUNTY MAYO

Ballycroy National Park

Ballycroy (098 49888, www.ballycroynationalpark.ie). Open visitor centre Mar-Oct 10am-5pm daily. Admission free.

This vast uninhabited wilderness, dominated by the remote Nelphin Beg mountain range, takes in one of the last intact Atlantic blanket bog areas in Ireland. There's plenty of wildlife to spot, from the rare golden plover to the common Irish hare, and walks aplenty, including the tough and isolated 29km Bangor Trail, which goes through the park following an old drovers' path from Bangor to Newport. The new visitor centre, with an information desk, nature trail and tearoom, is on the N59 in the village of Ballycroy.

Céide Fields ★

8km west of Ballycastle (096 43325, www.ceide fields.com). Open June-Sept 10am-6pm daily. Easter-May, Oct 10am-5pm daily. Admission €4; €2-€3 reuctions; €10 family. No credit cards.

The Céide Fields is the oldest intact field and farm system in the world. Preserved beneath the bog for over 5,000 years, the site was discovered in the 1930s by local schoolteacher Patrick Caulfield but only properly excavated 40 years later by his son, Seamus. It's a remarkably exposed and isolated place, at the edge of dramatic, 115m-high seacliffs. The westerly winds sweep across the fields and the sound of birds and crashing waves below are the only signs of life. There are guided tours around the stone-walled fields, and the visitor centre – a pyramid-shaped building that fits deftly into the landscape – explains the archaeological background as well as the natural history of the site. There are magnificent views from the rooftop platform.

Museum of Country Life ★

Turlough Park, Turlough (094 903 1755, www.museum.ie). Open 10am-5pm Tue-Sat; 2-5pm Sun. Admission free.

Opened in 2001, this impressive modern building is one of the four museums that make up the National Museum of Ireland, and is devoted to the history of rural life in Ireland from 1850 to 1950 (the others, in Dublin, cover the country's archeology, decorative arts and natural history). Spread over four floors, the museum is admirably comprehensive, looking at the political and social history of the period, agriculture and fishing, rural crafts, domestic life and folklore. Forget any idea of a romantic, rural idyll – for most people in the Irish countryside, life was nasty, brutish and short. Make a day of it: the exhibitions are well-laid out and informative, and green and lovely Turlough Park is tailor-made for picnics. The shop (selling crafts, textiles and books) and café are inside Turlough Park House, a grand Victorian residence; the drawing room and library are also open to visitors.

Westport House

Westport (098 27766, www.westporthouse.ie). Open House & gardens July, Aug 10am-7pm daily. Mid Apr-June 10am-6pm daily. Early Apr, Sept 10am-4pm daily. Dec 10am-6pm Sat, Sun. Mar, Oct 10am-4pm Sat, Sun. Nov 10am-4pm Sun. Pirate Adventure Park July, Aug noon-7pm daily. June 11am-6pm daily. Mid-late Apr 10am-6pm daily. May 11am-6pm Sun. Admission House, Gardens & Pirate Adventure Park €24; €16.50-€18 reductions; €17 family. House & gardens only €12; free-€8.50 reductions.

This large, handsome limestone mansion, set in parkland overlooking Clew Bay, was built in the 18th century on the ruins of a 16th-century castle belonging to notorious Irish pirate Grace O'Malley. It remains in the hands of her direct descendents, the Brownes. Adults may want to explore the house and gardens, but youngsters will inevitably head straight for the Pirate Adventure Park, equipped with slides, bouncy castles, flume rides, tennis courts, a pitch and putt course, and even camping facilities – all hidden neatly away out of immediate view.

Westport House

House Hotel

Nun's Island Theatre around the corner inside a converted church. If you're interested in buying some art, check out two small gallery-cum-shops – the long-established Kenny Gallery (091 709350, www.thekennygallery.ie) and the White Room Gallery (091 757699, www.whiteroom.ie). Both are located in Liosbaun retail park on Tuam Road on the city's outskirts.

Outside the city

Just to the south of the city is the bustling, noisy seaside resort of Salthill. In summer, Galwegians and tourists stroll the two-kilometre promenade, picnic and bathe at the beach (or the indoor Leisureland complex, if the weather's bad), or visit the aquarium, Galway Atlantaquaria (091 585100, www.nationalaquarium.ie). By night, revellers in their gladrags descend upon the many bars, discos and casinos dispersed along the streets.

Sixteen kilometres to the east is Clarenbridge, most famous for the three-day Clarenbridge Oyster Festival (www.clarenbridge.com) at the beginning of September. It's been running for more than 50 years and is the best place to sample some of Ireland's finest oysters.

Further south, Kinvara is a picturesque harbour town, teeming with leisure and fishing boats and backed by a row of colourful buildings. Overlooking the bay, perched dramatically on a rocky outcrop, is Dunguaire Castle (www.shannonheritage.com/attractions/dunguairecastle, closed Oct-Apr), a four-storey tower house dating from 1520. Oliver St John Gogarty, the famous Irish literary figure (and the model for Buck Mulligan in James Joyce's *Ulysses*), bought the property in 1924 and began restoring it. It became the meeting place for writers involved in the great revival of Celtic literature, including WB Yeats, JM Synge and George Bernard Shaw.

The Gathering of the Boats in August sees Galway Hookers with their rust-coloured sails racing across the bay, while traditional musicians descend on the village in May for the Cuckoo Festival.

Where to eat & drink

What Galway City may lack in major sights, it makes up for with great restaurants and bars. Most of the best cafés are located in the Latin Quarter. Revive Café (35 Eyre Street, 091 533779) is a bright spot with crêpes and cakes, while the lemon meringues at Goyas (091 567010, www.goyas.ie, closed Sun) on Kirwan's Lane look like works of art. McCambridge's (38-39 Shop Street, 091 562259, www.mccambridges.com) is an upmarket deli with olives, cheese, meat, fresh veg and lots of goodies.

And you can't visit Galway without popping into McDonagh's (22 Quay Street, 091 565001, www.mcdonaghs.net). Established in 1902, it serves the best fish and chips in town to eat in or take away.

Bars in the Latin Quarter are often traditional and cosy; cross over the river to Galway's West End for more modern choices. There are several notable restaurants, such as Oscars seafood bistro (Lower Dominick Street, 091 582180, closed Sun), but the area is known mainly for its nightlife (*see p74*).

Kinvara has plenty of good pubs and restaurants too. The Pier Head bar-restaurant (091 638188) is blessed with beautiful views over the bay and draws a big crowd, especially at weekends. The Pizza Café (091 638129) serves scrumptious pizza in a casual setting – a refreshing change from the fishy menus that you find everywhere else. Both are on the quay.

Ard Bia at Nimmos ★

Spanish Arch, Long Walk (091 539897, www.ardbia. com). Food served 9am-3.30pm, dinner served 6-10pm Tue-Sun.

Café by day, restaurant by night, Ard Bia has built an excellent reputation in the past few years. The look is eclectic chic – Laura Ashley wallpaper, Cath Kidston teapots, souvenirs from the owners' trips to Asia – and the atmosphere homely. Organic and local produce is used in the hearty, modern Irish dishes. The menu changes seasonally, as does the wine list, which includes organic wines sourced from small vineyards. Own-made chutneys, jams and breads can be bought to take home.

Artisan Restaurant

2 Quay Street (091 532655, www.artisangalway.com). Lunch served noon-3pm Fri, Sat. Dinner served 6-10pm daily.

Artisan specialises in imaginative Irish cuisine with a French twist. The use of local, seasonal produce (organic too, if possible) is admirable, as is the friendly service and intimate atmosphere. It's a good-looking spot, with dark wood tables and chairs, art on the walls and a quirky centrepiece on the bar.

Cava

51 Lower Dominick Street (091 539884, www.cavarestaurant.ie). Food served noon-10.30pm Mon-Wed, Sun; noon-midnight Thur-Sat.

Lovers of Spanish food won't be disappointed by Cava, where authentic, delicious tapas are served throughout the day, alongside an extensive, all-Spanish array of wines, beers, ciders and sherries. The weekend brunch menu includes Irish, Spanish and vegetarian breakfasts. The welcome is warm, and the atmosphere lively.

Martine's Wine Bar

21 Quay Street (091 565662, www.winebar.ie). Open 5-10pm Mon-Fri, Sun; 3-10.30pm Sat.

Martine McDonagh (the first woman in Ireland to open a wine bar) runs this friendly, laid-back venue. Inside, a small bar leads to two dining rooms, offering a tasty, fairly priced bistro-style menu. The pavement tables are the ideal people-watching spot come summer.

Where to stay

Low-cost accommodation includes the popular, 200-bed Sleepzone hostel (091 566999, www.sleepzone.ie), just off Eyre Square, and self-catering or B&B rooms at Galway University's Corrib Village (Newcastle Road, 091 527112, www.corribvillage.com) – outside the city centre and summer holidays only.

Mid-priced options include the bright, modern Harbour Hotel (New Dock Road, 091 894800, www.harbour.ie) overlooking the waterfront; the older but very comfortable Park House Hotel (Foster Street, 091 564924, www.parkhousehotel.ie); and reliable chain hotel Jurys Inn (091 566444, http://galwayhotels.jurysinns.com) on Quay Street. On the south side of Eyre Square is the four-star Hotel Meyrick (091 564041, www.hotelmeyrick.ie). Behind the formidable Victorian exterior is a modern establishment containing 97 rooms, assorted bars and restaurants, and a spa.

Most of the B&Bs are on the outskirts of the city, as is the five-star Glenlo Abbey Hotel (091 526666, www.glenlo.com), a historic residence with attached golf course, set on 138 acres of land near Lough Corrib.

G Hotel

Wellpark, Galway City (091 865200, www.theghotel.ie). Rates €140-€450 double incl breakfast.

Despite a somewhat obscure location on the outskirts of the city beside an industrial estate, the G Hotel is a glamorous five-star hotel. The ultra-modern interior – the creation of famous hat designer Philip Treacy, who was born in Galway – is flamboyant and eye-popping. Bright colours, wall-to-ceiling windows, velvet-lined seats and statement lighting await beyond the moodily dark reception area. The 114 bedrooms and suites are slightly more understated, and supremely elegant and comfortable. The spa is popular with locals at the weekend, as is the afternoon tea.

Heron's Rest

16 Long Walk, Galway City (091 539574, www.theheronsrest.com). Rates €130-€160 double incl breakfast.

Sorcha Molloy has converted her charming house into one of Galway's most popular B&Bs. It's centrally located but remarkably peaceful, with stunning views over the River Corrib. The six rooms are stylish and very comfortable. Renowned for her delicious, award-winning breakfasts and welcoming service, Sorcha has worked hard to ensure her guests experience a wonderful stay.

House Hotel

Lower Merchants Road, Galway City (091 538900, www.thehousehotel.ie). Rates €99-€165 double incl breakfast.

Quirky, welcoming and stylish sums up this boutique hotel near the Spanish Arch. The 40 rooms are swish and relaxing. A 'peckish' menu is served during the day and can be enjoyed in the lounge with its brightly coloured couches or in the restaurant, which has a reasonably priced bistro menu for dinner. The hotel is a popular spot for cocktails, with live music and a late bar at weekends. You can book into cocktail-making classes on a Saturday if you're eager to get the party started early.

Twelve Hotel

Bearna Village (091 597000, www.thetwelvehotel.ie). Rates €120-€185 double incl breakfast.

Located west of the city in the suburb of Bearna, the Twelve Hotel is named after the Twelve Bens mountains. Dark wooden floors, earthy tones and candles create a calming and elegant atmosphere. A similar look is followed in the 47 guest rooms, which offer luxury without the high price tag. The Pins bar-bistro specialises in gourmet pizzas, and there's also an in-house bakery. Traditional music sessions and jazz nights combined with delicious cocktails mean you may never want to leave.

ARAN ISLANDS ★

The Aran Islands – Inis Mór, Inis Meáin and Inis Oírr – are situated at the mouth of Galway Bay and are visible from both the Galway and Clare coasts. The islands' remoteness and starkly rugged landscape have lured travellers for years, and they remain relatively untouched by the passage of time, particularly Inis Meáin. The islanders continue to make their living from the land and sea, although these days tourism is also crucial to the economy. The main language spoken is Irish, and traditional crafts – woven baskets and, most famously, knitted Aran sweaters – still thrive.

The karst limestone landscape, although flat and desolate, has a windswept beauty, and a huge number of wild flowers manage to survive the harsh terrain and often grim weather. Scattered across the islands are pre-Christian, early Christian and Celtic mythological monuments, including seven forts, some believed to date from 1100 BC.

In summer, ferries transport thousands of visitors from the mainland, primarily to Inis Mór. Aran Island Ferries (091 568903, www.aranislandferries.com) operates year round from Rossaveal (an hour west of Galway City), but there are also seasonal services from Doolin in County Clare. You can also fly from Connemara Airport with Aer Arann (091 593034, www.aerarannislands.ie).

Furthest from the mainland, Inis Mór is also the largest of the islands (the name means Big Island) with around 900 inhabitants. Kilronan, the main settlement and where the ferry docks, has developed significantly in response to the increasing number of visitors. The facilities here are the best out of the three islands, with good hotels, B&Bs, hostels, campsites, bars and restaurants. The tourist office (099 61263, closed Mon, Sun Sept-Mar) is next to the pier. The Inis Mór Way – a 50-kilometre signposted route around the island – can be tackled on foot, or by bike (from Aran Bicycle Hire). The less energetic can take a guided tour by minibus or traditional horse and cart. The main sight is Dun Aengus (*see p76*), a prehistoric ring fort balancing precariously above the steep sea cliffs on the island's western edge.

Inis Meáin (Middle Island) is less visited than Inis Mór, but no less beautiful. Sandy coves sit beneath weather-beaten sea cliffs; green fields pocket the limestone terrain; and stone walls criss-cross the land like necklaces. It's the least populated island, with only 200 or so residents, and has attracted many artists over the years. JM Synge spent time here at the turn of the 20th century, living the life of the people and gathering material for his plays and stories. Teach Synge (099 73036, closed Oct-May), the 300-year-old cottage where he lived, and was visited by WB Yeats, Lady Gregory and Patrick Pearse, is open to the public in summer. Just up the road is the impressive fifth-century fort of Dún Conchúir. The Inis Meáin Way, an eight-kilometre walking circuit of the island, takes in most of the sights.

Inis Oírr (East Island) is the smallest of the trio, only three kilometres by three kilometres, and perhaps the least intriguing, though it does have a lovely beach east of the pier on the north coast, around which most of the activity on the island takes place. The Inis Oírr Co-operative (099 75008, closed Sat, Sun) can provide information, and maps of the ten-kilometre circular Inis Oírr Way.

Where to eat & drink

On Inis Mór, O'Malley's at Bay View (099 61041, www.bayviewaran.com, closed Nov-Jan) is a welcome sight near Kilronan pier, a modern wine and tapas bar. It's owned by the same brothers who run the very fine Pier House restaurant (099 61417, www.pierhouserestaurant.com, closed Oct-Easter). Tigh Fitz's and Joe Watty's are popular watering holes at night.

The stylish dining room at Inis Meáin Restaurant & Suites (*see below*) specialises in local seafood, especially lobster and crayfish, and island-grown vegetables. It's open for dinner only, in summer.

Fisherman's Cottage
Inis Oírr (099 75073, www.southaran.com). Open Apr-Oct. Lunch served 10am-3pm, dinner served 7-9.30pm daily.
This casual restaurant inside a pretty white cottage has much in common with the Slow Food movement. Dishes are healthy and tasty, and many of the ingredients – fish, lamb and vegetables – come from the Aran Islands. The owners also offer yoga, kayaking, cookery and language classes, and accommodation at South Aran House (*see below*).

Where to stay

The Aran Islands Hotel (087 121 2036 mobile, www.aranislandshotel.com, closed Nov-Jan, Mon-Fri Mar, Apr) is the most modern hotel on Inis Mór, yet with only 22 bedrooms has a homely feel. Pier House Guest House (099 61417, www.pierhouse aran.com, closed Nov-March) is located right by the pier – you can hop off the boat and through the front door in seconds. Also near the pier, located above popular bar Tigh Jo Mac, Kilronan Hostel (099 61255, www.kilronanhostel.com) has en-suite dorms sleeping four, five or six.

On Inis Meáin, halfway along the island near Dún Conchúir fort, is Kilmurvey House (099 61218, www.kilmurveyhouse.com, closed Nov-Easter), a 150-year-old stone building with 12 en-suite rooms.

There's only one hotel on Inis Oírr, Ostan Inis Oírr (099 75020, closed Oct-mid Mar), but there are a number of B&Bs. One of the best is South Aran House (099 75073, www.southaran.com, closed Nov-Mar), situated at the south of the island.

Inis Meáin Restaurant & Suites
Inis Meáin (mobile 086 826 6026, www.inismeain.com). Rates €250-€350 suite incl breakfast.
Inis Meáin native Ruairí de Blacam and his Cork-born wife Marie-Thérèse have created the most stylish place to stay on the islands. The striking, cut-stone building blends beautifully into the landscape, despite being ultra-modern. There are four suites and one huge apartment suite (all designed for two), simply decorated in natural colours and materials, and with marvellous views. Breakfast is delivered to each suite, and bikes and fishing rods are also provided. The on-site restaurant is open for dinner only (Apr-Oct). The family also runs an upmarket knitwear company, with a shop on the island.

Man of Aran Cottage
Inis Mór (099 61301, www.manofarancottage.com). Open Mar-Oct. Rates €80-€90 double incl breakfast. No credit cards.
The 1934 docu-drama *The Man of Aran* was filmed at this thatched cottage, tucked next to Kilmurvey Beach and surrounded by a surprisingly luxuriant garden. Joe and Maura Wolfe are marvellous hosts; Joe grows organic veg to feed the guests, while Maura is a fantastic chef (and has worked at Buckingham Palace). The three rooms are small, but authentic and charming.

Inis Mór

CONNEMARA

Oughterard & Roundstone

Jutting out into the Atlantic, west of Galway City, Connemara is dotted with countless loughs, too many even to have all been named. Barren bogland sprawls beneath the towering Maam Turks and Twelve Bens, which dominate the skyline. The region has always been lightly populated and its isolation has helped protect its rich culture and Ireland's largest Irish-speaking area. The seaside towns are extremely popular holiday destinations – for visitors from the east coast or coachloads of daytrippers – and are rather overrun with holiday home developments. But driving along the winding roads, through the boglands in the shadow of the mountains, it's easy to see why the region's remoteness and wild beauty has attracted so many.

Oughterard, less than 30 kilometres from Galway City, is the main centre for those wanting to explore Lough Corrib, Ireland's largest lake. The main street has dozens of angling shops, as well as the tourist office (091 552808, www.connemarabegins.com, closed Sat, Sun winter), which can provide information on the best fishing, picnicking and boating spots. The lough contains more than 300 islands, the largest of which, Inchagoill, has 12th- and 13th-century monastic ruins. Corrib Tours (091 592447, www.corribprincess.ie, closed Nov-Mar) runs boat trips from Galway City along the River Corrib to the lough, while Corrib Cruises (091 557798, www.corribcruises.com) operates between Oughterard, Inchagoill and Ashford Castle on the northern shore.

Nearby attractions include Brigit's Garden (091 550905, www.brigitsgarden.ie, closed Nov-Jan, Sat Feb, Mar, Oct) in Roscahill. The Celtic-inspired gardens are great for families, with fairy hills, forts and crannógs (artificial islands) to amuse the youngsters, while the lovely tearoom will keep the adults happy. A short drive away is Aughnanure Castle (091 552214, www.heritageireland.ie, closed Nov-Mar), a well-preserved example of an Irish tower house, built around 1500. It sits on the edge of a river and is approached via a wooded pathway and a drawbridge. The recently restored Glengowla Mines (091 552360, http://glengowla.goegi.com. closed Nov-mid Mar) offer a change of scene from lakes and castles. Lead and silver were mined here until 1865; the tour goes underground to explore marble chambers and caverns studded with precious minerals.

At Maam Cross, 16 kilometres west along the main N59, you can cut north along the R336 into the interior of Connemara for a bleak, but strangely beautiful drive to Leenane. Alternatively, if the jagged coast – trimmed with white sand beaches, deep inlets and quaint seaside hamlets – appeals, then continue along the N59 towards Clifden. Joyce's Craft Shop (095 34658) is a popular stop-off at Recess. Established in 1928, the shop sells a broad selection of Irish-made crafts, clothes, pottery and other products.

A left turn on to the R341 leads to the pretty and deservedly acclaimed fishing village of Roundstone ★. Tucked in at the base of Errisbeg Mountain, it has colourful terraced houses and a picturesque harbour with views over beautiful Bertraghboy Bay. It's a wonderful base from which to explore the Connemara coast, including two lovely beaches at Dog's Bay and Gurteen Bay. There are a couple of hotels and a surprising number of quality craft shops for such a small village, as well as several bars and places serving freshly caught fish. Annual events include the Roundstone Connemara Pony Fair and the Regatta (www.roundstoneregatta.com), both in July.

Ballyconneely, a 15-minute drive west around the coast, lacks the facilities of Roundstone, but has just as much charm and beauty. A tranquil spot, it's said to be the home of the Connemara pony;

you can go trekking along the sand with the Point Pony Trekking & Horse Riding Centre (087 246 8294 mobile, www.thepointpony trekkingcentre.com). The beaches are good for bathing and fishing. For top-quality, traditionally smoked fish, visit the family-run Connemara Smoke House (095 23739, www.smokehouse.ie, closed Sat, Sun). It's situated at the very tip of west Connemara, by Bunowen Pier.

Clifden to Leenane

Sitting at the edge of the ocean beneath the Twelve Bens mountain range, Clifden is the largest town in Connemara. Main Street is crammed with shops, restaurants and cafés. The Clifden Bookshop (095 22020, www.clifdenbookshop.com, closed Sun Nov, Jan) specialises in local history, guides and maps, while the Whitehorn Gallery (095 30703, www.thewhitethorngallery.ie, closed Jan, Feb) and the Lavelle Art Gallery (095 21882 mobile, www.connemara.net/lavelleartgallery) both exhibit and sell work by local artists and have some beautiful pieces. On Market Street, Prendergast Antiques (087 629 6195 mobile, www.clifden.biz) is a small, quirky shop that's worth a browse. The old railway station is now a hotel with a courtyard containing the Station House Museum (095 21699, closed Oct-Mar), devoted to the history of the Connemara pony, and a collection of small boutiques, the best of which is Ohh! By Gum (095 21334, closed Jan, Sun winter), selling old-style sweets and unusual, organic and Fairtrade fashion.

An eight-kilometre bike trail runs south from town to the Connemara History & Heritage Centre (095 21808, www.connemaraheritage.com, closed Nov-Mar), where Dan O'Hara's Homestead provides an insight into 19th-century farming life. There is a craft shop and a restaurant on site too. You can also cycle the spectacular Sky Road, a signposted 13-kilometre loop north of town, with panoramic views across the island-studded coastline. The road is narrow and winding and gets very busy with cars in summer, so care should be taken. Bicycles can be rented from John Mannion's on Bridge Street. The Clifden Arts Festival (www.clifdenartsweek.ie), a week-long event in September featuring theatre, music and dance, is well worth attending.

A short drive north, off the N59, is the fishing village of Cleggan, where you can catch a boat over to the island of Inishbofin (see p85), a scenic little place with good facilities for visitors. The N59 continues to the main entrance and visitor centre for Connemara National Park (see p76). Many people walk through the stunning forests to picturesque Kylemore Abbey (see p77). Between the two is the small village of Letterfrack, whose main attraction is a branch of Avoca (095 41058, www.avoca.ie), a very popular Irish chain selling crafts, gifts, clothes and household items.

Just north of Letterfrack is the Ocean & Country Visitor Centre (095 43473, closed Nov-Mar), on the edge of Ballinakill Bay. There's a maritime museum and a café, plus fishing and scenic boat trips. Nearby is Tully Hill, which can be climbed in

under three hours; the reward is stunning views across Renvyle peninsula. Driving along the small, bumpy roads offers fine views out to the islands. There are some lovely stretches of beach – perfect for swimming – several of which have caravan and camping sites.

From Kylemore Abbey, the N59 climbs steeply, eventually opening up to what must be Connemara's most beautiful view: Killary Harbour, Irelands only fjord. Here, the sea weaves a narrow route around the sheer seacliffs of Mweelrea, the region's highest mountains, topping out at 819 metres. The black water cuts inland for 16 kilometres, forming a natural divide between Galway and Mayo counties. You can view the ominous cliffs from below with Killary Cruises (091 566736, www.killarycruises.com, Apr-Oct); boats leave from Nancy's Point, just west of Leenane.

Killary Adventure Centre (095 43411, www.killaryadventure.com), located on the top of the hill before the village, organises activities for young and old, from kayaking to bungee jumping, and also has decent accommodation. There's not much to the sleepy village of Leenane, except for its heavenly location. The drive in and out of the village is an awe-inspiring sight.

Where to eat & drink

No matter how small the village, you should find a cosy, traditional pub in which to enjoy a drink and most likely a wholesome bowl of soup and some sort of fish dish. Local mussels, oysters and fresh fish appear frequently.

Clifden has a range of good restaurants, being a tourist hotspot. Mularkey's Bar inside Foyles Hotel (095 21801, www.foyleshotel.com) on Main Street is an excellent venue for live music.

Connemara Hamper

Market Street, Clifden (095 21054, www.connemara hamper.com). Open Jan, Feb 10am-5pm Thur-Sat. Mar-Dec 10am-5.30pm Mon-Sat.
A fantastic deli selling own-made chutneys and jams, plus breads, cakes, Irish cheeses, pâtés and wines. Most products are sourced in and around the region. The perfect place to stock up for a gourmet picnic.

Kylemore Abbey Mitchell Café

Kylemore (095 41146, www.kylemoreabbeytourism.ie). Open Summer 9.30am-5.30pm Mon-Fri; 9.30am-6pm Sat, Sun. Winter 10am-4.30pm daily.
Under the watchful eye of the nuns, Kylemore's café has grown from a small teahouse to a spacious, bright and heaving eaterie serving a wide range of dishes, salads and sandwiches made from fresh. There's also a tearoom in the walled garden, open May-Sept.

Mitchell's Restaurant

Market Street, Clifden (095 21867). Food served Mid Mar-Oct noon-10pm daily.
Mitchell's (20 years old in 2011) is an informal spot for lunch, with wraps, sandwiches and chowder. Dinner is a convivial affair, featuring consistently good, homely dishes – naturally, the seafood is a highlight.

O'Dowd's Seafood Bar & Restaurant
*Roundstone (095 35809, www.odowdsbar.com). Open
Bar 10am-midnight daily. Food served Restaurant
10am-10pm daily.*
Run by the O'Dowd family for almost a century, this is one
of Roundstone's most popular and traditional bars, with
wonderful harbour views. The well-priced menu is noted for
its sumptuous fish dishes, such as Aran Bay prawns in
garlic butter and seafood chowder. A similar menu is served
in the slightly more formal restaurant next door.

Where to stay
Despite its relative isolation and rural nature,
Connemara is well supplied with accommodation,
especially B&Bs – check www.connemara
accommodation.com.

The Oughterard area has no shortage of options.
Lovely places overlooking the lough include the
small Victorian manor Currarevagh House (091
552312, www.currarevagh.com, closed mid Oct-
mid Mar), which has just 12 bedrooms and serves
fantastic meals. Further south, near Roscahill,
is elegant Ross Lake House Hotel (091 550109,
www.rosslakehotel.com, closed Nov-mid Mar).

Emlaghmore Lodge (095 23529,
www.emlaghmore.com, closed Nov-Easter) lies
between Roundstone and the Connemara Golf
Club just outside Ballyconneely. A modest house
with three bedrooms, it's idyllically situated on
conservation land with a little stream running
through the garden.

Clifden has numerous hotels and B&Bs, many of
the latter on the Sky Road. Best is the wonderful
Dolphin Beach House (095 21204, www.dolphin
beachhouse.com, closed Nov-mid Feb), run by the
industrious Foyle family, who own many hotels in
the area. There are also several very upmarket
options. Abbeyglen Castle Hotel (095 21201,
www.abbeyglen.ie, closed Jan) sits into the hillside
on the Sky Road overlooking Clifden. Beautiful
grounds, complimentary afternoon tea, wonderful
service and the in-house parrot make it a charming
place to stay. A 15-minute drive east of Clifden,
four-star Ballynahinch Castle Hotel (095 31006,
www.ballynahinch-castle.com, closed Feb) has a
truly stunning location overlooking the Ballynahinch
River, a renowned salmon fishery. The hotel is
surrounded by 350 acres of wooded land with
wonderful walks on its doorstep and, of course,
superb fly fishing.

Budget travellers should head to Sleepzone (095
42929, www.sleepzone.ie, closed Mon-Fri Nov-Feb),
a well-established hostel near Killary Adventure
Centre, with 100 beds in private rooms and dorms.

Anglers Return
*Toombeola, Roundstone (095 31091, www.anglers
return.com). Open Mar-Nov. Rates from €90 double
incl breakfast. No credit cards.*
This charming 18th-century house a few kilometres outside
Roundstone was built as a sporting lodge, but its new life
as a B&B appears prosperous. It's very popular with fishing
enthusiasts, painters and those looking for an informal and
restorative place to stay. The five rooms are comfortable,
although not all are en suite.

Cashel House Hotel ★
*Cashel (095 31001, www.cashel-house-hotel.com).
Open Feb-Dec. Rates €150-€190 double incl breakfast.*
The McEvilly family were one of the first to open a country
house hotel in Ireland, back in 1968. The 19th-century
building, furnished in a cosy, old-fashioned manner, is set
in 50 acres of gorgeous gardens and woodland at the head

Ashford Castle. See p89.

Things to do

CONNEMARA

Inishbofin

Located 10km off the western tip of Connemara, Inishbofin ('Island of the white cow') makes a perfect daytrip. Ferries (095 44878, www.inishbofin islanddiscovery.com) take half an hour to reach the island from Cleggan harbour, a 15-minute drive from Clifden. The 8km-by-5km island is easily explored on foot or by bike (which can be hired at the pier). The west side is dominated by a jagged rocky outcrop called the Stags, while the centre cradles swan-filled Lough Bofin. There are small, pretty coves with sandy beaches – ideal for swimming, snorkelling and diving – plus plenty of birdlife (including the rare corncrake) and seals. there's a hostel, three hotels and assorted B&Bs. Details on the useful website www.inishbofin.com.

COUNTY MAYO

Clare Island & Inishturk

Sitting at the mouth of Clew Bay, mountainous Clare Island is a striking sight from the mainland. The resident population of 130 swells in summer, when visitors arrive by the ferryload from Roonagh Quay – it's only a 20-minute trip (098 23737, www.clareislandferry.com; 098 25045, www.omalley ferries.com). A manageable 8km by 5km, the island offers a post office-cum-shop, a community centre, a few eating options and assorted B&Bs – though many places are open only between June several September. There's good walking and cycling and some historic sights, including a Cistercian abbey with medieval wall paintings, and a 16th-century tower house that was once the home of pirate queen Grace O'Malley. Prehistoric remains scatter the craggy landscape, and the spectacular seacliffs on the north and west attract a huge variety of birds. Next to the harbour is a large sandy beach with Blue Flag status.

Ferries also run to Inishturk, midway between Clare Island and Inishbofin. It's tiny, just 5km by 2.5km, with a population of 65, a couple of B&Bs and one shop – though they manage to hold a traditional music festival in June and a regatta in August. There are a couple of sandy swimming beaches and a few historical ruins.

Croagh Patrick

Murrisk (098 64114 visitor centre, www.museums ofmayo.com/croaghpatrick.htm).

Famous for its annual pilgrimage on the last Sunday of July ('Reek Sunday'), when thousands of penitents climb the hill barefoot, this 754m mountain is said to have been where St Patrick fasted for 40 days in 441. Legend says that it was from the south side that he threw all the snakes, thereby ridding Ireland of the creatures for good. The visitor centre on the R335 at the base of the mountain provides all the information needed for the ascent, and also has a cafeteria and shop. The walk takes about three and a half hours there and back; while a moderate climb in general, it is very steep in parts and the ground is extremely rocky. It's advisable to wear solid footwear and warm clothing (weather conditions can change quickly) and to carry a stick and mobile phone. There's a statue of St Patrick en route, and a small chapel at the top.

Great Western Greenway

www.discoverireland.ie/great-western-greenway.aspx.

This traffic-free cycling and walking trail runs for 18km along the northern edge of Clew Bay, mainly following the disused Newport-Mulrany railway line. You can hire bikes, including child trailers and tagalongs, from Newport Bicycle (098 42900, www.newport-bicycle.com) on the Westport Road on the edge of Newport. Extensions to either end of the trail (from Westport and Newport, and from Mulrany to Achill Island) should be completed by the end of 2011.

Enthusiasts can also tackle six loop bike routes, ranging in length from 12km to 44km – three around Achill Island and three around Westport. The Discover Ireland website has downloadable maps, but the routes are well signposted.

River Moy

Co Mayo (www.rivermoy.com).

The River Moy is the most productive salmon fishery in western Europe, with anglers coming from all over to fish in the area. Many local hotels provide fishing packages that include equipment hire, permits and guides. The northern Mayo towns of Ballina and Foxford are the most popular bases for visitors, but there are numerous beautiful and peaceful fishing spots.

---

of Cashel Bay, with its own private beach. Food is top-quality; the lavish breakfasts are well worth getting up for. With only 30 rooms, this place feels like a home away from home. The McEvillys also offer gardening courses and run a Connemara pony stud farm.

Quay House

Beach Road, Clifden (095 21369, www.thequayhouse. com). Open Apr-Oct. Rates from €125 double incl breakfast.

The oldest building in Clifden, the Quay House (c1820) is located away from the hustle and bustle of the town, next to the harbour. It's been run as a hotel by the Foyles for nearly 30 years. The 14 rooms – almost all with harbour views – differ in decor. Most contain period furniture, gilt-edged mirrors and four-poster beds; others are more modern with 'African' or 'parrot' themes. Breakfast (possibly the best in Connemara) is served in the conservatory surrounded by palm trees, flowers and creepers.

Rosleague Manor

Letterfrack (095 41101, www.rosleague.com). Open Easter-Oct. Rates €140-€210 double incl breakfast.

A 200-year-old, pink-painted Regency house with superb views over Ballinakill Bay, Rosleague (also part of the Foyle family empire) offers the intimate atmosphere of a country house, but without any stuffiness – it feels like staying at the home of a wealthy relative. Great food served in the brightly painted dining room, followed by a nightcap on the lawn, or in the conservatory or drawing room, makes for the perfect evening. The 20 rooms vary in design, but most are very spacious with period furnishings.

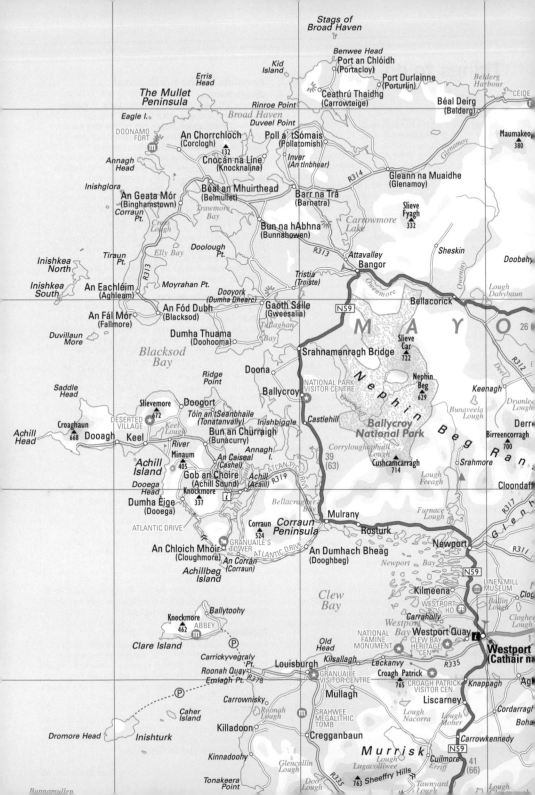

COUNTY MAYO

Leenane to the north coast

From Leenane, it's worth resisting the N59 and turning left on to the R335 to Louisberg. Hugging the edge of the still, dark water of Killaray Harbour (look for the salmon nets), the road moves inland after a couple of kilometres. It then weaves between the majestic Mweelrea massif and the Sheefry Hills, passing mirror-like lakes and small cascading waterfalls. The surrounding bogland is dotted with roaming sheep, birds wheel overhead, and the stillness is breathtaking.

The small town of Louisberg has little to hold you, although boat trips to Clare Island and Inishturk (see p85) depart from Roonagh Quay, a few minutes west of the town. Surf Mayo (087 621 2508, www.surfmayo.com) on Bridge Street can arrange surfing lessons on a local beach. Unpretentious Hudson's Pantry (Long Street, 098 23747, open Thur-Sat, other times vary) in the centre of town is a fine spot for lunch, with a menu that embraces international flavours and local seafood.

The road from Louisberg to Westport passes the famous holy mountain of Croagh Patrick (see p85), one of the most important Catholic pilgrimage destinations in Ireland. Opposite the visitor centre is the An Górta Mór monument, commemorating the millions who died or emigrated during the Great Famine of 1845-49. Designed by Irish artist John Behan, it's a bronze sculpture of a coffin ship, with eerie skeletons floating beside the sails. Below is ruined 15th-century Murrisk Abbey (the traditional starting point for the Croagh Patrick pilgrimage), offering wide-open views over Clew Bay. The bay is studded with what looks like the humped green backs of whales – in fact, they are half-submerged glacial hills, known as drumlins – and is a formidable sight as you descend the road towards Westport.

There are two parts to Westport: the more picturesque end by the harbour, and the main town centre, which lies slightly inland along the Carrowbeg River. The two are connected by a road lined with B&Bs. It's neat and trim place, the streets packed with shops, cafés, restaurants and more pubs than you could care to count. The town positively buzzes in summer, but continues to attract visitors throughout the winter, mainly for the nightlife. Clew Bay Heritage Centre (098 26852, closed Sat July, Aug; Sat, Sun Jan-June, Aug-Dec) near the harbour is devoted to the history of the area, with a small collection of objects and photos. Families should head to Westport House (see p77), which combines the attractions of a stately home with a theme park.

If you're interested in rural history, venture east on the N5 to Turlough on the other side of the county seat of Castlebar – it's about half an hour's drive. Here you'll find the Museum of Country Life (see p77), in a beautiful setting in Turlough Park.

Alternatively, head north from Westport for ten minutes to diminutive Newport, where you can join

the Great Western Greenway (*see p85*), an off-road cycling and walking route along the edge of Clew Bay to Mulrany. For an unusual souvenir, visit award-winning artisan butcher Dominick Kelly's (Main Street, 098 41149, www.kellysbutchers.com, closed Sun) to pick up traditional Irish sausages and black pudding.

At Mulrany, the N59 turns north towards Ballycroy National Park (*see p77*). From there, it's another hour to the Céide Fields (*see p77*). Perched on the north coast, this neolithic site has the oldest-known stone-walled fields in the world. If you want to get a real feeling for north Mayo, a landscape of bleak and uninhabited bogland, drive to the Fields by turning left at Bangor on to the R313, then right on to the R314. The latter continues east from the Fields, to the village of Ballycastle, where Mary's Bakery & Tea Rooms makes a good lunch stop.

Half an hour south of Ballycastle is Ballina, Mayo's largest town. There's not much to see here, but it's a good place to pick up supplies before heading to more remote parts, and it does have one of the county's most splendid places to stay, the Ice House Hotel (*see p92*). Most visitors are anglers who come from far and wide to fish the River Moy, world-famous for its salmon. A number of fishing lodges are scattered along the river.

Achill Island ★

Positioned just off Mayo's north-west coast, Achill is Ireland's largest island, about 20 kilometres long and 19 kilometres at its widest point and with a population of about 2,700. The east part of Achill is a Gaeltacht area and most islanders speak Irish. You reach it via the R319 from Mulrany, which also forms part of the Atlantic Drive, a scenic route around the Corraun peninsula and the island itself. At times it's chaotically bumpy and narrow, but the breathtaking panoramic views are worth the jolts. After crossing the bridge over Achill Sound (the stretch of water between the peninsula and Achill), you reach the main town, also called Achill Sound.

The island's curved, white sand beaches (five of which are designated Blue Flag) are swamped in summer. There are plenty of German visitors, inspired by Heinrich Böll's descriptions of the island's haunting, magical beauty and tranquillity in his book *An Irish Journal*. Böll visited regularly in the 1950s and '60s, and the cottage in which he stayed is now used as a residence for artists and writers.

Achill Sound is the only town with ATM facilities. There's a tourist office beside McLaughlin's pub, a few shops and a couple of bars – the liveliest is Óstan Oileán Acla – though many visitors use the town merely as a springboard on their way to the northern villages.

You can follow the Atlantic Drive by car or, as many do, by bike. Near the southernmost tip of the island you'll find a three-storey, 15th-century tower house, known locally as Grace O'Malley's Castle after the lengendary pirate queen. Nearby are the ruins of a 12th-century church with attached graveyard, and the holy well of Saint Damhnait. The road then turns north, offering ocean views towards Clare Island, before reaching Dooega beach, a stunning stretch of white sand that's safe for swimming and perfect for picnics. The road then turns inland to the centre of the island (there's a viewing point at Minaun Heights) and on to the village of Cashel, where there's another tourist office.

You're now back on the main R319. A short drive west is the small, pretty village of Keel. Tucked in behind a marvellous, three-kilometre stretch of golden sand, it's one of the most popular villages from which to explore the island, with plenty of places to stay. On the way in, look out for colourful and bustling Blackfield coffee shop and surf school (098 43590, www.black field.com, closed Oct-Easter). Art Gallery Keel is also worth a browse.

Just north of Keel, at the foot of Slievemore mountain, is the Deserted Village, a cluster of about 100 derelict stone dwellings, last inhabited at the beginning of the 20th century. The settlement was used as a 'booley' – locals would live in the cottages in summer while grazing their cattle on nearby pasture – but the reason for its final abandonment is unclear. Dugort on the north coast has yet another beautiful Blue Flag beach, and it's from here that coastal boat trips aboard the *Lady Slievemore* depart.

Outdoor adventurers will love Achill. There are numerous walks in the mountainous interior, and watersports galore to try, from surfing and diving to sea-kayaking. Novice windsurfers should head to the calmer waters of Keel Lough. Sea fishing, from the shore or by boat, is also popular. Achill Dive Centre (mobile 087 234 9884, www.achill divecentre.com), based near Keel, runs PADI courses and takes boats to dive sites off the southern coast, while Achill Outdoor Education Centre (098 47253, www.achilloutdoor.com) in Cashel offers assorted activities in high season and has dormitory accommodation.

There's always plenty going on over the summer, including the delectable Seafood Festival in mid July and the Walks Festival on the August bank holiday weekend. The Yawls Festival is a series of weekly races during July and August, using traditional wooden sailing boats.

Website www.achilltourism.com pretty much covers everything you'll need to know.

Cong

In the far south of Mayo, adjacent to the border with Galway, is the quaint village of Cong. Set on the northern shore of Lough Corrib and almost surrounded by water, it's best known for being the home of Ashford Castle (094 954 6003, www.ashford.ie), an opulent five-star hotel complete with crenellations and surrounded by wonderful gardens and woodland. Non-residents can wander around the grounds and take a guided boat trip – for a price.

The town is also a tourist draw for being the location for the 1952 Oscar-winning film *The Quiet Man*, starring John Wayne and Maureen

Cong Abbey. See p91.

Achill Island. See p88.

O'Hara. Fans of the movie can pay homage (quietly, of course) at the small, thatched Quiet Man Cottage Museum (094 954 6089, www. museumsofmayo.com/quietman.htm, closed Nov-Feb), where the ground floor has been turned into a replica of the film's White-o-Morn cottage. There are also guided tours to the key filming spots.

At the heart of the village is a ruined Augustinian abbey, founded in the 12th century by Turlough O'Connor, the last High King of Ireland, on the site of an older church. On the nearby riverbank is a former monks' fishing house. A picturesque path leads behind the abbey, along the river and through beautiful woodland, or you can hire a bike from David O'Loughlin Cycles on the main street and set off to Lough Mask, which has some of the most beautiful scenery in south Mayo. The road heads towards Clonbur and then Finny, continuing around the lough in an 80-kilometre loop, with water views for much of the way and a number of viewing points.

Where to eat & drink

Although Castlebar is the county town, Westport is the livelier spot for evening entertainment. An Port Mór (Bridge Street, 098 26730, www. anportmor.com, closed Mon winter) is probably the town's most popular restaurant, serving hearty Irish dishes made with admirably local ingredients, while La Bella Vita (High Street, 098 29771, closed Mon, Tue winter) offers Italian fare in cosy surroundings.

There's plenty of choice by the harbour, including reliable pub grub in the Asgard (098 25319), the Helm Bar (098 26398, www.thehelm.ie) and the atmospheric Towers Bar (098 26534). Fish is the focus at the new, modern Fishworks Café, part of the Carlton Atlantic Coast Hotel (098 29000, www.atlanticcoasthotel.com).

In Keel, on Achill Island, the best options are the beachside Beehive (mobile 086 854 2009, closed Dec-Feb), where you can dine on traditional nettle soup or try the own-made scones; or idiosyncratic Ferndale (098 43908, www.ferndale-achill.com), where the immense menu offers a culinary world tour, with dishes from India, South America, Scandinavia and the Caribbean. In winter, it's open by appointment only.

Matt Molloy's Bar
Bridge Street, Westport (098 26655, www.matt molloy.com). Open Summer 12.30-11.30pm daily. Winter 3-11.30pm Mon-Fri; 12.30-11.30pm Sat, Sun. No credit cards.
You can't go to Westport and not drop into Matt's. On first impression, it's a typical Irish pub, with a small front bar filled with the smell of hops and the sound of chatter. Further in, there may be a group playing traditional music, pints before them on the table. Finally, enter what looks like a converted barn – where musicians play up a storm while the young of the town dance, drink and sing along. The pub is owned by Matt Molloy, flute player in the Chieftains; if he's not on tour, you might find him performing here.

Sage
10 High Street, Westport (098 56700, www.sage westport.ie). Open Feb-Dec 5.30-10pm Mon-Sat.
A simply decorated place with dark wood furniture and floors, serving uncomplicated and delicious food with an Italian twist. Bruschetta, aubergine parmigiana and sage and sausage ravioli are typical dishes, and all the pasta is made in-house daily. In keeping with the 'small is beautiful' ethos, wine comes from family vineyards.

Tavern Bar & Restaurant
Murrisk (098 64060, www.tavernmurrisk.com). Open Bar 12.30-11.30pm Mon-Thur, Sun; 12.30pm-12.30am Fri, Sat. Food served Restaurant Summer 12.30-10pm Mon-Thur, Sun; 12.30pm-10.30pm Fri, Sat. Winter 12.30pm-9pm Mon-Thur, Sun; 12.30-9.30pm Fri, Sat.
This bright pink pub is the ideal spot after – or, for the less athletic, instead of – a hike up Croagh Patrick. The lengthy bar menu features burgers and chips, lasagne, sandwiches and soup, and also daily specials. Upstairs is a more formal dining room specialising in fish and seafood, including mussels and oysters from Clew Bay. Quality is consistently high and the place is packed with locals at weekends.

Where to stay

There's a surplus of B&Bs and guesthouses in Mayo, as well as a number of excellent country house hotels. For example, there's Newport House (098 41222, www.newporthouse.ie, closed Nov-Mar), in Newport, overlooking the river and quay. Mount Falcon (096 74472, www.mount falcon.com) and Enniscoe House (096 31112, www.enniscoe.com, closed Nov-Mar) are both in north Mayo. The former is on the N26, five kilometres south of Ballina; the latter on the other side of Lough Conn on the R315, four kilometres south of Crossmolina.

Hidden in the Delphi valley, en route to Louisberg, is a 19th-century house once owned by the Marquis of Sligo, now Delphi Lodge (095 42222, www.delphilodge.ie). There are 12 B&B rooms in the main house (available mid Mar-mid Oct), as well as five self-catering cottages (available year round) dotted around the estate.

Sitting above Westport harbour is the lovely Ardmore Country House Hotel (098 25994, www.ardmorecountryhouse.com, closed Nov-Feb), an intimate establishment with 13 well-appointed rooms and a good restaurant. Smaller and more homely is Boffin Lodge B&B (098 26092, www.boffinlodge.com)

Achill Island has every kind of accommodation: campsites, hostels, B&Bs, guesthouses, self-catering cottages and hotels. Gray's Guesthouse (098 43244) is a legendary guesthouse in Dugort, in business since 1970.

Bervie
Keel, Achill Island (098 43114, www.bervie-guesthouse-achill.com). Rates €90-130 double incl breakfast.
Once a coastguard building, this sprawling, single-storey guesthouse is magically positioned overlooking the Atlantic, only a few feet from Keel beach. Owners Elisabeth and John Barrett are gracious and welcoming hosts. Achill lamb and

Delphi Mountain Resort

beef, local seafood and organic veg feature in the top-quality meals served in the dining room, which looks on to the cliffs of Minaun. Packed lunches and afternoon tea can also be provided. The 14 en suite rooms are simply decorated, with lots of wood, calming pale colours and plenty of blankets to keep you warm; most have sea views.

Delphi Mountain Resort

Delphi (095 42208, www.delphimountainresort.com).
Rates €138-€198 double incl breakfast.
Husband-and-wife team Rory and Aileen Concannon run this eco-conscious hotel set against the Mweelrea and Twelve Ben mountains. It's built of stone and wood to blend into the landscape, and fresh mountain waters flows from the taps. You can spend the day enjoying the stunning surroundings – the resort offers guided hill walks, kayaking in Killary fjord, surfing on Cross Beach and other activities – then retreat to the luxury of the on-site spa and smart restaurant. Sleeping options include large one-and two-bedroom suites, split-level doubles and family rooms, and dorm accommodation.

Ice House Hotel ★

The Quay, Ballina (096 23500, www.icehousehotel.ie).
Rates €140-€220 double incl breakfast.
A restored 19th-century ice store with striking modern additions, the 32-room Ice House Hotel is so close to the River Moy you're almost in the water. Natural timber and whitewashed walls mix with contemporary furniture and work by leading Irish artists. It's hard to choose between the elegantly traditional 'heritage' rooms in the original building, and the ultra-modern riverside rooms with their floor-to-ceiling windows. The glassed-in Pier Restaurant (open to non-residents) offers excellent modern Irish cooking in a smart waterside setting. To top it all, there's also a spa, with a steam room, various treatments and outdoor hot tubs.

Lisloughrey Lodge

Cong (0949 545400 , www.lisloughrey.ie).
Rates €150-€170 double incl breakfast.
Next to Ashford Castle, perched atop a hill overlooking Lisloughrey Quay and Lough Corrib, this period house has been transformed into an upmarket modern hotel. Dark leather upholstery and bare floorboards contrast with chairs, curtains and wallpaper in vibrant colours and bold patterns. Fifty rooms are discreetly tucked behind the main house around a neat, landscaped courtyard. Inside the original house are two restaurants: the trendy Malt Bar & Brasserie and, upstairs, the more formal Salt Restaurant with views over Lough Corrib.

Stella Maris ★

Ballycastle (096 43322, www.stellamarisireland.com).
Rates €200-€250 double incl breakfast. No credit cards.
Built in the 1850s as a coastguard headquarters and later used as a convent, this four-star hotel sits on the north Mayo coast just north of Ballycastle. The long white building is mere yards from the water, guaranteeing uninterrupted views of Bunatrahir Bay. There are just 11 en suite bedrooms (almost all with sea views), a comfortable lounge and a beautiful conservatory. Food (overseen by owner Frances Kelly) is a highlight, from the lavish breakfasts to superior dinners with own-made bread and local meat, cheese and fish. The hotel is closed from early October to late April.

Counties Limerick & Clare

Limerick is often used simply as a stepping stone for visitors, providing a lunch stop or, at best, a bed for the night. However, the county has some of the most ancient ruins in the country, at Lough Gur. Limerick city is trying hard to shake off its poor reputation, and both the recent development along the quays and the arrival of upmarket hotels and restaurants are making it a more attractive destination. South-west of the city, towards Kerry, is the pretty tourist hotspot of Adare, with its fine collection of restaurants and hotels.

Clare, on the other hand, has it all. The shores of Lough Derg are a focus for boaters, anglers and watersports enthusiasts, while the coastline is blessed with sandy coves, lively seaside villages and some of the best surf in the country. To the north-west of the county is the near-mystical limestone landscape known as the Burren. Traditional music and dance is at the very heart of the county – no matter where you go in Clare, you're likely to hear the sound of a fiddle, a whistle and the rhythmic beating of the bodhrán.

COUNTY LIMERICK

Limerick city

Limerick city gets a bad press and, unfortunately, it's not all undeserved. It can be rough in parts (one nickname is 'Stab City'), but there are signs of economic improvement, with the quays being redeveloped and new hotels built. There's also a fair sprinkling of good restaurants and some interesting sights.

The River Shannon flows through the city on the last leg of its journey before it reaches the Atlantic. The Vikings sailed up the Shannon and established what is now Ireland's fourth largest city. King's Island (Englishtown) was the original settlement and the centre of the medieval city; it is here that the bulk of the sights can be found. The arched Thomand bridge traverses the Shannon beside impressive King John's Castle (see p98). A short walk away is the Limerick Museum (Castle Lane, 061 417826, closed Mon, Sun), which has a collection of more than 40,000 items dating as far back as 2000 BC. Limerick's oldest building is St Mary's Cathedral (Nicholas Street, 061 310293, www.cathedral.limerick.anglican.org), constructed in 1168 on the grounds of a royal palace. The interior is wonderfully ornate in parts, with Gothic stained-glass windows and an ancient west door that was said to be the entrance to the former palace.

After the cathedral, turn right on to Bridge Street and cross the river to reach the Hunt Museum (see p98), which houses a superb collection of art, sculpture and antiquities. Southwards, along Arthur's Quay, is Limerick Tourist Office (061 317522, closed Sun); ask about the walking tours that start from here. East of Patrick Street is another medieval section; while little of historic interest remains, one 19th-century institution has survived. Tucked away on Ellen Street, the Milk Market (Cornmarket Row, mobile 086 028 1828, www.milkmarketlimerick.ie) has been running since 1852. The market is in full swing from Friday to Sunday (some stalls and shops also open on Wednesday and Thursday), with sellers of meat, fruit and vegetables, cheese, cakes, flowers and crafts. The emphasis varies by the day, with the Riverside Variety market on Sunday having stalls packed with art, crafts and jewellery. There's always a buzz about the place, and it's perfect for lunch or coffee and cake.

The city's main drag is O'Connell Street, which is lined with all the usual high-street names, though the little side streets house independent cafés, bars and shops. At the south end of the street is the Belltable Arts Centre (061 319866, www.belltable.ie, closed Sat, Sun), which has an eclectic cultural programme. Heading east up Hartstongue Street, you reach Pery Square, home to the Georgian House & Garden (061 314130, www.limerickcivictrust.ie, closed Sat, Sun), carefully restored as a typical urban Georgian residence.

North of the square is the entrance to the People's Park, beside which is the beautiful Carnegie Building, once the city library and museum, and now the Limerick City Gallery of Art (LCGA, 061 310633, http://gallery.limerick.ie). The permanent collection covers Irish art from the 1800s to the present, and contemporary art shows

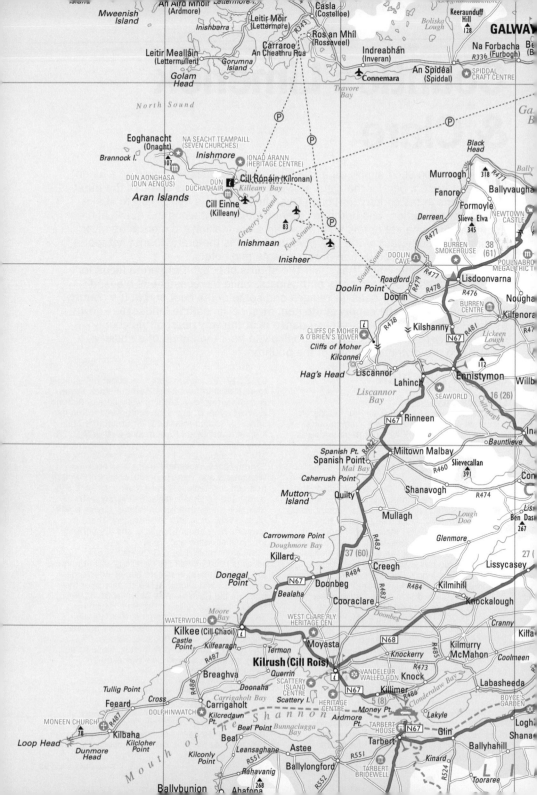

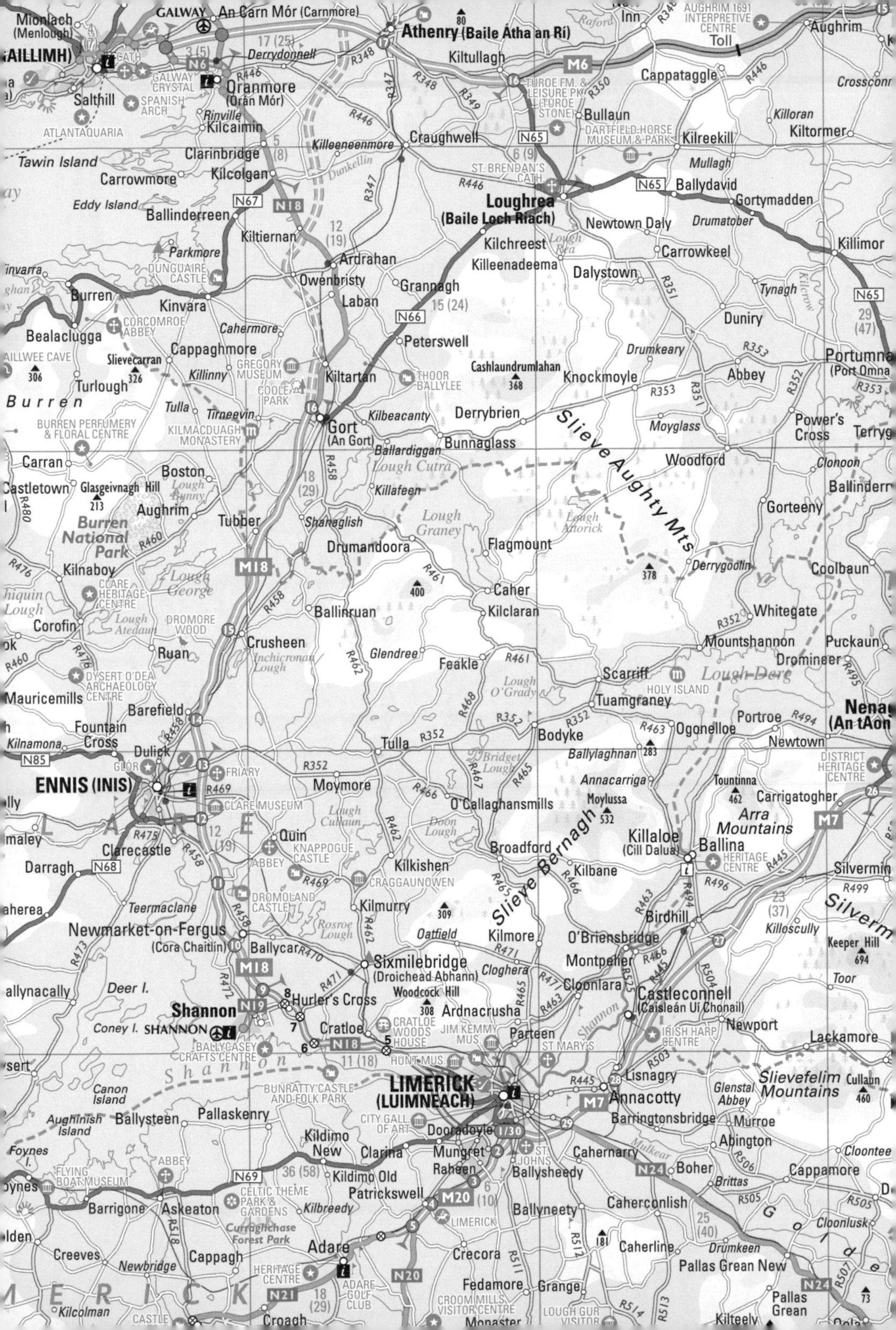

GALWAY An Carn Mór (Carnmore)

(AILLIMH)
(Menlough)
Mionlach

Salthill
ATLANTAQUARIA
SPANISH ARCH
GALWAY CRYSTAL

Oranmore (Órán Mór)
Rinville
Kilcaimin

Athenry (Baile Átha an Rí)
Kiltullagh
Cappataggle
Crossconn
Aughrim
AUGHRIM 1691 INTERPRETIVE CENTRE
Toll

Derrydonnell
Killoran
Kilreekill
Kiltormer
Killimor

Clarinbridge
Kilcolgan
Killeeneenmore
Craughwell
TUROE FM. & LEISURE PK & STONE
DARTFIELD HORSE MUSEUM & PARK
Bullaun
Mullagh
Ballydavid
Gortymadden

Carrowmore
Ballinderreen
Kiltiernan
Ardrahan
Owenbristy
St Brendan's Cath
Loughrea (Baile Loch Riach)
Newtown Daly
Drumatober
Killimor

Eddy Island
Parkmore
Kilchreest
Killeenadeema
Dalystown
Carrowkeel

Burren
Kinvara
Cahermore
Grannagh
Laban
Petersvell
Drumkeary
Tynagh
Duniry

Bealaclugga
CORCOMROE ABBEY
DUNGUAIRE CASTLE
Cappaghmore
Cashlaundrumlahan
Knockmoyle
Abbey
Power's Cross
Portumna (Port Omna)
Terryg

AILLWEE CAVE
Slievecarran
Killinny
GREGORY MUSEUM COOLE PARK
Kiltartan
THOOR BALLYLEE
Derrybrien
Moyglass
Clonoon

Burren
Castletown
Glasgeivnagh Hill
Aughrim
Tulla
Tirneevin
Gort (An Gort)
Kilbeacanty
Ballardiggan
Lough Cutra
Bunnaglass
Slieve Aughty Mts
Woodford
Ballinderr
Gorteeny
Coolbaun
Whitegate

Carran
Boston
Killafeen
Shanaglish
Lough Graney
Flagmount
Derrygoolin
Mountshannon
Dromineer
Puckaun

BURREN NATIONAL PARK
Kilnaboy
Tubber
Drumandoora
Caher
Kilclaran
Holy Island
Scarriff
Lough Derg
Nena (An tAon

Corofin
DROMORE WOOD
Ballinruan
Feakle
Tuamgraney
Portroe
Newtown

Mauricemills
DYSERT O'DEA ARCHAEOLOGY CENTRE
Crusheen
Glendree
Lough O'Grady
Bodyke
Ogonelloe
DISTRICT HERITAGE CENTRE

Kilnamona
Barefield
Dulick
FRIARY
Moymore
Tulla
Ballylaghnan
Tountinna
Carrigatogher

ENNIS (INIS)
CLARE MUSEUM
O'Callaghansmills
Annacarriga
Moylussa
Arra Mountains
Ballina

Darragh
Quin
KNAPPOGUE CASTLE
Broadford
Kilbane
Killaloe (Cill Dalua)
Silvermin

Clarecastle
CRAGGAUNOWEN
DROMOLAND CASTLE
Kilkishen
Birdhill
HERITAGE CENTRE
R499

Teermaclane
Kilmurry
ROSROE Lough
Kilmore
O'Briensbridge
Killoscully
Keeper Hill 694
Toor

Newmarket-on-Fergus (Cora Chaitlin)
Ballycar
Oatfield
Montpelier
Cloonlara
Castleconnell (Caisleán Uí Chonaill)
Newport
Lackamore

Deer I.
Sixmilebridge (Droichead Abhann)
Cloghera
IRISH HARP CENTRE

SHANNON
Hurler's Cross
Woodcock Hill
Ardnacrusha
Parteen
Slievefelim Mountains
Cullatin

Coney I.
Cratloe
CRATLOE WOODS HOUSE
JIM KEMMY MUS
ST MARY'S
Lisnagry
GLENSTAL ABBEY
Murroe

Canon Island
BUNRATTY CASTLE AND FOLK PARK
LIMERICK (LUIMNEACH)
Annacotty
Barringtonsbridge
Abington

Aughinish Island
Ballysteen
Pallaskenry
Kildimo New
CITY GALL OF ART
Dooradoyle
Cahernarry
Boher
Cappamore

Foynes
FLYING BOAT MUSEUM
Clarina
Mungret
Raheen
Ballysheedy
Brittas
R505

Barrigone
Askeaton
CELTIC THEME PARK & GARDENS
Kildimo Old
Patrickswell
Ballyneety
Cahirconlish
Cloontee

Creeves
Newbridge
Cappagh
Kilbreedy
CURRAGHCHASE FOREST PARK
Crecora
Caherline
Drumkeen
Cloonlusk

Kilcolman
Adare
ADARE GOLF CLUB
HERITAGE CENTRE
Fedamore
Grange
Pallas Green New

Croagh
CROOM MILLS VISITOR CENTRE
LOUGH GUR VISITOR CENTRE
Monaster
Pallas Green
Kilteely

are held throughout the year. LCGA also participates in ev+a (www.eva.ie), a festival of national and international contemporary art, with work displayed around the city from March to June.

Limerick has its fair share of festivals, the most popular being the Limerick International Music Festival (www.mbnaicofestival.com) in May, when a series of concerts are given by the Irish Chamber Orchestra and their guests. Many take place in the University Concert Hall (061 331549, www.uch.ie), which also has an annual programme of music and dance. For two weeks in late June/early July, the city is full of traditional music and dance – not only performances, but also workshops and masterclasses – for BLAS, the International Summer School of Traditional Music & Dance (www.ul.ie/~iwmc/blas).

Lough Gur & Adare
Leave the city on the R512 and in 25 kilometres you come to Lough Gur (*see p98*). Scattered around the scenic shores are various archaeological sites, some dating back to 3000 BC, which have provided much of what we know about Neolithic Ireland. Stop first at the Heritage Centre to get your bearings.

Another popular destination is the village of Adare, 16 kilometres west of Limerick city. It grew up around the impressive Adare Manor (*see p100*); in the 19th century, the Earl of Dunraven lined the wide main street with thatched cottages and neat, brightly coloured buildings, creating one of Ireland's prettiest villages. For such a small place, it has a surprising number of restaurants and pubs, plus a luxury hotel and a golf club.

Adare Heritage Centre (Main Street, 061 396666, www.adareheritagecentre.ie) has a helpful tourist office, a craft shop and an interesting exhibition on the village's history. Staff also run guided tours of nearby ruined Desmond Castle on the edge of the Maigue River. Next door to the Heritage Centre is Trinitarian Priory (061 396177), founded in 1230, and one of several ecclesiastical buildings in and around Adare: there's also 13th-century St Nicholas Church and Chantry Chapel in the grounds of Adare Manor; a 14th-century Augustinian priory (now a church and school) to the south of Maigue Bridge; and the remains of a 15th-century Franciscan friary in the grounds of the golf club (but visible from the road).

Where to eat & drink
One of the best hangouts in Limerick city is the Sage Café (Catherine Street, 061 409458, www.thesagecafe.com, closed Sun), a bright, cheery place with an appealing menu that runs from breakfasts to sandwiches and soups, plus a few hot mains. Café Noir (Robert Street, 061 411222, www.cafenoir.ie, closed Sun) is an airy eaterie with great pastries, salads and sandwiches that opens late at weekends to become more of a tapas bar. Fusion food is served at sleek restaurant Chocolat (O'Connell Street, 061 609709, www.chocolatrestaurant.ie), while sister

establishment Jasmine Palace (O'Connell Street, 061 412484, www.jasminepalace.ie) has a modern oriental menu. Copper & Spice (061 313620, www.copperandspice.com) on Cornmarket Row serves Indian and Thai cuisine. More classic dishes can be found at Freddy's Bistro (Theatre Lane, 061 418749, www.freddysbistro.com, closed Mon, Sun), where the likes of steaks, tagliatelle carbonara and wild mushroom risotto are served in a beautifully restored 19th-century building. The Corn Store (Thomas Street, 061 609000, www.cornstorelimerick.com), sister restaurant of the Corn Store in Cork, is a bustling cocktail bar and restaurant with a brasserie-style menu.

Aubars (061 317799, www.aubars.com, closed Sun) is a busy modern bar on Thomas Street serving decent food. For something more traditional, try the music sessions or poetry evenings at the cosy White House Bar (O'Connell Street, 061 412377, www.whitehousebarlimerick.com), or Nancy Blake's (Upper Denmark Street, 061 416443), which always has a lively crowd encompassing all ages. Limerick-born rugby player Peter Clohessy owns the ever popular Peter Clohessy's Bar (Howley's Quay, 061 468100, www.peterclohessy.ie), which has three different bars, and DJs playing into the wee hours at weekends.

There's plenty of choice in Adare, including the reasonably priced Blue Door Restaurant (Main Street, 061 396481, www.bluedooradare.com), set in a charming thatched cottage and serving bistro-style fare. Music sessions are held in many of the bars, the majority of which are traditional. The Mustard Seed restaurant at Echo Lodge (*see p100*), in business for more than 25 years, has a deserved reputation for fine cooking.

French Table
Steamboat Quay, Limerick (061 609274, www.frenchtable.ie). Lunch served noon-3pm Tue-Fri. Dinner served 6-9.30pm Tue-Sun.
A popular French restaurant with an informal atmosphere and a classic menu. Start with onion soup or foie gras terrine with red onion marmalade and toasted brioche, then move on to duck à l'orange, or seven-hour shoulder of lamb with field mushrooms, smoked bacon and red wine jus. Leave room for chocolate mousse and chantilly cream or a selection of French cheeses.

White Sage
Main Street, Adare (061 396004, www.whitesage restaurant.com). Dinner served 5.30-9.30pm Tue-Fri; 5.30-10pm Sat.
Housed in one of the pretty thatched cottages on the main street, the White Sage has a pleasing country-chic interior. Dishes on the seasonally changing menu are sophisticated: ragout of wild rabbit and prune with hickory smoked bacon might be followed by slow-cooked saddleback of pork with lightly spiced puy lentils, or shallot tarte tatin with st tola goat's cheese and white onion soubise. Most ingredients come from small, local producers. One of the dining rooms overlooks an outdoor terrace, where there are tables for warm evenings.

Places to visit

Bunratty Castle

COUNTY LIMERICK

Hunt Museum ★
Rutland Street, Limerick (061 312833, www. huntmuseum.com). Open 9am-5pm Mon-Sat; 2-5pm Sun. Admission €5; €2.50-€3.50 reductions; €12 family.
Located on the riverfront in the restored 18th-century Customs House building, the Hunt Museum holds the art and antiquities assembled over a lifetime by antiques dealers John and Gertrude Hunt. The collection runs from the Neolithic period to the 20th century, and includes works by Picasso, Renoir and Jack B Yeats, as well as weapons, tools, jewellery, ceramics and statuary. The museum also has changing exhibitions by contemporary national and international artists. The lovely café has a riverside terrace.

King John's Castle
Nicholas Street, Limerick (061 711200). Open times vary; phone for details. Admission €9; €5.50-€6.65 reductions; €20.60 family.
Work on the castle started in 1200 and took over ten years to complete (though much of what remains today was added over the centuries). Built for King John, 'Lord of Ireland', the castle was constructed on top of the original Viking settlement – remains of houses dating from this period were discovered during excavation and are on display in the castle grounds. Explore the towers and rooms, admire the historic artefacts, and then take a walk along the battlements to view the whole city. The interpretive centre tells the history of the castle, with special attention given to the many attacks it suffered during the Great Siege of 1642.

Lough Gur ★
Bruff (061 385386, www.loughgur.com). Open Heritage Centre May-Oct 10am-5.30pm daily. Admission €5; €2.50 reductions. No credit cards.
As well as being beautiful, the Lough Gur area has an extraordinary history: the picturesque shores are peppered with ancient sites, and a guided tour by local historian Michael Quinlan (mobile 087 285 2022, www.loughgurdevelopment.ie, closed mid Nov-mid Feb) is a great way to see them. Alternatively, there are a couple of hour-long trails that take in the most spectacular sites – download them from the website on to a smartphone, or pick up maps from the Heritage Centre or Limerick Tourist Office. The Grange Stone Circle (the largest and most complete of its kind in Ireland) consists of 113 large stones and dates from 2200 BC. It's thought to have been both a ritual site and an astronomical calendar. Nearby, the wedge-shaped Gallery Grave (2500 BC) has four cap stones covering a chamber in which animal and human bones have been discovered. The Heritage Centre – designed to resemble Neolithic huts – houses original and replica artefacts, and an exhibition about the pre-Celtic settlers.

SOUTH CLARE

Bunratty Castle & Folk Park
Bunratty (061 360788, www.shannonheritage. com). Open Castle 9.30am-4pm daily. Folk Park July, Aug 9.30am-6pm daily. Sept-June 9.30am-5pm daily. Admission €15.75; €9-€10 reductions; €33.60 family.
Built in 1425, Bunratty Castle has been restored to its former glory and is furnished with 15th- and 16th- century tapestries, art and furniture. In the evenings, medieval banquets are held in the keep for tourists who want to experience the food, music and atmosphere of old Ireland. The surrounding Folk Park consists of a life-size reconstruction of a 19th-century village; there are more than 30 buildings including farmhouses, a church, a watermill and a walled garden. Costumed 'villagers' interact with visitors. There's a tearoom and a pub on site.

Craggaunowen Project

Sixmilebridge (061 360788, www.shannonheritage. com). Open Easter-Aug 10am-5pm daily. Admission €9; €5.50-€6.85 reductions; €21.50 family.
Using the knowledge gained from the prehistoric sites at Lough Gur, John Hunt (of Hunt Museum fame, *see p98*) set about re-creating ancient life at Craggaunowen. The 50-acre site contains crannogs (ancient dwellings), a ring fort, and even part of an original Iron Age wooden track. The reconstructed hunting sites and farmsteads convey life during the early Christian period; there is also a restored 16th-century keep. The curragh was built and used by Tim Severin, who crossed the Atlantic in it in 1976. Picnic benches are dotted about the beautiful grounds, and there's also a tearoom.

Scattery Island

Near Kilrush (065 905 1327). Ferries Mid June-Aug daily. Apr-mid June subject to demand. Return fare €12; €7 reductions. No credit cards.
A monastery was founded on this small uninhabited island in the sixth century by St Senan, and it quickly became an important ecclesiastical centre. A visitor centre explains Scattery's history and the location of various ruins. There are free guided tours, or you can roam over the remains of six churches and marvel at the 37metre-high round tower and holy well (reputedly with healing powers) by yourself. The trip from Kilrush marina takes about 20 minutes; boats run throughout the day in summer – timings are tide-dependent.

NORTH CLARE

Ailwee Cave

Ballyvaughan (065 707 7036, www.aillweecave.ie). Open times vary; phone for details. Admission €17; €10-€15 reductions; €39 family.
Over two million years ago, glacial meltwaters carved out a subterranean river beneath Ailwee Mountain; as the waters receded, they left behind a series of caverns and passageways. A fascinating guided tour takes you into the underground caverns, which are adorned with peculiar rock formations, stalactites and stalagmites and were once the lair of ancient bears. The centre also has a lovely tearoom, a craft shop and a food shop specialising in local produce.

Burren Centre

Kilfenora (065 708 8030, www.theburrencentre.ie). Open June-Aug 9.30am-5.30pm daily. Mar-May, Sept, Oct 10am-5pm daily. Admission €6; €3.80-€5 reductions; €20 family.
Starting at the Burren Centre will help you get the most out of the area. An exhibition explains the geography and geology of the Burren, shows how people survived the inhospitable terrain, and illustrates that, while the land appears barren, it is in fact a treasure trove of wildlife and unusual vegetation. The history of the many megalithic tombs and monuments is explained, and there's a café and a craft shop.

Cliffs of Moher ★

065 708 6141, www.cliffsofmoher.ie. Open times vary; phone for details. Admission Visitor centre €6; free-€4 reductions. O'Brien's Tower €2; €1 reductions.
The Cliffs of Moher rise at Hag's Head, and run for 8km as far as Doolin to the north. However, as most of the land backing the cliffs is private, you can only gain access via the visitor centre. It's an eco-friendly building, tucked into the landscape and with a grass roof, and provides information on the area's geology and natural history; there's a café and a restaurant too. From here, it's a short walk to O'Brien's Tower, a 19th-century castle on the highest point of the cliffs: there are amazing panoramic views from the top of the tower. You can also follow the path along the cliff edge, peer down at the pounding waves and listen to the cries of the thousands of seabirds nesting below. For another perspective, view the cliffs by boat. Cliffs & Aran Cruises (065 707 5949, closed Sept-Mar) runs trips from Doolin pier.

Burren National Park

Wild Geese

Main Street, Adare (061 396451, www.thewild-geese.com). Lunch served 12.30-3pm Sun. Dinner served 6.30-10pm Tue-Sat.

A few doors along from the White Sage, and housed within a similarly quaint thatched cottage, but with altogether more traditional decor. The restaurant has been in business for more than a decade, producing dishes such as roast breast of corn-fed chicken stuffed with buffalo mozzarella and chorizo wrapped in parma ham, served with rosti, spinach and a sun-dried tomato dressing – again with a commitment to Irish suppliers.

Where to stay

Accommodation in Limerick has improved over the years and a number of sleek, modern hotels have emerged in the centre of the city: Absolute Hotel (061 463600, www.absolutehotel.com) on Sir Harry's Mall has a small spa and a riverside restaurant and bar; and the Savoy Hotel (Henry Street, 061 448700, www.savoylimerick.com) contains the popular Market Square Brasserie. More boutique in style, but just as contemporary, is the George Hotel (O'Connell Street, 061 460400, www.lynchotels.com). Chains include the Clarion Hotel (061 444100, www.clarionhotellimerick.com) on Steamboat Quay and, a little outside the centre, the Radisson Blu Hotel & Spa (Ennis Road, 061 326666, www.limerick.radissonsas.com).

In Adare, the Dunraven Arms (Main Street, 061 605900, www.dunravenhotel.com) was established in 1792 and is a lovely mix of traditional (four-poster beds, antique furniture) and modern (flatscreen TVs and deluxe linen). The bar is equally popular with guests and non-residents; there's bar food, and a smart restaurant too.

Adare Manor Hotel & Golf Resort

Main Street, Adare (061 605200, www.adare manor.com). Rates B&B €290-€493 double incl breakfast. Self-catering €2,310-€4,200 per week.

The family seat of the Dunravens until 1982, this palatial property is now a luxury hotel. Originally a Georgian country manor, it was thoroughly reworked over the years as a neo-Gothic 'calendar' house (365 stained windows, 52 chimneys and so on). There are more than 800 acres of parkland, and a championship golf course. Accommodation comes in the form of 62 rooms (with antique furniture and splendid bathrooms) and 46 modern self-catering houses. Formal dining is offered in the Oak Room, more casual meals in the Carriage House, and afternoon tea in the spacious drawing room. Activities include archery, fishing and horse riding, as well as golf, and there are bikes for hire. Indoors, there's a swimming pool, and spa treatments are also offered.

Mustard Seed at Echo Lodge ★

Ballingarry (069 68508, www.mustardseed.ie). Rates €130-€330 double incl breakfast.

Echo Lodge, a Victorian mansion set amid ten acres of manicured lawns, dotted with trees and wild flowers, is 8km outside Adare. There are 18 classic rooms in the main building, while the renovated schoolhouse in the garden has three suites designed in a more contemporary style. Guests and locals dine at the hotel's award-winning restaurant, the Mustard Seed, to experience the four-course, seasonally changing dinner menu. A typical meal might consist of st tola's goat's cheese and basil fritters with tangy fig relish and garden salad, then apple and calvados sorbet, followed by pan-fried guinea fowl and wood pigeon with crisp pancetta and a butternut squash and broad bean risotto, and finally, dessert and petits fours.

SOUTH CLARE

Ennis & around

As well as being an excellent base for exploring the surrounding countryside, Clare's largest town, Ennis (www.visitennis.ie), has a flourishing art and music scene, and some good restaurants. The heart of the town is to the east of the River Fergus. O'Connell Square, where there's a statue of political leader Daniel O'Connell, marks the town centre. Several streets feed out from the square, one of which, Arthur's Row, holds the Tourist Office (065 682 8366, closed Sept-June Mon, Sun). Guided walking tours (mobile 087 648 3714, www.enniswalking tours.com) leave from here, and the building also houses the small Clare Museum (065 682 3382, www.clarelibrary.ie, closed Mon, Sun), which illustrates the history of the county. O'Connell Street, High Street and Abbey Street are narrow thoroughfares lined with bars, cafés and shops (including a growing number of independents). At the far end of Abbey Street is the town's main sight, Ennis Friary (065 682 9100, www.heritage ireland.ie), a 13th-century Franciscan Friary with cloisters, belfry, nave and chancel all intact. At the time of writing, it was closed for conservation work, so phone or check the website for the latest information.

Beside the River Fergus there's a Riverside Sculpture walk (the tourist office can supply a map). The river is also known for its salmon and trout fishing; Tierney Cycles & Fishing (Abbey Street, 065 682 9433, www.clarebikehire.com, closed Sun) has fishing gear and also rents out bicycles.

Ennis is renowned for traditional music and the main arts venue, Glór (Causeway Link, 065 684 3103, www.glor.ie, closed Sun), hosts regular concerts as part of its vibrant programme of drama, comedy, music and film. Annual festivals also demonstrate the importance of music to the community: at the five-day Ennis Trad Festival (www.ennistradfestival.com), in November, gigs are held in venues all over town, with workshops and céilís drawing big crowds. In May, the wonderful Fleadh Nua (www.fleadhnua.com) is a week of ceilidhs, concerts, street entertainment, and workshops in dance, music and song – and is undoubtedly the best time to visit. Non-music celebrations include the Book Club Festival (www.ennisbookclubfestival.com), which brings together many of Ireland's best writers for readings, workshops and discussions in March, and the Clare County Show (www.clarecountyshow.com), in July, where the entertainment runs from show-jumping to food and craft fairs.

Poulnabrone Dolmen. See p106.

Nine kilometres south of Ennis on the R469 are the beautiful ruins of 15th-century Quin Abbey, surrounded by fields and wild flowers. From here it's a short drive to imposing Knappogue Castle (061 360788, www.shannon heritage.com, closed Nov-Apr) and its Victorian gardens. The castle is open to the public; banquets are held in the restored dining room, and a state apartment is available for self-catering groups of up to ten people. A few kilometres off the R462, and even further into the past, is the Craggaunowen Project (see p99), a re-creation of life in prehistoric Ireland. A further eight kilometres south is Bunratty Castle & Folk Park (see p98), and just to the west, Shannon Airport (061 712000, www.shannonairport.com).

Kilrush & the Loop Head peninsula

Kilrush sits at the mouth of the River Shannon, about 45 kilometres south-west of Ennis. Bottle-nosed dolphins have made the estuary their home, and boat trips depart from the busy marina several times a day in summer, cruising the waters for glimpses of the playful creatures; contact Dolphin Discovery (065 905 1327, www.discoverdolphins.ie, closed Nov-Mar) for more information. Boats also leave here for nearby Scattery Island (see p99).

Kilrush was a 'landlord' town, owned by the Vandeleur family, and suffered badly during the Great Famine. Part of the family's estate is now the Vandeleur Walled Garden (Killimer Road, 065 905 1760, www.vandeleurwalledgarden.ie, closed Oct-Mar Sat, Sun), which has a lovely café in the grounds. Explore further by hiring bicycles from Gleeson's Cycle Hire (Main Street, 065 905 1127, closed Sun), or on horseback: the West Clare Equestrian Centre (065 905 9115, www. westclareequestrian.com) can arrange treks.

Kilkee (www.kilkee.ie), 13 kilometres west of Kilrush towards the Loop Head peninsula, has the best beach in the south-west, with a 1.5-kilometre stretch of sand. The tourist office (065 905 6112, www.kilkee.ie, open June, July daily; Sept Mon-Sat; Oct-May Tue-Sat) is on O'Connell Street. Most activities here are water-based, and for one weekend in September the town is taken over by the Cois Fharraige Surf & Music Festival (www.coisfharraige.com). Surf lessons are given on the beach, and the Kilkee Diving & Watersports Centre (East End Pier, 065 905 6707, www.oceanlife.ie) organises dives.

BEST GOLF COURSES

Ireland is paradise for golfers, with hundreds of spectacular courses across the county, with links courses a speciality. There's plenty of useful information on www.golf.discover ireland.ie, including an annual guide, available to download, by post or from tourist offices.

Ballybunnion Golf Course
Sandhill Road, Ballybunion, Co Kerry (www.ballybuniongolfclub.ie).
With two of the most spectacularly located links courses on the west coast of Ireland, Ballybunion is one of Ireland's most popular clubs for visitors. The scenic and challenging Old Course and Cashen Course are both world-class.

County Louth Golf Club
Drogheda, Co Louth (www.countylouthgolfclub.com).
Situated at the mouth of the River Boyne, with the Irish Sea to the east, this is an unusual and very scenic links course. Also known as Baltray, it's been listed as one of the top 25 courses in the British Isles.

Dun Laoghaire Golf Club
Bray, Co Wicklow (www.dunlaoghairegolfclub.ie).
Sitting in beautiful Ballyman Glen, against the backdrop of the Wicklow Mountains, Dun Laoghaire is a championship parkland course. It has three nine-hole courses, designed so that different combinations of the 27 holes can be played.

European Club
Brittas Bay, Co Wicklow (www.theeuropeanclub.com).
Located beside sand dunes, the top-ranked European is a superb links course, less than an hour's drive from Dublin. Guests are welcome on a daily basis.

Killarney Golf & Fishing Club
Killarney, Co Kerry (www.killarney-golf.com).
Founded in 1893, Killarney Golf Club is situated in one of the most stunning regions of Ireland, adjacent to Killarney's Lower Lake. The club has hosted the Irish Open Championships and has three championship courses – Mahony's Point, Lackabane and Killeen.

Nevsail Watersports (The Strand, mobile 086 330 8236, www.nevsailwatersports.com) offers any number of activities including kayaking, windsurfing and powerboating. Otherwise, there's always golf, of course – at Kilkee Golf Club (065 905 6048, www.kilkeegolfclub.ie) or Kilrush Golf Club (065 905 1138, www.kilrushgolfclub.com) – and a spectacular cliff walk either side of the strand. You can cycle from Kilkee to the end of the peninsula; bikes can be hired from William's Bike Hire (Circular Road, 065 905 6041, closed Sun).

The Loop Head peninsula is the remotest part of Clare, a place where winds howl over sheer cliff edges. Sea stacks abound: Diarmaid and Grainne's rock, on the western side of the headland, is the highest, at over 100 metres. The cliffs are inhabited by thousands of birds; peregrines, razorbills, guillemots, fulmars, choughs and rock doves. To the east of the peninsula is a conservation area with a diverse range of bird and sea life; there's plenty of useful information on www.loophead.ie. En route to the tip, on the east coast, is Carrigaholt, from where dolphin-watching boat trips (065 905 8156, www.dolphin watch.ie, closed Nov-Mar) leave throughout the day. The Long Dock Pub (West Street, 065 905 8106, www.thelongdock.com) serves good food and has frequent traditional music sessions.

Close to the headland is the village of Kilbaha, where you can stay at the Lighthouse Inn (065 905 8358, www.thelighthouseinn.ie). It's on a pebble beach, and has wonderful sea views, as well as a restaurant specialising in seafood. If you want to rent a bicycle to go around the loop drive, or hire fishing rods, contact Mike Barnes at Loop Head Adventures (065 905 9233, closed Oct-Apr); he can arrange day excursions or simply equip you and point you in the right direction. A cliff walk leads from Kilbaha out to the headland as far as the lighthouse, with glorious views across to Kerry. Alternatively, drive to the car park – it's then a short walk to the tip.

Where to eat & drink

Ennis Farmers' Market is held every Friday on Upper Market Street; if you miss this, the Ennis Gourmet Store (Barrack Street, 065 684 3314) sells many of the same artisan products and also has a lovely café. Another great little café is Food Heaven (Market Street, 065 682 2722, closed Sun), which does takeaway lunches and has a deli counter. A good, if formal, dinner venue is the Town Hall restaurant in the Old Ground Hotel (*see p103*). It also does more relaxed breakfasts and lunches, and the bar has traditional music sessions on Thursday nights. Knox's (Abbey Street, 065 682 9264, www.knoxs.ie) has a bistro and a lively modern bar with bands at weekends, while traditional music can be heard at Cruises Bar inside the Queens Hotel (065 682 8963, www.queenshotelennis.com), also on Abbey Street. Don't miss Durty Nelly's (061 364861, www.durtynellys.ie), right beside Bunratty Castle, which has a great atmosphere in its different styled bars; there's also a restaurant. Kilrush has a good farmers' market on Thursdays (for cakes, head to Minihan's stall) and, as befits a popular seaside town, Kilkee boasts several excellent fish and seafood restaurants.

Morrissey's Seafood Bar & Grill
Doonbeg (065 905 5304, www.morrisseysdoonbeg.com). Open 6pm-midnight Tue-Sun. Dinner served 6-9.30pm Tue-Sun.
In the summer, diners start the evening here with a drink on the deck, enjoying the river views. Inside, the once traditional bar has been revamped with cream walls, dark wood furniture and burgundy banquettes. The menu lists numerous fish and seafood dishes (Carrigaholt crab claws with garlic and herb butter, salmon and cod fish cake with vermouth cream; fish and chips with mint and pea purée), plus the likes of steaks and southern fried chicken. Morrissey's also has seven neat, modern B&B rooms (€90 double including breakfast). Doonbeg is around 11km north-east of Kilkee on the main N67.

Naughton's Bar
O'Curry Street, Kilkee (065 905 6597, www.naughtons bar.com). Open June-Aug 6pm-1am daily. Easter-May, Sept, Oct 6pm-1am Sat, Sun. Dinner served June-Aug 6-10pm daily. Easter-June, Sept, Oct 6-10pm Sat, Sun.
Open brickwork, dark wood and cosy fires welcome you into Naughton's Bar, one of Kilkee's best. The atmosphere is friendly and laid-back, with holidaymakers piling in to enjoy a drink inside or on the terrace. The menu is strong on fish and seafood – the specials board features the daily catch from the harbour – but there are also steaks, burgers, sandwiches and salads.

Strand Restaurant & Guesthouse
Strand Line, Kilkee (065 905 6177, www.thestrand kilkee.com). Dinner served Mar-Oct 5.30-9.30pm daily.
The Strand is located right on the beach, and the floor-to-ceiling windows make the most of the view. The airy dining room has a straightforward menu with a bias towards fish: seafood chowder or Carrigaholt crabs claws in garlic and chilli cream sauce, say, followed by stir-fried Atlantic monkfish or fish and chips; there are burgers and steaks too. Six comfortable double bedrooms cost €74-€90 per night, including breakfast.

Where to stay
Ennis has a decent number of mid-range hotels. These include the convenient Temple Gate Hotel (The Square, 065 682 3300, www.templegate hotel.com), which has a good bistro and comfortable rooms; and the more upmarket Old Ground Hotel (O'Connell Street, 065 682 8127, www.flynnhotels.com), which has a smart restaurant and an atmospheric bar (*see p102*). Decent budget accommodation can be found at the Rowan Tree Hostel (Harmony Row, 065 686 8687, www.rowantreehostel.ie), centrally located in a Georgian house on the river.
Bunratty is a popular place for an overnight stay as it's only a few kilometres from Shannon Airport. Bunratty Castle Hotel (061 478700, www.bunratty castlehotel.com) has spacious, stylish modern

Lahinch Golf Club
Lahinch, Co Clare (www.lahinchgolf.com).
Another of Ireland's top links courses, Lahinch was rated by Phil Mickelson as one of his favourite links layouts. The championship golf course hosts the South of Ireland Championships, and is much loved for its picturesque beachside location.

Lough Erne Golf Course
Enniskillen, Co Fermanagh (www.lougheirnegolfresort.com).
This championship golf course, positioned on a spit of land between Lough Hume and Lower Lough Erne, was designed by Nick Faldo. Exciting and challenging, with beautiful lakeside views, it has become one of Ireland's top golf courses.

Mount Juliet
Thomastown, Co Kilkenny (www.mountjuliet.ie).
Said to be the best parkland course in Ireland, Mount Juliet was designed by Jack Nicklaus and opened in 1991. It has hosted the Irish Open, Presidents Cup and the WGC-American Express Golf Championship. The luxury hotel (*see p187*) is pretty special too.

Portmarnock Golf Club
Portmarnock, Co Dublin (www.portmarnockgolfclub.ie).
A short drive from Dublin, Portmarnock is another links course in a fantastic setting, and rated one of the world's top courses. A range of events have been played here, including the Irish Open and the Walker Cup.

Royal Portrush Golf Club
Portrush, Co Down (www.royalportrushgolfclub.com).
Royal Portrush has two courses – the Valley Links and the Dunluce Links, the latter considered one of the most challenging links courses in Europe. It's the only club in Ireland to have hosted the Open (aka the British Open), the only major held outside the US.

Waterville Golf Club
Waterville, Co Kerry (www.watervillegolfclub.ie).
Over 100 years old, Waterville Golf Club is located in the gorgeous Ring of Kerry, bang next to the Atlantic. It's another championship links course with a first-class reputation, and has been voted among the top five courses in Ireland and the top 25 in the world.

Burren Perfumery. See p106.

rooms, a leisure centre and a small spa. In Kilkee, the family-run Stella Maris Hotel (065 905 6455, www.stellamarishotel.com) is a lovely gabled Victorian house with a bar and restaurant that's just a three-minute walk from the beach.

Doonbeg Lodge ★
Doonbeg (065 905 5600, www.doonbeggolfclub.com). Rates €155-€355 double incl breakfast.
There's an almost New England feel to Doonbeg Lodge. Built of local stone, with slate roofs, it overlooks a crescent-shaped beach, and the salty Atlantic air whips across the lawns. Decor is understated and contemporary, with open fires in the public areas. It's a large place, with 60 rooms, plus six self-catering cottages and 64 suites, all spacious, with marble bathrooms, Wi-Fi and underfloor heating. Assorted drinking and dining choices range from the relaxed Darby's Bar to fine dining in the Long Room. If the stunning beach is not distraction enough, there's the spa and a Greg Norman-designed golf course.

NORTH CLARE
Visitors are lured to north Clare by its long, sandy beaches and one of Ireland's most unusual landscapes, the Burren – not to mention the region's musical heritage. Notable music hotspots include the small villages of Tulla, known for the traditional music played in McCarthy's and Torpey's Bar, and Feakle, where the Feakle Festival (www.feaklefestival.ie) of traditional Irish music is held in August.

Lough Derg
In the north-east of Clare, the pretty town of Mountshannon sits beside Lough Derg. Boating, kayaking and fishing are all popular pursuits. In May/June, the Iniscealtra Festival of Arts (www.iniscealtra-artsfestival.org) presents a diverse programme of dance, theatre, music and other events.

About 25 kilometres further south is the hillside town of Killaloe. The town is built around the 13th-century St Flannan's Cathedral, with the narrow streets rising steeply from the lake. Killaloe is the hometown of Brian Boru, Ireland's High King who united the country against the Vikings at the end of the tenth century. The Brian Boru Heritage Centre (Bridge Street, 061 360788, www.shannonheritage.com, closed Oct-Apr) recounts his legendary past, as well as dealing with local history and folklore. The tourist office is also located here and can help with booking watersports and other activities. The annual festival in Brian Boru's memory, Feile Brian Boru (086 358 6293 www.feilebrianboru.killaloe.ie), held in June, is a week of music, entertainment, sport and general craic. Killaloe is linked to Ballina, just across the lake in County Tipperary, by a long, arched bridge – a short walk there brings more dining options.

The coast & the Burren
Along the coast west of Ennis are several popular surfing spots, with crashing Atlantic waves and raucous sessions in the local bars. Lahinch, while not the loveliest of towns, has a decent selection of accommodation and a fantastic stretch of golden sand that's safe for swimming and surfing. Learn the relevant skills at Lahinch Surf School (Main Street, mobile 087 960 9667, www.lahinchsurfschool.com), based in a beach hut on the promenade, or hire boards at the Lahinch Surf Shop (Old Promenade, 065 708 1543, www.lahinchsurfshop.com). There's also the championship course at Lahinch Golf Club (Liscannor Road, 065 708 1003, www.lahinchgolf.com), and an aquarium and swimming pool at Lahinch Seaworld & Leisure Centre (The Promenade, 065 708 1900, www.lahinchseaworld.com). The tourist office (The Dell, 065 708 2082, www.lahinchfailte.com, closed Nov-Feb) can help with bookings for deep-sea angling, guided hikes and day trips incorporating the Cliffs of Moher and the Burren.

A five-minute drive inland is the market town of Ennistymon (www.ennistymon.net). The cascading waters of the River Cullenagh pass beneath a pretty arched bridge, and a walk down the quaint main street, with its old-fashioned shopfronts, is an exercise in nostalgia. Bars such as Cooley's House (065 707 1712) or Daly's (065 707 1919), both on Main Street, are equally lost in time, and often have music sessions.

The R478 north from Lahinch follows the coastline to charming Liscannor, where a small harbour is overlooked by the Logues Liscannor Hotel (065 708 6000, www.loguesliscannorhotel.com, closed Nov-Mar). It's a sedate place, with little going on, but makes a good overnight stop for visitors heading to the Cliffs of Moher (*see p99*). One of Ireland's most famous sights, drawing hundreds of thousands of visitors a year, the cliffs are named after 'Mothar', a ruined fort demolished during the Napoleonic wars. Extending along the coast for eight kilometres and dropping vertically down to the wild ocean below, they are a vertigo-inducing 213 metres at their highest.

At the north end of the cliffs, set back slightly from the sea, is Doolin (www.doolin-tourism.com) – it's popular with surfers for the nearby waves and with tourists for the music. Micho Russell is largely responsible for the town's musical reputation. He had an international career with his tin whistle, becoming Ireland's most famous traditional musician in the latter part of the 20th century. McDermott's (065 707 4328, www.mcdermottspubdoolin.com), McGanns (Main Street, 065 707 4133, www.mcgannspubdoolin.com) and O'Connors (Fisher Street, 065 707 4168, www.gusoconnorsdoolin.com) are likely spots for a night of music and fun. Every February, the town celebrates Micho's legacy by hosting the music fest that is the Micho Russell Memorial Weekend (www.michorussellweekend.ie).

Five minutes' drive from Doolin is another local attraction, Doolin Cave (065 707 5761, www.doolincave.ie). A guided tour heads 24 metres underground to emerge in an enormous cavern where a gigantic glistening stalactite hangs above the floor.

The Burren – from the Irish word 'Boíreann' meaning a rocky place – stretches across the north-west of Clare. A vast karst limestone pavement, marked by deep fissures and pocketed by bogs, it covers about 250 square kilometres and reaches all the way to the sea. There is nothing quite like it elsewhere, and the area attracts geologists, hikers and the curious. Although the terrain seems barren and desolate, there is plenty of evidence of past settlers, in the form of scattered megalithic ruins. Burren National Park (01 888, 2000, www.burrennationalpark.ie) is a conservation area within the Burren. Note that there are no marked trails, and it is important to have a proper map of the area before setting off on a walk. Start any trip at the Burren Centre (see p99), in Kilfenora. This village is another favourite spot for traditional music, and boasts Ireland's oldest céilí band, Kilfenora Céilí Band (www.kilfenoraceiliband.com). Music can be heard at Linnane's (065 708 8157) while Vaughan's Pub (065 708 8004, www.vaughanspub.ie) has Irish dancing on Thursday and Sunday nights.

Nearby Lisdoonvarna is known for its Matchmaker Ireland festival (www.matchmakerireland.com) in September, when, over the course of a month, thousands are drawn to the small town in the hope of finding love; there's plenty of music and street entertainment too. At other times, it's still a busy town with plenty of bars and places to stay, but a more picturesque base is the seaside village of Ballyvaughan, 16 kilometres north along the N67. It's more or less one street, with a pretty harbour, a handful of shops (including an excellent butcher) and several pubs, but for such a small spot it has a number of decent dining and sleeping options. }It's a spectacular 15-minute drive – with the mountains on one side and the sea on the other – to Fanore and its lovely Blue Flag beach. You can also get there by bike: hire one in Ballyvaughan from Burren Bike (mobile 086 341 2875), which also offers cycle tours of the area.

The main sights of the Burren are within easy reach of Ballyvaughan. One of the most popular is very close: the impressive Ailwee Cave (see p99). A little further south, along the R480, is the Gleninsheen Wedge Tomb, dating from around 2500 BC. It was near here, in 1932, that a farm boy found the famous Gleninsheen Collar (a gold gorget probably used as a neck ornament), dating from the late Bronze Age (about 700 BC); it's now on display in the National Museum of Ireland in Dublin. Further south from Gleninsheen is the Poulnabrone Dolmen, a dramatic site consisting of a thin cap stone sitting on two portal stones. Excavation here has revealed human remains, jewellery and other artefacts.

The Caherconnell Stone Fort (065 708 9999, www.burrenforts.ie) is the Burren's most significant ancient remains. The visitor centre (closed Nov-mid Mar) has information on the life of the fort and its inhabitants, as well as a brief history on the other megalithic sites in the immediate area.

The tiny hamlet of Carron, with Cassidy's pub (see right) and Clare's Rock hostel (see p108),

makes a remote but atmospheric base in the heart of the Burren. A couple of kilometres north is the wonderful Burren Perfumery (065 708 9102, www.burrenperfumery.com). Tucked away down a bumpy lane, it's housed in an old building, where a range of perfumes, soaps, candles and other delightfully scented items are made. The tearoom has a small terrace out front beneath towering trees, where you can enjoy home-baked goods, soups and light lunches.

Where to eat & drink

In Tulla, Flapper's Restaurant (Main Street, 065 683 5711, closed Sun) serves good, homely dishes both day and evening. Mountshannon has a wider selection of bars and restaurants: the quaint An Cupán Caifé (061 927275, closed Mon, Tue) overlooks the lough and offers soups, sandwiches and cooked lunches, and a more formal dinner menu, while Keane's Pub (Main Street, 061 927214) is an atmospheric bar. Killaloe is a lively spot in the summer; close to the bridge, Gooser's (061 376791, www.goosers.ie) is housed in a thatched building, and has a traditional bar (with an outdoor terrace) plus a more modern dining area where decent bistro-style food is served. The popular Cherry Tree restaurant (Lakeside Drive, 061 375688, closed June-Aug Mon; Sept-May Mon, Sun), across the bridge in Ballina, serves excellent contemporary food and has wonderful views over the lake.

On the coast, in Lahinch, there's the Shamrock Inn (065 708 1700, www.shamrockinn.ie) for pub grub and music at the weekends; Danny Mac's (065 708 1020) is in a similar vein. Both are on Main Street. In Doolin, intimate Cullinan's (065 707 4183, www.cullinansdoolin.com, closed Wed, Sun) specialises in top-notch seafood dishes, and also has eight B&B rooms. Roadford House Restaurant (065 707 5050, www.roadfordrestaurant.com, closed July, Aug Mon; Sept-June Mon, Thur) on the edge of Doolin is a smart joint serving modern Irish cuisine in a welcoming setting; it also has five simply decorated B&B rooms. There are plenty of traditional music pubs in Lisdoonvarna, some of which serve fine food too: try the Roadside Tavern (Doolin Road, 065 707 4084, www.roadside tavern.ie) or the atmospheric Wild Honey Inn (Kincora Road, 065 707 4300, www.wildhoney inn.com, closed Jan; Nov-Apr Mon-Wed).

For a genuine, cosy Irish bar, head to O'Loclainn's Bar (065 707 7006) in Ballyvaughan; alternatively, Monks Bar (065 707 7059), opposite the pier, does good food. The lovely Tea & Garden Rooms (065 707 7157, www.tearoomsballyvaughan. com, closed Nov-Mar) has glorious views over Ballyvaughan harbour and pretty gardens out the back. It's worth dropping by Vasco (065 707 6020, www.vasco.ie, open June-Aug daily; Apr, May, Sept, Oct Fri-Sun) in Fanore for beach picnic supplies, or you could stay and make the most of its restaurant and wine bar. In Carron, Cassidy's (065 708 9109, www.cassidyspub.com) serves excellent food, including delicious

Gregans Castle Hotel. See p108.

gluten-free pizzas and has an outdoor terrace where people gather for a pint of Guinness and a chat.

An Fulacht Fia
Coast Road, Ballyvaughan (065 707 7300, www.an fulachtfia.com). Lunch served 12.30-4pm Sun. Dinner served 5-9pm daily. Closed mid Jan-mid Feb.
Behind the Burren slate is a contemporary interior, with a bar area at the front, and beyond that the dining room, where the neutral carpet and walls are brightened by red velvet chairs and colourful artwork. The restaurant has a loyal local following for dishes such as wild halibut roasted in Sicilian butter, with pea and watercress purée, or pan-roasted breast of chicken stuffed with mushrooms and smoked pancetta, served with crushed chive potatoes and Madeira jus. You'll need to book during the summer.

Barrtra Seafood Restaurant
Nr Lahinch (065 708 1280, www.barrtra.com). Food served June-Aug 1-10pm daily. Sept 1-10pm Wed-Sun. May 1-10pm Thur-Sun.
Set on the cliffs several kilometres outside Lahinch, with views out over Liscannor Bay, this unassuming restaurant – housed within a neat white building, focuses on fresh local fish and shellfish. The menu changes according to what is available, but dishes are always simply, and perfectly, cooked. The lack of airs and graces, and the friendly service, make Barrtra a popular spot.

Vaughans Anchor Inn
Main Street, Liscannor (065 708 1548, www.vaughans.ie). Open 10am-11.30pm daily. Food served noon-9.30pm daily.
A traditional bar leads into a nautically themed restaurant area – both are informal. During the day, expect dishes such as creamy seafood chowder or a hearty burger. The evening menu has a more sophisticated selection, such as spring roll of Liscannor crab or sautéed foie gras with caramelised apple to start, and mains such as a seafood platter or roast saddle of rabbit. In addition, there are seven bright bedrooms (€70 double including breakfast).

Where to stay
At Lough Derg, the Mountshannon Hotel (Main Street, 061 927162, www.mountshannon-hotel.ie) is popular with anglers and boaters, as is the campsite just outside Mountshannon at Lakeside Holiday Park (061 927225, www.lakesideireland.com, closed Oct-Apr). Further south in Killaloe, the Lakeside Hotel (061 376122, www.lakesidehotel.ie) has a good location with comfortable rooms.

Seaside Lahinch has no shortage of accommodation, with numerous self-catering cottages and B&Bs. Grander establishments include the extensive Lahinch Golf & Leisure Hotel (065 708 1100, www.lahinchgolfhotel.com, closed Oct-Apr) or, for a more intimate option, Vaughan Lodge (Ennistymon Road, 065 708 1111, www.vaughanlodge.ie), a contemporary hotel with 22 bedrooms and an excellent restaurant. For more budget beds, Lahinch Hostel (Church Street, 065 708 1040, www.visitlahinch.com) is located in the centre of town.

Doolin is similarly well supplied; Hotel Doolin (065 707 4111, www.hoteldoolin.ie) and Tir Gan Éan (065 707 5726, www.tirganean.ie, closed Nov-Feb) both have comfortable modern rooms, while Ballinalacken Castle Hotel (065 707 4025, www.ballinalackencastle.com, closed Nov-Easter) has more upmarket accommodation and a traditional restaurant. B&Bs in Ballyvaughan include Drumcreehy House (Bishop's Quarter, 065 707 7377, www.drumcreehyhouse.com), which has attractive rooms; and the Hylands Burren hotel (Main Street, 065 707 7037, www.hylandsburren.com, closed Jan), which is central and popular with walkers.

In the heart of the Burren, in Carron, Clare's Rock (065 708 9129, www.claresrock.com, closed Oct-Apr) is a family-friendly hostel and B&B, which also hires bikes.

Gregans Castle Hotel ★
Ballyvaughan (065 707 7005, www.gregans.ie). Rates €195-€245 double incl breakfast. Closed Nov-mid Feb.
A truly lovely 18th-century manor, run with great flair as a country-house hotel for more than 30 years by the Haden family. The 20 elegantly modern bedrooms have views over the surrounding countryside (you can see Galway Bay from some). There are turf fires in the drawing room and the casually stylish Corkscrew bar. The hotel restaurant, overseen by chef Mickael Viljanen, has won countless awards. Guests can look foward to the likes of pan-fried hand-dived scallop, with smoked eel, citrus, pumpkin and liquorice, followed by loin of young wild Wicklow venison roasted in juniper butter, with braised shin, beetroot, walnut, date, chicory and game jus.

Moy House
Lahinch (065 708 2800, www.moyhouse.com). Rates €220-€280 double incl breakfast. Closed Oct-Feb.
Moy House has a marvellous location, set in 15 acres containing a river and woodland, and with lawns sweeping down to the sea. The nine-room hotel is a nice blend of contemporary and traditional, and very comfortable thoughout. The drawing room has a crackling fire, and old portraits in keeping with the 18th-century building. There are stunning views over Lahinch Bay from the dining room, which serves modern Irish dishes: start, perhaps, with Liscannor Bay lobster, with bisque risotto, coconut and lemongrass, then move on to fillet of beef, with mushroom and onion pie, asparagus and light pepper jus.

Sheedy's Country House Hotel
Lisdoonvarna (065 707 4026, www.sheedys.com). Rates €99-€170 double incl breakfast. Closed Nov-Mar.
John and Martina Sheedy run their hotel with passion. The 11 rooms and suites are comfortably furnished and have spacious bathrooms, while the public areas have turf fires and plenty of places to lounge. John is responsible for the restaurant, and uses vegetables from the garden and local cheeses, meats and fish in dishes such as st tola goat's cheese tart on caramelised onions and roasted peppers, or roast rack of Burren lamb with pearl barley, baby onions and smoked bacon. Dining at Sheedy's is a grand affair in a relaxed and jovial atmosphere, an experience that keeps guests coming back for more.

County Kerry

The Kingdom of Kerry is one of the most magical places in Ireland, thanks to its wild and windswept beauty. Glistening lakes, majestic mountains, white-sand beaches, sheer sea cliffs and remote, ravaged islands – there are many natural wonders to admire. The beautiful Killarney Lakes and the Gap of Dunloe have been attracting visitors since Victorian times, while the Ring of Kerry, the route around the Iveragh peninsula, attracts thousands of visitors a year. Further north, the Dingle peninsula is smaller but equally stunning, and is a stronghold of Gaelic folklore and culture. The ocean is ever-present, and there's an abundance of small, charming fishing villages, offering watersports of all kinds, and restaurants serving some of the freshest seafood in the country. Kerry also has some of Ireland's most appealing towns: Killarney, gateway to Killarney National Park; Kenmare, the self-confessed culinary capital of Ireland; and Dingle, where the vibrant nightlife is a match for the colourful buildings.

KILLARNEY & AROUND

At the base of Ireland's largest mountain range, the MacGillycuddy's Reeks, lies Killarney National Park, which incorporates three scintillating lakes: Muckross, Leane and Upper Lake. The region has attracted tourists for centuries, who come to admire the towering peaks and tranquil waters, and visit the castles and abbeys dotted along the shores. Wooded walkways are lined with rhododendrons, azaleas and startling red strawberry trees. Running beside the park is the Gap of Dunloe, a stark glacial valley between Purple Mountain and Bull Mountain, pocketed with lakes and trickling rivers traversed by stone bridges.

At the edge of all this beauty is the town of Killarney (www.killarney.ie), its compact centre filled with hotels, guesthouses, B&Bs and hostels to accommodate the thousands of annual visitors. It's a thriving town, lively and friendly, with all the facilities a traveller might need conveniently at hand – but inevitably something of a tourist trap. Eating and drinking places are numerous, and several craft galleries and shops sell traditional Irish sweaters and other Irish-made items. Dozens of companies offer trips around the spectacular Ring of Kerry (*see p116*) and other sights on the well-trodden south-west tourist trail. The Tourist Information Centre (064 66 37928, www.killarney.ie) is just west of the town centre, on Beech Road.

Annual highlights include the Summerfest (www.killarneysummerfest.com), held over the last week of July, which brings large concerts and small gigs, workshops, street entertainers, and lots of family-oriented activities to venues all over town. Killarney Racecourse (www.killarneyraces.com) has a packed fixture list in July and August, and there are some exceptional golf courses in the vicinity, such as the Killarney Golf & Fishing Club (064 663 1034, www.killarney-golf.com) and Beaufort Golf Resort (064 664 4440, www.beaufortgolfresort.com).

Killarney National Park ★ (www.killarneynational park.ie) lies just outside Killarney, to the south-

Ross Castle. See p118.

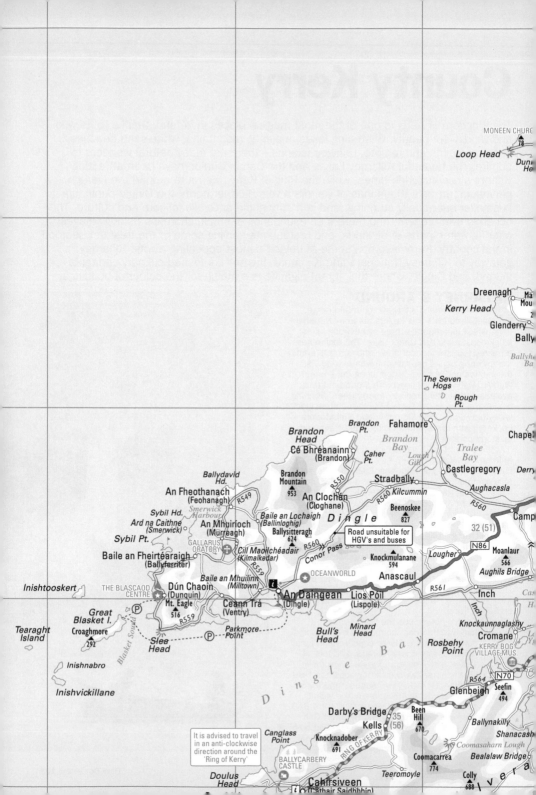

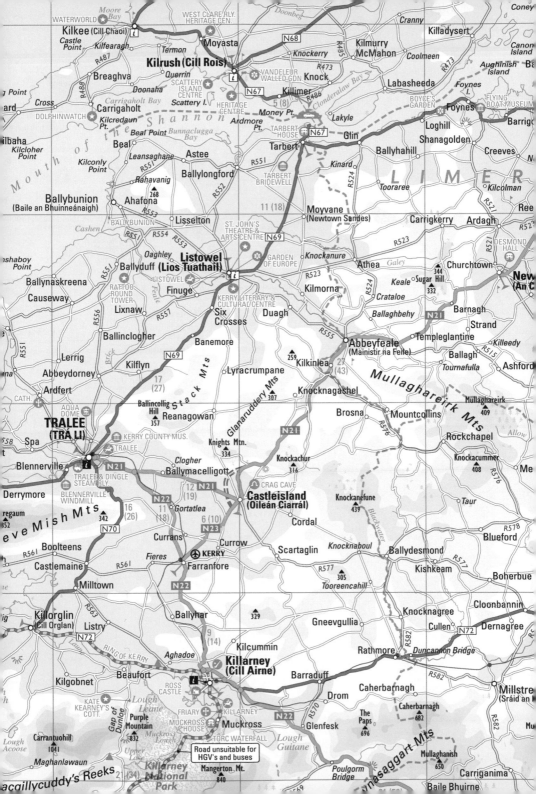

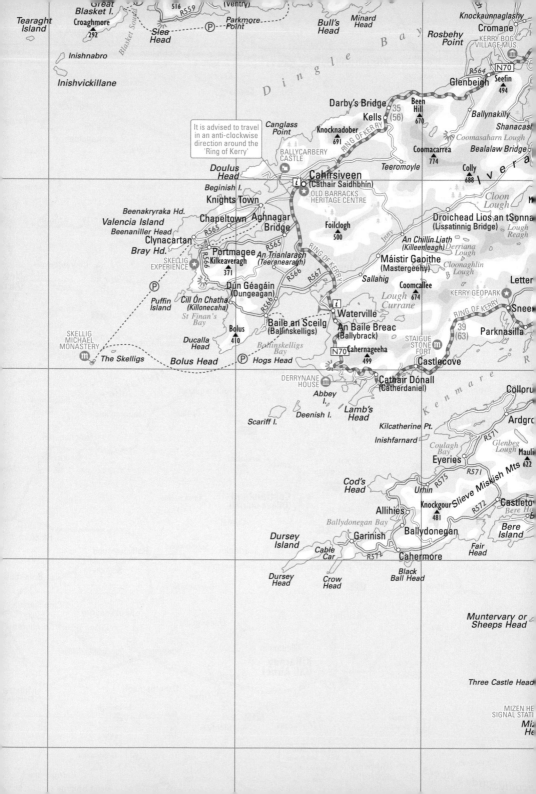

Bricin

west. The park's visitor centre (064 663 1440, www.heritageireland.ie) is located at Muckross House & Gardens (*see p118*), six kilometres from town off the N71. You can pick up information on the park's key sights, boat trips and fishing, and detailed maps of walking and cycling routes. Among the wildlife in the park are red deer, red squirrels, foxes, otters and over 100 species of birds.

Numerous paths lead around Muckross Lake or Lough Leane, and to impressive Muckross Friary, a 15th-century Franciscan friary with cloisters and a tower. Killarney Guided Walks (mobile 087 639 4362, www.killarneyguidedwalks.com, closed Nov-Feb) runs daily two-hours walks of the park, departing from Killarney town at 11am.

The park can also be approached from the west, through the Knockreer estate, which once belonged to the Earls of Kenmare. Access is via the Deenagh Lodge gate, opposite St Mary's Cathedral, an impressive Roman-Catholic church designed in 1870 by Augustus Pugin. The lodge now functions as a tearoom, and the main house is a field study centre. Visitors can wander the formal gardens and wooded walks overlooking Lough Leane. Ross Castle (*see p118*) is located in the demesne, at the edge of Lough Leane. Boats leave from Ross Pier to Lord Brandon's Cottage on Upper Lake – the trips are popular, so book ahead in summer.

West of the National Park, the Gap of Dunloe cuts through the MacGillycuddy's Reeks. A ten-kilometre stretch of road leads through the barren, glacial valley, past a series of five lakes, with rocky purple mountains on either side (the limestone has a peculiar purple sheen). The Gap is accessible on foot, or by bicycle, horse or pony and cart – but not by car. Access is from two points: Kate Kearney's Cottage (064 664 4146, www.katekearneys cottage.com) or Lord Brandon's Cottage on Upper Lake. Starting at Kate's means you can have

refreshments before tackling the hike, and descending into the forbidding Black Valley. From Lord Brandon's Cottage, you can hop on a boat across Upper Lake and into Lough Leane to Ross's Castle.

Daytrips incorporating a walk or pony-and-trap ride through the Gap of Dunloe, a boat trip across the lakes and then a bus ride back into town is a fantastic way to see the area if your time is limited; details from Killarney Day Tour (064 663 1068, www.killarneydaytour.com). The more energetic can rent bikes (064 663 1282, www.killarneyrentabike.com) and cycle around Muckross Lake to Torc Waterfall or through the Gap of Dunloe, returning by boat to Ross Castle. 'Jaunting cars', as the pony and traps are called, are lined up at various points around the National Park.

Where to eat & drink

Killarney has a thriving dining scene, and many of the upmarket hotels have smart restaurants that are open to non-guests.

Head to Jam (Old Market Lane, 064 663 7716, www.jam.ie, closed Sun) for tasty wraps, plus sandwiches, soups and lots of sweet treats made in its bakery. Chapter Forty (New Street, 064 667 1833, www.chapter40.ie, closed Mon, Sun) prides itself on providing high-end cuisine and service. The menu is modern Irish, with a fusion twist. Gaby's Seafood Restaurant (High Street, 064 663 2519, www.gabysireland.com, closed Sun) serves some of the best fish around. Lobster, oysters, and shellfish platters with rich, creamy sauces are house specialities.

For lively music sessions, head to the Danny Mann (064 663 1640, www.evistonhouse.com), part of the Best Western hotel on New Street, or the more modern Granary (064 662 0075) on Beech Road.

Bricín

High Street, Killarney (064 663 4902, www.bricin.com).
Dinner served June, July 6-9pm Mon-Sat. Aug-May
6-9pm Tue-Sat.
Bricín was established more than 20 years ago by two Kerry
brothers, Paddy and Johnny McGuire. On the ground floor
there is an Irish craft shop, stocked with pottery, lace and
knitwear. Above is a spacious dining room of traditional
design, including stained-glass windows – it's old-fashioned
in the best possible way. The food is good, honest home
cooking, with boxty (potato pancakes) a house speciality.

Miss Courtney's Tearoom ★

College Street, Killarney (mobile 087 610 9500,
www.misscourtneys.com). Open 10am-6pm Mon-Sat;
noon-6pm Sun. No credit cards.
Miss Courtney's has been serving Killarney's best afternoon
tea since 1909, and is still run by the same family. Owner
Sandra Dunlea (great-niece of the original Miss Courtney)
has created the perfect blend of decadence and nostalgia,
with comfortable chairs, sparkling chandeliers, embroidered
tablecloths, traditional tea sets, and pale pink panelled walls.
Dainty sandwiches, own-baked scones and sumptuous
cream cakes are piled high on tiered cake stands, and black
and white family photos adorn the walls. A gem.

Smoke House

8 High Street, Killarney (064 662 0801, www.the
smokehouse.ie). Open/food served 8am-10pm daily.
Newcomer the Smoke House (also owned by Sandra Dunlea)
is quickly becoming a firm favourite. Fashionable good
looks – dark wood, black and white photos, booths – and
excellent music combine with tasty food to make it a funky
place any time of day. Pop in for a traditional, vegetarian or
champagne breakfast, choose from the all-day menu of open
sandwiches, salads and nibbles, or come for a chic, laid-back
dinner. Charcoal-grilled meat and fish are the mainstays.

Where to stay

Although Killarney is bursting with hotels and
B&Bs, it's best to book during the summer months,
especially for the smarter hotels, which are very
popular with tour groups.

The five-star Killarney Park Hotel (064 663 5555,
www.killarneyparkhotel.ie) in the centre of town
is an old favourite, while four-star sister hotel the
Malton (064 663 8000, www.themalton.com)
occupies a grand, creeper-clad Victorian building set
in six acres of land. Upmarket spa hotels include
the Aghadoe Heights Hotel & Spa (064 663 1766,
www.aghadoeheights.com, closed Nov-Apr Mon-
Thur), perched on a hill behind the town with
stunning views; the Brehon (Muckross Road,
064 663 0700, www.thebrehon.com); and the
Killarney Plaza Hotel (Kenmare Place, 064 662
1111, www.killarneyplaza.com, closed Jan, Dec),
complete with a wonderful Molton Brown spa.

The smaller hotels might offer fewer facilities,
but tend to have more character. Good examples
include the Ross (064 663 1855, www.theross.ie),
a contemporary, boutique-style place with a small
spa and a very good restaurant; the more traditional
Arbutus Hotel (College Street, 064 663 1037,
www.arbutuskillarney.com, closed Jan, Dec); and

the excellent Muckross Park Hotel (064 662 3400,
www.muckrosspark.com, closed Nov-Jan Mon-Thur),
just outside the town centre.

Cahernane House Hotel

Muckross Road, Killarney (064 663 1895, www.
cahernane.com). Rates €130-€250 double incl
breakfast. Closed Nov-Mar.
A ten-minute walk from town, Cahernane House Hotel offers
old-fashioned grandeur in a peaceful setting. The 19th-
century house is set in its own lakeside estate, approached
along a tree-lined driveway. There are 38 bedrooms: those
in the old part of the house are particularly smart, while the
newer rooms provide a more contemporary style of elegance.
There's a cellar bar for late-night tipples, and the graceful
Herbert Room for formal dining.

Miss Courtney's Tearoom

Europe Hotel & Resort

Fossa (064 667 1300, www.theeurope.com).
Rates €220-€290 double incl breakfast.
Don't forget your bathing suit when you visit the Europe. After a massive refurbishment, it now has one of Ireland's most stunning spas. Loungers surround the large, pristine pool, with picture windows providing views over Lough Leane to the MacGillycuddy's Reeks. Pottering between pool, steam room and relaxation room will revive your windswept body after a morning of mountain walking. The hotel is smart and contemporary in design, and large (187 rooms and suites). There's plenty of comfortable seating in the public areas, plus a library, bar, brasserie and restaurant – all maximising the superb views.

Killarney Royal Hotel

College Street, Killarney (064 663 1853, www.killarney royal.ie). Rates €75-€180 double incl breakfast.
With so many large, modern hotels in town, it's nice to have the choice of a small, elegant, country-style hotel. The 29 rooms, each with its own seating area and large marble bathroom, are decorated with swagged curtains, smart wallpaper and a mix of antique and new furniture. The drawing room, with its plump armchairs, open fire and fresh flowers, is very inviting. There's a bistro for casual meals and a more formal restaurant.

IVERAGH PENINSULA

The Iveragh peninsula is one of Ireland's most visited areas. This comes as no surprise to those who have experienced the Ring of Kerry, the 170-kilometre scenic loop drive around the peninsula. The dramatic coastline is fringed with pristine beaches and dotted with charming villages, with mirror-like lakes reflecting the towering mountains of the interior. Rhododendrons – smatterings of colour against the weatherworn terrain – line the narrow, winding loop road (N70). A sprinkling of islands entice visitors off the mainland, across the often choppy Atlantic, to witness the extreme isolation the islands' inhabitants once endured.

If time is short, consider taking a day tour around the Ring of Kerry, departing from Killarney (numerous bus companies run tours).The excursion takes a full day and entails a lot of jumping on and off the bus, rapid photo opportunities and a mere surface view of the peninsula, but you will enjoy some spectacular views and see the coast's highlights, without having to negotiate the often alarmingly narrow road. If you're travelling in a more leisurely fashion, it's a good idea to base yourself in more than one town, so you can properly experience the different areas.

Plenty of useful information is available on www.ringofkerrytourism.com.

Kenmare to Waterville

The tour buses drive anti-clockwise around the Ring of Kerry, and most car drivers do the same – to get the best views and avoid traffic snarl-ups. But you can also drive clockwise, which is the route described below.

Kerry's culinary capital, Kenmare, is nestled at the head of Kenmare Bay, 33 kilometres south of Killarney along the N71. Occupying a strategic position at the start of the Ring of Kerry, the town has a collection of fine hotels and some of the best restaurants in the county. The neat streets lined with pastel-coloured buildings and the leafy square are the creation of the 1st Marquis of Lansdowne, who rebuilt the town in 1775. It's a bright, bustling place, with several enticing shops, bars and eateries to keep you busy for a couple of days. Many visitors stay here when exploring the Iveragh peninsula, and also the Beara peninsula to the south (part of which is in County Cork).

The tourist office (064 664 1233, www.kenmare.ie, open July, Aug daily; Apr-June Mon-Sat; Sept, Oct Mon-Fri) is located off Market Street in the Heritage Centre, where there is an exhibition on local history and the Great Famine. On the second floor is Kenmare Lace (064 664 2978, www.kenmarelace.ie, closed Nov-mid Apr), started in the 19th century when a group of nuns arrived in Kenmare in the wake of the Famine. In an attempt to provide some industry, they set about teaching lace-making to the townsfolk. The results were sold in the Lansdowne Arms on Main Street, which still stands today.

Kenmare has few 'sights', except for the Druid's Circle, a Bronze Age monument tucked away on a small hillock behind Market Square. Fifteen boulders are positioned in a tight circle around a central boulder that's engraved with ceremonial markings. However, it's easy to while away a day in the town, window-shopping, taking tea or scouring the excellent farmers' market (Wed-Sun). It's possible to walk (or drive) the 11 kilometres from Kenmare to Moll's Gap, at the junction of the N71 and R568, for stunning views across the lakes mountains – get a map from the tourist office. There's an Avoca shop and café at Moll's Gap.

The village of Caherdaniel is 48 kilometres from Kenmare along the Ring of Kerry road; many visitors use it as a base for exploring the peninsula. Part of the appeal is nearby Derrynane Bay, with its curved, sandy Blue Flag beach and perfect bathing waters. The bay falls within the boundaries of Derrynane National Park (*see p119*), which also contains the former home of Irish hero Daniel O'Connell. There's plenty to do in and around Caherdaniel. There are several walks in the vicinity, including the long-distance Kerry Way (*see p123*). You could book a trek with Eagle Rock Equestrian Centre (066 947 5145, www.eaglerockcentre.com, closed Sun) or take a lesson (sailing, canoeing, windsurfing, waterskiing) with Derrynane Sea Sports (mobile 087 908 1208, www.derrynaneseasports.com, closed Oct-Apr). West from Caherdaniel, the road climbs up to the Coomakista Pass; at the top is a lookout with some of the south-west's finest views.

Waterville sits between Ballinskelligs Bay and Lough Currane, with mountains to the east – giving the town a little bit of everything. It's a popular seaside resort, boasting one of the country's finest links courses at Waterville Golf Club (066 947 4102, www.watervillegolfclub.ie), plus a handful of good pubs and a couple of restaurants. The pebbled beach has a promenade, and a statue of Charlie

Killarney National Park. See p109.

Places to visit

Great Blasket Island

KILLARNEY & AROUND

Muckross House & Gardens

Off N71, Killarney National Park (064 667 0144, www.muckross-house.ie). Open House & Gardens July, Aug 9am-7pm daily. Sept-June 9am-5.30pm daily. Farms June-Aug 10am-6pm daily. May, Sept 1-6pm daily. Apr, Oct 1-6pm Sat, Sun. Admission House, Gardens & Farms €12; €6-€10 reductions; €30 family. House & Gardens only €7; €3-€5.50 reductions; €17.50 family. Farms only €7.50; €4-€6 reductions; €20 family.

This beautiful mansion on the shores of Muckross Lake was built in 1843 for the Herbert family. Inside, it's decorated with 19th-century furniture and items that belonged to the former residents; downstairs, the old kitchen and servants' quarters are on display. Outside are a series of formal gardens, including a Stream Garden, Sunken Garden and Rock Garden. There are also three traditional farms, containing livestock and manned by costumed actors to portray agricultural life in the 1930s and '40s. The walled garden houses a workshop for potters and weavers, who work away while visitors watch; the results can be purchased in the craft shop. The Garden Restaurant is a lovely place for lunch.

Ross Castle

Knockreer Estate, Killarney (064 663 5851, www.heritageireland.ie). Open Apr-Sept 9am-5.45pm daily. Mar, Oct 9.30am-5.45pm daily. Admission €6; €2-€4 reductions; €14 family. No credit cards.

Ross Castle was built in the 15th century by the O'Donoghue Ross clan, who surrounded the castle with a high curtain wall flanked by round towers – still standing. Several rooms have been restored, including the Great Hall, with its flagstones and reproduction 15th- and 16th-century objects. The informative guide recounts the history of the castle and its former residents, as well as the legend of the ghost of O'Donoghue, who sleeps beneath the lake. Every seven years, on 1 May, he reappears on a white horse – good fortune comes to anyone who sees him.

IVERAGH PENINSULA

Derrynane National Park ★
Caherdaniel (066 947 5113, www.heritageireland.ie).
Open House May-Sept 10.30am-6pm daily. Apr,
Oct, Nov 10.30am-5pm Wed-Sun. Grounds 24hrs
daily. Admission €3; €1-€2 reductions; €8 family.
No credit cards.
Within Derrynane National Park is Derrynane House,
the ancestral home of Ireland's great hero Daniel
O'Connell (1775-1847). O'Connell achieved Catholic
Emancipation for the Irish, earning him the title of 'the
Great Liberator', and he remains one of Ireland's most
important historical figures. The house has been a
museum since the late 1960s. Family portraits hang
from the walls, and there are documents and writings
by and about O'Connell. Some of the more interesting
artefacts are the duelling pistols he used to shoot rival
John D'Esterre in 1815, and the black glove he wore
in remembrance of his death. In the courtyard is the
opulent gold chariot in which he rode through Dublin
after his release from prison.

A café serves light lunches and cakes in summer.
From here, several waymarked trails lead through
the grounds. One of the more beautiful heads west
of Derrynane Harbour, up a rocky hill, past tree-shaded
spots and wild flowers, and with stunning views
over the craggy coastline. Also within the park is
a gorgeous Blue Flag beach, where many head for
a swim in fine weather.

Skellig Experience
Valentia Island (066 947 6306, www.skellig
experience.com). Open July, Aug 10am-7pm daily.
Mar-June, Sept-Nov 10am-5pm days vary, phone for
details. Admission €5; €3-€4 reductions; €14 family.
Housed within a stone-clad, grass-roofed building
overlooking the Atlantic, the Skellig Experience centre
follows in the steps of the sixth-century monks who
made the Skellig Islands their home, explaining how
they constructed their dwellings and what their lives
were like. There are also displays about the islands'
lighthouses and seabirds, and a decent café. The
centre runs daily two-hour cruises around the islands
(Apr-Sept), but without going ashore.

Skellig Michael ★
About 14km from the Kerry coast, amid the
choppy Atlantic waters, lie the Skellig Islands,
their jagged peaks visible for miles. These are
among Ireland's most fascinating islands, and
the uncertainty of visiting them, due to the
unpredictable sea conditions, make them all the
more mysterious. The smaller of the islands, Little
Skellig, is a bird sanctuary and cannot be visited
– though boats usually pass near enough that
you can see some of the 27,000 pairs of gannets
that nest on rocky cliffs island. The larger island,
Skellig Michael (or Great Skellig) can be visited:
it's famous for being one of Ireland's earliest
monastic settlements, dating from the seventh
century, and is now a UNESCO World Heritage
Site. The monastic remains are astoundingly
well preserved, considering their age and the
extreme conditions. At the top of a flight of
670 steep steps is a cluster of small beehive

huts (clochans), a refectory and a church. The monks
constructed the huts so that rain would not penetrate
the thick stone walls, and angled them in such a
way as provide shelter from the harsh Atlantic winds.
The buildings have stood on the summit of Skellig
Michael for over 1,300 years, housing the monks
until the 13th century, allowing them to live off
fish from the sea and to trade with passing ships.

The journey to Skellig Michael takes over an
hour, and can be gruelling if the sea is choppy, so
be prepared. Proper walking shoes and water are
essential, and vertigo-sufferers or the unfit should
not attempt the perilous climb to the peak. Boats
depart from various points: Ballinskelligs with
Ballinskelligs Watersports (066 947 9182, closed
Nov-Mar), Portmagee with Skellig Boat Trips (066
947 2437, closed Nov-Mar), and various other
operators on Valentia Island. Book at least a day
or two in advance.

DINGLE PENINSULA

Dunbeg Fort
Slea Head Drive, Fahan (066 9159755,
www.dunbegfort.com).
The remains of Dunbeg Fort perch precariously on a
sheer cliff edge, overlooking Dingle Bay and across
to the Iveragh peninsula. Dating back to the Iron Age,
it's one of Ireland's best preserved promontory forts.
The visitor centre above the Stone House Restaurant
has some displays on the history of the fort.

Gallarus Oratory
Ballydavid (066 915 5333). Open Oratory 24hrs
daily. Visitor centre 9am-8pm daily. Admission
Oratory free. Visitor centre €3; €2.50 reductions.
This tiny church dates from around the seventh
century, and is a perfect example of the dry-stone
building technique of the period. Shaped like an
upturned boat, it has a low doorway and a tiny window
at the opposite end – and that's about it. However,
it's fascinating to get a close look at the structure,
which has withstood centuries of the south-west's
formidable weather, as well as numerous invaders.
The small visitor centre across the road has
information on local history, and a café.

Great Blasket Island ★
www.dingle-peninsula.ie/blaskets.html.
Lying 3km off the Dingle coast, rocky Great Blasket
Island has a rich literary history that achieved
worldwide renown thanks to the books written by the
islanders at the beginning of the 20th century. The
island was abandoned in 1953, and today only day-
trippers clamber ashore to wander the grassy paths
and peer at the long-deserted homes. At the eastern
end is a small, beautiful, sandy beach called Trá Bán
(White Beach). Trips leave from Dingle and Dunquin,
and usually incorporate a cruise around the other
Blasket islands, where thousands of puffins, fulmars,
shearwaters and other seabirds nest. Seals, dolphins,
whales and basking sharks are sometimes spotted.
You can buy tickets at the timber huts at Dunquin pier,
from either of the two boat companies; both run eco
marine tours too. The sea can be rough, so the boats
aren't always running.

Great Blasket Visitor Centre

Dunquin (066 915 6444). Open Easter-Oct 10am-5.15pm Mon-Sat; 11am-5.15pm Sun. Admission €4; €2-€3 reductions. No credit cards.

Whether or not you are planning a trip to Great Blasket, don't miss the visitor centre, where you'll discover the astonishing literary history of the Island. Harsh and inhospitable, for many centuries it was home to an Irish-speaking population of up to 200, many of whom were great storytellers. A visit from English scholar and philosopher George Thomson in the 1920s kick-started the islanders' publishing career. Thomson stayed, became fluent in the language and encouraged the islanders to write down their stories; over the next 20 years, their tales of living at the edge of the world were read all over the world. You can purchase some of their books, then have a read in the café with a cup of tea.

NORTH KERRY

Kerry Literary & Cultural Centre

24 The Square, Listowel (068 22212, www.kerry writersmuseum.com). Open May-Sept 10am-5.30pm Mon-Fri. Oct-Apr 11am-4pm Mon-Fri. Admission €5; €4 reductions; €12 family.

Housed in a restored Georgian building, the Kerry Literary & Cultural Centre chronicles and portrays the lives and words of the town's most famous authors: John B Keane, Maurice Walsh, Bryan MacMahon, Brendan Kennelly and George Fitzmaurice. Statues of the writers adorn the rooms, the hallways are lined with their works, and their books are sold in the adjoining bookshop. The centre also hosts storytelling evenings, along with other artistic performances.

Skellig Michael. See p119.

Chaplin, who is said to have spent his holidays here. Mór Active (mobile 086 389 0171, www.activityireland.ie) organises a huge range of outdoor activities, from rock climbing, kayaking and coasteering to camp craft and rambles along the seashore. For horse riding, contact the Ring of Kerry Equestrian Centre (mobile 086 608 9856, open Apr-Sept Tue-Sun; Oct-Mar by appointment).

Ring of Skellig & Valentia Island

From Waterville, you can continue inland along the N70 or take the more scenic route via the R567/R566. Commonly known as the Ring of Skellig, this is a remote, winding and sometimes heart-pounding drive. Ballinskelligs has a lovely Blue Flag beach, where Skellig Surf (mobile 087 917 8808, www.skelligsurf.com, open May-Oct daily; Nov-Apr by appointment) offers surfing, windsurfing and kayaking classes and trips. This is a Gaeltacht area and is busy in summer with students perfecting their Irish.

There are boat trips to the remote Skellig Islands, and the Cill Rialaig Artists Retreat (066 947 9277, open June-Aug daily) displays and sells work by visiting artists, and has a lovely café with a turf fire. To the delight of many travellers, Skelligs Chocolate Company (066 947 9119, www.skellig chocolate.com, closed Jan; Sept-May Sat, Sun) is nearby; you can watch the chocolate being made, Willy Wonka style, and taste the results. Annual events include Féile Barr na Sráide (mobile 087 978 7434), a traditional music and dance festival in June, and the long-running Ballinskelligs Rowing Regatta in July.

The twisting road reaches great heights between Ballinskelligs and the fishing village of Portmagee, with yet more spectacular views over St Finian's Bay. Colourful buildings adorn Portmagee's seafront, and it's a departure point for trips to Skellig Michael (see p119), the largest of the two Skellig islands and the site of a sixth-century monastic settlement. Portmagee has some some lively pubs, many of which hold traditional music nights in summer.

A bridge from Portmagee leads to Valentia Island (www.visitvalentiaisland.ie), the most westerly point in Europe. The wonderful Skellig Experience (see p119), on the waterfront just across the bridge, is well worth a visit. The island is just three kilometres wide and 11 long; most facilities and services are in Knightstown, at the eastern tip. It was from Valentia that the first transatlantic cable was laid in 1857, the history of which is covered in the small Valentia Heritage Centre (School Road, 066 947 6411, www.vhc.cablehistory.org, closed Oct-Mar) in Knightstown. The island is also famous for the discovery, in 1993, of the oldest fossilised footprints in the northern hemisphere. Some 150 footprints made almost 400 million years ago by a tetrapod, a lizard-like creature, are visible at the Tetrapod Trackway, a rock platform near the lifeboat station at Dohilla.

The best way to appreciate the island's stark beauty is on foot or by bike: try Casey's Bicycle Hire in Portmagee (New Street, 066 947 2474, closed

Sept-June Sun). At Glanleam, there's a lighthouse facing the worst of the Atlantic waves, the island's only sandy beach, and the lovely tropical gardens at Glanleam House & Gardens (see p126). Deep-sea angling and diving are popular pursuits; Valentia Island Sea Sports (066 947 6204, closed Sept-June) arranges dives and other water-based activities.

Cahersiveen to Killorglin

The next town on the mainland is Cahersiveen. The Old Barracks Heritage Centre (066 947 2777, www.theoldbarracks.com, closed Dec-Feb) is set in an unusual whitewashed Victorian structure, complete with turreted tower (formerly a RUC barracks) that dominates the town. Assorted exhibitions relate the history of the peninsula and other particulars, such as the Fenian Rising and the Great Southern & Western Railway. The centre also contains the tourist office, a shop selling local crafts and a café. If you're visiting on a Thursday, the farmers' market is an ideal place to pick up picnic supplies. The Cahersiveen Festival of Music & the Arts (www.celticmusic festival.com) brings music, family fun and fireworks over the August bank holiday weekend. Boats leave from Renard Point to Valentia Island.

From Cahersiveen, the N70 wends its way north, sometimes hugging the coastline, at other times weaving through valleys, but never losing sight of the mountains. Rhododendrons and fuschia line the roadside. Just before is Rossbeigh Strand, a splendid long sandy beach that's perfect for swimming. Push north for a few kilometres and turn inland to Caragh Lake to find luxurious accommodation at Carrig Country House (see p126).

Killorglin, 40 kilometres from Caherisiveen, is the final town on the peninsula, and has several good restaurants. It's most noted for the Puck Fair (www.puckfair.ie), held in August, which originated in the early 17th century. Tradition says that a goat is hunted in the mountains, captured and brought to town, then crowned king and placed on a platform for the three days of the festival. Thousands come to join in the celebrations, including music, dancing, street entertainment and a cattle fair. If you're starting the Ring of Kerry from this end, Killorglin tourist office (School Road, 066 976 1451, closed Sat, Sun), housed in the council offices, is a good place to start.

Where to eat & drink

Kenmare rivals Kinsale in County Cork for the title of gourmet capital of Ireland. Jam Café (064 664 1591, closed winter Sun) is part of the Kerry bakery chain, with shelves of baked goods, and sandwiches and snacks to eat in or take away. Cupán Tae (064 664 2001, closed Jan-Easter) serves a variety of teas in pretty, bone-china cups, as well as finger sandwiches, tempting scones and cream cakes. The Pantry (064 664 2233, www.kenmare.eu/thepantry, closed Sun) is a healthfood shop, with organic fruit and veg, organic wines and gluten-free foods. All three are located on Henry Street. Relaxed, traditional pubs with good food include the Horseshoe (Main Street, 064 664 1553, www.thehorseshoekenmare.com, closed Nov-May Tue, Wed); PF McCarthy's (Main Street, 064 664 1516); and the Purple Heather (Henry Street, 064 664 1016, closed Sun).

The Lime Tree Restaurant & Art Gallery (Shelbourne Street, 064 664 1225, www.lime treerestaurant.com, open June-Aug daily; other times phone for details) is a fantastic spot on the edge of town, with an inventive menu of modern Irish food, plus a gallery showcasing and selling work by local artists. For simply but expertly cooked fish and shellfish, plus some classics such as Irish stew, there's Packie's (Henry Street, 064 664 1508, closed June-Sept Mon; Oct-May Mon, Sun). It's a cosy spot, with candles, wooden booths and smiling staff. For good pizza and pasta, head to Prego (064 664 2350), also on Henry Street.

In Waterville, Peter's Café (087 995 0199, closed mid Nov-mid Mar) serves sandwiches and soups, while the Huntsman Oyster Bar & Restaurant (Cliff Road, 066 947 4124) is a contemporary joint specialising in fish dishes. For quality fare in a casual setting, try the Smuggler's Inn (066 947 4330, www.the-smugglers-inn.com, closed Nov-Easter) on Cliff Road. Many ingredients are organic or sourced locally (Cromane oysters, Dingle Bay prawns) and it also has 14 comfortable B&B rooms.

In Cahirsiveen, QC's Seafood Bar & Restaurant (Main Street, 066 947 2244, www.qcbar.com, closed Mon, Tue winter) majors on chargrills and fresh seafood. The Point Bar (066 947 2165,

Jack's Coastguard Restaurant

closed Nov, Dec; Mon-Fri Jan-Easter), next to the boat dock at Renard Point, also serves excellent seafood. On Valentia Island, the Royal Pier Bar (066 947 6144) in Knightstown is a popular local watering hole with good views.

For such a small town, Killorglin has a surprising number of fine eateries, and live music seems to be a way of life. Bringing a touch of Spanish flair is Sol y Sombra (066 976 2347, www.solysombra.ie, closed Mon, Tue). Located in a converted church off Lower Bridge Street, it offers delicious tapas, and the stained-glass windows, stone pillars and high-beamed ceilings make for an atmospheric setting for the regular music nights.

Jack's Coastguard Restaurant
Cromane Lower (066 976 9102, www.jacks coastguardstation.ie). Dinner served Mar-Oct 6-9.30pm Mon, Wed-Sun. Jan, Feb, Nov, Dec 6-9pm Thur-Sun.
This winning venue is located in the former coastguard station next to Cromane's beach, a 15-minute drive west of Killorglin. Start with a pint in the traditional bar before moving to the bright, split-level restaurant, where delectable seafood dishes (oven-roasted hake with wild mushroom riosotto and black truffle oil, or paella with local seafood) come with spectacular views over Inch peninsula. Then return to the bar for a nightcap, where you're almost guaranteed some traditional Irish music or a local band. Jack's also offers B&B accommodation nearby.

Mulcahy's Restaurant
Henry Street, Kenmare (064 664 2383). Dinner served 6-10pm Mon, Wed-Sun.
Chef Bruce Mulcahy uses local ingredients to create food with Asian flair, having learned his trade in Thailand and Japan. So expect high-quality sushi and sashimi, as well as the likes of Kerry lamb served with a cep and pistachio crust. The atmosphere in the smartish dining room (leather seating and plenty of polished wood) is relaxed, and staff are friendly.

Nick's Seafood Restaurant & Piano Bar ★
Lower Bridge Street, Killorglin (066 976 1219). Open Bar 5-11.30pm Wed-Fri, Sun; 5.30-11.30pm Sat. Food served Restaurant 5.30-10pm Wed-Sun.
A Kerry stalwart – and famed throughout Ireland – Nick Foley's restaurant has been serving classic seafood dishes for more than 25 years. Two handsome townhouses contain a bar (complete with pianist) and a characterful restaurant, with white tablecloths and a dark-timbered ceiling. Succulent Kerry lamb and beef are available for non-fish eaters, but it's the lobster thermidor and top-quality oysters (from the family farm) that most diners are after. The extensive and unusual wine list will please connoisseurs. End the evening with a singalong around the piano.

Number 35
Main Street, Kenmare (064 664 1559, www.no35 kenmare.com). Dinner served July-Sept 6-9.30pm daily. Jan-June, Oct-Dec 6-9.30pm Sat, Sun.
An accommodating, relaxed establishment, Number 35 is spread over two floors, with bare limestone walls, wooden ceilings, floorboards and furniture, and low lighting. The seasonal, brasserie-style menu is a class act, with Irish beef

and local seafood put to good use in such dishes as Kenmare mussels in a cream, white wine and dill sauce (a starter), slow-cooked lamb stew or tomato and basil pasta (both mains). Inventive own-made pizzas (pork belly, black pudding and caramelised onion; chicken curry) feature too. Finish with local ice-cream or strawberry pavlova.

Where to stay

There's a wide choice of accommodation in Kenmare (www.kenmare.com): affordable B&Bs, cosy guesthouses and luxury five-star hotels. For budget beds, try the Kenmare Hostel (064 664 2333, www.kenmarehostels.com, closed mid

Things to do

Muckross House & Gardens. See p118.

Gaelic football
www.kerrygaa.ie.
The two most popular spectator sports in Ireland are Gaelic football and hurling, the national sport. Kerry's Gaelic football team, known as the Kingdom, are the most successful team in the sport's history, having won the All-Ireland Senior Football Championship a record 36 times (and contested the final 55 times). As a result, the game – something like a blend of rugby and soccer, played by a 15-strong team – is very popular in the county. You can watch matches of a high standard during the championship season (Apr-Sept) at Fitzgerald Stadium in Killarney and Austin Stack Park in Tralee.

KILLARNEY & AROUND

Muckross Circuit Walk
Starting at Muckross House (*see p118*), this 10km walk around Muckross Lake is mainly on a paved path through woodland, with a short stint along a road. It skirts Lough Leane, where there are fine views, and passes Dinis Cottage, a hunting lodge that is open for refreshments in summer. It also takes in the Meeting of the Waters, where the waters of Lough Leane converge with those of Muckross Lake, and the 20m cascade that is Torc Waterfall. There are plenty of picnic places. The whole thing takes about three hours, and can also be done by bike.

IVERAGH PENINSULA

Kerry Way
www.kerryway.net.
This 200km waymarked trail, starting and finishing in Killarney, takes in the mountain, farms, villages and

coastline of the Iveragh peninsula – it's one of Ireland's most popular long-distance paths. The walk is divided into nine stages; those looking for a challenge should put aside ten to 12 days for the whole walk. The website is packed with useful information on services and accommodation en route.

DINGLE PENINSULA

Dingle Way
www.dingleway.net.
A 179km trail circumnavigating the Dingle peninsula. It traditionally departs from Tralee, passing through mountains, headlands (Brandon Head, Slea Head), villages and towns (including Dunquin and Ballyferriter and Dingle itself), with views to die for. The terrain is very diverse, taking in cliff edges, quiet country lanes, farmland and remote beaches, but is only moderately difficult.

NORTH KERRY

River Walk
Listowel.
Leaving from the Town Square, take the path to the right of the castle down to the river. From here, a pathway follows the grassy bank northwards (with one diversion up to the road to cross a bridge). A sign for the Gardens of Europe points the way from the river, through a wooded park, eventually arriving at the gardens, which are divided into segments representing the 12 countries that joined the European Union in 1992. There's also a Holocaust memorial. It's a peaceful spot for a rest, and only a five-minute walk along the main road back to the centre of Listowel.

BEST ISLANDS

There are hundreds of islands off Ireland's lengthy coastline; here are some of the most enticing. For more, see www.irishislands.info.

Achill Island

www.achilltourism.com.
Ireland's largest island, Achill is easy to get to: it's connected to the mainland of County Mayo by road. Heinrich Böll wrote about Achill's stark beauty, while artists such as Paul Henry and Charles Lamb tried to capture it all on canvas. It's still very popular, with visitors drawn by the sandy beaches, heather-clad hills and rugged coastline. *See p88.*

Cape Clear Island

www.capeclearisland.eu.
Ireland's most southerly island, diminutive Cape Clear is a 45-minute boat trip from the coast of County Cork. A Gaeltacht area, it has a pub, holiday cottages, Irish classes in summer and a storytelling festival in September. *See p142.*

Great Blasket Island

www.blasketislands.ie.
A 20-minute ferry ride brings you to Great Blasket Island, located off County Kerry's Dingle peninsula. Pristine white beaches, walking trails, an abundance of wildlife (including a colony of grey seals) and a rich literary history are just some of its attractions. *See p119.*

Rathlin Island

www.rathlincommunity.org
Five miles off the north Antrim coast, Rathlin is a designated conservation area, containing the RSPB Seabird Centre, because it supports Ireland's largest seabird colony – kittiwakes, razorbills, fulmars, puffins and other species. The rugged island is edged with spectacular cliffs, and crowned at each end with a lighthouse. There's a pub, shop, a couple of churches and accommodation if you want to stay over. *See p283.*

Skellig Michael

A UNESCO World Heritage site, Skellig Michael contains the redoubtable remains of a seventh-century monastic settlement – reached by a climbing a steep staircase to the island's spiny peak. It's an hour's boat ride from Kerry's Iveragh peninsula. *See p119.*

Tory Island

www.oileanthorai.com.
Remote, weather-lashed Tory Island, off the north coast of Donegal, has natural and man-made charms, notably a large bird population and a long-established artists' scene. Combine birdwatching with a scenic walk around the island – it's pretty small – to experience its particular atmosphere. *See p35.*

Oct-mid May) in the centre of town, or, a few kilometres away, the campsite and hostel at Faungorth Activity Centre (064 664 1770, www.faungorth.com, closed Nov-Mar). Brooklane Hotel (Sneem Road, 064 664 2077, www.brook lanehotel.com) on the edge of town has modern rooms and suites, and a popular bar and restaurant, while Muxnaw Lodge (Castletown Bere Road, 064 664 1252, www.kenmare.eu/ muxnaw) is a gabled Victorian mansion overlooking Kenmare River, with five delightful B&B rooms and mature gardens.

If money's no object, handsome Shelburne Lodge (Cork Road, 064 664 1013, www.shelburne lodge.com, closed Nov-Mar) is an ivy-covered, 18th-century stone house just outside Kenmare. Ten elegant bedrooms are split between the main house and the former coachhouse, and there's also a cosy drawing room and expansive gardens. Upmarket Sheen Falls Lodge (064 664 1600, www.sheenfallslodge.ie, closed Jan) is much bigger, with 66 exquisitely decorated rooms, plus a spa, golf course and fine-dining restaurant.

In Caherdaniel, the Derrynane Hotel (066 947 5136, www.derrynane.com, hotel closed Oct-Apr), in a prime position beside the bay, has 50 hotel rooms and eight self-catering holiday homes (open all year round). Facilities include a sauna and steam room, tennis court, seaweed baths and an outdoor heated pool for those not wanting to brave the Atlantic. Self-caterers should try quirky Iskeroon (066 947 5119, www.iskeroon.com, closed Oct-Apr). For more choices, visit www.caherdanielonline.com.

In Waterville, the Old Cable House (066 947 4233, www.oldcablehouse.com) is a popular B&B with a small restaurant, while the Butler Arms Hotel (066 947 4144, www.butlerarms.com, closed mid Oct-Easter) is a large, homely place, if rather old-fashioned, with a wonderful waterfront location and friendly staff.

Ballinskelligs has some B&Bs (listed on www.visit ballinskelligs.ie) and the budget Skellig Hostel (066 947 9942, www.skellighostel.com). In Portmagee, there are self-catering cottages and farmhouses (066 947 7151, www.portmageeseasidecottages.com), Portmagee Hostel (066 948 0018, www.port mageehostel.com) and several B&Bs. Moorings Guesthouse (066 947 7108, www.moorings.ie), overlooking the harbour, has 16 comfortable rooms, a popular bar with regular Irish music and dancing sessions, and a good seafood restaurant.

A number of B&Bs are scattered around Valentia Island, though the bulk of the accommodation is concentrated in Knightstown (www.visitvalentia island.ie), including the Royal Hotel (066 947 6144, www.theroyalvalentia.com). The sole hostel and campsite, Ring Lyne (066 947 6103), is near Chapeltown.

Ard na Sidhe (066 976 9105, www.ardna sidhe.com, closed Nov-Apr) means 'Hill of the Fairies' and this grand sandstone house has a magical hilltop location next to Caragh Lake. It's just been refurbished in a modish country style, with modern four-poster beds and stylish fabrics.

Europe Hotel & Resort. See p116.

Carrig Country House ★

Caragh Lake, nr Glenbeigh (066 976 9100, www.carrig house.com). Rates €150-€250 double incl breakfast.
You can't help but fall in love with Frank and Mary Slattery's yellow-painted Victorian house on the banks of Caragh Lake. The 17 bedrooms are decorated with antique furniture and floral curtains, and most have large windows with views over the lake's placid waters. There's a comfortable drawing room, a fine restaurant (popular with locals) with a piano player in one corner, and plenty of nooks and crannies. Fresh flowers are displayed everywhere, while azaleas, rhododendrons, hydrangeas, wisteria and clematis bring colour to the charming lakeside gardens.

Glanleam House & Gardens ★

Glanleam, Valentia Island (066 947 6176). Rates €80-€200 double incl breakfast.
In the 1830s, Sir Peter George Fitzgerald, the 19th Knight of Kerry, created the spectacular subtropical gardens at Glanleam – taking advantage of the mild microclimate to feature rare and subtropical plants, many from Australasia. Today, it's an exotic, lush wonderland, with paths weaving through the thick foliage, streams and water features. The 40-acre gardens are open to the public, but guests at Fitzgerald's former home (originally a linen mill) can visit them for free. The seven bedrooms are delightful, combining antique and contemporary furnishings, and with views over the gardens or out to sea. A large library serves as a reading room, and there's also a walled kitchen garden.

Park Hotel Kenmare ★

Kenmare (064 664 1200, www.parkkenmare.com). Rates €290-€360 double incl breakfast.
At the top of Kenmare town, iron gates and dense hedges conceal the five-star Park Hotel. While rooms don't come cheap here, you can expect only the best of everything. The 46 rooms – with views across the manicured lawns, gardens and Kenmare Bay – are individually decorated, with rich fabrics, period furniture and artwork. There's a drawing room, a glorious garden lounge and, for film buffs, an in-house cinema. Come evening, drop into the cellar bar to taste the array of malts, or get dressed up for dinner in the excellent restaurant. The Park is renowned for having one of Ireland's best spas (open to hotel guests only), featuring a 25m lap pool, gym, sauna, yoga room, fitness classes and numerous indulgent treatments. The other facilities – including a golf course, croquet lawn and tennis court – are superb, and cycling, riding and fishing can be arranged.

DINGLE PENINSULA

Too often, visitors follow the yellow brick road that is the Ring of Kerry and forget about the other Kerry peninsula to the north. They're missing out. The Dingle peninsula (www.dingle-peninsula.ie) juts out nearly 50 kilometres into the Atlantic, which crashes against the high cliffs and laps upon the white sand beaches. Wide Dingle Bay is a playground for anglers, surfers and leisure boaters – and one very special inhabitant: Fungi the dolphin, who has made the bay his home for 25 years. The land is littered with ancient sites, some among the finest in all Ireland. Off the southernmost tip rise the pinnacles of the Blasket Islands, which have a ravaged beauty thanks to the scouring effects of wind and water. The

peninsula's key town is Dingle. A vibrant spot with colourful building lining the waterfront, it's extremely popular in summer, when crowds congregate in the numerous bars and a festive atmosphere prevails. This is a strongly Gaeltacht area, so many signposts are in Irish and many locals speak Irish.

Dingle & the south coast

The R561 runs along the south coast, parallel to the Slieve Mish Mountains. From Castlemaine, it's about 18 kilometres to Inch, a tiny hamlet with a few buildings perched above the peninsula's finest beach: Inch Strand, featured in the famous David Lean movie *Ryan's Daughter*. Backed by undulating dunes that provide shelter on windy days, the sand spit reaches across Dingle Bay for five kilometres. Perched above, with truly wonderful views across the bay, is Inch Beach House (*see p131*) offering B&B accommodation, some self-catering cottages and Sammy's Bar, Restaurant & Café (*see p129*) – all under the same ownership. The water is dotted with kite-surfers, windsurfers and bathers; surfboards can be rented at the shop next to Sammy's.

Eight kilometres further on, at the junction with the N86, is the town of Annascaul. It's good fishing territory, thanks to the Annascaul River, and there are marked walking trails leading into the mountains. Hikers aplenty take part in the Annascaul & Inch Walking Festival, held over the October bank holiday weekend. The South Pole Inn (066 915 7388) is an atmospheric pub, founded by the renowned Antarctic explorer Tom Crean, who was born in the town and took part in both Scott and Shackleton's expeditions to the South Pole.

The N86 then turns inland and runs beside the mountain range, until the sight of brightly painted façades – orange, turquoise, green, all the colours of the rainbow – signals your arrival in Dingle town ★. The attractive harbour, lined with neat buildings, shelters fishing and leisure boats. Narrow streets rise steeply from the harbour to link with the main drag, which is set back from the water. Cafés, boutiques and knick-knack shops abound, alongside characterful pubs and seafood restaurants that ensure many a lively evening.

Driving and parking can be problematic in the small town, so it's best to abandon your car for the duration of your stay. The car park is at the harbour, on Strand Street, where the helpful Tourist Information Centre (066 915 1188, closed Oct-Apr Sun) is also located. Staff should be able to help with accommodation – though it's best to book before you arrive. Also on Strand Street is Dingle Oceanworld (066 915 2111, www.dingle-oceanworld.ie), home to a colourful array of exotic fish, including sharks, stingrays, turtles, clown fish and piranhas.

Boats (066 915 2626, www.dingledolphin.com) depart from the pier all day throughout the year, in the hope of catching a glimpse of Fungi the bottlenose dolphin, who has lived in Dingle Bay since 1983. Fungi seems to love all the attention, and is likely to make a grand appearance, splashing about playfully. Many people want to get in the water with Fungi; two-hour swimming trips are offered in

Park Hotel Kenmare

the mornings. Booking is necessary for all trips: phone in advance or pop into the office on the pier next to the tourist centre. Ferries also run from the harbour to Great Blasket Island (see p119) – a fantastic day out.

A farmers' market takes place at the harbour every Friday and is a hub for local food producers. Plenty of gift shops sell Fungi memorabilia, of course. There are also artisan food shops, such as the Little Cheese Shop (Grey's Lane, mobile 087 625 5788, www.thelittlecheeseshop.net, closed Sun). Wonderful wall hangings, throws and other textiles, made by weaver Lisbeth Mulcahy, are available in her smart shop on Green Street (066 915 1688, www.lisbethmulcahy.com, closed Oct-June Sun) – as well as pottery by her husband, Louis, and other gift items. Díseart Visitor Centre (066 915 2476, www.diseart.ie, closed Sat, Sun), located in a former convent on Green Street, calls itself an 'Institute of Irish Spirituality and Culture' and runs all manner of courses and workshops (in archaeology, Irish language, folklore and music, among others). Visitors can admire the 12 stained-glass windows designed and installed by the famed Irish artist Harry Clarke.

The reason many people come to Dingle is to take advantage of the numerous outdoor activities on offer. By boat, surfboard, bicycle, horse or on foot: whatever your preferred mode of transport, it's catered for. Bikes can be rented at Foxy Johns (Main Street, 066 915 1316) – one half is a pub, the other a hardware/bike hire shop – while Man in the Mountains Outdoor Shop (Strand Street, 066 915 2400, www.themountainmanshop.com, closed Oct-May Sun) can arrange mountain biking, horse riding, hiking and bus tours. Wannabe surf dudes can book lessons with West Coast Surf School (Green Street, mobile 086 836 0271, www.westcoastsurf school.ie), while the more experienced should head to Finn McCools surf shop (066 915 0833, www. finnmccools.ie) on Lower Green Street.

Dingle buzzes throughout the summer, and even in winter you'll find a crowd enjoying a pint or two, especially during festivals. The Dingle Walking Festival (http://dinglewalkingfestival.com) in February arranges guided walks in the locality and other parts of the peninsula, while the flourishing arts scene in the town is celebrated at the beginning of May with the week-long Pan Celtic

Dingle. See p126.

Dingle peninsula. See p126.

Festival (www.panceltic.ie). August brings three days of racing at the Dingle Horse Racing Festival (www.dingleraces.ie) and the wonderful Dingle Regatta. September is also a busy month, with the Dingle Trad/Fusion Festival (www.dingletrad fest.com), a mix of traditional and contemporary musicians from Ireland and abroad, and the Dingle Food & Drink Festival (www.dinglefood.com).

Slea Head to Castlegregory

The R559 heading west from Dingle is known as the Slea Head Drive; as you cross the headland, the views over Ventry harbour are a taste of what's to come. Ventry is a fishing village with a beautiful, crescent-shaped beach. Outside the village, the small Celtic & Prehistoric Museum (066 915 9191, closed Nov-mid Mar) has a fantastic collection of items from the Stone and Bronze Ages, and Celtic and Viking periods.

In the shadow of Mount Eagle is Fahan, famed for the ancient clifftop site of Dunbeg Fort (see p119). Close by are the Fahan beehive huts, early Christian stone huts believed to have been built to shelter pilgrims. The road then narrows and follows the sheer cliffs closely around the headland. You can pull into a viewpoint to fully appreciate the panoramic view across to the Blasket Islands. The road descends into Dunquin, another small fishing settlement, from where boats leave frequently for Great Blasket Island. The Great Blasket Visitor Centre (Ionad an Bhlascaoid Mhóir – see p120) to the north of Dunquin is packed with interest.

A few kilometres further, on the tip of Clochar Head, is the idyllic Tig Áine (066 915 6214, www.tigaine.com, open daily late May-Aug; rest of the year by appointment): it's a multipurpose set-up, with an art gallery, traditional crafts shop, café and restaurant. It also functions as a writers' centre. Further on towards Ballyferriter is the popular Louis Mulcahy shop (Clogher, 066 915 6229, www.louismulcahy.com), husband of Lisbeth and one of Ireland's most famous potters. You can watch potters at work, purchase items or even take a course.

Ballyferriter nestles between the jagged peaks of Sybil Head and the Three Sisters to the north, and Croaghmurhin to the south. It's a small place, with several good pubs hosting traditional music sessions, such as Tigh an tSaorsaigh or Tigh Uí Catháin, which has an outdoor terrace. The village is at its most vibrant during the five-day traditional music festival Scoil Cheoil an Earraigh (www.scoilcheoil.com) in February. Heritage walks are arranged at Músaem Chorca Dhuibhne (066 915 6333, www.westkerrymuseum.com, open daily June-mid Sept; rest of the year by appointment), an intriguing museum with displays about the peninsula's geology, archaeology, and social and cultural history. There's also a little café.

Next comes Ballydavid, where attractive Wine Strand beach is a great place for a dip on a warm day. A surprising number of historic sites are within striking distance. The most remarkable is probably the Gallarus Oratory (see p119); nearby is Gallarus Castle, a 15th-century tower house once belonging

to the Fitzgeralds, the lords of West Kerry. The four-storey rectangular building has recently been restored and is open to visitors. To the south-east, and not easy to find, is the monastic site of Riasc. A fifth- or sixth-century stone wall surrounds the foundations of six monks' huts, a square oratory and some astoundingly well-preserved standing stones, carved with words and decorative symbols.

Brandon Mountain occupies the north-west corner of the peninsula, and is great for walkers, with the long-distance Dingle Way (see p123) passing scenic Brandon Head. Extending out of the mainland east of Brandon Head is a sand spit known as the Maharees, where surfers of all description (board, kite, wind) flock for some of the best conditions around. It's also perfect for those seeking blustery walks along sandy beaches or energising sports. Jamie Knox Watersports (066 713 9411, www.jamieknox.com) offers equipment hire, lessons and plenty of advice. At the top of the peninsula, on Scraggane pier, is dive centre Waterworld (066 713 9292, www.waterworld.ie). Accommodation is available in Harbour House, and other activities can also be arranged.

From Dingle, it's 25 kilometres via the R560 to the only town on the north side of the peninsula, Castlegregory. It's a twisting, narrow, sometimes terrifying drive, climbing 400 metres up to Conor Pass. At the top is a car park, with truly stupendous views across the peninsula north and south. Castlegregory has a tourist office, a couple of pubs, and basic accommodation in Fitzgerald's Euro Hostel (066 713 9951) on Strand Road or Anchor Caravan Park (066 713 9157, closed Oct-Easter). A wonderful Blue Flag beach is close by, near Castlegregory Golf Club (066 713 9444, www.castlegregorygolflinks.com). From Castlegregory, the road follows the coastline, with beautiful views towards County Clare as you approach Tralee.

Where to eat & drink

At Inch beach, there are panoramic views and great food at Sammy's Bar, Restaurant & Café (066 915 8118, www.inchbeach.ie, closed mid Jan-mid Feb, mid Nov-mid Dec). Toasted sandwiches, soup and snacks are served in the café, while the restaurant offers the likes of Dingle Bay oysters, seafood pasta and steaks.

Dingle town, as you might expect, is overloaded with eating and drinking places. Astonishingly, there are around 50 pubs, mostly traditional in style, so good Guinness and a friendly atmosphere aren't hard to find. Lord Bakers (066 915 1277, www.lordbakers.ie) on Main Street is thought to be the town's oldest pub; drop in for a pint or to partake of the food (Dingle Bay seafood a speciality, though roasts and other meat dishes are available). Traditional music is the pulse of Dingle, and there will always be a session or two on any given night. An Droichead Beag (Small Bridge Bar) on Main Street, and O'Flahertys on Bridge Street are the most famous venues.

Gallarus Oratory. See p119.

There are some excellent, funky cafés for casual meals. The Goat Street Café (066 915 2770, www.thegoatstreetcafe.com, closed Sun), located on – you've guessed it – Goat Street, is open from breakfast to dinner. Thai green curry or vegetarian tagine might feature at lunch, while the evening menu varies depending on the catch of the day. For the tastiest fish and chips, it has to be Reel Dingle Fish (Bridge Street, 066 915 1713, closed Jan Mon-Wed). Local ice-cream maker Murphy's (Strand Street, 066 915 2644, www.murphysice cream.ie) offers a medley of scrumptious flavours, including sea salt, and Kerry cream.

Global Village (Main Street, 066 915 2325, www.globalvillagedingle.com, closed Tue) on the Main Street is a bright, relaxed restaurant with a more formal menu, and a well-deserved reputation. It's open only in the evenings. Ashe's Bar (Main Street, 066 915 0989, www.ashesbar.ie) continues to be a favourite with locals for drinks and excellent seafood; it also has B&B rooms. For fantastic home cooking, it's hard to beat the Garden Café (Green Street, mobile 087 781 5126, www.thegarden cafedingle.eu, closed Tue). It's a proper community venture, supporting local food producers, artists and craftspeople, with an eco-conscious vibe and a small back garden.

Seafood is the speciality at the Old Pier (Feothanach, 066 915 5242, www.oldpier.com, closed Jan-Apr Mon-Fri; May, June, Oct Mon-Wed) in Ballydavid, which also has B&B rooms. The friendly local pub, Tigh TP (066 915 5300, www.tigh-tp.ie) does good food and hosts music sessions. After a bracing walk on the windy beach at the Maharees, head to Spillane's (066 713 9125, www.spillanes bar.com) for delicious steaks, burgers and fish dishes. To experience a proper local Irish bar with plenty of charm and character, stop in Camp (on the N86, between Castlegregory and Tralee) at Ashe's Bar (066 713 0133) or the Railway Tavern (066 713 0188), where traditional music is played most nights.

Chart House
The Mall, Dingle (066 915 2255, www.thecharthouse dingle.com). Dinner served June-Sept 6-10pm daily. Mid Feb-May, Oct-Dec 6-10pm Wed-Sun.
It's hard to say which is the best restaurant in Dingle as the quality everywhere is high, but currently the Chart House appears to have established itself as number one. The dining room is an atmospheric setting for some fine cuisine that focuses, as you would expect, on local ingredients. Try the Blasket Island lamb, Annascaul black pudding wrapped in filo pastry, or Dingle Bay crabmeat and seafood bisque. The wine list is just as carefully chosen, with many wines imported directly from South Africa.

Dick Mack's ★
Green Street, Dingle (066 915 1960, www.dickmacks. homestead.com). Open varies; phone for details.
Dick Mack's pub is a Dingle institution. Run by an eccentric Kerry man who prowls the bar wearing a cowboy hat, it's both traditional and quirky – as all good Irish bars should be. Golden stars embedded in the pavement outside immortalise the famous people who have popped in over the years, among them Julia Roberts. The place was once a cobbler's, as is evident in the front room, with tools and shoes seemingly deserted and stools pulled up to the counter, now the bar. Behind is a series of little rooms, complete with an Aga and a piano. Open fires, random paraphernalia and the county's best snug – all contribute to make this one of the most charming pubs in Kerry.

Out of the Blue ★
Strand Street, Dingle (066 915 0811, www.outoftheblue.ie). Lunch served 12.30-3pm Sun. Dinner served 5-9.30pm Mon-Sat; 5.30-9.30pm Sun.
It is indeed blue – and yellow and red and orange. This unassuming restaurant resembles a Caribbean beach shack; inside, the laid-back vibe, friendly staff and bright decor can only make you smile. There's no menu as such: it depends on what comes in off the boat that day, as seafood is the thing here. Dishes are written up daily on the blackboard, and there's usually plenty of choice. Only the best and

freshest of the sea's delicacies are served, cooked simply but perfectly. Sit outside on a bench and watch the boats sail into the marina, trying to ignore the people in the queue, willing you to give them your table.

Where to stay
Inch Beach House (066 915 8118, www.inchbeach.ie) is a wonderful place to stay in Inch. Overlooking Dingle Bay and mere steps from the strand, it has 11 smart, modern rooms and superb sea views from the glass-walled dining room, plus nine well-equipped self-catering cottages. Dingle Gate Hostel (066 915 7150, www.dingle gatehostel.com), a hostel with camping facilities is a couple of kilometres outside Annascaul.

Dingle town has plenty of accommodation to suit all budgets; check listings on www.dingle-peninsula.ie. Luxury guesthouses include Castlewood House (The Wood, 066 915 2788, www.castlewooddingle.com, closed Jan), which has a boutique-hotel vibe, with the 12 bedrooms varying in design, and many overlooking the bay. Under the same ownership is waterside Heatons House (The Wood, 066 915 2288, www.heatons dingle.com). Both have restaurants. Tucked above town on the hillside, Greenmount House (Gortonora, 066 915 1414, www.greenmount-house.com) has bright, spacious rooms with wooden floors and beautiful views.

The capacious Dingle Skellig Hotel (066 915 0200, www.dingleskellig.com, closed Jan-mid Feb; Nov, Dec Mon-Fri) is popular with families as it has good facilities, including a swimming pool, crèche and kids' club. For more basic, and cheaper, accommodation, try the Grapevine Hostel (Dykegate Lane, 066 915 1434, www.grapevinedingle.com, closed Jan, Dec Mon-Fri) in the town centre, which has dorms and twin rooms; or the Rainbow Hostel (066 915 1044, www.rainbowhosteldingle.com), just outside town, where you can also pitch a tent.

Out of the Blue

Accommodation elsewhere on the peninsula is mainly in B&Bs, though Ballydavid has the Smerwick Harbour Hotel (066 915 6470, www.smerwick hotel.ie, closed Oct-Easter), with a bar, restaurant and en suite rooms. Alternatively, there's the Dingle Activities Centre (066 915 5143, www.dingle activities.com, closed Oct-Mar), which has a campsite and self-catering accommodation.

Emlagh House ★
Dingle (066 915 2345, www.emlaghhouse.com). Rates €130-€220 double incl breakfast. Closed Dec-Feb.
Emlagh House provides a tranquil escape from the hustle and bustle of lively Dingle town. It's immaculately maintained, with gleaming marble floors and a mix of antique and contemporary furniture. The ten bedrooms are elegantly decorated and very spacious. Breakfast is a hearty affair, with fresh fruit, cold meats and the option of a hot meal to set you up for a day's exploration.

Gorman's Clifftop House & Restaurant
Ballydavid (066 915 5162, www.gormans-clifftop house.com). Rates €99-€150 double incl breakfast.
Located a few minutes from Ballydavid, Gorman's Clifftop House is, as its name suggests, positioned high above the sea, overlooking Smerwick Harbour. It has eight simply furnished but very comfortable rooms, some with jacuzzi baths, and all with either a sea or mountain view. Open fires, scattered books and a comfortable sitting room make guests feel at home. Dinner brings delicious home cooking – perhaps Dingle Bay prawns or a lovely salad to start, followed by Kerry lamb or freshly caught fish – served in the colourful, laid-back restaurant.

NORTH KERRY
North Kerry lacks the appeal of the rest of the county, though Tralee, the county town, pulls in the crowds for the annual extravaganza that is the Rose of Tralee (www.roseoftralee.ie) in August. Inspired by the 19th-century ballad of the same name, it's one of the biggest festivals in Ireland, centred around choosing a young woman from a host of international contenders to be the winning 'Rose'. There's a carnival atmosphere through the town, and accommodation must be booked months in advance. Kerry folk know how to throw a party, and the celebrations continue with several days of action at the Tralee Races.

The main commercial centre in Kerry, Tralee is a typical market town, its main street lined with cafés, pubs and the usual high-street names. The tourist office (066 712 1288, closed Jan, Feb Sat, Sun; Mar-June, Sept-Dec Sun) is located in Ashe Memorial Hall, a grand sandstone building on Denny Street. In the same buiding is the Kerry County Museum (066 712 7777, www.kerry museum.ie, closed Jan-Apr, Sept-Dec Mon, Sun), which has a collection of more than 4,000 items, from the Stone Age to the present. Adjacent is the Town Park, a green and pleasant space with lovely rosebeds, which is also home to Siamsa Tíre, the National Folk Theatre of Ireland (066 712 3055, www.siamsatire.com). Dedicated to supporting and encouraging Irish folk culture, the centre presents a packed programme of music, dance, theatre and literary events throughout the year.

Just outside town, in a picturesque position on the edge of Tralee Bay, is Blennerville Mill, a renovated 19th-century windmill with an exhibition on Irish emigration, a restaurant and a craft shop. You can climb to the top of the windmill to see the sails in motion. Opposite is a bird viewing hide; the mudflats and saltmarshes of Tralee Bay Nature Reserve are important feeding grounds for seasonal seabirds.

Golfers will enjoy the area, thanks to the Arnold Palmer-designed links course at Tralee Golf Club (066 713 6379, www.traleegolfclub.com) on the coast at West Barrow, and, further north, the world-renowned Ballybunion Golf Club (Sandhill Road, 068 27146, www.ballybuniongolfclub.ie).

About 30 kilometres north of Tralee via the N69 is the pretty riverside town of Listowel. It has a distinguished literary heritage – the famous 20th-century playwright John B Keane hailed from here – that is celebrated in the popular Writers' Week festival (www.writersweek.ie) in June. The Kerry Literary & Cultural Centre (aka the Seanchaí – see p120) is a museum celebrating the lives and works of the county's five most famous authors. It's on the market square, a large open space surrounded by gaily painted Georgian buildings. The large church in the middle has been converted into St John's Theatre & Arts Centre (068 22566, www.stjohnstheatrelistowel.com), which presents plays, dance events, concerts and art exhibitions.

Set back from the square, overlooking the River Feale, is 15th-century Listowel Castle (mobile 086 385 7201, www.heritageireland.ie, closed Sept-mid May). Two large square towers survive, and guided tours are given. The path leading behind the castle brings you along the River Walk – a good way to explore the town. Children will enjoy the Lartigue Monorailway (mobile 068 24393, www.lartiguemonorail.com, closed Oct-Apr). You can take a short journey on a replica of the original steam-powered monorail, which was designed by Frenchman Charles Lartigue and operated from 1888 to 1924, carrying passengers between Listowel and Ballybunion

The latter is a popular seaside resort some 15 kilometres north-west of Listowel, with a wonderful Blue Flag beach that is also popular with surfers.

Where to eat & drink

Tralee has a wide choice of cafés and restaurants. Denny Lane (11 Denny Street, 066 719 4319, www.dennylane.ie, closed Sun) is a great café for breakfast (porridge, buttermilk pancakes), a casual lunch (toasties, quiche, salads) or Saturday brunch (bagels, eggs benedict). A short drive outside Tralee, en route to Killarney in the Ballyseedy Garden Centre, is bright and airy Jam Café (066 719 2580, www.jam.ie). Part of the small Kerry chain, it serves fresh salads, scrummy cakes and inventive savoury dishes. For flavoursome pizza

and pasta dishes, visit the bustling Bella Bia's (Ivy Terrace, 066 714 4896, www.bellabia.com); for excellent steak, the Holy Cow, inside Benners Hotel, (Castle Street, 066 712 1877, www.benners hoteltralee.ie) is the spot.

There are also bars aplenty, including Bailey's Corner (Castle Street, 066 712 6230) and the Mall Tavern (The Mall, 066 712 1370) – both favourites for daytime food and late-night drinks – plus the ever-popular Blaskets (Castle Street, 066 712 3313), which has music and a late licence at weekends. For a traditional Irish bar with traditional music, head to Sean Og's (Bridge Street, 066 712 8822, www.sean-ogs.com). Keep an eye out for posters for Club Head Bang Bang, usually run on an ad hoc basis at the rear of the Greyhound Bar: it's a great night of bands and DJs.

Listowel's nightlife consists of mainly traditional bars with music sessions and a lively local clientele. The John B Keane bar or Tankard's, both on William Street, are atmospheric traditional pubs, the former owned by the late author's family. Allos café-bar (Church Street, mobile 068 22880, closed Mon, Sun) is much loved for its excellent bistro-style cooking and decent pints; it has accommodation upstairs too.

Station House

Blennerville (066 714 9980 www.thestationhouse.ie). Open 12.30-11.30pm Mon-Thur; 12.30pm-midnight Fri; 12.30pm-12.30am Sat; 12.30-11pm Sun.
Located across the road from Blennerville Mill, the Station House has built a reputation for its 'latino lounge' vibe and bistro-style cooking. There's also tapas and a weekend brunch menu. Dark wood, stone walls and candelabras create a sultry ambience, and a pianist and jazz musicians play regularly.

Where to stay

Tralee has limited accommodation compared to Killarney. The best hotel in the area is Ballyseede Castle (Ballyseede, 066 712 5799, www.ballyseede castle.com, closed Jan, Feb), five kilometres east of Tralee on the N21. Surrounded by extensive parkland, it has 23 rooms decorated in a slightly old-fashioned country house style, plus a bar and restaurant. Listowel is an incredibly hospitable town, with plenty of locals opening their homes for visitors on a B&B basis; check listings at www.listowel.ie.

Listowel Arms

The Square, Listowel (068 21500, www.listowelarms. com). Rates €120-€140 double incl breakfast.
In business since the 19th century and cointinuing ot mi its high standards over the years, the Listowel Arms, set on the main square, has bundles of old world charm. Renovations have modernised facilities, and the 42 bedrooms are spacious and comfortable, some with views over the River Feale. The public areas are airy, with open fires and sofas, while the lively pub serves a very popular carvery lunch, and has an terrace overlooking the river. The hotel is a key venue for Writers' Week, so booking is essential in June.

County Cork

Cork is one of Ireland's most visited counties, with daily flights from the UK and mainland Europe into its cosmopolitan main city. Cork city is a thriving cultural centre, boasting a busy festival calendar and some great bars and restaurants. Inland, rich farmland and undulating hills provide the county with an abundance of natural produce, while the craggy coastline and its busy fishing villages are the source of excellent seafood. As a result, the county has become a major foodie destination, with an astounding number of high-quality restaurants catering for the growing influx of holidaymakers.

West from Cork city, the bohemian harbour village of Kinsale draws summer crowds, thanks to its fine seafood restaurants, lively drinking holes and the prospect of numerous watersports and activities. Further west, the landscape becomes more dramatic, especially on the Mizen, Sheep's Head and Beara peninsulas, with their charming villages, remote islands and staggering weathered beauty.

CORK CITY

Corcaigh – Gaelic for Cork – means 'marsh', so it's no surprise that Cork city is surrounded by water. The River Lee divides the city into north and south, with an island in the middle, and the quays of the waterways on either side are lined with old warehouses. Dozens of bridges traverse the river connecting the central island with the north and south. The river feeds into Cork harbour, one of the world's largest natural harbours. It remains a busy industrial port, but the heart of the city lies on the island, and it is here that tourists will find the vibrant, diverse and increasingly cosmopolitan atmosphere for which Cork has become known. Cork was City of Culture in 2005 and the legacy of the money and energy poured into the arts during this period is an exciting and dynamic cultural life. Also, in recent years, the city and surrounding areas have developed a flourishing culinary scene.

Cork is Ireland's second city – although any Corconian will claim that it is number one. Locals are proud of the county's rebellious reputation, which stems from Cork being the base for the National Fenian Movement in the 19th century.

The history of Cork began in the seventh century when St Finbarre founded a monastery on the banks of the Lee, but it was another 300 years before the Vikings arrived and developed a settlement on the island marshes. The arrival of the Anglo-Normans saw the erection of a city wall and the reclaiming of some of the marshlands. By the 18th century, Cork had become a prosperous trading centre and the wide waterways were busy with boats.

These days, waterways once used to moor boats on the island have been transformed into roads. The wide Grand Parade is one such. The Tourist Information Centre (021 425 5100, closed winter Sun) is located at the south end of the street; historical walking and open bus tours of the city can be arranged here. Also at this end of Grand Parade is the National Monument in memory of those who died in rebellions between 1798 and 1867.

St Patrick's Street curves into Grand Parade and both are a hive of activity, with shops, cafés, bars and restaurants occupying the many Georgian buildings. Tucked in between the two streets is the English Market (see p141), a historic covered food market.

Off these major thoroughfares are smaller streets, such as lively Paul Street, and French Church Street and Carey's Lane, narrow cobbled alleys that formed the French Quarter where Huguenots lived in the 18th century. Just east on Emmet Place is the Crawford Art Gallery (see p140) beside which is the glass-fronted Opera House (021 427 0022, www.corkoperahouse.ie), which has a diverse programme of theatre, music, comedy and dance throughout the year.

South of here is Cork's business district; South Mall, dotted with modern cafés and restaurants overlooking the river, caters for the working lunch. From here there are views across to City Hall, an impressive limestone building topped with a copper domed clock tower.

To the west of the island is Fitzgerald Park, several acres of formal gardens spreading out from the River Lee. In the grounds is Cork Public Museum (021 427 0679, www.corkcity.ie, closed Oct-Mar Sun), where the city's political, social, economic, and sporting history is depicted. A kilometre west of the park is the fascinating Cork City Gaol (see p140).

The area to the north of the island is known as Shandon; here the streets, lined with a mix of Georgian buildings and more modern residential housing, rise steeply away from the river. It's rather reminiscent of the streets of San Francisco. Cork's most famous landmark is perched on the hillside watching over the city – St Anne's Shandon (021 450 5906, Church Street, www.shandon bells.org). Built in 1722, the church is a blend of red sandstone and limestone, and it is from this landmark that the city colours of red and white were adopted. The four clocks on the steeple

Tournafulla • Ashford • Broadford • Milford • Newtownshandrum

Lyracrumpane • Kilkinlea • (43) • Mullaghareirk Mts • R522 • R515 • R515

Knocknagashel • Mullaghareirk 409 • Drumcollogher • R578 • R515

Glanaruddery Mts 307 • Brosna • Mountcollins • R576 • Rockchapel • Allow • R579 • Tullylease • R572 • R578 • Dromina • Newtown (An Baile Nua)

Knights Mtn. 334 • N21 • Knockachur 316 • Knockacummer 408 • Meelin • R578 • Freemount • Liscarroll • R580 • Churchtown • N2

CRAG CAVE • Knockanefune 439 • Knocknagree • Taur • 266 • R576 • Newmarket (Áth Trasna) • Bawn Cross Roads • DONKEY SANCTUARY • Kilbrin • Castlecor • R522

Castleisland (Oileán Ciarrál) • Cordal • Blueford • R578 • Kanturk (Ceann Toirc) • R576 • Cecilstown • New Twopothouse Village • Ballyclough

KERRY • Currow • Scartaglin • Knocknaboul • Ballydesmond • R577 • Boherbue • R579 • R576 • Castlecor

Farranfore • R577 305 • Kishkeam • Tooreencahill

Kilcummin • 329 • Knocknagree • Cloonbannin • 41 (66) • Banteer • N72 • CORK

Killarney (Cill Airne) • Gneevgullia • Cullen • N72 • Dernagree • Dromagh • Rathcool • Lombardstown • Glantane • R621 • Drommahar

Barraduff • Rathmore • Duncannon Bridge • R582 • Rathcool • Lyre • R579 • R619

Drom • Caherbarnagh • Millstreet (Sráid an Mhuilinn) • Kilcorney • Nad • Bweeng

MUCKROSS • The Paps 696 • Caherbarnagh 682 • MILLSTREET • Boggeragh Mts • R579

TORC WATERFALL • Glenfesk • Musheramore 646 • Carrigagulla • Stuake • Donoughmc

Road unsuitable for HGV's and buses • Lough Guitane • Mullaghanish 650 • Carriganima • Ballinagree • Rylane • Crean's Cross Ro

Mangerton Mt. 840 • Poulgorm Bridge • Derrynasaggart Mts • Aghabullogue • R619 • Berrings • Model Village • Clogh

Morley's Bridge • Coomagearlahy 508 • Baile Bhuirne (Ballyvourney) • PRINCE-AUGUST TOY SOLDIER FACTORY • Clondrohid • Peake • Dripsey • Inishca

Kilgarvan • Cúil Aodha (Coolea) • Baile Mhic Íre (Ballymakeery) • Macroom (Maigh Chromtha) • Coachford • Farran • N22

Cleady • STONE CIRCLE • CALLAN 1261 • Mweelin 487 • Ré na nDoirí (Reananeree) • Sullane • N22 • R618 • Farnanes • Killumney • Aherla

Road unsuitable for HGV's and buses • Carran 606 • Coomataggart 541 • Béal Átha an Ghaorthaidh (Ballingeary) • Cill na Martra (Kilnamartyra) • Kilbarry • Toames • Kilmurry • Cloughduv • Crookstown

Coolnagoppoge 639 • Gougane Barra Forest Park • Lee • R584 • Inchigeelagh • Kilmichael • Poulanargid • Bealnablath • Templemartin • Cross Ba

Knockboy 706 • Doughill Mountain 572 • 473 • Lough Allua • Teerelton • Cappeen • R585 • R590

Shehy Mts • 546 • Togher • Shanlaragh • Castletown • Newcestown • Kilpatric

BAMBOO PARK • R585 • Bandon • R587 • Ballineen • Enniskean • Bandon (Droichead na Bandan) • WEST CO HERITAGE

Kealkill • Derrynacaheragh • R586 • R588 • Kilcolman • N71 • Ballin

Snave Bridge • R584 • Nowen Hill 537 • Dunmanway (Dún Mánmhaí) • Ballynacarriga • 13 (21) • Ballinascarthy • R603

Ballylickey • Mullaghmeesha 487 • Castledonovan • R586 • R599 • Lyre • Ballingurteen • MICHAEL COLLINS ABBEY CENTRE • R602

BANTRY HOUSE & GARDENS • R637 • Rossmore • R588 • Timoleague • R600 • Courtmac

Bantry (Beantraí) • Aghaville • Drimoleague • Drinagh • R599 • Carrigfadda 313 • Bealad • Clonakilty (Cloich na Coillte) • LISSELAN GARDENS • R600 • R601

Dromore • N71 • R586 • Killeenleagh • R593 • Caheragh • Reanascreena • REGIONAL MUS • MODEL RAILWAY VILLAGE • North Ring • Lislevane • Ba

Pt. kboolteenagh 218 • Durrus • Mount Kid 298 • Derreeny Bridge • Connonagh • 19 (31) • Lisavaird • Castlefreke • Ardgehane • Butlerstow

N71 • 23 (37) • Bridge • Leap • N71 • Rosscarbery • Sey Heads

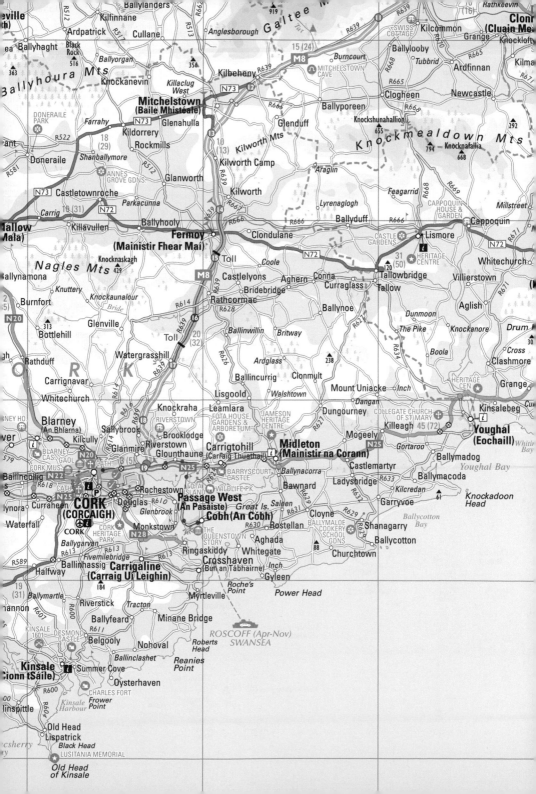

River Lee, Cork

have earned the church the nickname 'four-faced liar' as they are notoriously inaccurate. Climb the steeple for glorious views across the city. A five-minute walk from the church on O'Connell Square is the Cork Butter Museum (*see p140*).

Leave the island, going south, to arrive at St Finbarre's Cathedral (Bishop Street, 021 496 3387, www.stfinbarres.wordpress.com) on the site of St Finbarre's original settlement. It's an striking 19th-century edifice, crowned with three majestic Gothic spires, designed by William Bruges and built from Cork limestone. An ornate interior includes rich mosaics, stained-glass windows, a gilded dome roof and walls lined with Cork red marble. The area surrounding the church, known as Finbarre's Quarter, is a maze of narrow residential streets behind which towers the 17th-century Elizabeth Fort on Barrack's Street, reputedly used by the Williamites when besieging the walled city.

To the east of here, past the warehouses and factories, a peaceful and pretty walkway follows the River Lee out of the city. It's under two kilometres to Blackrock harbour, where there is a little café. From here, you can walk to Blackrock Castle Observatory (*see p140*).

Culture & festivals

The arts scene in Cork is thriving – there's a constant stream of exhibitions, concerts and events. The Firkin Crane Theatre (021 450 7487, www.firkincrane.ie) in Shandon is both a dance school and a theatre for the performing arts. A diverse programme of theatre, dance and music is held in the beautiful Victorian Everyman

Palace (MacCurtain Street, 021 450 1673, www.everymanpalace.com), while the Cork Arts Theatre (Camden Court, 021 450 5624, www.corkartstheatre.com) runs smaller scale performances supporting contemporary, emerging playwrights. The Crane Lane Theatre (Phoenix Street, 021 427 8487, www.cranelanetheatre.ie) is located in a converted old gentlemen's club and hosts a range of modern musical events. On nearby St Patrick's Street, the Savoy Theatre (021 422 3910, www.savoytheatre.ie) has gigs and concerts throughout the week and runs a nightclub at weekends. In the west of the city, at the entrance to the University, the Glucksman Gallery (021 490 1844, www.glucksman.org, closed Mon) is housed in one of Cork's most interesting contemporary buildings, a wooden, glass, limestone and steel construction. As well as a number of modern art exhibitions throughout the year, there's also a lovely café on the premises.

Cork has many festivals: in June, the atmosphere is electric for the Cork Midsummer Festival (www.corkmidsummer.com), two weeks of music, dance, theatre, visual arts and street entertainment in venues throughout the city. At the end of October, the Cork Jazz Festival (www.guinnessjazzfestival.com) draws thousands of jazz lovers from around the world to see national and international musicians perform. Other events of note include the Irish International Folk Dance Festival (www.damhsafest.ie, July); the Cork Folk Festival (www.corkfolkfestival.com, late September/early October); the East Coast Early Music Festival (www.eastcorkearlymusic.ie, October); and the Cork Film Festival (www.corkfilmfest.org, November).

Where to eat & drink

Cork has a host of specialist food shops, and a vibrant dining scene. The narrow streets on the island are full of attractive options: Amicus (Paul Street, 021 427 6455, www.amicusrestaurant.ie) serves a range of international dishes in a bright and contemporary dining room, and the café in the Crawford Art Gallery (see p140) serves delicious Ballymaloe-style dishes, including salads, breads and delicious tarts. In the English Market is the atmospheric Farmgate Café (021 427 8134, www.farmgate.ie, closed Sun), which creates moreish, wholesome dishes using the best of the market's ingredients. The nearby Market Lane Restaurant & Bar (Oliver Plunkett Street, 021 427 4710, www.marketlane.ie) has a tempting menu at a reasonable price, and is also a popular spot for evening drinks. Café Gusto (Washington Street, 021 425 4446, www.cafegusto.com, closed Sun) is good for meze plates and antipasti platters, and also has a BYO policy. Sister restaurant Liberty Grill (Washington Street, 021 427 1049, www.libertygrillcork.com, closed Sun) has a good menu of burgers and grills, plus a great brunch. For pancakes and snacks, try Idaho (021 427 6376, closed Sun) on Caroline Street. Robust Irish cuisine is served at Nash 19 (Prince's Street, 021 427 0880, www.nash19.com, closed Sat, Sun).

Along the quays are a number of restaurants worth investigating, such as Club Brasserie (Lapps Quay, 021 427 3987, closed Sun), a contemporary restaurant equally good for lunch or dinner, while the Boardwalk Bar & Grill (Lapps Quay, 021 427 9990, www.theboardwalkbarandgrill.com, closed Sun) serves great steak with a pianist or DJ playing in the background. Meat is also the order of the day at funky An Crúibín on Union Quay (021 431 0071, www.themeatcentre.com, closed Mon).

Head north off the island to Bridge Street for classic tapas and Spanish wines at the characterful Boqueria (021 455 9049, www.boqueria.ie, closed winter Sun) or to Star Anise (021 455 1635, closed Mon, Sun) for Mediterranean-style food. Follow this with a drink in Dan Lowrey's (021 450 5071), a traditional bar on MacCurtain Street. Also here is Cork institution Isaac's (MacCurtain Street, 021 450 3805), situated in a converted 18th-century warehouse and serving an uncomplicated menu of Irish and international dishes.

Four kilometres out of town is the beautiful Fleming's Restaurant (Tivoli, 021 482 1621, www.flemingsrestaurant.ie), set in a Georgian house and serving classic French cuisine. It also has three charming rooms available for B&B.

Cork has plenty of atmospheric bars; for the best, see p144.

Café Paradiso

Café Paradiso ★

Lancaster Quay (021 427 7939, www.cafeparadiso.ie). Lunch served noon-3pm Fri, Sat. Dinner served 5.30-10pm Tue-Sat.

Vegetarian restaurant Café Paradiso has built up a sterling reputation around the country for its excellent food. Mouthwatering creations include blood orange, fennel and Knockalara sheep's cheese salad with pistachio crumb and

Places to visit

Blackrock Castle Observatory

CORK CITY

Blackrock Castle Observatory

Blackrock (021 435 7917, www.bco.ie). Open 10am-5pm Mon-Fri; 11am-5pm Sat, Sun. Castle tour 3.30pm Mon-Fri; 1.30pm, 3.30pm Sat, Sun. Admission €6; €4 reductions; €16 family. No credit cards.

Blackrock Castle was constructed in the late 16th century as a watchtower and fort guarding the River Lee entrance to Cork. Rebuilt in the 1820s following a fire, it looks like a proper castle – round towers, battlements, thick stone walls overhanging the river – and now houses an astronomy centre. It's a visually stimulating and educational experience: visitors can explore the past on a guided tour, visiting the castle dungeons and turret observatory, then step into the future with interactive exhibitions about the planets. Scientifically minded children will enjoy Comet Chaser, an interactive film in which participants attempt to prevent a comet from destroying Earth. There's also a café and a shop.

Cork Butter Museum

O'Connell Square (021 430 0600, www.cork butter.museum). Open July, Aug 10am-6pm daily. Mar-May, Sept, Oct 10am-5pm daily. Nov-Feb by appointment only. Admission €4; free-€3 reductions. No credit cards.

The Butter Museum is more captivating than you might expect. It explores the history and social impact of Ireland's dairy culture, from the medieval practice of preserving butter in bogs, via Cork's development as a trading centre in the 1700s and the establishment of the Cork Butter Exchange (the world's largest butter market), to the modern-day success of the Kerrygold brand.

Cork City Gaol

Convent Avenue, Sunday's Well (021 430 5022, www.corkcitygaol.com). Open Mar-Oct 9.30am-5pm daily. Nov-Feb 10am-4pm daily. Admission €8; €4.50-€7 reductions; €24 family. No credit cards.

With its turrets, battlements and gate tower, Cork City Gaol looks more like a stately home-cum-castle than a prison. Completed in 1824, it's a fine example of the Georgian-Gothic style, designed by local star architect Sir Thomas Deane. It stopped functioning as a prison in 1923 after the Irish Civil War, and gradually became derelict until it was restored in the 1990s. Life-like wax figures now occupy the refurbished cells, offices and rooms, illustrating what life was like in the gaol, backed up by an exhibition and audio-visual display. It's worth listening to the audio guide as you wander the cold corridors. Visitors wanting to experience the jail in a more sinister light should book one of the night tours.

Crawford Art Gallery ★

Emmet Place (021 480 5042, www.crawford artgallery.ie). Open 10am-5pm Mon-Wed, Fri, Sat; 10am-8pm Thur. Admission free.

This handsome red-brick 18th-century building, once the city's Custom House, became a school of design in 1850. Arts patron William Horatio Crawford provided the means to extend the building to incorporate galleries for sculpture and painting. Today, the main collection contains more than 2,000 pieces, and is particularly strong in 19th- and early 20th-century Irish art. Artists featured include Jack B Yeats, Joan Miró and Picasso. The modern extension displays temporary shows of Irish and European contemporary art. You could easily pass several hours touring the galleries, followed by lunch in the excellent café.

English Market

Entrances on Princess Street, Grand Parade & Oliver Plunkett Street (www.corkenglishmarket.ie). Open 8am-6pm Mon-Sat.

Cork's huge covered food market was voted one of the best food markets in Europe by *Observer Food Monthly*, and epitomises the very essence of Cork's thriving culinary scene; fresh, vibrant, innovative and organic. It was established in 1788 as a simple fruit and vegetable market. Nowadays, alongside traditional stalls selling local meat and fresh fish, you'll find exciting artisan food producers offering handmade chocolates, speciality cheeses, gourmet sausages, fancy olives and organic veg. Carnivores should check out Kathleen Noonan's pig meat stall, which sells traditional favourites such as pigs' tails and crubbeens (pigs' feet). Others might prefer the unusual loaves of the Alternative Bread Company or Ballycotton Seafood's amazing array of fish. Foodies, beware: you may never want to leave.

EAST CORK

Fota House, Aboretum & Gardens

Fota Island (021 481 5543, www.fotahouse.com). Open House Apr-Oct 10am-5pm Mon-Sat; 11am-5pm Sun. Arboretum & Gardens 9am-5pm daily. Admission House €6; €3-€4 reductions; €15 family. Arboretum & Gardens free.

Originally a hunting lodge, Fota House was extended to become the residence of the Smith Barry family in the 1820s; two new wings and a servants' quarter were added. The 45-minute guided tour (check the website for timings) takes in everything from the library to the game larder, plus an impressive collection of Irish art, and visitors also learn about the history of the family and the architecture of the house. The glorious gardens and arboretum, full of magnificent trees and including the lovely Orangery, are free to explore. Finish in the café (in what was once the long gallery and billiard room), where there's a range of baked goods and hot meals, plus a view over the gardens.

Fota Wildlife Park

Fota Island (021 481 2678, www.fotawildlife.ie). Open 10am-6pm Mon-Sat; 11am-6pm Sun. Admission €14; €9 reductions; €44-€56 family.

Fota Wildlife Park

Set on 70 acres of the former Smith Barry estate, this wildlife park contains more than 70 species of animals. Visitors follow paths that weave through the grounds, where animals ranging from flamingos and kangaroos to rabbits and red squirrels roam freely. Fencing surrounds the African Savannah area, in which you'll find cheetahs, giraffes and other animals, while the lakes are dotted with islands, home to assorted monkeys. Feeding sessions and wildlife talks happen daily. Bring a picnic (benches are numerous), or make use of the two cafés.

Jameson Experience

Old Distillery Walk, Midleton (021 461 3594, www.tours.jamesonwhiskey.com). Tours Apr-Oct 10am-4.30pm daily. Nov-Mar 11.30am, 1.15pm, 2.30pm, 4pm daily. Rates €13.50; €8-€11 reductions; €30 family.

Midleton is where the Jameson whiskey empire began, more than 200 years ago. Whiskey is no longer distilled on the site, but you can take a guided tour of the old distillery, visiting the mills, maltings, warehouses and kilns, and finishing with a tipple of the good stuff.

KINSALE & AROUND

Charles Fort

Summercove (021 477 2263, www.heritage ireland.ie). Open Mid Mar-Oct 10am-6pm daily. Nov-mid Mar 10am-5pm daily. Admission €4; €2-€3 reductions; €10 family. No credit cards.

Located 3km outside Kinsale, with panoramic views over the harbour and out to sea, this classic, 17th-century, star-shaped fort has been the site of many a battle. Once housing around 450 soldiers, the empty buildings are home to only pigeons and crows today, with the exception of one building that has been restored as an exhibition space.

You can reach the fort via the Scilly Walk, a 2km paved route along the water's edge that runs from the centre of Kinsale. It then continues to the headland. For short stretches, pedestrians must walk on the road. Maps are available at the tourist office in Kinsale.

Desmond Castle

Cork Street, Kinsale (021 477 4855, www.heritage ireland.ie). Open Easter-mid Sept 10am-6pm daily. Admission €3; €1-€2 reductions; €8 family. No credit cards.

A neat, three-storey tower house built at the beginning of the 16th century by the Earl of Desmond. Originally used as a Customs House, it became a prison in the 18th century; during the Great Famine, it functioned as a workhouse. Today, it holds the International Museum of Wine, which documents the link between the Irish and wine-making around the world.

WEST CORK: CLONAKILTY TO BALTIMORE

Drombeg Stone Circle

Between Rosscarbery & Glandore.

Located about 2.5km from Glandore, this ancient site comprises 17 stones ranging in height, standing together to form a tight circle. Flanked by two portal stones, they are said to orientate the monument in the direction of the setting sun during the winter solstice. A few yards away are the remains of what is known as a *fulacht fiadh*, a ritual cooking site.

Lisselan
Nr Clonakilty (023 883 3249, www.lisselan.com).
Gardens Open June-Aug 8am-9pm daily. May,
Sept 8am-8pm daily. Mar, Apr, Oct 8am-6pm
daily. Nov-Feb 8am-5pm daily. Admission €6;
free-€5 reductions.
Golf club Open June-Aug 8am-9pm daily. May,
Sept 8am-8pm daily. Mar, Apr, Oct 8am-6pm daily.
Nov-Feb 8am-5pm daily. Green fees €10-€25.
Fishing Open Mid Feb-Sept 8am-dusk daily.
Rates €30; €20 reductions.
A short drive outside Clonakilty is the wonderful Lisselan estate, with a 19th-century, French-style chateau and more than 30 acres of gardens. Only the gardens are open to the public, though there are plans to set up an art gallery and a vintage car museum too. Designed in the 1850s, the grounds contain a rockery, an azalea and a rhododendron garden, intercut by rambling paths and dotted with water features, bridges, statues. There's also a beautifully sited golf course, and fishing is permitted on the Argideen River – one of the best rivers for salmon and sea trout – which runs through the estate.

Lough Hyne
5km south-west of Skibbereen.
Lough Hyne was Ireland's first Marine Nature Reserve and is an inland saltwater lake, meaning it is fed by the Atlantic and is tidal. The lake is small, but is home to many species of fish, including cod, monkfish and mackerel. Small islands speckle the water – on one of these are the ruins of Cloghane castle, where, it is said, the king with the 'donkey's ears' once lived. Swimming is possible, but watch out for jellyfish. Various signed cycle routes run between Baltimore and the lake; alternatively, drive to the lake, park and then follow the Knockomagh Wood Nature trail for spectacular views across the lake to Baltimore. For information on kayaking or diving, ask in Skibbereen or at Baltimore Tourist Office.

WEST CORK: MIZEN HEAD & BEARA PENINSULAS

Bantry House
Bantry (027 50047, www.bantryhouse.com).
Open Mid Mar-Oct 10am-6pm daily. Admission
€10; €3-€8 reductions; €24 family.
Bantry House has one of the most beautiful locations in Ireland, sitting on a hilltop above Bantry Bay and surrounded by acres of grounds, including formal terraced gardens. The house was built in the 19th century by Richard White, 1st Earl of Bantry, and remains the private residence of his descendants today. Much of it is open to the public; the house, with its antique furniture, ornate tapestries and numerous paintings and sculptures, is kept in immaculate condition and makes for a fascinating visit. There are frequent events (concerts, talks, plant sales) too. The tearoom, located in what

was once the kitchen, serves light lunches and cakes. Accommodation is also available (*see p158*).

Cape Clear Island
028 39153, www.capeclearisland.eu.
This small rocky island, 5km long and 2.5km wide, is Ireland's most southerly inhabited point. Cape Clear is a Gaeltacht area, with a population of around 120. Come summer, the island is alive with daytrippers making the 45-minute boat journey from Baltimore or Schull. They come to walk or cycle round the island; bikes can be rented in Skibbereen and taken on the boat. Birdwatchers are drawn to the large breeding colonies of black guillemots and thousands of shearwaters. There's also a bird observatory (028 39181, closed Nov-Easter) at North Harbour, and it's common to see dolphins, whales, basking sharks and seals too. Cape Clear also known for the International Storytelling Festival (www.capeclear storytelling.com) in September.

Accommodation is available at a handful of basic B&Bs, a campsite and Cape Clear Hostel (028 41968, www.capeclearhostel.com, booking compulsory Oct-Apr), housed in the old coastguard station. The craft shop at North Harbour has information on the island and on guided walks. Other facilities include a pub serving food and a little shop.

Ilnacullin/Garinish Island
In Bantry Bay, near Glengarriff (027 63040,
www.heritageireland.ie). Open June-Aug 10am-
6.30pm Mon-Sat; 11am-6.30pm Sun. May, Sept
10am-6.30pm Mon-Sat; noon-6.30pm Sun. Apr
10am-6.30pm Mon-Sat; 1-6.30pm Sun. Oct 10am-
4pm Mon-Sat; 1-4pm Sun. Admission €4; €2-€3
reductions; €10 family.
Architect and garden designer Henry Peto created this lovely island garden before World War I. The mild microclimate means it's one of Ireland's most lush and varied gardens, and a destination for horticulturists from all over. Paths are lined with hundreds of different trees, shrubs and plants from Australia, China, South America and elsewhere. The Italianate garden and Grecian temple are highlights, and there's also an abandoned Martello tower on the island. A coffee shop serves light refreshments.

Mizen Head
Mizen Head (028 35115, www.mizenhead.net).
Open June-Sept 10am-6pm daily. Mid Mar-Apr, Oct
10.30am-5pm daily. Nov-mid Mar 11am-4pm Sat,
Sun. Admission €6; €3.50-€4.50; €18 family.
Located 8km from Goleen, the Mizen Head signal station was built on Cloghane Island in 1906. The link to the mainland was by an arched bridge, which withstood over 100 years of storms until it was replaced by a new, sturdier bridge, opened on St Patrick's Day 2011. The visitor centre tells the history of the signal station, and of the Fastnet Lighthouse off the coast. A paved walkway leads to the signal station, which holds some exhibits as well as information on Marconi, who came to Crookhaven in the hopes of getting the first signal across the Atlantic Ocean. The views over the crashing waves and back to the weathered cliffs are breathtaking – and certainly worth the trip to the most southern point in Ireland.

Les Gourmandises. See p144.

Pavilion

FIVE CORK CITY BARS

Crane Lane
*Phoenix Street (021 427 8487,
www.cranelanetheatre.ie). Open
2pm-2am daily.*
The Crane Lane Theatre styles itself as
'a house of jazz, blues and burlesque'.
It has three bars, there's always some
form of musical event happening, and
they serve till late.

Hi-B Bar
*Oliver Plunkett Street (021 427 2758).
Open 4-11.30pm Mon-Thur, Sun; 2pm-
12.30am Fri, Sat. No credit cards.*
If you're looking for something a little
different, try the quirky Hi-B – it's a Cork
institution. Walk up a narrow, creaking
staircase to enter the tiny room, usually
buzzing with a mixed crowd.

Mutton Lane
*Mutton Lane (021 427 3471). Open
10.30am-11.30pm Mon-Thur; 10.30am-
12.30am Fri, Sat; 10.30am-11pm Sun.*
Tucked down an alleyway off St Patrick's
Street is this intimate, traditional bar.
Oodles of character and plenty of
candlelight make it a cosy place for
a drink or two.

Pavilion
*Carey's Lane (021 427 6230,
www.pavilioncork.com). Open Bar
11am-11.30pm Mon-Wed; 11am-2am
Thur-Sat; 5-11.30pm Sun. Club times
& admission see website for details.*
Down a cobbled lane in the old French
Quarter, the Pavilion has a popular bar
downstairs (with frequent musicians
and DJs), while upstairs in the old
cinema room, there are concerts
and other events. At weekends, its
operates as a nightclub.

Sin é
*Coburg Street, Cork (021 450 2266).
Open 12.30-11.30pm Mon-Thur, Sun;
12.30pm-12.30am Fri, Sat.*
A small piece of classic Ireland, this
is a busy bar with traditional music
sessions most weekend nights.

pomegranate citrus dressing, or sweet chilli-glazed pan-
fried tofu with asian greens in a coconut and lemongrass
broth, with soba noodles and a gingered aduki bean
wonton. Stay the night in two spacious, modern en suite
rooms above the restaurant.

Cornstore
*40A Cornmarket Street (021 427 4777,
www.cornstorecork.com). Lunch served noon-3pm
Mon-Fri; noon-4pm Sat, Sun. Dinner served 5-10pm
Mon-Thur; 5-10.30pm Fri, Sat; 5-9pm Sun.*
Housed in a two-storey converted granite mill, the Cornstore
has a New York bistro vibe, with faded, brown leather
seating, cosy booths and oak panelling, and accessoried with
glitzy chandeliers, mirrors and contemporary furniture. The
relaxed ambience is a nice match for the steak and seafood
menu. There's a popular wine and cocktail bar on the
premises too.

Les Gourmandises
*17 Cook Street (021 425 1959, www.les
gourmandises.ie). Lunch served 12.30-3pm Sun.
Dinner served 6-9.30pm Tue-Sat.*
The small but sophisticated shop front perfectly reflects
the style of this French restaurant, run by Patrick and Soizic
Kiely. Inside the decor is elegantly modern, as is the menu:
roasted mackerel with apple, watercress and lemon crème
fraîche might be followed by braised lamb shoulder with
baby peas, pomme fondant, broad beans and rosemary jus.
Vanilla crème brûlée with pink grapefruit jelly and
shortbread biscuit is a typical pudding, and there are
French cheeses too.

Jacobs on the Mall
*30 South Mall (021 425 1530, www.jacobsonthemall.
com). Dinner served 5.30-10pm Mon-Sat.*
The dining room at Jacobs, in what was once Turkish baths,
has high ceilings and a glass roof, and potted greenery
hangs from the ceiling, giving the place the air of a modern
greenhouse. A seasonal menu lists the likes of seafood
chowder or Jack McCarthy's black pudding on a potato and
caramelised onion tortilla with apple salad to start. Mains
run from venison sausage and champ with buttered kale,
roast root vegetables and onion jus to Thai-style green
chicken curry.

Jacques
*9 Phoenix Street (021 427 7387, www.jacques
restaurant.ie). Dinner served 6-9.30pm Mon-Sat.*
Quality, imaginative dishes at reasonable prices, served in
a stylish and relaxed dining room, make Jacques a prized
destination. The restaurant has been around for more than
30 years, and a strong local following knows and loves
dishes such as figs stuffed with Ardsallagh cheese and
caramelised nuts, or tagine of hake with cumin, coriander
and fresh tomatoes.

Where to stay
Centrally located hotels include the very modern
and slick Clarion Hotel (021 422 4900,
www.clarionhotelcorkcity.com) on Lapps Quay,
and the comfortable Jurys Inn Cork Hotel (021
494 3000, http://corkhotels.jurysinns.com)
on Anderson's Quay. On MacCurtain Street, the

smart Gresham Metropole Hotel (MacCurtain Street, 021 464 3700, www.gresham-hotels-cork.com) is right beside the Everyman Theatre, while Hotel Isaacs (021 450 0011, www.isaacscork.com) has both standard rooms and apartments, and a popular restaurant next to a pretty waterfall. Fashionable Lancaster Lodge (Lancaster Quay, 021 425 1125, www.lancasterlodge.com) offers vibrantly decorated, spacious rooms, and is a short walk from the city centre.

Hayfield Manor Hotel
Perrott Avenue, College Road (021 484 5900, www.hayfieldmanor.ie). Rates €149-€209 double incl breakfast.
Hayfield Manor is the perfect country retreat, even though it's only a kilometre from the centre of Cork. Hidden away at the top of a leafy avenue, this handsome red-brick mansion is surrounded by two acres of land. From the moment you arrive, you're made to feel welcome and relaxed; there are open fires in the reception area, and next door a traditional bar with excellent bar food. The 88 rooms vary in size, but all are traditional in design with plenty of plush fabrics, heavy curtains and antique furniture. Orchids Restaurant is a fine dining restaurant, with extravagant floral displays and views over the gardens. There's also a spa, with a pool, relaxation room and treatment rooms. A luxurious stay is guaranteed – even for dogs, who get their own private kennel and gourmet menu.

Imperial Hotel
South Mall (021 427 4040, www.flynnhotels.com). Rates €110-€250 double incl breakfast.
Located in the business district, the Imperial is Cork's oldest hotel, dating from 1813. Famous past guests include Irish revolutionary Michael Collins, who spent his last night here in 1922 before being killed in the Irish Civil War. After recent renovations, the place has lost its old-world airs and now provides upmarket contemporary accommodation, complete with a posh spa with pool, thermal suites and treatment rooms. The 126 well-appointed rooms range from 'classic' to suites, with a penthouse for high-rollers. There's a bar and a trio of eateries, including the swish Pembroke restaurant, specialising in seafood.

EAST CORK
There are numerous islands, inhabited and uninhabited, in Cork's sizeable harbour. Some are linked to the mainland by causeways and well served by public transport. One of these is Fota Island (www.visitfota.com), encompassing 116 acres of parkland that belonged to the Smith Barry family until the 1970s, when it was handed over to the state. The island is now a major attraction: as well as the parkland, there's glorious, 19th-century Fota House (*see p141*) with its gardens and arboretum, Fota Wildlife Park (*see p141* – the only one in Ireland), and Fota Island Resort (*see p149*), which includes a golf course, a hotel and self-catering accommodation. The island is only 15 kilometres from Cork city, so it's possible to see it all in a daytrip.

A causeway leads south from Fota Island to Great Island, the setting for the pretty town of Cobh (www.visitcobh.com). The town prides itself on its rich seafaring history; it was the final port of call for the *Titanic* on her maiden voyage, and a major departure point for Irish emigrants to North America during the Great Famine – a staggering 2.5 million people left from Cobh. The town remains an important port today, with a constant stream of cruise liners docking in the harbour throughout the summer, which means plenty of trade for the many bars and restaurants.

Cobh (pronounced 'Cove') is set on a steep hill with stunning vistas over Cork harbour, and a seafront lined with brightly coloured Victorian houses. The skyline is dominated by imposing St Colman's Cathedral (021 481 3222, www.cobhcathedralparish.ie). The neo-Gothic design appears rather out of place, but is impressive nonetheless, and if the spectacular 90-foot spire doesn't catch your attention, the sound of the cathedral's 49 bells certainly will.

Cobh Tourist Office (021 481 3301, www.cobhharbourchamber.ie) – set in the old Royal Cork Yacht club, a magnificent Italianate building from the 1850s – has plenty of information on the area and can advise on accommodation.

Cork City Gaol. See p140.

Ballyvolane House. See p149.

RABBIT CONTROL
PLEASE SHUT GATE !

Also here is the multidisciplinary Sirius Arts Centre (021 481 3790, www.siriusartscentre.ie), which hosts changing art exhibitions throughout the year.

The town's former Victorian railway station houses the Queenstown Story (021 481 3591, www.cobhheritage.com), which illustrates the history of Cobh, particularly the Great Famine and subsequent mass emigration, through a series of exhibitions. Cobh Museum (High Road, 021 481 4240, www.cobhmuseum.com, closed Nov-Apr), located in a former Presbyterian church, has old-fashioned glass display cases, paintings and other items exploring the social, cultural and maritime history of Cobh and Great Island. For more on the town's history, join the Titanic Trail Heritage Walk (021 481 5211, www.titanic-trail.com), an informative guided tour of the town that leaves from the Commodore Hotel at 11am daily.

Boat trips around the harbour run daily, and Whale of a Time Sea Adventures (mobile 086 328 3250) offers whale watching trips. Fishing expeditons are plentiful, and can be booked through the tourist office. Watersports are a major feature too; Sail Cork (021 481 1237, www.sailcork.com) organises sailing courses and boat hire.

The town commemorates the sinking of the *Titanic* (in April) and the *Lusitania* (in May). The South of Ireland Piping & Drumming Contest (mobile 087 684 9565) brings massed bands to the town in June, while the Cobh People's Regatta (www.cobhpeoplesregatta.com) is a three-day festival in August with music and entertainment throughout the town. Closing the season in September is the Blues Festival (www.cobhblues festival.com) and the long-running International Sea Angling Festival (021 481 2167).

Further east, in a marvellous clifftop location facing the Atlantic and overlooking a small island topped with a lighthouse, is the fishing village of Ballycotton (www.ballycotton.com). It's smaller, more sedate and more relaxed than Cobh. The Ballycotton Cliffwalk (*see p148*) is a great way to stretch your legs, while the local beach at Garryvoe is fine for swimming. Sea-angling and birdwatching are very popular pastimes, and boat trips to Ballycotton Island can be arranged.

North of Cork harbour, about 20 kilometres from Cork city via the N25, is the market town of Midleton. Visitors come here for a taste of Ireland at the Jameson Experience (*see p141*). It's something of a culinary hub, in fact, with several decent eateries nearby, notably Ballymaloe House (*see p148*), ten kilometres to the south-east. A fabulous farmers' market is held on Hospital Road on Saturday mornings, and the Midleton Food & Drink Festival (www.midletonfood festival.ie) in September sees the town packed with food stalls. A short drive from Midleton, near Carrigtwohill, is Barryscourt Castle (021 488 2218, www.heritageireland.ie, closed Oct-late May), the 16th-century seat of the Barry family. It's a fine example of an Irish tower house, and much of the interior has been restored to the original 16th-century design. Admission is free.

Continue east along the N25 for less than 30 kilometres to reach Youghal, which lies on the River Blackwater estuary, the border between County Cork and County Waterford. Reputedly the second-largest port in Europe during the medieval period, it was once a powerful walled city, though only remnants of the wall can be seen today. The narrow Main Street is lined with brightly coloured buildings; the attractive sandstone clocktower on South Main Street stands on the site of the old town gateway, and served as a gaol and public gallows. North from here, past the many shops, cafés and bars, is the unusual Red House, a Dutch-style mansion built in 1710 as the residence of a wealthy merchant family. Opposite is Tynte's Castle (www.tyntescastle.com), a four-storey, late 15th-century tower house – only the exterior can be viewed. Off North Main Street, at the top of Church Street, is the picturesque Collegiate Church of St Mary, the north transept of which dates from AD 680. Close by is 16th-century Myrtle Grove,

the former home of Sir Walter Raleigh, who was granted land in the area by Elizabeth I. The house is privately owned. Guided historical walks can be arranged by the Youghal Tourist Information Centre (024 20170, www.youghal.ie, closed Oct-Apr Sat, Sun), located on Market Square on the waterfront.

The town has an excellent Blue Flag beach, and a wide range of water activities are available, including powerboating, sailing and boat trips along the River Blackwater. For details, contact the tourist office or try Aqua Trek (024 90542, www.aquatrek.ie).

Where to eat & drink

The lovely café at Fota House (see p141) serves light lunches, cakes, teas and coffees. Cobh has plenty of bars and cafés; the Quays bar-restaurant (Westbourne Place, 021 481 3539, www.the quays.ie) has particularly fine views over the harbour from its outdoor terrace. Seafood dishes are the attraction at the Herring Gull (The Pier, 021 464 6768, closed mid June-mid Sept Mon; mid Sept-mid June Mon-Wed) in Ballycotton.

In Midleton, the Jameson Experience (see p141) has a useful café; nearby is Mediterranean restaurant Raymond's (Distillery Walk, 021 463 5235, www.raymonds.ie). On the Main Street, O'Donovan's (021 463 1255, closed Mon, Sun) is an elegant, intimate establishment serving excellent modern Irish food.

In Youghal, steaks, salads, pasta dishes and a lunchtime carvery are available at the Red Store (Main Street, 024 90144, www.redstore.ie); there's also a large sunny courtyard. The best place for seafood is Ahearne's (North Main Street, 024 92424, www.ahernes.net), which also offers modest but comfortable B&B rooms. The Nook (North Main Street, 024 92225, www.findthe nook.ie) is a fine traditional bar with musical entertainment on some evenings. The Walter Raleigh Hotel (O'Brien's Place, 024 92011, www.walterraleighhotel.com) has retained its old-fashioned bar, and there are frequent traditional music sessions here too.

Ballymaloe House ★

Shanagarry (021 465 2531, www.ballymaloe.com). Restaurant Lunch served 1-2pm, dinner served 7-9.30pm daily. Café Open 10am-5pm daily.
A country house hotel with a splendid restaurant and, two miles away, an internationally renowned cookery school. The heart of Ballymaloe is the rambling house set on 400 acres, most of which is farmed – much of the farm's produce is used in the café and restaurant. Within the main house, lunch and dinner are served in elegant, interconnecting dining rooms. The evening menu is five courses (with plenty of choice), and might start with soup, followed by Ballymaloe pork, spinach and herb terrine, a main such as grilled Ballycotton hake with crab, tomato and ginger beurre blanc and courgettes, and then Irish cheeses and dessert. There's also a café behind the house, and a crafts and food shop. Accommodation consists of 30 prettily decorated bedrooms (€170-€250 double incl breakfast), and some attractive self-catering cottages and chalets.

Things to do

EAST CORK

Ballycotton Cliffwalk
Ballycotton (www.ballycotton.com/ leisure_walking.htm).
Starting at the car park above the cliffs, this 5km loop walk follows a recently refurbished path, with stunning views across the sea out to Ballycotton Island. It's an easy stroll, with plenty of grassy picnic spots along the way. Walkers should keep an eye out for nesting birds and wild flowers.

WEST CORK: MIZEN HEAD & BEARA PENINSULAS

Beara Way
Beara peninsula (www.bearatourism.com/ bearaway.html).
The Beara Way circles the Beara peninsula for 200km, following mainly side roads, country tracks and bog roads. It passes through the towns of Kenmare, Glengarriff and Castletownbere, as well as assorted villages, including Allihies, Ardgroom, Adrigole and Eyeries – you can download pdfs of each section from the website. The trail is open to walkers and bike riders, but dogs aren't allowed.

Sheep's Head Way & Cycle Route
Sheep's Head peninsula (www.thesheepsheadway.ie).
Two long-distance trails for walkers and cyclists, around the stunning and isolated Sheep's Head peninsula. Foot travellers can attempt the 88km Sheep's Head Way, from Bantry to the headland and back, in its entirety or do it in shorter stints. The trail follows quiet roads, across moorland, mountains and cliffs, with spectacular views over Dunmanus and Bantry Bay. There are some villages en route for overnight stays. The 120km signposted cycle route starts in Ballylickey, travels down the northern side of the peninsula and back to Durrus, ending in Roaringwater Bay, near Ballydehob.

Ballymaloe House

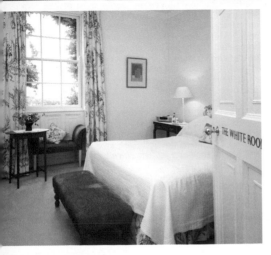
THE WHITE ROOM

Farmgate
Coolbawn (021 463 2771, www.farmgate.ie).
Lunch served noon-3.30pm Tue-Sat. Dinner served
6.30-9.30pm Thur-Sat.
Maróg O'Brien opened Farmgate more than 25 years ago. The front area is crammed with Cork's finest produce and is one of the best food emporiums in the county (open 9am-6pm Tue-Sat). The country-chic feel is carried through to the café at the back, the whitewashed walls, foliage and bronze sculptures creating an interesting space. During the day the menu lists salads, soups and tarts, as well as freshly baked cakes and breads (cakes, scones, coffees and teas are served 9am-5pm Tue-Sat). On certain evenings, the space is transformed: white linen and flickering candlelight create the backdrop for more formal meals, where crab crostini with chilli and lemon might be followed by roast duck with sage and onion stuffing and apple sauce.

Where to stay
Families and golfers flock to the Fota Island Resort (021 488 3700, www.fotaisland.ie), which boasts a hotel, leisure centre, golf course, self-catering houses, and both formal and casual dining. Knockeven House (021 481 1778, www.knockeven house.com) on the edge of Cobh has spacious, traditionally decorated B&B rooms. In Midleton, accommodation is limited: the best options are the mid-range Midleton Park Hotel & Spa (Old Cork Road, 021 463 5100, www.midletonpark. com) or, a few kilometres outside town, pleasant Loughcarrig House (021 463 1952, www.lough carrig.com). In Youghal, La Petite Auberge (The Mall, 024 85906, www.lapetiteauberge.ie, closed Jan) is a stylish B&B. For a real treat, there's also Ballymaloe House (*see left*).

Ballyvolane House ★
Castlelyons (025 36349, www.ballyvolanehouse.ie).
Rates €170-€260 double incl breakfast.
A 40-minute drive from Cork city, Ballyvolane sits off the M8 in the lush Blackwater Valley. The 18th-century mansion is surrounded by acres of woodland, with ornamental lakes and wild flowers. The Greene family has run Ballyvolane for the past quarter-century, and their personal touch is much in evidence. The house is immaculately maintained, with a grand lounge area, and six bedrooms that blend the old with the new to delightful effect. Equal care is taken with the food, which comes from no further than the local area, and often from the estate. The walled garden supplies the vegetables, bread is freshly made, and roaming hens lay eggs for breakfast. Guests eat a four-course dinner by candlelight, around the large, mahogany table. A typcial menu might have wild garlic soup followed by roast rib of McGrath's Hereford beef with sauce béarnaise, new potatoes, roast spring onions and ruby chard, plus cheeses and dessert. There are walks in the woods or private fishing on the River Blackwater.

Bayview Hotel
Ballycotton (021 464 6746, www.thebayview
hotel.com). Rates €105-€179 double incl breakfast.
Closed Nov-Easter.
Ballycotton remains an unspoilt fishing village, slightly off the beaten track, which makes Bayview Hotel ideal for a

Kinsale harbour

quiet getaway. The 35 rooms are handsomely decorated and many have lovely sea views; a pathway leads from the hotel to a private beach. The excellent restaurant specialises in contemporary French dishes using local produce, as in roast fillet of hake with carrot and coriander purée, pea and broad bean fricassée and grain mustard froth. Guests may use the leisure facilities – including gym, sauna and pool – at sister hotel, the Garryvoe (021 464 6718, www.garryvoehotel.com), a five-minute drive away.

Castlemartyr Resort

Castlemartyr (021 421 9000, www.castlemartyr resort.ie). Rates €210-€245 double incl breakfast. Closed Oct-Jan Mon-Wed, Sun.
The ruins of a 13th-century castle once belonging to the Knights Templar stand beside this grand mansion built by Richard Boyle in the 17th century, and the complex is surrounded by several hundred acres of land, including rolling lawns and a lake. The hotel is luxurious, yet nicely understated. It's a large establishment, with 168 rooms – these vary in size and design, but all are spacious and well kitted out. The public areas include a number of eating options, from a formal dining room to the casual Club House; there's also the Knights Bar, which has a fire and is open all day. Extras include a glass-surrounded spa area with a large pool, and a golf course.

KINSALE & AROUND

A half-hour drive south of Cork city, at the mouth of the River Bandon, with green headlands stretching either side, is Kinsale ★. Its maze of narrow streets are tightly packed with brightly painted buildings housing art galleries, boutiques, bars, restaurants and cafés. The harbour is thronged with fishing trawlers and leisure boats, and no matter the time of year, it's an upbeat place to visit. Not only is Kinsale one of Ireland's most beautiful towns, it's also a gourmet destination. And it's not just tourists who appreciate the town; at weekends, Corconians are drawn by the nearby beaches, forts, castles and spectacular headland walks. Festivals pull in the crowds too: in October, there's a Gourmet Festival and a Jazz Festival (for both, see www.kinsale.ie), and a week-long arts festival (www.kinsalearts week.com) in July.

Kinsale's history is mainly as a prosperous trading centre; it was also the site of the arrival of James II to Ireland. In 1915, just off the coast, 1,200 people drowned when the *Lusitania* was sunk by a German U-boat.

Nowadays, tourism holds sway, with hotels (all with great views over the harbour) lining Pier Road.

Also here is the Tourist Office (021 477 2234, www.kinsale.ie, closed Sept-June Sun), which has a mass of information on water-based activities in the area, including sea and river excursions, surfing, windsurfing, sailing, canoeing, waterskiing and deep-sea angling trips. Staff can arrange accommodation, and guided historical walking tours leave from outside the office every day.

At this end of Pier Road, small streets converge at Market Place, the site of 16th-century Market House. It became a courthouse in the 20th century, and today houses the Kinsale Regional Museum (021 477 7930, closed Mon-Fri). At the top of Chairmans Lane, past the picture-perfect fishermen's cottages, is Desmond Castle (see p141), an exemplary urban tower house. Main Street is choc-a-bloc with pretty shops, including the contemporary Enibas Jewellery (021 477 7022, www.enibas.com, closed Nov-Feb Tue, Wed) and the more old-school Linda's Antiques (021 477 4754), which sells antique jewellery, porcelain and other treasures. New and vintage books can be bought at the colourful Bookstór (021 477 4966, www.bookstor.ie) on Newman's Mall, while Kinsale Bookshop (Main Street, 021 477 4244) has up-to-date titles for beach-reading. There are a handful of galleries, including the popular Giles Norman (Main Street, 021 477 4373, www.gilesnorman.com) photography gallery. Kinsale Crystal (Market Street, 021 477 4493, www.kinsalecrystal.ie, closed Sun) offers visitors the opportunity to see crystal being cut and to purchase some intricate pieces.

Kinsale Equestrian Centre (mobile 086 853 0894, www.kinsale-equestrian.com) offers treks around the Kinsale area and along the River Bandon. The area is good for cycling too – there's a pleasant jaunt to Charles Fort (see p141), via the beautiful hamlet Summercove – bikes can be rented at Mylie Murphy Fish Tackle & Cycle Hire (021 477 2703, closed Oct-Apr Sun) on Pearse Street. And although there's no major stretch of beach in town, there's a good swimming spot at the Dock. Head west out of Kinsale, cross over the bridge and take a left turn to the Dock Inn, beside which there's a car park and a path leading to a little beach overlooking Charles Fort. From here, you can walk across the headland to 16th-century James Fort.

From Kinsale, the R600 heads west towards Clonakilty. A turn-off goes to Old Head, a rugged headland capped with a lighthouse, and home to the famous Old Head Golf Club (021 477 8444, www.oldhead.com, closed mid Nov-mid Apr). About five kilometres from Kinsale is Garrettstown Strand, a Blue Flag beach that's great for swimming and bracing walks, while also being a popular windsurfing and surfing spot. G Town Surf School (021 477 8884, www.surfgtown.com, www.gtown adventures.com) runs beginner surf classes throughout the year, and arranges canoeing trips, mountain biking and other outdoor activities.

Deep inlets cut into the coastline along the R600, resulting in some striking views, particularly at Harbour View beach. Timoleague (www.timoleague.ie) is tucked at the top of one of the inlets; here a large, grey abbey dominates the village's small, colourful buildings. Timoleague Abbey was founded in 1240 by a Franciscan order and remains in relatively good shape, with its cloisters and nave still intact. Courtmacsherry Water Sports Centre (023 884 4464, www. courtmacsherrywatersports.com, open summer Mon-Fri, Sun; winter by appointment) is at the tip of the peninsula. The beach is popular with families, and there's plenty to do.

Timoleague Abbey

BEST TOWNS & VILLAGES

Arthurstown
Co Wexford.
There's nothing better than sitting outside this picturesque hamlet's one and only bar, watching the sun go down over the bay on a summer's evening. *See p194.*

Ballyvaughan
Co Clare.
This tiny, attractive harbour village, perched on the edge of the bleak but beautiful landscape of the Burren, has a surprising number of excellent eating and accommodation options, and a laid-back vibe. *See p106.*

Cong
Co Mayo.
Nestled between Lough Corrib and Lough Mask, and surrounded by water and woodland, Cong contains the atmospheric remains of an old abbey and a supremely luxurious hotel, Ashford Castle. *See p89.*

Cushendun
Co Antrim.
Known as Northern Ireland's quaintest village, Cushendun has neat little cottages, stunning views and a white-sand beach. *See p280.*

Dalkey
Co Dublin.
Dalkey's twisting main street is lined with some of Co Dublin's finest eateries, bars, boutiques and artisan shops. There's a reason why some of Ireland's most famous names call this village home. *See p233.*

Dingle
Co Kerry.
This jaunty town in the rugged Dingle peninsula is much loved for its resident dolphin Fungi, beautiful views, variety of outdoor activities, and vibrant music and bar scene. *See p126.*

Where to eat & drink

Seafood is, inevitably, a big focus, but, such is the foodie nature of Kinsale, there are plenty of other edible delights. Of the town's many cafés, the bright and airy Lemon Leaf Café (Main Street, 021 470 9792) serves everything from morning fry-ups to open sandwiches, salads and cakes. The menu at Jo's Café (mobile 087 948 1026, www.joskinsale.com), also on Main Street, includes Irish ice-creams in several flavours. The cheap and cheerful Seaview Café (Pier Road, 021 470 9953) has lovely views and a lively ambience. Crackpots (Cork Street, 021 477 2847, www.crackpots.ie, closed Jan-Mar Mon-Fri) serves a short menu of modern dishes in a space decorated with ceramics made by the owner. Shanghai Express (Lower O'Connell Street, 021 477 7100, open mid Mar-mid Jan Mon, Wed-Sun) offers a change from Irish cuisine.

Plenty of the pubs serve food: the White House (021 477 2125, www.whitehouse-kinsale.ie), at the top of Pearse Street, has a chic dining room serving open sandwiches and fish dishes; Jim Edwards (Market Quay, 021 477 2541, www.jimedwardskinsale.com) is a nautical-themed bar, specialising in fish dishes. Behind the 800-year-old red façade of Max's (Main Street, 021 477 2443, www.maxs.ie, open June-Sept daily; Mar, Apr, Oct-mid Dec Mon, Wed-Sun), classic dishes are served in a relaxed dining room.

Upbeat and traditional An Seanachai (Main Street, 021 477 2209) has music sessions and a nightclub upstairs. Around the corner on Guardwell, local bands play most nights at the Folk House Inn (021 477 2382, www.folk housevenue.com), which also has a popular nightclub, Bacchus (open Thur-Sat).

For a quiet pint with bundles of character, head to the Greyhound (Market Square, 021 477 2889). One of Kinsale's best haunts, it has a tiny front bar, usually packed with locals, plus another small room with booths, low lighting and a fire. Dalton's Bar (021 477 7957) is another low-key traditional bar on the same street. The Spaniard (021 477 2436, www.thespaniard.ie), along Scilly Walk has decent food and is a fine spot for sunset drinks – the outdoor seating area has fantastic harbour views. Regular Irish music sessions feature too.

In Timoleague, Dillons Restaurant (023 884 6390, closed Nov-Feb Mon-Wed) on the main street is a good spot for lunch.

Bulman

Summercove (021 477 2131, www.thebulman.ie). Open 12.30pm-12.30am daily. Lunch served 12.30-4pm, dinner served 6-10pm Tue-Sun.
People come here in droves, for the wonderful atmosphere, and to watch the sun go down over the harbour outside the orange-painted pub. Inside, the traditional bar is cosy, with open fires and snugs. Bar food is served, and there's often music in the evenings, with sessions lasting until the early hours. Upstairs is a more modern, nautically decorated restaurant, Toddie's. Excellent seafood such as local lobster, oysters and fish of the day is served, alongside other dishes.

Fishy Fishy ★

Pier Road, Kinsale (021 470 0415, www.fishyfishy.ie). Food served Apr-Sept noon-9pm daily. Oct-Mar noon-4pm Mon-Wed; noon-9pm Thur-Sat; noon-5pm Sun.

A casual, relaxed seafood restaurant that's known across the country. A small bar area leads into a bright restaurant, where pieces of fish-shaped metal, artworks and photographs of local fishermen leave diners in no doubt about the content of the menu. Choose your lobster from the tank, or opt for the catch of the day. The food is classic stuff: seafood chowder, fish pie and so on. There's a buzzy atmosphere, friendly service and a covetable outdoor seating area. Fishy Fishy also runs a chippie in the centre of town (open noon-4.30pm Tue-Sat)

Jola's

Lower O'Connell Street, Kinsale (021 477 3322, www.jolasrestaurant.com). Dinner served June-Sept 6-10pm daily. Oct-May 6-10pm Wed-Sat.

Jola's offers something a little different to the Kinsale norm. The smart dining room is located in the basement of an old building, and exposed brick, flickering candles, white linen tablecloths and old-fashioned carver chairs make it the perfect place for a romantic meal. There's fish aplenty, but also dishes such as pierogi stuffed with Clonakilty black pudding, served with crispy bacon and pear purée, or Irish lamb cutlets with basil and walnut pesto, sautéed new potatoes, and cashew nuts. There's also a lovely outdoor terrace, and an extensive wine list. Jola's is a special place, for a special occasion.

Where to stay

Kinsale has plenty of places to stay, but demand is high, so it's best to book in advance. Favourites include Pier House B&B (Pier Road, 021 477 4169, www.pierhousekinsale.com) on the waterfront, and stylish Blindgate House (Blindgate, 021 477 7858, www.blindgatehouse.com, closed Dec-Feb), just outside the town centre. Glebe Country House (021 477 8294, www.glebecountryhouse.com), formerly a Georgian rectory that now offers B&B and self-catering accommodation, is about 12 kilometres west of Kinsale, in Ballinadee.

If you'd prefer a larger hotel, but still want to be in town, try the 73-room Actons Hotel (Pier Road, 021 477 9900, www.actonshotelkinsale.com). A few kilometres outside town is the modern Carlton Kinsale Hotel (Rathmore Road, 021 470 6000, www.carltonkinsalehotel.com). Part of the Charlton Hotel chain, it has a leisure centre with spa.

The best camping is at Garrettstown in the peaceful grounds of an 18th-century estate: Garrettstown House (021 477 8156, www. garrettstownhouse.com, closed mid Sept-Apr).

Blue Haven Hotel

Pearse Street, Kinsale (021 477 2209, www.bluehaven kinsale.com). Rates €80-€160 double incl breakfast.

A popular and central hotel with 17 comfortable rooms, a busy restaurant and Hamlet's cocktail bar. If it's peace you're after, you may not get it here, although the rooms on the top floor are relatively quiet. Alternatively, the owners have another hotel a few doors down – the Old Bank House (www.oldbankhousekinsale.com), with another 17 rooms.

Enniskerry
Co Wicklow.
The most charming village in Co Wicklow, with an array of sweet cafés, antiques shops and galleries. Splendid Powerscourt House & Gardens is within walking distance. See p209.

Inistioge
Co Kilkenny.
One of Ireland's prettiest riverside towns, with trim houses and shops surrounding a leafy town square. Up the narrow twisting hill, Woodbrook demesne offers spectacular views over the lush valley. See p182.

Kenmare
Co Kerry.
The gateway to the awe-inspiring Iveragh peninsula and the culinary capital of Kerry. Kenmare's wide streets are packed with top eating spots and the outskirts sprinkled with some of Ireland's most luxurious hotels. See p116.

Kinsale
Co Cork.
Colourful buildings, excellent restaurants and a stunning waterside location have made Kinsale one of the most loved towns in the south, with a year-round festive atmosphere. See p150.

Rathmullan
Co Donegal.
Perfectly placed for exploring Donegal's peninsulas, Rathmullan sits on Lough Swilly, with sweeping views towards Malin. Good restaurants, lively bars and plentiful watersports add to its appeal. See p43.

Roundstone
Co Galway.
This small fishing village sits on the remote Connemara coastline, near the foot of Errigal Mountain. It's a spirited summer town, renowned for its scenic walks, watersports and buzzing nightlife. See p82.

Cobh harbour. See p145.

Bedrooms in both are tastefully designed, with a mix of new and antique furniture, and are of a good size for such a prime location. The Old Bank House also has a little café.

Perryville House

Long Quay, Kinsale (021 477 2731, www.perryville house.com). Rates €150-€300 double incl breakfast. Closed Nov-mid Apr.

Located in the heart of Kinsale, Perryville's painted Victorian façade is easy to spot. The 24 classic rooms (some with four-poster beds) vary in design; some have views over the harbour. Owners Laura and Andrew Corcoran know how to make guests feel at home, with little touches such as scented candles, fresh flowers, and books and papers in the two lounge areas. Breakfast is a hearty affair, with freshly baked bread, fruit and a traditional fry-up. The Corcorans recently opened a tearoom serving cakes and light lunches. Despite its central location, Perryville is a quiet spot with a country house ambience.

WEST CORK: CLONAKILTY TO BALTIMORE

From Kinsale, it's 35 kilometres via the R600 or slightly further by the main N71 to Clonakilty, a busy market town, with colourfully painted houses and traditional shopfronts. Popular with tourists, it has a number of good eateries, and plenty of bars showcasing traditional music in the evening. There are several boutiques and bookshops, including Kerr's Bookshop (Ashe Street, 023 883 4342, closed Sun) and Coughlan Bookshop (Rossa Street, 023 883 3068, closed Sun). On Spiller's Lane, just off Bridge Street, you'll find a surf shop, an antiques emporium and a wholefood store. On the other side of the lane is Recorder's Alley, where the Clonakilty Food & Craft Market (www.clonakilty market.com) takes place on Friday from 9am to 2pm. The Clonakilty International Guitar Festival (www.clonguitarfest.com) in September is a great time to experience the town. There's plenty of useful information on http://clonakilty.ie.

Clonakilty is famous for being the birthplace of Irish revolutionary Michael Collins. There's a statue of the 'Big Fella' on Emmet Square, and, three kilometres outside town towards Timoleague, the Michael Collins Centre (023 884 6107, www.michaelcollinscentre.com, open mid June-mid Sept Mon-Sat) has been set up in his honour. Other attractions include the West Cork Model Railway Village (Inchydoney Road, 023 883 3224, www.modelvillage.ie), sited on the edge of town in a garden. Reflecting local life in the 1940s, the model includes a teeny Clonakilty town, a railway line and a copy of Charles Fort, together with miniature people and animals. Also nearby, off the N71 heading west, are the lovely gardens at Lisselan (*see p142*). You can also fish and play golf here.

Most people visit Clonakilty to pick up supplies, stay overnight for an evening of traditional music and then hit the stunning Blue Flag beach at Inchydoney Island (linked to the mainland via causeways). The curved strand is the area's most popular for swimming, surfing and walking. There's a beachside car park, but this fills up fast in summer; an alternative is to hire bikes at MTM Cycles (023 883 3584, closed Sun) on Ashe Street in Clonakilty, and cycle the four kilometres to the beach – there's only one or two little hills to negotiate along the way. Inchydoney Lodge & Spa (*see p156*) serves lunch, and drinks throughout the day. Novice waveriders can book a lesson with the West Cork Surf School (mobile 086 869 5396, www.westcorksurfing.com) during the summer.

Fishing on the nearby River Bandon (www.bandon river.com) is another popular pastime; pick up supplies and advice from Clontackle & Leisure (023 883 5580, www.clontackle.com, closed Wed, Sun) on Pearse Street.

Heading west, Rosscarbery sits atop a small hill at the edge of yet another deep sea inlet. It has a pretty square with two good cafés – Gossip Bistro (023 883 1950, closed Mon) and Pilgrims Rest (023 883 1796, closed Sept-May Tue) – and one or other of the pubs is likely to have a traditional music session. The Lagoon Activity Centre (www.lagoonactivitycentre.ie, open June-Aug daily; Sept-May by appointment) runs kayaking, and other boating activities on the lagoon, though the best place to swim is east of town at Owenahincha Beach. The most popular attraction in the vicinity is Drombeg Stone Circle (see p141), a megalithic site near Glandore.

It's a 20-minute drive west from Rosscarbery to the market town of Skibbereen. Facilities include banks, large supermarkets, a medical centre and some gift shops, and it's a good place for an amble. Traffic can be a problem, especially on Fridays during the Cattle Market – although this is also an interesting time to visit. In September, A Taste of West Cork Food Festival (www.atasteofwestcork.com) is a week-long mix of food, drink and music.

The tourist office (028 21766, www.skibbereen.ie, closed Jan-May Sat, Sun) is on North Street, which is where the West Cork Arts Centre (028 22090, www.westcorkartscentre.com, closed Sun) can also be found. The centre has a gallery running contemporary exhibits of local and international artists, and hosts workshops and film screenings.

The devastating effects of the Great Famine on Skibbereen is conveyed in the Skibbereen Heritage Centre (028 40900, www.skibbheritage.com, closed Mar-mid May, mid Sept-Oct Mon, Sun; all Nov-mid Mar). It's located in a converted gasworks on Upper Bridge Street. The Lough Hyne Visitor Centre is also here; it tells the history of Lough Hyne (see p142), a scenic saltwater lake a few kilometres south-west of town, and has maps of local walks. An aquarium contains some of the species found in the lake.

Atlantic Seakayaking (028 21058, www.atlanticseakayaking.com), based in Skibbereen, offers a variety of guided kayak trips, including half-day, full-day and seaweed foraging excursions – it's a wonderful way to see the coastline. The company provides lessons too; note that children need to be at least nine years old.

From Skibbereen, take the R595 south to reach the village of Baltimore (www.baltimore.ie), on the very tip of the peninsula. The focus is the harbour, busy with fishing boats, and leisure boats taking visitors to Cape Clear Island (see p142) and Sherkin Island. Overlooking the pier, on a little square, are a handful of pubs, a bistro and two B&Bs – all surrounded by a disproportionate number of holiday homes. The place is heaving throughout the summer; off-season, it's quiet and relatively unexciting. Watching over the village from a rocky outcrop is Dún na Séad (028 20735, closed Oct-May), a beautifully restored fortified castle, originally constructed in the 13th century but altered over the centuries. It's open to the public.

Baltimore is where to come if you want to sail, dive or island-hop. Baltimore Diving Centre (Harbour Drive, 028 20300, www.baltimorediving.com) can arrange diving trips and accommodation, while

Whale Watch West Cork (mobile 086 120 0027, www.whalewatchwestcork.com, closed Dec-Mar) organises whale and dolphin sightseeing trips. Minke, fin and humpback whales visit the coastal waters off west Cork, and there are resident groups of common dolphins and porpoises.

Assorted events and festivals take place through the summer. At the end of May comes the Seafood Festival, with street entertainment, music and dozens of stalls stacked with seafood (and cheeses). The Wooden Boat Festival, a celebration of traditional sailing boats alongside much partying, is held the same weekend. The Sherkin Island Regatta (July), Baltimore Regatta (July/Aug) and the Deep Sea Angling Competition (Aug) help swell visitor numbers too.

Where to eat & drink

Clonakilty is home to the famous Clonakilty pudding, a black pudding that is sold in all the local butchers and features on many restaurant menus, including at the contemporary Costelloes Malthouse (Ashe Street, 023 883 4355, www.clonakiltyrestaurant.com, closed Oct-Feb Mon, Sun). Mio Restaurant (Connolly Street, 023 885 8571, www.mio.ie, closed Sept-May Mon) does good pizza and pasta dishes, while the Winery (Astna Square, 023 883 4580, www.thewinery.ie, closed Nov-Feb Sun) is a pleasant spot for coffee and a sandwich during the day, or some tapas and a glass of wine in the evening. Most of the pubs have traditional music at weekends; try the Clonakilty Wrestler (Pearse Street, 023 882 1455) or De Barra's (Pearse Street, 023 883 3381, www.debarra.ie).

Near Clonakilty, in Ring village, is Deasy's Harbour Bar & Seafood Restaurant (023 883 5741, closed Oct-May Mon, Tue), a traditional fishing village eaterie, serving very fresh seafood. There's also an excellent, casual seafood restaurant – O'Callaghan Walshe (023 884 8125, www.ocallaghanwalshe.com) – on the town square in Rosscarbery.

Baltimore's main strip is dominated by the Waterfront (028 20600, www.waterfronthotel.ie), which operates as a guesthouse, and a modern bar and restaurant. Next door, the more traditional Bushe's Bar (028 20125, www.bushesbar.com) gets packed in summer, as does the Algiers Inn around the corner.

Remotely located on Hare Island – but worth the trip – is the Island Cottage restaurant and cookery school (028 38102, www.islandcottage.com, open mid June-mid Sept Wed-Sun).

An Sugan

Wolfe Tone Street, Clonakilty (023 883 3719, www.ansugan.com). Open noon-11pm daily.
Food served noon-9.30pm daily.
The best part of An Sugan is the front bar area, adorned with random pieces of delftware, whiskey jugs and, in the corner, an old piano begging to be played. The pub has a reputation for having plenty of character and serving excellent food. The bar menu lists seafood chowder and open sandwiches alongside more substantial dishes such as

steaks or fish and chips. Two more modern dining rooms are used as overspill areas, or for private dining. The owners also run a B&B with seven modern rooms (€90 double).

Glebe Gardens

Baltimore (028 20232, www.glebegardens.com). Restaurant Breakfast served 10am-11.30am, lunch served noon-3pm, dinner 7-10pm Wed-Sat. Food served 10am-6pm Sun. Gardens 10am-6pm daily. Admission €5. Closed Sept-Easter. No credit cards.
Situated on the edge of the village, this is a beautiful spot with a wonderful café run by three sisters. Dishes are simple and delicious; expect the likes of pan-fried plaice with capers and lemon butter, and elderflower pannacotta. Produce is as local as can be – much of it comes from the gorgeous surrounding gardens, which feature a series of areas, including vegetable and herb plots, a flower garden and an old hay meadow. Gardening courses are also held.

Riverside Café

North Street, Skibbereen (028 40090, www.riverside skibbereen.ie). Open 9am-5pm Mon-Thur; 9am-9pm Fri, Sat.
The modern, airy café makes the most of its lovely location, with an outdoor terrace near the water. Large windows allow in plenty of light. The Riverside serves generous portions of down-to-earth dishes, including salads, soups, sandwiches and hamburgers, and Mediterranean-style tapas on Friday and Saturday nights. It's a friendly place, and the perfect pitstop before hitting the peninsula.

Where to stay

In the centre of Clonakilty, on a Georgian square, is the family-run O'Keeffe's Emmet Hotel (Emmet Square, 023 883 3394, www.emmethotel.com). The traditional bedrooms are very comfortable, and there's also a good bistro-style restaurant, as well as a bar and nightclub. Outside town, at Muckruss, the Dunmore House Hotel (028 883 3352, www.dunmorehousehotel.ie, closed mid Jan-mid Mar) overlooks the ocean. Contemporary in style, it has 29 bright and spacious rooms, plus a cosy bar and a decent restaurant.

Baltimore has no shortage of accommodation; the best of several hotels are Casey's (028 20197, www.caseysofbaltimore.com), which also has self-catering houses, and Rolfs (Baltimore Hill, §028 20289, www.rolfscountryhouse.eu), a resort hotel with self-catering accommodation too.

Inchydoney Lodge & Spa

Inchydoney Island (023 883 3143, www.inchydoney island.com). Rates €190-€250 double incl breakfast.
Located on one of Cork's most beautiful beaches, Inchydoney is blessed with fantastic views and the perfect swimming hole on its doorstep. Guests are welcomed with a big smile, and the offer of a glass of Irish Mist whiskey and a rest in front of the fire. The 67-room hotel offers contemporary luxury, with airy, spacious public areas including a lounge area with dozens of couches to slouch on, a children's playroom and a fantastic pool, steam room and sauna. The bar serves food day and night, and is busy with both guests and daytrippers. A fine-dining restaurant serves classic dishes, and has beautiful views over the sea.

WEST CORK: MIZEN HEAD & BEARA PENINSULAS

West of Skibbereen, the landscape begins to get wilder; gorse and heather appear and the coastline becomes more jagged. The small coastal town of Schull (www.schull.ie), 24 kilometres west of Skibbereen, is the main town on the Mizen peninsula ★. It's a laid-back place, close to several stunning beaches. Main Street is inhabited by several jewellery shops, Chapter One Bookstore (028 27606, closed Jan-Mar Mon, Sun), several cafés and a wonderful chocolatier: Gwen's Chocolates (028 27853, www.gwenschocolate. com, open Mar-Sept, Dec Tue-Sat).

Many Irish families have summer homes here, attracted by the welcoming community, the pretty bay and the excellent Schull Harbour Sailing Club. The club runs a number of regattas, the most popular of which is Calves Week in early August. Boat trips to the islands of Clear, Fastnet and Sherkin operate from the harbour – information is available at the Tourist Office (Main Street, 028 28600, closed mid Sept-May Mon-Wed) – while kayaking, windsurfing and other activities are organised by the Schull Watersports Centre (The Pier, 028 28554, open Mar-Oct Mon-Sat). Away from the water, there's Schull Planetarium (028 28315, www.westcorkweb.ie/planetarium), housed in the local community college.

The town also has an active artistic community, which organises the Art in Schull Festival in July, with exhibitions, drama and film events, and workshops. A dynamic roster of Irish and international films are shown at the Fastnet Short Film Festival (www.fastnetshortfilmfestival.com) in May. Schull Country Market (www.schullmarket. com, mid Apr-Sept) brings food and craft stalls to the Pier Road car park on Sunday mornings.

The drive from Schull to Mizen Head at the end of the peninsula is a beautiful one, passing through small villages. After Goleen, there's the promontory of Rock Island, capped by an old communications building (now converted into self-catering accommodation). Spanish Point, on the far side of Rock Island, attracts advanced surfers. The hamlet of Crookhaven was once a major refuelling point for ships travelling between the US and northern Europe. These days, the attractive harbour is quiet, but two atmospheric, traditional bars – the Crookhaven Inn (028 35309, www.the crookhaveninn.com, closed Oct-Easter) and O'Sullivan's (028 35319) – have outdoor benches with views to the promontory. Both bars serve food, and are popular after a day on the beach. There's little accommodation except for a few self-catering cottages; for these, try Galley Cove B&B (www.galleycovehouse.com) or Schull Tourist Office.

Continue around Brow Head to reach the area's most beautiful beach, Barley Cove. It's sandy, perfect for swimming and overlooked by the modern Barley Cove Hotel (028 35234, www.barleycovebeachhotel.com, closed Sept-May except Easter), which also has a restaurant. The road then ascends, offering spectacular views, until you reach Ireland's most southerly point, Mizen Head.

The next promontory provides a dramatic drive to weatherbeaten Sheep's Head. Go through Durrus, and the coastal road rises above Dunmanus Bay, bordered by hills coated in heather. At the foot of Seefin Mountain is Kilcrohane, a quiet but useful overnight stop for those attempting the Sheep's Head Way or Cycle Route (see p148). At the end of the road, at Toreen, is the Sheep's Head Café (027 67136, closed Nov-Feb) and an information point.

Returning on the coast road on the west side, there are striking views across Bantry Bay. Bantry itself has charming harbour, and plenty of amenities. Magnificent Bantry House (see p142) is perched above, with yet more glorious views. Information on sailing classes, kayaking trips, boat excursions and local walks, including the town's heritage trail, can be found at the Tourist Office (027 50229, open June, July daily; Apr, May, Aug, Sept times vary), located in the old courthouse on Bantry Square. Bantry is busy during the West Cork Chamber Music Festival (www.westcorkmusic.ie) in late June and the West Cork Literary Festival (www.westcorkliteraryfestival.ie) in July.

A few kilometres north of Bantry along the N71, the tiny village of Ballylickey has a wonderful food shop, Manning's Emporium (027 50456), which sells local cheeses, cured meats, chutneys and wines – it's ideal for picnic supplies.

Further north, Glengarriff is the starting point for the wild Beara Peninsula. Tucked into the north side of Bantry Bay, the town has a mild climate, sterling views and has been a tourist destination for years – witness the attractive 18th-century Eccles Hotel (see p158). There are several bars and some craft shops such as Quill's Woollen Market (027 63488). As well as a pretty beach, visitor attractions include the tropical gardens at Bamboo Park (027 63007, www.bamboo-park.com). More horticultural delights lie a 15-minute boat ride away on the small island of Ilnacullin, also called Garinish Island (see p142).

Rising from the centre of the peninsula are the barren Caha Mountains, which can be crossed via the twisty, sometimes fearsome road known as Healy Pass. Awe-inspiring vistas await at the viewpoint on top. The R572 coast road from Ardigole to Castletownbere has plenty of snapshot moments too, especially when approaching Bere Island. Castletownbere is an important fishing town, and has Ireland's second largest natural harbour. It's a sizeable place, considerably larger than Glengarriff, with plenty to do. There are boat trips to Bere Island, diving with Beara Diving (mobile 087 699 3793, www.bearadiving.com, closed Oct-Apr), and walks, including the long-distance Beara Way (see p148). For maps and information, visit the tourist office (The Square, 027 70054, www.bearatourism.com, closed Apr-Sept Sat, Sun; Oct-Mar Mon, Fri-Sun).

The tip of the peninsula juts out towards Dursey Island and a cable car runs across the channel between the two. Crossings are limited; check with the tourist offices in Castletownbere or Glengarriff. The small island is empty, but it's enough to walk around enjoying the atmosphere and the crashing waves. Round the headland is the town of Allihies, dramatically set, with a small sandy beach. Nearby is the Dzogchen Beara Tibetan Buddist Retreat Centre (027 73032, www.dzogchenbeara.org), which holds meditation classes and offers accommodation. The road from Allihies along the western side of the peninsula is perhaps even more beautiful than the eastern side, with incredible views across Kenmare River; after Ardgroom, you enter County Kerry.

Bantry House. See p142 and p158.

Where to eat & drink

Hudson's Wholefoods (Main Street, 028 37565, closed Sun) in Ballydehob is useful for picnic supplies or a coffee and a snack. In Schull, Paradise Crêpe (Main Street, mobile 087 743 7427, closed Oct-Apr) offers savoury and sweet crêpes, and has a pleasant rear terrace. There are several traditional bars in the town, including Hackett's (028 28625, closed Oct-May Sat, Sun), while TJ Newman's (028 27776, www.tjnewmans. com) is a bright, modern café-wine bar with an all-day menu. Both are on Main Street.

Bantry has a small selection of restaurants. The Brick Oven on Proby's Quay (021 432 2699) serves good pizzas – afterwards, head straight to Ma Murphy's (New Street, 027 50242). This is a proper Irish bar, with a small grocery shop at the front and, behind glass doors, a cosy bar, followed by another room with an open fire. Locals drink here, and at the Anchor, also on New Street, which often has music sessions.

McCarthy's Bar (The Square, 027 70014) in Castletownbere is pictured on the cover of the bestselling Irish travelogue of the same name, written by Pete McCarthy. It's worth dropping into the bar for a pint and a chat with the locals.

Fish Kitchen

New Street, Bantry (027 56651, www.thefishkitchen.ie). Lunch served noon-3.30pm, dinner served 5.30-9pm Tue-Sat.
Situated above the Central Fish Market (the source of much of the menu), this is a sweet dining room, with candles balanced in large clam shells and a happy buzz of satisfied customers. Starters include oyster, chorizo, garlic and chilli prawns, or an open crab sandwich; more substantial dishes are fish cakes with tomato salsa, smoked salmon tagliatelle or catch of the day.

Good Things Café

Ahakista Road, Durrus (027 61426, www.thegood thingscafe.com). Lunch served 12.30-3pm, dinner served 6.30-8.30pm daily.
Carmel Somers is an accomplished chef, using local produce to create simple but sumptuous dishes, to much acclaim. Beyond the pristine white exterior is a small, bright dining room. The menu varies with the days and seasons, but a typical meal might see salad of beetroot, broad beans and peas, with walnut and herb dressing, followed by new season shoulder of lamb and prune tagine, then warm poached cherries with vanilla ice-cream to finish. Carmel also runs a cookery school here, covering everything from fish preparation to baking; check the website for details.

Heron's Cove

The Harbour, Goleen (028 35225, www.heronscove.com). Dinner served May-Sept 7-9.30pm daily; Oct-April by advance booking only.
The dining room is casual, decked out with pine tables and chairs, and with views of Goleen harbour. Sue Hill's menu features the likes of Dunmannus Bay scallops with smoked bacon cream sauce, Heron's Cove crab cakes, and Goleen lamb chops with rosemary jus and organic vegetables. There are also five simple B&B rooms, with terracotta walls and large windows (€70 double).

Where to stay

Schull has plenty of self-catering lodgings and several B&Bs – for details, see www.schull.ie. Particularly charming is Grove House (028 28067, www.grovehouseschull.com) on the Corra Road: set in an ivy-clad Georgian manor, it has five bedrooms and a restaurant. B&B and self-catering accommodation is available at Rock Cottage (028 35538, www.rockcottage.ie), a handsomely restored, ex-hunting lodge on the way from Schull to Toormore. Beautiful Blairscove House (027 61127, www.blairscove.ie, closed Nov-mid Mar), near Durrus, offers stylish suites for B&B and a few self-catering apartments, plus a popular restaurant.

Bantry has a new hotel, the Maritime (The Quay, 027 54700, www.themaritime.ie). Not so pretty on the outside, it has a chic interior and a leisure centre. The more traditional Bantry Bay Hotel (027 50062, www.bantrybayhotel.ie) has a handy location on Wolfe Tone Square. In Ballylickey, there are 25 elegant bedrooms, plus a living room, library, verandah and a good restaurant, at Seaview House Hotel (027 50073, www.seaviewhouse hotel.com, closed mid Nov-mid Mar).

On the Beara peninsula, most rooms are in mid-range hotels and B&Bs. In Glengarriff, the venerable Eccles Hotel (Glengarriff Harbour, 027 63003, www.eccleshotel.com, closed Nov-Feb) has comfortable rooms and beautiful views over the harbour, while family-run Casey's (027 63072, www.caseyshotelglengarriff.ie, closed Jan, Dec) offers simple modern rooms and good pub food. Between Glengarriff and Castletownbere, Ulusker (027 60606, closed Oct-Mar) is a lovely guesthouse overlooking Bantry Bay. Allihies has a handful of B&Bs (details on www.visitallihies.com), the nicely priced Allihies Village Hostel (027 73107, www.allihieshostel.net, closed Nov-Mar) and Anthony's Campsite (027 73002, closed Oct-Apr) next to the beach.

Ballylickey House

Ballylickey (027 50071, www.ballylickeymanorhouse.com). Rates €90-€180 double incl breakfast. Closed Oct-Mar.
This graceful white manor overlooking Bantry Bay was built by Lord Kenmare in 1650 as a hunting lodge. The Graves family has lived here for four generations, and the present incumbents know how to make guests feel welcome. Accommodation is divided between the manor house and a few cottages; the comfortable rooms are in keeping with the surrounds, and have views over the immaculate and extensive gardens. There's an outdoor swimming pool too.

Bantry House ★

Bantry (027 50047, www.bantryhouse.com). Rates €160-€240 double incl breakfast. Closed Nov-Feb.
Bantry House is one of Ireland's most handsome historic houses (*see p142*). One wing holds seven guest rooms, decorated with a mix of antique and new furniture, and with modern bathrooms. Relax with a drink from the honesty bar in the spacious billiard room, or the drawing room with open fire. A substantial breakfast is served, after which guests can take a tour of the main house or wander the extensive gardens. The combination of a relaxed atmosphere and grand surroundings makes this a special place to stay.

Counties Tipperary & Waterford

Much of Tipperary is countryside, with green hills and valleys and a few towering mountain ranges. Dotted about the county are well-preserved monastic ruins, including the imposing Rock of Cashel, Hore Abbey and Cahir Castle. The Knockmealdown and Comeragh Mountains border Tipperary and Waterford, and excellent waymarked trails can be accessed from either side of the border. To the south of the heather-covered mountains, Waterford's coastline is fringed with several fine beaches, and there are thriving coastal communities such as Ardmore, Dunmore East and Waterford city.

These are good counties for food-lovers, as the growth of organic farming enterprises and artisan food producers has helped encourage a large number of farmers' markets, restaurants and even food festivals such as the Waterford Festival of Food in Dungarvan.

NORTH TIPPERARY

At the very north of the county is the town of Roscrea, situated along the N7 on the banks of the River Bunnow. In the centre is the Roscrea Heritage Centre (Castle Street, 0505 21850, www.heritageireland.ie, closed Oct-mid Apr) – a complex consisting of Roscrea Castle and Damer House. The castle dates from the 13th century, while the mansion was built in 1722; guided tours are available. Tickets for Roscrea Castle also give access to the restored Black Mills building (0505 21850, closed Oct-Easter) on Church Street, which houses St Cronan's High Cross and the Roscrea Pillar Stone. Other ruins include those of a 15th-century Franciscan Friary on Abbey Street. The best way to see Roscrea's historical remnants is to pick up the heritage trail maps available in the Heritage Centre.

Lying 30 kilometres west of Roscrea is north Tipperary's largest town, Nenagh. It's a busy market town, and a handy stop-off for those making their way to Lough Derg. Once a prominent Anglo-Norman stronghold, all that remains of the castle are the keep, a tower and part of the gatehouse, surrounded by a small park. Nenagh Heritage Centre (Kickham Street, 067 33850, closed mid May-mid Sept Sun; mid Sept-mid May Sat, Sun) is housed in two Georgian buildings that were once the governor's house, and a gatehouse for the former jail complex. The centre is a bit of a mixture, comprising a reconstruction of an old schoolroom and dairy, changing art exhibits, an agricultural museum and, in the gatehouse, the old jail cells.

Nenagh has several good eateries, and on Saturday mornings there is an excellent farmers' market at Teach an Leinn, the town's traditional market house on Kenyon Street.

A few kilometres west is Lough Derg. While the western shore (in County Clare) is more popular, there are several pretty towns on the Tipperary side, which serve as good bases for water activities. Dromineer, ten kilometres north-east of Nenagh, has an attractive harbour; boat trips leave from here, while walkers often start or finish the Lough Derg Way (see p162) in the town. Also of note is the Dromineer Literary Festival (www.dromineer literaryfestival.ie) in September/October. Just north of Dromineer is Terryglass, another attractive lakeside town, best known for the lively music sessions held during the summer in the local pubs.

South of Roscrea, five kilometres west of Thurles and just outside the small village of Ballycahill, is Ballynahow Castle (067 31610). Built by the Purcells in the 16th century, this is one of few round castles in Ireland. A few kilometres further south is the atmospheric Holy Cross Abbey (see p170).

However, the big draw in this area is the Rock of Cashel (see p170), a 12th-century monastic site resplendent on a grassy knoll. Many visitors stay overnight in the lively town of Cashel, in order to see the magical sight of the floodlit Rock, and so there's an abundance of hotels, cafés and bars.

Lesser sights include the ruins of 13th-century Hore Abbey; set in a field on the outskirts of town, it retains the original nave, chapter house and vaulted sacristy. The abbey can be approached on foot along Bishop's Walk, at the back of the gardens of Cashel Palace Hotel (see p164), once the home of the Bishop. St John's Cathedral on John Street dates from the mid 18th century; beside it is the Bolton Library, home to a collection of antiquarian books and manuscripts from as far back as the 12th century. For more on all these, visit the tourist office in the Heritage Centre (062 62511, www.cashel.ie, closed Nov-Feb Sat, Sun),

where you can also see the town's original charters and a model of Cashel in 1640.

At the foot of the Rock of Cashel is the Brú Ború Cultural Centre (062 61122, http://comhaltas.ie, closed Sat, Sun), which holds a theatre, restaurant, craft centre and genealogy suite, as well as hosting a variety of traditional Irish music shows, theatre and dance from June to August. Also in the summer, the Cashel Cultural Festival stages a range of street theatre, comedy, music and dance events over four days.

Just outside Cashel is Golden. Surrounded by the fertile land known as the Golden Vale, the town is the site of the remains of Ireland's largest medieval priory, Athassel Priory (see p170).

Where to eat & drink

Eateries in Roscrea are limited. Nenagh, however, has a wealth of them. For example, Country Choice (25 Kenyon Street, 067 32596, www. countrychoice.ie, closed Sun) has a deli with a fine array of organic vegetables, local cheeses, meats and breads. The small café at the back serves tarts, salads, sandwiches and other delectable items. Also on Kenyon Street, the bright, modern Pepper Mill (067 34598, www.the peppermill.ie, closed Mon) combines a ground-floor wine bar with an upper-level restaurant. The traditional Fairways Bar & Orchard Restaurant (Ballymagree, 067 41444, www.thefairwaysbar.ie), a five-minute drive outside Nenagh town, has an

Things to do

NORTH TIPPERARY

Lough Derg Way
www.discoverloughderg.ie.
The Lough Derg Way runs north-east from the city of Limerick to Killaloe (26km), and then follows the eastern edge of the lake to Dromineer (32km). Passing through lakeside towns, the Arra Mountains and along rural waymarked paths, it's a popular walk in summer for those wanting an alternative means of transport to cars and boats. A map of the route is available from nearby tourist offices.

SOUTH TIPPERARY

Glen of Aherlow Walks
www.aherlow.com.
There are two national loop walk trails in the Glen of Aherlow – Christ the King and Lisvarrinane Village – both of which take in woodland, quiet country roads and grassy fields. There are also circular walks through Slievenamuck, which range from 30 minutes to four hours. For more advanced walkers, the two lake walks – Lough Curra and Lake Muskry – are recommended: the trails lead into the Galtee Mountains offering superb views over the corrie lakes, through wooded foothills, mountain streams and open moorland. The Galtee Walking Club meets at different points every Sunday and welcomes visitors; its quarterly schedule is available from the Glen of Aherlow Fáilte Society (062 56331). The society can also arrange guided walks in the area.

Slievenamon Mountains
Famed in old songs and poems, Slievenamon means the 'Mountain of the Women', and legend has it that the local women raced to the top of the mountain to claim the hand of the warrior Fionn Mac Cumhail; he wanted Grainne, the daughter of the High King of Ireland, to win, so he advised her on the best route. The walk to the summit is an easy one, along a broad path, with panoramic views on clear days. A series of heather hillocks surround the mountain, some of which are crowned by ancient burial grounds, the highest of which is said to be the entrance into the Celtic underworld. The easy route is clearly signposted from Kilcash, while more experienced hill walkers can do a loop walk around the mountain. Information is available at the tourist offices in Cashel or Cahir.

WATERFORD CITY & AROUND

Waterford & Suir Valley Railway
Kilmeaden (www.wsvrailway.ie).
Originally laid in 1872, the narrow-gauge railway has been out of use since 1987, apart from this 17km stretch. The 50-minute journey, in a 19th-century train, runs along the River Suir, with stunning views across to Kilkenny and the surrounding countryside.

WEST & NORTH WATERFORD

Ardmore Cliff Walk
Ardmore.
This 5km trail starts just past the Cliff House Hotel (see p178); while not difficult, it's not for vertigo sufferers. It leads over Ardmore and Ram Head, past a shipwreck and up to the remains of St Declan's Cathedral and Round Tower, with stunning views to the east and west. Maps and details of the trail are provided in the Ardmore Tourist Information Centre (024 94444) in the village or Dungarvan Tourist Information Centre (058 44000).

Comeragh Mountains Walking Trail
Kilcooney Wood.
Leaving from Kilconey Wood car park on the R676, the trail goes into the Comeragh Mountains and is steep in parts. The climb leads to a ridge overlooking Coushingaun Lough and offers stunning views over the Nire Valley. You can either return the way you came, or continue on across the heather-covered mountain to Fauscoum, where a small cairn marks the peak, and then over to Crotty's Rock. From here there are incredible views of tranquil Crotty's Lake. The whole route will take up to five hours, but note that detailed maps are essential.

Whale watching
Migrating whales pass close to Waterford's coastline from June to February, but sightings are all but guaranteed from December to February. You can watch from the shore, the best points being Helvic and Ardmore Head; all you need are binoculars and patience. The Irish Whale & Dolphin Group (www.iwdg.ie) provides information on where and when to go, and locations of recent sightings. Boat trips can be arranged with several companies; try South East Angling (www.seatours.ie).

enterprising menu of modern Irish and international dishes available in the bar and restaurant.

Bars are dotted along the shores of Lough Derg: among them, a white thatched cottage that houses Larkin's Bar & Restaurant (067 23232, www.larkinspub.com) in Garrykennedy. Classic Irish cooking is served, and traditional music sessions take place most nights. In Dromineer, the Whiskey Still (067 24129, closed Oct-Mar Tue) has a lovely deck overlooking the harbour, and serves pub grub. One of the best-known places is the Derg Inn (067 22037, www.derginn.ie) in Terryglass, where outdoor tables get packed with sailors and day-trippers enjoying a pint and a hearty meal. In the evening the place is hopping with music and craic.

Cashel has all a visitor needs in terms of cafés, bars and restaurants. For a fine lunch, head straight for cheerful Café Hans (Moor Lane, 062 63660, closed Mon, Sun), sibling of Chez Hans (*see below*); here, delicious salads, open sandwiches, and a few hot dishes such as poached salmon are served in a buzzy atmosphere. If you can't get a table, return later for tea and cake. The Spearman (Main Street, 062 61143, closed Sun) is a pleasant little bakery and café. For an old-fashioned vibe, make your way to Ryan's (062 61431) or Dowlings (062 62956) – both are on Main Street and have cosy snugs and good Guinness – while the Brian Boru (062 63381) across the road is more modern, with DJs and bands playing at weekends.

Chez Hans ★
Moor Lane, Cashel (062 61177, www.chezhans.net).
Dinner served 6-9.30pm Tue-Sat.
Built as a public lecture hall in 1861, this beautiful stone building now houses Cashel's best restaurant, owned and run by the Matthiae family since 1968. The dining room is formal, with white tablecloths and silverware, and light streaming in through stained-glass windows. Typical starters are Dunmore East lobster baked with butter, herbs and samphire, and truffle, wild mushroom and spinach risotto; mains might feature rack of Tipperary lamb with ratatouille and lamb jus or the ever-popular seafood cassoulet. Next there's a tricky choice between the tasting plate of desserts or the platter of Irish cheeses. People travel for miles to eat here, so booking is advisable.

Fiacri House
Boulerea (0505 43017, www.fiacrihouse.com).
Dinner served 6.30-9.15pm Wed-Sat.
Enda and Ailish Hennessy run a restaurant and cookery school from their pretty pink farmhouse, located 10km from Roscrea. Drinks are served in a cosy lounge with an open fire, before guests sit down to a five-course dinner. The menu changes seasonally, but might include crispy bacon salad with black pudding and Fiacri House free-range poached egg, followed by soup, then sorbet of the day, and then honey roast supreme of duck with herb potato stuffing, caramelised onion and wild berry sauce. To finish, there's a range of indulgent puddings or Irish cheeses. The cookery classes cover all abilities – see the website for details.

Pantry Café
Qunetin's Way, Nenagh (067 31237, www.thepantry cafe.ie). Open 8.30am-6pm Mon-Sat.

Dunmore East. See p172.

An excellent deli and café, where much is made of breakfast. Sit in a light-filled room and enjoy full Irish breakfasts, pancakes, bagels or muffins. Later in the day, there are pasta dishes, salads and the must-try 'hot belly' sandwiches. Stacked with a range of fillings and served warm, they are delicious. The deli is just as appealing, and an ideal place to buy picnic supplies.

Where to stay
Cashel has several good B&Bs, such as Hill House (Palmershill, 062 61277, www.hillhousecashel. com). At Cashel Lodge & Camping Park (062 61003, www.cashel-lodge.com), just outside town, there's well-priced accommodation in a restored farmhouse, as well as a campsite. Bailey's Hotel (Main Street, 062 61937, www.baileyshotel cashel.com) has a contemporary interior inside an 18th-century shell. There are 19 comfortable bedrooms, and a good bar and restaurant.

Ashley Park House
Ardcroney (067 38223, www.ashleypark.com).
Rates €70-€100 double incl breakfast. No credit cards.
Slightly north of Nenagh along the N52 is one of Ireland's prettiest 18th-century houses, set in 80 acres of gardens on the banks of Lough Ourna. The five bedrooms vary in size, but all are traditionally decorated and very comfortable, with impressive views. Breakfast is a hearty affair that will set you up for the day; dinner can be provided by arrangement. A charming, old-world guesthouse with a welcoming atmosphere.

Cashel Palace Hotel

Main Street, Cashel (062 62707, www.cashel-palace.ie).
Rates from €130 double incl breakfast.
Once a manor house (built in 1730) and formerly the
Bishop's residence, the Cashel Palace Hotel has retained
many of its original features. The 20 well-appointed rooms
are in keeping with a country house hotel, and some have
views looking out to the Rock of Cashel. There's a pretty
drawing room too. In the basement, the Bishop's Buttery is
a lively spot serving a modern Irish menu, frequented by
locals and tourists.

Coolbawn Quay

Coolbawn Quay (067 28158, www.coolbawnquay.com).
Rates €170 double incl breakfast.
This lakeside resort, 20km north of Nenagh, is styled in the
manner of a 19th-century Irish village, with 47 bedrooms
spread out through cottages, suites and rooms. The largest
sleep up to eight: useful for groups. Interiors are country-
minimalist, with all mod-cons; some rooms have turf-
burning stoves. Guests can dine in the informal clubhouse,
where there's also a small traditional bar. A spa offers a
variety of treatments, plus a relaxation area with a small
pool. There's a marina where guests can moor their boats –
handy for those taking a break from cruising the Shannon;
trips on the lake can also be arranged.

Inch House ★

Nenagh Road, Thurles (0504 51348, www.inchhouse.ie).
Rates €90-€110 double incl breakfast.
This country house B&B and restaurant is owned and run
by the Egan family, who have lovingly restored the 18th-
century manor over the years. Accommodation comprises
five comfortable, elegant rooms. Open fires warm the
drawing room and library bar. The restaurant, which opens
in the evenings to guests and non-residents, focuses on
quality local ingredients, as seen in mains such as fillet of
Crowe's Farm pork, rolled and stuffed with apricot and

herbs, served with red wine jus and Inch House apple chutney. The house is on a working farm, and there are many attractive walks nearby.

SOUTH TIPPERARY

Cahir is a bustling market town and, like so many towns in the south-east, grew up around an Anglo-Norman stronghold. The name means 'fort'; Cahir was a well-defended medieval town and Cahir Castle (see p170) an important base for the powerful Butler family. On Church Street there's a beautifully restored 19th-century mill: the Craft Granary (052 744 1473, www.craftgranary.com, closed Jan-June, Sept-Nov Sun), where crafts made in the area are sold. On Saturday morning, Tipperary's food artisans sell their wares at the farmers' market. From the castle car park you can walk along the River Suir for roughly two kilometres on the Swiss Cottage Walk, which leads to the picturesque Swiss Cottage (see p170).

West of Cahir are the rolling plains of the Glen of Aherlow ★, tucked in between Ireland's highest inland range, the Galtee Mountains, and Slievenamuck Ridge. Leave Cahir on the N24 and turn left at Bansha on to the R663 to access the glen. The scenery is breathtaking, and there are plenty of things to do, including cycling, horse riding at the Hillcrest Riding Centre in Galbally (062 37915), fishing in the River Aherlow (052 618 0055) or golfing at the four surrounding golf courses. Visit the Aherlow Tourist Office (062 56331, www.aherlow.com, closed summer Sun, winter Sat, Sun) adjacent to the Coach Road Inn on the R663, for more information.

The glen also has many glorious walks (see p162), and a Walking Festival takes place each June: guides lead three hikes each day and walkers return to music and dance in the evening. The Glen of Aherlow Nature Park (www.aherlow.com) also offers a series of woodland trails for all abilities, with picnic benches dotted throughout. Beside the entrance to the park on the R664 is the statue of Christ the King, erected in 1950 to bless the glen and all those who pass through it. The statue marks the glen's most scenic point, and the views are exceptional.

Around eight kilometres from the glen of Aherlow is the small market town of Tipperary, made famous by the popular World War I song 'It's a Long Way to Tipperary' (the lyrics appear on signs along the N24). The Tipperary Excel Arts & Cultural Centre (Mitchell Street, 062 80520, www.tipperary-excel.com) houses a family history research centre, three cinemas, a theatre, a small local art gallery and a café. You can pick up tourist information here too. Also in the area, on the other side of the Galtee Mountains to the Glen of Aherlow, are the Mitchelstown Caves (see p170).

Some 16 kilometres east of Cahir, on the River Suir, is Tipperary's main town, Clonmel. Once an important medieval trading centre, it is now a busy, administrative town, famous for the brewing of Bulmers cider (known as Magners outside Ireland). The original brewery in the centre of the town is still operational; in season you can see the mountains of apples being prepared for brewing, and the aroma lingers over the town.

There's a mix of family-run shops and chain stores along O'Connell Street. Standing astride O'Connell Street is West Gate, built in 1831 and one of the three entry points into Clonmel. At the eastern end of O'Connell Street is the Main Guard (052 612 7484, www.heritageireland.ie, closed Oct-mid Apr), an 18th-century sandstone building fronted by a loggia of open arches. Built as a courthouse, it fell into disuse, and the open arches were converted into shops. Restored to its former glory, it has a small exhibition inside on the history of the building.

Down by the quays is a Franciscan friary, remodelled in the 18th century, but retaining a 15th-century tower and containing several tombs belonging to the Butler family. Just off New Quay is Nelson Street, where the South Tipperary Arts

Cahir Castle

Old Convent

Centre (052 612 7877, www.southtipparts.com, closed Mon, Sun) hosts exhibitions and music, theatre and dance performances. In July, the town celebrates the nine-day Clonmel Junction Festival (www.junctionfestival.com), with stalls and entertainment throughout the town.

East of Clonmel on the N24, Carrick-on-Suir is worth visiting for charming Ormond Castle (*see p170*). Either side of the town are two gardens of interest: Killurney Gardens (mobile 087 944 4662, open by appointment only) in Ballypatrick, and Fairbrook House & Museum of Contemporary Figurative Art in Kilmeaden (051 384 657, www.fairbrook-house.com, open by appointment only May-Sept). North of Carrick-on-Suir are the Slievenamon Mountains (*see p162*). A number of walks lead to the summit, from where there are panoramic views across the south-east.

The Knockmealdown Mountains dominate the skyline on the final approach to County Waterford. The most scenic drive south is the 20-kilometre section of the R668 from Cahir to Lismore. Known as the Vee, the twisting road is lined with rhododendrons. The climb into the mountains is dotted with viewpoints, where you can stop and picnic before descending into Waterford.

Where to eat & drink

Choice is limited in Cahir, but the River House (Castle Street, 052 744 1951, www.riverhouse.ie) has a great location, right across from the castle. It's a bright, airy, and modern space where food is served all day; there are also outdoor tables. Most people opt for a picnic in the Glen of Aherlow, having stocked up in either Cashel or Cahir, but there's also the option of the Coach Road Inn on the R633.

As well as the excellent farmers' market on Saturday mornings in the primary school car park, Clonmel has a number of reliable cafés and restaurants. Have a coffee and cake or savoury snack in Hickey's Bakery (052 612 1587, www.hickeysbakery.com, closed Sun) on Westgate, which has been perfecting its baked goods for over 100 years and is known for its barm brack (fruit loaf). For an atmospheric drink with good pub grub, head to Sean Tierney's (052 612 4467) on O'Connell Street. Spread over four floors, it has plenty of places for a quiet pint.

Between Clonmel and Carrick-on-Suir, the Dove Hill shopping complex houses Lily Mai's Café (051 645603), worth a visit even if you're not interested in the retail possibilities.

Befani's

Sarsfield Street, Clonmel (052 617 7893, www.befani. com). Breakfast served 9-11am Mon-Sat. Lunch served 12.30-2.30pm Mon-Sat; 12.30-4pm Sun. Dinner served 5.30-9.30pm daily.
Serving a range of Mediterranean dishes, Befani's has justly become a local favourite. Located in a restored listed building near the quays, the dining room is often packed with people tucking into tapas with a twist: fried calamares with smoked paprika and chilli aioli, say, or spicy Italian

meatballs. Larger dishes are also available, such as a platter of fresh seafood. Simple, comfortable B&B rooms are available in the adjacent Townhouse.

Kilkieran Cottage ★

Castletown (051 642388, www.kilkierancottage.com). Lunch served 12.30-3.30pm Sun. Dinner served 6-9.30pm Wed-Sun.
The restaurant's location – a few kilometres north of Carrick, on a hillside overlooking the Nier Valley – is reason enough to visit, even without the top-notch food. The modest dining room is set within a traditional whitewashed cottage; vibrant artwork lines the stark white walls, and linen cloths give an air of elegance to an otherwise casual room. Chef and owner Michael Mee uses local ingredients such as Comeragh lamb, Tipperary beef and seafood from Dunmore East on a seasonal menu. Staff are friendly and attentive, and guests can dine outdoors in summer. Booking is essential.

Where to stay

There are plenty of B&Bs and self-catering cottages in the Glen of Aherlow; find details on www.aherlow.com. Camping is possible at the ideally located Ballinacourty House (062 56559, www.camping.ie, closed Oct-mid Mar) or the Glen of Aherlow Camping & Caravan Park (062 56555, www.tipperarycamping.com) in Newtown. For a little more luxury, try Aherlow House Hotel (062 56153, www.aherlowhouse.ie). Among the trees in the Galtee Mountains, 16 kilometres from Cahir, is the Mountain Lodge Hostel (052 746 7277, www.anoige.ie, closed Oct-Mar) nicely placed for hill walkers.

Pitch your tent or pull up your campervan at lovely Apple Farm (052 744 1459, www.theapple farm.com), where you'll be surrounded by apple trees – there's even a complimentary bottle of their juice on arrival. The campsite is just off the N24 between Cahir and Clonmel. Five minutes outside Clonmel, Hotel Minella (Coleville Road, 052 612 2388, www.hotelminella.ie) has an admirable location on the River Suir.

North of Clonmel is Mobarnane House (052 613 1962, www.mobarnanehouse.com, closed Nov-Feb), an 18th-century manor set in tranquil grounds and perfect for those walking in the Slievenamon Mountains. South of Clonmel, pretty Kilmaneen Farmhouse (052 613 6231, www.kilmaneen.com) offers B&B or a self-catering cottage. The owners can also arrange guided walks in the area and are a font of knowledge on things to do in Tipperary.

In Carrick-on-Suir, the Carraig Hotel (051 641455, www.carraighotel.com) on Main Street offers simple B&B accommodation.

Old Convent ★

Mount Anglesby, Clogheen (052 746 5565, www.theoldconvent.ie). Rates €170 double incl breakfast. Closed Christmas-mid Feb.
The Old Convent calls itself a 'gourmet hideaway', so guests know that food will be as important as the stylish rooms. Located at the foot of the Knockmealdown Mountains, the neat convent façade hides a modern interior. The seven

bedrooms are all different – a four-poster bed in one, a legged slipper tub in another – but all are supremely comfortable retreats with views over the mountains and gardens. The restaurant (in what was the chapel, and which still has stained-glass windows) is the scene for a nine-course dinner.

WATERFORD CITY & AROUND

Waterford city

The Vikings first recognised the strategic position of this sheltered spot in the estuary, with direct access to three major rivers serving much of the south-east of Ireland. Here they built their walled city, which rapidly grew into a major trading centre, Waterford. In 1170, Strongbow's men assaulted the city and laid claim over the land. Henry II raised the status of Waterford to a royal city, acknowledging its importance as a major stronghold in Ireland. English and French merchants flocked to the city, and Waterford became the country's main importer of wine, and exporter of wool and hides. In 1650, it was taken by Ireton's troops and many of the Catholic merchants were expelled from the city; with William of Orange's accession the city became predominantly Protestant. Under the direction of John Roberts, the city underwent architectural rejuvenation, and many of his buildings survive today. Shipbuilding became a major industry and Waterford continued to thrive until the latter half of the 20th century, which saw the closure of many factories and the end of the shipbuilding industry.

Although the city's outer ring, interspersed with industrial parks, does not make a good first impression, some visitors will appreciate the quay lined with cranes and ships, and all will love the centre, with its medieval layout of narrow roads and laneways, remnants of the old city wall and the occasional grand Georgian building.

The one-hour guided Waterford City Walking Tour is the best way to orient yourself and learn the history of the city. Contact the Tourist Office (The Granary, Merchants Quay, 051 875823, closed Oct-June Sun) for details, or pick up a map and set out on your own. The quays here are generally used as a marina for leisure boats; walking east from the Granary, you come to the Victorian clocktower perched on the edge of the quays facing Barronstrand Street. A few metres up the street is Holy Trinity Cathedral (051 875166, www.waterford-cathedral.com), Ireland's oldest Roman Catholic cathedral, constructed in 1793. Designed by John Roberts, the building has undergone many renovations, leaving it with an ornate interior.

Off Barronstrand Street, George's Street is lined with period buildings, the ground floors converted into shops and businesses. Barronstrand Street turns into Michael Street and further up, into John Street: this is the main shopping strip in Waterford and the place to find all the familiar high-street names plus a few boutiques. One of the city's most famous sites is east of the shopping district, located at the bottom of the Mall. Reginald's

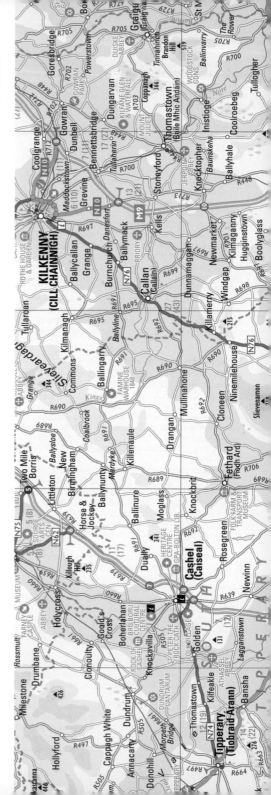

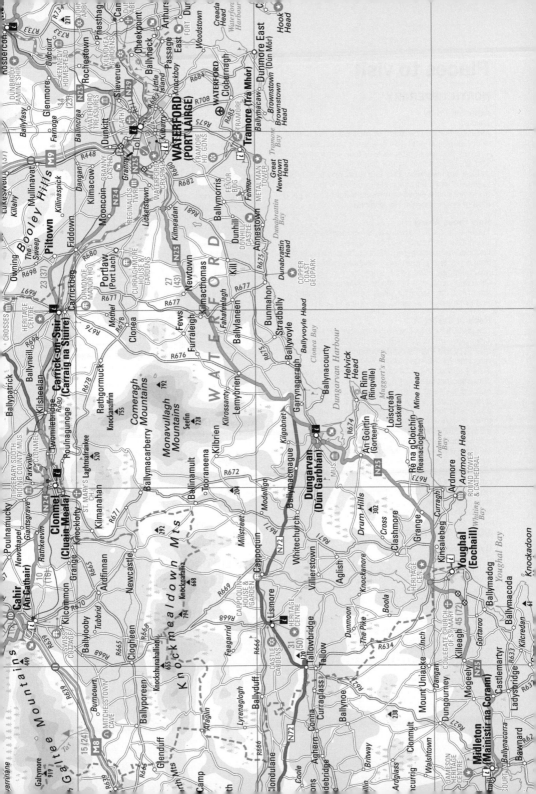

Places to visit

NORTH TIPPERARY

Athassel Priory
Golden.
Athassel Priory is believed to have been the largest priory in Ireland until 1447, when it burnt down. The remains are scattered over four acres of land and are approached over a grass-covered bridge and through a gatehouse. This is a quiet and beautiful spot, and while some ruins are no more than rubble, there are some significant remains that give a good idea of how extensive the site was.

Holy Cross Abbey
Thurles (0504 43118, www.holycrossabbey.ie). Open 9am-8pm daily. Admission free.
Founded as a monastery in the 12th century, and long a place of pilgrimage, the abbey gained many new buildings after 1414, when the 4th Earl of Ormonde became a benefactor. Now owned by the state, the Holy Cross has been fully restored, and once again functions as a place of worship.

Rock of Cashel ★
Cashel (062 61437, www.heritageireland.ie). Open June-mid Sept 9am-7pm daily. Mid Mar-May, mid Sept-mid Oct 9am-5.30pm daily. Mid Oct-mid Mar 9am-4.40pm daily. Admission €6; €2-€4 reductions; €14 family. No credit cards.
This spectacular set of buildings high on a limestone outcrop is one of Ireland's most visited attractions – a large car park at the foot of the hill caters for the endless stream of visitors during the summer; from there it's a five-minute walk uphill to the site. Originally a castle, the Rock of Cashel was gifted to the church and became a powerful religious centre until the 17th century. The site was added to over the years, but includes a 12th-century round tower, the High Cross and Romanesque chapel, a 13th-century Gothic cathedral, a 15th-century castle and the restored Hall of the Vicars Choral. There's an audio-visual tour, or an informative guided tour, which runs hourly and lasts about 45 minutes.

SOUTH TIPPERARY

Cahir Castle ★
Castle Street, Cahir (052 744 1011, www.heritage ireland.ie). Open Mid June-Aug 9am-6.30pm daily. Mid Mar-mid June, Sept-mid Oct 9.30am-5.30pm daily. Mid Oct-mid Mar 9.30am-4.30pm daily. Admission €3; €1-€2 reductions; €8 family. No credit cards.
Cahir Castle was built on an island in the middle of the River Suir in 1142 by Conor O'Brien and later granted to James Butler, 1st Earl of Ormond, in 1375. Despite being sacked on numerous occasions, it stayed in the possession of the Butler family until the 1960s, when the state took over and began major restoration work. Cahir is one of Ireland's largest and best preserved castles; the keep, tower, wall and battlements all remain, and the portcullis is in working order. There are guided tours, plus an audio-visual display of the history of the town and castle, and a scale model of what the castle looked like in medieval times.

Mitchelstown Caves
Burncourt (052 746 7246, www.mitchelstown cave.com). Open Apr-Sept 10am-5.30pm daily. Oct-Mar 10am-4pm daily. Admission €7; €2 reductions. No credit cards.
The Mitchelstown Caves are a network of caverns and chambers, linked by long passageways for some 3km underground. They were discovered by accident in 1833 by a labourer. Since then, the caves have been open to visitors, though paths and lights were only installed in the 1970s. The 30-minute guided tour visits three caverns where there are exceptional calcite formations, one of which is named the Tower of Babel.

Ormond Castle
Castle Park, Carrick-on-Suir (051 640787, www.heritageireland.ie). Open Late Apr-early Oct 10am-6pm daily. Admission free.
Carefully integrating two 15th-century towers, this Elizabethan manor was constructed in the 1560s by Thomas Butler, the 10th Earl of Ormonde. He is said to have built it in anticipation of a visit from his cousin Elizabeth I; within the house are stucco representations of the Queen, flanked by Equity and Justice. The detailed stucco ceiling and ornately carved fireplaces in the Long Gallery have been carefully restored. It is the finest example of a Tudor manor house in Ireland and is the only unfortified dwelling in Ireland to have survived that period. There are guided tours of the house, and visitors can roam the surrounding gardens.

Swiss Cottage
Kilcommon (052 744 1144, www.heritage ireland.ie). Open Apr-late Oct 10am-6pm daily. Admission €3; €1-€2 reductions; €8 family. No credit cards.
The Swiss Cottage can be reached by car along the R670 Ardfinnan Road; on foot, it's 2km alongside the river from Cahir town. The picturesque thatched cottage was designed in 1810 by John Nash, Regency architect, for Richard Butler, 1st Earl of Glengall. The cottage has been fully restored: inside, the guided tour reveals hand-painted wallpaper, antique furniture and a spiral staircase to the master bedroom.

WATERFORD CITY & AROUND

Reginald's Tower
The Mall, Waterford (051 304220, www.heritage ireland.ie). Open June-mid Sept 10am-6pm daily. Easter-May 10am-5pm daily. Mid Sept-Easter 10am-5pm Wed-Sun. Admission €3; €1-€2 reductions; €8 family. No credit cards.
The Vikings built a fort on this site in 914, and when the Anglo-Normans attacked Waterford in 1170, the capture of the tower heralded the fall of the city. Ragnall MacGillemaire, who was the Irish-Viking ruler of the city, was imprisoned by the Anglo-Normans in the tower and it is from him that the tower takes its name. The tower has a colourful and varied history, functioning as a royal castle, a jail, a store for ammunition, and, today, as a museum. There are a number of exhibits in the tower, including some Viking artefacts.

Waterford Crystal Visitor Centre

The Mall, Waterford (051 317000, www.waterford visitorcentre.com). Open Apr-Oct 9am-4.15pm Mon-Sat; 10am-4.15pm Sun. Jan-Mar 9am-3.15pm Mon-Sat; 10am-3.15pm Sun. Nov, Dec 10am-3.15pm Mon-Fri. Admission €11.50; €4-€8.50 reductions; €29.50 family.

The first glass factory in Waterford was established in 1783, when brothers George and William Penrose set up shop. Their business flourished until heavy taxation forced the company to close in 1851. In 1947, the Waterford Crystal factory opened and, despite considerable competition, the glass continues to be recognised and sold throughout the world. The centre has recently moved to new premises on the Mall: visitors can tour the workshops and see the entire process, from the making of the moulds to glassblowing, cutting and engraving. A shop sells the finished crystal and glass items.

WEST & NORTH WATERFORD

Dungarvan Castle

Castle Street, Dungarvan (058 48144, www.heritage ireland.ie). Open Late May-late Sept 10am-6pm daily. Admission free.

Hidden behind the well-preserved curtain wall is a gate tower, corner tower and a shell keep. Strategically built in 1185 by the Anglo-Normans, the castle sits on the mouth of the River Colligan, providing shelter and access inland for trading. The 18th-century military barracks in the castle courtyard have been restored and now house an exhibition about the castle's past.

Lismore Castle ★

Lismore (058 54061, www.lismorecastlearts.ie). Open Gardens & Gallery Mid Mar-mid Sept 11am-4.45pm daily. Admission Gardens & Gallery €8; €4-€6 reductions; €20 family.

Lismore Castle sits beside the River Blackwater, amid trees and parkland. The original castle was built in 1185 by King John, who then passed it to the church, and it remained a bishop's residence until 1589. Later the property of the Dukes of Devonshire, it was much altered and added to in the mid 19th century; it remains their private residence. Much of the castle is private, but visitors can stroll in the beautiful gardens or visit Lismore Castle Arts (www.lismorecastlearts.ie), a contemporary art gallery in the converted west wing. Sculptures are dotted around the seven acres of land surrounding the castle, and the yew-tree walk is said to be where Edmund Spenser wrote *The Faerie Queen.*

Rock of Cashel

Tower (see p170) is one of six remaining towers interspersed along the city wall (there were 17) and is also the largest remaining structure of the medieval walled city.

Just along the Mall is City Hall, another of John Roberts's designs, and behind it a further example of his work: Christchurch Cathedral (051 858958, www.christchurchwaterford.com, closed Sun and Nov-May). The cathedral, built on the site of a tenth-century church, was finally completed in 1773. It is Ireland's only neo-classical Georgian cathedral and hosts many concerts and other cultural events.

A recent initiative by Waterford Tourism is a Viking Triangle on the Mall, using artefacts from the now-closed Waterford Treasure Museum. The 'triangle' comprises Reginald's Tower and the recently renovated Bishop's Palace (a museum covering Waterford's history from the 1700s to the 20th century), plus the Medieval Museum (due to be completed in June 2012). The Mall is also home to the well-known Waterford Crystal Visitor Centre (see p171).

Waterford has quite a few cultural hubs: the Garter Lane Arts Centre (O'Connell Street, 051 855038, www.garterlane.ie, closed Mon, Sun), shows art exhibitions, films and music, dance and theatre performances. The Greyfriars Gallery (Greyfriars Street, 051 849856, closed Mon, Sun), set in a beautiful 19th-century Gothic church, contains the municipal art collection featuring works by Jack B Yeats, Charles Lamb and Louis Le Brocquy, among others. Temporary exhibitions are held throughout the year. The Waterford Film Festival (www.waterfordfilmfestival.com) is held here, as are a number of smaller festivals.

The Theatre Royal (The Mall, 051 874402, www.theatreroyal.ie, closed Sun) is an impressive space hosting some of the biggest music and drama events in the area, including performances during the Waterford International Music Festival (www.waterfordintlmusicfestival.com). Held each autumn, this is Waterford's biggest festival and the town resounds with everything from gospel and opera to contemporary music. Other popular festivals include the Spraoi Festival (www.spraoi. com), a street festival held over the August bank holiday weekend; and the Imagine Arts Festival (www.imagineartsfestival.com), which features up to 80 events over ten days.

The coastal towns

Waterford's coastal towns provide scenic locations from which to explore the county. Passage East lies 12 kilometres east of the city; from here you can take the car ferry to Ballyhack on the Hook peninsula in Wexford. Dunmore East, 18 kilometres south of Waterford, is a quaint fishing village, much loved for its neat thatched cottages, pretty harbour and sandy coves. There are a handful of lively pubs and restaurants, plus plenty of activities (water sports, golfing). The village is split in two: the west side centred around the harbour; the east side where the Strand Inn overlooks a sandy cove. Along Dock Road, which links the two sides of the village, are a number of secluded beaches. Although the village is busy all summer, the liveliest weekend is in August, when the Dunmore East Bluegrass Festival (www.waterford-dunmore. com) attracts bluegrass lovers for a weekend of music, dance and fun.

Tramore, 16 kilometres west of Dunmore East, is full of takeaways, arcades and housing developments; it's not a patch on Dunmore East. What it does have is good waves, and there's a large range of surf shops where you can hire equipment and arrange lessons. Try Oceanics (051 390944, www.oceanics.ie, open daily Mar-Dec; by appointment Jan, Feb).

Where to eat & drink

There is plenty of choice in Waterford. The Granary Café (Merchants Quay, 051 860977) is in a handsome old building and serves savoury tarts, salads and comforting hot dishes such as chicken pie. Harlequin Café & Winebar (Stephen Street, 051 877552, www.harlequin-cafe.com, closed Sun) is open throughout the day, serving excellent coffee and Italian dishes at reasonable prices. Berfranks (Coal Quay, 051 306032, closed Sun) is a little deli and café serving delicious cakes and good coffee. A favourite with the locals, Bodega (John's Street, 051 844177, www. bodegawaterford.com, closed Sun) is a friendly restaurant with an eclectic menu. La Boheme (George's Street, 051 875645, www.laboheme restaurant.ie, closed Mon, Sun), located in the basement of the Chamber of Commerce, serves classic French dishes in an elegant dining room. Also on George's Street is Doolan's Pub (051 841504, www.tandhdoolans.com), which has a great atmosphere in the evening, and also serves food in the day. The excellent farmers' market (10am-4pm Sat) on Jenkins Lane sells a huge array of foodstuffs.

Around ten kilometres east of Wexford in Cheekpoint is the 300-year-old Suir Inn (051 382220, www.mcalpins.com, closed winter Mon-Wed, Sun), a popular spot for a drink or pub food in traditional surroundings. The Spinnaker (051 383133, www.thespinnakerbar.com) and the Strand Inn (051 383174, www.thestrandinn.com) in Dunmore East are side by side; both deserve a visit for their food and drink. The Lemon Tree (Convent Road, 051 383164, www.lemontree catering.ie, closed Mon) on the edge of Dunmore East serves tasty lunch dishes and morning baked goods (and also has a new branch in the Theatre Royal in Waterford).

L'Atmosphere

Henrietta Street, Waterford (051 858426, www.restaurant-latmosphere.com). Lunch served 12.30-2.30pm Mon-Fri. Dinner served 5.30pm-midnight daily.
L'Atmosphere is the perfect name for this casual French bistro, with its bare brick walls, blackboards scrawled with daily specials and smiling staff. The menu is classic stuff – foie gras to start, followed by cassoulet or beef bourguignon. Finish with a cheese platter or chocolate profiteroles.

Tannery. See p178.

Downes Bar
Thomas Street, Waterford (051 874118). Open 5-11.30pm Mon-Thur; 5pm-12.30am Fri, Sat; 6-11pm Sun.
You can't go to Waterford and not visit Downes Bar – it's the city's most characterful establishment. Open since 1759, it has remained in the hands of the same family for six generations. This is traditional at its best, with various nooks and crannies and unexpected features (such as a squash court), as well as friendly staff. As a memento, Downes sells its own bottled whiskey.

La Palma on the Mall ★
The Mall, Waterford (051 879823, www.lapalma.ie). Dinner served 5.30-9.30pm Mon-Sat.
A Georgian building, with a modern interior, housing a chic cocktail lounge and an equally smart Italian restaurant. The menu lists the likes of pan-fried duck breast with mostarda fruits, sautéed pear and pomegranate sauce. For more casual dining, try sister restaurant Espresso (Parnell Street, 051 874141, www.espresso.ie), which serves great pizzas.

Where to stay
The choices in Waterford include the slightly corporate-looking, 135-room Tower Hotel (The Mall, 051 862300, www.towerhotelwaterford. com) overlooking the marina, or the more old-fashioned 100-room Granville Hotel (051 305555, www.granville-hotel.ie) on the Quay. Athenaeum House Hotel (051 833999, www.athenaeumhousehotel.com, closed Jan) is just outside Waterford but is more individual, while, nine kilometres east of the city, Faithlegg House (051 382000, www.faithlegg.com, closed Jan; Feb, Mar Mon-Thur, Sun) is set on the Suir. The Georgian building has a spa and a championship golf course.

Dunmore East has plenty of B&Bs and self-catering accommodation (details on www.discover dunmore.com) and two hotels: the family-run Haven Hotel (Dock Road, 051 383150, www.the havenhotel.com, closed Mar-Oct) and the small Ocean Hotel (www.theoceanhotel.com). Designed by John Roberts as a hunting lodge, the charming Gaultier Lodge (051 382549, www.gaultier-lodge. com) now operates as a guesthouse. It's six kilometres outside Dunmore East, in a great location beside a beach.

Foxmount Country House
Passage East Road, nr Waterford (051 874308, www.foxmountcountryhouse.com). Rates €110 double incl breakfast. Closed Nov-Feb.
Only a ten-minute drive from Waterford is the delightful Foxmount Country House, run as a guesthouse by the Kent family for more than 40 years. The four bedrooms are prettily decorated, and have views over the surrounding gardens and countryside. The drawing room has a roaring fire and is the perfect place to enjoy an afternoon tea of warm scones and cake.

Sion Hill House
Sion Hill, Ferrybank, Waterford (051 851558). Rates €70-€96 double incl breakfast.

Dunmore East. See p172.

This Georgian edifice sits on a hillside overlooking Waterford, surrounded by flower-filled gardens. The house has classic old-world charm, with plenty of antique furniture. The four handsome rooms have wonderful views; guests can take tea in the welcoming lounge. A great base just a couple of minutes' drive from the city.

Waterford Castle
The Island, Waterford (051 878203, www.waterford castle.com). Rates Hotel €140-€340 double incl breakfast. Castle lodges €400-€750 per week.
A 15th-century castle on its own island, surrounded by 300 acres of woodland and accessed by private ferry – all just one minute down river from Waterford. Guests may choose from 19 traditional rooms in the castle or 48 modern self-catering cottages (with three or four bedrooms) nearby. A pianist accompanies dinner in the oak-panelled Munster Room restaurant. Further attractions are an 18-hole golf course, tennis, boules and various nature trails.

WEST & NORTH WATERFORD

Dungarvan & around
The Copper Coast – so called because it was heavily mined for copper in the 19th century – runs along the R675 from Tramore to Dungarvan and is a designated UNESCO Geopark; for more, see www.copper-coast.com. The spectacular cliffs along this stretch are of geological interest, and information panels are dotted about on beaches, caves and cliff edges. The Geopark Information Centre in Bunmahon (Monksland Centre, 051 292828, www.europeangeoparks.org, closed Sat, Sun) provides maps and information on the archaeology, geology and history of the area. Even if you have no interest in the creation of the Copper Coast, it makes for an incredibly scenic drive. The best of several standout beaches are Stradbally Cove in the quaint village of Stradbally, and the popular Blue Flag beach Clonea Strand.

The route brings you to the flourishing coastal town of Dungarvan, a good base for those visiting the south coast. Sitting on either side of the River Colligan, which enters the sea here, Dungarvan has a large bay, best seen from the road heading west out of town. The town centre is compact, with much of the activity revolving around the main square. A burgeoning food scene has resulted in some excellent cafés and restaurants, and a cookery school, as well as fine food festivals, such as the Waterford Festival of Food (www.waterfordfestivaloffood.com) in April. The farmers' market, held in the Eurospar car park (11am-3pm Fri), has goods from some of the county's best food producers, including livestock.

While most tourists come to see the darkened ruins of Dungarvan Castle (*see p171*), perched on the bay, whale watching (*see p162*) is a further attraction. Migrating whales can be seen off the coast from June to February, though December to February are the best months for sightings. Visitors also flock to the town during May's Feile Na Deise Festival (www.feilenandeise.com), a traditional Irish music and culture festival held over a weekend.

Cliff House Hotel. See p178.

Golfers are well served by three golf courses: Dungarvan Golf Club (Knocknagranagh, 058 41605, www.dungarvangolfclub.com); West Waterford Golf & Country Club (058 43216, www.westwaterford golf.com); and Gold Coast Golf Club (058 44055, www.goldcoastgolfclub.com).

In town, the Waterford County Museum (St Augustine Street, 058 45960, www.waterford countymuseum.org, closed summer Sun; winter Sat, Sun) deals with the maritime and local history of County Waterford, while art exhibitions are held in the Old Market House Arts Centre (Lower Main Street, 058 48944, closed Mon, Sun), a handsome black and white building dating from the 17th century.

An Rinn (Ring in English), is a Gaeltacht area six kilometres south of Dungarvan on Helvick Head. It's ruggedly picturesque country, with a number of scattered villages, and the community is steeped in a rich music and dance culture. Walk out on An Coinnigéar, a sand spit protruding from the mainland towards Dungarvan, for panoramic views across the bay. In nearby Mweelahorna, the Joan Clancy Gallery (058 46205, www.joanclancy gallery.com, open daily during exhibitions) shows work by established and emerging Irish artists.

Further along the coast, and tucked in between two grassy headlands, is the village of Ardmore. The long stretch of sand here is well sheltered, making it popular with families. There's also a stunning walk around the headland (see p162), and plenty more energetic activities; Ardmore Adventures (Main Street, mobile 083 374 3889, www.ardmoreadventures.ie) organises sea kayaking, surf lessons, rock climbing and powerboating trips.

Ardmore is also the site of an early Christian settlement – possibly the earliest in Ireland: St Declan reputedly set up a monastery here 30 years before St Patrick came to the country. The ecclesiastical remains are located on a hilltop overlooking the town; here, St Declan's Cathedral and a 30-foot-high Round Tower stand within the graveyard where St Declan is said to be buried. Just outside the village, as the hill rises towards the western headland, the ruins of St Declan's church and well can be explored too.

North Waterford

Hill walkers and nature lovers come to North Waterford for the walking trails in the Comeragh and Knockmealdown Mountains. The Comeragh Scenic Drive takes you from the sleepy village of Ballymacarbry through the lush Nire Valley, where there are more good walks (see p162).

West from here off the N73, at the foot of the Knockmealdown Mountains, is the pretty riverside town of Lismore in the Blackwater Valley ★. The town itself is of some interest, and the Lismore Heritage Centre & Tourism Office (Main Street, 058 54975, www.discoverlismore.com, closed Nov-Apr Sat, Sun) is the best place to start an exploration. A series of displays depict the town's history, from the monastic settlement of St Carthage in 636 (the cathedral is dedicated to

him) and the Anglo-Norman arrival in 1172, through to the 19th century. The centre runs informative historical walking tours every day. Enquiries about river fishing should also be made here.

Lismore is a lovely place to pass a day, with plenty of good places to eat, plus Lismore Castle (see p171) to wander round. For those wanting to see the Blackwater Valley from the river itself, Blackwater Touring (mobile 087 683 2872, www.blackwaterboating.ie) in nearby Cappoquin organises canoeing and kayaking trips, with the option of overnight camping on the riverbank.

Where to eat & drink

Along the Copper Coast, Harney's Bar (051 396180) in Dunhill and Mother McHugh's (051 390303) in Fenor are traditional Irish bars, serving decent pub food. While Annestown is the only village in Ireland without a pub, Dungarvan has no such shortage. Cheery Ormond Café (Grattan Square, 058 41153, closed Sun) is popular with locals for a casual bite, while the buzzing Nude Food Café (O'Connell Street, 058 24594, www.nudefood.ie, closed Sun) has an extensive menu running from meze plates to meatballs in a spicy tomato sauce. The recently revamped Quealy's Café Bar (O'Connell Street, 058 24555, closed Tue) is a trendy and popular bar that also serves food, while Dungarvan's oldest bar, the Lady Belle (Grattan Square, 058 44222) is the perfect place for a few quiet pints. The Anchor Bar (Davitts Quay, 058 41249), overlooking the harbour, does good pub grub and is popular with the weekend crowd, as is Merry's (058 24488, www.merrys.ie) on Main Street, known for a high standard of food, and music on weekends.

In Ring, the best bar for traditional music is Mooney's (058 46204), located on the R674, or there's the Marine Bar (058 46520, www. marinebar.com) in Pulla, which holds traditional music sessions and ceilidh nights. Main Street in Ardmore has the Old Forge (024 94750) for reliable meals, or An Tobar (024 94166) for casual drinks and pub food.

The Glencairn Inn & Pastis Bistro (058 56232, www.glencairninn.com), near Lismore in Glencairn, is a cosy lodge serving French bistro food such as coq au vin and baked mussels in garlic butter. It also has four charming en-suite rooms available for B&B. South of Lismore in Tallow, located on the river, is the Brideview Bar & Restaurant (Tallow Bridge, 058 56522, www.brideviewbar.com, closed Mon), a fine place to stop for a drink or some seafood.

O'Brien Chop House ★

Main Street, Lismore (058 53810, www.obrien chophouse.ie). Lunch served 12.30-3pm Wed-Sat; noon-4pm Sun. Dinner served 6.30-8.30pm Wed, Thur; 6.30-9.30pm Fri, Sat.
The charming Victorian frontage at O'Brien's is typical of this simple yet beautiful restaurant, and inside there are quirky touches such as mix-and-match cups and saucers. Local really does mean local here: their own walled garden

supplies vegetables, fruit and herbs, while honey comes from a nearby beekeeper, and meat from McGrath's down the road. The bar menu features antipasti and charcuterie platters, while more substantial meals are preceded by freshly baked bread. Robust Irish dishes might include fish or game pie, or roast breast of woodpigeon on fried bread with blaeberry sauce, or McGrath's hanger steak, baked bone marrow, chips, and béarnaise sauce. Top quality food, cooked with care, in unpretentious surroundings. The restaurant is sometimes open on Mondays and Tuesdays in summer; call ahead to check.

Tannery ★
10 Quay Street, Dungarvan (058 45420, www.tannery.ie). Lunch served 12.30-2.30pm Fri; 12.30-2.45pm Sun. Dinner served 6-9.30pm Tue-Sat.
As the name suggests, this restaurant is housed in an old tannery, but behind the brick façade, some original tanning vats are the only evidence of the building's former life. The bright contemporary restaurant sports fashionable wallpaper and fresh flowers, and chef-proprietor Paul Flynn is passionate about locally sourced produce in his take on modern Irish cuisine. Service is efficient and jovial, bringing starters such as crab crème brûlée with pickled cucumber and melba toast or crispy onion rolls with Ardsallagh goat's cheese mousse and sweet potato fondant. Pleasing mains include seafood stew with saffron and rosemary broth and garlic bread, or slow-cooked pork platter with maple baked beans and crushed root vegetables. Down the road from the restaurant is a cookery school, which runs day and weekend courses. There are also two townhouses just around the corner, with stylish rooms available for B&B.

White Horses
Main Street, Ardmore (024 94040). Open May-Sept 11am-11pm Tue-Sun. Oct-Dec 6-11pm Fri-Sun. Food served May-Sept 11am-10.30pm Tue-Sun. Oct-Dec 6-10.30pm Fri-Sun.
This welcoming restaurant is a favourite with holidaymakers, for coffee and baked goods, a light lunch of open sandwiches or seafood chowder, or a hearty dinner. Seafood features strongly on the menu, served simply with a variety of sauces, though there are meat and vegetarian dishes too. Note that during the summer months it can be difficult to get a table, so it's wise to book for lunch or dinner.

Where to stay
Dungarvan and the surrounding area has plenty of cheap and cheerful B&Bs that can be booked through the Dungarvan tourist office (Court House, 058 41741, www.dungarvantourism.com, closed summer Sun; winter Sat, Sun). At the riverside Park Hotel (058 42899, www.flynnhotels.com), leisure facilities include a swimming pool, while Lawlors Hotel (Bridge Street, 058 41122, www.lawlors hotel.com) has smart comfortable rooms. A ten-minute walk outside town is Cairbre House (058 42338, www.cairbrehouse.com, closed mid Dec-mid Jan), set within several acres on the banks of the River Colligan, and with four traditionally designed rooms. Powersfield House (058 45594, www.powersfield.com) is a lovely guesthouse outside Dungarvan with four equally trad rooms.

Casey's Caravan & Camping Park (058 41919, closed mid Sept-mid Apr) at Clonea beach has very good facilities on a glorious beach. For those wanting to stay in the Irish-speaking area, Gortnadiha Lodge (058 46142, www.gortnadiha lodge.com) is the best option, with views over Dungarvan Bay.

A fine base for walking in the mountains, Glasha (052 613 6108, www.glashafarmhouse. com) is a lovely farmhouse in Ballymacarbry with six upmarket rooms, four of them with Jacuzzis.

Cliff House Hotel ★
Ardmore (024 87800, www.thecliffhousehotel.com). Rates €225-€470 double incl breakfast.
Built into the cliffs overlooking Ardmore Bay, the Cliff House Hotel has one of the most beautiful locations in the south-east. Tastefully designed to blend in with the dark cliffs, it has grass roofs, stacked dark slate walls, polished wooden floors and light streaming in through the floor-to-ceiling windows. The 39 bedrooms vary in size and design, but all have a natural, sometimes nautical feel. All rooms maximise the view across the bay to the grassy headland, and some even have showers with a vista. A bar area serves food and drink; a large deck caters for sunny days, and the spa features an outdoor jacuzzi, as well as a pool, sauna and steam room with panoramic views over the sea. The intimate restaurant, run by Dutch chef Martijn Kajuiter, has a Michelin star for dishes such as roast fillet of Helvick turbot with Dingle Bay crab ravioli, trumpet mushrooms, leeks, rosemary oil and white wine sauce. The Cliff House is also good at the little touches – wellington boots are lined up at the door, ready for walkers, and there's an area stacked with books waiting to be read.

Hanora's Cottage
Ballymacarbry (052 613 6134, www.hanoras cottage.com). Rates €160-€200 double incl breakfast & dinner.
Hanora's is a homely place, known for its hospitality and peace and quiet, where guests can head out into the mountains, explore the Nire Valley or simply sit back and relax. The ten bedrooms are traditionally decorated but each comes with a jacuzzi bath (there's also a hot tub in the conservatory overlooking the gardens). The food served in the restaurant draws non-residents too: expect dishes such as oven-baked Dunmore East mussels with garlic and lemon crust, served with garlic mayonnaise, followed by pork fillet with Clonakilty black pudding and stewed apple sauce; there's also a separate vegetarian menu.

Richmond House
Cappoquin (058 54278, www.richmondhouse.net). Rates €100-€120 double incl breakfast.
The Deevy's 18th-century country house is both elegant and relaxing, with a spacious drawing room where guests unwind in front of the fire. The nine bedrooms are individually designed, but all have antique furniture and fine views over the surrounding parkland. The restaurant is open to non-residents, and dinner is a lively affair, where roulade of locally smoked salmon served on pickled cucumber with a coriander dressing might be followed by roast fillet of West Waterford lamb with tapenade, sun-dried tomatoes and rosemary jus. Options on the vegetarian menu include twice-baked emmental soufflé.

Counties Kilkenny & Wexford

South-east Ireland's strategic position and close proximity to England meant it was the main landing point for the Vikings and, later, the Anglo-Normans. The remains of castles and other ancient buildings scattered across the countryside are a reminder of how important the counties of Kilkenny and Wexford were at the time. Jerpoint Abbey and Kells Priory in Kilkenny are two splendid examples, both picturesquely sited by flowing rivers. Kilkenny Castle is located in Kilkenny, Ireland's most attractive inland city, while the bustling port town of Wexford has the remnants of the city wall and Selskar Abbey as mementoes. Today, Wexford is more famous for its annual International Opera Festival.

The land in the south-east is low-lying and largely farmed, while the coastal areas of Wexford have long, secluded stretches of beach, pretty fishing villages such as Rosslare, Kilmore Quay and Duncannon, and the stunningly rugged Hook peninsula.

COUNTY KILKENNY

The main attractions of the county are located in and around the medieval city of Kilkenny. This is one of Ireland's most appealing inland cities, and has a vibrant nightlife. The surrounding countryside is gently undulating, dotted with ancient sites and crossed by the gushing waters of the Nore and Barrow rivers, on which sit the attractive towns of Inistioge and Thomastown.

Kilkenny city

No matter which direction you approach Kilkenny from, you're rewarded with a view of Kilkenny Castle (see p184), perched prominently above the River Nore. The entrance to the castle is on the Parade, and this makes a good point from which to start a tour of the compact city centre.

Kilkenny is well known for its high standard of craftsmanship; the Kilkenny Design Centre (Castle Yard, 056 772 2188, www.kilkennydesign.com), a shop selling Irish-designed pottery, clothing and jewellery, is housed within the converted 18th-century stables across from the castle. Adjacent is the National Craft Gallery (Castle Yard, 056 779 6147, www.ccoi.ie, closed Jan-Mar Sun; Mar-Dec Mon), which holds exhibitions of furniture, ceramics, stonework and jewellery by local and national craftspeople. There are several craft workshops tucked in behind, all of which are part of Trail Kilkenny (www.madeinkilkenny.ie), which links craft centres across the county. Leaflets on this and many other attractions are available at the Kilkenny Tourist Centre (056 775 1500, closed Sun) on Rose Inn Street, just off the Parade.

To the west of the castle, the warren of tightly packed streets is a reminder of medieval town planning. The High Street forms the main strip, and is occupied by a mix of old and new façades fronting both small, family-run businesses and major high-street stores. There are also a number of cafés here and on St Kieran's Street, a narrow lane running north of the High Street.

Both streets merge into Parliament Street, site of the beautifully restored 17th-century merchant townhouse, Rothe House (056 772 2893, www.rothehouse.com, closed Nov-Mar Sun). Across from here is St Francis Abbey Brewery (see p184).

Continuing west down Parliament Street, turn right on to Abbey Street for Black Abbey. Founded in 1225, the name comes from the black habits worn by the Dominican monks. The abbey became a courthouse in 1543 and wasn't restored as a place of worship until the 19th century. Parliament Street then turns into Irishtown, which is overlooked by St Canice's Cathedral (see p184).

Kilkenny gets very lively in summer, when assorted festivals draw in the crowds. In early May, Smithwick's Kilkenny Rhythm & Roots Festival (www.rootsmusic.info) fills pubs and music venues with a classy line-up of Americana, folk and roots musicians, while June brings the Cat Laughs Comedy Festival (www.thecatlaughs.com). The Kilkenny Arts Festival (www.kilkennyarts.ie) sees ten days of music, theatre, dance, film and literary events in August.

A once-a-week treat is the Kilkenny Farmers' Market every Thursday morning in the Market Yard (close to Parliament Street). More than 20 stalls brim with fruit, vegetables and foodstuffs grown or made by locals.

Around Kilkenny city

North of the city are a couple of places to visit: about ten kilometres away is Dunmore Cave

(Castlecomer Road, 056 776 7726, www.heritage ireland.ie, closed Nov-Mar Mon, Tue), where a series of caverns are packed full of stalagmites and stalactites. An exhibition in the visitor centre also tells of a brutal Viking massacre at the caves. Just north of here is Castlecomer Discovery Park (see p184), a popular weekend spot for locals.

South of Kilkenny, the Barrow and Nore rivers meander through the countryside. Stop off in Bennettsbridge to visit the Nicholas Mosse Pottery (056 772 7505, www.nicholasmosse.com). A shop beside the studio sells beautifully crafted homewares and textiles as well as pottery, and the café has a tasty selection of cakes, desserts and snacks. Further south on the R700 is Thomastown, an attractive market town on the banks of the River Nore. In recent years, the town has seen the opening of several galleries and gift shops, such as Gorgeous (056 775 4700, closed Mon-Wed, Sun) on Pipe Street, which sells imaginative gifts, as well as designer wallpapers and fabrics. Contemporary ceramics are made and sold at Karen Morgan Porcelain (Market Street, mobile 086 166 3691, www.karenmorganceramics.com, closed Sun), as they are at Brid Lyons Studio & Gallery (056 772 4977, closed Mon, Sun) on Low Street. Thomastown makes for a nice lunch break on the way to one of the county's major attractions, Jerpoint Abbey (see p184), which lies a couple of kilometres from the town.

The R700 south-east out of Thomastown runs along the River Nore and is breathtakingly scenic; after eight kilometres you reach Inistioge, Kilkenny's prettiest town. It was the film location for the movie *Circle of Friends*, yet the stunning riverside setting, quaint village square and colourful buildings serve as an attraction in their own right. Lovely Woodstock Gardens (see p184) is worth a visit too.

A 15-minute drive due south of Kilkenny is Kells, a pleasant market town beside King's River and the home of one of Ireland's largest and most remarkable monastic sites, Kells Priory (see p184).

Where to eat & drink

Kilkenny city is full of decent bars, cafés and restaurants. For a riverside picnic, pick up soups, meats and cheeses from Blueberry Larder (056 776 1456, www.blueberrykilkenny.com, closed Mon, Sun) on Market Yard. Café Sol (William Street, 056 776 4987, www.restaurants kilkenny.com) serves a Mediterranean-style menu – as does Sol Bistro (056 775 4945), its sister establishment in Thomastown. The Kilkenny Design Centre (Castle Road, 056 772 2118, www.kilkennydesign.com) has a popular café serving wholesome tarts, casseroles, sandwiches and soups. For a treat, visit Campagne (The Arches, 5 Gashouse Lane, 056 777 2858, www.campagne.ie, closed Mon): this buzzing, contemporary restaurant uses local produce in a French-inspired menu. Zuni hotel (see p187) also has a modern Irish restaurant.

You can't walk far in Kilkenny without coming across a good pub. Characterful Tynan's Bridge House (056 772 1291) on John's Bridge is the city's oldest pub, while the Left Bank (The Parade, 056 775 0016, www.leftbank.ie) is more modern. The Marble City Bar is one of several top-notch bars in Langton House Hotel (see p187).

In Inistioge, the Circle of Friends café (closed Mon) serves soups, sandwiches and pizza, or there's the Woodstock Arms (056 775 8440, www.woodstockarms.com) for a pint. In nearby Graiguenamanagh, Boats Bistro (059 972 5075, www.boatsbistro.com, open June-Sept Wed-Sun; Mar-May Sat, Sun) on the River Barrow buzzes with groups from river cruises. Dining is on two floors, and dishes include plenty of fish.

Bassett's

Inistioge (056 775 8820, www.bassetts.ie). Lunch served noon-4pm Wed-Sat; 1-5pm Sun. Dinner served 7.30-10pm Wed-Sat.
Perched on a hill overlooking the Nore valley, Bassett's provides one of the best views in the county. The bright, airy restaurant serves food throughout the day: soups, sandwiches, burgers, omelettes and so on at lunch, and a more formal menu at dinner, featuring local produce such as wild Nore salmon and Kilkenny beef. On Saturday nights, diners can try a succession of starter-sized dishes.

Blackberry Café ★

Market Street, Thomastown (mobile 086 775 5303, www.theblackberrycafe.ie). Open Summer 9.30am-5.30pm Mon-Fri; 10am-5.30pm Sat; 11am-5pm Sun. Winter 9.30am-5.30pm Mon-Fri; 10am-5.30pm Sun. No credit cards.
Originally a shoemaker's, the Blackberry has been lovingly and extensively restored. It retains its 18th-century frontage, with the characteristic large Georgian windows now painted a fresh tea green, and adorned with a magnificent sculptural blackberry. Cakes, tarts and scones (freshly baked daily) are on display inside; the menu also includes soups, sandwiches, quiches, local cheese and meat platters, and salads.

Things to do

COUNTY KILKENNY

Hole in the Wall
High Street, Kilkenny (mobile 087 807 5650, www.holeinthewall.ie). Open 8pm-midnight Mon, Wed-Sun. No credit cards.
A charming venue, the Hole in the Wall is a renovated 16th-century townhouse that hosts concerts, lectures and readings. Drinks are served in a tiny, atmospheric 18th-century tavern.

WEXFORD TOWN & AROUND

Slieveboy Loop Walk
Askamore (www.askamore.com).
This 12km circular walk starts in the small town of Askamore and follows a well-marked trail out of the town, through woodland and up Slieveboy mountain, offering glorious views north to the peaks of the Wicklow Mountains and east to the Irish Sea. The website also has details of two shorter loop walks in the vicinity.

Kilkenny Castle. See p184.

Places to visit

COUNTY KILKENNY

Castlecomer Discovery Park
The Estate Yard, Castlecomer (056 444 0707, www.discoverypark.ie). Open May-Aug 9.30am-5.30pm daily. Mar, Apr 9.30am-5pm daily. Sept-Feb 10am-5pm daily. Admission €7; €5-€6 reductions; €20 family.
Castlecomer Discovery Park has a range of outdoor activities for adults and children. There is a network of woodland trails, enlivened by wooden sculptures. Picnic tables are scattered around the park, so visitors can sit and enjoy lunch by the river. The two lakes are both stocked with rainbow trout, which can be fished for a reasonable fee. The park was once part of a big estate; the house is no more, but the farmyard and kitchen gardens have been turned into a visitor centre (where Castlecomer's coal mining history is explored). Old outbuildings have been converted into craft workshops – pottery, paintings and jewellery are for sale. The Jarrow Café serves breakfast and lunch.

Jerpoint Abbey
Thomastown (056 772 4623, www.heritageireland.ie). Open Mar-Sept 9am-5.30pm daily. Oct-Nov 9am-5pm daily. Dec-Feb 9am-4pm Mon-Fri. Admission €3; €1-€2 reductions; €8 family. No credit cards.
Located next to the R448, just outside Thomastown, this imposing Cistercian abbey was founded in the latter half of the 12th century. The ruins of the Romanesque church dating from that period are impressive enough, but the most beautiful remains are the 15th-century tower and the cloister with its unusual carvings. The visitor centre explains the history of the abbey.

Kells Priory ★
Kells. Admission free.
Visitors enter through a gatehouse into an expansive site where the ruins of a chapel, church and a number of domestic buildings illustrate the former purpose, importance and size of the priory. One of the largest medieval monuments in Ireland, Kells was founded in 1193 by Baron Geoffrey FitzRobert. The priory suffered a violent history – hence the fortified walls – and was eventually dissolved by Henry VIII in 1540. The wall encircling the three-acre site is interspersed by seven tower houses, giving it the local name 'seven castles'.

Kilkenny Castle ★
The Parade, Kilkenny (056 770 4100, www.kilkenny castle.ie). Open June-Aug 9am-5.30pm daily. Apr, May, Sept 9.30am-5.30pm daily. Mar 9.30am-5pm daily. Oct-Feb 9.30am-4pm daily. Admission €6; €2.50-€4 reductions; €14 family.
James Butler, 3rd Earl of Ormonde, purchased the 12th-century castle on the site above the River Nore in 1391, and it remained in the hands of the same family until 1935. Acquired by the Irish State in 1967 for a token payment of £50, the castle has now been restored to its former splendour, with the interior reflecting the decor of the 1830s. A guided tour includes the library, drawing room, a number of bedrooms and the impressive Long Gallery, which occupies an entire wing of the castle. The servants' quarters are now occupied by the Butler Gallery, which holds exhibitions of contemporary art.

St Canice's Cathedral & Round Tower
The Close, Coach Road, Kilkenny (056 776 4971, www.stcanicescathedral.com). Open June-Aug 9am-6pm Mon-Sat; 2-6pm Sun. Apr, May, Sept 10am-1pm, 2-5pm Mon-Sat; 2-5pm Sun. Oct-Mar 10am-1pm, 2-4pm Mon-Sat; 2-4pm Sun. Admission Cathedral €4; €3 reductions. Round Tower €3; €2.50 reductions. Cathedral & Round Tower €6; €5.50 reductions; €12 family.
There has been a church on this site since the sixth century, though the present cathedral dates from the 13th; it underwent major renovations in the 17th following extensive damage during Cromwell's invasion of Kilkenny. The 30m-high Round Tower – particular to Ireland and a common feature at religious sites – was built in the ninth century, and is the oldest standing structure in the city of Kilkenny. If you can cope with the numerous stairs and assorted ladders to reach the top, you'll be rewarded with glorious 360° views.

St Francis Abbey Brewery
Parliament Street, Kilkenny (056 779 6498, www.smithwicks.com). Open June-Aug 11am-4.15pm Tue-Sat. Sept-May 11.30am-3.30pm Tue-Sat. Tours 12.30pm, 1pm, 3pm, 3.30pm Tue-Sat. Admission €8. No credit cards.
During the 13th century, the Franciscans established an abbey with its own well on the banks of the River Nore in Kilkenny. The monks brewed a light ale for visitors, using water from the well – and thus started the strong brewing tradition that still exists in the city. The premises are now the home of Smithwicks Ale, established by John Smithwick in the early 18th century. A tour of the premises includes the brewery and the remains of the abbey.

Woodstock Gardens & Arboretum ★
Inistioge (056 779 4033, www.woodstock.ie). Open Apr-mid Oct 9am-7pm daily. Mid Oct-Mar 10am-4.30pm daily. Admission €4 per car. No credit cards.
Reached along a steep, winding road out of Inistioge village, these gardens surround the ruined shell of a Georgian house. While the house remains untouched, the county council has been restoring the land for the past few years. There are beautiful rose, terraced and walled gardens, a grotto, and avenues lined with trees. The arboretum has been stocked with trees from Asia and South America, and new species are constantly being added. There's also a charming tearoom, but opening times are limited, particularly outside the summer months, so call ahead to check.

WEXFORD TOWN & AROUND

Irish Agricultural Museum & Johnstown Castle Gardens
Murntown (053 914 2888, www.irishagrimuseum.ie). Open Museum & Grounds Apr-Oct 9am-5pm Mon-Fri; 11am-5pm Sat, Sun. Nov-Mar 9am-12.30pm, 1.30-5pm Mon-Fri. Walled Gardens May-Sept 9am-5pm Mon-Fri; 11am-5pm Sat, Sun. Admission Museum, Grounds & Walled Gardens €6; €4 reductions; €20 family. No credit cards.

Jerpoint Abbey

Johnstown Castle, a stunning 19th-century Gothic Revival mansion, lies 6km south-west of Wexford. While the house is, sadly, not open to the public, the 50 acres of formal gardens and woodland are, and you can sit by the lake or walk along forest trails. The Irish Agricultural Museum is located in the converted stables and explores Irish country life from the 18th century to the middle of the 20th. There is also a section on Johnstown Castle, and an attractive tearoom.

Irish National Heritage Park
Ferrycarrig (053 912 0733, www.inhp.com). Open May-Aug 9.30am-6.30pm daily. Sept-Apr 9.30am-5.30pm daily. Admission €8; €4-€6.50 reductions; €20 family.
An open-air museum set in 35 acres of beautiful woodland, covering Irish history from the Stone Age to the Normans. Among the impressive reconstructions are a ringfort, a Viking ship and monastic sites. The park itself supports a variety of wildlife, including otters and kingfishers. There is also a shop and a good self-service restaurant overlooking the lake.

National 1798 Rebellion Visitor Centre
Enniscorthy (053 923 7596, www.1798centre.ie). Open 9.30am-5pm Mon-Fri; noon-5pm Sat. Admission €6; €3.50 reductions; €16 family. No credit cards.
A series of audio-visual exhibitions depict the 1798 Rebellion, while also placing it in the context of European and global political events of the time, including the French Revolution and American Independence. Wexford experienced 11 of the 23 Rebellion battles, with a loss of 20,000 lives over a four-week period.

SOUTH & WEST WEXFORD

Duncannon Fort
Duncannon (051 389454, www.duncannonfort.com). Open June-Aug 10am-5.30pm daily. Sept-May 10am-4.30pm Mon-Fri. Guided tours 10.30am, 12.30pm, 2pm, 3pm, 4.30pm. Admission €5; €3 reductions; €12 family. No credit cards.
In anticipation of an attack by the Spanish Armada, this star-shaped fort was built on a promontory in Waterford Harbour. A 10m moat surrounds the fort and an open parade area is encircled by military

buildings. On the lower level, at the tip of the fort, is the 'croppy boy' cell, where the rebels of the 1798 Rebellion were held before their trial. There's also a Maritime Museum, and a coffee shop with views out to sea.

John F Kennedy Arboretum
12km south of New Ross (051 388171, www.heritageireland.ie). Open May-Aug 10am-8pm daily. Apr, Sept 10am-6.30pm daily. Oct-Mar 10am-5pm daily. Admission €3; €1-€2 reductions; €8 family. No credit cards.
Visitors could easily spend a day wandering these 600 acres on the southern slopes of Slievecoiltia. There are more than 4,500 types of trees and shrubs laid out here; the stunning Ericaceous Garden has 500 different rhododendrons, and many varieties of azaleas and heathers. The lake is a haven for waterfowl, and a popular picnic spot in summer. There's a road to the summit of Slievecoiltia, from where there are panoramic views across south Wexford. Start your trip at the visitor centre, where there are maps of the park and trails, plus a number of displays. The tearoom is open from May to September.

Kilmokea Gardens
Great Island (051 388109, www.kilmokea.com). Open Mar-Nov 10am-6pm daily. Admission €7; €4-€6 reductions.
Surrounding the pretty Georgian guesthouse (*see p195*) are seven acres of formal gardens and woodland, which are open to the public. Stroll through the large water garden, kitchen garden or rose garden, or follow the boardwalk around the duck pond. For anglers, there is a lake stocked with trout. There's also a craft shop and café adjacent to the house, where soups, sandwiches and snacks are served.

Saltee Islands ★
www.salteeislands.info.
The privately owned Saltee Islands, 5km off the coast of Kilmore Quay, comprise Great and Little Saltee, and together form one of Ireland's most famous bird sanctuaries. Spring and autumn see thousands of migrating birds, while puffins, gannets, gulls and razorbills inhabit the islands all year. There is also a breeding colony of grey seals on Great Saltee; pups can be seen during the summer. Visitors are allowed on Great Saltee between 11am and 4.30pm; boat trips can be arranged from Kilmore Quay.

Tintern Abbey ★
Saltmills (051 562650, www.heritageireland.ie). Open Mid May-Sept 10am-6pm daily. Admission €3; €1-€2 reductions; €8 family.
This secluded abbey, surrounded by acres of woodland, was founded by William Marshall, Earl of Pembroke, around 1200. The considerable remains include the nave, chancel, cloister and chapel. The abbey was dissolved in 1536 and granted by Henry VIII to one Anthony Colclough. It remained in the Colclough family until the 1960s and is now owned by the state. An exhibition depicts Tintern's history, and there is a small tearoom.

Mount Juliet

Chez Pierre

17 Parliament Street, Kilkenny (056 776 4655).
Lunch served 10am-4pm Mon-Sat. Dinner served
7-10.30pm Sat.
A cosy French restaurant with an uncomplicated bistro menu. Friendly staff bring starters such as goat's cheese tartlet and scallop salad, and mains of duck magret or fish of the day, both served with locally grown vegetables. Finish with a French cheese platter and a glass of port.

The Motte

Inistioge (056 775 8655). Dinner served 7-11pm
Thur-Sat.
On the outskirts of Inistioge, within an ivy-clad lodge, the Motte is an intimate restaurant, its walls adorned with art and the room warmed by an open fire. Owners Rodney and Deirdre Doyle maintain a relaxed atmosphere, in which diners enjoy the likes of warm salad of sautéed duck livers, followed by slow-braised beef in Guinness, or red chilli and lime herb-crusted cod.

Ristorante Rinuccini

1 The Parade, Kilkenny (056 776 1575, www.rinuccini.
com). Lunch served noon-3pm Mon-Fri; noon-3.30pm
Sat, Sun. Dinner served 5-10pm Mon-Sat; 5-9.30pm
Sun.
Situated opposite Kilkenny Castle, Rinuccini's is a smart Italian restaurant, with lively staff and an extensive wine list. The menu includes plenty of classic pasta dishes, as well as fresh fish (mixed seafood salad, say) and local meat (such as braised rack of Wexford lamb, cooked in wine, on porcini and forest mushroom risotto with truffle oil).

Where to stay

Kilkenny is well supplied with hotels and B&Bs. Hotel Kilkenny (College Road, 056 776 2000, www.hotelkilkenny.ie) is a slick, contemporary hotel in the city centre. Also popular are the Kilkenny Ormonde Hotel (Ormonde Street, 056 775 0200, www.kilkennyormonde.com) with its excellent spa and leisure facilities; and smart Langton House Hotel (John Street, 056 776 5133, www.langtons. ie), which has 34 stylish bedrooms. Laragh House (Waterford Road, 056 776 4674, www.laragh house.com) is a reliable B&B with eight bedrooms.

Outside the city, accommodation is more limited. Ballyduff House (056 775 8488, www. ballyduffhouse.com) is a lovely guesthouse six kilometres from Thomastown. Close to Kells, Lawcus Farm Guesthouse (Stoneyford, 086 603 1667, www.lawcusfarmguesthouse.com), a beautifully renovated 200-year-old farmhouse on the banks of the King's River, is ideal for fishing enthusiasts and those after a tranquil retreat.

Inistioge has B&B rooms in the comfortable Woodstock Arms (*see p182*). The four well-appointed rooms at Ballyogan House (059 972 5969, www.ballyoganhouse.com, closed Nov-Mar), in Graiguenamanagh, all have views of the Blackstairs Mountains.

Butler House

16 Patrick Street, Kilkenny (056 776 5707, www.
butler.ie). Rates €130-€180 double incl breakfast.
The old Dower House of Kilkenny Castle, Butler House has been much restored, and the 13 bedrooms modernised with contemporary furnishings and fittings, though many Georgian features remain. There are beautiful gardens too. Breakfast – an extensive hot and cold buffet – is served in the converted stable block (which also houses the Kilkenny Design Centre).

Mount Juliet

Thomastown (056 777 3000, www.mountjuliet.ie). Rates
€129-€329 double incl breakfast. Self-catering €1,250-
€1,700 per week. Closed Jan-Mar Mon-Wed, Sun.
This stunning Georgian mansion, set in 1,500 acres of farm and woodland just outside Thomastown, is now a luxurious hotel. There are 47 rooms and ten self-catering lodges; rooms in the main house retain a traditional, country manor feel, while the Clubhouse rooms are more modern in design and handy for the golf course. Rose Garden Lodges and the Paddocks provide spacious self-catering accommodation. There are several dining options, from the casual President's Bar to the elegant Lady Helen Dining Room. In addition, Mount Juliet has a championship golf course, a spa and leisure centre, an equestrian and activity centre, fishing, and endless paths to walk or cycle along.

Zuni

26 Patrick Street, Kilkenny (056 772 3999, www.
zuni.ie). Rates €80-€130 double incl breakfast.
An intimate townhouse hotel and restaurant in central Kilkenny. The 13 bedrooms are contemporary in design, though not the most spacious in town. Zuni is a popular spot with locals, both for tapas in the café and for the modern Irish menu in the restaurant. There's also a small bar.

WEXFORD TOWN & AROUND

Wexford town

The main town along the coast is Wexford. Founded by the Vikings, Wexford was an important port by the 19th century. While the quays remain and boats still bob on the waters, today it's more of a leisure marina than port, thanks to the increased silting of the harbour. Rosslare Europort (www.iarnrodeireann.ie/rosslare), 20 kilometres away, now serves as the commercial and passenger port from and to the UK, Wales and France. However, Wexford remains a busy coastal town.

Once a walled city, the only remnant of the structure is one of the five original gates, Westgate Tower, which acts as Wexford's Heritage Centre. There's an audio-visual display giving the history of the town, and access to the old stone rooms upstairs. A battlements walk brings you to the ruins of the 12th-century Selskar Abbey nearby.

Wexford's central thoroughfare, Main Street, is threaded around by narrow alleys and lanes, a legacy of the Viking settlement. Main Street plays host to chain stores, cafés and bars. At the north of the street is Bull Ring, named for the bull-baiting that took place here in Norman times. More blood was shed in the square when Cromwell's men murdered citizens here in 1649. A little further up, on North Main Street, the Westgate Design Centre (053 912 3787, www.westgatedesign.ie,

Dunbrody House. See p195.

closed Sun) showcases a range of Irish-made products from glassware to clothing.

Wexford has a thriving arts scene, and the Wexford Arts Centre (Cornmarket, 053 912 3764, www.wexfordartscentre.ie, closed Mon, Sun) holds art exhibitions and theatrical, musical, literary events and workshops throughout the year. Nearby, the newly built Wexford Opera House (High Street, 053 912 2400, www.wexfordopera.com) hosts the internationally acclaimed Wexford Festival Opera over 18 days in October/November.

Down along the Quays, leisure boats and smaller fishing trawlers are moored. Boat trips around Wexford Harbour and up to the seal colonies and birds at Raven Point depart from here (Anthony Kuhn, mobile 085 732 9787, closed Oct-late Mar). Also on the Quays, the Wexford Farmers' Market (www.wexfordfarmersmarkets.com) has plenty of stalls every Friday morning, in the SuperValu car park at the Key West centre.

For an organised stroll around town, look up Wexford Walking Tours (mobile 086 107 9497, www.wexfordwalkingtours.com, closed Nov-Feb), which offers historical, ghostly or tavern walks.

Near Wexford

Just west of Wexford on Newtown Road is Wexford Racecourse (www.wexfordraces.ie), which has a number of meets each year. Slightly further to the west is the open-air museum, the Irish National Heritage Park (*see p185*), while eight kilometres

south-west of Wexford is the Irish Agricultural Museum (*see p184*) with its beautiful Johnstown Castle Gardens.

A few kilometres north of town, in what is commonly known as the 'north slob lands', is Wexford Wildfowl Reserve (Ardcavan Lane, 053 912 3406, www.wexfordwildfowlreserve.ie). Ten thousand white-fronted geese fly here from Greenland for the winter months, among many other migratory birds. There are several hides and an observation tower.

On warm days, locals jump into their cars and make for the sands of Rosslare, just south of Wexford. The seaside resort has maintained its popularity despite its close proximity (eight kilometres) to Rosslare Europort. Activities in Rosslare are mainly based on the beach or at the local golf course (053 913 2032, www.rosslare golf.com). Windsurfing, kayaking and sailing can be arranged through the Rosslare Water Sports Centre (053 913 2202, closed Sept-June) on the Strand. Those not brave enough for a dip in the cool waters will appreciate the spa and pool at Kelly's hotel (*see p192*).

Ten kilometres north of Wexford, just past the small town of Curracloe, is the stunning Ballinesker Beach. With its miles of sand backed by dunes, it was used as the location for the D-Day sequence in *Saving Private Ryan*.

North-west from here along the N11, straddling the River Slaney, is the quaint town of Enniscorthy.

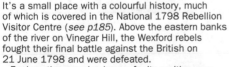

It's a small place with a colourful history, much of which is covered in the National 1798 Rebellion Visitor Centre (*see p185*). Above the eastern banks of the river on Vinegar Hill, the Wexford rebels fought their final battle against the British on 21 June 1798 and were defeated.

Enniscorthy was also known for its malthouses: in 1796, there were 29 of them and they played a crucial role in the town's economy. Today you can see what remains of this heritage in ex-malthouse the Bailey (Barrack Street, 053 923 0353, www.thebailey.ie), a bar, restaurant and nightclub that hosts the Blackstairs Blues Festival (www.blackstairsblues.com) in September.

West of the River Slaney, the striking 13th-century Enniscorthy Castle presides over the town. (It holds the Wexford County Museum, but this is currently closed with no sign of a date for reopening.) Just east of the castle is Abbey Square, where there's a farmers' market on Saturday mornings; as well as fresh produce, a small number of stalls sell soups, crêpes and sandwiches. West of the castle, Castle Street turns into Main street, which is lined with independent shops and cafés. The road becomes Cathedral Street, the site of St Aidan's Cathedral, designed by Augustus Pugin and built in 1843.

Enniscorthy sits in the shadows of the Blackstairs Mountains; for information on walks, visit Enniscorthy Tourist Office (Mill Park Road, 053 923 4699, closed winter Sat, Sun). On the back roads a couple of kilometres west of Enniscorthy is Kiltrea Bridge Pottery (053 923 5107, www.kiltreapottery.com, closed Sun), where you can watch potters in action and purchase ceramics.

Where to eat & drink

Wexford has plenty of eating and drinking options. Stable Diet (South Main Street, 053 914 9012, www.stablediet.com, closed Sun) is a stylish pâtisserie and café serving breakfasts (french toast with bacon and maple syrup) and lunches (soups, sandwiches, tartines and salads) alongside cakes and scones. D'Lush Café (053 912 3795, www.dlushcafe.ie, closed Sun) in the Wexford Arts Centre has own-made dishes and cakes as well as delicious hot chocolate. The café inside the Westgate Design Centre (*see p187*) serves soups, sandwiches, quiche and salads in a modern space.

Reliable bar options include Maggie May's (Monck Street, 053 914 5776), which has a decent beer garden, plus traditional music sessions several nights a week. On South Main Street, the Sky & the Ground (053 912 1273) is a characterful bar with top-notch bar food and traditional music nights, while South 51 (053 917 4559) has a roof garden and music sessions. Centenary Stores (Charlotte Street, 053 912 4424, www.thestores.ie) has a modern, popular bar downstairs and DJs playing into the wee hours upstairs.

In Enniscorthy, Via Veneto (053 923 6929, www.viaveneto.ie, closed Tue) on Weafer Street is

Duncannon Harbour. See p194.

a friendly, old-school Italian restaurant. The tiny Antique Tavern (14 Slaney Street, 053 923 3428, www.theantiquetavern.com) hangs on the edge of town overlooking the River Slaney. Its interior is dotted with memorabilia and photos.

Rosslare has a small selection of watering holes, the best being La Marine bar at Kelly's hotel (*see p192*) or Brady's (053 913 2433) on the Strand Road.

La Dolce Vita
Trimmers Lane, Wexford (053 917 0806). Open 9am-5.30pm Mon-Fri; noon-9pm Sat. No credit cards.

A classic Italian restaurant and deli, and a popular hangout for locals. Panini and coffee are served, as well as dishes such as calf's liver with onions and thyme, or own-made sausage with braised lentils. The coffee is excellent, especially when enjoyed at one of the outdoor tables.

Lobster Pot
Ballyfane (053 913 1110). Open noon-11.30pm Tue-Sat; 12.30-10.30pm Sun. Food served noon-9pm Tue-Sat; 12.30-8pm Sun.

On a sunny day the outdoor tables at the Lobster Pot are packed with people enjoying platters of seafood and pints. Inside is a maze of interconnecting rooms and cosy snugs,

Clement and Kevin Carley. Bouillabaisse or confit of rabbit might be followed by pan-fried sea bass in a vodka and lemon sauce or rack of Irish lamb with a blue cheese sauce. An extensive wine list, and a relaxed but sophisticated atmosphere complete the picture.

The Yard ★

3 Lower Georges Street, Wexford (053 914 4083, www.theyard.ie). Open Café 9am-5pm Mon-Sat. Restaurant Lunch served noon-3pm Mon-Sat. Dinner served 6-9pm Mon-Wed; 6-10pm Thur-Sat.

A chic, modern addition to Wexford's restaurant scene. Imaginative, beautifully presented dishes include starters of Kilmore scallops and roast pork belly with a salad of sugar snap peas and citrus dressing, or smoked mackerel pâté with soda bread and red onion relish. Mains feature roast fillet of turbot with potatoes, tomato and fennel salad and salsa verde, and honey-glazed goat's cheese and beetroot tartlette with lambs lettuce, and a walnut and balsamic dressing. The daytime café at the front is a pleasant spot to sit back with a glass of wine from a well-selected list and soak up the good-natured atmosphere.

Where to stay

There's a lot of choice in Wexford town: among the smarter hotels is the contemporary Whites of Wexford (Abbey Street, 053 912 2311, www.whitesofwexford.ie), while the Riverbank House Hotel (Wexford Bridge, 053 912 3611, www.riverbankhousehotel.com) is reasonably priced. On the edge of town, the modern Whitford Hotel (New Line Road, 053 914 3444, www.whitford.ie) has a swimming pool. There are several B&B options; upmarket ones include Rosemount House (Spawell Road, 053 912 4609, www.wexfordbedandbreakfast.ie) and McMenamin's Townhouse (6 Glena Terrace, Spawell Road, 053 914 6442, www.wexford-bedandbreakfast.com). The sleek Ferrycarrig Hotel (053 912 0999, www.ferrycarrighotel.ie) is a ten-minute drive from Wexford. It's on the River Slaney, so there are beautiful views from many of the public areas and some of the rooms.

En route to Rosslare, in Drinagh, is secluded Killiane Castle (053 915 8885, www.killiane castle.com, closed Nov-Feb). It's a working farm in a stunning setting, which provides B&B lodging in an elegant house and self-catering in courtyard apartments. Rosslare has a swathe of B&Bs catering for those heading to and from the port; for a list see www.wexfordweb.com. Just outside Rosslare, in Tagoat, Churchtown House (053 913 2555, www.churchtownhouse.com, closed Nov-Mar) is a gracious 18th-century house with 12 B&B rooms.

Enniscorthy is short on places to stay, apart from the Riverside Park Hotel (The Promenade, 053 923 7800, www.riversideparkhotel.com, closed Jan), which has a leisure club and an attractive waterside location. In the surrounding countryside, Woodbrook House (Woodbrook, 053 925 5114, www.woodbrookhouse.ie, closed Oct-Apr), a Georgian house in the shadow of the Blackstairs Mountains, has four B&B rooms.

and the place oozes character and charm. Dishes are simple, but good: local fish, battered and served with chips, or pan-fried in butter; or Carne crab claws and crab salads and lavish seafood platters. There are salads and a few meat options too. Prepare to wait for a table, as the Lobster Pot has quite a reputation.

Le Tire Bouchon

South Main Street, Wexford (053 912 4877, www.letirebouchon.ie). Dinner served 6-9pm Mon-Thur, Sun; 6-10pm Fri, Sat.

Upstairs from the Sky & the Ground bar, this smart French restaurant is run by ex-Dunbrody House chefs Arnaud

BEST MUSIC FESTIVALS

Ireland has hundreds of music festivals throughout the year, covering jazz, rock, pop, blues, folk and, especially, traditional music. Here are some of the best; for more, see pp11-21.

Ballyshannon Folk & Traditional Music Festival
www.ballyshannonfolkfestival.com. Venue Ballyshannon, Co Donegal. Date late July.
Now in its fourth decade, the Ballyshannon festival has built a sterling reputation for its diverse and exciting programme, with plenty of top performers from Ireland, as well as guests from abroad.

Castle Palooza
www.castlepalooza.com. Venue Tullamore, Co Offaly. Date end July.
Nominated for the best small festival in Europe, this little gem takes place in the grounds of 17th-century Charleville Castle. Enjoy gigs, dance, workshops, art exhibitions and short films, all in the shadows of the magical woodland and atmospheric castle.

Cois Fharraige Surf & Music Festival
www.coisfharraige.com. Venue Kilkee, Co Clare. Date mid Sept.
A relative newcomer (launched in 2007), this three-day music festival by the sea brings in surfers and music fans from all over, with beach parties running through the weekend. Seasick Steve, Supergrass, the Zutons and Stereo MCs have played at past events.

Cork Jazz Festival
www.guinnessjazzfestival.com. Venue Cork, Co Cork. Date end Oct.
Three days of the very best of national and international jazz, held in one of Ireland's most vibrant cities. It's big, loud and brassy – bring your dancing shoes.

North of Enniscorthy, near Gorey, is the contemporary Seafield Hotel (Ballymoney, 053 942 4000, www.seafieldhotel.com). Close to Ballymoney Beach, the hotel is popular for golf and spa weekends.

Ballinkeele House
Ballymurn (053 913 8105, www.ballinkeele.com). Rates €150-€170 double incl breakfast. Closed Jan, Dec.
This 19th-century manor surrounded by 300 acres of farmland and woods has been in the Maher family since 1840. It remains a working farm, but with five upmarket rooms available for guests. Downstairs there are open fireplaces and a drawing room to relax in. A four-course meal is served in an elegant dining room. Guests can wander the grounds, sit by the lake and soak up the tranquillity. Ballymurn is 10km south-east of Enniscorthy.

Kelly's
Rosslare Strand, Rosslare (053 913 2114, www. kellys.ie). Rates €176-€198 double incl breakfast. Closed Dec-mid Feb.
Situated on the beach, with uninterrupted views across the Irish Sea, Kelly's resort hotel (with 118 rooms) has been open since 1895 and is something of an institution. Recent improvements include the addition of leisure facilities and treatment rooms. Families book well in advance for the spacious family rooms, plus the use of the in-house babysitting service and the playground. (However, the hotel restricts the number of families to ensure it is not dominated by children.) Spa and golf weekends are popular too. There are two restaurants: Beaches is more formal; La Marine is more of a bistro and bar.

Marlfield House Hotel
Courtown Road, Gorey (053 942 1124, www. marlfieldhouse.com). Rates €160-€570 double incl breakfast.
Run by Mary and Ray Bowe for more than 30 years, this is one of Wexford's foremost country house hotels. The approach to the Georgian house is along a tree-lined drive; the surrounding gardens are lovely, and include a lake and a wildfowl reserve. The 19 bedrooms are decorated with antique furnishings; the public rooms sport paintings, chandeliers, antiques and open fires. Marlfield built its reputation on its restaurant. Seasonal menus feature produce from the kitchen garden, Wexford lamb and beef, and Bannow Bay oysters.

Monart Spa & Lodge ★
The Still, nr Enniscorthy (053 923 8999, www. monart.ie). Rates €190-€240 double incl breakfast.
One of Ireland's best spas, Monart hides its up-to-the-minute design behind an 18th-century façade. The main house is decorated in traditional style, with a games room and reading room; a glass tunnel links this with the spacious reception and modern building. The 68 rooms are contemporary, but very comfortable, and decorated in neutral tones; all have terraces that overlook either the duck pond or the forest. The thermal spa includes a salt grotto, a pool, an aromatic steam room, and indoor and outdoor saunas; numerous treatments are available. There's a bar, with a decked terrace, which also serves food, and a fine dining restaurant. It's all understated and tranquil, and makes for a wonderful getaway.

SOUTH & WEST WEXFORD

Dubliners tend not to venture as far as Wexford's south coast beaches, leaving them blissfully uncrowded. Kilmore Quay, a picturesque fishing village, comes to life during the summer months. It's known for its beautiful thatched cottages, which line the main street. The small harbour is the heart of the town; boats leave from here on trips to the Saltee Islands (*see p185*) or on fishing expeditions; try *Celtic Lady II* (mobile 087 292 6469) or *Autumn Dream* (mobile 087 213 5308, www.kilmoreangling.com). An old lightship bobs on the calm waters of the harbour. Bicycles can be hired at the Harbour Masters Office at the marina, and there's a Blue Flag beach for swimming. For refreshments, there's a good bar, several excellent fish and chip shops and a couple of decent restaurants. The best time to visit the village is in July during the Kilmore Quay Seafood Festival (www.kilmorequayseafoodfestival.com), a weekend of music, street entertainment and platters of very fresh seafood.

West of Kilmore Quay is Hook peninsula ★, Wexford's most rugged and scenic stretch of coastline. While the east coast of the peninsula is fringed with sandy beaches, the west side looks out over Bannow Bay. Just before the peninsula is Carrig-on-Bannow, a small town famous for the traditional and contemporary music sessions in Colfers pub (051 561159) and festivals such as the Phil Murphy Memorial Weekend (www.philmurphyweekend.com), when Irish music sessions, workshops and other events are held. Driving on to the peninsula via the R733, look out for signs for Tintern Abbey (*see p185*), a 13th-century Cistercian abbey tucked away on a quiet country road.

Turning on to the R734, heading south, you come to Fethard, a small village where you can pick up maps and information from the tourist office (Main Street, 051 397502, www.hooktourism.com, closed June-Aug Sun; Sept-May Sat, Sun). The beaches south of the town are delightfully secluded: Grange Strand just outside the town is perfect for families, while Baginbun Beach and Carnivan Beach are also popular. On the headland in between is something of a secret: an open-air swimming pool where waves spill in over the rocks.

Towards the tip of the peninsula there are spectacular views across the Irish Sea. Before the very end, take the inconspicuous turn-off for Slade – the village is worth the short detour. Overlooking the harbour are the ruins of the late 15th- or early 16th-century Slade Castle. You can walk from Slade around the headland to Hook Lighthouse (051 397055, www.hookheritage.ie), the world's oldest operational lighthouse. Alternatively, there's a car park beside the lighthouse, as well as a small café serving snacks in the visitor centre. A guided tour takes visitors to the top of the lighthouse; you'll learn that it was built by William Marshall, Earl of Pembroke, to guide the ships into Waterford Harbour and that it was first operated by monks. Nature enthusiasts should walk around the rocks and headland, where the waves pound

Electric Picnic
electricpicnic.ie. Venue Stradbally Estate, Co Laois. Date early Sept.
A vibrant and eclectic three-day programme of music, art, theatre and comedy. It's a relatively small affair, but manages to attract some major national and international bands (Arcade Fire, Pulp, Chemical Brothers). The laid-back, family-friendly vibe is a big part of the appeal.

Fleadh Cheoil
www.fleadh2011cavan.ie. Date Aug.
Technically not a festival, but a showcase of Ireland's traditional music and dance through competition, taking place in a different city every year (Cavan in 2011). If it's traditional culture you're after, there is no better place.

Fleadh Nua
www.fleadhnua.com. Venue Ennis, Co Clare. Date May.
Running since 1970, this week-long festival brings the best traditional bands to Ennis for a fine mix of concerts, ceilidhs, music, song and dance workshops, Irish language lessons, street entertainment and more.

Oxegen
www.oxegen.ie. Venue Punchestown Racecourse, Naas, Co Kildare. Date mid July.
Ireland's largest pop music festival pulls out all the stops with a line-up of top international bands. Pop, rock, hip hop, indie – it's all there. Come prepared with wellies, rain jackets, sunscreen and tents for a fun-fuelled weekend.

Sligo Live
www.sligolive.ie. Venue Sligo, Co Sligo. Date end Oct.
Labelled as a folk, roots and indie festival, there's a little bit of everything at this mellow five-day jamboree. Sligo town comes alive with music, food and dance, and the atmosphere is always fantastic.

on blustery days: there are plenty of birds and occasional sightings of dolphins and whales.

The west coast of Hook peninsula has yet more lovely views, and many small bays that are good for fishing. The best swimming is off the long stretch of fine, white sand at Duncannon. Traditionally a fishing village, it's a great place for anglers, who can either fish from the shore or by boat. A Sand Sculpting Festival (051 389216) is held in August, when a weekend is given over to sand creations (professional and amateur) along with music, dance and street theatre. Presiding over the village on the headland is impressive Duncannon Fort (*see p185*).

Further along, there's little to do in the picturesque village of Arthurstown except sit and admire the views across the harbour, have a pint in the old-world King's Bay Inn or take part in a cookery class at the luxury hotel Dunbrody House (*see right*). Close by is Ballyhack, where the car ferry to Passage East in Waterford leaves every 15-20 minutes. Ballyhack Castle (051 389468, www.heritageireland.ie, closed Sept-mid June), a large tower house built by the Knights Templar around 1450, is the only attraction here.

A few kilometres north, on the banks of the Barrow estuary, is Dunbrody Abbey (www.dunbrody abbey.com, closed mid Sept-Apr). The ruins of the 13th-century Cistercian abbey can be explored and there's a hedge maze, crazy golf, a craft shop and a café. From here it's a short drive to Kilmokea Gardens (*see p185*).

There are more beautiful gardens at the John F Kennedy Arboretum (*see p185*). Nearby is the farm where JFK's great-grandfather Patrick Kennedy was born. The Kennedy Homestead (Dunganstown, 035 388264, www.kennedyhomestead.com, closed Oct-Apr) remains a working farm run by descendants of the Kennedys. There's a visitor centre in the grounds of the farm, with JFK memorabilia, an audio-visual display and a souvenir shop.

Just north of the Arboretum, New Ross sits astride the River Barrow and is one of the oldest towns in the country. It was once a busy port; nowadays the quays are the location of the Dunbrody Famine Ship (051 425239, www.dunbrody.com), a replica of the original 1845 vessel that carried 3,000 people from Ireland to America during the Great Famine. An exhibition outlines the history of the Great Famine and the story behind the 'coffin ships', in particular the *Dunbrody*. The town's history is also explored by the Ros Tapestry (Priory Court, The Quay, 051 445396, www.rostapestry.com, closed winter). Fifteen intricately stitched modern tapestries depict the story of the Norman settlement in Ireland and the founding of New Ross. Tapestry demonstrations are held and there's a pastry shop for snacks.

The streets of New Ross climb upwards from the harbour. Steep and lined with old buildings, in contrast to the new constructions around the quays, these narrow lanes are pleasant to stroll around, and contain a few decent eateries. On Saturdays, there's a farmers' market on the quays from 9am.

In July the town is taken over by the JFK Dunbrody Festival (www.jfkdunbrodyfestival.org), a three-day music extravaganza.

Hook Lighthouse. See p193.

Where to eat & drink

Excellent seafood can be found at Kilmore Quay, as trawlers sell their daily catch to the nearby restaurants. The Saltee Chipper (053 912 9911, closed winter Mon) is a contender for the best fish and chip shop in Co Wexford, while the Silver Fox restaurant (053 912 9888, www.silverfox.ie, closed Nov-Feb Mon-Wed) specialises in sparkling fresh seafood.

On the east side of Hook peninsula, the best options for lunch are the cafés at Tintern Abbey (*see p185*) or Hook Lighthouse (*see p193*). The Templars Inn (051 397162, www.templarsinn.com, closed Nov-mid Mar), a couple of kilometres from Hook Head on the west of the peninsula, serves excellent seafood and has outdoor tables.

Duncannon has two good pubs: the Strand Tavern (051 389109) and Roche's (051 389188). At the latter, food is served in the atmospheric and traditional front bar, but there's also a bright, contemporary restaurant, Sqigl, which serves modern Irish cuisine with an emphasis on fish.

There's a handful of bars in New Ross, the best of which is the Hillside Bar (051 421155), where a carvery lunch is an option.

Aldridge Lodge ★

Duncannon (051 389116, www.aldridgelodge.com). Dinner served 5.30-9.30pm Wed-Sun.
Locals deem Aldridge Lodge the best place to eat on Hook peninsula. The dining room is small, so you may need to book well ahead. On approach, it looks as if you're about to dine at someone's home, so the smart restaurant with white linen tablecloths, brown leather chairs and wooden floors is a surprise. Fish features prominently, in dishes such as steamed crock of Kerry mussels with white wine, herb and garlic cream, but there are meat dishes too: roast wild Tipperary venison with braised organic beetroot and goat's cheese mash, perhaps, or a tasting plate of Irish pork. The Lodge is also a guesthouse, with three en suite rooms (€80-€90 double incl breakfast), simply and stylishly decorated.

Café Nutshell

South Street, New Ross (051 422777). Open July, Aug 9am-5.30pm Mon-Sat. Sept-June 9am-5.30pm Tue-Sat.
A pleasant deli and café where Philip and Patsy Rogers serve organic, home-cooked food using local produce where possible. The coffee is excellent and the smell of freshly baked goods in the morning is irresistible. Lunch sees a selection of soups, sandwiches, quiches, salads and so on.

Crazy Crab Café & Bistro

Kilmore Quay (053 914 8848, www.crazycrab.ie). Open Apr-Oct noon-9pm daily. Feb, Mar, Nov, Dec noon-9pm Thur-Sun. Closed Jan.
The Crazy Crab excels at supplying generous portions of fresh and affordable seafood. Start with langoustines or crab cooked in garlic butter, say, and then move on to share the big seafood platter or lightly battered fish of the day with chips. There are a few other dishes too, such as warm chicken salad or beefburger. It's a no-frills establishment, with simple white walls and furniture, stripped floorboards and local art displayed on the walls.

Where to stay

Kilmore Quay is a busy summer hub with an abundance of self-catering cottages and B&Bs; the Wexford Tourist Office (Quay Front, Wexford, 053 912 3111, closed Sept-June Sun) has details. Campers and caravanners will find excellent facilities at Ocean Island Caravan & Camping Park (051 397148, www.oceanislandmobilehomes.com, closed Oct-Easter) near Fethard. Aldridge Lodge restaurant (*see left*), just outside Duncannon, also has rooms. In nearby Arthurstown is the lovely Glendine Country House (051 389500, www.glendinehouse.com), which has six spacious, elegant rooms and a wonderful view across the Barrow Estuary. In New Ross, the Brandon House Hotel (051 421703, www.brandonhousehotel.ie) has a fine location on a hillside overlooking the River Slaney, plus comfortable, modern rooms and a leisure centre.

Dunbrody House

Arthurstown (051 389600, www.dunbrodyhouse.com). Rates €245-€360 double incl breakfast.
Surrounded by 300 acres of parkland, Dunbrody is an opulent retreat on the Hook peninsula. The Georgian house retains many of its original features, while furnishings are a happy blend of old and new, and there are fresh flowers throughout. All 22 bedrooms are elegantly designed, spacious and have countryside views. Dundon's Champagne Seafood Bar is a chic, all-day bar and restaurant that's an informal alternative to the Harvest Room, where the table d'hôte (rillette of pork belly with apple and cider chutney, for example, followed by pan-seared salmon with broad beans and asparagus tips, and caper and shallot sauce) is supplemented by seasonal and tasting menus. Outbuildings have been converted into a cookery school, and classes run throughout the year. There's also a spa, which is open to non-residents.

Kilmokea Country Manor

Great Island (051 388109, www.kilmokea.com). Rates €150-€280 double incl breakfast. Closed Jan.
This handsome former rectory offers a lived-in grandeur. Guests receive a warm welcome from owners Mark and Emma Hewlett. There are just six bedrooms, all named after flowers and individually furnished, plus self-catering suites in the converted coach house and granary. Dinner and breakfast are served in the small dining room, and there's also a cosy drawing room. Guests can stroll around the gardens (also open to the public – *see p185*), fish in the lake, visit the pool and spa area, play croquet or tennis, or simply enjoy the peace and quiet.

Marsh Mere Lodge

Arthurstown (051 389186, www.marshmerelodge.com). Rates €90 double incl breakfast.
Marsh Mere Lodge is tucked into the side of the hill overlooking King's Bay at the edge of Arthurstown and has an *Anne of Green Gables* look to it. Guests are welcomed with a big smile, a cup of tea and a slice of cake in the second-floor sitting room, where there's a roaring fire and views over the bay. There are four attractive bedrooms, each with an individual look. The front porch is perfect for sunset viewing. A hearty breakfast, including fresh eggs from the house hens, will set you up for the day.

Counties Kildare & Wicklow

The sandy soil of the Curragh in County Kildare is ideally suited to horse-breeding and racing, so it's no surprise that Ireland's two major racecourses are here. To get really close to some thoroughbreds, you can visit the Irish National Stud, which is also home to world-famous Japanese gardens. In contrast to the open plains of Kildare, County Wicklow is all mountains, lakes and coastal towns. Known as 'the Garden of Ireland', the terrain is wilder and more beautiful than that epithet suggests. In a 30-minute drive from Dublin, you can be at the foot of the Wicklow Mountains, walking the cliff path between Bray and Greystones, meditating on the monastic ruins of Glendalough or strolling around the picturesque village of Enniskerry.

Bordering the Dublin suburbs and furnished with good public transport and roads, both Kildare and Wicklow have become major commuter areas, providing far more affordable living space than the Irish capital. This also makes their attractions ideal for day-trippers who are based in Dublin. However, each county also has exceptional hotels and plenty of self-catering or camping opportunities should you wish to explore them at a slower pace.

COUNTY KILDARE

North Kildare

The main visitor attractions are to the north of the county, an area of relatively flat and fertile land. Kildare town is quiet, with little to see except the impressive Cathedral of St Brigid, built by the Normans in 1221 on the site where St Brigid is believed to have founded a religious house in the fifth century. The grounds have one of the tallest round towers in Ireland (it's almost 33 metres high), beside which is a high cross and the foundations of an ancient, but restored fire temple. There are also some wonderful early Christian stone carvings inside the cathedral. Occupying a restored 18th-century market house, the Kildare Heritage Centre (045 530672, www.kildare.ie, closed Sun) is across from St Brigid's. An audio-visual exhibition gives Kildare's history from the fifth century to the present. The centre also contains a tourist office.

Just south-west of town, Kildare Village (Nurney Road, 045 520501, www.kildarevillage.ie) is a

Irish National Stud. See p200.

Castletown House. See p200.

suburban mall, usually packed with locals and Dubliners hunting for discounts and high-street brands such as Coast, Le Creuset and Reiss. The main reason to stop in nearby Newbridge is also to shop, either in the rather soulless Whitewater Shopping Centre or, more appealing, at Newbridge Silverware (045 431301, www.newbridge silverware.com), where you'll also find a Museum of Style Icons that features clothes worn by such screen stars as Marilyn Monroe and Audrey Hepburn, movie memorabilia and a jewellery range inspired by the actresses.

Between Kildare and Newbridge lie the plains of the Curragh. Thought to be the oldest and largest area of semi-natural grassland in Europe, the 4,870 acres of sandy soil support a number of rare species of plant. The land is also perfectly suited to feeding horses, hence the area's role as a centre of Irish horse-breeding. The Irish National Stud (see p200) is a major tourist draw, giving visitors a privileged glimpse into this multi-million-euro trade, as well as the chance to wander in a delightful Japanese garden. The Curragh Racecourse, headquarters of flat racing in Ireland, hosts all five Irish Classic races (see p210), including the Derby, Oaks and St Leger.

North of Kildare town is a different type of landscape altogether: the Bog of Allen – wellies recommended. The quiet town of Lullymore is home to the Bog of Allen Nature Centre (045 860133, www.ipcc.ie, closed Sat, Sun). Dedicated to the conservation of peatland – over 80 per cent of which has been lost across Ireland due to, among other things, afforestation and overgrazing – the centre contains a traditional Irish cottage, displays about Irish bog land and a delightful wildlife garden.

East is the livelier community of Naas, its good road connections and close proximity to Dublin (just over 30 kilometres away) having made it popular with commuters. Barker & Jones bookshop (Main Street, 045 856130, www.barkerandjones.ie)

is worth a browse, and each Friday from 10am, a Country Market (http://naascountrymarkets. bluewaterroad.ie) is held in the Town Hall, a building that was the local jail until 1833. The market, in business since 1952, sells freshly baked goods, homegrown vegetables, free-range local eggs and fresh flowers. Nearby Punchestown Racecourse (045 897704, www.punchestown.com) hosts the four-day Irish National Hunt Festival in May; if that's insufficiently adrenalin-pumped for you, there's motor-racing at the Mondello Park circuit (045 860200, www.mondello.ie).

Twelve kilometres north of Naas along winding country roads, Straffan is a quaint town with some of Ireland's best golf facilities: both courses at the Kildare Hotel & Country Club (016 017200, www.kclub.ie), which hosted the Ryder Cup in 2006, were designed by Arnold Palmer. If knocking a little white ball around for hours isn't your thing, the Lodge Park Heritage Centre (016 288412, www.steam-museum.ie, open June-Aug Wed-Sun) might appeal. It has old steam engines (some still working) from breweries, distilleries and ships. Outside are well-tended walled gardens, and there's also a café. Ireland's oldest and largest Palladian country home – Castletown House (see p200) – is a short drive away.

North again, across the M4 motorway and near the border with County Meath, the thriving university town of Maynooth is home to St Patrick's College, founded as a seminary in 1795. The college remains an educational establishment, but also houses the National Science Museum (017 086000, www.nuim.ie/museum, open May-Sept Tue, Thur, Sun). It displays religious artefacts (chalices, vestments, rosaries), as well as objects relating to Marconi's first telegraph transmission and scientific apparatus owned by Nicholas Callan, the inventor of the induction coil. Maynooth's other main attraction is its castle (016 286744, www.heritageireland.ie, closed Oct-May), home in the 12th century of the Kildare

Fitzgeralds, one of Ireland's most powerful families. An exhibition in the keep tells the place's history; you can also arrange guided tours. Golfers will gravitate towards the K Club (see p203), one of Ireland's best golf resorts.

A little east of Maynooth, towards Dublin, is the reborn Village at Lyons. Settlements emerged along the busy Grand Canal from the early 19th century to supply goods and services to travellers, with the village at Lyons just one example. When the canal lost its commercial significance, the village fell into decline. It was reborn as a foodie destination in the mid 1990s. Within beautifully restored grey stone buildings, you'll now find a café and restaurant (for both, see p203) and a few shops – like the eateries, open Wednesday to Sunday only. Work up an appetite walking the beautiful towpaths (you can also hire bicycles in summer), or learn how it's all done at one of cook and author Clodagh McKenna's cookery classes.

South Kildare

There is less to interest visitors in the south of County Kildare, but you will chance on a few attractive towns. Athy is one: a historic market town at the junction of the Grand Canal and the River Barrow. Founded as an Anglo-Norman settlement in the 12th century, it gained new significance in late medieval times as a military holding on the boundary of the English-controlled Pale. The bridge approach to Athy gives full view of the impressive turrets of White's Castle, built in the 15th century and now a private residence. Information about the castle and the rest of the town can be found at the Athy Heritage Centre (059 863 3075, www.athyheritagecentre-museum. ie, closed winter Sat, Sun), where the audio-visual displays are supported by an unusual range of artefacts, notably a sledge harness used by Ernest Shackleton during his Antarctic expedition in 1908-09. There are also some lovely walks along the towpaths of the late 18th-century Grand Canal (maps are available at the Heritage Centre).

On Sundays, the Farmers' Market & Craft Fair (www.kildare.ie/athyfarmersmarket) in Emily Square sells mouth-watering delicacies, local produce and handicrafts. Alternatively, take a ten-minute drive out of town to the Castlefarm Shop (059 863 6948, www.castlefarmshop.ie, open last Fri and Sat of mth) to buy cheese, jam, organic meat, vegetables and even wine, produced on the farm or in the local area. There are enjoyable guided tours of the farm too.

South-east of Athy, beyond the M9 motorway, is Castledermot, a tiny town on the banks of the River Lerr. Barely set back from the main thoroughfare is what remains of the walls of a 13th-century abbey, with an associated 15th-century building known as the Abbey Castle – it's probably where the monks lived until the friary was destroyed in the mid 16th century. The old graveyard contains a tenth-century round tower (in remarkably good shape apart from lacking its coned roof) and two high crosses, intricately carved with biblical scenes, that may date from the ninth century.

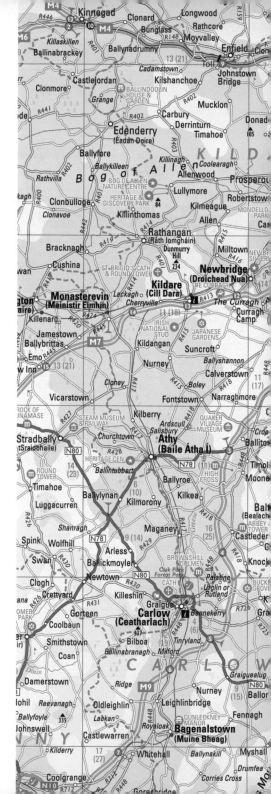

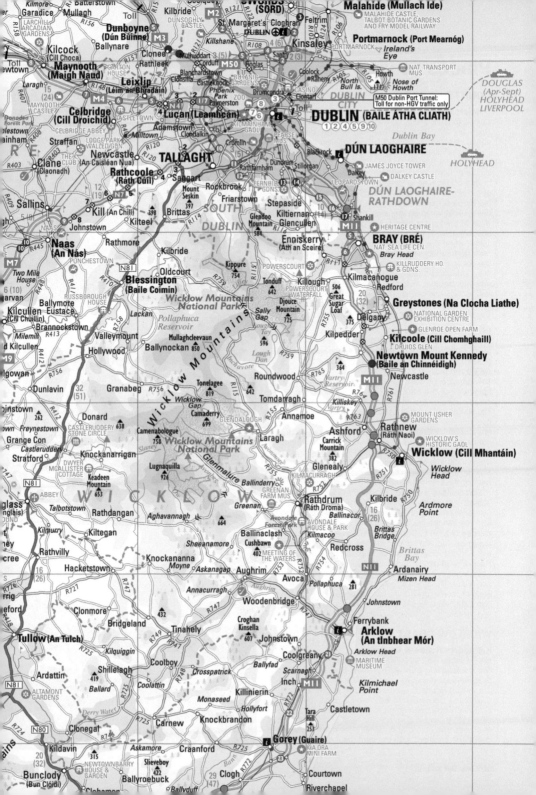

Places to visit

COUNTY KILDARE

Castletown House

Celbridge (016 288252, www.castletownhouse.ie).
Open Apr-Oct 10am-6pm Tue-Sun. Guided tour €4.50;
€3.50 reductions; €12.50 family. No credit cards.
This huge Palladian house was built between 1722
and 1729 for William Conolly, Speaker of the Irish
House of Commons – and Ireland's wealthiest man
by dint of dabbling in forfeited estates after the Battle
of the Boyne. Lady Louisa Conolly further enlivened
the property from 1759, as she set about the interior
design with Venetian glass chandeliers and, along the
walls of the long gallery, busts of Greek and Roman
philosophers. The house remained in the family until
1967, when it was bought by Desmond Guinness;
after restoration work, Castletown was opened to
the public in 1968. It's now under state ownership.
The guided tour takes you through a series of stately
reception rooms, including the celebrated long gallery,
and various bedrooms. There is also extensive
parkland, still laid out as in the 18th century.
There's also a lovely restaurant in the west wing.

Irish National Stud

Tully (045 522963, www.irish-national-stud.ie).
Open Feb-Dec 9.30am-5pm daily. Tours noon,
2.30pm, 4pm daily. Admission (incl tour) €11;
€6-€8 reductions; €27 family.
The land around Tully has been used for breeding
horses since the 1300s, when, it is claimed, the
steeds used by the Knights of Malta were bred here.
The National Stud was established in 1946, and
continues to provide a home to some of Ireland's
finest thoroughbreds; they can be admired at close
quarters on the informative, behind-the-scenes guided
tour. There are also Thoroughbred Trail weekends,
which include a close-up view of some races. The
Stud's Horse Museum tells the story of Ireland's long-
running passion for horses and the 'sport of kings'.
　　Surprisingly, a visit to the Stud isn't just about
horses – there are also two gardens. The Japanese
Gardens, probably the finest in Europe, are charming,
with a small tea house and a little bridge. They were
created between 1906 and 1910 by Japanese
designer Eida and his son Minoru, at the behest of
rich Scottish brewer Colonel William Hall-Walker. St
Fiachra's Garden is approached via a subterranean
tunnel that pops you out into a landscape of woods
and water. Designed to reflect the inspiration Ireland's
earliest monks drew from natural beauty, the garden
has trails where you'll see limestone monastic cells
and Waterford Crystal ornamental gardens.

WICKLOW COAST

Killruddery House & Gardens

Bray (mobile 087 419 8674, www.killruddery.com).
Open House July-Sept 1-5pm daily. Gardens May-Sept
9.30am-5pm daily. Apr, Oct 9.30am-5pm Sat, Sun.
Admission House & Gardens €10; €3-€8 reductions;
€20 family Gardens only €6; free-€5 reductions.
Killruddery has been home to the Brabazon family
since 1618, and is currently the seat of the 15th Earl
of Meath. The house and gardens are open to visitors
during the summer, with the gardens – designed by

Mount Usher Gardens

French landscape architect Bonet in 1682 – especially impressive. Visitors walk through formal entertainment gardens, lined with disciplined lime, hornbeam and beech hedges; peek at the Orangery; or explore the sections of wooded wilderness. Of additions made in the 18th and 19th centuries, the most notable is the Sylvan Theatre, laid out in a classical style with terraced banks and a high bay hedge. The Brabazons are an enterprising family: in addition to renting out the estate as a film location (*PS I Love You*, *Angela's Ashes* and *The Tudors* television series were all shot here), they sell produce from their working farm. Garden parties, events for children, concerts and film festivals are all hosted here.

Mount Usher Gardens ★
Ashford (040 440205, www.mountushergardens.ie). Open Gardens Mar-Oct 10.30am-6pm daily. Café 10am-4pm daily. Admission €7.50; free-€6 reductions.
Laid out along the banks of the River Vartry, Mount Usher Gardens blends trees, shrubs and flowers from all over the world to create a magical haven. Narrow pathways weave through the gardens, with benches and lawns to stretch out on and bask in the sounds of the flowing river and breathe in the wonderful scents. Magnolias, azaleas and rhododendrons are a highlight in spring, while the maples provide a stunning red-gold display in autumn. Outside the gardens are shops, a garden centre and the excellent Avoca Garden Café.

Wicklow's Historic Gaol
Wicklow Town (040 461599, www.wicklows historicgaol.com). Open 10.30am-4.30pm Mon-Sat; 11am-4.30pm Sun. Night tours (adults only) 7pm last Fri of mth. Admission €7.30; €4.50-€6 reductions; €19 family. Night tours €15. No credit cards.
If ghosts are your thing, you'll love being in Wicklow Gaol – ghost hunters Angie Freedland and her husband Keith claim it is one of the most haunted buildings they've visited. From 1702 until 1924, this was the last mortal abode for many hardened criminals, and now audio-visual displays, life-sized dolls and actors recreate their last miserable years on earth. For those brave enough, there are evening ghost tours; more timid types can take a day tour, browse the craft shop and have a snack in the café. The Gaol also contains a small museum dedicated to Robert Halpin, the Wicklow-born sailor who laid the first transatlantic telegraph cables in 1866 as captain of Brunel's mighty steamship SS *Great Eastern*.

INLAND WICKLOW

Glendalough ★
Laragh (040 445352, www.glendalough.ie). Open Visitor centre Mid Mar-mid Oct 9.30am-6pm daily. Mid Oct-mid Mar 9.30am-5pm daily. Tours by appointment. Admission Visitor centre €3; €1-€2 reductions; €8 family. Tours free. No credit cards.
Glendalough, meaning 'the valley of two lakes', is a glacial valley sheltered by tree-covered mountains, and a tranquil and stunning setting for one of Ireland's most famous monastic sites. The remains of the monastic 'city' established in the sixth century by St Kevin are extensive. Most impressive is a 30m-high round tower that rises from the ancient graveyard. Further remains include the ninth-century cathedral (the roof is missing, but the chancel, nave and sacristy are still visible), the smaller St Kevin's Church (thought to date from the 12th century) and, among weathered gravestones, St Kevin's Cross. The visitor centre beside the Glendalough Hotel is the best place to start your exploration: use the model of the ancient Christian site as it's thought to have been to plan your visit. The centre arranges guided tours, but access is free if you're happy to wander on your own. It's a 20-minute walk from the visitor centre to the beautiful upper lake, where there is also a car park. Here you'll find the tiny, tenth-century Reefert Church, from which a pathway leads to a beehive-shaped stone structure, St Kevin's Cell, overlooking the lake.

Powerscourt House & Gardens ★
Enniskerry (012 046000, www.powerscourt.ie). Open Gardens 9.30am-5.30pm/dusk daily. House May-Sept 9.30am-1.30pm Mon, Sun. Oct-Apr 9.30am-1.30pm Sun. Café 9.30am-4.30pm daily. Waterfall May-Aug 9.30am-7pm daily. Mar, Apr, Sept, Oct 10.30am-5.30pm daily. Nov-Feb 10.30am-4pm daily. Admission House & Gardens €8; free-€7 reductions. Waterfall €5; free-€4.50 reductions.
Powerscourt was an important Anglo-Norman site, with a castle erected here in the 13th century. It passed through many owners, before it fell in 1603 to Richard Wingfield, whose family retained it for 350 years. The building underwent significant changes in the 18th century, when a Palladian mansion was built around the ancient castle. Acres of impressive gardens were laid out, creating formal gardens, a walled garden, lily ponds, a Japanese garden, wooded land and Italian terraces. Although much of the interior of the building was destroyed by fire in 1974, the restored ballroom shows the grandeur of the building at its best. The estate also has Ireland's largest waterfall, cascading down a 120m rockface; it makes for a marvellous picnic spot. Access is through a different entrance than the gardens, a kilometre south of the house.
The Avoca Café (012 046066, www.avoca.ie) with its large outdoor terrace serves freshly made salads and hot dishes; there's also an Avoca shop.

Russborough House
Blessington (045 865239, www.russborough.ie). Open (guided tour only) May-Sept 10am-6pm daily. Apr, Oct 10am-6pm Sun. Other times by appointment. Admission House €10; €5-€8 reductions; €25 family. Maze €3.
Russborough House was built in 1741, by Joseph Leeson, the son of a wealthy Dublin brewer. It took ten years to build and its façade is the longest in Ireland, with the main house attached by colonnades to the east and west wings. You can only admire the ornate interior on one of the hourly guided tours, which will glide you over polished limestone and Italian marble floors, under baroque plasterwork and chandeliers, past rugs and tapestries dating from the 18th century. There's an impressive art collection – which has been burgled on four occasions. In the gardens, children can get lost in the beech hedge maze, while a short trail around the grounds gives you an opportunity to admire the exterior of the building. There's a café.

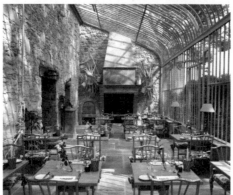

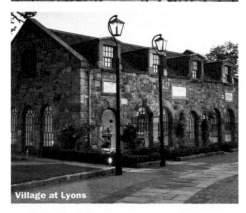
Village at Lyons

Where to eat & drink

In Kildare town, the Silken Thomas (The Square, 045 522232, www.silkenthomas.com) is an all-rounder, with bars, a restaurant, a nightclub and even accommodation.

Naas has some good-quality restaurants and cafés, among them Harvest Kitchen (Sallins Road, 045 881793, www.harvestkitchen.ie), serving tasty sandwiches, wraps and soup; and Missy Moo's (Chapel Lane, 045 871130, closed Sun), which offers unusual ice-cream flavours, as well as scrumptious brownies and cakes. Beside the canal dock, Vie de Châteaux Wine Bar & Grill (045 888478, www.viedechateaux.ie) has tightly packed tables, a lively atmosphere and an accommodating menu mostly made up of French classics, including charcuterie, moules frites, snails, cheese and, of course, excellent wines. For evening entertainment, try Fletcher's (Main Street, 045 897328), which is perfect for quiet drinks and a chat; locals' favourite Hayden's (Poplar Square, 045 866544); or the bar and lounge at the modern Osprey Hotel (045 881222, www.ospreyhotel.ie).

Being a student town, Maynooth has plenty of pubs. The best restaurant, located in the Glenroyal Hotel (016 290909, www.glenroyalhotelkildare.ie), is Lan Tania, which serves Thai and Japanese dishes to eat in or take away. The Mad Hatter Café (Keenan's Lane, mobile 085 714 8085, www.madhattercafe.ie, closed Sun) is a lovely spot for lunch in Castledermot. It serves own-made salads, soups, sandwiches and wraps, as well as good coffee, cupcakes and brownies.

L'Officina

Kildare Village (045 535850, www.officina.ie).
Open/food served 9.30am-6pm Mon-Wed; 9.30am-7pm Thur, Fri; 9.30am-8pm Sat; 10.30am-6pm Sun.
Don't let its location in the Kildare Village shopping mall put you off: L'Officina has become a destination in itself. The premises are large and bright, and the place has a relaxed bustle about it. It's popular, so you may have to wait for a table at weekends. Expect great, reasonably priced Italian food – everything from garlic-laden bruschetta to pasta with freshly made, simply executed sauces – and a well-chosen wine list. The outdoor tables, overlooking the ruins of Grey Abbey, are perfect for sipping a summery glass of pinot grigio.

Village at Lyons ★

Celbridge (01 630 3500, www.villageatlyons.com).
Food served Restaurant noon-3pm, 6-9.30pm Wed-Sat; noon-7pm Sun. Café 11am-5pm Wed-Sun.
The Canal Café provides soups, savoury tarts, pizza, and meat and cheese platters, while La Serre Restaurant is a proper fine-dining affair. Set within a large conservatory, the restaurant creates uncomplicated, tasty Modern European dishes using high-quality, seasonal produce. There's also accommodation for those who want to spend more time exploring the village: two elegant, traditionally designed double rooms in Shackleton House; the one-bedroom Shackleton Apartment; and 14 suites spread across two other properties, with lake and garden views, four-poster beds and en suite bathrooms. A double room costs €180, including breakfast.

Where to stay

County Kildare has plenty of fine places to stay, generally outside the towns, including the Village at Lyons (*see p203*). Martinstown House (The Curragh, 045 441269, www.martinstownhouse. com) is a lovely retreat with murals in pastel shades and antique furniture; the communal dinners are an endearingly informal touch. The county is also well furnished with castles, several of which have been turned into hotels. One of the best is Killashee House Hotel (045 879277, www.killasheehouse.com), just outside Naas. Set in 200 acres of land, it has authentic-feeling old buildings and a tasteful modern extension containing a spa and leisure centre.

Some of Kildare's leading hotels also have world-renowned golf courses, including Palmerstown House (045 906901, www.palmerstownhouse. com), near Naas, and Carton House (015 052000, www.cartonhouse.ie), outside Maynooth. Both are surrounded by lovely grounds that will appeal to non-golfers too.

Barberstown Castle

Straffan (016 288157, www.barberstowncastle.ie).
Rates €230 double incl breakfast.
The keep of Barberstown Castle dates from 1288, to which has been added a series of large whitewashed Edwardian and Victorian buildings. Eric Clapton purchased the hotel in 1979, selling it to the current owners in 1987. They turned what had been a ten-room guesthouse into a 58-room, four-star hotel. Each room is individually decorated (and named after a former owner of the property, all the way back to the first: Nicholas Barby) and the castle's unusual mix of periods is reflected in the interior decor. There are two elegant drawing rooms and a fine-dining restaurant.

K Club

Straffan (016 017200, www.kclub.ie).
Rates €295-€395 double incl breakfast.
The K Club is home to two championship golf courses. Set in formal gardens, the opulent building looks like an 18th-century French château, but was, in fact, built in 1831; it opened as a hotel, after lavish renovations, in 1991. The 69 traditionally styled rooms (including nine suites) are divided between the main house, a newer extension and garden cottages. Original paintings by Jack Yeats adorn the walls (one room is dedicated to the artist's work), and there's also a spa. For dinner, you can choose between the relatively formal Legends Restaurant in the clubhouse and the River Room in the main house, or opt for a more relaxed meal in one of the hotel's three bars.

WICKLOW COAST

Lying south of Dublin, 'the Garden of Ireland' is not a county of manicured lawns and tidy floral beds, but of mountains, lakes, open expanses, cascading waterfalls and forests. The N11/M11 runs the length of the coast from Bray down to Arklow, through fertile farmland and quaint villages and towns, and past Blue Flag beaches and fading promenades.

Starting at the county's northern border, Bray was once a thriving seaside resort. The seafront

is lined with tall Victorian buildings, their façades now somewhat dishevelled and forlorn. Many of the bottom floors have been converted into amusement arcades, bars and cheap restaurants, while the upper floors have been left to decay. An appealing promenade runs the length of the pebbly beach (which is protected from strong winds by Bray Head) and a funfair is set up here in summer. Day-trippers still come to enjoy an ice-cream and a stroll along the front, while a braver minority take on the cool, rocky waters. Visitors who take the steep trek up Bray Head will be rewarded with superb 360-degree views. From the top, a cliff path leads south to Greystones, a walk of roughly two hours (*see p207*).

Bray's main attraction is the National Sea Life Aquarium (012 866939, www.visitsealife.com), which has more than 150 species of fish, as well as crabs and starfish that can be touched. Off the promenade, the new Mermaid Arts Centre (012 724030, www.mermaidartscentre.ie) offers music, theatre, drama and visual art events. The tourist office (Civic Offices, Main Street, 012 867128, www.braytourism.ie, closed Sun) can help with details of the town's two key annual events: the Bray Jazz Festival (www.brayjazz.com), which takes place over the May Day bank holiday, and the multi-purpose Summer Fest, which runs through July and August.

Just south of Bray is Killruddery House & Gardens (*see p200*). The stately home and lovely grounds are open to visitors, and assorted events are held here, from concerts to film festivals.

The old fishing community of Greystones is now a popular sleeper town for Dublin, with quick connections via the DART (Dublin Area Rapid Transport). The high street has some pretty boutiques, gift shops and cafés; standout shops include Toil & Glitter and Juju's for designer clothes, and the Goddess Room for vintage and second-hand fashion. Greystones Theatre (012 871755, www.greystonestheatre.com) has performances all year. There are also the considerable attractions of a Blue Flag beach.

Leave Greystones on the R761 – a bumpy, windy back road – to drive through a number of small towns. Children will enjoy the petting animals and playground at Glenroe Open Farm (012 872288, www.glenroefarm.com, open May-Aug daily; Mar, Apr, Sept, Oct Sat & Sun), located on a side road just before Kilcoole. Nearby, the National Garden Exhibition Centre (012 819890, www.gardenexhibition.ie) has almost two dozen different show-gardens, plus a garden centre where you can buy plants, and a little café. Inland of the M11, the Mount Usher Gardens (*see p201*) in Ashford are a worthwhile diversion.

About 20 kilometres south of Greystones is Wicklow town. It's a typical country town, set around a fine harbour, with the broken remains of a castle perched on a rocky promontory. The Black Castle was built in the second half of the 12th century by the Fitzgerald family, on land granted to them by Strongbow, an Anglo-Norman lord. It didn't last long: in 1301, it was burned down by the O'Byrne and O'Toole clans, mortal enemies of the Fitzgeralds.

K Club. See p203.

From the pier, you can walk south across Dunbur Head to Wicklow Lighthouse (*see p209*), an impressively situated, octagonal tower that dates from the 18th century and is now an intriguing place to stay.

The town's main point of interest is Wicklow's Historic Gaol (*see p201*). Other attractions include the Dominican Farm & Ecology Centre (0404 61833, www.ecocentrewicklow.ie, open Tue, Thur-Sat), part of the Dominican Convent on Kilmantin Hill; and Shuttle Knit (0404 25641, www.shuttleknit.com), a community enterprise in Crinion Park where you can watch a weaver in action – phone to check the best days to visit. Wicklow Tourist Office (Fitzwilliam Square, 0404 69117, closed summer Sun; winter Sat, Sun) can provide maps of local walks, including the Halpin Trail, which leads to buildings and locations around town that are associated with the 19th-century mariner Captain Robert Halpin. Halpin captained Isambard Kingdom Brunel's monstrous ocean-steamer SS *Great Eastern* during its second life laying the first international telegraph cables in the 1860s.

Strung along the R750 coast road are a sequence of pristine, white-sand beaches – a magnet for holidaying Dubliners in summer. Maghermore Beach, around three kilometres south of Wicklow town, has good surfing; further south, Silver Strand Beach, Jack's Hole and Brittas Bay are ideal for swimming. Brittas Bay, also a Blue Flag beach, is particularly stunning, with three kilometres of powdery sand backed by grassy dunes. Vans sell ice-cream and fish and chips; there's also a surf school van in the school holidays. The R750 continues to Arklow, which grew up around the fishing port and has a Maritime Museum (mobile 086 384 3283, www.arklowmaritimemuseum.com, closed Mon, Sun).

Where to eat & drink
Bray is a fish-and-chips kind of place: try one of the chip shops along the seafront or Henry & Rose (Florence Road, 012 829342), across from the train station. Alternatively, on the seafront there's an outpost of the Porterhouse microbrewery chain (012 860668, www.porterhousebrewco.com), which serves good pub grub and has a beer garden.

For a small town, Greystones has a terrific range of food options. The Three Qs (Gweedore Church Road, 012 875477, closed Mon) serves sandwiches, soups and hot dishes for lunch, and a mix of fish and chips and more impressive dishes, such as duck confit or Wicklow game casserole, for dinner; booking advised. Cavistons (Glasthule Road, 012 809120, www.cavistons.com, closed Sun) is a first-class food shop with an appetising display of cheeses and olives for the picnic basket, plus a lovely café for light meals. Towards the harbour on Trafalgar Road, the Summerville café (012 874228) offers good country-style cooking and has a charming garden. Chakra by Jaipur (012 017222, www.jaipur.ie), a branch of a small national chain in the Meridian

shopping centre, serves the best (albeit pricey) Indian food for miles. For drinks, the Burnaby (012 874015) on the main street and the Beach House (aka Dan's, 012 874623) on the seafront are always packed with locals; Dan's hosts gigs at the weekends.

For lunch in Wicklow town, try Halpin's Bridge Cafe (Bridge Street, 040 432677, www.halpins cafe.com) or the Mezzanine Cafe (Abbey Street, 040 467521, closed Sun).

Happy Pear ★
Church Road, Greystones (012 873655, www.the happypear.ie). Open Café 9am-6pm Mon-Sat; 10.30am-6pm Sun. Food market 9am-6pm Mon-Sat.
With its bright orange exterior, wooden tables out front, stalls of fresh vegetables, and smiling young staff in shorts and flip-flops, this is a place that's as fun as it is passionate about food. Owners Steven and David started off with an organic food market, but expanded into an all-encompassing organic food centre to meet demand. Buy some veg, grab a smoothie (to take away or drink in – there's also a seating area upstairs) or enjoy a daily changing menu of delicious own-made salads, vegetarian hot dishes, soups and gluten-free breads. The Happy Pear's funky reputation ensures that the place is always packed.

Hungry Monk
Church Road, Greystones (restaurant 012 875759, wine bar 012 010710, www.thehungrymonk.ie). Restaurant Lunch served 12.30-7pm Sun. Dinner served 5.30-11pm Thur-Sat. Wine bar Open/food served 5-11pm Mon-Sat; 12.30-9pm Sun.
This family-run restaurant has been a local favourite for years. Candlelit tables, red velvet curtains and bottles of wine lining the walls create a welcoming and intimate venue. In winter, the menu offers wholesome dishes focused on local game, as well as the likes of honey-roasted pork belly. Summer brings lighter dishes, including plenty of fish – perhaps Kilmore Quay scallops or dover sole. Vegetables come from a local farm and the meat (such as the wild venison) from elsewhere in County Wicklow. The relaxed bar also serves food, and there's another comfortable dining area downstairs.

Where to stay
While Bray has a number of B&Bs, Greystones lacks accommodation for visitors; those who wish to stay nearby could try the modern and spacious Marriott Druids Glen Resort (012 870800, www.druidsglenresort.com), which has a golf course and spa. More atmospheric is Tinakilly House (040 469724, www.tinakilly.ie), a handsome Victorian mansion built by Captain Robert Halpin, set in beautiful grounds and with a fine restaurant; it's located in Rathnew, a few kilometres inland from Wicklow town. Captain Halpin's Bunkhouse (Bachelor's Walk, 040 469126, www.wicklow townhostel.ie) is a new hostel on the riverfront in the middle of Wicklow town.

For campers and caravanners, there's River Valley Caravan Park (040 441647, www.river valleypark.com, open Mar-Oct) at Redcross village, near Brittas Beach.

Things to do

Sally Gap

COUNTY KILDARE

Horse racing

Those who enjoy the sound of pounding hooves on turf and the roar of a cheering crowd are especially well catered for in County Kildare, which hosts some of the best annual race meets in Ireland. Highlights are the Irish Derby, which takes place on the last weekend of June at the Curragh Racecourse (045 441205, www.curragh.ie) and the Punchestown Irish National Hunt Festival (045 897704, www.punchestown.com), held usually in the last week of April. For other key events on Ireland's racing calendar, *see p210*.

Royal & Grand Canals

The Royal and Grand Canals were opened in the early 19th century for the commercial transport of goods and passengers between Dublin's River Liffey and the River Shannon. The passenger services were discontinued by the 1850s and, although freight was still carried for another century, the canals were commercially defunct by 1960. Today, however, they are being reborn as part of the tourist industry, with towpaths providing peaceful walks – some over short stretches, others continuing for up to 28km. Information, maps and guided history leaflets can be downloaded from www.kildare.ie/tourism/waterways/grand-canal.asp.

Daytime boat trips or the weekly rental of narrowboats is possible on both canals; visit the website of the Inland Waterways Association of Ireland (www.iwai.ie) for details. The IWAI is a great source of information on all activities relating to the canals.

WICKLOW COAST

Bray to Greystones Cliff Walk

www.visitwicklow.ie/attractions/bray-greystones-cliff-walk.htm.
Start either at the southern end of Bray promenade or from Greystones harbour. The 8km walk takes approximately two hours, but is relatively flat, with only a few steep sections; nonetheless, you should carry refreshments and wear solid walking shoes. The path hugs the cliff edge, somewhat precariously, above the train track that runs between the two towns, with the rocky ledges below providing a home for thousands of seabirds, which squeal loudly as the waves pound the beaches below. The lack of crowds and uninterrupted views across the Irish Sea make this a lovely peaceful excursion, with Bray Head one of many terrific picnic spots. If you're lucky, you might glimpse dolphins playing down below.

INLAND WICKLOW

Great Sugar Loaf

Between Killough & Kilmacanogue.
The Great Sugar Loaf is the volcano-like mountain that dominates the skyline as you drive south from Dublin. The 501m-high peak itself is not well signposted. If you're approaching on the N11 from Kilmacanogue, follow the road until you reach a quarry on your left. Take the next left turn, and continue until you see a car park on your left. The initial part of the walk is through boggy land, so it can be messy when wet, and the peak itself is rocky and quite steep. But the rigours of the short climb are redeemed immediately by the views at the top, a spectacular panorama stretching all the way north to Dublin and south across Wicklow. There's useful route information on http://mountainviews.ie/summit/455/.

Wicklow Way

www.wicklowway.com.
Inland Wicklow is marvellous walking territory, and the Wicklow Way – the first waymarked trail established in Ireland – is one of the county's most scenic routes. It's traditionally walked from north to south, starting in Marlay Park in south Dublin and ending in Clonegal, just over the border in County Carlow. It goes through the desolate bogs of the Sally Gap, descends into the glacial valley at Glendalough, and passes through the mountains of Wicklow. Although a mighty 127km in total, it can be tackled in sections – suggested divisions are indicated on the website.

Powerscourt House & Gardens. See p201.

Ballyknocken House

Glenealy, Ashford (040 444627, www.ballyknocken.com). Rates €118 double incl breakfast.
This Victorian farmhouse located on 350 acres of farmland is owned and run by television chef Catherine Fulvio. It's primarily a cookery school, but also a guesthouse, with seven handsome bedrooms available for B&B; dinner is also served at weekends. Food is a definite highlight – with ingredients fresh from the farm – but there is also some great hiking in the surrounding country, and walking holidays can be arranged.

Hunter's Hotel

Newrath Bridge, Rathnew (040 440106, www.hunters.ie). Rates €130-€180 double incl breakfast.
Hunter's is not only Ireland's oldest coaching inn, dating from the early 1700s, but has been run by the Gelletlie family since 1820. The building oozes charm: step outside and you almost have to stop yourself trying to summon a horse and trap. The 16 small bedrooms have views over the beautiful rear gardens; on a cold night, a hot water bottle awaits you, and some rooms also have open fires. There's a modest-sized bar area with an open fire and lounge chairs, and a dining room, where guests can have evening meals (joined by locals for lunch at the weekends). All the food is own-made, with some produce coming from the hotel gardens. Hunter's isn't the height of luxury, but for pure, idiosyncratic atmosphere it's hard to beat – that previous guests range from the king and queen of Sweden to novelist Maeve Binchy and actor Daniel Day-Lewis is testament to the place's appeal.

Wicklow Lighthouse ★

Wicklow Head, nr Wicklow town (016 704733, www.irishlandmark.com). Rates €1,260-€1,400 per week.
For a room with a view, you can't do better than this former lighthouse, perched on the Wicklow coast with the sea on three sides. Built in the 1780s, it's now owned and managed by the Irish Landmark Trust, which converts historic buildings into self-catering holiday accommodation. The 29m-high octagonal tower contains two double bedrooms, a bathroom and a small kitchen – note that the latter is at the top of the building, requiring a climb of 109 steps.

INLAND WICKLOW

Enniskerry to Rathdrum

Starting just outside the suburbs of Dublin, the long-distance Wicklow Way (*see p207*) traces the peaks, valleys and forests of the Wicklow Mountains. Part of the mountain range, which runs north–south through County Wicklow and into County Wexford, has been designated a National Park. It's the perfect setting for outdoor activities such as kayaking, mountain biking and hiking.

Just inland of Bray, Enniskerry ★ is at the northern end of the range, less than ten kilometres south of Dublin. It's one of Wicklow's most appealing villages, with multicoloured buildings along the main street that house attractive cafés, gift shops and galleries. Enniskerry Gallery is one lovely find, a jungle of antique jewellery, books and other desirables. Although small, Enniskerry has a decent array of accommodation, so it's a

good base from which to explore inland Wicklow. For walkers, Hilltoptreks (mobile 087 784 9599, www.hilltoptreks.ie) has a 10.20am daily pick-up outside the Powerscourt Arms for guided day walks in the region.

Don't miss Powerscourt House & Gardens (*see p201*), just outside the village, with its magnificent landscaped gardens and acres of lawn, plus the added attraction of Powerscourt Falls.

When leaving Enniskerry, you can take one of two routes. Heading south, the R760 joins the R755 – a narrow road that twists through forested mountains – at Killough. At this point, you can head east towards Kilmacanogue to reach the Great Sugar Loaf (*see p207*) or continue south towards Roundwood, a pretty town on the shores of the Vartry Reservoir. En route to Roundwood is the Ballinastoe Mountain Bike Trail (www.coillte outdoors.ie), 13 kilometres of forest riding for mountain bikers. For something more sedate, the Ballinastoe Golf Club (012 818480, www. ballinastoegolfclub.com) is directly across from the forest, with spectacular valley views. Roundwood – the highest village in Ireland, according to the village sign – has a couple of acceptable eateries. It's a popular base for walkers, with excellent trekking around the reservoir and in the surrounding mountains.

The alternative route out of Enniskerry – and perhaps the more spectacular drive – is to head west until you can turn south on the R115. You'll find yourself in a vast area of blanket bog, threading through one of the passes across the Wicklow Mountains. The tiny village of Glencree is the first and last settlement on the road. It contains a German graveyard for those who lost their lives in World War II, when Ireland maintained its neutrality, and also the Glencree Reconciliation Centre (012 829711, www.glencree.ie), established to help bring together the two sides of the Troubles in Northern Ireland. The centre has exhibitions telling the history of the conflict, and a café.

The wild, desolate and starkly beautiful countryside surrounding the Sally Gap (at the junction with the R759) has, unsurprisingly, been the setting for many movies, including *Braveheart*. If you head south-east on the R759 – skirting pretty, glistening Lough Tay, with Lough Dan in the distance – the road then joins the R755, running past the Vartry Reservoir and into Roundwood. Alternatively, if you stay on the R115, the scenery changes dramatically as you descend into a lush, forested glacial valley – this is where you'll find one of Ireland's most important monastic sites: Glendalough (*see p201*).

This area is part of Wicklow Mountains National Park and there are fabulous walks in the vicinity. The National Park Information Centre (040 445800, www.wicklowmountainsnationalpark.ie, closed Mon-Fri Oct-Easter) in Glendalough is the best place to pick up information on local walking trails.

More of a crossroads than a village, Laragh has a healthy number of B&Bs, a couple of restaurants and a hotel. A few kilometres away is an outdoor adventure centre for children: Clara

BEST HORSE RACING EVENTS

Five Irish Classics
Curragh Racecourse, Curragh,
Co Kildare (045 441205,
www.curragh.ie).
The five flat-racing Classics are held
over the course of the year at the world-
famous Curragh Racecourse: the Irish
Derby, the Irish Oaks, the Irish 1,000
Guineas, the Irish 2,000 Guineas and
the St Leger. The Irish Derby is the
most popular, with a busy fixture list,
plenty of entertainment and a boisterous
atmosphere. Ireland's equivalent of
the Epsom Derby, it takes place three
weeks after the English event, usually
in late June or July.

Irish Grand National
Fairyhouse Racecourse, Ratoath,
Co Meath (01 825 6167,
www.fairyhouse.ie).
The first Grand National to be held in
Ireland was in 1870 at the Fairyhouse
Racecourse; it's been run here every
year since (except for breaks in 1919
and 1941 due to World War I and II).
An array of steeplechase races are
held over the Easter weekend, with
the Grand National as the main fixture.
Like the English Grand National, it's a
great weekend for horse-racing novices
as well as die-hard fans.

Leopardstown Christmas Festival
Leopardstown Racecourse,
Leopardstown, Dublin (01 289
0500, www.leopardstown.com).
Kicking off on St Stephen's Day
(Boxing Day), the four-day Leopardstown
Christmas Festival has long been a
popular social event. Punters come to
see some of Ireland's best National
Hunt racing and to continue the
Christmas cheer.

Lara (040 446161, www.claralara.com, open
June-Aug daily; May Sat, Sun). Kids might also
enjoy the Trout Fishery (040 445470, closed
Oct-Mar Wed) in the nearby village of Annamoe.

A 15-minute drive south of Laragh is the quiet
town of Rathdrum, best known for its association
with Charles Stewart Parnell. Avondale House
(040 446111, closed Nov-Easter; May, Sept Mon),
just outside the town, is where Ireland's greatest
political leader and key advocate of Home Rule
grew up. In addition to tours of the house, there are
splendid self-guided walks (from 30 minutes to five
hours) through 500 acres of woodland, and a café.

Slightly further south, the Avonmore and Avonbeg
rivers converge at a delicious spot that inspired
the Irish Romantic songwriter and poet Thomas
Moore to compose 'The Meeting of the Waters'.
The Meetings Pub (040 235226, www.the
meetingsavoca.com) by the bridge overlooks the
lush greenery of the banks. This gorgeous part
of Wicklow, known as the Vale of Avoca, contains
several delightful towns, including Woodenbridge
and Macreddin, but the most famous is Avoca ★
itself, next to the river of the same name. It was
the setting for the popular TV series *Ballykissangel*,
and many visitors come in search of the
Ballykissangel street – a small tourist information
point in the local library can direct you.

On the outskirts of the village is an 18th-century
mill, where Avoca Handweavers set up as a farmers'
co-operative in 1723. It still produces hand-woven
goods, following Avoca's rebirth in the 1970s and
transformation into the very successful national
chain of today, encompassing woollen goods,
clothing, homewares and cafés. The whitewashed
mill cottages house an Avoca shop and café.

West to Blessington
It's also worth driving further inland from Laragh,
along the R756. It's just over 30 kilometres,
past the large Pollaphuca Reservoir, to Blessington,
a useful place to pick up supplies and a thriving
hub for outdoor activities of all sorts. Many such
activities, including rock climbing, orienteering
and fishing, and on-site accommodation, are
offered at Avon Ri resort (Burgage, 045 900670,
www.avonri.com). Active breaks and walking
holidays, again with accommodation, can be
arranged at Kippure Estate (014 582889,
www.kippure.com), a few kilometres east of
Blessington. A more cultural attraction is
Russborough House (*see p201*), a large Palladian
mansion designed by Richard Cassells, who
was also the architect of Powerscourt House.

Where to eat & drink
Enniskerry has plenty of places to eat and drink.
Poppies (012 828869, www.poppies.ie) has
been producing wholesome, rustic cooking
since 1982 – it's the best lunch venue in town.
Kennedy's (www.kennedysofenniskerry.com) is
a superior deli with baked goods, bagels, salads
and hot drinks, while Chez Cocobelle (Church Hill)
serves panini, salads and heartier meals such

as fish and chips, chicken pie and full Irish breakfasts. Next door, Nancy Murphy's Bar (012 868333) offers proper bar food and hosts gigs at the weekends. The Powerscourt Arms (012 828903, www.powerscourtarmscountry house.com) is more traditional, and has recently opened an evening bistro to supplement its longstanding all-day lunch menu.

Roundwood has several atmospheric bars, including the Coach House (012 818157, www.thecoachhouse.ie) and the Roundwood Inn (mobile 087 686 0976), which serves bar food and, in its restaurant, modern Irish cuisine.

There's a wonderful old-world bar in Laragh, Lynham's Hotel (040 445345, www.lynhams oflaragh.ie), which has been open since 1776. It also has 12 bedrooms, hires out bikes and prepares packed lunches for walkers.

Further south, in Rathdrum, is the well-regarded Bates Restaurant (Market Square, 040 429988, www.batesrestaurant.ie), specialising in nicely priced Italian food. The several eating options at BrookLodge (*see p212*) draw gourmets to the little village of Macreddin. For a nice pint in Avoca, try Fitzgerald's Bar (Main Street, 040 235108) – frequently the scene for scandal in *Ballykissangel*.

In Blessington, the excellent Grangecon Café (Kilbride Road, 045 8578920, closed Sun) cooks everything on the premises.

Byrne & Woods Restaurant

Roundwood (012 817078). Lunch served 1-3.30pm Tue-Sun (May-Sept 1-3.30pm Sun). Dinner served 6-10pm Tue-Fri; 5.30-10pm Sat; 6-9.30pm Sun.
Owned by Marino Monterisi of Rathdrum's Bates Restaurant, Byrne & Woods is a newcomer to Roundwood. Decked out with dark wood, stoutly upholstered chairs and stacks of wine bottles, it follows Bates in using local, seasonal produce in Italian-influenced dishes. Starters such as ricotta and spinach ravioli are joined by Kiltrea smoked trout and Wexford beef salad, while mains range from risotto to Tipperary pork belly and plenty of fish dishes. There are reasonably priced menu deals and excellent vegetarian options. The restaurant is vibrant at weekends, with a bar perfectly situated next door for ending the night.

Conservatory Tearooms & Restaurant

The Old Schoolhouse, Laragh (040 445302). Open 10am-6pm Thur-Sun.
Lisa de la Haye has tastefully renovated this stone building, the former schoolhouse, at the edge of Laragh village. The restaurant occupies a bright and airy conservatory, while the country-style kitchen has a communal table for those who wish to dine near the heart of the culinary action. There's a short list of starters and main courses – all own-made, of course – and a delectable selection of desserts; at teatime, treat yourself to scones, cakes and homemade jams and breads. The bits and bobs scattered about – pretty cups and saucers, cake stands and so on – are available to purchase. A charming spot.

Fern House Café

Avoca Handweavers, Kilmacanogue (012 746990, www.avoca.ie). Food served 9.30am-4.30pm Mon-Sat; 9.30am-5pm Sun. Dinner served 5.30-9.30pm Thur-Sat.

Punchestown Irish National Hunt Festival

Punchestown Racecourse, Naas, Co Kildare (045 897704, www.punchestown.com).
The jump season ends with a bang at Punchestown's Irish National Hunt Festival, held over five days in late April/early May, with the highlight being the Gold Cup Day. Ladies sport their finery, and crowds descend from Dublin and throughout the country to take part in the jollities.

Summer Festival Race Meeting

Galway Racecourse, Ballybrit, Co Galway (091 753870, www.galwayraces.com).
Galway City's week-long Summer Festival Race Meeting starts on the last Monday in July. Thousands turn up, dressed to the nines, to join in the revelries and have a flutter. Galway's pubs are packed before and after the races, and the atmosphere is electric in the city throughout the week.

Ulster Derby Race Day

Down Royal Racecourse, Maze, Lisburn, Co Down (028 9262 1256, www.downroyal.com).
The Down Royal is Northern Ireland's most famous and prestigious racecourse, with a history stretching back to the 17th century. The most popular meet is the Ulster Derby Race Day in mid June, which combines the glitz and glamour of Ladies Day with some high-class thoroughbred action.

Avoca seems to have outposts all over Ireland – largely because they do what they do so well – but nowhere is better than this site, off the N11 at Kilmacanogue. It's the company headquarters, and there's also a foodhall, a shop, a garden nursery and two cafés – the self-service Sugar Tree and the table-service Fern House. The latter is set in a conservatory decked out with ferns and miniature orange trees; outside is a paved terrace. Dishes are fresh and own-made, as in the standard Avoca cafés, but more sophisticated: starters include sea trout gravadlax and Italian-style antipasti platters, while mains run from a house bouillabaisse of salmon, sea bass, mussels and clams to Moroccan mezze.

Where to stay

Reasonably priced and comfortable B&Bs are plentiful, though it's advisable to book in summer. Check www.wicklow-bnb.com for detailed listings.

In Enniskerry, the Powerscourt Arms (*see p211*) offers the most affordable overnight stay in town, with 12 B&B rooms. At the very top end of the scale for luxury and price, the Ritz-Carlton Powerscourt (012 748888, www.ritzcarlton.com/en/properties/powerscourt), in the grounds of Powerscourt House, has a spa, a Gordon Ramsay restaurant and incredible views over Wicklow. A more affordable option is Summer Hill House Hotel (012 867928, www.summerhillhouse hotel.com), just at the edge of Enniskerry.

Further south, the Glendaloch International hostel (040 445342, www.anoige.ie/directory/wicklow) is right at the edge of the Glendalough monastic site, while the Wicklow Way Hostel (mobile 087 092 0612, www.thewicklowwayhostel.ie) is next to Lynham's Hotel (*see p211*) in Laragh.

There are plenty of self-catering options on the lakeside near Blessington. The best luxury option is Tulfarris House Hotel (045 867600, www.tulfarrishotel.com, closed Nov-Mar Mon-Thur, Sun), with adjoining championship golf course.

BrookLodge

Macreddin (040 236444, www.brooklodge.com).
Rates €110-€250 double incl breakfast.
While hardly a secret, BrookLodge and blossoming Macreddin village are a delight. The original country house stands serene in its robe of ivy, and a stream runs through the well-kept grounds. A cluster of separate buildings house restaurants, a bar and the Wells Spa. There are 90 bedrooms in all, from standard rooms to expansive suites. The three brothers responsible for BrookLodge are passionate about organic food, and this is a destination for foodies: fine-dining restaurant the Strawberry Tree is one of the best in Wicklow, while at La Taverna Armento – a more recent addition – southern Italian dishes are created with organic ingredients sourced from Armento in Italy. Actons Pub, set away from the hotel, serves stout from its own microbrewery and hosts traditional music sessions at weekends. There's something for everyone here.

Rathsallagh House ★

Dunlavin (045 403112, www.rathsallagh.com).
Rates €190-€220 double incl breakfast.
The approach along the tree-lined driveway to this lovely-looking hotel will relax you into a country pace of life. The

low-slung building originally housed stables (clearly, a grand affair during Queen Anne's reign) and was converted into a formal residence when the first manor house was destroyed during the 1798 rebellion. The drawing rooms, library and reading rooms are warmed by open fires, and the old-fashioned bar hosts evening music sessions. The 29 rooms are split between the rambling main house and the courtyard, and vary in size. There is also a fine restaurant and, in the 530 acres of surrounding park, a golf course and walled garden. Dunlavin is on the western edge of County Wicklow, about 18km south-west of Blessington.

Glendalough. See p201.

Dublin

Dublin is a city that everyone raves about. Displaced locals get all misty-eyed about the pubs, the craic and the friendly people they left behind; recently returned visitors wax lyrical about everything from the architecture to the seafood; tourist brochures conjure visions of a Celtic utopia where historic, cobbled streets always lead to a pint of Guinness and a traditional sing-song, and where charming shops and first-class restaurants are to be found on every corner. But, while much of that is true, don't be surprised if you still find yourself feeling a little disappointed by what you find. The fact of the matter is that nowhere, not even the mythical 'fair city' of Ireland, can live up to that much hype. Dublin is no theme park to 'oirishness', nor is it some quaint provincial backwater where every second person is bubbling over with blarney and bonhomie. It is a modern, hard-working centre of commerce and industry; it is a cultural capital, reflected in its new status as a UNESCO City of Literature; and it is home to some of Europe's most accomplished artists and academics. It is a city that deserves to be taken seriously. And, for those who do, it is a richly rewarding, fascinating place.

Dublin is surprisingly diminutive in scale. The centre comprises just a few manageably sized neighbourhoods, bisected by the River Liffey, and you'll find that it's no distance at all from the top of O'Connell Street, north of the river, to the peaceful Grand Canal, on the south side. By far the best way to explore the place is on foot. Despite its compact layout, Dublin manages to pack in a good deal of variety. There are historic buildings by the dozen, plenty of green spaces and quiet squares, and enough shops, bars and restaurants to gobble up your holiday allowance ten times over. The city has a strong sense of its past (it seems that every few steps brings you to another statue or heritage plaque); and yet, an equal portion of its landscape has been consigned to the future, with a crop of modern structures (mainly north of the river) contending with the Georgian terraces and ancient bell towers.

TEMPLE BAR & THE OLD CITY

South of the Liffey, the maze of cobbled streets that forms the Temple Bar quarter is the dynamo at the heart of Dublin; it's always at the frontline of new developments, be they architectural, cultural, touristic or simply part of the tireless evolution of new music venues, hotels, drinking dens and clubs. Meeting House Square is the heart of the area's cultural entertainment programme. Open-air film screenings – mainly of old classics – alternate with concerts, puppet shows, circus performers and dance events during the summer. Throughout the year, the Square is also home to a hugely popular Saturday food market and a Sunday craft and furniture market. Also here is the Gallery of Photography (671 4654, www.irish-photography. com, closed Mon), which has a permanent collection of modern Irish photography, regular

Guinness Storehouse. See p216.

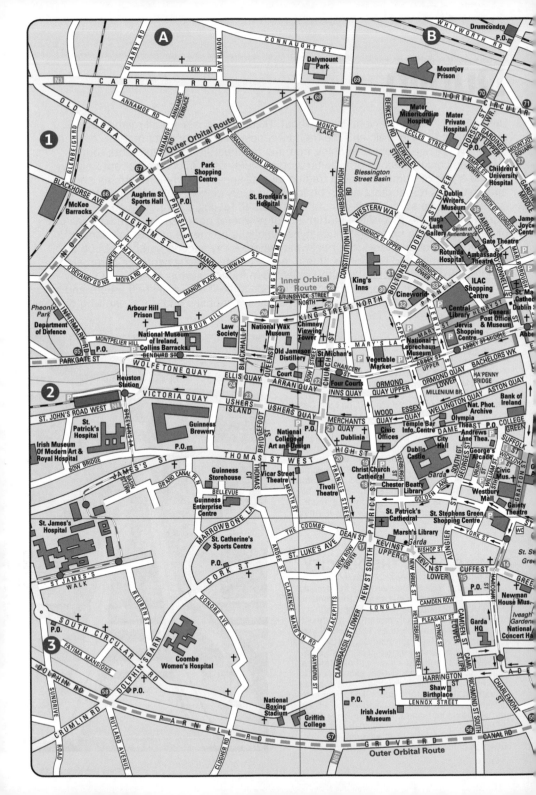

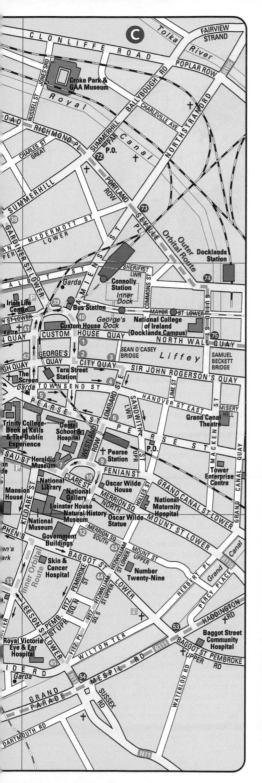

exhibitions of contemporary local work and touring shows, and the red-brick, zinc-punctuated National Photographic Archive, full of excellent, often poignant photographic records of Irish life.

Around the corner, on Temple Bar itself, the Original Print Gallery (no.4, 677 3657, www.originalprint.ie) and Temple Bar Gallery & Studios (nos.5-9, 671 0073, www.templebargallery.com, closed Mon, Sun) stand side by side. The Original Print specialises in limited-edition prints, and these increasingly come from the Black Church Print Studios upstairs, making this something of a success story for an area that has a designated role in the promotion of culture. The Temple Bar Gallery shows work that is innovative and – if not always appealing – usually local.

The small second-hand book fair on Temple Bar Square (held every weekend) is also worth a visit: you won't find rare manuscripts or first editions, but if you're looking for vintage paperback editions of favourite classics, your chances of a hit are high. Here too, on Sundays from 2pm to 6pm, is Speaker's Square. This is an opportunity for anyone with a grievance, grudge or passion to get it off their chest. All are welcome, and, as with London's Hyde Park equivalent, the ranting can be top-class. Just around the corner, on Eustace Street, is the Irish Film Institute (IFI, 6 Eustace Street, 679 5744, www.irishfilm.ie), which shows foreign and arthouse movies. Nearby, the Button Factory (see p228) is one of Dublin's hottest music venues.

Head west along East Essex Street to discover the Project Arts Centre (881 9613, www.project artscentre.ie, closed Sun), a venue for all manner of events, from art exhibitions to music, dance and theatre productions. On the other side of Parliament Street are a series of narrow lanes that have

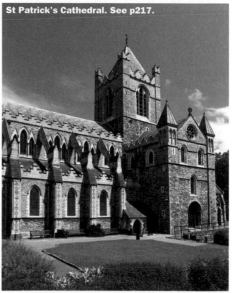

St Patrick's Cathedral. See p217.

Places to visit

TEMPLE BAR & THE OLD CITY

Chester Beatty Library ★

*Clock Tower Building, Dublin Castle, Dame Street
(407 0750, www.cbl.ie). Open May-Sept 10am-5pm
Mon-Fri; 11am-5pm Sat; 1-5pm Sun. Oct-Apr 10am-
5pm Tue-Fri; 11am-5pm Sat; 1-5pm Sun. Guided
tours 1pm Wed; 3pm, 4pm Sun. Admission free;
donations welcome.*

Many of the finest works from Sir Alfred Chester
Beatty's priceless art collection are housed in this
purpose-built museum in Dublin Castle. An Irish-
American mining magnate with a passion for the
East, Chester Beatty settled here in the 1950s and
bequeathed his life's collection to the Irish people
in 1969. Manuscripts, icons, miniature paintings,
early prints and objets d'art from Europe and the
Far East take you through the differing traditions of
belief and learning in the Western, Islamic and East
Asian worlds. Upstairs is a Zen roof garden, while
on the ground floor is the Silk Road café.

Christ Church Cathedral

*Christ Church Place (677 8099, www.cccdub.ie).
Open June-Aug 9.30am-7pm Mon-Sat; 12.30-2.30pm,
4.30-7pm Sun. Apr, May, Sept, Oct 9.30am-6pm
Mon-Sat; 12.30-2.30pm Sun. Nov-Mar 9.30am-5pm
Mon-Sat; 12.30-2.30pm Sun. Admission €6; €4
reductions; €14 family.*

Dubliners chiefly know Christ Church as a place to
hear the bells ring out on New Year's Eve and for the
beautiful choral evensongs (Wednesday and Thursday
at 6pm, Saturday at 5pm and Sunday at 3.30pm).
The building dates from the 1180s and, with its
many subsequent restorations (including some over-
enthusiastic Victorian work), is handsome rather than
spectacular. Look for the heart-shaped iron box said
to contain the heart of St Laurence O'Toole, and for
the mummified rat and cat – supposedly found in an
organ pipe and displayed mid-chase.

Dublin Castle

*Dame Street (677 7129, www.dublincastle.ie).
Open (guided tour only) 10am-4.45pm Mon-Sat; noon-
4.45pm Sun. Admission €4.50; €2-€3.50 reductions.*

Formerly the seat of British power in Ireland, and
efficiently infiltrated by spies during the Michael
Collins era, this isn't really a castle – no moat, no
drawbridge, no turrets – more a collection of 18th-
century administrative buildings, albeit very fine
ones, built on a medieval plan of two courtyards.
A figure of Justice stands over the main entrance,
dating from the time of British rule, and is something
of a sardonic joke – she stands with her back to the
city, wears no blindfold and her scales tilt when filled
with water. These days the Castle provides a venue
for grand state functions and the occasional concert
recital. The interior, including the beautiful State
Rooms, is operated on a pay-per-view basis, but
you can wander freely around the exterior.

Dublinia

*Christ Church, St Michael's Hill (679 4611,
www.dublinia.ie). Open Apr-Sept 10am-5.45pm
daily. Oct-Mar 11am-4.30pm daily. Admission
€7.50; €5-€6.50 reductions; €23 family.*

Chester Beatty Library

The crudely interactive features of this exhibition on
the world of medieval Dublin seem to date from a
pre-digital age, but overall this exhibition is the best
of its kind in the city. A scale model of medieval Dublin
helps place the two cathedrals in their geographical
context, while a reconstructed archaeological dig is
probably most interesting for the newspaper clippings
that accompany it – they chart the history of the noble
but doomed protest to save the site of one of Viking
Europe's most significant settlements at Wood Quay
from destruction at the hands of Dublin Corporation.
St Michael's Tower, although no match for the Gravity
Bar in the Guinness Storehouse (*see below*), provides
a fine view of the heart of old Dublin.

Guinness Storehouse ★

*St James's Gate (408 4800, www.guinness-
storehouse.com). Open July, Aug 9.30am-7pm
daily. Sept-June 9.30am-5pm daily. Admission
€15; €9-€11 reductions; €34 family; free under-6s.*

It may no longer be part of the active brewery, but
this 'visitor experience', housed in a six-storey listed
building dating from 1904, has become the popular
public face of what is undoubtedly Ireland's most
recognisable brand. The building is designed around
a pint glass-shaped atrium and incorporates an
exhibition space, function rooms, a restaurant and
two bars. Much of the vast floor space is taken up
with presentations on the history and making of the
humble pint, which, although self-congratulatory in
tone, are magnificently realised. Most entertaining,
perhaps, is the advertising section – a testament
to the company's famously imaginative marketing.
The Storehouse tour includes a complimentary pint
of the best Guinness you are likely to taste, and

there's nowhere better to drink it than in the Gravity Bar, located at the very top of the building with a 360° view over Dublin.

Irish Museum of Modern Art ★
Royal Hospital, Military Road (612 9900, www.imma. ie). Open 10am-5.30pm Tue, Thur-Sat; 10.30am-5.30pm Wed; noon-5.30pm Sun. Admission free.
One of the most important 17th-century buildings in Ireland, the Royal Hospital was designed by Sir William Robinson in 1684 to serve as a nursing home for retired soldiers. Famously, he modelled it on Les Invalides in Paris. In 1991, the place was reopened as a modern art museum, with superb exhibition spaces distributed around a peaceful square. The displays are usually temporary shows, combined with a selection from the small permanent collection. On the ground floor, the Heritage section provides some fascinating and (in the case of the Gallipoli accounts) occasionally horrifying background on the Royal Hospital and the pensioners who lived there. The grounds include a beautifully restored baroque formal garden.

Kilmainham Gaol
Inchicore Road (453 5984, www.heritageireland.ie). Open (guided tour only) Apr-Sept 9.30am-5pm daily. Oct-Mar 9.30am-4pm Mon-Sat; 10am-5pm Sun. Admission €6; €2-€4 reductions; €14 family.
Although it ceased to be used as a prison in 1924, this remains the best-known Irish lock-up and one of the most fascinating buildings in the country. It was here that the leaders of the 1916 Easter Rising, along with many others, were executed. If you harbour an interest in the 1916 Rising or, indeed, any previous rebellions in Ireland from the 18th century onwards, you'll find Kilmainham Gaol a lot more informative and evocative than the National Museum. The multimedia displays documenting the atrocious prison conditions are grimly informative, but it is the lively guided tours that steal the show. Groups are led through the dank corridors, past bleak cells and into the atmospheric main hall (where some of the opening scenes of the original *Italian Job* were filmed). The sites of various executions, vigils, injustices and condemnations are conjured to vivid life, leaving you with a curious conflict of guilt and relief as you walk back out through the gates and into the free world.

St Patrick's Cathedral
St Patrick's Close (453 9472, www.stpatricks cathedral.ie). Open Mar-Oct 9am-5pm Mon-Fri; 9am-6pm Sat; 9-10.30am, 12.30-2.30pm, 4.30-6pm Sun. Nov-Feb 9am-5pm Mon-Sat; 9-10.30am, 12.30-2.30pm Sun. Admission €5.50; €4.50 reductions; €15 family.
This, the largest church in Ireland, dates from the 13th century, but was founded on a far older religious site associated with St Patrick and dating from the fifth century. As a memorial to Anglo-Irish life in Ireland, it tells a more interesting tale than Christ Church (*see left*), and its many plaques and monuments commemorate various celebrated figures of the Anglican Ascendancy. That said, St Patrick's remains most famous for its association with the celebrated writer and satirist Jonathan Swift. Most of his best-known works were written while he was dean here from 1713 to 1745. Swift's savage criticisms of the cronyism and ineptitude that marked England's colonial administration of its largest island neighbour were powerful enough to bring down governments.

TRINITY COLLEGE & ST STEPHEN'S GREEN

Book of Kells & Old Library
Trinity College (896 1000, www.tcd.ie/library). Open May-Sept 9.30am-5pm Mon-Sat; 9.30am-4.30pm Sun. Oct-Apr 9.30am-5pm Mon-Sat; noon-4.30pm Sun. Admission €9; €8 reductions; €18 family; free under-12s.
'Kelly's Book', as it still gets called occasionally, is Trinity's most famous artefact, but it suffers slightly from *Mona Lisa* syndrome: it's so endlessly reproduced that it seems underwhelming in real life. The book, designed around the ninth century, is an illuminated copy of the Gospels in Latin, lovingly created by early Christian monks; at any one time, four pages are on display – two illustrated and two text – inside a bullet-proof glass case. Alongside is the Book of Durrow, an even earlier illuminated manuscript of the Gospels, made in about 675. There's also a multimedia exhibition to take you through the process of creating such texts – for die-hard bibliophiles only – but most people just come to gawp at the texts. Each summer, around 3,000 people a day troop through the Old Library, designed by Thomas Burgh and built between 1712 and 1732. The Long Room, a vaulted, echoing, dimly lit expanse, is the city's most beautiful room: a perfect panelled chamber with rows of double-facing shelves holding about 200,000 old volumes, accessed by antique ladders and guarded by busts of literary giants (and, of course, by actual security guards).

National Gallery of Ireland
Merrion Square West (661 5133, www.national gallery.ie). Open 9.30am-5.30pm Mon-Wed, Fri, Sat; 9.30am-8.30pm Thur; noon-5.30pm Sun. Admission free; donations welcome.
This gallery houses a small but fine collection of European works from the 14th to the 20th centuries, including paintings by Caravaggio, Tintoretto, Titian, Monet, Degas, Goya, Vermeer and Picasso. A room is also devoted to painter Jack B Yeats, who developed an impressionistic style particularly suited to the Irish landscape. The smaller British collection is also impressive, with works by Hogarth, Landseer and Gainsborough; every January an exhibition of Turner's watercolours draws art lovers from all over the world. Giovanni Lanfranco's magnificent *Last Supper* is a sight worth goggling at, as many do on a daily basis. The gallery's fabulous Millennium Wing has also been a big draw since its opening.

National Museum of Ireland – Archaeology
Kildare Street (677 7444, www.museum.ie). Open 10am-5pm Tue-Sat; 2-5pm Sun. Admission free. Tours €2.
The National Museum is deservedly one of Dublin's most popular attractions. The 19th-century building designed by Thomas Newenham Deane is squeezed into a site to the side of the impassive façade of

▶

Spectacle Parade Opticians

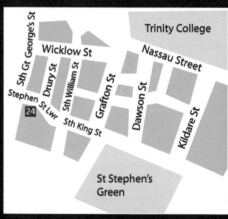

Places to visit

Leinster House (seat of the Irish Parliament). Its domed entrance hall, or Rotunda, looks like a Victorian reworking of the Pantheon, with windows on the upper gallery that jut inwards, so that the space appears to cave in towards the spectator. The most striking exhibition among its many excellent pieces is Ór, a collection of Bronze Age Irish gold displayed in vast glass cases on the ground floor. There are also several examples of extraordinarily intricate sacred and secular metalwork dating from the Iron Age to the Middle Ages; well-preserved artefacts from prehistoric and Viking Ireland; and ancient Egyptian relics.

Science Gallery

Trinity College, Pearse Street (896 4091, www.sciencegallery.ie). Open varies. Admission free.
The newest and most innovative museum to open its doors on Trinity campus, the Science Gallery takes a fresh, fun and lively look at the applications of science across a number of walks of life. For example, there's techno-thread clothing (togs that respond, think, even grows on its own) and displays of robotic art (that is, robots that are built to create art). The Science Gallery is a completely fascinating, laudable venture, and anyone with even a passing interest in the appliance of science should take a look.

O'CONNELL STREET & THE NORTH BANK OF THE LIFFEY

Hugh Lane Gallery

Parnell Square North (222 5550, www.hughlane.ie). Open 10am-6pm Tue-Thur; 10am-5pm Fri, Sat; 11am-5pm Sun. Admission free.
The Hugh Lane Gallery first opened its doors to the public in 1908. Art patron Hugh Lane's collection of Manets, Coubets and Renoirs is on the ground floor (but don't miss Irish artists Walter Osbourne and Roderic O'Conor), as are Harry Clarke's marvellous stained-glass windows. A highlight is the London studio of Irish-born Francis Bacon, which, in a Herculean feat of excavation, was moved piece by piece from South Kensingon and reconstructed here behind glass. Visitors gape at its half-completed canvases, dirty paintbrushes, bottles of booze, books, dust, magazines and sublime filth. The gallery has also upped its collection of paintings by Bacon. The Sean Scully Room is the only space in Ireland dedicated to this major Irish-American contemporary artist. Also a big draw for the gallery is its highly successful 'Sundays at Noon' programme of free musical concerts (check the website for dates).

James Joyce Centre

35 North Great George's Street (878 8547, www.jamesjoyce.ie). Open Apr-Sept 10am-5pm Mon-Sat; noon-5pm Sun. Oct-Mar 10am-5pm Tue-Sat; noon-5pm Sun. Admission €5; €4 reductions; free under-14s. Walking tours €10; €8 reductions.
Joyce never lived here, nor did Leopold Bloom, though a minor character in *Ulysses* – Denis Maginni – held dance classes here (but then in what building in central Dublin did a minor character in *Ulysses* not do something in?). The house, which opened as the James Joyce Centre in the mid 1980s, took 14 years to renovate and, through careful adherence to old

Science Gallery

photos, it now looks just as it did in 1904, when Maginni would have been holding his classes. The top floor has a re-creation of Joyce's room in Zurich and a touch-screen history of the publication of *Ulysses*, while the terrace holds the door of 7 Eccles Street (Bloom's house). The centre organises Joycean walking tours every Saturday, at 11am and 2pm.

National Museum of Ireland – Decorative Arts & History

Collins Barracks, Benburb Street (677 7444, www.museum.ie). Open 10am-5pm Tue-Sat; 2-5pm Sun. Admission free.
Within the commanding neoclassical military barracks once used by the British Army, this branch of the National Museum of Ireland contains the nation's most significant collection of decorative arts, as well as displays devoted to Ireland's social, political and cultural history. Highlights include Soldiers & Chiefs, which documents the impact of four and a half centuries of warfare on the ordinary Irishman, and an exhibition about Irish designer Eileen Gray.

Phoenix Park ★

www.phoenixpark.ie.
The largest city park in Europe, covering almost eight square kilometres, Phoenix Park contains an invigorating blend of formal gardens, casual meadows, sports fields and wild undergrowth, as well as herds of deer. A good way to cover it thoroughly is by rented bike (www.phoenixparkbikehire.com). The visitor centre (677 0095, closed Nov-Feb Mon, Tue) has an exhibition about the park's history and wildlife. Aras an Uachtarán, the official residence of the Irish president, is also here. Guided tours (get tickets at the visitor centre) allow you to see some of the building, a Palladian lodge that originally served as the seat of the Lord Lieutenant of Ireland. Other attractions include the much-improved Dublin Zoo (474 8900, www.dublinzoo.ie) and Farmleigh (815 5900, www.farmleigh.ie, closed Jan), an 18th-century mansion that belonged to the Guinness family until the early 1990s. It's now owned by the state and is used to house visiting dignitaries, but tours of the house and gardens are generally available.

become something of a designer hub. The Exchange (Exchange Street Upper, 677 9264, www.exchange dublin.ie), a quirky, volunteer-run arts centre, sets the pace for the area, with theatre, readings, concerts and other happenings throughout the week. Cows Lane is speckled with furniture, craft and clothes shops, several cafés and the wonderful Gutter Bookshop (Cows Lane, 679 9206, www.gutterbookshop.com), which hosts frequent readings by national and international authors. On Saturdays, the street fills with stalls for the Cows Lane Fashion & Design Market – the best place to find original clothing, jewellery and accessories by up-and-coming designers. Opposite is City Hall (222 2204, closed Sun), a fine example of the Georgian architecture that Dublin is famed for, with a spectacular domed roof.

Heading further west brings you to the Old City and the intersection point of Dublin's two historic Golden Ages: the medieval period, when Dublin was a significant stop-off on the great Viking trade routes that stretched from the Baltic to North Africa; and the 18th century, when Ireland's capital briefly flowered as the second city of what was at that time the burgeoning British Empire. Memorials in both Christ Church Cathedral (see p216) and St Patrick's Cathedral (see p217) to the many Irishmen who lost their lives fighting Britain's colonial wars; the French Huguenot presence in both St Patrick's Cathedral and Marsh's Library; and the assortment of languages spoken in Dublin during the Middle Ages (colourfully recreated in the audio accompaniment to the Dublinia exhibition, see p216) are all proof of something that many Dubliners seem unaware of – namely, that the city experienced both periods of great wealth and large influxes of foreign nationals long before that of the late 1990s.

As you round the top of Lord Edward Street, the Anglo-Norman Christ Church Cathedral seems less impressive than you might expect, almost dwarfed by the surrounding buildings. Tucked away down a spindly side street behind City Hall, Dublin Castle (see p216), bastion of British rule in Ireland since the time of King John, has a faintly hangdog air, as if unsure of its role and uncomfortable with its colonial associations. The Dubh Linn gardens at the back are a reliably peaceful retreat. Head south up busy Nicholas Street and you will find St Patrick's Cathedral, perhaps the most telling memorial to Anglo-Irish life in the city.

Further west still, the Liberties is a frequently overlooked, although fast-gentrifying, part of the city: its markets, vibrant street life and association with the Guinness family (it's home to the Guinness Storehouse visitor attraction, see p216) all lending it character. Beyond lies the villagey district of Kilmainham, worth a trip for Kilmainham Gaol (see p217), now very familiar from various films, which harbours a rich history of Ireland's independence struggles within its fortified walls.

Where to eat & drink

Temple Bar has its fair share of good places for a quick snack, café fare and no-nonsense, good-value cooking, as well as upscale dining. But beware: this is an area that has a huge tourist footfall (and correspondingly few locals), and some establishments have been known to cut corners on quality and service, safe in the knowledge that you're unlikely to be returning.

Il Baccaro

Meeting House Square (671 4597). Dinner served 5.30-10.30pm daily.
You'll not find the same quality of regional Italian cucina in this cute little restaurant as you would at some of the city's more serious joints, but that's not to say that Il Baccaro is a dud. Far from it. This is a genuinely cheap, cheerful and fun spot before a night on the town. Bruschetta, crostini, bresaola and all the usual suspects are to be found among the starters, pastas, polentas and cutlets among the mains. Wicker-clad chianti bottles, exposed brickwork, the odd mural and sunny tiles set the scene.

Brazen Head

20 Bridge Street Lower (677 9549, www.brazenhead. com). Open 10.30am-midnight Mon-Thur, Sun; 10.30am-12.30am Fri, Sat. Food served 10.30am-9.30pm daily.
A number of places claim to be Ireland's oldest pub – and the Brazen Head, dating from 1198, is certainly in the running for the title. It's been the drinking haunt of many a famous Irishman, from revolutionaries Daniel O'Connell and

Clarence. See p222.

Trinity College

Michael Collins, to writers Jonathan Swift, Brendan Behan and James Joyce. Old-world charm, Irish food and music sessions continue to draw Dubliners and visitors.

Foggy Dew

1 Fownes Street Upper (677 9328). Open noon-11.30pm Mon, Tue; 11am-12.30am Wed; 11am-1am Thur; 11am-2am Fri, Sat; 1pm-midnight Sun. No credit cards.
Sitting adjacent to the looming Central Bank and named after an old Irish ballad, this is one of the rare pubs in Temple Bar that draws a healthy mix of tourists and Dubliners. Indeed, since its refurbishment, it has attracted some of the same jokers who once dubbed it the 'Dodgy Few'. You'll hear the best of Irish and international alternative music playing at night. Arrive early and lay claim to one of the charming snugs.

Queen of Tarts ★

Cows Lane (633 4681, www.queenoftarts.ie). Open 8am-7pm Mon-Fri; 9am-7pm Sat; 10am-6pm Sun.
Possibly Dublin's best café, the Queen of Tarts has been run for more than a decade by sisters Yvonne and Regina Fallon. It has two branches: the original on Dame Street, and the newest on Cows Lane, just around the corner. The latter has comfortable nooks and crannies decorated with floral cushions and mismatched crockery, plus a balcony. Visit for breakfast, lunch or weekend brunch; there's a takeaway service too. Choose from a cornucopia of sweet goodies (victoria sponge, New York-style raspberry cheesecake, chocolate chip cookies) or try one of the delicious savoury tarts (spinach, brie and pecan nuts, say) served with own-made bread and salad.

Where to stay

The Temple Bar area is not that well supplied with hotels, but one of the city's chicest addresses, the Clarence (*see right*) is here. There are also some reasonable deals to be had at the charmingly shabby Central Hotel (*see right*). You might be better off looking to O'Connell Street and the North Quays (*see p231*) for accommodation, especially as the streets of Temple Bar can be noisy at night.

Central Hotel

1-5 Exchequer Street (679 7302, www.centralhotel.ie). Rates €88-€169 double incl beakfast.
This comfortable, 187-year-old hotel is unique in that it's a prime piece of real estate (right off Dame Street near Temple Bar) that the designers haven't yet got their hands on. The 70 spacious rooms have wonderful architectural touches and big, old sash windows. The cosy Library Bar is a haven of civility with its leather armchairs, blazing fires, wood panelling and books: it's the thinking Dubliner's trendy hangout. The restaurant is attractive and particularly pleasant at breakfast time, when light streams through its huge windows.

Clarence

6-8 Wellington Quay (407 0800, www.theclarence.ie). Rates €179-€309 double incl breakfast.
If you are curious to see what the soon-to-be 'old Clarence' looks like, then this might be your last chance, as the building that has enshrined the U2 frontmen's hip hotel for the last 12 years is slated for demolition. But until then – no official date for the commencement of work had been set at the time of writing – it will be business as usual at this swish address. The large, sound-proofed guest rooms (49 in total) are elegantly decorated and luxuriously appointed (crisp sheets with four-digit thread-counts are topped by soft duvets; tiled bathrooms are filled with covetable bath products). If you can tear yourself away from the views of the Liffey from the big windows in your room, the Tea Room restaurant and the Octagon Bar downstairs are well worth your time and money (although no longer quite as trendy as they once were). There's also a spa for pampering.

Paramount

Parliament Street & Essex Gate (417 9900, www.paramounthotel.ie). Rates €69-€200 double incl breakfast.
You'd never guess it from sitting in the Turk's Head bar on a Saturday night, but this hotel is something of a hidden gem. It's not a peaceful place – the aforementioned bar and nightclub packs in revellers most nights – but it looks quite good. The 64 bedrooms are reminiscent of 1930s chic, done up in subtle tobacco tones, with leather headboards, dark

wood furnishings and soft lighting. The spacious rooms are equally popular with raucous pleasure-seekers and low-key weekenders, but ask for rooms on the upper floors if you're not keen on earplugs.

TRINITY COLLEGE & ST STEPHEN'S GREEN

There's a great atmosphere surrounding the sprawling, leafy campus of Trinity College – a blend of lofty academia and the vibrant traffic of students who move about the place in noisy gaggles or occupy the tree-shaded perimeters of the green. As you enter Front Square you'll see Sir William Chambers' neoclassical Chapel and Examination Hall. The Chapel interior – elegant, with a stuccoed ceiling – looks rather like a mini Houses of Parliament, with two rows of pews facing each other rather than the altar. The extremely pretty campanile, designed by Charles Lanyon, rises up directly opposite the main portico, framing beautiful, mature maple trees.

The Museum Building, close by the Old Library where the famous Book of Kells is housed (*see p217*), was inspired by John Ruskin's celebration of Venetian Gothic and designed by Benjamin Woodward and Thomas Deane in 1852. Although the elevation from Nassau Street doesn't look like much, it is worth making a detour to check out the exterior and atrium of the new Ussher Library, adjacent to the Arts Block, and the adjoining Berkeley Library, two fine examples of 1970s brutalism. Outside the Berkeley is Arnaldo Pomodoro's golden sculpture 'Sphere within a Sphere'. The Pavilion, a drab enough building at the edge of the cricket pitch, comes into its own every summer because it gets the sun longer than almost anywhere else in the city.

If you're in need of maps or tourist information, stop at the Dublin Tourism Centre (605 7700, www.visitdublin.com), which is next to the campus inside a converted church on Suffolk Street.

Cross Nassau Street, past the statue of Molly Malone, to reach pedestrianised Grafton Street, Dublin's shopping heartland. There are all the standard high-street names, as well as the more refined Brown Thomas (605 6666, www.brown thomas.com), housing designer brands. The small streets off Grafton Street are where you're likely to find independent boutiques; Powerscourt Townhouse Shopping Centre (679 4144) and the atmospheric Georges Street Arcade (South Great George's Street, 283 6077, www.georgesstreet arcade.ie) are also worth a browse.

At the end of Grafton Street is St Stephen's Green, once a well-to-do residential neighbourhood, as is evident from the rows of grey Georgian townhouses that line up around its lush squares. These days, however, it's the city's commercial hub, where most of Dublin's major offices are to be found. In the vicinity are several important institutions, including the highly regarded National Gallery of Ireland (*see p217*), the National Museum of Ireland – Archaeology (*see p217*), the recently renovated Royal Hibernian Academy (Ely Place, 661 2558, www.royalhibernianacademy.ie) and the National Concert Hall (Earlsfort Terrace, 417 0000, www.nch.ie). Just off the Green is the Gaiety Theatre (South King Street, 679 5622, www.gaietytheatre.ie), established in 1871 and one of Dublin's oldest playhouses. It turns into a nightclub at weekends.

This is a beautiful neighbourhood in which to lose yourself on a long, meandering walk – around the Green itself, through the Iveagh Gardens behind the National Concert Hall, or along the historic streets that lead to the quiet waters of the Grand Canal. Many visitors see little beyond Merrion Square (where it seems every famous 19th-century Dubliner – including Oscar Wilde – lived at one time or another), and where the

St Stephen's Green

Stay with us in

Generator
DUBLIN

Dublin

Great City

Live Music

Central Location VIP Suite with Jacuzzi
Generator Bar Live Music
En-Suites Available Free Wi-Fi
Female-only Dorms

GENERATORhostels.com/Dublin

National Parliament, the Oireachtas (618 3000, www.oireachtas.ie) is located. But it's worth stretching your legs a little further and taking a walk along the canal if you have the time.

Where to eat & drink

The streets around St Stephen's Green are unsurprisingly well-stocked with expensive lunchtime venues for business people. Shanahan's (119 St Stephen's Green West, 407 0939, www.shanahans.ie, closed Sun) is a prime – and admittedly very good – example. If your budget doesn't stretch this far and your tastes wander further, try the French cuisine at Pearl (20 Merrion Street Upper, 661 3627, www.pearl-brasserie.com, closed Sun) or the excellent Thai menu at Diep Le Shaker (55 Pembroke Lane, 661 1829, www.diep.net, closed Mon, Sun).

South Great George's Street is lined with bars and restaurants, and gets hectic at the weekend. Newcomer the Rustic Stone (707 9596, www.rusticstone.ie), run by celebrity chef Dylan McGrath, has won an enviable reputation for its succulent steaks and meats served at the table on hot stones. Long-running Yamamori (no.72, 475 5001, www.yamamorinoodles.ie) is probably the best Japanese restaurant in town. Just off the main drag, on Exchequer Street, is one of Dublin's best-loved gastropubs, the Exchequer (nos.3-5, 670 6787, www.theexchequer.ie) and, a few doors away, the top-notch food emporium Fallon & Byrne (nos.11-17, 472 1010, www.fallonand byrne.com, closed Sun restaurant). The latter is an ambitious set-up, with an excellent contemporary restaurant upstairs, a lavish food hall on the ground floor, and a wine bar and casual eatery in the basement.

One block south, Fade Street is home to Hogan's (677 5904), a slightly grungy, laid-back pub with bands playing downstairs and a lively ambience, and the excellent brasserie L'Gueuleton (see p227). Nearby, the South William (52 William Street South, 672 5946, www.southwilliam.ie) is a cool if crowded hangout, with DJs and music seven nights a week.

South of Nassau Street and a couple of minutes from Trinity, classic Italian restaurant Dunne & Crescenzi (16-18 South Frederick Street, 675 9892, www.dunneandcrescenzi.com) is part of the growing food empire run by husband-and-wife team Eileen Dunne and Stefano Crescenzi. They also own Nonna Valentina (Portobello Road, 454 9866, www.nonnavalentina.ie, closed Mon), a more upmarket Italian restaurant at the edge of Dublin along the Grand Canal, and L'Officina (see p203) in County Kildare.

For late-night drinks and some of Dublin's best live music, head for Camden Street and Wexford Street. Whelans and the Village (for both, see p229) are crucial music venues, while Solas (31 Wexford Street, www.solasbars.com) dispenses great cocktails. Green Nineteen (19 Camden Street Lower, 478 9626, www.green19.ie) is a popular spot thanks to its budget-priced international menu (posh sarnies, burgers, red lentil curry, burritos) and buzzing atmosphere.

If you're after a traditional Dublin bar, try Grogans (South William Street, www.grogans pub.ie), Kehoe's (South Anne Street, 677 8312, www.louisfitzgerald.com), the Long Hall (George's Street, 475 1590), Neary's Pub (Chatham Street, 677 8596), O'Donoghues (Baggot Street, 660 7194, www.odonoghues.ie), Peter's Pub (Johnson Place, 679 3347, www.peterspub.ie) or the Stag's Head (Dame Court, 679 3687, www.louisfitzgerald.com).

Bang Restaurant

11 Merrion Row (400 4229, www.bangrestaurant.com). Lunch served 12.30-3pm Mon-Sat. Dinner served 6-10.30pm Mon-Wed; 5.30-11pm Thur-Sat.
A cool minimalist interior, with vivid art, and a menu that is full of dishes you want to eat. Start, perhaps, with slow-cooked oxtail, with potato and herb gnocchi and gremolata, or roast butternut squash soup with pan-seared scallop and wild garlic foam. Continue with grilled gurnard with sautéed hispi cabbage, brown shrimps and squid ink, or maybe the dry-aged sirloin steak, with onion purée, pickled mushrooms and dauphinoise potato. Dress stylishly and you'll fit right in.

Cornucopia

Wicklow Street (677 7583, www.cornucopia.ie). Food served 8.30am-9pm Mon-Wed; 8.30am-10.30pm Thur-Sat; noon-8.30pm Sun.
In business for 30 years, casual and earthy Cornucopia is one of Ireland's best vegetarian restaurants. The daily changing menu features two soups, ten delicious salads, five main courses and and assorted desserts. Vegan, wheat-free, gluten-free – you name it, they have it. Mains might be Thai green curry, Moroccan chickpea tagine or quiche of the day, the ingredients varying with the seasons, but all are exceptionally tasty and very healthy.

L'Ecrivain

109A Lower Baggot Street (661 1919, www.lecrivain. com). Lunch served 12.30-2pm Thur, Fri. Dinner served 6.30-10.30pm Mon-Sat.

L'Gueuleton. See p227.

Classic Irish dishes get a truly gourmet twist at this stalwart of Dublin's fine-dining scene. Located in the heart of the business and media district, it attracts many suits at lunch, but in the evening it's the perfect spot for a romantic dinner or family celebration. Any note of formality is truly Irish (that is, non-existent), and a good time is encouraged, often via the piano downstairs in the bar. The cooking is highly accomplished: wild sea bass with razor clams, gnocchi, carrot purée and bisque foam, say. On a sunny day, try for a terrace table.

L'Gueuleton

Fade Street (675 3708). Lunch served 12.30-3pm Mon-Fri; 1-4pm Sun. Brunch served 12.30-4pm Sat. Dinner served 6-10pm Mon-Sat; 6-9pm Sun.

Superb, unpretentious brasserie cooking has earned this charming little restaurant a good reputation over the years, and the owners have had the sense not to go tinkering with a winning formula. The signature french onion soup is still on the menu (alongside a revolving cast of grilled ribeye, slow-roast pork belly, and other tried and tasty favourites). Le Gueuleton has a New York vibe, and doesn't take reservations, such is the demand for the simple, no-nonsense dishes. The food and wine are keenly priced. Eating here is good fun – it's the perfect place for a loud and opinionated group of friends.

Peploe's

St Stephen's Green (676 3144, www.peploes.com). Open noon-10.30pm daily.

There are several reasons why Peploe's is considered the best wine bar in town. First, it's a truly sophisticated joint. Its rooms (decked out with wood, murals and crisp table linen) are patrolled by smartly kitted-out staff and resonate to the low hum of intelligent conversation and quietly swinging jazz. It's also a firm favourite for a fun Friday lunch, and for the city's cultured set to have casual evening meals. Chef Sebastian Scheer turns out dishes such as prawn linguine with cherry tomatoes, basil and chilli; roast rack of lamb with tomato and fennel gratin and parmesan mash; and fish pie made with monkfish and Dublin Bay prawns. The wine list is very good and very long – do check it out, even if it's just for a glass of wine at the bar.

Thornton's ★

Fitzwilliam Hotel, St Stephen's Green West (478 7008, www.fitzwilliamhotel.com). Lunch served noon-1.30pm Thur-Sat. Dinner served 6-9.30pm Tue-Sat.

One of the most talked-about fine-dining restaurants in Dublin, Thornton's is the culinary seat of celebrity chef Kevin Thornton, whose fiery appearances on RTÉ1's cook-off show *Heat* have put him firmly in the spotlight. The restaurant (which is affiliated to, but has a separate entrance from, the Fitzwilliam Hotel – *see right*) is a stylishly sombre medley of burgundy upholstered chairs, dark chocolate-coloured carpets and thick white tablecloths, with striking modern photography brightening the walls. It's very comfortable and the staff are an attentive, knowledgeable lot, but the real reason to visit is to experience Thornton's exquisitely refined seasonal cooking: fillet of black sole with parmesan crust, shellfish tortellini, lemon confit and parsley purée, for example. Or you could plump for the 'surprise menu', a spread of eight unannounced courses served at the dramatic chef's table. Wines are, of course, sublime – but, like the food, they ain't cheap.

Where to stay

As with the eating scene, this upmarket, central area is not short of stylish – and in some cases overpriced – accommodation. At the top end of the scale, and both located on St Stephen's Green, are the Shelbourne Hotel (663 4500, www.marriott.co.uk) and the Fitzwilliam Hotel (478 7008, www.fitzwilliamhotel.com). The Westin Dublin (*see p228*) is also very swish, and has a popular bar and restaurant.

For those on a budget who want to stay central, it's useful to know that Trinity College (896 1177, www.tcd.ie) opens up its on-campus halls of residence during the summer holidays. Kelly's Hotel (South Great George's Street, 648 0010, www.kellysdublin.com) has small, boutique-style rooms, often at good rates.

Dylan ★

Eastmoreland Place (660 3000, www.dylan.ie). Rates €189-€259 double incl breakfast.

Cool enough to stay in the Dylan? You wish. Everything at this stylish boutique hotel – from the oversized lanterns strewn around the entrance to the iPods in the bedrooms – has been carefully thought out. The guests who breeze in and out of the swish lobby and cocktail bar (check out the funky zinc counter) are the kind of well-dressed hipsters who seem entirely at home among the sumptuously upholstered furniture, trendy wallpaper and the minimalism of the bright, white terrace. The 44 guest rooms are a triumph of understated style blended with flashes of boldness (the bedheads are stunning). Bathrooms are loaded with gorgeous Ren products, the in-room safes are laptop-compatible – you get the picture.

Kilronan House

70 Adelaide Road (475 5266, www.kilronanhouse.com). Rates €85-€149 double incl breakfast.

It may look like just another B&B from its modest terraced façade, but the 12-room Kilronan House is an elegant and, above all, welcoming place that has been renovated with real class. Some of the rooms in the handsome Victorian building still have original period features and high ceilings; newer bedrooms do not (although they do have a bit more space). The massive, varied breakfasts served in the sunny front dining area will set you up for the day. Staff are never short on enthusiasm.

Merrion Hotel ★

Upper Merrion Street (603 0600, www.merrion hotel.com). Rates €230-€280 double incl breakfast.

Spread over four listed Georgian houses, the Merrion Hotel is a refined and elegant place to lay your head. The spacious guest rooms (123 rooms and 19 suites, found in the main building or in the garden wing) make much use of calming neutral tones, mixing period features with more modern furnishings to stylish effect. The large bathrooms feature plenty of Italian marble, and all have separate bath tubs. There's also a stately drawing room (the setting for a lavish afternoon tea), a couple of bars, and two classy restaurants: the Cellar Restaurant is a striking vaulted space serving Irish cuisine, while Patrick Guilbaud is Dublin's finest French restaurant. The hotel also has a fine collection of 19th- and 20th-century art. The basement houses a spa with a swimming pool, steam room, gym and treatment rooms.

Sugar Club

BEST LIVE MUSIC VENUES

The roll-call of big-name Irish musicians is seemingly endless, and, thanks to a generous tax-exemption system for artists, Dublin is still full of young musos eager to make their big break. Rock and traditional Irish music fans are best catered for; the classical music scene is largely undistinguished. It's also worth checking out the website of Irish music promoter Comhaltas (http://comhaltas.ie).

Button Factory
Curved Street (670 9202, ww2.button factory.ie). Music 7.30pm, days vary.
The Button Factory is the rebranded and refurbished version of what was once the Temple Bar Music Centre, a home to hard rock bands where sound quality and atmosphere mattered less than beer and decibels. With a new layout, decor and sound system since 2007, the venue is a useful addition to the Dublin music scene. There are traditional and folk sessions every second Tuesday of the month.

Crawdaddy
Hatch Street Upper, off Harcourt Street (478 0166, www.crawdaddy.ie). Music times vary.
Medium-sized Crawdaddy is an exciting venue with an impressively varied roster of rock, funk, indie, dance, soul, electro, jazz, folk and world music. It can hold about 300 people, and ticket prices tend to be higher than average, but the place has the atmosphere of an intimate club.

International Bar
23 Wicklow Street (677 9250, www.international-bar.com). Music from 9pm Tue-Sun.
A quaint old pub with a small but charming venue upstairs. In recent years, it's become more of a comedy space, with stand-up acts every night, but it still has trad music sessions in the bar on Sunday afternoons and evenings.

Number 31
31 Leeson Close (676 5011, www.number31.ie). Rates €150-€320 double incl breakfast.
Set in one of the city's most fashionable locales, this guesthouse is a real find, combining modern design with an almost rural tranquillity. Most of the soothingly decorated bedrooms (there are 21) occupy a Georgian townhouse, although a few are in the beautifully designed modern mews building, where delicious own-made breakfasts are served. Warm yourself in front of the peat fire in the sunken lounge or wander through the lush gardens for some green therapy.

Westin Dublin
Westmoreland Street (645 1000, www.thewestindublin. com). Rates €179-€489 double incl breakfast.
The Westin's imposing 19th-century façade (the building was once a bank) suggests an interior of traditional grandeur and exclusivity, and the reality does not disappoint. The elegant reception area is all marble columns and exquisite plasterwork; a hall of mirrors lines the Westmoreland Street entrance. The 163 rooms are decorated in mahogany and neutral shades, with comfortable beds, soft linen and modern dataports; many have sweeping views of the city. The hotel's bar, aptly called the Mint, is located in the old bank vaults.

O'CONNELL STREET & THE NORTH BANK OF THE LIFFEY

Any Dubliner worth his or her salt will proudly tell you that O'Connell Street is a very wide street (46 metres) and its buildings are tall (for Dublin). Bookended by sculptures of Ireland's two great constitutional nationalists – Daniel O'Connell and Charles Stewart Parnell – it is, without question, the most imposing thoroughfare in the city, and although it doesn't hold the Parliament, it seems to be to focal point for every political rally. But until recently it was going to seed: it had become a lucrative beat for petty criminals and junkies, its pavements mired in litter, half its buildings leased to burger joints, the other half knocked down.

These days, all that has changed. Garda patrol tirelessly, and developments include the widening of footpaths, the restoration of monuments, the creation of a plaza in front of the General Post Office (a potent symbol of Irish independence) and, of course, the Spire, an enormous stainless-steel shard that jabs 120 metres into the sky. All this met with the usual barrage of criticism but the street now looks leafy, prosperous, much tidier, more pedestrian-friendly – in short, much more like the main street of a European capital should.

Off the bottom end of O'Connell Street, on Lower Abbey Street, is the Abbey Theatre (Abbey Street, 878 7222, www.abbeytheatre.ie, closed Sun). It has been a cultural hub since it opened its doors in 1906 under the directorship of WB Yeats, JM Synge and Lady Gregory, and continues to play a pivotal role in Irish theatre. At the other end of O'Connell Street, on Parnell Square, is the prestigious Gate Theatre (874 4045, www.gate-theatre.ie), in business since 1928. Just to the north, past the tranquil Garden of Rembrance, dedicated to those who lost their lives during the fight for Irish Independence, is the Hugh Lane Gallery (*see p219*). Sir Hugh Lane (a nephew of Lady Gregory) persuaded some famous Irish artists to donate their work to the gallery and then himself purchased work by other international names. The gallery now houses artists' work including Yeats, Renoir, Degas and a whole area dedicated to Francis Bacon.

Parnell Square also houses the Dublin Writers Museum (872 2077, www.writersmuseum.com), which celebrates Dublin's literary heroes from the past 300 years, including Oscar Wilde and Samuel Beckett. Portraits, personal belongings and some of the writers' works are displayed in the restored Georgian mansion. Another Irish literary great is celebrated nearby at the James Joyce Centre (*see p219*) on North Great George's Street.

Stretching along the north bank of the Liffey, the North Quays is the collective name for the series of streets that run to the west of the Docklands' Custom House (the 18th-century, neoclassical building that now houses various government departments and a visitor centre) all the way to Phoenix Park (*see p219*), the city's biggest green space. Although it appears as one long street, the names change every block or so – Eden Quay, Bachelors Walk, Ormond Quay, Inns Quay – as do the individual characters of the discrete residential hubs that are scattered along this mile-long stretch. The newly developed 'Italian Quarter' along Ormond Quay features some fine Italian eateries and wine bars. There are also several markets, including the remnants of the fabled Smithfield horse-trading fair, to be explored: it's busy, bustling and interesting.

Just north of Arran Quay is the Old Jameson Distillery (Bow Street, 807 2348, www.tours.jamesonwhiskey.com), where John Jameson established his whiskey distillery in 1780. Tours are available. A short walk west, housed within the former Collins Barracks, is the National Museum of Ireland – Decorative Arts & History (*see p219*).

To the other (east) side of the Custom House and spanning 1,300 acres of land north and south of the river, Dublin's Docklands once languished in a semi-derelict state. But all that changed when the Dublin Docklands Development Authority was created in 1997. Now the area has been transformed into the city's financial district. Smart office blocks, restaurants, wine bars and pubs have all flung open their doors. What makes Dublin's dockside regeneration different from similar projects across Europe is the emphasis that has been placed on quality of design, and some world-famous architects have been involved.

A short stroll from the financial district is Dublin's largest concert venue, the O2 (North Wall Quay, 819 8888, www.theo2.ie). The surrounding area has been developed into Point Village (www.pointvillage.ie), containing restaurants, bars and a hotel, with a good outdoor market at the weekend. It's also home to the 60-metre-high Dublin Wheel (855 9204), Ireland's answer to London's observation wheel.

Sugar Club
8 Leeson Street Lower (678 7188, www.thesugarclub.com). Open 8pm-midnight Mon-Thur; 8pm-2.30am Fri-Sun.
One of Dublin's most stylish venues, the Sugar Club has the feel of a hip US jazz bar. The audience gazes down on the musicians from tiered seats with tables. The programme ranges from cabaret and rock to jazz or singer-songwriter sets.

Vicar Street
99 Vicar Street, off Thomas Street West (775 5800, www.vicarstreet. com). Music from 7.30pm daily.
A modern venue with an old-style feel, Vicar Street has comfortable seating, sensitive lighting and a great sound system. It's been expanded to hold 1,000 punters, but has lost none of its intimate atmosphere. The spacious pub in the front and the little bars hidden in the corridors are handy too. Acts have included Rufus Wainwright, Calexico and Al Green, as well as big-name jazz and comedy acts and top local musicians.

Village
26 Wexford Street (475 8555, www. thevillagevenue.com). Open 11am-2.30am Mon-Fri; 3pm-2.30am Sat; 5pm-2.30am Sun.
This shiny bar/restaurant/club has become central to Dublin nightlife. Everyone from Scissor Sisters to Pere Ubu has played here, and there's a different club every night of the week.

Whelan's
25 Wexford Street (478 0766, www.whelanslive.com). Music from 8.30pm Mon-Sat.
One of the city's most prestigious venues, Whelan's has built an unassailable reputation among Dublin music fans. It's the stomping ground for most of the city's up-and-coming bands: Damien Rice, David Kitt, the Frames, Paddy Casey and Gemma Hayes all made their first appearances here. With a line-up that takes in Irish trad, English folk and American roots, it's a vital Dublin venue.

Vicar Street

Discover the city from your back pocket

Essential for your weekend break, 30 top cities available.

POCKET SIZED
from £6.99 / $11.95

**TIME OUT GUIDES
WRITTEN BY
LOCAL EXPERTS**
Visit timeout.com/shop

Where to eat & drink

There's plenty of choice to suit all budgets along and around bustling O'Connell Street, from burger joints to haute cuisine. The riverfront around Lower Ormond Quay and the Capel Building is also a focus for new, high-quality restaurants and aspiring, entrepreneurial chefs.

Chapter One ★

18-19 Parnell Square (873 2266, www.chapterone restaurant.com). Open Lunch served 12.30-2pm Tue-Fri. Dinner served 6-10.30pm Tue-Sat.
The critics love it, the punters love it and so will you: a meal at Chapter One is easily the most accessible, affordable and enjoyable fine-dining experience in Dublin. The dining room is warm and tasteful and, as for the cooking, it is nothing short of spectacular. A starter of pea soup might be served with crème fraîche dumplings and sorrel; among the mains, hake might be cooked with seaweed and Japanese salt, and accompanied by broccoli purée, lemon emulsion and crab beignet. All followed, perhaps, by warm chocolate mousse, with caramel jelly, espresso mousse, lime ice-cream and honeycomb. Needless to say, the wine list is excellent, and the list of top-flight local meat, fish and vegetable suppliers speaks for itself.

Enoteca delle Langhe

24 Lower Ormond Quay (888 0834). Food served noon-midnight Mon-Sat; 12.30pm-midnight Sun.
The cuisine and wines of Piedmont (or more specifically the Langhe region of Piedmont) are at the heart of this excellent operation. If you love beautiful Italian wine, fresh, moreish cooking, and the convivial atmosphere of a group of Italian foodies doing what they love, then you should pay a visit. Cheese, tapenade, olives and salamis are served with plenty of bread (great to share, and cheap too). With an Italian deli, coffee shop and two more Italian restaurants in the same development, not for nothing is this area known as the Italian Quarter.

101 Talbot

101 Talbot Street (874 5011, www.101talbot.ie). Lunch served noon-3pm, dinner served 5-11pm Tue-Sat.
This long-running restaurant nourishes wise locals who pay little attention to food fads. Don't expect any razzmatazz, just straightforward, honest cooking geared to everyone from vegans to carnivores. Dishes run from roast rump of Lough Erne lamb with nectarine salsa, minted crushed new potatoes and broccoli to Moroccan-style vegetable and chickpea tagine with toasted almonds, couscous and pitta bread. Chocoholics rave about the chocolate tart, while 101's proximity to theatreland also makes it an ideal spot pre- or post-performance.

Winding Stair

40 Lower Ormond Quay (872 7320, www.winding-stair.com). Food served noon-10.30pm Mon-Thur, Sun. Lunch served noon-3.30pm, dinner served 5.30-10.30pm Fri, Sat.
With its steel H-beams and darkwood floorboards, white-painted brick walls and old service elevator, bookshelves and river-facing windows, the Winding Stair looks a little like a Tribeca loft apartment or some arty atelier in Berlin. The bookshop is well-loved and the restaurant is one of the

capital's most popular, with a reputation for putting well-sourced, high-quality ingredients to imaginatively good use. The menu is changed very regularly, and might include starters such as Irish charcuterie with own-made bread, pickles and relish, and mains such as Kilkeel hake with smashed lemon and crab potatoes, capers, roasted spring onion and a buttery sauce. The global wine list runs to several pages, including great selections by the glass. Staff are enthusiastic about what they do, as are their customers.

Where to stay

The North Quays, which are just a short hop away over the Millennium Bridge, make a decent central alternative to the noisy lanes of Temple Bar. Further east, the Docklands is more the preserve of chain hotels, but you may still find a decent, riverside room among them – the Clarion (*see below*) being an excellent example. At the north end of O'Connell Street, the august Gresham Hotel (23 Upper O'Connell Street, 874 6881, www.gresham-hotels.com) has been in operation for 200 years.

Abode Apartments

Quay Apartments, Eden Quay (814 7000, www.abodedublin.com). Rates €590-€650 per week for 2 people. €690-€750 per week for 4 people.
One in a string of locations around the city, these smart riverside apartments are a nice alternative to a hotel (especially for longer stays or for those with kids). Situated on the top two floors of a modern block, the apartments have floor-to-ceiling windows and make the most of the views. The street-level video intercom provides the peace of mind that is sometimes missing in Dublin's self-catering sector. Kitchens are perfectly serviceable and the staff (who are contactable 24/7) are helpful and pleasant. Other locations include the very central Adelaide Square and the award-winning Wooden Building in Temple Bar.

Clarion Dublin IFSC

International Financial Services Centre (433 8800, www.clarionhotelifsc.com). Rates €135-€180 double incl breakfast.

Chapter One

Dalkey

Yes, it's a chain hotel, and big with business travellers; but don't be put off. This is an excellent place: great-looking, well run, with a fabulous location, decent prices and lots of extras. The 179 rooms are spacious, with sweeping views of the Liffey. Decorated in soothing neutral colours, all cream and taupe, they feature Egyptian cotton duvets, large TVs, free broadband and even video-game consoles.

Morrison
Ormond Quay (887 2400, www.morrisonhotel.ie).
Rates €165-€285 double incl breakfast.
With an interior designed by John Rocha and every fancy boutique touch from in-room iPod docks to gorgeous bathrooms with aromatherapy toiletries and sunken baths, the 138-room Morrison lives up to its reputation for sophisticated luxury. It has a great site across the river from Temple Bar – just a few steps from the action, but with a pleasingly sequestered feel. A lot of work has been done on the interior, and the results are stunning. The two bars (especially the intimate Morrison Bar) and the Halo restaurant are design-literate, good-quality operations.

AROUND DUBLIN
A fair city it may be, but Dublin also has a more outdoorsy side to it, thanks to its natural advantages of sea and mountains. They lend the city beauty whatever the weather, and, on a good day, provide some really stunning views.

The cheapest way to see the coast is still the best: take a DART train from the north end of the line, Howth, to the south end at the Greystones (or vice versa). Much of the trip is along the constantly changing seashore; the stretch from Sandycove to Bray is especially attractive.

Popular day-trip destinations include Dun Laoghaire, which has two attractive piers and some decent shops. A little more upmarket is Dalkey ★, village to the stars – Bono, Lisa Stansfield and Neil Jordan have all chosen to live here. The main street is packed with good bars, eateries and shops, and it's also the starting point for some glorious coastal walks. A walk along the main street (start at Coliemore Road, then turn on to Sorrento Road and finally Vico Road) gives views of a section of coastline endlessly likened to the Bay of Naples. First is Coliemore Harbour, the launchpad for boats to Dalkey Island in summer. Past Coliemore Harbour on the left is Dillon's Park, a grassy space with views out to sea and two larger-than-life-size goat statues. Next up is Sorrento Terrace, the city's most exclusive address, on a clifftop above the sea. From there, turn on to Vico Road (the rocky Vico bathing spot is unashamedly nudist), then turn towards Killiney Hill, on top of which stands a wishing stone and Queen Victoria's obelisk. From here you can explore the small forest above Burmah Road. Alternatively, follow Vico Road down to Killiney beach, which is a safe swimming spot.

North of Dublin, Howth has a harbour lined with fish shops and restaurants, with gulls honking above and seals barking below. A wonderful eight-kilometre cliff walk leads to a lighthouse, offering spectacular views back to Dublin city and the southern coastline.

Where to eat & drink

Alexis Bar & Grill
St Patrick Street, Dun Laoghaire (280 8872, www.alexis. ie). Lunch served 12.30-2.30pm Tue-Fri; 12.30-3pm Sun. Dinner served 5.30-10pm Tue-Sat; 5.30-9pm Sun.
Set away from the seafront, Alexis has built up a loyal local following. The seasonal dinner menu features hearty, rustic dishes such as roast Wicklow rabbit with root vegetables, and wood pigeon tart with braised onions, as well as lighter fare such as pan-fried Kilmore Quay scallops with cauliflower purée and pea shoot salad. Lunch is a lighter affair, with a shorter menu. The atmosphere is casual and buzzing, and the place is usually packed with a merry crowd.

Hartley's
Harbour Road, Dun Laoghaire (280 6767, www.hartleys. ie). Lunch served noon-3.30pm, dinner served 5.30-10pm Tue-Thur. Food served noon-10pm Fri, Sat; noon-9pm Sun.
The current hotspot in Dun Laoghaire, located in the old railway terminal. While the exterior and some internal period features have been preserved, Hartley's has a bright, contemporary feel. If the weather is good, book a table on the large outdoor terrace for views of the harbour. The easy-going menu includes barbecue beef spare ribs, beer-battered halibut and chips, fancy burgers and steaks. It's not cheap, but you're guaranteed an enjoyable time.

King Sitric ★
East Pier, Howth (832 5235, www.kingsitric.ie). Food served Summer 6.30-10pm Mon, Wed-Sat; 1-7pm Sun. Winter 6.30-10.30pm Wed-Sat; 1-7pm Sun.
If you ask any Dubliner to name the best local seafood restaurants, they'll probably mention King Sitric. Run by Aidan and Joan MacManus and in operation since 1971, it deserves every award it receives. Most of the fish and seafood is extremely local – much of it landed in Howth itself. Lobster and crab come from Balscadden Bay, and the salmon is smoked in Howth's last remaining traditional smokehouse. Game appears on the menu in winter, and Irish farmhouse cheeses are always a great way to finish.

Ragazzi
109 Coliemore Road, Dalkey (284 7280). Dinner served 5.15pm-10.15pm Mon-Sat; 4-9.30pm Sun.
It's not posh or fancy, but if you're looking for a warm, welcoming atmosphere and tasty pizzas, then Ragazzi hits the spot. Thin, crispy bases and plenty of delicious toppings will make you feel like you just landed in Naples.

Where to stay
Most people visit the coast for the day, and return to Dublin at night, but there are options if you want to stay over. The Victorian-era Marine Hotel (Marine Road, 230 0030, www.royalmarine.ie) in Dun Laoghaire has been thoroughly renovated, and now has 228 rooms and excellent, modern facilities. Just outside Dalkey is the Fitzpatrick Castle Hotel (230 5400, www.fitzpatrickcastle. com), a large, red and white crenellated affair with comfortable rooms. In Howth, the King Sitric (*see above*) has eight simply decorated B&B rooms, all named after Irish lighthouses.

Counties Louth & Meath

Medieval abbeys, high crosses and round towers are concentrated within a few kilometres of the walled city of Drogheda, on the eastern coastline of County Louth. A short distance inland, the ruins of Monasterboice and Mellifont Abbey are highlights of the region, while to the far north of the county, Carlingford Lough is a beautiful setting for mountain walks or just propping up one of the many bars. The River Boyne, which divides Drogheda, has cut a fertile valley right through County Meath, inland from County Leath. Hidden within this green landscape are some of Ireland's most important ancient monuments: there are the Neolithic passage tombs of Brú na Bóinne, which contain Europe's most significant prehistoric art, and the Hill of Tara, steeped in ancient tales of goddesses and palaces.

COUNTY LOUTH

Drogheda

Drogheda is Louth's major town and the gateway to the Boyne Valley. With historic buildings, a thriving arts scene and lively nightlife, it's a pleasant base from which to explore the area. For a long period, the city was two separate – often rival – settlements astride the river. A wall was built around them in the mid 13th century and, in 1412, they finally merged into a single entity, creating one of Ireland's mightiest Anglo-Norman strongholds.

Most of Drogheda's key sights are north of the river. St Laurence's Gate, originally the east gate into town, is pretty much all that remains of the city walls. To its west, the Tholsel, a rather sedate limestone building dating from 1770, was a meeting place for the Drogheda Corporation, used for court sessions and as a holding place for petty criminals; the landmark clocktower was added in 1810. At the top of Peter Street, St Peter's Church of Ireland is on the site of an old church, burned to the ground by Cromwell's troops in 1649 at the end of the notoriously savage siege of Drogheda. More than 100 people who had been sheltering in the steeple died in the fire. It was not until 1752 that the ruins were replaced by a new Renaissance-style church, to which a beautiful porch and steeple were added in the 1830s. This church should not be confused with St Peter's Roman Catholic Church (see p240) on West Street, which contains the head of Oliver Plunkett, a 17th-century Archbishop of Armagh who was canonised after his execution for treason by the English.

The oldest surviving structure in Drogheda is south of the river. Some believe Millmount was an ancient passage tomb, others claim it as the grave of ancient Celtic poet Amergin, but the Anglo-Normans – displaying their characteristic lack of sentimentality – recognised a good defensive position and plonked a motte on top of the raised mound. This was later destroyed and replaced by a Martello Tower. Adjacent to the tower, within the former barracks, is the Millmount Museum (041 983 3097, www.millmount.net), with displays that include a Victorian kitchen dresser, an exploration of Drogheda's role as a centre of manufacturing, and sundry other geological and archaeological details; the museum also arranges tours of the tower, from which there are splendid views.

On Laurence Street, the Highlanes Gallery (041 980 3311, www.highlanes.ie, closed Sun) is in a 19th-century Franciscan friary. Stained-glass windows and plain whitewashed walls create a bright, welcoming space where the permanent collection of paintings is often joined by visiting exhibitions. There's also a craft shop and a café serving soups, sandwiches, pâtés and cheese.

The Drogheda authorities have invested in the arts in recent years, opening the wonderful Droicheah Arts Centre (041 983 3946, www.droicheadarts centre.com, box office closed Mon, Sun) on Stockwell Lane. It hosts exhibitions, workshops and a broad programme of comedy, music and theatre. If you're visiting in May, the Drogheda Arts Festival (www.droghedaartsfestival.ie) provides six days of music, dance, theatre and visual arts.

A short distance north of Drogheda on the coastal road, just outside Clogherhead, is a Blue Flag beach with fantastic views up to the Cooley Peninsula and Mourne Mountains. On the way back to Drogheda, stop at Beaulieu House, Gardens & Car Museum (see p240) to wander in the walled garden or admire the collection of vintage racing cars. A few kilometres inland to the north-west of Drogheda are the magnificent ruins of Mellifont Abbey and Monasterboice (for both, see p240). Both are signposted off the M1.

Dundalk & Carlingford Lough ★

Further north, the industrial town of Dundalk is less attractive than Drogheda, but is home to the Louth County Museum (Carroll Centre, Roden Place, Jocelyn Street, 042 932 7056, www. dundalkmuseum.ie, closed Mon, Sun). Within an 18th-century warehouse, the museum traces the county's history and development with artefacts from the Stone Age to the present. For fresh air and pretty countryside, head east of Dundalk along the Cooley Peninsula, which forms the south bank of Carlingford Lough. The lough is surrounded by mountains with some great walking trails: the well-serviced circular routes Common's Loop, Slieve Foye Loop and Barnavave Loop are the most popular. For information on these walks, contact the Carlingford Tourist Information Centre (042 937 3033, www.carlingford.ie); the centre was closed due to flood damage as we went to press, but an email form is provided on the website.

The town of Carlingford is located on the southern bank of the lough. Here Carlingford Adventure Centre (Tholsel Street, 042 937 3100, www .carlingfordadventure.com) can arrange sailing, abseiling, cycling, walking and canoeing, as well as walking tours. The town is also popular with weekend hen and stag parties, which accounts for the numerous bars and restaurants in what is a rather small, medieval town. Some remnants of Carlingford's past can still be seen, notably the ruins of King John's Castle. Perched on a rocky outcrop overlooking the lough, it was built by Hugh de Lacy and extended by King John, brother of Richard the Lionheart. Of Carlingford's ancient gates, the Tholsel still stands, a three-storey structure that remains impressive, albeit a little bedraggled. There are also a couple of tower houses: the 15th-century fortified Mint, which predates Taaffe's Castle, thought to have been built in the 1700s. Both were built by wealthy merchants when Carlingford was at its peak of prosperity. The Tourist Information Centre arranges informative guided walks around the town's historic buildings, and there are local history exhibitions in the Heritage Centre (042 937 3888, www. carlingfordheritagecentre.com, closed Sat, Sun), formerly Holy Trinity Church.

In spring, the Táin Walking Festival (042 937 3033) uses a series of themed walks through the town and around Cooley Peninsula to investigate the area's history, while the recently revived Carlingford Oyster Festival (mobile 086 197 3797) in August is a weekend of oyster-tasting, street entertainment and live music, combined with a regatta.

Where to eat & drink

In recent years, Drogheda's bars and restaurants have been flourishing. On Dyer Street, the laid-back D'Vine Wine Bar & Restaurant (041 980 0440, closed Mon, Tue), in the quirky setting of the Distillery House, serves great, simple Italian food. For an olde-worlde bar, try McPhails (Laurence Street, 041 983 7371), which has gigs most nights; music fans should also check out McHugh's (041 983 5995) on Chord Street.

In Dundalk, McKeown's Bar & Lounge (042 933 7931) on Clanbrassil Street is a typical Irish pub with great character. For good food served in cosy surroundings, try Restaurant Number 32 (Chapel Street, 042 933 1113, www.no32.ie, closed Sun), which serves a mix of Asian-influenced dishes (spiced lamb kofta, Asian-style salmon) and hearty mains (confit of duck, garlic and rosemary lamb's loin). The popular Quaglinos at the Century (Roden Place, 042 933 8567), housed in a fine listed building, uses local and seasonal produce.

Carlingford has a stack of eateries and bars. Favourites include Magees Seafood Bistro (Tholsel Street, 042 937 3751, www.mageesbistro.com), serving gastropub staples in an old stone building; and the BayTree (Newry Street, 042 938 3848, www.belvederehouse.ie, closed Mon-Wed winter; Mon summer), with its emphasis on fresh, local fish and seafood. There's more seafood at the restaurant at Carlingford Marina. For a quiet drink, try Lily Finnegans (Whitestown, 042 937 3730, closed Mon-Wed); for somewhere livelier, there's PJ O'Hare's (Tholsel Street, 042 937 3106, www.pjoharescarlingford.com).

Newgrange, at Brú na Bóinne. See p240.

Milltown
Ardlougher
Lough Oughter
Butlers Bridge
Ballyhaise
Drung
Lisboduff
Cootehill
Lough Avaghon
Lough Eglish
Broomfield
R192
R181
Shantonagh
Laragh
22 (35)
Killeshandra
Annalee
R188
Tullyvin
Kill
Drumgoon
R191
Maudabawn
Lough Tacker
Corduff
Donaghmoyne
Drumbroagh
R180
Killykeen Forest Park
CATH. OF SS PATRICK & FELIM
Cavan (An Cabhán)
Poles
Stradone
Canningstown
Corraneary
Sheercock
Lough Sillan
Northlands
R178
Corvally
Carrickmacross (Carrig Mhachaire)
R99
R198
Derrylane
ST FEIDHLIMIDH'S CATH
CAVAN CRYSTAL
Crossdoney
Lavey
Clifferna
Tonyduff
Drumkeens Lough
Skeagh Lough Upper
Drumerscloone
Gleaghnane Lough
Magheracloone
Carrickashedog
Cornafean
Corlismore
Cashel
Ballinagh
Carrickaboy
Cross Keys
Termon
New Inn
Moylett
Drumanespick
Leiter
R165
Bailieborough (Coillan Chollaigh)
Moyer
Ballynamona
Dún an Rí Forest Park
Kingscourt (Dún an Rí)
Coolderry
Drumcon
Arvagh
Gorteen
N55
R154
Graddum Lough
Nadreegeel Lough
N3
31 (50)
Killinkere
Lisgrea
R178
Relagh Beg
Crossreagh
Kilmainhamwood
Erve Lough
Teevurcher
R162
Dee
Aghnacliff
Inchmore
Dring
Bunlahy
Granard
Lough Gowna
Cloonagh
Kilcogy
Ballymachugh
Ballynarry
R394
Crosserlough
Kilnaleck
COUNTY MUSEUM
Ballyjamesduff
R194
Virginia
Mount Nugent
Castlerahan
Eighter
Knockatemple
Lough Ramor
R194
R191
Mullagh Lough
Mullagh
Whitewood Lough
R164
Nobber
Woodt
Lough Sheelin
Ryefield
Lisduff
ST. KILIAN'S HERITAGE CENTRE
Thomastown
19 (31)
Castl
Lough Kinale
Finnea
Ross
R195
Derver
Moynalty
N55
Abbeylara
Derragh Lough
Mullaghmeen
LOUGHCREW CAIRNS
Carnaross
Carlanstown
R162
Lisryan
Lismacaffry
Castletown
Ballymanus
Oldcastle
Millbrook
Naneagh Lough
Slieve na Calliagh
Ballinlough
Kells (Ceanannus Mór)
HERITAGE CEN
Baile Órthaí (Oristown)
Kilbe
Street
Coole
LOUGHCREW GARDENS
Murrens
Drumone
Slieve Gullion
Crossakeel
R163
M3
Marty
Baile Ghib (Gibstown)
R163
NAVA
Rathowen
18 (29)
Ballinalack
TULLYNALLY CAS.
Ilnagh Glore
ABBEY
Fore
Lough Bane
Kilskeer
R154
14 (23)
HIGH CROSSES
Cortown
10 (16)
Navan (An Uaimh)
N4
Ballinalack
Castlepollard
Lough Lene
Archerstown
Clonmellon
N52
Fordstown
Bohermeen
Toll
Multyfarnham
Collinstown
Drumcree
R395
Ballinlig
Cloran
Martinstown
N51
Boyerstown
Kilc
Knockeyon 214
Lough Analla
Delvin
BALLINLOUGH CASTLE GARDENS
Athboy (Baile Átha Buí)
19 (31)
Tullaghanstown
Halltown
Dunderry
Ballycorkey
Crookedwood
Robinstown
Ballynacarrigy
Monilea
Crazy Corner
Tevrin
N52
Bracklyn
Cloghbrack
Kildalkey
Kilbride (Cill Bhríde)
CATH.
Skeagh
Monroe
R393
Lough Owel
13 (21)
Cloghan
R156
Ballivor
Trim (Baile Átha Troim)
HOSPITA ST. JOHN BAPTIST
Slanemore
Rathconrath
11
10
Mullingar (An Muileann gCearr)
Bellview
Killucan
Raharney
Rathwire
DONORE CASTLE
R160
R158
Laracor
R154
B
Mount Dalton Lough
R390
9
N52
R156
Thomastown
Correllstown
Hill of Down
Rathmolyon
Summerhill
Mo
Uisneach
184
Killare
Loughanavally
Dysart
BELVEDERE HO. GDNS. & PK.
The Downs
Gainestown
11 (18)
Castlerickard
Togher
Agher
Ga
Castletown Geoghegan
Gaybrook
15 (24)
Kinnegad
M4
Clonard
Longwood
R159
M4
10
Bunglass
Rathcore
Enfield
Cloncurry
Newtown
Streamstown
Milltownpass
R446
Moyvalley
R148
Toll
7 (11)
Spittaltown
N52
Dalystown
Rochfortbridge
M6
Killaskillen
Ballinabrackey
R401
Ballynadrumny
13 (21)
Johnstown Bridge
Toll
KILBEGGAN
Horseleap
Ballinagore
Ardmorney
Tyrrellspass
19 (31)
Garr
Castlejordan
Kilshanchoe
Cadamstown
Mucklon
Donadea
Donadea Forest Pa
Newtownlow
Kilbeggan
Coppanrush
Clonmore
Grange
BALLINDOOLIN HOUSE & GARDEN
Carbury
Derrinturn
Timahoe
Staplestown
Mainham
LOCKE'S DISTILLERY MUSEUM
5
Croghan
R441
R400
Rhode
R402
Edenderry (Éadan Doire)
R403
Derrygolan
Kilclonfert
Killeshill
Ballyfore
Killinagh
Cooleragh
Prosperous
7 (11)
ABBEY
Durrow
14 (23)
N52
R420
Ardan
DEW HERITAGE CENTRE
Derrygrogan
Daingean
Rathvilla
BOG OF ALLEN
Ballykilleen
Allenwood
KILDAR
Corndarragh
Bog of Allen

Bru Bar Bistro
Unit 8, Haymarket Northbank, Drogheda (041 987 2784, www.bru.ie). Restaurant Food served noon-10pm daily. Bar Open 6pm-1.30am Fri, Sat.
This busy modern establishment with its striking glass frontage ranges across two floors. On the ground-floor is a restaurant – offering alfresco dining and a menu of crowd-pleasers (pasta, steak, burgers, stir-fries) – with a late-opening weekend cocktail bar above it. The bar has live music and DJs.

Eastern Seaboard Bar & Grill ★
Bryanstown Centre, Dublin Road, Drogheda (041 980 2570, www.easternseaboard.ie). Food served noon-10pm Mon-Sat; noon-8pm Sun.
This quirkily contemporary restaurant has a New York industrial-luxe feel, its walls adorned with animal heads, a vintage US flag, unusual wall paintings and a mixture of antique and new furniture. The menu offers pails of deep-fried shrimp, delicious crab cakes and slow-roasted pork belly; good, simple but tasty food at a reasonable price. The staff are friendly and relaxed and on any given night of the week the atmosphere is buzzing. The outside smoking area is decked out with comfy sofas, heaters and foliage to keep the puffers happy.

Where to stay
In Drogheda, the small, family-run Scholars Townhouse Hotel (King Street, 041 983 5410, www.scholarshotel.com) offers comfortable, affordable accommodation. There's also the Best Western Boyne Valley Hotel (Dublin Road, 041 983 7737, www.boyne-valley-hotel.ie) on the outskirts of town, close to the M1. For Dundalk, the Crowne Plaza Hotel (042 939 4900, www.cpireland.crowneplaza.com) is most comfortable. There are plenty of B&Bs and self-catering places in Carlingford: Beaufort House (Ghan Road, 042 937 3879, www.beaufort house.net) has lovely sea views, and Belvedere House (Newry Street, 042 938 3848, www. belvederehouse.ie, closed Mon-Wed winter; Mon summer), home to the BayTree restaurant (*see p235*), is another possibility. The website www.carlingford.ie has accommodation listings.

D Hotel
Scotch Hall, Drogheda (041 987 7700, www.thedhotel. com). Rates €89-€100 double incl breakfast.
Drogheda's trendiest hotel, the D is playfully business-chic in style, with a good river setting. The 100-plus bedrooms are neatly contemporary and many have views over the water, as does the hotel's informal 'bistro-style' restaurant. There's also a bar that serves cocktails and hosts weekend gigs. A good, modern choice, with reasonable room rates.

Ghan House
Carlingford (042 937 3682, www.ghanhouse.com). Rates €105-€130 double incl breakfast & dinner.
This Georgian family home on the shore of Carlingford Lough is a relaxing and special place to stay. The four characterful bedrooms in the main house have views of either the mountains or the sea, while the eight comfortable rooms in the new section have good sight of the mountains.

Trim Castle. See p241.

Places to visit

COUNTY LOUTH

Beaulieu House, Gardens & Car Museum

*Beaulieu, Drogheda (041 983 8557, www.beaulieu.ie).
Open July, Aug 11am-5pm Mon-Fri; 1-5pm Sat, Sun.
May, June, Sept 11am-5pm Mon-Fri. Admission
Museum €6. House (guided tour only) €8. Gardens
€6. No credit cards.*

The first unfortified house of its kind in Ireland,
Beaulieu House was built in 1628 on land previously
owned by the family of Oliver Plunkett. The brick used
in the house was imported from the Netherlands,
which gives the exterior a distinctly Dutch flavour.
Remaining in the hands of the Tichbourne family to
this day, Beaulieu's interior has been impeccably
maintained and is full of family portraits and antique
furniture. Guided tours of the house and the lovely
walled gardens are offered. The Car Museum's
collection of racing cars, which date from the early
20th century, was amassed by the current owner,
Gabriel DeFreitas, who had a very successful motor-
racing career in the 1960s.

Mellifont Abbey

*Tullyallen (041 982 6459, www.heritageireland.ie).
Open Visitor centre May-Sept 10am-6pm daily.
Admission €3; €1-€2 reductions; €8 family.
No credit cards.*

Founded in 1142, Mellifont Abbey was the first
Cistercian monastery in Ireland – and quickly became
one of the wealthiest and most important abbeys
in the country, with more than 20 Cistercian houses
founded either directly or indirectly by Mellifont.
The abbey was dissolved in 1539, passing into the
hands of Sir Edward Moore, who made it his personal
residence. Thereafter, it played various roles in Irish
history. Here Hugh O'Neill, Earl of Tyrone, submitted
to Lord Mountjoy and signed the Treaty of Mellifont.
The abbey was also headquarters for William III during
the Battle of the Boyne. After that, the place fell into
disrepair. Much of the vast abbey is little more than
rubble now, but there are enough significant ruins to
give a sense of it all. The visitor centre has a small
historical exhibition that includes a model of the
abbey as it is thought to have been.

Monasterboice

*9km north of Drogheda, just north of junction 11
of the M1 motorway. Open sunrise-sunset daily.
Admission free.*

Tucked away in the Boyne Valley, Monasterboice
– consisting of the remains of a pair of churches,
a round tower and two of the finest remaining
high crosses in Ireland – is one of the country's
earliest Christian sites. Standing on the site of a
monastery, supposedly founded by St Buithe in
the fifth century, the South Cross and West Cross
date back to the ninth century. They are the finest
examples of religious art from that time, with intricate
carvings that illustrate scenes from both the Old and
New Testaments. The 5.5m-tall South Cross, also
called Muirdach's Cross, is near the entrance to
the site and is the better preserved of the two, with
images and even an inscription at its base clearly
visible. The 7m-tall West Cross (also called Tall Cross)
is the highest in Ireland. The 30m-high round tower,

Hill of Tara

which is in remarkable shape given the site was
burned in 1097, is the second tallest in Ireland.

St Peter's Roman Catholic Church

*West Street, Drogheda (041 983 8537,
www.saintpetersdrogheda.ie). Open Summer
7.30am-8pm daily. Winter 7.30am-6pm daily.*

This imposing Gothic-style church was built in
1791, but only part of the original building survived
reconstruction in 1884. Inside, you'll find a shrine
containing the head of St Oliver Plunkett; other parts
of his body are housed elsewhere in the church.
Plunkett was Archbishop of Armagh and spent a lot
of time in Drogheda prior to his arrest by the English.
Convicted of treason, the priest was hanged, drawn
and quartered in London, but his dismembered body
was returned to Ireland.

COUNTY MEATH

Battle of the Boyne Visitor Centre

*Oldbridge (041 980 9950, www.battleoftheboyne.ie).
Open May-Sept 10am-6pm daily. Mar, Apr 9.30am-
5.30pm daily. Oct-Feb 9am-5pm daily. Admission €4;
€2-€3 reductions; €10 family.*

The centre, its entrance guarded by cannon, tells
the story of the Battle of the Boyne using artefacts
(original and replica 17th-century helmets, bayonets,
pistols and swords) and audio-visual displays. There
are a number of marked walks around the battle-site
(maps are available from the centre), as well as
pleasant walled gardens. Drinks and snacks are
available in the Tearoom Pavillion.

Brú na Bóinne ★

*Donore (041 988 0300, www.heritageireland.ie).
Newgrange Open June-Sept 9am-7pm daily. May
9am-6.30pm daily. Feb-Apr, Oct 9.30am-5.30pm*

daily. Nov-Jan 9am-5pm daily. Admission €6; €3-€5 reductions; €15 family.
Knowth June-Sept 9am-7pm daily. May 9am-6.30pm daily. Open Easter-late April, Oct 9.30am-5.30pm daily. Admission €5; €2-€3 reductions; €13 family. Both Last tours & shuttle bus 1hr 45mins before closing.
Visitor centre Open June-Sept 9am-7pm daily. May 9am-6.30pm daily. Feb-Apr, Oct 9.30am-5.30pm daily. Nov-Jan 9am-5pm daily. Admission €3; €2 reductions; €8 family.
Brú na Bóinne is one of Ireland's most popular sites, so it's best to arrive in the morning during the summer – otherwise you run the risk of all the tours selling out. The area has three superb examples of New Stone Age passage tombs, built some 5,000 years ago. These tombs are on the tops of hills a short distance from one another, with Knowth the largest of the three and Newgrange the best preserved (albeit enhanced with a little modern restoration). It is thought the tombs were built around 3200 BC, making them 500 years older than the Egyptian pyramids and 1,000 years older than Stonehenge. Public access to Knowth and Newgrange is only possible by guided tour arranged through the Brú na Bóinne visitor centre, which also has a very thorough exhibition detailing what is known about the sites. There's a canteen-style café for refreshments before you take the shuttle bus to these rather claustrophobic and immensely fascinating stone chambers.

When you arrive at Newgrange, the pristine exterior is rather unexpected. Indeed, the earth mound is decorated with stones of white quartz, the placement of which has caused some dispute – even though the stones themselves are original and from this site. The 97 kerbstones at the base of the structure are also authentic, and some – notably those guarding the entrance to the tomb – have impressive ancient engravings. The interior is narrow and the roof is packed with strategically stacked stones that have kept the small chamber dry for millennia. The precision of the tomb's designers is demonstrated by the small opening (called a roof-box) at the entrance of the tomb, which is carefully aligned to allow the first rays of sunlight on the winter solstice (21 December) to stream along the stone passageway and illuminate the chamber. An annual ballot is organised to determine the few lucky people who will be taken into the chamber on that day to experience the solstice.

Hill of Tara ★
Navan (046 902 5903, www.heritageireland.ie). Open Visitor centre Late May-mid Sept 10am-6pm daily. Admission €3; €1-€2 reductions; €8 family. No credit cards.
Once the seat of Ireland's High Kings, this low-lying ridge – believed to have been a site of ritual all the way back to the late Stone Age – is deeply seeded with the country's ancient myths. The grassy hill is distinctively indented with rounded-off, circular ridges and from the top, given clear weather, you can see 13 counties. There are more than 30 monuments here, including the Lia Fail (Stone of Destiny), a standing stone said to have been the coronation stone of the Kings of Tara. According

to legend, when a true Irish or Scottish king stands upon the stone, it cries out, announcing the legitimacy of his reign. The visitor centre provides information on all the monuments, as well as detailing the history and mythology relating to the Hill.

Loughcrew Cairns ★
Oldcastle (049 854 1356, www.loughcrew.com). Open 10am-4pm daily. Admission free.
A very different experience to Newgrange, Loughcrew has been left in its original state, giving it a ruggedly ancient feel. The approach to the summit is along grassy paths up the hillside, with great views of the surrounding countryside. Through a simple latched gate, you are free to explore the protruding earth-mounds, patches of sunken ground and tablets of stone that are littered around the summit, some dating back to 4000 BC. The central cairn has an entrance between standing stones; if you request the key and a torch from the café, you can unlock the gate and squeeze along the narrow passageway into the tiny stone chamber. Because it is unrestored, Loughcrew seems much more ancient than the much older Newgrange – an undiscovered treasure rather than a reverently preserved and carefully presented national monument.

Loughcrew Gardens
Oldcastle (049 854 1356, www.loughcrew.com). Open Mar-Oct noon-6pm daily. Admission €6; €3-€5 reductions; €20 family. Guided tour €20.
As well as the megalithic Cairns, Loughcrew has six acres of gardens and woodland, painstakingly cared for by the Naper family since the 1600s. Formal gardens, sweet porticos, water features and the ruins of St Oliver Plunkett's family church and tower house can all be explored. There's also an adventure course with activities for all ages, and B&B accommodation (€110-€130 double incl breakfast) is offered in Loughcrew House. The café serves snacks and hot drinks.

Trim Castle
Trim (046 943 8619, www.heritageireland.ie). Open Easter-Sept 10am-6pm daily. Oct 9.30am-5.30pm daily. Nov-Jan 9am-7pm Sat, Sun. Feb-Easter 9.30am-5.30pm Sat, Sun. Admission Castle & keep tour €4; €2-€3 reductions; €10 family. Castle only €3; €1-€2 reductions; €8 family.
On the bank of the River Boyne, the remains of Trim Castle are in surprisingly good shape – so much so, they were used in the filming of Braveheart. The place has a long history: in 1172, Henry II granted Hugh de Lacy the Liberty of Meath in an attempt to deter Richard de Clare (aka Strongbow) from setting up an independent Anglo-Norman kingdom of Ireland. Hugh built a wooden castle, which was later burned to the ground and, in 1176, replaced by a stone keep. The site was then secured by building a curtain wall and a moat, crossed by a bridge to the north. The castle was extended again by Walter de Lacy, Hugh's son, with the construction of fore-buildings and a new, more impressive entrance, which still stands today. The site is well preserved, and there's an intriguing guided tour that includes entry to the keep – there are panoramic views from the top.

Loughcrew Gardens. See p241.

There's an open fire in the drawing room, and a cosy bar area. Operating one of Ireland's first cookery schools, Ghan House provides wonderful, home-cooked dinners and breakfasts, using home-grown produce, local beef and Cooley lamb, and oysters and fish from the lough.

COUNTY MEATH

The River Boyne intersects County Meath, winding its way through rich, fertile pastures. The Boyne Valley contains not only some of Ireland's finest farmland, but also the country's finest ancient site: Brú na Bóinne is an area of Neolithic passage tombs so important it has been made a UNESCO World Heritage Site. Castles are strewn along the banks of the Boyne – Trim Castle, Slane Castle and Talbot's Castle – and the river gave its name to Ireland's largest battle, the Battle of the Boyne.

Oldbridge, Brú na Bóinne & Slane

Just west of Drogheda at the junction with the M1 is the site of the Battle of the Boyne. On 1 July 1690 (but, due to a change in calendars, celebrated by the controversial Orangemen marches on the days running up to 12 July), battle was joined between the reigning British king, William III, and his deposed uncle and father-in-law James II. William and his 36,000 men lined up north of the river, while James took up positions to the south with some 25,000 troops, mainly Irish Catholics but supported by some French soldiers. By the end of the day, 1,500 men were dead, and William had confirmed his status as the Protestant King William III. The Battle of the Boyne Visitor Centre (see p240) is at Oldbridge, the point where William's troops crossed the river.

A five-minute drive south of Oldbridge is one of Ireland's most ancient sacred sites. Brú na Bóinne (see p240; 'Bend in the Boyne' – also known by the names of its two key sites: Newgrange and Knowth)

is one of Ireland's most visited monuments. There is no access to the site without a guide, and guided tours can only be arranged through the visitor centre. Knowth is the less developed of the two, and has a large number of ornately engraved stones. The two passages in the tomb are aligned with sunrise and sunset on the equinoxes in March and September.

About ten kilometres west of Oldbridge, along the N51, is Slane. At the foot of the village, where the River Boyne flows over weirs and under a single-lane bridge, stands an imposing Gothic gateway. Through this entrance King George IV rode to visit his mistress, Lady Conyngham, at Slane Castle (041 982 0643, www.slanecastle.ie, open June-Aug Mon-Thur, Sun). Long the ancestral home of the Conynghams, the castle was built by the Normans but redesigned as an imposing Georgian edifice surrounded by precise gardens. After a fire in 1991 destroyed more than a third of the building, it took almost ten years to restore the place, but the castle is now open for guided tours – as well as weddings and conferences. Each summer, Slane Castle hosts a music concert with a big headline act.

Slane village is set on the old main road from Dublin to Belfast, and has four identical grey-stone Georgian houses on the corners of the main intersection. These were built by the Conynghams in the late 19th century. Behind the village, the Hill of Slane is where St Patrick defiantly lit the Easter Fire for the first time in 433, the symbolic event that marks the arrival of Christianity to Ireland. It's an easy ramble to the top of the hill, where you'll find an old church and college that date from 1512.

Slane was the birthplace of war poet Francis Ledwidge. On the way out of town along the N51, the tiny cottage where he was born in 1887 is now the Francis Ledwidge Museum (041 982 4544, www.francisledwidge.com, closed Nov-Mar Mon-Fri).

It has examples of Ledwidge's work and some of his belongings, with detailed boards recounting the events of his life up to his death in World War I.

Navan & Kells

Continue west along the N51 for about 12 kilometres to reach Navan, best known as the birthplace of actor Pierce Brosnan. Perhaps more interestingly, the town was also the birthplace of Francis Beaufort, inventor of the Beaufort Scale for wind force. Uneven development has meant Navan isn't the prettiest place, but it does have a few good restaurants and the Solstice Arts Centre (Railway Street, 046 909 2300, www. solsticeartscentre.com, box office closed Sun), housed in an eye-catching contemporary building and programming local and international music, theatre, dance and comedy.

Kells lies 16 kilometres north-west of Navan. This was where St Colmcille (more famous as St Columba) established a religious settlement, prior to his departure for Iona. In the ninth century, the community of St Columba's monastery were forced out of Iona by violent Viking raids and returned to Kells for refuge. The monks built a monastery there, where they created the Book of Kells, a lavishly illuminated Latin version of the four gospels. The Book survived almost intact despite numerous raids on the monastery, and is now kept at Trinity College Dublin. A copy of it is housed in Kells Tourist Office (Kells Civic Offices, Hedford Place, 046 924 8856, www.meath.ie/tourism, closed Sat, Sun).

Most of the main sights are in the grounds of St Columba's Church. Built on the site of the original monastery, the church burned down in 918 and was rebuilt in 1152 – of this medieval version only the old bell tower remains – and again in 1578. Beside the church is a 25m-tall round tower, said to have been the site of the murder of one of the men who fought for the High Kingship of Ireland in 1076, with three ornately carved high crosses around it. On the lane approaching the church, St Columba's House is the oldest surviving structure in Kells, dating from the ninth century. The small, stone building with its steep roof and tiny chambers is usually closed, but occasionally the keeper is on hand to let you in.

Just over 20 kilometres west of Kells is the megalithic cemetery, Loughcrew Cairns (see p241). Of the 30 or so passage tombs dug into the summit of Slieve na Callaigh, one is accessible to the public. The keys to the tomb are held at the Loughcrew Gardens (see p241), about a kilometre past the turn for the Cairns, and well worth a visit in themselves.

Trim & around

Fifteen kilometres south-west of Navan is Trim. It's a bustling little town with a colourful history, reflected by the grand remains of a number of historic buildings, including the formidable Trim Castle (see p241). Across the river, perched on the banks of the Boyne, is Talbot's Castle. Built in 1415 by Sir John Talbot, Lord Lieutenant of Ireland, it was bought, modernised and turned into a boys' Latin school by Jonathan Swift. There's no public access, but there are wonderful views of the house from the grounds of Trim Castle. Behind Talbot's are the remains of a fifth-century

Bellinter House. See p244.

Augustine abbey, St Mary's, with a crumbling belfry. It's known as Yellow Steeple.

If you cross the footbridge from Trim Castle and pass under Sheep's Gate, then follow the river path for a kilometre, you'll eventually arrive at the remains of St Peter's and St Paul's Cathedral, which was Ireland's largest Gothic cathedral. From here, cross over the beautiful St Peter's Bridge for the ruins of the Priory of St John the Baptist. Both the cathedral and the priory were founded by Simon de Rochfort in the early 13th century, with the priory used as a hospital and guesthouse by Augustinian monks.

Bective Abbey is eight kilometres from Trim along the R161. A signpost leads you off the road to this beautifully located Cistercian abbey, founded in 1147. Hugh de Lacy, founder of Trim Castle, was buried here, but his remains were later moved to Dublin. The abbey has been extended and modernised over the years, but most of the remains date from the 15th century. There's a well-preserved round tower at the entrance, as well as various arches and the cloister.

Continue along the road from the abbey to find the mythologically resonant Hill of Tara (*see p241*), its 30 monuments having given rise to considerable archaeological speculation.

Where to eat & drink

Slane has limited options for eating and drinking, but traditional cakeshop Georges Pâtisserie (Chapel Street, 041 982 4493, closed Mon, Sun) on the main street serves hot drinks, snacks and freshly baked goods, and Boyle's Bar (Main Street, 041 982 0729, www.boylesofslane.com) is a lively spot with music most nights. Navan has a better selection, including the Loft Restaurant (26 Trimgate Street, 046 907 1755), with its ground-floor tapas bar, and the Russell Restaurant (15-16 Ludlow Street, 046 903 1690, www.russell restaurant.com, closed Mon, Tue). The Loft has a sister restaurant in Kells: the Ground Floor restaurant (Bective Square, 046 924 9688, closed Mon, Tue) is also airy, casual and contemporary in style. Still in Kells, the Vanilla Pod Restaurant (046 924 0084, www.headfortarms.ie) in the Headfort Arms Hotel is a good choice for dinner, its dishes made using locally sourced produce.

Just outside Trim, busy Marcie Regan's (Newtown Bridge, mobile 087 310 4304) offers traditional music, while O'Connells (046 902 5122), a few kilometres from the Hill of Tara, is a traditional, no-frills bar with plenty of atmosphere. Closer to the Hill of Tara, Maguire's Coffee Shop (046 902 5534) has been serving home-made snacks since the time of Daniel O'Connell, while Franzini O'Briens (046 943 1002, closed Mon winter) on French's Lane is the best restaurant in Trim, overlooking Trim Castle.

Brabazon Restaurant ★
Tankardstown House, Slane (041 982 4621, www.tankardstown.ie). Dinner served 6-10pm Thur-Sat. Food served noon-8pm Sun.

The Brabazon, a former cowshed, is tucked away in a wood 5km from Slane. Carefully restored original brickwork is prettified by modern chandeliers and floaty curtains, and there's a large stove-fire. The menu is seasonal and reasonably priced, using local products in dishes such as Lough Erne lamb or succulent pork belly and cheek. The wine list is well chosen, and the friendly, relaxed staff help create a pleasant atmosphere.

Where to stay

County Meath has a number of lovely country-house options, including the Millhouse (Old Mill, mobile 083 364 1612, www.themillhouse.ie) in Slane, which overlooks the river; it's only open for small groups and special occasions, such as Valentine's Day. Just outside Slane, Rossnaree House (041 982 0975, www.rossnaree.ie, closed Nov-Feb), a fine Victorian building, offers B&B in four stunning themed rooms. Artistic retreats are also offered.

In Trim, hotels include the Trim Castle Hotel (Castle Street, 046 948 3000, www.trimcastle hotel.com) in the centre of town and, a kilometre or so outside the town, the more popular Knightsbrook Hotel & Golf Resort (Dublin Road, 046 948 2100, www.knightsbrook.com). There's also a lovely guesthouse in Athboy, west of Trim: Frankville House (O'Growney Street, 046 948 7961, www.bluedoorguesthouse.ie).

Bellinter House
Nr Navan (046 903 0900, www.bellinterhouse.com). Rates €198-€358 double incl breakfast & dinner.
A few kilometres south of Trim, this 18th-century Palladian mansion is surrounded by acres of land. The interior is surprising: although the house was restored in keeping with the original design, the decor is very contemporary, with cow-skin chairs and funky lampshades giving a minimal, almost shabby-chic feel. The 34 bedrooms – some in the two wings of the main house, others in converted outbuildings – all blend old-style and contemporary, and there is a spacious drawing room, a games room and a library. Relaxing and friendly, this hotel is a favourite with Dubliners, but some rooms in the main house are a bit poky and, although there's a beautiful pool, some other facilities were not working at the time of our visit. The basement Eden restaurant has excellent service, good food and is popular with locals at the weekend.

Tankardstown House ★
Slane (041 982 4621, www.tankardstown.ie). Rates €315-€350 double incl breakfast. Cottages from €200 incl breakfast.
Set in 80 acres of land, Tankardstown is Patricia Conroy's elegantly restored home, turning original features and traditional styling into something utterly luxurious. As well as the six bedrooms, there are two drawing rooms with an open fire, where guests can help themselves to drinks from the honour bar. Dinner is served in a gorgeous restaurant room or the courtyard. For families or other groups, there are 12 further rooms in the spacious cottages (not self-catering), from which guests are still invited to come up to the house for pre-dinner drinks and breakfast. The grounds include an open-air hot tub, and a walled garden.

The Midlands

The mostly inland areas straddling the M6 between Dublin and Galway contain many surprises. Lovers of beautiful countryside can enjoy the lakes and waterways of County Cavan, explore Longford's pretty villages, and walk among the distinctive grass-topped hillocks in County Monaghan or in the Slieve Bloom Mountains. Those with a feel for history should certainly venture to Clonmacnoise, one of Ireland's most important monastic sites, with significant ruins remaining, and the Iron Age paths at Corlea Trackway archaeological site, preserved for millennia under bogland, are worth a detour. Monaghan was also home to poet Patrick Kavanagh, who would doubtless have made time to visit the Tullamore whiskey distillery. After a few drams, you might find yourself in the mood for the Seven Wonders of Fore and the legend of the Children of Lir.

COUNTY CAVAN

The rolling, watery landscape of Cavan is very scenic, and the county's many lakes and rivers also provide excellent fishing for trout, pike, bream, rudd, perch and eel. The waterways are terrific fun for leisure boating too.

Cavan is the county town. It's a busy market town, with a compact centre – Main Street will furnish you with any supplies you need for further exploration of the area. The tourist office (049 433 1942, www.cavantourism.com, open June-Sept Mon-Fri) is located in Farnham Street's Johnstown Library & Farnham Centre, which also functions as an art gallery. A new theatre has recently opened at the Imperial on Main Street: the Gonzo Theatre (mobile 087 168 9430, www.thegonzotheatre.com) programmes gigs and comedy as well as theatre. It has a weekly alternative cinema, the Picture Lounge. Lovers of traditional music should head to Main Street to the Farnham Arms Hotel (049 433 2577, www.farnhamarmshotel.com) or Cruiscín Lán (049 436 5702), which both host weekly sessions.

About six kilometres west of Cavan, the new Blue Wall Gallery (049 436 1627, www.bluewallgallery.com, closed Mon, Sun) in Corracanvy hosts contemporary art shows and has a sculpture garden. The bustling market town of Ballyjamesduff, about 15 kilometres south-east of Cavan, is home to the Cavan County Museum (see p50), while a few kilometres further south, Lough Sheelin is a favourite spot for fly-fishing in May.

North of Cavan town, lakes and rivers dominate the landscape. A complex cluster of lakes at Lough Oughter is linked by the River Erne to Upper Lough Erne, about 30 kilometres to the north. Cruisers can be hired from Emerald Star (071 962 7633, www.emeraldstar.ie) at Belturbet, halfway between Lough Oughter and the Upper Erne. Visitors can putter further north into Lower Lough Erne, or turn the tiller west on the Shannon–Erne Waterway towards Leitrim. The green hills and fields also make this a good area for walking and cycling: the Cavan Way (see p249) and Kingfisher Cycle Trail (see p249) are very picturesque.

Where to eat & drink

The Oak Room (32 Main Street, 049 437 1414, www.theoakroom.ie, closed Mon) is the best place for dinner in Cavan, serving a menu of international greatest hits – including some serious steaks made from local beef. Just outside town, the popular Side Door (049 433 1819, closed Mon, Tue) dishes up burgers, pizza and pasta, while the lovely Olde Post Inn (047 55555, www.theoldepostinn.com, closed Mon), a cosy restaurant in Cloverhill, nine kilometres north of Cavan, offers hearty food, and seven B&B rooms. In Ballyconnell, Pól O'D Restaurant (049 952 6228, closed Mon-Wed) is a country-style affair serving home-cooked dinners (Thur-Sun). In Belturbet, the Seven Horseshoes (Main Street, 049 952 2166, www.theseven horseshoes.com) has a lively bar, a restaurant and ten rooms for B&B.

MacNean House & Restaurant ★

Main Street, Blacklion (071 985 3022, www.macnean restaurant.com). Lunch served 12.30-3.30pm Sun. Dinner served 6-9.30pm Wed-Sat; 7-8.30pm Sun.
Irish celebrity chef Neven Maguire's commitment to using the best of local and seasonal produce has made his establishment, in tiny Blacklion village in the north-west of the county, a foodie destination – booking is essential. You can expect exquisite cooking, faultless and friendly service, and accommodatingly priced menus – from the €39 Sunday lunch to a nine-course tasting menu blowout for €85 (€125 with wine pairings). The relaxed atmosphere extends to the 18 rooms offered for B&B (€140-€200 double incl breakfast).

Where to stay

Those exploring the River Erne or Shannon–Erne Waterway, do best to stay in Ballyconnell or Belturbet. The International Fishing Centre (049 952 2616, open Mar-May, Oct, Nov) in Belturbet offers residential fishing holidays and wooden cabins for rent, as well as a good bar and restaurant; for B&B, try the Seven Horseshoes (see above). Near Ballyconnell, the Slieve Russell Hotel & Country Club (049 952 6444, www.slieverussell.ie) is a four-star

LEITRIM
FERMANAGH
MONAGHAN
CAVAN
LONGFORD
Iron Mountains
Manorhamilton
Glenboy
Blacklion
Belcoo
Bellanaleck
Arney
Maguiresbridge
Eshnadarragh
Scotstown
Monaghan (Muineachán)
Tyholland
Keady
Tassagh
Darkley
Glenfarne
Drummacabranagher
Wheathill
Swallow Holes
Marble Arch Caves
Florence Court (NT)
Florence Court Forest Park
Mackan
Ballindarragh
Drumcard
Castle Balfour
Lisnaskea
Knocks
Bunneil
Rosslea
Smithborough
Castleshane
Clontibret
Gubaveeny
Killarga
Coollegreane
Tiltinbane
Cuilcagh
Mullan
Kinawley
Upper Lough Erne
Tully
Donagh
Derrynawilt
Three Mile House
Cavanagarven
Braddocks
Tawnylea
Dowra
Glengavlen
Slievenakilla
Swanlinbar
Derrylin
Derryad
Magheraveely
Clones (Cluain Eois)
Killeevan
Scotch Corner
Newtownhamilton
Creaghanroe
Corry
Altbrean
Bellavally Gap
Derrynacreeve
Slieve Rushen
Gortmullan
Teemore
Newtownbutler
Crom Estate (NT)
Anlore
Newbliss
Crossreagh
Latnamard
Stranooden
Creevagh
Swan's Cross Roads
Ballybay (Béal Átha Beithe)
Annayalla
Cullyhanna
Drumkeeran
Drumnafinnila
Lough Allen
Corlough
Slieve Russell
Wattlebridge
Aghalane
Rockcorry
Doohamlet
Castleblayney (Baile na Lorgan)
Corglass
Altagowlan
Slieve Anierin
Corraleehan
Bawnboy
Ballyconnell
Templeport Lough
Belturbet
Redhills
Scotshouse
Drum
Aghnamullen
Arigna
Arigna Mining Experience
Mountallen
Aghacashel
Aughnasheelan
Arts & Cultural Cen.
Ballyhugh
Milltown
Cloverhill
Treehoo
Lisboduff
Cootehill
Latton
Lough Morne
Kilkit
Lough Eglish
Broomfield
Ballyfarnon
Keadew
Drumshanbo
Ballinamore
Drumlonan
Newtown Gore
Ardlougher
Lough Oughter
Butlers Bridge
Ballyhaise
Drung
Tullyvin
Drumgoon
Shantonagh
Laragh
Drumcong
Keshcarrigan
Fenagh
Glenview Folk Mus.
Drumlea
Doogary
Killegar
Corrawaleen
Killeshandra
Kill
Maudabawn
Donaghmoyne
Knockvicar
Cootehall
Leitrim
Heritage Centre
Greagh
Garvagh
Kilnagross
Cavan (An Cabhán)
Cath. of SS Patrick & Felim
Tullcoe
Corraneary
Shercock
Corduff
Drumbroagh
Carrickmacross (Carrig Mhachaire)
Carrigallen
Arghavas
Derrylane
Cavan Crystal
Crossdoney
Poles
Stradone
Lavey
Canningstown
Northlands
Capragh
Corcreeghy
Costello Chapel
Carrick-on-Shannon (Cora Droma Rúisc)
Lisduff
Cloone
Corriga
Cornafean
Corlismore
Ballinagh
Cashel
Grousehall
Moylett
Drumanespick
Magheracloone
Carrickashedoge
Killukin
Jamestown
Drumsna
Mohill
Moyne
Arvagh
Gorteen
Carrickaboy
Cross Keys
Termon
New Inn
Bailieborough (Coillan Chollaigh)
Moyer
Kingscourt (Dún an Rí)
Reaghstown
Aghamore
Clogher
Annaghmore
Leggagh
Carrigan
Crosserlough
Ballyjamesduff
Lisgrea
Killinkere
Ballynamona
Teevurcher
Hillstreet
Rodeen
Dromod
Cavan & Leitrim Railway
Cornageeha
Farnaght
Ballinamuck
Lough Gowna
Loughduff
Kilnaleck
Relagh Beg
Crossreagh
Kilmainhamwood
Drumcondra
Elphin
Drummullin
Roosky
Clooneagh
Aghnacliff
Cloonagh
Aghadowry
Inchmore
Kilcogy
Ballynarry
Ballymachugh
County Museum
Mount Nugent
Virginia
Ballymakane
Mullagh
Nobber
Woodtown
Strokestown Park House & Famine Museum
Kilglass
Pipers Town
Drumlish
Corn Hill
Dring
Bunlahy
Castlerahan
Eighter
Knockatemple
Lisduff
Ryefield
Thomastown
Moynalty
Lobinstown
Roscommon Heritage & Genealogy Centre
Strokestown
Scramoge
Whitehall
Newtown Forbes
Ennybegs
Esker
Ballinalee
Granard
Finnea
Ross
Mullaghmeen
Oldcastle
Loughcrew Cairns
Derver
Castletown
Carlanstown
Termonbarry
Cloondara
Cullyfad
Abbeylara
Castletown
Millbrook
Slieve na Calliagh
Carnaross
Kells (Ceanannus Mór)
Baile Órthai (Oristown)
Wilkinstown
Tully
Lackan
Curraghroe
Longford (An Longfort)
Ferraghfad
Lisryan
Lismacaffry
Ballymanus
Murrens
Loughcrew Gardens
Drumone
Slieve Gullion
Ballinlough
Kilberry
Aghamuck
Ballagh
Ballyleague
Killashee
Stonepark
St. Mel's Cath.
Edgeworthstown
Ardagh
Street
Coole
Tullynally Cas.
Castlepollard
Abbey
Fore
Crossakeel
Kilskeer
Clonmellon
Cortown
High Crosses
Fordstown
Baile Ghib (Gibstown)
Navan
Stackallan
Blackcastle

Roscommon (Ros Comáin)
Athlone (Baile Átha Luain)
Mullingar (An Muileann gCearr)
Trim (Baile Átha Troim)
Athboy (Baile Átha Buí)
Delvin
Kinnegad
Rochfortbridge
Tyrrellspass
Kilbeggan
Moate (An Móta)
Clara (Clóirtheach)
Tullamore (Tulach Mhór)
Edenderry (Éadan Doire)
Enfield
Clane (Claonadh)
Prosperous
Sallins
Rathangan (Ráth Iomgháin)
Newbridge (Droichead Nua)
Kildare (Cill Dara)
Monasterevin (Mainistir Eimhín)
Portarlington (Cúil an tSúdaire)
Mountmellick (Móinteach Milic)
Portlaoise (Port Laoise)
Stradbally (An tSraidbhaile)
Athy (Baile Átha Í)
Kilcullen (Cill Chuillin)
Mountrath (Maighean Rátha)
Birr (Biorra)
Banagher (Beannchar)
Ferbane (An Féar Bán)
Shannonbridge
Ballymahon
Kilcormac
Geashill
Daingean
Clonbullogue
W E S T M E A T H
M E A T H
O F F A L Y
K I L D A R E
Bog of Allen
Slieve Bloom Mts
Lough Ree
N O R T H

hotel with a spa and 18-hole championship golf course. In the pretty town of Virginia, south-east of Ballyjamesduff, the Park Hotel (049 854 6100, www.parkhotelvirginia.com, closed mid Dec-Feb) has fine views over Lough Ramor and another golf course. There are further B&B options at Cloverhill's Olde Post Inn (*see p245*) and MacNean House (*see p245*) in Blacklion.

Farnham Estate Hotel
Farnham Estate, Cavan (049 437 7700, www.farnham estate.com). Rates €130-€220 double incl breakfast.
Set in 1,300 acres of park and woodland, this hotel is a 19th-century mansion with a modern extension, providing a total of 158 rooms. Within the original house, you'll find stripped wood and marble floors, contemporary furniture and spaciously minimalist public areas. Guests can dine in the casual Wine Goose Bar or the more formal Botanica Restaurant, and relax for drinks in any of several drawing rooms. The spa has a thermal suite and indoor and outdoor pools. In addition, there are plenty of walks around the estate, and a golf course.

COUNTY MONAGHAN
It is in this county that the drumlin belt becomes most evident, hence the county's name: *muineachain* means 'little hills' in Irish. Monaghan is full of the characteristically whale-shaped grassy hillocks, interspersed with lakes and small market towns. The county town, also called Monaghan, is a bustling affair, the heart of which – the Diamond – is dominated by the Rossmore Memorial. The town centre has some attractive buildings, including the old Market House and Courthouse, while the County Museum (Hill Street, 047 82928, www.monaghan.ie, closed Sun) provides some social, cultural and economic context.

Just outside town is Rossmore Forest Park, once part of the Rossmore family estate. Little is left of the impressive mansion, though you can still see the walls and garden. There are wooded walking trails and five fishing lakes. Maps are available from www.coillteoutdoors.ie.

A short drive north-east through hilly countryside from Monaghan town is the pretty estate village of Glaslough. Since the 17th century this has been the demesne of the Leslie family, a clan renowned for a history of eccentricity and mischievousness. Castle Leslie (*see right*) is now a luxurious hotel.

At Castleblayney, south-east of Monaghan town, Lough Muckno is surrounded by woodland and shaded walks. Adrenalin-seekers can waterski or wakeboard at the adventure centre (mobile 087 740 2806, www.skimuckno.com, closed Nov-Mar) in the Forest Park. By contrast, busy Carrickmacross and Clones are towns with strong traditions of lace-making; you can still buy fine examples of the craft.

County Monaghan is also the birthplace of Irish writer Patrick Kavanagh. He was born in the small town of Inniskeen, in the south of the county, where you can visit his grave and the Patrick Kavanagh Rural & Literary Resource Centre (*see p250*).

The best time to visit is during the wonderful Flat Lakes Literary & Arts Festival (www.theflatlake

Things to do

COUNTY CAVAN

Cavan Way
www.walkireland.ie.
This 26km walk in the west of Cavan threads its way between the small villages of Blacklion and Dowra, following the river valley before heading into the hills to the Shannon 'Pot', source of the river. You can download maps from the Walk Ireland website.

Kingfisher Cycle Trail
www.sustrans.org.uk.
The first long-distance cycle trail in Ireland, the Kingfisher Trail covers 386km through Cavan, Donegal, Fermanagh, Leitrim, Monaghan and Roscommon counties, but can be broken into smaller, more manageable sections.

COUNTY WESTMEATH

Lilliput Jonathan Swift Amenity Park
Lough Ennell, Mullingar (044 922 6141).
The park – on the south-west bank, near Dysart – has plenty to enjoy. You can hire boats for leisure or angling (044 922 6329, www.lilliputboathire.com, closed Nov-Feb) or get stuck into outdoor activities with Lilliput Adventure Centre (044 922 6789, www.lilliputadventure.com). Otherwise, there's golf, swimming, walking in the woods, or just chilling out over lunch in the café.

festival.com), held in the grounds of Hilton Park (*see p251*) over one weekend in June. In addition to appearances from poets and novelists, there's plenty of music and comedy.

Where to eat & drink
The best place to eat in Monaghan town is Andy's Bar & Restaurant (12 Market Street, 047 82277, www.andysmonaghan.com, closed Mon).

Where to stay
In Carrickmacross, the Nuremore Hotel & Country Club (042 966 1438, www.nuremore.com) is a fine country hotel with an 18-hole golf course.

Castle Leslie ★
Glaslough (047 88100, www.castleleslie.com). Rates B&B €160-€190 double incl breakfast. Self-catering €830-€1,050 per week.
Owned by the Leslie family since 1660, the castle is set in 1,000 acres of woodland, gardens, lakes and hills, with deer, hare, squirrels and foxes roaming about. There are 20 guest rooms, each individually styled and retaining their old-world elegance. There's a pool room, a warm and welcoming drawing room, and a grand dining room, all luxuriously appointed. A stylish extension to the renovated hunting lodge incorporates a further 29 rooms, as well as a traditional Irish bar and brasserie. Self-catering cottages, a spa, equestrian centre, fishery and dozens of walks around the picturesque estate complete the picture.

Places to visit

Clonmacnoise

COUNTY CAVAN

Cavan County Museum

Virginia Road, Ballyjamesduff (049 854 4070, www.cavanmuseum.ie). Open June-Sept 10am-5pm Tue-Sat; 2-6pm Sun. Oct-May 10am-5pm Tue-Sat. Admission €3; €1.50 reductions; €8 family.
The social, economic and cultural history of the county is illustrated with artefacts such as Sheela-na-gigs (mysterious medieval sculptures of women), a solid-silver mace from the 1700s, and 17th-century weapons. Exhibits cover the Great Famine, traditional Irish sports such as hurling and Gaelic football, and even Percy French, composer of the song 'Come Back Paddy Reilly to Ballyjamesduff'.

COUNTY MONAGHAN

Patrick Kavanagh Rural & Literary Resource Centre

Inniskeen (042 937 8560, www.patrickkavanagh country.com). Open 11am-4.30pm Tue-Fri. Admission €5; €3 reductions.
As well as exhibitions on the history of the area, the centre has examples of Kavanagh's writing and items relating to his life. A collection of paintings depicts his epic poem *The Great Hunger*. On the Kavanagh Country Tour, a guide leads groups around the town and surroundings to places immortalised in Kavanagh poems.

COUNTY LONGFORD

Corlea Trackway Visitor Centre

Kenagh Road, Kenagh (043 332 2386, www.heritageireland.ie). Open Mid Apr-Sept 10am-6pm daily. Admission free.
Buried under the bogs at Corlea for more than 2,000 years, a togher (Iron Age road) was discovered here in 1984. Excavation revealed a series of trackways that dated from 148 BC. The interpretive centre includes an 18m stretch of trackway, as well as explaining bogland ecology. A guided tour then takes you outside to where a wooden walkway overlays a remaining trackway.

COUNTY WESTMEATH

Belvedere House ★

Mullingar (044 934 9060, www.belvedere-house.ie). Open May-Aug House, café & garden market 9.30am-5pm daily. Grounds 9.30am-8pm daily. Mar, Apr, Sept, Oct House, café & garden market 9.30am-5pm daily. Grounds 9.30am-6pm daily. Nov-Feb House, café & garden market 9.30am-4pm daily. Grounds 9.30am-4.30pm daily. Admission €8.75; €4.75-€6.25 reductions; €21-€24 family. Guided tours €1.
Visitors can tour this immaculately restored, 18th-century Palladian mansion (designed by eminent architect Richard Cassells), set on the eastern shores of Lough Ennell. The house has fine period features and furniture, and is surrounded by 160 acres of woodland and formal gardens. There are frequent concerts and festivals at the house, but it's a joy simply to stroll in the Victorian walled garden and through the extensive grounds.

COUNTIES OFFALY, LAOIS & CARLOW

Birr Castle Demesne ★

Birr, Co Offaly (057 912 0336, www.birrcastle.com). Open Mid Mar-Oct 9am-6pm daily. Nov-mid Mar 10am-4pm daily. Admission €9; €5-€7.50 reductions; €25 family.
Residence of the Earls of Rosse since 1640, Birr Castle remains the family home, so the interior isn't open to the public. However, the castle is well worth visiting for its lovely grounds. There are many rare trees and plants, the world's tallest box hedges, and plentiful wildlife in the rivers, lakes and woods, including otters, herons, kingfishers and red squirrels. Hours can be lost wandering the grounds, but do save some time for the Historical Science Centre, which showcases the family's astronomical research work over the centuries: a wooden telescope was built here by the 3rd Earl of Rosse in the 1840s – at the time, the largest telescope in the world. There's also a shop and café.

Clonmacnoise ★
Shannonbridge (090 967 4195,
www.heritageireland.ie). Open June-Aug 9am-7pm
daily. Mid Mar-May, Sept, Oct 10am-6pm daily.
Nov-mid Mar 10am-5.30pm daily. Admission €6;
€2-€4 reductions; €14 family. No credit cards.
In a peaceful location on the Shannon riverside,
this impressively extensive monastic site consists
of the ruins of two round towers, a cathedral, seven
churches (the earliest dating from the tenth century),
three high crosses and many ancient grave slabs.
Founded in around 560 by St Ciarán, Clonmacnoise
became over time one of the most significant centres
of ecclesiastical education in Ireland. The visitor
centre covers St Ciarán's arrival and biography,
and the subsequent growth of the monastery,
and there are displays of graveslabs and local
plants and animals.

Emo Court ★
Emo, Co Laois (057 862 6573, www.heritage
ireland.ie). Open House guided tour Easter-Sept
10am-6pm daily. Gardens dawn-dusk daily.
Admission €3; €1-€2 reductions; €8 family.
The 1st Earl of Portarlington began work on this
grand neo-classical building in 1790, but the current
building is the result of the interventions of several
generations – including the Jesuits, who made the
place their home in 1930. Today, Emo Court has
been restored as far as possible to its former
grandeur. The obligatory guided tour (held hourly)
is interesting and useful. Within the grounds of the
estate, there are walks through the formal gardens
and down to the lake, and a lovely tearoom.

Birr Castle Demesne

Hilton Park
Clones (047 56007, www.hiltonpark.ie). Rates
€190-€270 double incl breakfast. Closed Nov-Feb.
Five kilometres outside Clones, Hilton Park is housed in a
Palladian mansion, wonderfully situated in 200 acres of
formal gardens, lakes and woodland. The six rooms have
been elegantly restored in country-manor style, with dinner
served to residents in an almost ecclesiastical dining room.
After a forest walk or fishing and boating on the private
lake, relax in the comfortable drawing room.

COUNTY LONGFORD
Landlocked Longford is a quiet sort of place, its
landscape a mixture of farms and bogland lakes.
Longford is a busy market town with the River
Camlin running through it; the riverside pathway
is ideal for walkers and cyclists. Anglers should
head to the tourist office on Market Square (043
334 2577, http://longfordtourism.ie, closed Sat,
Sun) to get information on the best fishing spots
and to arrange permits, while golfers can enjoy
themselves at County Longford Golf Club (043
334 6310, www.countylongfordgolfclub.com).

There are several places to explore, including
Ardagh, a charming village south-east of Longford.
Those wanting to investigate the Royal Canal should
head south-west to Richmond Harbour in Clondra.
From here, you can follow the towpath – all the way
to Dublin, if you want – along the Royal Canal Way.

Don't miss the excellent archaeological exhibits
at Corlea Trackway Visitor Centre (*see p250*),
15 kilometres south of Longford town.

Where to eat & drink
In Longford, get lunch at Torc Café & Food Hall
(New Street, 043 334 8277, www.torccafe.com,
closed Sun), which has sandwiches, pizza, cakes,
great coffee and a chocolate fountain.

Where to stay

Viewmount House
Dublin Road, Longford (043 334 1919, www.view
mounthouse.com). Rates €100 double incl breakfast.
Viewmount House is an 18th-century country manor that
once belonged to Lord Longford. The open fires, antique
furniture and warm hosts make it a charming place to stay.
The dozen bedrooms in the original manor are comfortable
and smartly furnished, while additional rooms in the
outbuildings maintain the flavour of the main house. The
restaurant in the old stables is an atmospheric place, with a
bit of buzz at the weekends when the locals descend. The
food combines Irish ingredients with Asian touches.

COUNTY WESTMEATH
Just off the N4, Mullingar is Westmeath's county
town. There are several decent eateries and a
tourist office on Market Square (044 934 8650,
closed July, Aug Sun; Sept-June Sat, Sun), but
the key attractions are Belvedere House (*see
p250*) and, just to the south, Lough Ennell,

glistening among green dairy pastures. Explore the lake from the Lilliput Jonathan Swift Amenity Park (see p249).

To the north of the county, wistful Lough Derravaragh is the legendary resting place of the Children of Lir, siblings who were turned into swans. Castlepollard is the most appealing of the towns in this part of Westmeath, and both Tullynally Castle and Fore are nearby.

Tullynally Castle (044 966 1159 , www.tullynally castle.com, open May-Aug Thur-Sun), a kilometre

Wineport Lodge

north of Castlepollard, was the seat of the Earls of Longford for more than 300 years. The grand Georgian mansion was remodelled into a sprawling Gothic Revival castle, now looking like something created by Disney. It remains the Longford family home, so the castle is only accessible through group tours booked in advance. However, the stunning gardens, which have manicured terraced lawns and Chinese and Tibetan gardens, are open to the public.

In a lush valley to the east of Castlepollard, the small village of Fore is known for its 'Seven Wonders'. On and around the seventh-century monastic site founded by St Féichín, where a 12th-century church and abbey still stand, the seven miraculous sights include the place where water flowed uphill, and the monastery itself, which was apparently built right in the middle of a bog.

At the western edge of the county, the small estate village of Glasson was written about by the poet Oliver Goldsmith as the 'Village of Roses'. Near the shore of beautiful Lough Ree, which is peppered with tiny islands, the village is an understandably popular place for an overnight stay.

South of Glasson, Athlone's prime location on the River Shannon has given rise to a flourishing leisure boating industry, with visitors able to enjoy the lively nightlife when they return their boats or tie up overnight. Dozens of boats head north into Lough Ree each day, or south to the monastic site of Clonmacnoise. You can book trips at the tourist office in the Church Street Civic Offices (090 649 4630, open June-Aug Mon-Sat; Apr, May, Sept Mon-Fri), where there's information on different cruise options that include longer rentals along the Shannon. Opposite the dock and on the riverbank, Athlone Castle (090 644 2100) is a 14th-century Anglo-Norman structure that is undergoing major renovation; it should reopen, with a new interpretation centre, in 2012. The town has a flourishing arts scene; theatres include the Dean Crowe Theatre (Chapel Street, 090 649 2129, www.deancrowetheatre.com, closed July, Aug) and the Passionfruit Theatre (Northgate Street, mobile 086 333 8457, www.passionfruittheatre.com).

Where to eat & drink

Mullingar has several good eateries. Lovely Ilia Coffee (28 Oliver Plunkett Street, 044 934 0300, www.ilia.ie, closed Sun) is a great spot for lunch, while its new sister establishment, Ilia Restaurant (37 Dominick Street, 044 934 5947, closed Mon), serves delicious tapas. In Glasson, Grogan's Pub (090 648 5158, www.grogansofglasson.com) is an atmospheric place, having changed little since it opened in the 18th century. There's also Glasson Village Restaurant (090 648 5001, closed Mon).

Athlone has plenty of good dining options. Try Kin Khao Thai (090 649 8805), a fabulous Thai restaurant on Abbey Lane, or the global flavours at the upbeat Leftbank Bistro (Fry Place, 090 649 4446, www.leftbankbistro.com, closed Mon, Sun). For great views over the River Shannon, there's the Olive Grove (Custume Pier, 090 647 6946, www.theolivegrove.ie); the menu focuses on Irish produce, with dishes including seafood chowder, steaks and black pudding. After dinner, grab a pint at Sean's Bar (090 649 2358, www.seansbar.ie) on Main Street. In operation since AD 900, Sean's is said to be the oldest bar in Ireland and Britain.

Where to stay
Decent options in Mullingar include Annebrook House Hotel (Austin Friar Street, 044 935 3300, www.annebrook.ie) and the Mullingar Park Hotel (Dublin Road, 044 933 7500, www.mullingarpark hotel.com). The tranquil country-house hotel Mornington House (044 937 2191, www.mornington. ie, closed Nov-Mar) in Multyfarnham is close to the shores of Lough Derravarragh. If you can't get a room at Wineport Lodge (see below) in Glasson village, there's always the Glasson Golf Hotel (090 648 5120, www.glassongolf.ie). Athlone has plenty of accommodation, from hostels and caravan parks up to the Radisson Blu Hotel (Northgate Street, 090 644 2600, www.radissonblu.ie/hotel-athlone). You can get more information on www.athlone.ie.

Wineport Lodge ★
Glasson (090 643 9010, www.wineport.ie).
Rates €178-€298 double incl breakfast.
Set in the reedy banks of Killinure lake, the Wineport is a funkily designed wooden lodge, with an airy bar and restaurant, a spa and appealing outdoor terraces. The 29 rooms are spacious, bright and modern, with balconies and lake views. The Wineport began life as a restaurant, so the food is excellent. It's an ideal countryside retreat.

COUNTIES OFFALY, LAOIS & CARLOW

If you're visiting the extensive monastic site of Clonmacnoise (see p251) in County Offaly, it's worth making a detour to Birr. A rather refined estate town, full of Georgian terraces, it is also home to Birr Castle Demesne (see p250). The lively Birr Theatre & Arts Centre (057 912 2911, www.birrtheatre.com) is in a handsome 19th-century hall, best enjoyed during Birr Vintage Week & Arts Festival (www.birrvintageweek.com) in August, when the entire town dresses up in vintage clothing to enjoy street entertainment, theatre and music.

Whiskey lovers make pilgrimages to Tullamore, where the Tullamore Dew Heritage Centre (Bury Quay, 057 932 5015, www.tullamore-dew.org) celebrates the history and manufacture of the golden liquor in a former distillery warehouse.

Much of Offaly is bog and farmland, but the south-east of the county is bordered by the low-lying Slieve Bloom Mountains (www.slievebloom.ie). It's good hiking country, and the Slieve Bloom Walking Festival is held in May. Among several self-guided loop walks, the most challenging is the Slieve Bloom Way, a waymarked trail across the range through scenic valleys, forests and bogland. The pretty village of Kinnitty is the best base.

The Slieve Bloom Mountains extend into County Laois, easily accessible on the busy Cork–Limerick road. The county's highlight is Emo Court (see p251), but the looming Rock of Dunamase, near Portlaoise, is also worth a look. An Iron Age ring fort on its summit was replaced by a 13th-century castle, the crumbling remains of which can be easily explored on foot.

Continuing south-east, Laois borders the small county of Carlow, which is traversed by rivers and looked down upon by the Blackstairs Mountains. Carlow town buzzes with students, and the college combines two cultural venues in a striking modern building: Visual – Centre for Contemporary Art & George Bernard Shaw Theatre (Old Dublin Road, 059 917 2400, www.visualcarlow.ie).

Due south of Carlow, Bagenalstown, perched on the banks of the River Barrow, is popular with anglers. Further south is the sleepy and serene village of St Mullins, delightfully set on the banks of the Barrow Canal, on the Kilkenny border. The towpaths make a fine walk.

Where to eat & drink
The Stables (057 912 0263, www.thestables birr.com, closed Mon, Sun) is a lovely tearoom, furniture shop and B&B in Birr. Just outside town in Crinkill, the Thatch Bar (Military Road, 057 912 0682, www.thethatchcrinkill.com) is indeed straw-roofed and serves good food with international influences. If you're in Carlow, head to the Rattlebag Café (202 Barrack Street, 059 913 9568, closed Sun) for lunch, or try Lennons@ Visual (059 917 9245, www.lennons.ie), a modern, canteen-style space in the Visual arts centre. It has an inventive brunch menu, and Irish produce is to the fore. In St Mullins, the canalside Old Grainstore (051 424440, www.oldgrainstore cottages.ie, closed Mon) has a pleasant café and three self-catering cottages.

Where to stay
In Offaly, there's B&B accommodation at the Stables (see above) in Birr. On the Laois side of the Slieve Bloom Mountains is 18th-century Roundwood House (057 873 2120, www.round woodhouse.com), a family-run affair with six charming B&B rooms. Castle Durrow (057 873 6555, www.castledurrow.com) is a grand property with formal gardens and plenty of character on the Dublin–Cork route, but golfers may prefer the Heritage Golf & Spa Resort (057 864 5500, www. theheritage.com), north-east of Portlaois. It has self-catering apartments as well as standard rooms.

Near Bagenalstown, Lorum Old Rectory (059 977 5282, www.lorum.com, closed Jan, Dec) is a grey-stone Victorian building, with rooms decorated in a modernised traditional style and fine home-cooked food, while Kilgraney House (059 977 5283, www.kilgraneyhouse.com, closed Nov-Feb) is a beautiful Georgian country manor, with excellent food and a serene setting. The Old Grainstore (see above) in St Mullins offers self-catering.

Northern Ireland

Giant's Causeway, County Antrim. See p284.

Belfast

The combination of the Great Famine and the Industrial Revolution brought about a massive boost to both Belfast's economy and population. As people flocked to the factories and docks, the city cashed in on the cheap, plentiful workforce and by the end of the 19th century, Belfast boasted the world's largest shipyard and linen production centre, alongside tobacco factories, rope-making works and heavy engineering. It rapidly became Ireland's biggest and richest city. These prosperous times left an indelible mark on the city in the shape of grandiose Victorian buildings, many of which still stand, even if their uses have changed in the interim.

World War II, the industrial downturn and more than 30 years of bombing as a result of the sectarian divide in Northern Ireland reduced much of Belfast to rubble by the 1990s. It was only after the IRA ceasefire in 1994 that billions of pounds were invested to restore the city to its former glory. These investments have paid off enormously, along with the effort of local communities to turn Belfast into a vibrant, culturally rich and safe place to visit.

The city centre around Donegall Square is a compact and easy place to explore on foot. North of the square is the main shopping district and some of Belfast's finest restaurants and bars. The area stretching east towards the River Lagan, once dominated by shipyards, now houses two of the city largest entertainment venues. And a 20-minute walk south of the square is the University quarter, home to some of Belfast's most popular attractions: Queen's University, the Botanic Gardens and the Ulster Museum. Fun, cheap bars and restaurants cater to the student hordes, and there's always a great buzz to the area.

CITY CENTRE

Belfast is both the capital of Northern Ireland, and its largest metropolis. The city centre is focused on Donegall Square and its environs, notably to the north and east. The square is dominated by the huge, copper-domed City Hall (*see p260*), built in 1906, and is dotted with assorted statues and memorials including one to the ill-fated RMS *Titanic*, which was built in Belfast. The surrounding lawns are much used in summer; in winter they are occupied by the Christmas Continental Market, a magical maze of stalls selling food, drink and festive gifts from across Europe. Encircling the square is a mish-mash of grand Victorian edifices and run-of-the-mill modern buildings housing banks, shops and restaurants. Of most interest is Linen Hall Library (*see p260*), Belfast's oldest library. Belfast City Tour buses (9032 1321, www.belfastcity sightseeing.com) and regular public buses servicing the city leave from the square.

The Belfast Welcome Centre (9024 6609, www.gotobelfast.com), the city's tourist office, is just off the square's north side at 47 Donegall Place. It offers a hotel booking service, internet café and left-luggage facility (which is hard to find elsewhere due to security issues).

The main shopping area stretches northwards: the key streets are Donegall Place, Royal Avenue, Castle Street and High Street. Many high-street shops have commandeered Victorian buildings and erected shiny new façades – but cast your eyes to the sky and you will see that the top floors, while slightly jaded, retain their original grandeur. In addition, there are two large shopping malls: Castlecourt and the new, glitzy Victoria Square.

Belfast's oldest district lies north of Ann Street, where you'll find a series of narrow alleyways, some cobbled, known as the Entries. Once the mercantile and industrial hub of the city, these give a proper feel of Victorian Belfast; Pottinger's Entry, with its wrought-iron entrance arches, is the most obvious. Adjoining the Entries, above Waring Street, is the Cathedral Quarter. Massive investment has been pumped into the area over the past few years, turning it into the centre of Belfast's arts and entertainment scene. New apartments, cafés, restaurants and bars have risen up around Belfast Cathedral (*see p260*), the city's main Church of Ireland (Protestant) place of worship, and there are some lovely hotels too.

This is also where you'll find Northern Ireland's most popular gay bar: Kremlin (96 Donegall Street, 9031 6060, www.kremlin-belfast.com, closed Mon, Wed). Spread over several floors, with kitsch, Soviet-inspired decor, the club features top DJs, live performances and themed nights. On Talbot Street, adjacent to the cathedral, you'll find the War Memorial building (9032 0392, www.niwarmemorial.org, closed Sat, Sun), which

City Hall

contains an exhibition about Northern Ireland's involvement in World War II.

The Albert Memorial Clock, a well-known landmark, stands on Queens Square at the river end of High Street. Completed in 1869 in memory of Prince Albert, the ornate, 113-foot sandstone tower is slightly askew as it was built on sinking wooden piles. From here it's a few steps to the River Lagan, once the industrial heart of Belfast. Look across the water to Queen's Island and you'll see the two huge yellow gantry cranes – fondly known as Samson and Goliath – that, along with the dark outline of the Antrim Mountains, dominate the Belfast skyline. They belong to Harland and Wolff, the shipbuilders famous for building the *Titanic* and a host of other vessels (including HMS *Belfast* in London). The company is still in business; the cranes, a symbol of the shipyard's survival in difficult times, were scheduled for preservation in 2003.

The industrial warehouses that once rang to the noise of clanging iron have been replaced with glossy new buildings whence the sound of music now emanates. Adjacent to Oxford Street is the internationally acclaimed Waterfront (box office

9033 4455, www.waterfront.co.uk), an arts, music and conference centre, and behind it, on the corner of Oxford and May Streets, is St George's Market (*see p260*), one of Belfast's oldest – and best – attractions.

Across the river is the Odyssey entertainment complex, which contains a 10,000-seat stadium (www.odysseyarena.com) that pulls in big-name bands, comedians and sports events, as well as cinemas, bars and restaurants. Queen's Island is also the site of the Titanic's Dock & Pump-House (9073 7813, www.titanicsdock.com). There's an exhibition about Belfast's shipbuilding history and a café, and you can also see the huge dry dock – the biggest in the world at the time it was constructed, and a marvel of Edwardian engineering – where the ship was built. The area has been designated the Titanic Quarter and much building work is under way; a brand-new visitor complex is due to open in 2012. Lagan Boat Co (9033 0844, www.lagan boatcompany.com) runs Titanic-themed boat tours from Donegall Quay along the river. You can also join one of the regular two-hour walks around the key sights with Titanic Walking Tours (07904 350339, www.titanicwalk.com).

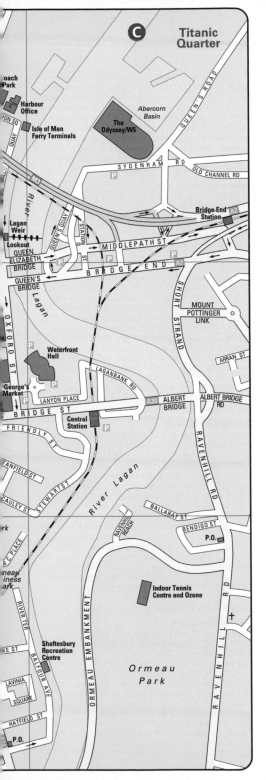

A couple of blocks west of Donegall Square is Great Victoria Street, which runs south towards the the University area. This stretch of road is known as the Golden Mile – a somewhat misleading name now, as it's mainly lined with dull office blocks, desolate buildings and empty lots. There are some places of note, however, such as the Grand Opera House (*see below*), a magnificent Victorian theatre that is indeed grand and does host opera productions. Across the road is the legendary Crown Bar (*see p264*), a landmark building, both inside and out.

Festivals

Belfast has an eclectic selection of festivals throughout the year, including the humorous street performers celebration Festival of Fools (www.foolsfestival.com) in spring; the more serious Féile an Phobail (www.feilebelfast.com) in West Belfast in August; and the extremely popular Belfast Festival at Queen's (www.belfastfestival.com) in October, featuring an impressive line-up of local and international artists across all genres. The Cathedral Quarter is a key hub for events, notably the Cathedral Quarter Arts Festival (www.cqaf.com) in May and the Open House Festival (www.open housefestival.com) of folk, traditional and bluegrass music in September. For more information on annual events, *see pp11-21*.

Where to eat & drink

Belfast knows how to do fabulous food and bars. The Entries and Cathedral Quarter have some of the best bars in the city centre, including the spacious, wood-panelled Cloth Ear, and Bert's, which is modelled on a 1930s New York jazz bar, with scarlet satin walls and velvet chairs. Both

Things to do

CITY CENTRE

Grand Opera House

Great Victoria Street, BT2 7HR (box office 9024 1919, www.goh.co.uk). Open Box office 9.30am-5.30pm Mon-Fri; noon-5pm Sat. Tickets £9.25-£36.
Opened in 1895, the Grand Opera House was designed by the great theatrical architect Frank Matcham, and is still a beauty. It has a gorgeous painted ceiling and ornate balconies decorated with figures of Hindu gods and other oriental motifs in celebration of Queen Victoria's latest title at the time, Empress of India. A success from the start, it was Belfast's entertainment epicentre for decades until a decline in the 1950s led to its closure in 1972. It became the first listed building in Belfast and reopened in 1980 after major restoration. More problems followed, including several IRA bombs, but it continues its long history of presenting opera, theatre, musicals and ballet. A modern extension houses a smaller performance space, a café and a restaurant. An exhibition has artefacts from past productions, including costumes and photos.

Places to visit

Linen Hall Library

CITY CENTRE

Belfast Cathedral
Donegall Street, BT1 2HB (9032 8332, www. belfastcathedral.org). Open 10am-4pm Mon-Sat. Tours by appointment. Admission free; donations appreciated. Tours suggested donation £3. No credit cards.
The Cathedral Church of St Anne has been the centrepoint for the area since its inception in 1899 – though it took another 80 years for the Romanesque building to be finally completed, thanks to extensive damage in World War II and delays that occurred as a result of the Troubles. The most beautiful feature is the mosaic roof above the baptistry, composed of 150,000 pieces of glass representing the Creation. The Cathedral Choir is renowned, singing in two services each Sunday and in summer and Christmas concerts.

City Hall
Donegall Square, BT1 5GF (9027 0456, www.belfastcity.gov.uk/cityhall/index.asp). Open 8.30am-5pm Mon-Thur; 8.30am-4.30pm Fri; 2-4pm Sat (tours only). Tours 11am, 2pm, 3pm Mon-Fri; 2pm, 3pm Sat. Admission free. Tours free.
Opened in 1906, this huge and imposing structure is built of light grey, almost white, Portland stone to a classical Renaissance design. It's looking particularly fine nowadays, thanks to an £11 million restoration

completed in 2009. The main entrance is certainly eye-catching with its black and white chequered floor, ornate plasterwork and Italian marble staircase. The 173ft-high dome, complete with whispering gallery, was modelled on St Paul's Cathedral and – as must have been the intention – creates a reverential atmosphere. To explore the building and learn about its history, join one of the regular free tours. There's a small coffee shop and exhibition area.

Linen Hall Library ★
17 Donegall Square, BT1 5GB (9032 1707, www.linenhall.com). Open Library 9.30am-5.30pm Mon-Fri; 9.30am-4pm Sat. Café 10am-4pm Mon-Fri; 10am-3.30pm Sat. Admission free; donations appreciated.
Founded in 1788, Linen Hall is the oldest library in Belfast and the last subscription library in Ireland. Walking up the old stairwell and into the high-ceilinged main library, you become aware of the importance of such an institution. Renowned for its unparalleled Irish and Local Studies Collection, it also contains the Northern Ireland Political Collection documenting the history of the Troubles, and containing everything from stickers to Christmas cards to books. Events include free readings and lectures, and the regularly changing exhibitions are usually intriguing (political posters from the Troubles, historic photos of Ulster). People chat quietly or read books in the wonderful café, where old-fashioned tables are spread over two rooms and the windows overlook Donegall Square. Hot drinks, pastries, baked potatoes and other snacks are served.

St George's Market
12-20 East Bridge Street, BT1 3NQ (9043 5704, www.belfastcity.gov.uk/markets). Open 6am-2pm Fri; 9am-3pm Sat; 10am-4pm Sun.
There's been a market on this site since 1604. It's now Belfast's last covered Victorian market, a handsome building of red-brick and green ironwork completed in 1896, and covers a whole city block. Friday brings the Variety Market, for which hundreds of stalls sell a vast array of goods, from coffee to fish, antiques to clothes. Saturday is the City Food & Garden Market, with fresh, local produce (fish, meat, vegetables, cheese) alongside foreign specialities. The Sunday market is a combination of the Friday and Saturday offerings, with an emphasis on local arts and crafts. Musicians play frequently, and assorted festivals and events are held here too.

UNIVERSITY AREA

Botanic Gardens ★
College Park, Botanic Avenue, BT7 1LP (9031 4762, www.belfastcity.gov.uk). Open 7.30am-dusk daily. Admission free.
Adjacent to Queens University is Belfast's largest green space. Established by a local horticultural society in 1828 and opened as a public park in 1895, the Botanic Gardens are a joy to wander. Admire the flowering borders, rose beds and old oak trees; peek into the Tropical Ravine, which houses a range of exotic plants; and visit the Palm House – designed by Charles Lanyon in the 1830s, it's an early (and very

fine) example of a curvilinear cast-iron glasshouse. Alternatively, simply rest on one of the many benches and soak up the serene atmosphere. Open-air concerts and events are held here in summer.

Ormeau Baths Gallery
18A Ormeau Avenue, BT2 8HS (9032 1402, www.ormeaubaths.co.uk). Open 10am-5.30pm Tue-Sat. Admission free.
Inside a red-brick Victorian building, once housing a swimming baths, are the modern, white-walled exhibition spaces of OBG. One of Northern Ireland's leading contemporary art galleries, it presents a stimulating roster of work by local and international artists, and also runs a popular children's art club on Saturday mornings. There's a good art bookshop, but no café.

Ulster Museum
Botanic Gardens, BT9 5AB (0845 608 0000, www.nmni.com/um). Open 10am-5pm Tue-Sun, bank hols. Admission free.
One of four establishments that make up the National Museums Northern Ireland, the Ulster Museum reopened in autumn 2009 after a three-year, £17 million redevelopment. The transformation is a big success: the new-look building is bright, spacious and open, with four floors containing well-laid-out displays devoted to art, nature and history. Each section has a 'discovery zone' where visitors are allowed to touch artefacts, try on costumes and get truly hands-on in a way that most museums don't allow. It's a fascinating place, with something for everyone – from Indonesian shadow puppets and 18th-century embroidered bedcovers to Egyptian mummies and Peter the stuffed polar bear – plus changing exhibitions that highlight elements of the museum's vast holdings. To top it all, admission is free. Allow yourself a good few hours; there's a pleasant café and the shop is worth a visit too.

AROUND BELFAST

Belfast Castle & Cave Hill Country Park
Antrim Road, BT15 5GR (9077 6925, www.belfastcity. gov.uk/belfastcastle). Open Visitor centre 9am-10pm Mon-Sat; 9am-5.30pm Sun. Admission free.
Built in the 1860s by the third Marquis of Donegal, in the Scottish baronial style popular at the time, Belfast Castle sits in a prime position overlooking the city. The visitor centre-cum-museum on the second floor provides information on the building and its gardens, along with maps of walks in the surrounding park. A marked trail leads past the caves (from which the area got its name), a fort and woodland to the top of Cave Hill, where you get spectacular views over Belfast. The outline of the hill has been likened to Napoleon sleeping on his side, and was nicknamed Napoleon's Nose – it's claimed it was the inspiration for Swift's satirical novel *Gulliver's Travels*.

Belfast Zoo
Antrim Road, BT36 7PN (9077 6277, www.belfast zoo.co.uk). Open Apr-Sept 10am-7pm daily (last admission 5pm). Jan-Mar, Oct-Dec 10am-4pm daily (last admission 2.30pm). Admission Apr-Sept £8.90; free-£4.70 reductions; £19 family. Jan-Mar, Oct-Dec £7.10; free-£3.60 reductions; £19 family.
Established in 1934, this council-run zoo is one of Belfast's oldest and most visited attractions. Within its attractive grounds atop Cave Hill you'll find more than 1,200 creatures representing 140 species, both native and exotic. Most of the animals are endangered in the wild, and the zoo is heavily involved in conservation and breeding projects. Highlights include the Asian elephants, Rothschild's giraffes and big cats (cheetahs, Barbary lions – now extinct in their native habitat – and a Sumatran tiger), but the penguins, kangaroos and numerous monkeys and apes are perennial faves.

Stormont
Upper Newtownards Road, BT4 3ST (9037 8263, www.niassembly.gov.uk). Open May-Aug 7.30am-9pm Mon-Fri; 9am-9pm Sat, Sun. Apr, Sept 7.30am-8pm Mon-Fri; 9am-8pm Sat, Sun. Oct-Mar 7.30am-6pm Mon-Fri; 9am-5pm Sat, Sun. Admission free.
This impressive Greek classical white building perched at the top of a hill is a familar sight from countless television news programmes. Home of the Northern Ireland Parliament until 1972, it now houses the Northern Ireland Assembly, which was created in 1998 as part of the Good Friday Agreement. Adjacent is baronial-style Stormont Castle, seat of the Northern Ireland Executive. There's limited public access to the buildings, but the estate's formal gardens and attractive woodland can be wandered freely – there's also an adventure playground. It's a pleasant way to spend a couple of hours, within the shadows of Belfast's political nerve centre.

Stormont

are part of the Merchant Hotel (*see right*). Across the road is new and popular bar-restaurant 21 Social (1 Hill Street, 9024 1415, www.21social. co.uk). One of the more intriguing establishments is the John Hewitt Bar (51 Donegall Street, 9023 3768, www.thejohnhewitt.com): run as a charity, it has an excellent range of beers, homely food and regular gigs.

South of here on Donegall Square, there's always a trendy crowd at the Apartment Bar (9050 9777, www.apartmentbelfast.com), which also has a brasserie-style dining room, and DJs at weekends. Robinson's (Great Victoria Street, 9024 7447, www.robinsonsbar.co.uk) is spread over four floors, with a modern bar, an old-fashioned saloon, a traditional Irish bar with traditional music sessions, a bistro, and a nightclub with DJs – something for everyone.

The in-store café at the Arthur Street branch of Avoca (9027 9955, www.avoca.ie) is dependable. There's cheap and cheerful Lebanese food at Byblos (Amelia Street, 9023 6266, closed Sun), plus a number of mid-range restaurants not far from the Grand Opera House. Try the Ginger Bistro (7-8 Hope Street, 9024 4421, www.gingerbistro. com, closed Sun) or Cayenne (Shaftesbury Square, 9033 1532, www.cayenne-restaurant.co.uk, closed Tue), the latter owned by local celeb chefs Paul and Jeanne Rankin and famed for its signature dishes of salt 'n'chilli squid, and pan-seared foie gras with roasted nectarines.

Another popular choice is the Bank Gallery (9032 2000, closed Sun), the first-floor restaurant at the Edge, though it's a bit out of the way, located next to the river on Laganbank Road.

For the pick of Belfast's historical watering holes, *see p264.*

Café Vaudeville

25-39 Arthur Street, BT1 4GQ (9043 9160, www.cafe vaudeville.com). Open 11.30am-1am Mon-Sat. Lunch served noon-3pm, dinner served 5-9pm Mon-Sat.
True to its name, this is as much a visual experience as a place to eat and drink. The elaborate, burlesque-like design is all velvet curtains, leopard-skin chairs, fancy chandeliers and embellished surfaces. Various levels in the former bank allow you to mingle with the late-night party crowd or seek refuge in the more tranquil balconies and corridors. There's live music most nights – jazz, Rat Pack, and DJs at the weekend – while the Mediterranean-style menu features lots of Irish beef, pork and venison. An almost theatrical experience, not to be missed.

Deanes ★

36-40 Howard Street, BT1 6PF (9033 1134, www.michaeldeane.co.uk/deanes.asp). Lunch served noon-3pm, dinner served 5.30-10pm Mon-Sat.
Michelin-starred chef Michael Deane is king of the Belfast dining scene, with six restaurants ranging from a shopping mall bistro to this, his flagship eatery. The simple styling of the space (orange walls, polished floorboards) is reflected in the unfussy, seasonal dishes that make the most of prime local ingredients. It's not at all exclusive, and the lunch/pre-theatre set menu is a steal for food of this quality. Next door is the more casual Deane's Seafood Bar; there's also a café/wine bar/bistro on nearby Bedford Street (Deanes Deli) and a restaurant near the university (Deanes at Queen's).

Made in Belfast

Wellington Street, BT1 6HT (9024 6712, www.made inbelfastni.com). Lunch served noon-3pm Mon-Sat; 12.30-4pm Sun. Dinner served 5.30-10pm Mon-Thur; 5.30-11pm Fri, Sat; 6-9pm Sun.
Come to MIB for quality food and decorative intrigue. Eclectic would be a tame description for this restaurant, with

Merchant Hotel

Queen's University. See p264.

its mismatched tables, chairs, sofas and lightshades, walls covered in newspaper, graffiti and random mirrors, and, to top it all, a giant towel rail-like construction of pipes in the middle of the room. Somehow, it manages to create a cosy, laid-back vibe that fits perfectly with the homely menu of international dishes, ranging from fish finger sandwiches to beef pie to scallops with black pudding. Sister restaurant Hooligan (23 Talbot Street, 9024 4107, www.beautiful hooligan.com) is equally charming, with a menu inspired by the varied cuisines of London's East End.

Mourne Seafood Bar
34-36 Bank Street, BT1 1HL (9024 8544, www.mourne seafood.com). Lunch served noon-5pm Mon; noon-4pm Fri, Sat; 1-6pm Sun. Food served noon-9pm Tue-Thur. Dinner served 5-10.30pm Fri, Sat.
This informal eaterie with its plain wooden tables and blackboard menu is deservedly popular for its fresh, top-quality fish and seafood at affordable prices. Mussels, oysters and cockles are sourced from Mourne's own shellfish beds in Carlingford Lough, while fish comes in daily from the local ports of Kilkeel and Annalong. Mourne Oyster Stout is the perfect accompaniment. For non-seafood lovers, there is a selection of steaks and chicken dishes.

Where to stay
The city centre is where you'll find most of the upmarket accommodation, including the slick, modern, 130-room Fitzwilliam Hotel (Great Victoria Street, 9044 2080, www.fitzwilliamhotelbelfast. com). There are also a few boutique hotels – often luxurious, but not ridiculously priced. Benedicts (7-21 Bradbury Place, Shaftesbury Square, 9059 1990, www.benedictshotel.co.uk) is a well-priced bolthole on the Golden Mile, with 32 rooms, a restaurant and a bar; check the website for deals.

Malmaison Belfast
34-38 Victoria Street, BT1 3GH (9022 0200, www.malmaison.com). Rates £85-£150 double.
The Malmaison chain has brought boutique-style opulence to a dozen UK cities; this is its only Irish outpost. Housed within a stunning Victorian building a short walk from City Hall, it's the perfect base from which to explore the city. Decor throughout is characterised by dark tones, sumptuous fabrics and low lighting. There are 62 sleek, modern bedrooms plus two expansive suites, named after the Harland and Wolff cranes; Samson has two plasma TVs, an open fire and a full-size purple snooker table. The atmospheric restaurant serves classic brasserie fare, and there's also a moody cocktail bar. Staff are notably cheery and friendly.

Merchant Hotel ★
14 Shipper Street, BT1 2DZ (9023 4888, www.themerchanthotel.com). Rates £115-£240 double incl breakfast.
A couple of streets from the cathedral, Belfast's most extravagant hotel occupies a handsome Italianate sandstone building, designed in the 1850s and originally the headquarters of Ulster Bank. The ornate main banking hall, with its central lantern dome, intricate plasterwork, gilt frieze and cherub-topped columns, is now the Great Room restaurant – a marvellous setting for superior Modern Irish cuisine and proper afternoon tea. The 62 rooms are lavish affairs, decorated in either a rich Victorian or cool art deco style, with bespoke furniture as well as original pieces – a theme found throughout the hotel. There are no less than three bars – for cocktails, jazz (with music nightly and at Sunday brunch) and a more traditional bar with food – plus a nightclub. The hotel underwent major renovations in 2010, adding a new wing with a rooftop terrace, gymnasium and spa. With its central location, stunning design and multiple entertainment options, the five-star Merchant is hard to beat.

FIVE HISTORIC BARS

Crown Bar
*46 Great Victoria Street, BT2 7BA
(9024 3187, www.crownbar.com).
Open 11.30am-11pm Mon-Thur;
11.30am-midnight Fri, Sat; 12.30-
10pm Sun.*
Belfast's most beautiful bar, without
question – and of such historic
importance that it's owned by the
National Trust. Every square inch is
elaborately decorated, from the colourful
windows (designed to shield those
within the saloon from prying eyes)
to the stunningly ornate ceiling, gorgeous
mosaic-tiled floors and intricately carved
woodwork. Much of it is the work of
Italian craftsmen who came to Ireland
in the 1880s to build new Catholic
churches. The huge casks, polished
brass taps and seemingly endless
granite-topped bar, with its heated
footrest, take second billing to the ten
elaborately carved wooden snugs, each
one unique. Grab one if you can, and be
transported to a place of cosy privacy,
where you can while away an afternoon
imagining the wheeling and dealing
that took place in the very same booths
over 100 years ago.

Crown Bar

Ten Square Hotel
*10 Donegall Square South, BT1 5JD (9024 1001,
www.tensquare.co.uk). Rates £89-£265 double incl
breakfast.*
The location, at the edge of Donegall Square overlooking
City Hall, could not be better. In fact, the Grade I-listed
building preceded City Hall and was once the home of the
Linen Mill Master. It's now a popular, buzzing hotel with 23
sleek, smart rooms spread over three floors. Bedrooms are
spacious and quiet, with large beds, statement wallpaper
and leather furniture. The brasserie-style Grill Room & Bar
is a favourite with non-residents. Having being named the
coolest hotel in Belfast, Ten Square works hard to lives up
to its reputation.

UNIVERSITY AREA
It's a 20-minute walk from the city centre to
Queen's University, and it's worth every step.
It's a heaving, vibrant part of the city and many
of Belfast's main sights are located here. The
main thoroughfares are University Road/Malone
Road, Botanic Avenue and Stranmillis Road, with
three churches on University Road (Crescent,
Moravian and Methodist), heralding the approach
to the university. Georgian buildings, now converted
into pubs, cafés, restaurants and bars, line the
streets, especially Botanic Avenue, where swarms
of students and tourists stroll the footpaths.
No Alibis Bookstore (83 Botanic Avenue, 9031
9601, www.noalibis.com, closed Sun) is a
friendly shop that specialises in crime, with new
and second-hand books, and regular readings
and music events.
   Named after Queen Victoria, Queen's University
was founded in 1845. The centrepiece of the
campus is the magnificent, red-brick Lanyon
Building, designed as a Gothic Revival remodelling
of Magdalen College, Oxford by Charles Lanyon,
the English-born architect responsible for many of
Belfast's key structures. Inside is a visitor centre
(9097 5252, www.qub.ac.uk/vcentre), where
you can arrange guided tours, and the Naughton
Gallery (9097 3580, www.naughtongallery.org,
closed Mon), which has a rolling programme of
art exhibitions. Lanyon also designed the Union
Theological College on the other side of Botanic
Avenue. This solid-looking, attractive building
housed the Northern Ireland Parliament until
Stormont was built in 1932.
   South of the university are the beautiful Botanic
Gardens (*see p260*), one of the few green areas
in Belfast and also home to the wonderful Ulster
Museum (*see p261*), devoted to art, history and
the natural sciences. Further south, off Lockview
Road, is the entrance to the Lagan Towpath,
which follows the river and canal network south
for 11 miles to Lisburn. A walk or cycle along here
is peaceful and often beautiful, passing locks,
meadows and woodland.
   Parallel to University Road is more salubrious
Lisburn Road, a haven for those in search of
independent boutiques, delis and good restaurants.
There are also several art galleries, including the
Taylor Gallery (no.471, 9068 7687, www.taylor

Beatrice Kennedy

gallery.co.uk, closed Sun), which has work by international big-hitters such as Andy Warhol and Damien Hirst, as well as Irish artists from Jack Yeats to Sean Scully. The Mullan Gallery (no.239, 9020 2434, www.mullangallery.com, closed Mon, Sun) specialises in contemporary Irish artists.

Where to eat & drink

University Road and Botanic Avenue are littered with cafés, restaurants and bars. Many are cheap and cheerful, and often packed out with students. The atmospheric Belfast Empire (9024 9276, www.thebelfastempire.com), housed in a Victorian church on the corner of Botanic Avenue and Cameron Street, is frequented by all-comers thanks to its mix of comedy shows, live music, quiz nights and big-screen football.

Beatrice Kennedy ★
44 University Road, BT7 1NJ (9020 2290, www. beatricekennedy.co.uk). Dinner served 5-10.30pm Mon-Sat. Food served 12.30-8.30pm Sun.
For fine dining in a rather unusual setting, try Beatrice Kennedy. Named after the former owner of this Victorian residence, the restaurant begins in what would have been the front room and stretches to the rear of the house. The open fireplace and array of random personal effects provide a cosy and authentic feel, while chef-patron Jim McCarthy has built up an excellent reputation for his regularly changing Modern European menu and use of high-quality, locally sourced produce. Meat is a speciality, with dishes such as honey-glazed dry-cured pork loin and belly with champ and chestnuts, but vegetarians do well too.

McHugh's Bar & Restaurant
29-31 Queen's Square, BT1 3FG (9050 9999, www.mchughsbar.com). Open noon-1am Mon-Sat; noon-midnight Sun.
Dating from 1711, McHugh's is said to be the oldest surviving building in Belfast. The sympathetically restored old bar, the walls adorned with maps and photos of Belfast of years past, has an authentic, characterful charm. The new café-bar blends in well with the original (and serves decent food), but it's the history and atmosphere of the old bar that the crowds come for.

Northern Whig
2-10 Bridge Street, BT1 1LU (9050 9888, www.thenorthern whig.com). Open noon-11pm Mon, Tue; noon-1am Wed-Sat; 1-11pm Sun.
Not a 'traditional' bar as such, but the high-ceilinged premises – the former offices of the *Northern Whig* newspaper – are impressive. You can't miss the huge granite statues that once graced the Communist headquarters in Prague. One of Belfast's most popular spots for drinks (especially cocktails and wine), reasonably priced food and a lively atmosphere.

Spaniard ★
3 Skipper Street, BT1 2DZ (9023 2448, www.thespaniard bar.com). Open noon-1am Mon-Sat; noon-midnight Sun.
'Tapas, music, good company' is the motto of the quirky Spaniard. The place oozes character, with its candlelight, rickety wooden tables, multicoloured cushions, and random rock/pop memorabilia plastered over the walls and hanging from the ceiling. An eclectic soundtrack, premium-brand spirits and snacky bites make it and intimate and fun place to spend an evening.

White's Tavern
2-4 Wine Cellar Entry, between Rosemary Street & High Street, BT1 2NQ (9024 3080, www.whites tavern.co.uk). Open noon-11pm Mon-Thur; noon-1am Fri, Sat; noon-midnight Sun.
Tucked down narrow Wine Cellar Entry, White's is Belfast's oldest hostelry, having received the first tavern licence in the city, way back in 1630. Decor is on the shabby side of shabby-chic, but if it's old-style and casual you're after, it's worth a stop-off. Traditional Irish musicians play downstairs, and Irish stew, fry-ups and burgers are among the food offerings.

Café Conor

*11A Stranmillis Road, BT9 5AF (9066 3266,
www.cafeconor.com). Open 9am-10pm Mon-Thur;
9am-11pm Fri, Sat; 9am-9pm Sun.*
Café Conor is a popular retreat after browsing the nearby
Ulster Museum. A bright, casual place with high ceilings
and art on the walls, it's open from breakfast (served until
5pm) to late, with tasty own-made cakes and snacks, plus a
full menu (hearty salads, burgers, Thai curry) at lunch and
dinner. In the 1940s and '50s, the building was the studio of
well-known local artist William Conor; the Ulster Museum
now owns some of his drawings and watercolours.

Where to stay

There's plenty of budget accommodation in the
University Area, including most of the city's
backpacker hostels. Reliable digs are Vagabonds
(9 University Road, 9543 8772, www.vagabonds
belfast.com), which offers double rooms as well
as dorms, and Kate's B&B (127 University Street,
9028 2091), which has a mix of single, double
and twin rooms, some en suite. During the summer
holidays, Queen's University (9097 4403) rents
reasonably priced en suite rooms in Elms Village
on the Malone Road. Mid-range choices include
Tara Lodge (36 Cromwell Road, 9059 0900,
www.taralodge.com), a modern hotel with 34
tastefully designed rooms; and the Crescent
Townhouse (Lower Crescent, 9032 3349,
www.crescenttownhouse.com), which has 17
bedrooms and its own brasserie and popular bar.

AROUND BELFAST

There are a few attractions on the outskirts of the
city. Four miles to the east, at the top of a long
driveway and surrounded by manicured lawns and
a cricket ground, is the formidable Stormont
(*see p261*), seat of Northern Ireland's government.

A similar distance north is Belfast Castle (*see
p261*), another of Charles Lanyon's designs. Now
a wedding and conference venue, the castle has
spectacular views over Belfast, and pathways lead
from it up to the summit of Cave Hill. Conveniently
for visitors, adjoining the castle on the Antrim Road
is Belfast Zoo (*see p261*).

West Belfast is itself of interest to visitors,
because it was the battlefield for sectarian groups
during the Troubles. During the 19th century,
as the city's shipbuilding and linen industries
prospered, cheap housing was erected in the area
to house the thousands arriving looking for work.
It was here that the sectarian divide emerged
and became most noticeable, as Catholics and
Protestants lived side by side in often unbearable
conditions, which only served to irritate existing
frictions. During the decades of conflict, West
Belfast was the fighting ground for Republican and
Loyalist militant groups, and heinous crimes were
committed both by and against Catholics and
Protestants. Today, new housing estates have
replaced the old and the district is much improved,
although Republican and Loyalist murals in the
(Catholic) Falls and (Protestant) Shankill areas are
a reminder of the hatred bred during the Troubles.
Republican ex-political prisoners lead walking tours
of the key sights, including the Falls Road and
Milltown Cemetery; details on www.coiste.ie.
Several black taxi companies also provide tours
– an interesting way of seeing the area.

For information on accommodation, eating and
drinking places, and things to see and do, consult
www.visitwestbelfast.com.

West Belfast mural

County Down

Wedged between Belfast and the border with the Republic is County Down, an area of undulating green fields and gorse-covered mountains, fringed with a fine coastline. It's also home to one of Northern Ireland's best museums – the Ulster Folk & Transport Museum – situated a few miles outside Belfast. Nearby is Strangford Lough, the largest sea inlet in the British Isles. Studded with half-submerged islands, the lough is a playground for yachters, canoeists and anglers, and a refuge for tens of thousands of waterbirds. Along the shore are picturesque towns and villages such as Strangford and Killyleagh, as well as a fine collection of castles, stately homes and early Christian sites. Presiding over the county are the hulking Mourne Mountains, which contain Northern Ireland's best hiking paths, while seaside towns such as Newcastle have seen a surge of investment in an attempt to restore popularity to these once-thriving Victorian resorts.

ARDS & LECALE PENINSULAS

Ards peninsula

It's to the south of the county that most visitors migrate, to the hulking mountains and the promise of golden sands. Many jump on the M1/A1 at Belfast and scoot down to Newry, where they believe the sights begin. But the best route for those wanting to get a real feel for Down is to head east on the A20 to the Ards peninsula – it's far more scenic and peaceful than the tooting horns and thundering trucks on the M1.

The first point of call is the fascinating Ulster Folk & Transport Museum (see p274), a 15-minute drive east of Belfast. Next comes Newtownards – a relatively unattractive town with little to offer tourists except for the Festival of the Peninsula (www.festivalofthepeninsula.info) in September and the International Guitar Festival (www.ards guitarfestival.co.uk) in October.

The A20 then curves along the eastern shore of Strangford Lough, past scattered boat moorings and a few settlements. This 20-mile-long tidal inlet is home to a vast variety of marine animal and plant life, with numerous small islands (drumlins) poking above the water like the backs of green whales. It's a conservation area and is of particular importance for its birdlife. Dense colonies of terns nest on the islands from May to July; more species arrive in summer to feast on the rich food sources; and between September and February, thousands of overwintering and migratory birds appear, including some 20,000 pale-bellied brent geese. The lough is also one of Ireland's most important breeding grounds for common seals; grey seals, porpoises and otters also visit. If you're interested in boating, fishing, birdwatching or walking, the area has much to offer. You'll find plenty of information on www.strangfordlough.org.

Mount Stewart House (see p274), an 18th-century mansion with beautiful Italianate gardens that now belongs to the National Trust, is five miles south of Newtownards. Just outside the town of Greyabbey are the impressive ruins of a Cistercian abbey (9181 1491, www.doeni.gov.uk, closed Mon-Sat Sept-Mar) founded in 1193. The grey-robed monks had a keen knowledge of plants and herbs; today, there's a recreated herb garden and attractive grounds. The town of Greyabbey itself has some antiques shops that are worth a browse.

At the mouth of the lough is the small town of Portaferry, where you can catch a car ferry (4488 1637, www.roadsni.gov.uk) to Strangford town on the opposite shore – it's a five-minute trip and boats run frequently. The tourist office (4272 9882, www.ards-council.gov.uk/visitor-information, closed Sept-Mar), located in former stables beside what was once Portaferry Castle on Castle Street, has information on accommodation, sights and walks. Also on Castle Street, the Exploris Aquarium (4272 8062, www.exploris.org.uk) showcases the diverse marine life of the lough and has a seal sanctuary. Three miles east of Portaferry is picturesque Kearney, a flourishing fishing community in the 19th century and now a showpiece village with a number of thatched white cottages restored by the National Trust. There are good walks in the area, notably along Knockinelde beach, where the panoramic views across the Irish Sea never fail to enchant.

West side of Strangford Lough

You can also drive from Belfast along the western edge of Strangford Lough; minor roads follow the shoreline, so the views are better than from the eastern shore. Castle Espie Wetland Centre (see p274), the only Wildfowl & Wetlands Trust (WWT) reserve in Ireland, is a marvellous place to appreciate the area's varied flora and fauna, and attracts Ireland's largest population of waterbirds. South of Castle Espie and accessed across several causeways, Mahee Island is a beautiful spot containing an ancient monastic site, Nendrum Monastery (www.doeni.gov.uk). Located at the top of a glacial hill, the site is thought to date from the fifth century, although the monastery was not established until the 12th. You can see the remains

of a round tower, a church and a more recently restored sundial, surrounded by three concentric stone enclosures. A small visitor centre is open sporadically. Also here are a ruined 16th-century tower-house, and the nine-hole Mahee Island Golf Club (9754 1234, www.maheegolf.com).

Small coves and islands punctuate the lough further south en route to Killyleagh, a small village that is dominated by Ireland's oldest inhabited castle. A romantic, Disney-like building with numerous turrets and round towers, Killyleagh Castle was constructed in the 12th century, then rebuilt in 1648 and again in 1850 by the Hamilton family. It's still the Hamilton family home and not open to the public, but peering through the iron gates is enough to transport you to *Fantasia*.

A mile beyond Killyleagh, bordering the lough, is Delamont Country Park (4482 8333, www.delamontcountrypark.com). As well as a visitor centre, a camping and caravanning site, a miniature railway and waymarked trails, the park encompasses Tyrella Beach, a wide sandy stretch more than a mile long, backed by sand dunes, that's ideal for swimming (lifeguards patrol in July and August). The Willowstone Festival (www.willowstonefestival.com) arrives at the park in July, bringing musical performances, interactive installations and events for adults and children.

A few miles to the south is the small waterside village of Strangford, where you'll find some cosy hotel bars and the eccentrically designed mansion of Castle Ward (*see p274*). The house is surrounded by great walks and in June opens its gates for the Castleward Opera Festival (www.castlewardopera.com).

Lecale peninsula

Once called the Island of Lecale, the Lecale peninsula stretches south from Strangford to Dundrum Bay and east to Ballynahinch. It's said that the area was once surrounded by water – by the Irish Sea, Strangford Lough and a series of waterways and ponds – until the waters were re-routed for industrial purposes.

The peninsula has strong associations with St Patrick, Ireland's patron saint. Born in Roman Britain in around 387 AD, he was captured and brought to Ireland as a slave at the age of 16. After six years, he escaped, and fled abroad, returning some years later, in 432, to spread Christianity. He's believed to have landed on the Lecale peninsula and his remains are said to be buried in Downpatrick, the main town. Some of the key points on St Patrick's Trail (www.discover northernireland.com/stpatrick/patrickstrail.aspx) – which features all the places associated with the saint in Northern Ireland – are on the peninsula. Saul, just outside Downpatrick, is one of the most important: it's reputedly where St Patrick first preached, in a barn given to him by the local lord. A church was built here in 1932 in commemoration of the saint's arrival 1,500 years earlier. A shrine was also erected on nearby Slieve Patrick; stations of the cross lead up the small hill to an imposing statue, built from local granite.

Downpatrick may be a forlorn-looking place, but it contains the impressive St Patrick Centre (53A Lower Market Street, 4461 9000, www.saintpatrickcentre.com, closed Sun Oct-Mar), which tells the story of the saint's life and influence on Ireland, and includes a state-of-the-art IMAX presentation. There's also a tourist information centre (4461 2233, www.downdc.gov.uk, closed Sun Sept-June). Uphill from the centre is Down Cathedral (*see p274*), site of St Patrick's grave. At Down County Museum (English Street, 4461 5218, www.downcountymuseum.com), housed in what was the Georgian county jail, you can examine a restored cellblock and view historic costumes, paintings, tools and other objects. There's a gallery of art relating to St Patrick, as well as early Christian objects and artefacts.

For a break from saintly encounters, there's the Downpatrick & County Down Railway (Market Street, www.downrail.co.uk, check website for opening hours), which runs short trips on old steam trains, and Downpatrick Racecourse (Ballydugan Road, 4461 2054, www.downpatrick racecourse.co.uk), where meetings take place throughout the year and have done so for over three centuries. Down Arts Centre (Irish Street, 4461 0747, www.downartscentre.com) is closed until September 2011 for renovations, but performances and events continue in alternative venues.

A mile north-west of town, in a spectacular setting on the banks of the River Quoile, lies atmospheric Inch Abbey (9181 1491, www.doeni.gov.uk), a ruined Cistercian abbey dating from the 12th century. Nearby, on an island in Loughinisland Lake, are the ruins of three churches built between the 13th and 17th centuries; it's a peaceful and islolated spot, ideal for picnics. A causeway leads to the island.

The final point on St Patrick's Trail is Struells Wells, just outside Downpatrick. From medieval times, pilgrims flocked to the four wells hidden within the rocky valley to pay penance or in search of cures for ailments – St Patrick is said to have blessed the waters. The tradition of Mass being said here on Midsummer's Eve is still upheld.

About six miles south-east of Downpatrick is the picturesque little town of Ardglass, a thriving fishing port for more than 2,000 years. Predictably, plenty of freshly caught fish appears on local menus, and the sea fishing is excellent. The town once contained seven 'castles' (actually fortified tower houses) built in the 14th and 15th centuries; most are in ruins now, though the remains of one has been used as the clubhouse for the local golf club since 1896. There are a few B&Bs and a pub that also has accommodation.

Killough, further west along the coast, is even quieter than Ardglass. There's a fine walk from the village to windswept St John's Point, where there's a lighthouse, a ruined church and superb sea views.

Where to eat & drink

Portaferry is short of good eating places, so consider lunch en route at the Bay Restaurant

Denvir's Hotel

at Mount Stewart House (*see p274*). Across the lough, in Strangford, the Cuan (4488 1222, www.thecuan.com) is a 200-year-old pub/hotel with tasty, own-made food that features plenty of local produce. In Killyleagh, you'll find the Dufferin Arms (35 High Street, 4482 1182, www.dufferinarms.co.uk), a traditional pub with Saturday afternoon folk music gigs. Picnic (47 High Street, 4482 8525, closed Sun winter) is a good place for a snack or sandwich, or to pick up picnic supplies.

In Dundrum, Mourne's Seafood Bar ★ (Main Street, 4375 1377, www.mourneseafood.com, closed Mon-Wed winter) is a casual restaurant/ fish shop – and sister of the Belfast restaurant (*see p263*) – where you're guaranteed delicious, uncomplicated fish and seafood dishes.

Curran's Bar & Seafood Steakhouse

83 Strangford Road, Chapeltown, BT30 7SP (4484 1332, www.curransbar.net). Open 11.30am-11.30pm Mon-Thur, Sun; 11.30am-1am Fri, Sat. Food served 12.30-8.30pm Mon-Thur, Sun; 12.30-9pm Fri, Sat.
Two miles north of Ardglass on the A2, this popular bar and restaurant has been run by the Curran family since 1791. High-beamed ceilings, wood panelling, a large fireplace and friendly service make for a cosy dining experience. The lengthy menu includes steaks, burgers and chicken dishes, but it's the freshly caught fish that appeals most, especially the seafood platter: prawns, crab claws, mussels, smoked mackerel, seafood chowder and other treats.

Denvir's Hotel

14 English Street, Downpatrick, BT30 6AB (4461 2012, www.denvirshotel.com). Open 11.30am-midnight Mon-Thur, Sun; 11.30am-1am Fri, Sat. Food served 8am-8pm Mon-Thur, Sun; 8am-9pm Fri, Sat.
Established in 1642, Denvirs Hotel is by far the best option for food and drink in Downpatrick. The restaurant and bar – with their rustic bare walls, low lighting and 17th-century fireplace – are full of character, and the menu highlights local ingredients (Dundrum Bay mussels, Irish

meat) in its wholesome dishes. The six B&B rooms (£70 double incl breakfast) have been recently renovated.

Where to stay

Belfast is so close to Strangford Lough that many visitors choose to stay there, but more rural retreats are available.

In Portaferry, the Portaferry Hotel (The Strand, 4272 8231, www.portaferryhotel.com) has 14 en suite rooms, some with marvellous lough views, while, a few miles to the south, Barr Hall Barns (Barr Hall Road, 4272 9895, www.barrhallbarns. com) provides self-catering facilities. There are campsites at Castle Ward (Apr-Oct, *see p274*) and Delamont Country Park (mid Mar-Oct, *see p269*).

The Cuan (*see left*) in Strangford has nine comfortable B&B rooms (£80-£90 double incl breakfast). In Killyleagh, the yellow-fronted Dufferin Coaching Inn (4482 1134, www.dufferin coachinginn.com) has seven en suite rooms (£65-£90 double incl breakfast).

In Downpatrick, there's accommodation at Denvir's Hotel (*see left*). Outside the town, Ballymote House (Killough Road, 4461 5500, www.ballymotehouse.com) offers B&B in a large Georgian house surrounded by wonderful parkland. It has the feel of a proper country home, with antique furnishings and four light-filled bedrooms.

Edenvale House ★
130 Portaferry Road, nr Newtownards, BT22 2AH (9181 4881, www.edenvalehouse.com). Rates £90 double incl breakfast.
Set beside Strangford Lough and surrounded by rolling green fields, this large, attractive Georgian house is the perfect getaway for those seeking respite from urban aggravation. There are just three rooms, all en suite and quite feminine in style, with floral fabrics and soothing pastel colours. The rambling gardens include a croquet lawn, and breakfast features eggs from the resident chickens, home-made bread and local bacon.

MOURNE MOUNTAINS, NEWCASTLE & NEWRY

The dramatic beauty of the Mourne Mountains ★ has captured the imaginations of artists for centuries. In 1896, a popular song by Percy French brought the mountains to the world's attention, and CS Lewis was inspired by the towering peaks and sweeping valleys when describing the magical landscape of Narnia. It's now an Area of Outstanding Natural Beauty, and owned in part by the National Trust.

Covering an area 15 miles long and eight miles wide, between Newcastle and Newry, the granite mountains are characterised by sharp peaks and ridges, dark mysterious valleys, racing rivers, tranquil lakes and acres of yellow gorse, and offer some of the best hiking in Ireland. Slieve Donard (2,789 feet) is the tallest of the peaks, and can be accessed by a trail that starts three miles outside Newcastle on the coast road near Bloody Bridge. The six-mile route follows a tumbling river, where locals lounge in pools on summer days. It's not a difficult climb, though steep in places, and there are sweeping views from the summit. The most famous – and challenging – walk is along the Mourne Wall, a drystone granite wall that forms a 22-mile circuit of the mountains, linking all the key summits.

The Mourne International Walking Festival (www.mournewalking.co.uk) in June is a marvellous time to visit, with organised walks in both the lower and upper mountains. The festival alternates between Newcastle and Warrenpoint, and is suited to all levels of hikers. The tourist office in Newcastle (10-14 Central Promenade, 4372 2222, www.downdc.gov.uk) can also provide maps and information on hiking.

Newcastle sits at the edge of the ocean, on Dundrum Bay, with the Mourne Mountains rearing behind. In its Victorian heyday it was a popular seaside resort where the well-to-do from Belfast

Things to do

ARDS & LECALE PENINSULAS

Lecale Way
www.walkni.com.
A 40-mile route for walkers and cyclists, from Downpatrick to Strangford and then south along the coast to Newcastle. It crosses National Trust property at Castle Ward, where an entrance fee must be paid. Maps and details are available on the Walk Northern Ireland website.

Strangford Lough Canoe Trail
Strangford Lough (9030 3930, www.canoeni.com/ strangford_lough.aspx).
Accessed from Delamont Country Park *(see p269)*, this trail is a paddling paradise for canoeists of all abilities, thanks to Strangford Lough's varied waters, picturesque islands and abundance of wildlife (including curious seals).

MOURNE MOUNTAINS, NEWCASTLE & NEWRY

Mourne Wall Walk
Definitely not for the unfit, this walk follows the Mourne Wall for some 22 miles, crossing the peaks of 15 mountains, including the tallest (Slieve Donard), offering some of the most spectacular views in Northern Ireland. It's possible – but challenging – to do the walk in a day; visit www.mournewall.co.uk for more information.

Newry Canal Towpath
www.cycleni.com.
A 20-mile route along the western towpath of the Newry Canal from Portadown to Newry, passing 14 lock gates, woodland and historical buildings. It's suitable for walkers and cyclists, and maps and details are available on the Cycle Northern Ireland website.

Mourne Mountains. See p271.

flocked for their summer holidays. After years of neglect, it has undergone major redevelopment in recent years; the pleasant promenade is now a popular strolling ground, and the beach is long and sandy. You'll find the usual amusement arcades, cheap caffs and bucket-and-spade shops, which cheapen the town to a certain extent, but it's handy if you need to pick up supplies, and the Royal County Down Golf Club (36 Golf Links Road, 4372 2419, www.royalcountydown.org) – a championship links course founded in 1889 – attracts plenty of golfers to the area.

Just inland from Newcastle is Tollymore Forest Park (*see right*), tailor-made for easy strolls and picnicking in leafy surroundings. The Mourne Trail

Riding Centre (96 Castlewellan Road, 4372 4351) can arrange treks through the forest (experienced equestrians only). Further inland is another Forest Park at Castlewellan (*see right*), said to have the best tree and shrub collection in Ireland. Blue Beans (67 Main Street, 4377 0414, www.blue beanscraft.co.uk, closed Sun) is a new craft shop in the town of Castlewellan. Textile artist Claire Warn has gathered a vast collection of traditional and contemporary Irish designs from more than 80 studios around the country, including vintage christening gowns, glassware, seaweed soap, linen tablecloths and jewellery.

The A2 road, wedged between the mountains and the sea, offers spectacular views as it winds

Places to visit

ARDS & LECALE PENINSULAS

Castle Espie Wetland Centre ★
78 Ballydrain Road, Comber, BT23 6EA (9187 4146, www.wwt.org.uk). Open July, Aug 10am-5.30pm daily. Mar-June, Sept, Oct 10am-5pm daily. Feb 10am-4pm Mon-Fri; 10am-5pm Sat, Sun. Nov-Jan 10am-4pm Mon-Fri; 10am-4.30pm Sat, Sun. Admission £6.50; free-£4.95 reductions; £17.50 family.
Castle Espie is a conservation area encompassing woodland, salt-marsh and reed beds, where Ireland's largest population of waterbirds gather. There's a range of walks and viewing points from where you can glimpse numerous birds – you can expect to see more than 50 species, depending on the time of year – and other wildlife such as otters, foxes and badgers.

Castle Ward ★
Strangford, BT30 7LS (4488 1204, www.national trust.org.uk). Open Grounds Apr-Sept 10am-8pm daily. Oct 10am-5pm daily. Nov-Mar 10am-4pm daily. House Mar-Oct 11am-5pm daily. Admission Grounds £5.45; £2.45 reductions; £13.35 family. House tour £4; £2 reductions; £10 family.
Long the home of the Ward family and now owned by the National Trust, Castle Ward is a fine example of a typical Irish demesne (country estate). The 18th-century mansion is unusual in that it incorporates two very different designs both inside and out; one half classical, the other neo-Gothic. There's a Victorian laundry, cornmill and sawmill, walking trails in the surrounding park and woodland, farmyard animals, an adventure centre and a wildlife centre – perfect for families. With so much to do, a day may not be enough; fortunately, there's camping on site.

Down Cathedral
English Street, Downpatrick, BT30 6AB (4461 4922, www.downcathedral.org). Open 9.30am-4.30pm Mon-Sat; 2-5pm Sun. Tours by appointment only. Admission free; tours £1.
Down Cathedral, with St Patrick's grave, is one of the most important points on St Patrick's Trail. The hilltop has been an ecclesiastical site for centuries; the current building was erected in the early 19th century but incorporates earlier remains. The white-walled interior includes an ancient granite font and a magnificent pipe organ, one of the finest in Ireland.

The supposed burial place of St Patrick is in the cemetery, marked by a large granite stone. Tradition has it that St Brigid and St Columcille are also buried in the grounds.

Mount Stewart House, Garden & Temple of the Winds ★
Portaferry, BT22 2AD (4278 8387, www.national trust.org.uk). Open Lakeside gardens 10am-6pm daily. Formal gardens Mar-Oct 10am-6pm daily. House Mar-Oct noon-6pm daily. Temple of the Winds Mar-Oct 2-5pm Sun. Admission House tour & gardens £7; £3.50 reductions; £17.50 family.
The former home of the Marquesses of Londonderry, this imposing neoclassical mansion was built in the 18th century, with adjoining wings and features added in the 19th. You can explore the lavish interiors (by guided tour only), but the real highlight lies outside. The impeccably maintained gardens, originally laid out in the 1920s by Lady Londonderry, are of international renown. Strangford Lough's mild microclimate allows much experimentation and diversity in planting, resulting in Mediterranean-style formal gardens with extravagant and colourful floral beds, and trees that grow to remarkable heights. The 90 acres also include a lake, lovely woodland and the Temple of the Winds, an octagonal belvedere and banqueting house built in the 1780s, from where there are fine views of the lough.

Ulster Folk & Transport Museum
Cultra, Holywood, BT18 0EU (9042 8428, www.nmni.com). Open Mar-Sept 10am-5pm Tue-Sun. Oct-Feb 10am-4pm Tue-Fri; 11am-4pm Sat, Sun. Admission £8; free-£4.50 reductions; £21.50 family.
Part of the National Museums Northern Ireland, this is really two museums in one. Set in 170 acres of parkland, the outdoor Folk Museum contains a marvellous series of original buildings from around Northern Ireland, some dating as far back as the 18th century. The Ballycultra town area contains whole streets, with shops, houses, churches, a pub, a tearoom and a school, all authentically furnished. There's also a rural area that includes assorted farms (with chickens, geese and pigs wandering about), a corn mill, a flax mill and a forge. With costumed guides, craft demonstrations and traditional

its way south from Newcastle. En route is Bloody Bridge – so named following a massacre during the 1641 Rebellion – a popular starting point for walks into the Mourne Mountains. At the foot of rugged Slieve Binnian (2,450 feet), the village of Annalong is a quieter and less developed alternative to Newcastle. It has a picturesque harbour and a working cornmill, though the main attraction is a mile inland: the Silent Valley Park (0845 744 0088, www.niwater.com/thesilent valley.asp), set at the edge of a huge reservoir built to provide water for Belfast and the Down region. The famous Mourne Wall, constructed in the early 20th century, marks the boundary of the reservoir's catchment area. Other walks in

the Silent Valley are over moorland and woodland. The car park has a visitor centre and café.

Ten minutes south of Annalong is Kilkeel, once the principal market town and fishing port in the 'Kingdom of Mourne'. It boasts Ireland's largest fishing fleet, and fishing is still the major industry – witness the sometimes overpowering stench and darkened skies as seagulls hover, waiting to dive upon the arriving trawlers. The harbourside Nautilus Centre sells an excellent selection of fresh fish and houses a restaurant with views over the bustling port. It's also home to the tourist office – with a reconstructed wheelhouse and an exhibition on the area's maritime heritage – and the Mourne Seafood Cookery School (4176 2525, www.mourneseafoodcookery school.com). South of town, at the entrance to Carlingford Lough, is the sunny, sandy expanse of Cranfield beach. Backed by grass-covered dunes, it has Blue Flag status and is great for families, with a children's play area and lifeguards in high season.

The A2 continues inland alongside Carlingford Lough to the picturesque settlements of Rostrevor and Warrenpoint. Both are relatively sedate, although things liven up in Warrenpoint in May during the Blues on the Bay Festival (www.blues onthebay.com) and again in August at the beauty pageant that is the Maiden of the Mournes Festival (www.maidenofthemournes.com). The Fiddlers Green Festival (www.fiddlersgreenfestival.co.uk) brings country, blues and folk music and family fun to Rostrevor for a week in July.

Mourne Textiles (86 Killowen Old Road, mobile 07717 175128, www.mournetextiles.com, open by appointment) in Restrevor is one of the last remaining handloom weaving workshops still in production in Northern Ireland. Established in 1950, the workshop creates beautiful fabrics inspired by the surrounding landscape and offers weaving courses. Shore-side Kilbroney Park has a range of woodland walks and is also the site of Cloughmore (aka 'The Big Stone'), a gigantic granite boulder, from where there are stunning views over the lough. According to legend, Finn MacCool threw the stone here during a fight with a Scottish giant.

Outside Warrenpoint, where the Newry River meets Carlingford Lough, is Narrow Water Castle, a fine example of a 16th-century tower-house and bawn (defensive wall). It's usually open to the public on Fridays in July and August, but you can also view it from the water on one of the boat trips around the lough.

A few miles inland is the region's main town, Newry. The Newry Heritage Trail takes in the main sights, many of which are near the twin waterways, the Newry Canal and River Clanrye, that run in adjacent channels through the town centre. Pick up a map at the Newry Tourist Information Centre (3031 3170, www.newryandmourne.gov.uk, closed Sun Apr-Sept; Sat, Sun Oct-Mar), housed in Bagenal's Castle on Castle Street. This 16th-century fortified house and adjacent 19th-century warehouse belonged to McCann's Bakery for 160 years, until the late 1990s. Also here is

crops growing in the fields, it's like walking through history. Permanent exhibitions explore farming skills and Victorian daily life in more depth.

The site also houses an impressively large transport collection, illustrating the different modes of travel used over the years in Ireland, including horse-drawn carriages, bicycles, trams, motorbikes, cars and aircraft. One gallery is devoted to the development of the Irish railway system; check out Maedb, Ireland's largest and most powerful steam locomotive.

There's a lot to see, so bring a picnic (or have lunch in the tearoom) and make a day of it.

MOURNE MOUNTAINS, NEWCASTLE & NEWRY

Castlewellan Forest Park
Castlewellan, BT31 9BU (4377 2240, www.nidirect.gov.uk/forests). Open 24hrs daily.
Adjoining Castlewellan town and set around mile-long Castlewellan Lake, this park mixes woodland areas with grassed areas and formal gardens. There are three marked trails, plus assorted ponds, a Moorish tower and Castlewellan Castle, a 19th-century, Scottish baronial-style building (not open to the public). Walled Annesley Garden contains the National Arboretum, one of Europe's finest collections of trees and shrubs. Designed in the 1850s, it's a mix of informal and formal planting, with terraces, flowerbeds, fountains, and some spectacular trees, including rare conifers and maples imported from Japan and many other unusual species. The park's newest attraction is a large hedge maze designed to represent the path to a peaceful future for Northern Ireland.

Tollymore Forest Park
Bryansford Road, Newcastle (4377 2240, www.nidirect.gov.uk/forests). Open 24hrs daily.
A Gothic arched gateway welcomes you to this beautiful park to the north of the Mourne Mountains. The one-time estate of the 8th Earl of Roden is dotted with a variety of trees – from oaks and Himalayan redwoods to eucalyptus and monkey-puzzles. Signposted walks weave through the woodlands and along the River Shimna. There's also a caravan and camping park.

the Newry & Mourne Museum (3031 3175, www.bagenalscastle.com), which has a diverse collection of local artefacts, including a grandfather clock, farming implements, maps and textiles.

Newry Town Hall is a striking red-brick structure located on a three-arched bridge over the River Clanrye, which once marked the border between County Down and County Armagh. Other sights include two large churches named after Ireland's patron saint – who reputedly planted a yew tree here in the fifth century. Dominating Hill Street, the main thoroughfare, is the Roman Catholic Cathedral of St Patrick & St Colman (3026 2586, open 8am-5pm daily), designed by local star architect Thomas Duff and built of grey Mourne granite. It was finished in 1829 – the year that Catholic emancipation was established. St Patrick's Church (3026 2621, www.downanddromore.org/newry, open Sun and by appointment) is on Steam Street. Founded in 1578 by Sir Nicholas Bagenal, it was the first Protestant church built in Ireland after the Reformation. Dean Jonathan Swift, the famous satirist, is believed to have preached here. The building has been restored and modernised, but the graveyard is full of historic headstones.

Newry has some large, modern shopping centres, but livelier and more idiosyncratic is the historic Newry Variety Market (Mary Street, 3026 3004, open Thur, Sat), where more than 70 stalls deal in clothes, fruit and veg, baked goods, flowers, bric-a-brac and household goods.

Where to eat & drink

Newcastle has plenty of affordable eateries, including the Sea Salt Delicatessen & Bistro (51 Central Promenade, 4372 5027), which runs theme nights at weekends. The Percy French bar at the Slieve Donard Resort & Spa (see right) does good pub grub and is one of the better bars in the town.

In Warrenpoint, the Duke Restaurant (7 Duke Street, 4175 2084) above the Duke pub has a good reputation for its fresh, locally sourced food.

In Newry, the Graduate Restaurant (Patrick Street, 3025 9611, closed Sat, Sun) is a one-off. Situated in Newry College, it's run by lecturers and staffed by training chefs and waiters. For drinking, the Bank (Trevor Hill, 3083 5501, www.thebanknewry.com) is probably the most popular 'trendy' bar/nightclub, while the Railway Bar (79-81 Monaghan Street, 3026 2498) has traditional music sessions on Thursday nights.

Copper Restaurant ★
9 Monaghan Street, Newry, BT35 6BB (3026 7772, www.copperrestaurant.co.uk). Lunch served noon-3pm Tue-Sat. Dinner served 5-9.30pm Tue-Thur; 5-10.30pm Fri, Sat. Food served noon-8.30pm Sun.
Recently moved to Newry from Warrenpoint, the Copper is hands down the best place to eat in town. The bistro-style menu includes Irish steaks, burgers and other meat dishes, but also features international flavours (beef bourguignon, grilled salmon teriyaki, Thai prawn and coconut curry). Ingredients are top-quality, and particular attention is paid to sauces and side dishes.

Restaurant 23
Balmoral Hotel, 13 Seaview, Warrenpoint, BT34 3NJ (4175 3222, www.restaurant23.com). Lunch served 12.30-2.30pm, dinner served 5.30-9.30pm Wed-Sun.
Smartly modern in style, with polished wood floors, banquette seating and funky wallpaper, Restaurant 23 has won a Michelin Bib Gourmand for its exciting, eclectic menu, the creation of chef Trevor Cunningham. Expect spiced duck wontons with mango salsa and curried cashew nuts or an assiette of locally caught fish and shellfish to start, followed by the likes of Mourne lamb, or hake with salt and pepper squid and a chorizo and tomato fondue. Vegetarians get their own menu. The carte isn't cheap, but the midweek set menus are a bargain.

Where to stay

At the end of the 19th century, the grand Slieve Donard Resort & Spa (1 Downs Road, 4372 1066, www.hastingshotels.com) was the jewel in Newcastle's crown. The red-brick façade is still magnificent, though a new extension does little to accentuate the character of the old place. It's large (178 bedrooms) and busy (especially with golfers), but has a lovely spa complete with sea views from the pool and sauna.

If your budget doesn't stretch that far, fear not: most villages and towns have B&Bs and pubs with rooms, and there's no shortage of camping and caravanning sites. The Forest Parks at Tollymore and Castlewellan (for both, *see p275*) offer camping, while, at the foot of the Mourne Mountains, Meelmore Lodge (52 Trassey Road, 4372 5949, www.meelmorelodge.com) has both a campsite (open Easter-Oct) and hostel accommodation (open all year).

In Warrenpoint, try the sea-facing Balmoral Hotel (4175 4093, www.balmoralhotel.biz), home of Restaurant 23 (*see above*). It has eight rooms, costing £80-£100 double including breakfast.

Carriage House
71 Main Street, Dundrum, BT33 0LU (4375 1635, www.carriagehousedundrum.com). Rates £75 double incl breakfast. No credit cards.
Located in the heart of Dundrum, this small B&B has three bedrooms thoughtfully designed with a mix of antique and retro pieces. A hearty breakfast is served overlooking the garden, where you'll find chickens and an intriguing metal sculpture of a horse. Owner Maureen Griffith is a warm and winning hostess, ensuring plenty of repeat custom.

Glassdrumman Lodge
85 Mill Road, Annalong, BT34 4RH (4376 8451, www.glassdrummanlodge.com). Rates £100-£180 double incl breakfast.
A smart, family-run hotel tucked away in blissful silence at the foothills of the Mourne Mountains, about a mile inland from Annalong. The ten comfortable, pleasantly styled rooms are often occupied by keen golfers, anglers or walkers; it's also a wedding and conference venue. The restaurant serves upmarket dishes using produce from the hotel's garden, and local fish and meat. Various package deals are offered; check the website for details.

Counties Antrim & Derry

The two northern counties of Northern Ireland have a lot to offer visitors, especially after huge investment to restore the region's reputation as a tourist destination. The Causeway Coastal Route, which follows the coastline from Belfast round to Derry, is one of the most scenic drives in the whole of Ireland, with breathtaking views across the sea to Scotland and attractive villages, such as Glenarm, Cushendall and Cushendun in County Antrim, to explore. Inland are the nine Glens of Antrim, a lush landscape of glacial valleys, dense forests and pretty waterfalls, best seen at Glenariff Forest Park. Also en route is the Giant's Causeway, Northern Ireland's most famous and most visited sight. At the end of the drive comes the city of Derry/Londonderry, once a major trouble spot for Northern Ireland's political problems. Its future looks more promising, and it is the UK's first European City of Culture in 2013.

CARRICKFERGUS TO FAIR HEAD

The 120-mile Causeway Coastal Route ★ runs all the way from Belfast to Londonderry, along the A2, with occasional detours inland – look for the brown signs. The drive is detailed on www.causewaycoastand glens.com, along with plenty of useful information on places, attractions and accommodation in the region. It has been rated one of the top ten road trips in the world. Unfortunately, such popularity has its drawbacks: the road, already narrow and winding, can be slow-going during the summer months. Bearing that in mind, it's best to take the road at your leisure, stopping off here and there to get a real feel for the coast and what it has to offer.

From Belfast, it's a 15-minute drive north to one of Ireland's oldest forts, Carrickfergus Castle (Marine Highway, 9335 1273, www.doeni.gov.uk), built more than 800 years ago. Its prominent position at the sea's edge clearly illustrates its important defensive role. Extremely well preserved, it contains a massive keep, three medieval courtyards and plenty of armour. There's nothing much else to see in Carrickfergus, and Larne, 13 miles further north, is an ugly industrial city notable only as being a port for regional and international ferries.

It is after Larne, when the views open out over the sea, that you will begin to understand the Coastal Route's appeal. It is also here that the Glens of Antrim rise from the interior, divided by fertile, green valleys. Sitting at the edge of the Glens, Glenarm is a sweet, sleepy village, consisting of not much more than an attractive high street, woodland and a castle. The main street is lined with houses and a few small shops, including contemporary jeweller the Steensons (Toberwine Street, 2884 1445, www.thesteensons.com, closed Sun). At the top of the street is the old castle entrance; you can drive through, park and then amble around the mature woodland of Glenarm Forest.

The family home of the Earls of Antrim for 400 years, Glenarm Castle (Castle Lane, 2884 1203, www.glenarmcastle.com, closed Oct-Apr) opens occasionally to the public, on bank holidays, and

for festivals and concerts in summer. However, the lovely Walled Garden, first laid out in the 18th century, is open daily from May to September. There's also a tearoom. At the top of the town, the road heads inland towards Slemish Mountain, which juts some 1,500 feet above the surrounding plain. The mountain is the central core of an extinct volcano, and is where St Patrick is reputed to have worked as a shepherd – hence the walk to the top is one that many pilgrims make in March. The round trip takes about an hour, though it's steep and rocky in parts; details on www.walkni.com.

Continue along the A2 for a few more miles of sea views and curving blacktop to reach Carnlough. The small town is surprisingly busy, with a maze of little streets and a rather beautiful harbour, which was used to export limestone from a local quarry until the 1950s. A bridge was built astride the main street to allow a train to bring the stone down to the harbour, and still stands today. George Shiels, one of Ireland's most famous playwrights, lived here until his death in 1945. Another famous name thrown about the town is Winston Churchill, who for a while owned what is now the Londonderry Arms (20 Harbour Road, 2888 5255, www.glensofantrim.com).

Beyond Carnlough, the high cliffs fall away and the landscape opens up to reveal a wide lush valley, scooped out of the green hills. At Glenariff (also called Waterfoot) – uneventful, but with a fine sandy beach – you can turn inland along the A43. It's a tight, twisting road skimming the edge of the hill above the valley; follow it until you see signs for Glenariff Forest Park (see p282).

Returning to the coast along either the A43 or the B14, in the shadow of the table-top Lurigethan Mountain and beside the River Dall, you will reach Cushendall ★. It's a pretty spot, popular with tourists as a base for exploring the county. Streets lined with gaily coloured buildings, interspersed with shops, bars and a couple of cafés, converge at the heart of the town, where Turnly's Tower stands. Otherwise known as the Curfew Tower, the four-storey red-sandstone building was built in 1809,

Ballygally Castle

at the behest of Francis Turnly, as 'a place of confinement for idlers and rioters'. Visit the tourist office (24 Mill Street, 2177 1180, closed winter afternoons) to gather information on local sights, walks, activities and places to stay. The town is busiest during the Heart of the Glens Festival (www.glensfestival.com), a long-running community celebration held in August. Lasting nine days, it brings music, dance, sports events, street parades and plenty of fun for all ages.

There's a nice beach close to Cushendall, and a beautiful cliff-top path with stunning views over the Sea of Moyle and across to Scotland. Start from the Cliff Path car park north of town; from here it's less than a mile to ruined Layde Church, hidden in a secluded valley. The names on the gravestones reflect the strong links between Cushendall and Scotland. A large Celtic cross marks the grave of Dr James McDonnell, founder of the Belfast School of Medicine, which later became Queen's University.

After Cushendall, the A2 cuts inland. Turn right to reach Cushendun, one of the best-loved and beautiful towns along the coast. Situated at the mouth of the River Dun, tucked between the Glens of Glendun and Glencorp, the town has a small harbour, a curved sandy beach and a picture-perfect town square. The latter, designed in 1912 by architect Clough Williams-Ellis (of Portmeirion in Wales fame), for the Baron of Cushendun, consists of a few neat, whitewashed buildings with slate roofs, decidedly Cornish in style. After the death of the Baron's wife, Maud, who came from Penzance, Ellis designed a row of picturesque white cottages in her memory. Known as Maud Cottages, these, along with the square, are now under the watchful eye of the National Trust and remain charmingly untouched. The town gets packed in July during its music and dance festival.

From Cushendun, the most scenic route north is along the coast road (not the A2) via Torr Head. Pay attention: it's a narrow, twisting road and not for the faint-hearted. But the wild, rocky landscape and crashing waves below are worth any heart palpitations, and on clear days there are stirring views across to the Mull of Kintyre, 12 miles away. Beyond Torr Head is Murlough Bay, the most beautiful bay in Antrim. A lush wooded hillside slopes down to the water's edge, and a narrow lane leads from the car park to the shore. On the far side of the bay is majestic Fair Head, with its vertical dolerite columns rising 600 feet above the shore – rock climbers flock here to tackle some of the best and most challenging sea climbs in Britain. The treacherous waters below hide many shipwrecks. There's a meandering path from Coolanlough car park to the headland, where you can gaze over to Rathlin Island and the Scottish isles.

Where to eat & drink

The tea shop (closed Oct-Apr) at Glenarm Castle (see p277) offers sandwiches, salads, savoury tarts and desserts. In Carnlough, the Londonderry Arms Hotel (20 Harbour Road, 2888 5255, www.glensofantrim.com) is somewhat dated, but does serve decent bar food and afternoon tea. It also has 35 B&B rooms. Cushendall has several good bars, including McCollam's (23 Mill Street, 2177 1992), aka Johnny Joe's. It hosts traditional music sessions and has the best eaterie in town, Upstairs at Joe's (2177 2630). Both pub and restaurant have limited opening hours in winter.

Laragh Lodge ★
120 Glen Road, Glenariff, BT44 0RG (2175 8221, www.laraghlodge.co.uk). Food served noon-9pm daily.

Laragh Lodge can be approached in two ways: along the A43 from Glenariff or, more enchantingly, through Glenariff Forest itself. Descend into the gorge, follow the turbulent waters to the beautiful Ess-Na-Grub waterfall, and you'll find a white lodge, surrounded by trees. The interior is simple: high-beamed ceilings, wooden floors, and glass windows spanning the length of the building. In winter, the room is adorned with fairy lights and the aroma of hot spiced port is enticing; in summer, you can bask outdoors under the canopy of trees. The hearty menu – own-made soup, deep-fried brie, traditional Sunday roasts – should satisfy a walker's hunger.

Mary McBride's
2 Main Street, Cushendun, BT44 0PH (2176 1511). Open noon-1am daily. Food served noon-7pm daily.
It's small and spartan – plain white walls, wooden tables and floor – but McBride's is the most atmospheric bar in Cushendun, if not along the whole Antrim coast. Expect impromptu singalongs, traditional music sessions and bundles of craic. Homely dishes include an excellent seafood chowder.

Where to stay
Glenarm has little in the way of accommodation. Cushendall is better provided for, with several B&Bs that can be booked via the tourist office. The Glens Hotel (6 Coast Road, 2177 1223, www.theglenshotel.com), with 14 en suite rooms, a bar and a restaurant, is probably the most comfortable option. Cushendun has a handful of B&Bs, plus self-catering cottages for stays of a week or longer. There are several camping sites along the coast, including Glenariff Forest Park

(*see p282*, open Easter-Sept), Cushendall Caravan Park (62 Coast Road, 2177 1699, open Apr-Oct) and Watertop Open Farm (188 Cushendall Road, 2076 2576, www.watertopfarm.co.uk, open Easter-Oct).

Ballygally Castle
Coast Road, Ballygally, BT40 2QZ (2858 1066, www.hastingshotels.com/ballygally-castle). Rates £165 double incl breakfast.
There are more luxurious hotels, but Ballygally Castle has spectacular views over Ballygally Bay, pretty gardens leading to a river and, intriguingly, is meant to be haunted. There are 44 rooms, spread between the original castle and a newer section. The castle was built as a residence in 1625 by James Shaw. French chateau in style, it retains many original features, including corner turrets, dormer windows and a steep roof. Inside, a spiral stone staircase leads to the atmospheric bedrooms (thick stonewalls, low beamed ceilings, small doorways), sympathetically designed to suit the historical feel. Guests should be prepared for the ghost of Mrs Shaw appearing at night. Legend says that after giving birth to a son, she was banished by her husband James to a tiny turret room. Some say she then jumped to her death from the window in desperation to get to her child; others say the evil Mr Shaw pushed her to her death.

BALLYCASTLE TO PORTRUSH
Perched on the northern coast, where two of the Glens of Antrim (Glentaisie and Glenshesk) converge, is the bustling seaside resort of Ballycastle. The central Diamond, surrounded by shops, cafés and restaurants, is typical of old market towns. The main street, Quay Road, leads down to the harbour, from where ferries

Giant's Causeway. See p282.

Places to visit

Glenariff Forest Park

CARRICKFERGUS TO FAIR HEAD

Glenariff Forest Park ★
Glenariff Road, Glenariff, BT44 0QX (2955 6001, www.nidirect.gov.uk/forests). Open dawn-dusk daily.
The nine Glens of Antrim provide some of Northern Ireland's most beautiful scenery. Glenariff is known as the 'Queen of the Glens', and Glenariff Forest Park, a short detour from the coast road, is a good introduction to its charms. Three trails within the park range in length from half a mile to five miles; the two-mile long Waterfall Trail has a boardwalk following a river through a deep, rocky gorge, past several lovely waterfalls. Elsewhere, there are marvellous views over the other Glens. There is also a large car park, a café and a visitor centre.

BALLYCASTLE TO PORTRUSH

Carrick-a-Rede Rope Bridge
119A Whitepark Road, Ballintoy, BT54 6LS (2076 9839, www.nationaltrust.org.uk). Open June-Aug 10am-7pm daily. Mar-May, Sept, Oct 10am-6pm daily. Nov-Feb 10.30am-3.30pm daily. Admission £5.09; £2.63 reductions; £12.45 family.
There's a car park, information centre and tearoom at the entrance, from where it's a 15-minute walk along a cliff path to the bridge. Originally erected by local salmon fishermen coming to check their nets, the rope suspension bridge links the mainland with Carrick-a-Rede island. You'll need a head for heights: the 65ft bridge traverses a 100ft chasm and tends to sway, so it feels very exposed. Still, people come in their thousands for the exhilaration of simply walking across it. Once on the tiny island, find a quiet perch to enjoy the view to Scotland and take a breather before recrossing the bridge.

Dunluce Castle ★
87 Dunluce Road, Bushmills, BT57 8UY (2073 1938, www.doeni.gov.uk). Open Easter-Sept 10am-6pm daily. Oct-Easter 10am-4pm daily. Admission £2; free-£1 reductions.
Now cared for by the Northern Ireland Environment Agency, this ruined medieval castle perches precariously on a high basalt outcrop, linked to the mainland only by a narrow archway. Parts may date from the 14th century, though the first record of the castle dates from 1513. It later became home to Sorley Boy MacDonnell, chief of the Clan MacDonnell (Earls of Antrim). When a ship from the Spanish Armada was wrecked nearby in 1602, the cannons were salvaged for use in the stronghold. The castle was abandoned about ten years later after, reputedly, the kitchens fell into the sea in the middle of a feast. You can climb down to the Mermaid's Cave beneath the castle – take care, it's rocky and steep.

Giant's Causeway ★
44A Causeway Road, Bushmills, BT57 8SU (2073 1855, www.nationaltrust.org.uk). Open Visitor centre July, Aug 9.30am-7pm daily. June, Sept 9.30am-6pm daily. Mar-May, Oct 9.30am-5pm daily. Nov-Jan 9.30am-4pm daily.
The Giant's Causeway is Northern Ireland's only UNESCO World Heritage Site. Legend claims that the outsized 'steps' were built by the Irish giant Finn MacCool as a way to Scotland, where he wanted to fight another giant. In fact, the hexagonal columns of layered black basalt – which are also likened to a pipe organ – resting on a rocky beach at the base of towering cliffs, are the result of volcanic activity over 60 million years ago. The Causeway attracts hundreds of thousands of visitors each year – and deservedly so. It's an impressive sight, despite the crowds milling

about. The weathered stones resemble other objects; look out for the Giant's Boots, the Camel's Hump and the Chimneystacks. For a quieter time, take a walk along the upper cliffs. A new visitor centre is due to open in spring 2012; in the meanwhile, there's a temporary information point next to the Causeway Hotel.

Old Bushmills Distillery
2 Distillery Road, Bushmills, BT57 8XH (2073 3218, www.bushmills.com). Open July, Aug 9.15am-5pm Mon-Sat; 11am-5pm Sun. Apr-June, Oct 9.15am-5pm Mon-Sat; noon-5pm Sun. Jan-Mar, Nov, Dec 9.15am-5pm Mon-Fri; 12.30-5pm Sat, Sun. Admission £7; £3.50-£6 reductions; £20 family.
Ireland's oldest whiskey distillery (King James I granted a royal licence to Sir Thomas Phillips to distill whiskey in Antrim in 1608) is filled with huge, gleaming copper stills and aged oak casks. Learn about the distilling process on the tour, then – the most important part – sample the product. Portion control is disappointingly rigid, but there is a shop.

Rathlin Island
www.rspb.org.uk.
This L-shaped island, sitting six miles off the Antrim coast and only 12 miles from the Mull of Kintyre, is serviced by ferries from Ballycastle (2076 9299, www.rathlinballycastleferry.com). Open to the winds, the isle is a rather bleak place, with little vegetation and steep cliffs, and is crowned at either end with a lighthouse. Measuring about six miles long and one mile wide, it's home to about 100 people and, between May and July, tens of thousands of breeding seabirds, including kittiwakes and puffins. As a result, it's a designated conservation area; the RSPB Seabird Centre is at the western tip. At the harbour, there's a

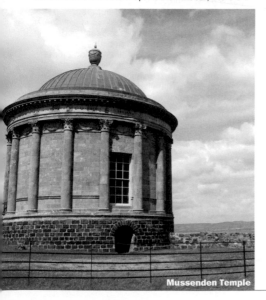
Mussenden Temple

pub, café, shop, guesthouse and the Rathlin Boathouse Visitor Centre (2076 2024, closed Oct-Apr), which can provide information on the stunning cliff walks, the best birdwatching spots and famous Bruce's Cave. According to legend, this is where Scottish hero Robert the Bruce retreated, after being defeated by the English, and saw a spider spinning a web. The sight inspired him to 'try and try again': he returned to Scotland, eventually beating the English. The numerous cliffside caves are accessible only by boat; trips can be arranged at the visitor centre.

COUNTY DERRY/LONDONDERRY

Downhill Demesne & Mussenden Temple ★
Mussenden Road, Castlerock, BT51 4RP (7084 8728, www.nationaltrust.org.uk). Open Grounds 24hrs daily. Hezlett House & Mussenden Temple Late Mar-Sept 10am-5pm daily. Admission £4.09; £2.04 reductions; £10.22 family. No credit cards.
The Downhill estate encompasses Hezlett House (*see p286*), as well as the ruins of a grandiose mansion built in the late 18th century by Frederick Augustus Hervey, Bishop of Derry. Wander around the well-preserved ruins, through the old stables and head towards the sea. Perched at the cliff edge is Mussendun Temple, which was used by Hervey as a library and is supposedly modelled on the Temple of Vesta in Rome. An inscription reads 'Tis pleasant, safely to behold from shore/The rolling ship, and hear the tempest roar' – a reference to the bewitching views from the large windows, over Downhill beach and as far as Donegal. Beware the stiff sea winds; there's little protection from the elements here.

St Columb's Cathedral
London Street, Derry, BT48 6RQ (7126 7313, www.stcolumbscathedral.org). Open 9am-5pm Mon-Sat. Tours by appointment. Admission free; donations appreciated. Tours £2; 50p reductions. No credit cards.
St Columb's Cathedral is the oldest building in Derry; its was built in 1633 in what became known as Planter Gothic style. The tower and main building are original, while the spire was added in the 19th century and the Chapter House in 1910. The Cathedral contains regimental flags, memorials and other historical items from the Siege of Derry. The attacking army catapulted a cannon shell into the building, with their terms of surrender attached to the shell – it's now displayed in the entrance. More relics are housed in the Chapter House Museum.

Tower Museum
Union Hall Place, Derry, BT48 6LU (7137 2411, www.derrycity.gov.uk/museums/tower-museum). Open July, Aug 10am-5pm daily. Sept-June 10am-5pm Tue-Sat. Admission £4.20; £2.65 reductions; £9.95 family.
There are two exhibitions here. One recounts the history of Derry from medieval times to present; the other examines the Armada ship *La Trinidad Valencera*, which sank off the coast of Donegal in 1588 and was discovered by a Derry scuba team in the 1970s. Don't forget to climb to the tower roof, to enjoy panoramic views across the city.

depart for the bird haven of Rathlin Island (*see p283*). Near the harbour is a memorial to Guglielmo Marconi, inventor of the wireless, who in 1898 sent a radio telegaph transmission from Ballycastle to Rathlin Island. The sandy beach draws plenty of holidaymakers in summer.

The busiest and most enjoyable time to visit is during the Auld Lammas Fair at the end of August. It's Ireland's oldest fair, in existence since 1606, and draw crowds of 250,000 over two days. The focus is on selling livestock and traditional foods such as dulce (an edible, dried, salted seaweed) and yellowman (a type of honeycomb manipulated into hard toffee). For details of this and other attractions, visit Ballycastle Tourist Information Centre (7 Mary Street, 2076 2024, www.moyle-council.org/tourism, closed Sept-June Sat, Sun).

On the outskirts of town are the remains of 13th-century Bonamargy Friary, idyllically set in lush pastures beside the River Margy. The well-preserved ruins consist of a chapel, vaults, gatehouse, cloisters, living quarters, and a graveyard where Sorley Boy MacDonnell, the chieftain and hero of Dunluce Castle further along the coast, is buried.

Leaving Ballycastle, it's worth taking the B15 (rather than the main A2) to see Carrick-a-Rede Rope Bridge (*see p282*), half a mile before the pretty village of Ballintoy. A few miles further on is the tiny hamlet of Portbraddon and marvellous Whitepark Bay, a mile-long arc of white sand backed by dunes,

Carrick-a-Rede Rope Bridge. See p282.

where you'll find one of the best located hostels (*see p286*) in Ireland. The excitement builds on approaching the next stop, the Giant's Causeway (*see p282*), probably the most famous sight in Northern Ireland. Expect to be greeted by a line of cars queuing for the car park – it is worth the wait.

From the Causeway, it's five miles to Bushmills, the name familiar to whiskey lovers worldwide – tours are available of the Old Bushmills Distillery (*see p283*). The small town has a few decent restaurants, a fantastic butcher's and a wonderful hotel, the Bushmills Inn (*see p286*). Fun, if touristy, is the Giant's Causeway & Bushmills Railway (2073 2844, www.giantscausewayrailway.webs.com), a gaily coloured, narrow-gauge steam train that runs for two miles to the Causeway. A good way to take in the scenery and beat the traffic, the train operates daily in July and Aug, weekends only Easter-June, Sept and Oct. The station is outside town, on the B146 Causeway Road.

From Bushmills, the A2 hugs the sea-ravaged limestone cliffs to Portrush. Pockmarked with caves and arches, the cliffs were once used as hideouts by smugglers and pirates. Don't make the mistake of bypassing Portballintrae, a tiny seaside village a mile from Bushmills. Stunning Runkerry Strand is perfect for a stroll, and the swell is favourable for surfing. The best secret is the coast path that runs from the end of the beach all the way to the Causeway. It's only a couple of miles and the panoramic ocean views are wonderful.

Further west, atop a rocky headland, the ruins of Dunluce Castle (*see p282*) rise precariously from the basalt cliffs. The site is dramatic and beautiful, and it's easy to figure out why the fortification was built in such a commanding position – Dunluce comes from the Irish for 'strong fort'. The castle is Antrim's most impressive ruin and has an intriguing history of chieftains, battles and heroes.

It's another three miles of scenic road to Portrush, a bustling town with two fantastic beaches. Before you reach the town, a lookout provides wonderful views back towards Dunluce, clearly showing the sea caves dug into the cliff. Eastwards, leading into Portrush, are the curving white sands of Whiterocks Beach. Families arrive in droves in high season to enjoy Portrush's clean beaches and seaside amusements; the raucousness may, however, be overwhelming for the more discerning visitor. Surfers prefer to visit in September and October, when the waves are bigger and better, the weather is still warm and the crowds have dispersed. On the Main Street, Troggs (no.88, 7082 5476, www.troggssurfshop.co.uk) and Woodies Surf Shop (no.102, 7082 3273, www.woodiessurfshop. co.uk, closed Feb Mon-Thur; Mar Tue) hire boards and wetsuits, provide lessons and can advise on where to go for the best breaks. On the harbour side of Portrush, west of Ramore headland, is West Strand Beach. It's extremely popular with families and kayakers as the water is quite shallow and the currents less severe than on Whiterocks Beach.

Child-friendly attractions include Waterworld (The Harbour, 7082 2001, www.colerainebc.gov.uk, closed Sept-May) with its slides, pirate playground

Central Wine Bar

and tenpin bowling alley; and the Coastal Zone (8 Bath Road, 7082 3600, www.doeni.gov.uk, closed winter Mon-Sat), a marine education centre. Maddybenny Riding Centre (7082 3394, www. maddybenny.com), located off the main road from Portrush to Coleraine, offers lessons and hacks from £18 for 45 minutes. Golfers will be drawn to the Royal Portrush Golf Club (Dunluce Road, 7082 3335, www.royalportrushgolfclub.com), established in 1888 and considered one of the best links courses in the world. It has limited availability for non-members, so you'll need to book well in advance.

Portrush is also famous for hosting Ireland's largest outdoor sporting event, the NorthWest 200 (www.northwest200.org), a motorbike road race between Portrush, Portstewart and Coleraine. It's held in May, while the NI International Air Show (www.niinternationalairshow.co.uk) is in early September. Thousands attend both events, and accommodation is in short supply.

Where to eat & drink

Ballycastle has an ever-expanding selection of restaurants and bars. Reliable pubs with plenty of character include O'Connors (9 Ann Street, 2076 2123) and the House of McDonnell (71 Castle Street, 2076 2975, closed winter Mon-Thur, Sun). The popular Cellar Restaurant (11B The Diamond, 2076 3037, www.thecellarrestaurant. co.uk) serves a consistently good, international menu in an atmospheric basement space, with a curved ceiling and church pews for seating.

Portrush has a plethora of cheap restaurants, takeaways and cafés, so you have to pick the good from the bad. Worth trying are Arrosto Cafe (17 Eglinton Street, 7082 5396) for generous bowls of soup and a wide range of drinks and sandwiches;

Ground Espresso bar (55 Main Street, 7082 5979, www.groundcoffee.net) for bagels, coffee and Wi-Fi; and 55° North (1 Causeway Street, 7082 2811, www.55-north.com) for stunning bay views and drinks at sunset. The Harbour Bar at Ramore Restaurants (*see below*) is the best bar in town – cosy and traditional downstairs, and modern with live bands upstairs. Kelly's Nightclub (Bushmills Road, 7082 6611, www.kellysportrush.co.uk, open Wed, Sat, other times vary) is one of Northern Ireland's largest clubs and heaving year-round, mainly because of the large student population.

Central Wine Bar

12 Ann Street, Ballycastle, BT54 6AD (2076 3877, www.centralwinebar.com). Open noon-1am daily. Food served noon-9pm daily.
This smart bar-restaurant has a clean modern look, with bare brick walls, wooden floors and furnishings, and trendy upholstered chairs. The menu suits all tastes, from fish and chips to crispy duck breast or more simple chicken and pasta dishes. It's popular with younger locals.

Ramore Restaurants

The Harbour, Portrush, BT56 8DF (Wine Bar 7082 4313, Coast 7082 3311, Harbour 7082 2430, www.ramorerestaurant.com). Open times vary; phone for details.
Located in the harbour in Portrush, Ramore encompasses four restaurants and two bars. The Wine Bar is the most popular, which, despite its name, offers a wide range of food, from classics like burgers, steaks and lasagne to fusion dishes such as Thai fish curry and Mexican chicken. Vegetarian options are limited, but the house salads are good. Coast serves pasta, stone-baked pizzas and other Italian dishes, and also has a cocktail bar. Prices are very reasonable throughout. You can't book and the waiting list can be long in summer, but you can always kill time with a pint of Guinness in the rustic Harbour Bar.

Tartine

140 Main Street, Bushmills, BT57 8QE (2073 1044, www.distillersarms.com). Lunch served noon-2.30pm Fri-Sun. Dinner served 5-7pm Wed-Sun.

Originally the home of the owners of the Bushmills distillery and then a pub, this building now houses one of the best restaurants in the area. The design mixes rough stone walls with smart leather chairs, white tablecloths and large windows to pleasing effect. The extensive modern Irish menu covers all bases; mains include several steak options (using local beef), seafood pie, and risotto with roasted Mediterranean vegetables, and venison casserole marinated in red wine and juniper berries. There's a set price menu for Sunday lunch, and a wine list to savour. Prices are very reasonable for food of this quality.

Where to stay

B&Bs and local hotels are plentiful along the north coast; Ballycastle Tourist Information Centre (*see p284*) has an accommodation booking service.

Gorgeous Whitepark Bay has two superbly located places to stay, both on Whitepark Road: the budget-priced Whitepark Bay Hostel (2073 1745, www.hini.org.uk, closed Nov-Mar), and wonderful Whitepark House (2073 1482, www.whitepark house.com), a guesthouse with just three double rooms. While most of the tourist sights are along the coast, upmarket Galgorm Resort & Spa (Fenaghy Road, 2588 1001, www.galgorm.com),

Tartine

inland near Ballymena, is renowned for its beautifully designed spa, modern rooms and lovely grounds.

Bushmills Inn ★

9 Dunluce Road, Bushmills, BT57 8QG (2073 3000, www.bushmillsinn.com). Rates £158-£298 double incl breakfast.

This 19th-century inn in the centre of Bushmills has been renovated and extended with loving care, resulting in one of the best places to stay in Antrim. The original part remains as it has done for years, with a cosy bar, turf fires, nooks, crannies and snugs to hide in, and weekend music sessions. A glass walkway leads to the new hotel – passing the appealing restaurant, with its brick walls, intimately placed tables and wholesome Irish food. The 41 bedrooms vary in size and style: all have the latest mod-cons , year are in keeping with the historic character of the place.

Links B&B

8 Bushmills Road, Portrush, BT56 8JF (7082 3769, www.linksviewportrush.co.uk). Rates £70-£80 double incl breakfast.

Unlike most local B&Bs, this is a brand-new building, with spacious, bright, well-designed rooms. It's proving a big hit with golfers who come to play the world-famous Royal Portrush links course, located just across the road. Best are the two deluxe rooms overlooking the golf course and the coast. There are also two family suites (two twin/double rooms) with their own bathroom.

COUNTY DERRY/LONDONDERRY

Portstewart to Derry

The final part of the Causeway Coastal Route is squeezed into the northernmost corner of County Derry. Three miles east of Portrush is the small town of Portstewart, a popular seaside resort in Victorian times. There's little reason to stop now, unless you want some award-winning sausages from Tom's Butchers, or an ice-cream from Morelli's. The road then swings inland, via the outskirts of the not-so-handsome town of Coleraine. Stay on the A2 and, after about six miles, turn left on to the Sea Coast Road at the Castlerock crossroads. Castlerock has a lovely, long white-sand beach, and a carefully restored 17th-century cottage, Hezlett House, where you can learn about rural life in the past. The house is part of the National Trust-owned Downhill Demesne (*see p283*), which also contains a picturesquely located clifftop temple. At the bottom of the hill is the tiny hamlet of Downhill, a peaceful and beautiful spot next to the sweeping curve of Magilligan Strand, a Blue Flag beach.

Further on, the B202 veers right towards the headland of Magilligan Point, which protrudes across the entrance of Lough Foyle. A restored Martello tower stands guard. Ferries (00 353 74 938 1903, www.loughfoyleferry.com) make the short crossing from the Point to Greencastle in County Donegal. The A2 then turns south, passing Binevenagh Mountain, now a nature reserve for birds of prey. It's possible to climb the mountain; for details, visit Limavady Tourist Centre (24 Main

Street, 7776 0650, www.limavady.gov.uk, closed Sun) in the next town. There's not much else of interest here, unless you're visiting in June, during the excellent Limavady Jazz & Blues Festival (www.limavadyjazzandblues.com).

Inland, about 20 miles south of Coleraine via the A29, is the lovely retreat that is Ardtara Country House (see p290).

Derry/Londonderry

Seventeen miles south of Limavady, at the mouth of Lough Foyle, is the city of Derry. That's the name the nationalists tend to call it; to unionists, it's Londonderry. While not the most picturesque of cities, Derry's location beside the River Foyle and rich cultural and architectural heritage make it an attractive place to visit. The name Derry derives from the Irish 'doire', a reference to the oak grove where St Columba founded a monastery in the sixth century. It was in the 17th century that the city was renamed Londonderry, and a wall built to protect it from raiding Irish chieftains; Derry remains one of the best-preserved examples of a walled city in Europe. The murals of Bogside have long been an attraction and remain so, but Derry's lively music, arts and nightlife scene are increasingly becoming its best assets. The city has rebuilt itself and its reputation, and now exudes a new, more positive energy – it will be the first UK City of Culture in 2013 (www.cityofculture2013.com).

Start your explorations at the Tourist Information Centre (no.44, 7126 7284, www.derryvisitor.com, closed winter Sun) on Foyle Street, at the edge of the walled city. The imposing, neo-Gothic building in red sandstone next to the wall is the Guildhall (7137 7335, www.derrycity.gov.uk, closed Sat, Sun), seat of local government. Built at the end of the 19th century, it was bombed and destroyed in the 1970s, but has been carefully restored; original features (such as the stained-glass windows depicting the city's history) have been reinstated. Visitors are welcome to wander through the building. Opposite is the Harbour Museum (Harbour Square, 7137 7331, www.derrycity.gov.uk/museums, closed Sat, Sun), which covers the maritime history of the region through maps, drawings and – best of all – a 30-foot curragh.

The circular city wall, 26 feet high and up to 30 feet wide, is a mile long and has seven gateways. The importance of the medieval city, and the extent to which is was defended, is evident from the 24 original cannons – many lined up along the wall at Shipquay Gate. Inside the gate, to the right, is the Tower Museum (see p283). Adjacent is the Craft Village (7126 0329, closed Sun), a replica of an 18th-century street and 19th-century square, with a craft shop and a café. At the centre of the walled city is the Diamond, marked by a 1927 war memorial, and Austin's department store, which has stood here for two centuries (it's supposedly the world's oldest independent department store).

Ferryquay Gate is on the east side, near the River Foyle. It was at this gate that the Siege of Derry, the city's most famous (and contentious)

Bushmills Inn

FIVE PARKS & GARDENS IN NORTHERN IRELAND

Carfunnock Country Park
Larne, Co Antrim BT40 2 QG (mobile 07745 570037, www.larne.gov.uk, www.carnfunnock.com). Open Park 24hrs daily. Family Fun Zone Mar-Oct 11am-5pm Sat, Sun; daily school hols. Admission Park £4 per car. Family Fun Zone prices vary per activity.
Located four miles north of Larne, Carfunnock Country Park is a great place to take the family. As well as woodland walks, formal gardens and a wildlife garden, there's an adventure centre with a miniature railway, bungee run and mini golf. Orienteering and other outdoor activities are organised too. The grounds include a campsite and coffee shop.

Dark Hedges
Bregagh Road, between Ballinlea Road & Ballykenver Road, nr Armoy, Co Antrim.
Neither a stately home nor a formal garden, the Dark Hedges are a stunning formation of beech trees along a quiet country road, a five-minute drive west of Armoy. Planted in 1750, the trees are now huge and majestic, their branches stretching across the road to form a tunnel. They are particularly spectacular in mist, and are said to be haunted by a grey lady, who wanders beneath them at night.

Mount Stewart House, Gardens & Temple of the Winds
National Trust-owned Mount Stewart is in County Down, five miles south of Newtownards next to Strangford Lough. The neoclassical house is impressive enough, but it's the gardens, laid out by Lady Londonderry in the 1920s and lovingly looked after ever since, that are the main draw. The notably mild microclimate allows a vast diversity of plants to thrive, and the results – reminiscent of an Italian villa landscape – are unusual and very special. *See p274.*

Seaforde Gardens

event took place, in 1689. By this time, King James II of England, Ireland and Scotland had imposed Catholic leaders on the Irish army and authorities, much to the dislike of mainly Protestant Ulster. Derry was one of the least loyal garrisons and Jacobite troops were sent to the city, but in December 1968, 13 young apprentice boys seized the city keys and locked the gates. Some 2,000 people were inside, a number that swelled to over 30,000 as Protestants sought refuge from the king's soldiers. City governor Robert Lundy fled, and from mid April until the end of July 1689, the city was besieged by King James and his troops, resulting in the deaths of around 8,000 citizens. The event is commemorated annually by the Apprentice Boys Parade, a flashpoint for sectarian violence in past years, but nowadays a much more peaceful affair.

The area around Ferryquay Gate houses several important arts venues. The Millennium Forum (New Market Street, 7126 4455, www.millenniumforum.co.uk) was the first purpose-built theatre in Derry, and has a vibrant roster of drama, music, dance and comedy. The Playhouse (5-7 Artillery Street, 7126 8027, www.derryplayhouse.co.uk) also presents theatre and dance performances. The same building also contains Derry's best contemporary art gallery, the Context Gallery (7137 3538, www.context gallery.co.uk, closed Mon, Sun) showing local and international work.

St Columb's Cathedral (*see p283*) stands beside Bishop's Gate. Outside the gate is the Fountain estate, so called because it was the original source

of fresh water for the city. Its current fame derives from it being the last remaining Protestant enclave on the west side of the river. As is common with many inland towns in Northern Ireland, the working-class area's Loyalist allegiance is evident from the kerbstones painted white, red and blue, and the predominance of Union Jacks.

Back inside the walled city is the Double Bastion, from where there are fine views over southern Derry and Bogside. Beneath it is the Verbal Arts Centre (Stable Lane, 7126 6946, www.verbalarts centre.co.uk, closed Sat, Sun), which promotes the arts of storytelling, poetry and song. Performances are held here, and the red-brick building, once a school, is an attraction in itself.

North-west, towards Butcher's Gate, is Derry's first Presbyterian Church, on Society Street. Adjacent is the Apprentice Boys Memorial Hall (7134 7630, www.apprenticeboys.co.uk, open Mon-Fri June-Oct), a handsome neo-Gothic building known to most locals as the 'Mem'. It is the headquarters of the Apprentice Boys organisation, and also houses a museum dedicated to the history and heritage of the Siege of Derry. The Nerve Centre (Magazine Street, 7126 0562, www.nerve-centre.org.uk, closed Sun) is an arthouse cinema and music venue that also contains editing suites and film studios.

Lying west of the walled city is the area commonly know as Bogside. As happened in Belfast, a huge increase in Derry's population during the Industrial Revolution, and the effects of the Great Famine, led to certain areas becoming overpopulated and desperately poor. Such was the case in Bogside,

Seaforde Gardens

Seaforde, Co Down BT30 8PG (4481 1225, www.seafordegardens.com). Open Easter-Sept 10am-5pm Mon-Sat; 1-5pm Sun. Admission Gardens or Butterfly House £4.70; £3.20 reductions; £13.90 family. Gardens & Butterfly House £8.10; £4.60 reductions; £21.90 family.
The Seaforde estate has been a family home for more than 400 years. The walled garden, dating from the early 18th century, has a stunning array of trees, flowers and vegetables, with the centrepiece being a hornbeam maze built in the 1970s. Peacocks roam freely in the outer gardens. The Butterfly House contains parrots, reptiles and hundreds of exotic, multicoloured butterflies.

Sir Thomas & Lady Dixon Park

Upper Malone Road, Belfast, BT17 9LA (9072 6345). Open dawn-dusk daily. Admission free.
Located on the outskirts of Belfast, Sir Thomas & Lady Dixon Park is best known for containing the City of Belfast International Rose Garden, at its most glorious in summer when some 45,000 blooms are on display. The main annual event is Rose Week in July. The park also has a Japanese garden, walled gardens and trails through meadows and woodland.

a predominantly Catholic district, which became a breeding ground for much discontent, hardship and, eventually, sectarian hatred. In August 1969, it was the scene of the 'Battle of the Bogside', a three-day clash between local nationalist youths and the Royal Ulster Constabulary (RUC), with British troops eventually called in to restore control. Bogside residents barricaded the streets, which were patrolled by with IRA members, and declared themselves independent of the civil authorities. 'Free Derry' remained a self-declared autonomous state until 1972.

The Museum of Free Derry (55-57 Glenfada Park, 7136 0880, www.museumoffreederry.org, closed winter Sat, Sun) recounts the history of the battle, the Free Derry movement and also the horrific events of Bloody Sunday on 30 January 1972 – when 14 civilians were killed by the British Army during a civil rights demonstration. There's a memorial to the massacre further south, on Rossville Street. South again is Free Derry Corner, where the iconic slogan 'You are now entering Free Derry' is painted on the side of a house. Nearby is the H-shaped Hunger Strikers' Memorial, commemorating the 1981 hunger strikes by republican prisoners in the H-Block of Long Kesh prison. Murals painted during the strikes, and one commemorating the death of a 14-year-old girl, are still evident in Bogside and serve as reminders of the area's bloody history. The People's Gallery (46 William Street, 7137 3842, www.freederrymurals.com) conducts thought-provoking tours by some of the mural artists; phone for details.

There's less to see on the east side of the River Foyle. For theatre fans, the huge Waterside Theatre (Glendermott Road, 7131 4000, www.waterside theatre.com) offers a mix of entertainment. The nearby Workhouse Museum & Library (Glendermott Road, 7131 8328, www.derrycity.gov.uk/museums, closed Fri, Sun) provides a glimpse into the appalling conditions of the Great Famine.

Any time of year is good for visiting Derry – events take place all year round – though the liveliest festival is probably the City of Derry Jazz & Big Band Festival (www.cityofderryjazz festival.com) in May.

Where to eat & drink

At Magilligan Point, the Point Bar (107 Point Road, 7775 0440) is a cosy, old-fashioned bar with food. It's a little off the beaten track unless you're catching the ferry to Donegal, but provides an excuse to visit the mouth of Lough Foyle.

In Limavady, the Lime Tree Restaurant (60 Catherine Street, 7776 4300, www.limetree rest.com, closed Mon, Sun) serves excellent homely food in a warm environment.

Derry's eating scene is nothing special, but it does have plenty of bars hosting traditional music sessions. Peadar O'Donnell's (59-63 Waterloo Street, 7126 7295, www.peadars-gweedorebar.com) is very popular, while the adjoining Gweedore Bar is more of a rock

music and DJ venue. For lunch and a quiet pint of Guinness, try Badger's Bar & Restaurant (16-18 Orchard Street, 7136 0763).

Browns Restaurant & Champagne Lounge

1 Bonds Hill, Derry, BT47 6DW (7134 5180, www.brownsrestaurant.com). Open noon-3pm, 5.30pm-1am Tue-Fri; 5.30pm-1am Sat; 10.30am-5pm Sun. Lunch served noon-2.30pm Tue-Fri. Dinner served 5.30-10pm Tue-Sat. Food served 10.30am-3pm Sun. Browns changed hands at the end of 2010, and now boasts a snazzy Champagne Lounge. The 1920s theme and art deco look is opulent, but the friendly staff and relaxed atmosphere prevent stuffiness. To match the setting, chef Ian Orr promises an ambitious but reasonably priced international menu; expect the likes of slow-braised shoulder of Lough Erne lamb with champ and cabbage, or salted Green Castle cod cakes with pork belly and lemon butter sauce.

Where to stay

Downhill Hostel (12 Mussenden Road, 7084 9077, www.downhillhostel.com) has a wonderful location at the base of a cliff, a stone's throw from stunning Castlerock Beach and within sight of Mussendun Temple.

The city of Derry is not lacking in B&Bs, but standards vary considerably. One of the nicest is the Merchant's House, (16 Queen Street, 7126 9691, www.thesaddlershouse.com, closed Jan, Feb), a Georgian townhouse with eight rooms spread over four floors. Tower Hotel Derry (Butcher Street, 7137 1000, www.towerhotelderry.com) is rather soulless, but it's the only hotel within the city walls. For budget travellers, there are several hostels; the largest is the Derry City Independent Hostel (44 Great James Street, 7128 0542, www.derry-hostel.co.uk).

Ardtara Country House ★

8 Gorteade Road, Upperlands, BT46 5SA (7964 4490, www.ardtara.com). Rates £90-£110 double incl breakfast.
It seems austere from the outside, but this is a very elegant country hotel, set in a restored 19th-century mansion, once the home of linen magnate Harry Clarke. The nine bedrooms differ in design, but follow a country-chic look, with open fires and all mod-cons, including flatscreen TVs and free Wi-Fi. The garden rooms are particularly large and bright, with views on to the extensive grounds. Other facilities include a bar, oak-panelled dining room, comfortable lounge and sunny conservatory.

Beech Hill Country House Hotel

32 Ardmore Road, Derry, BT47 3QP (7134 9279, www.beech-hill.com). Rates £95-£115 double incl breakfast.
A couple of miles south of the city centre, Beech Hill is probably the best place to stay in the area. The striking 18th-century mansion sits within a 32-acre estate of woodland, lawns and lakes. There are just 27 rooms, resulting in a relaxed, friendly atmosphere; the master suites are smartest and most spacious, but the rooms in the original house have more character. The Ardmore restaurant is much liked for its modern Irish cuisine.

Counties Fermanagh, Tyrone & Armagh

The inland counties of Northern Ireland are unfairly neglected by visitors. Their natural beauty is reason enough to visit: the green hills of Fermanagh snooze on the shore of Lough Erne, with its scattering of wooded islands, while the Clogher Valley Scenic Drive unlocks lovely southern Armagh. The mountainous north of County Tyrone, dominated by the Sperrin Range, is terrific hiking territory, but the county is also speckled with megalithic sites, pre-eminent among them the Beaghmore Stone Circles. Lough Neagh, the largest lake in the British Isles, is a favourite of anglers, walkers, boaters and nature enthusiasts. South of the lake, you can follow St Patrick's Trail to the city of Armagh, the bustling ecclesiastical capital of Ireland, presided over by a pair of cathedrals and also home to a fine planetarium. Fermanagh also has a lively town in the shape of Enniskillen, which features good dining options and more key attractions: the Marble Arch Caves and Florence Court.

COUNTY FERMANAGH

Fermanagh is sometimes referred to as the 'forgotten county', but those who do make it here are unlikely to forget the county's rolling hills, lush pastureland, lakes and rivers. Much of the county is taken up by extensive Lough Erne ★, whose shores are dotted with small towns and woodland, while the water is peppered with hundreds of tree-covered islands that, in May, resemble dazzling emeralds as the new leaves bloom. Watersports – kayaking, windsurfing and boating – abound, while those wishing to stick to dry land can cycle the weaving lakeside lanes.

Positioned between the Upper and Lower sections of the lough, the county town of Enniskillen has worked hard to confront and shake off the bad associations of the IRA bomb that killed 11 people in 1987, and has since emerged as a pretty and spirited town. The nearby countryside is leafy and green, and the town centre has plenty of shops, cafés and a riverside walkway. Much of the activity happens up on Church Street, which turns into High Street and then Townhall Street. The skyline is pierced by the steeples of the town's three churches. To the north of Church Street is the Buttermarket, otherwise known as Enniskillen Craft & Design (no phone, closed Sun), where craft studios and shops are housed within the beautifully restored 19th-century dairy market building.

The lake near Enniskillen becomes a major focus in summer, when boats ply the waters, anglers line the banks, and walkers stroll the pathways. Enniskillen Castle, once a strategic fortress of the Maguire family, sits on the west bank. It was rebuilt by Anglo-Irish landowner William Cole in the early 17th century and its rectangular, three-storey keep now houses the Inniskilling Museum (6632 3142, www.inniskillingsmuseum.com), which tells the story of the town's two regiments: the Royal Inniskilling Fusiliers and the 5th Royal Inniskilling Dragoon Guards. Also in the castle, Fermanagh County Museum (6632 5000, www.enniskillen castle.co.uk, closed Apr-June, Sept, Oct Sun; Nov-Mar Sat, Sun) relates the county's economic, social and cultural history. Further east, along Wellington Road, is the tourist office (6632 3110, www.fermanagh.gov.uk, closed Oct-Mar Sat, Sun), where you can pre-book lake cruises. For a panoramic view of the town, climb the 108 spiral steps of Coles Monument on Forthill, built in memory of Sir Lowry Cole, one of Wellington's generals.

Golfers come in droves for the three excellent courses nearby: Enniskillen Golf Club (6632 5250, www.enniskillengolfclub.com); Castle Hume Golf Club (Bleak Road, 6632 7077, www.castlehume golf.com); and the superb, Faldo-designed course at Lough Erne Golf Resort (see p295).

Just south of the town is Palladian gem Castle Coole (see p296), while further from Enniskillen, along the eastern shore of Upper Lough Erne, is the wildlife haven of the Crom Estate (see p296). The best point from which to explore the Upper Lough is Share Holiday Village (Smith's Strand, 6772 2122, www.sharevillage.org), which organises canoeing, kayaking, jet-boating and sailing trips, as well as land archery and fishing. It also has an arts centre offering courses in filmmaking, pottery, silk painting and even circus skills. The camping and caravan site is well equipped.

West of Enniskillen, the landscape becomes more mountainous and is popular with walkers. Eight miles south-west of Enniskillen is 18th-century Florence Court (6634 8249, www.nationaltrust.org.uk, check website for opening times), the former home of the Earls of Enniskillen. A captivating guided tour takes in the house and meandering

Lough Erne. See p291.

climbing up Magho Cliffs and providing spectacular views of Lough Erne and across to Donegal Bay.

At the northernmost point of Lower Lough Erne is the town of Belleek, home of the famous Belleek Pottery (see p296). East of town, next to the lough, is Castle Caldwell Forest, a nature reserve and bird sanctuary with a ruined castle and a series of walkways through the trees. The Fiddler's Stone at the entrance to the castle is an oversized carved fiddle, erected in memory of local musician Denis McCabe, who drowned nearby in 1770.

Continue along the northern/eastern shore of the Lower Lough to find Castle Archdale Country Park (6862 1588, www.doeni.gov.uk). There are nature trails and lakeside walks, a butterfly garden and deer. You can hire boats to explore White Island, which contains the remnants of an early monastic settlement. The 12th-century church has a fine Romanesque doorway, and eight well-preserved carved figures, which are thought to date from between the ninth and 11th centuries.

Where to eat & drink

Enniskillen has several good places to eat and drink, such as Scoffs Restaurant (Belmore Street, 6634 2622), which also has a lively wine bar. For a quick bite, pop into the wonderful Russell & Donnelly (6632 0111, www.russelland donnelly.com) on Darling Street for its fantastic array of local cheeses, meats, speciality wines and other delicacies. Franco's Restaurant (Queen Elizabeth Road, 6632 4424) is a local favourite for casual dining, and serves everything from pasta and pizza to steak and seafood. In the nearby village of Bellanaleck is the dainty Sheelin Tea Shop (Derrlin Road, 6634 8232), adjacent to the Sheelin Lace Shop & Museum (see p296). In Belleek, the Thatch (Main Street, 6865 8181, closed Sun), set in an 18th-century thatched cottage, serves wholesome café fare.

Blakes of the 'Hollow' & Café Merlot

6 Church Street, Enniskillen, BT74 7EJ (6632 0918). Blakes 11.30am-1am Mon-Sat; noon-midnight Sun. Atrium Bar 7pm-1am Thur-Sun. Café Merlot Lunch served 11am-3pm, dinner served 5.30-9.30pm daily. Number 6 Dinner served 5.30-9.30pm Fri, Sat. No credit cards (Blakes & Atrium Bar).
Blakes is a charmingly traditional bar that's been run by the same family since 1887. As well as the lovely old front room, which has stayed pretty much the same for over a century, there's also the new and bustling Atrium Bar, and the very popular Café Merlot, which has an excellent bistro menu and frequent jazz nights. For a slightly more formal atmosphere, climb to the top of the building to Number 6 restaurant, which serves superb contemporary cuisine.

Watermill ★

Kilmore Quay, Lisnakea, BT92 0DT (6772 4369, www.watermillrestaurant.org). Open/food served noon-11pm daily.
This wonderful old thatched building sits beside Upper Lough Erne, commanding stunning views of the lake. The open fires and cosy bar, coupled with a warm welcome,

grounds, including a sawmill and ice house. To the west are Marble Arch Caves (see p296), part of a nature reserve that stretches into the more mountainous County Cavan. There are several wonderful walks in the surrounding mountains: the Legnabrocky Trail starts from the caves and heads up Cuilcagh Mountain, while the long-distance Ulster Way (www.walkni.com/ulsterway) can be accessed north of the caves. Alternatively, follow the Marlbank Scenic Loop, a 32-mile drive via Derrylin, Kinawley, Florence Court and the caves, and back to Enniskillen.

North of Enniskillen is Lower Lough Erne. Some of the numerous islands can be visited, including Devenish Island (see p296). Erne Tours (6632 2882, www.ernetoursltd.com, closed Dec-Feb) runs cruises from Brook Park on the A46, or you can hire your own boat.

Seven miles north-west of Enniskillen on the B81 sit the substantial remains of Monea Castle (6632 3110), in the middle of a field. There are two large, nearly intact round towers at one end of the rectangular building. It dates from 1618, but was abandoned in the 18th century and has not been restored. Five miles further north, next to the lough, is another ruined fortress, Tully Castle, surrounded by formal gardens (tours are sometimes available; details on 6862 1588). A six-mile scenic drive heads west from here,

tempt diners from miles around. Chef-proprietor Pascal Brissaud's Irish-French cuisine is imaginative; starters might include classic French dishes (snails and frogs' legs, for instance) alongside more local produce – Fivemiletown goat's cheese or Kilkeel Bay lobster salads. Mains feature local beef, pork and fish dishes. The wine list is also excellent. Finish with French apple tart or crème brûlée. There are also 40 rooms (£79 double incl breakfast).

Where to stay

Killyhevlin Hotel (Dublin Road, 6632 3481, www.killyhevlin.com) is the smartest place to stay in Enniskillen, with spacious rooms and a spa and leisure centre. The lovely Manor House Resort Hotel (Killadeas, 6862 2200, www.manor-house-hotel.com), six miles from town, occupies a Victorian lakeside building, and also has good spa and leisure facilities. For a truly tranquil retreat, check into Lusty Beg Island (6863 3300, www.lustybegisland.com), a 75-acre private island with luxury wooden cabins for self-catering as well as lakeside suites for B&B. Accommodation is also available in the grand surroundings of Crom Castle, on the Crom Estate (*see p296*).

Belle Isle Castle ★

Lisbellaw, BT94 5HG (6638 7231, www.belleisle castle.com). Rates B&B £150-£180 double incl breakfast. Self-catering cottages £310-£650 per week.

Tucked away on a wooded island on Upper Lough Erne, Belle Isle is a beautiful retreat for those seeking a relaxed self-catering holiday. The 17th-century castle is a homely, rambling affair, with a large dining and drawing room, a do-it-yourself kitchen (complete with Aga) and eight bedrooms, varying in size and decor. Other options include three cottages, and spacious, well-equipped apartments in the former stables and coach house – these can be rented by the weekend or week. The estate has a walled kitchen garden, chickens (providing breakfast eggs), BBQ areas, a tennis court and a croquet lawn. Many guests come specially to take a course with the excellent Belle Isle Cookery School.

Lough Erne Golf Resort ★

Belleek Road, Enniskillen, BT93 7ED (6632 3230, www.loughernegolfresort.com). Rates £150-£276 double incl breakfast.

A few miles outside Enniskillen is this golfers' hotel, with Castle Hume Golf Course at the entrance and the Faldo Course backing on to Lough Erne. Accommodation (120 rooms in all) is divided between the hotel (where the decor is elegantly classic, and many rooms have lake views), and a range of luxurious 'lodge suites' consisting of two or three bedrooms and self-catering facilities. The Catalina restaurant serves excellent contemporary cuisine, using local, seasonal ingredients. If golf isn't your thing, there are plenty of other activities, including watersports, helicopter rides, fishing trips and a Thai spa.

COUNTY TYRONE

Tyrone is Northern Ireland's largest county. The northern part is dominated by the ominous Sperrin Mountains (www.sperrinstourism.com), which stretch into County Derry/Londonderry. Hikers

come here in search of challenging and often remote treks. The most challenging is the Ulster Way (www.walkni.com/ulsterway), a 625-mile circular path that traverse much of Northern Ireland. Easier, and much shorter, is the Central Sperrins Way, a 25-mile waymarked trail beginning and ending at Barnes Gap, near the small town of Plumbridge, a popular base with a handful of shops and pubs. There are also several cycle routes, ranging in length from ten to 40 miles, and the mountains' rivers make it a popular angling destination.

Gortin, four miles south of Plumbridge, is slightly bigger and has an Activity Centre (62 Main Street, 8164 8346, www.gortin.net) that organises walks into the mountains, as well as horse riding, canoeing and other outdoor activities. It also offers self-catering and hostel accommodation. Head east from Gortin (on the B46, the A505 and then minor roads) to reach the Beaghmore Stone Circles. The extensive Neolithic site consists of seven stone circles, ten stone rows and 12 cairns, all scattered around a remote field and thought to date from 2600 BC. The exact purpose of the site remains unknown. To the south is the Creagán Visitor Centre (*see p296*).

Ten miles south of Gortin is Omagh, the county town. It's a bustling place, with a good multi-purpose arts venue, Strule Arts Centre (Town Hall Square, 8224 7831, www.struleartscentre.co.uk, closed Sun), which also houses the tourist office (8224 7831, closed Sun). The Ulster American Folk

Watermill

Places to visit

COUNTY FERMANAGH

Belleek Pottery
3 Main Street, Belleek, BT93 3FY (6865 8501, www.belleek.ie). Open 9am-5.30pm Mon-Fri; 10am-5.30pm Sat; sometimes open Sun (phone to check). Admission free. Tours £4; free-£2 reductions.
This imposing 19th-century building on the banks of the River Erne is where Belleek's world-renowned pottery was produced until 1988. Today, it's a museum and showroom, telling the history of the company from early sanitaryware to fine porcelain.

Castle Coole
Enniskillen, BT74 6JY (6632 2690, www.national trust.org.uk). Open Grounds Mar-Oct 10am-7pm daily. Nov-Feb 10am-4pm daily. House, tearoom & shop July, Aug 11am-5pm daily. June 11am-5pm Mon-Wed, Fri-Sun. Mar-May, Sept 11am-5pm Sat, Sun. Admission Grounds £2.50; £1.25 reductions; £6.25 family. House £4.54; £1.81 reductions; £10.90 family.
One of the finest Palladian buildings in the north of Ireland, this grand mansion was built in 1798 by the 1st Earl of Belmore. It was so expensive that he nearly bankrupted himself, and it was not until the 2nd Earl's time that the interior, replete with ornate plasterwork, marble fireplaces and sumptuous Regency furnishings, was completed. The landscaped park and wooded grounds are ideal for long strolls.

Crom Estate
Upper Lough Erne, BT92 8AP (6773 8118, www.nationaltrust.org.uk). Open Visitor centre Mid Mar-Sept 11am-5pm daily. Oct 11am-5pm Sat, Sun. Grounds June-Aug 10am-7pm daily. Mid Mar-May, Sept, Oct 10am-6pm daily. Admission £2.95; 90p reductions; £6.81 family.
This 1,900-acre estate beside Upper Lough Erne has been the home of the Earls of Erne for over 350 years, and is one of the most important nature conservation areas in Northern Ireland. The estate is a flourishing wildlife habitat, home to wild deer, unusual butterflies, pine martens and multiple birdlife. It's a great place for walks and picnics, and you can also hire boats and try your hand at fishing for pike. Accommodation is available in the the west wing of the castle (the rest is still occupied by Lord and Lady Erne) or one of the estate cottages; visit www.cromcastle.com for details.

Devenish Island
St Molaise established a monastery on Devenish Island in the sixth century that grew into an important ecclesiastical centre until its demise in the 17th. The ruins include a church, graves and, most impressive of all, a 12th-century round tower – 98ft tall – that you can climb to snatch views from its narrow windows. A small museum contains some relics and displays illustrating the island's history. Erne Tours (*see p294*) runs trips to the island between May and October.

Marble Arch Caves ★
Marlbank, BT92 1EW (6634 8855, www.marble archcaves.net). Open July, Aug 10am-5pm daily. Mid Mar-June, Sept 10am-4.30pm daily. Admission £8.50; £5.50-£5.75 reductions; £19 family.

Armagh Planetarium

The Marble Arch Caves Global Geopark stretches from west Fermanagh into County Cavan, and is a nature reserve with some wonderful mountain hikes. The Marble Arch Caves are located in the Fermanagh part of the park. The 75-minute guided tour includes a walk through narrow passageways into lofty caverns adorned with stalactites and glistening calcite walls, as well as a boat journey along a subterranean river.

Sheelin Lace Shop & Museum
Bellanaleck, BT92 2BA (6634 8052, www.irishlace museum.com). Open Shop 10am-6pm Mon-Sat. Museum Apr-Oct 10am-6pm Mon-Sat. Admission Museum £2.50.
Learn about the art and history of Irish lace making at this little museum housed in a charming thatched cottage; the exquisite pieces come from across Ireland and all date from 1850 to 1900. Next door, the shop sells examples of antique lace, including wedding dresses and bonnets, more modern accessories and handmade soap and jewellery.

COUNTY TYRONE

Creagán Visitor Centre
Creggan, BT79 9AF (8076 1112, www.an-creagan.com). Open 9am-5.30pm daily. Exhibition 11am-5.30pm daily. Admission free.
Tucked into the Creggán landscape of raised and blanket bogland, this stone building is designed to mirror the archaeological sites in the area. You'll find historical information on the sites, as well as details of several local walking and cycling routes. The centre also hosts assorted events, featuring storytelling, traditional music and dancing, and arts and crafts.

Ulster American Folk Park ★
2 Mellon Road, Castletown, BT78 5QU (8224 3292, www.nmni.com/uafp). Open Mar-Sept 10am-5pm Tue-Sun. Oct-Feb 10am-4pm Tue-Fri; 11am-4pm Sat, Sun. Admission £6.50; £4 reductions; £13-£18.50 family.
This fascinating open-air 'living history' park spread over 40 acres has more than enough to keep you occupied for a whole day. Over 30 buildings (some original, some replicas) illustrate life in Ulster in the 18th and 19th centuries. They vary from prosperous

homesteads to tiny one-roomed homes, to entire re-created streets, featuring churches, shops and a schoolhouse, and also include some American structures, such as a log cabin and a Pennsylvania farmhouse. The Emigrants exhibition explores the history of mass Irish emigration to America. Agricultural trades, crafts, textiles, clothing and domestic life are also covered. There's a picnic area and a café.

COUNTY ARMAGH

Armagh Planetarium ★
College Hill, Armagh, BT61 9DB (3752 3689, www.armaghplanet.com). Open July, Aug 10am-5pm daily. Sept-June 10am-5pm Mon-Sat. Show times vary; check website for details. Admission £6; £5 reductions; £20 family.
There's not much you won't learn about the universe at the Armagh Planetarium. You can take a trip into space in a 3-D theatre, get up-to-date space exploration news, touch Ireland's largest meteorite, or take a walk through a scale model of the universe in the very cool Astro Park in the gardens. Adjacent to the planetarium is the original Armagh Observatory, founded in 1790.

Lough Neagh Discovery Centre & Oxford Island Nature Reserve ★
Craigavon, BT66 6NJ (3832 2205, www.oxford island.com). Open July, Aug 10am-5pm Mon-Sat; 10am-6pm Sun. Sept-June 10am-5pm daily. Admission free.
The Discovery Centre has masses of information on Lough Neagh and its wildlife. Several nature trails leave from the centre, and there are birdwatching hides for spotting the many birds on the lake. Fishing is possible off the jetties, and a marina offers boat trips. For those wanting to stay overnight, the Kinnego caravan/campsite has good facilities.

Navan Centre & Fort
81 Killylea Road, Armagh, BT60 4LD (3752 9644, www.armagh.co.uk/navancentre.aspx). Open Apr-Sept 10am-7pm daily. Oct-Mar 10am-4pm daily. Admission Apr-Sept £6; £4-£4.75 reductions; £16.50 family. Oct-Mar £5; £3-£3.75 reductions; £14.50 family.
Navan Fort (Emain Macha) was the seat of the pre-Christian Kings of Ulster for more than 700 years, making it one of the most important archaeological sites in Ireland. The circular plan of the earthwork is evident today, with ditches up to 13ft deep, and embankments 50ft wide and 13ft high. Enclosed within are two monuments, one a ring barrow (an Iron Age burial site) and the other a mound dating from 95 BC. The Navan Centre houses exhibitions on the site's place in legend, and the artefacts discovered here. Cooking, weaving and farming demos are held, and there's plenty to entertain kids.

St Patrick's Church of Ireland Cathedral
43 Abbey Street, Armagh, BT61 7DY (3752 3142, www.stpatricks-cathedral.org). Open Apr-Oct 9am-5pm daily. Nov-Mar 9am-4pm daily. Admission £3; free-£2 reductions.

In the mid fifth century, St Patrick founded a church in what is now Armagh. Over the centuries, the monastic settlement became an important European centre of learning – so much so that by the 12th century it was said that only those who had studied at Armagh could teach theology. The Cathedral has undergone numerous renovations and rebuilds, with significant interior work carried out in the 19th century. The basic shape remains 12th-century, however, with the slight tilt of the medieval chancel supposedly intended to mirror the tilted head of Jesus while dying on the cross. Inside, among the grand memorials, is part of an 11th-century Celtic cross. Brian Ború, tenth-century High King of Ireland, is buried here, as was his dying wish – a plaque marks the spot.

Slieve Gullion Forest Park
Off B113, near Forkhill (9052 4480, www.nidirect.gov.uk/forests).
Slieve Gullion is a mountain cloaked in mist as well as mythology. It's capped by a small lake, to the south of which lies a huge burial tomb known as the Calliagh Berras House – the highest surviving passage tomb in Ireland. You can crawl into the chamber, which has a skylight. The tomb is associated with the legendary witch Cailleach Beara, who tricked Finn MacCool, the Irish giant, into jumping into the lake. He emerged old and withered; the witch restored his youth, but his hair remained white. It is said that anyone who swims in the lake will also have their hair turned white. The park has assorted walking trails through broadleaf woodland, a walled garden and a café.

Ulster American Folk Park

Belle Isle Castle. See p295.

Park (see p296), a ten-minute drive north, is probably the most popular attraction in the county.

In the east of Tyrone (and forming the border with several counties) is massive Lough Neagh, covering 151 square miles – it's the largest lake in the British Isles. According to legend, it was created by Irish giant Finn MacCool (who was also responsible for the Giant's Causeway in County Antrim); during a fight with a Scottish rival, he scooped up a clod of land and threw it across the Irish Channel, thus forming the Isle of Man. The gaping hole that was left filled with water and became Lough Neagh.

The lake contains Europe's largest commercial eel fishery, and is also paradise for birdwatchers, thanks to the 100,000 wildfowl that overwinter here. Anglers take to the banks from spring onwards, fishing for eel, bream and perch. Cyclists can follow the Loughshore Trail (www.loughshore trail.com), a 113-mile cycle route that circles the lake. You can learn about local ecology and get out on to the water at the Lough Neagh Discovery Centre (see p297), and there's lots of useful information on www.discoverloughneagh.com.

Cookstown, 25 miles east of Omagh towards Lough Neagh, is famed for having the longest main street in Ireland. It stretches for over a mile, and on Saturdays holds a lively market. The countryside around the town is scattered with Neolithic and early Christian monuments, such as the tenth-century Ardboe High Cross, located on the lake edge. Twenty feet high, it was the first high cross built in Ulster. Cookstown tourist office (Burn Road, 8676 9949, www.cookstown.gov.uk, closed Sept-June Sun) can provide information and maps.

The prettiest village in the area is Benburb, a half-hour drive south of Cookstown via the A29. It's something of a hub for artists and craft makers, and the main street is lined with tiny cottages that were once apple-peeling sheds. Standing on a high rock, overlooking the Blackwater River, is Benburb Castle (Main Street, 3754 8241). A 17th-century 'Plantation' castle, it has been restored and is open to the public by arrangement. The surrounding grounds have some wonderful paths that lead through woodland towards the river.

Eastwards is the pretty Clogher Valley, a gentle and forgiving landscape of fertile fields and grazing cows. The 20-mile Clogher Valley Scenic Drive starts at the small town of Fivemiletown, 17 miles south of Omagh. Signposts along the Drive are sparse, but a map is available from the tourist office in Omagh. The route leads south towards Slieve Beagh, passing through remote moorland before descending into Fardross Forest. A few miles on is a three-tiered hilltop tower known as Brackenridge's Folly, a mausoleum built in the late 19th century by one George Brackenridge.

Where to eat & drink

On Main Street in Gortin, there's tasty, home-cooked food at the Pedlars Rest (8164 7942), and standard pub grub at the Foot Hills Bar (8164 8157, www.foothills.org.uk, closed Mon). In Omagh, the best places for lunch and snacks are the Riverfront Coffee House (Market Street, 8225 0011, closed Sun) and Thyme Restaurant & Café (19 High Street, 8226 8066, closed Sun). Pub fare is available at the Coach Inn (Railway Terrace, 8224 3330).

Deli on the Green

30 The Linen Green, Moygashel, BT71 7HB (8775 1775, www.deliononthegreen.com). Breakfast served 8-11am Mon-Sat. Lunch served noon-3pm Mon-Fri; noon-4pm Sat. Dinner served 5-9.30pm Thur, Fri; 6-9.30pm Sat.
Deli on the Green, located in the Linen Green discount designer shopping village just south of Dungannon, is a cheerfully decorated modern bistro and deli that serves a wide range of breakfast, lunch and dinner dishes to eat in or take away. Among the lunchtime options are Kettyle Irish steak burger, cajun chicken caesar salad, and fish and chips.

Where to stay

Outside Dungannon is Grange Lodge (7 Grange Road, 8778 4212, www.grangelodgecountryhouse. com), situated in 20 acres of wooded gardens, with five very comfortable single and double rooms. Stangmore Town House (24 Killyman Road, 8772 5600, www.stangmoretownhouse.com), also in Dungannon, has spacious B&B rooms and a popular restaurant. Visit www.flavouroftyrone.com for further accommodation suggestions, including campsites, B&Bs and hotels.

COUNTY ARMAGH

A county of both dramatic mountain scenery (to the south) and ugly sprawling industry (to the north), County Armagh is a place where it pays to be selective in your exploration. The county town, Armagh, is a good place to start. Given city status in 1994, it is one of Ireland's oldest settlements, its narrow streets running in a circular pattern around the key building of St Patrick's Church of Ireland Cathedral (*see p297*). The saint is said to have come here in 445, and founded a church on the small hillock where the Cathedral now stands. Across the city on another hill is another large religious edifice, the twin-spired St Patrick's Roman Catholic Cathedral (www.armagharchdiocese.org/stpatrickscathedral), constructed in the 19th century. As a result, Armagh is known as the ecclesiastical centre of Ireland.

The streets are a blend of prim stone cottages and elegant Georgian terraces. The main drag, English Street, which runs into Thomas Street to the west, is packed with high-street shops, cafés and bars. Armagh Tourist Office (English Street, 3752 1800) is in St Patrick's Trian Centre, a heritage centre containing three exhibitions. Two cover the history of Armagh, and St Patrick's association with the town; the third is 'The Land of Lilliput', based on Jonathan Swift's *Gulliver's Travels*, a first edition of which sits in the City

Library (43 Abbey Street, 3752 3142, http://armaghpubliclibrary.arm.ac.uk, closed Sat, Sun). North-east of the Cathedral on Market Street is the Market Place Arts Theatre (box office 3752 1821, www.marketplacearmagh.com, closed Sun), devoted to comedy, theatre, music, art and dance.

The Mall, the city's main green space, fringed with mature trees, is to the south. North of the park is the Courthouse, a relatively simple building designed by architect Francis Johnston, best known for building the General Post Office in Dublin. On Mall East, the Armagh County Museum (3752 3070, www.nmni.com, closed Sun) has collections covering social and cultural life, as well as an art gallery with work by some notable local artists, including the poet George Russell and JB Vallely. On nearby College Hill is the city's key attraction, the Armagh Planetarium (*see p297*).

Sights near Armagh include the ruins of Armagh Franciscan Friary (Friary Road, 3885 1102), founded in the 13th century, and the ancient royal site of Navan Centre & Fort (*see p297*).

In the south-east corner of the county, beautiful Slieve Gullion mountain rises above the low-lying landscape. It's at the heart of what is known as the Ring of Gullion, an unusual geological formation called a ring dyke (a circle of lower hills) that has been designated an Area of Outstanding Natural Beauty (AONB). The region has many megalithic sites and ruins, and appears in numerous Irish myths. The main access to the mountain is via Slieve Gullion Forest Park (*see p297*).

The only real attraction in the north of Armagh is Lough Neagh (*see left*).

Beaghmore Stone Circles. See p295.

Newforge House

Where to eat & drink

In Armagh city, beside the Planetarium, Manor Park Restaurant (www.manorparkrestaurant.co.uk) serves very good contemporary cuisine in an atmospheric dining room lit by candles, with walls of bare brick and stone. English Street has several bars, and there's also the friendly Hole in the Wall bar (9 Market Street, 3752 3515, www.the holeinthewallbar.com), housed in a 17th-century building on Market Street.

Not far from Lough Neagh, in Moira, is the Tannery (6 Chestnut Hill Road, 9261 1409, www.tannery bar.com), a stylish all-rounder with a casual bistro, a smarter, dinner-only restaurant, a bar and a nightclub. The steaks and burgers are excellent, and there are frequent gigs. In Lurgan, the Brindle Beam Tea Rooms (20 Winter Avenue, 3832 1721, closed Sun) serves hearty, homely food.

Uluru Bistro ★

16 Market Street, Armagh, BT61 7BX (3751 8051, www.ulurubistro.co.uk). Lunch served noon-3pm Tue-Sat. Dinner served 5-9pm Tue-Sun.
Australian duo Dean and Sarah Coppard's passion for good food shines through at this bistro, where many ingredients are sourced locally (some from the on-site garden) and the menu changes seasonally. The food is an imaginative mix of Asian and Antipodean influences (including marinated kangaroo and braised medallion of ostrich, as well as honey-glazed duck breast or slow-roasted shoulder of lamb). The drinks list features Australian beer and wine.

Yellow Door Deli

74 Woodhouse Street, Portadown, BT62 1JL (3835 3528, www.yellowdoordeli.co.uk). Open 9am-5pm Mon-Thur; 8am-5pm Fri, Sat.
Simon Dougan is one of the best-known chefs in Northern Ireland, and his café produces divine breads, cakes and own-made jams and chutneys, in addition to hearty stews of succulent lamb and wholesome salads. The menu changes daily, and there's also an extensive wine list.

Where to stay

Centrally located Armagh City Hotel (2 Friary Road, 3751 8888, www.armaghcityhotel.com) is corporate in style and feel, but with comfortable, modern rooms. Equally convenient is the historical Charlemont Arms Hotel (English Street, 3752 2028, www.charlemontarmshotel.com), with 30 rooms and a brasserie-cum-wine bar.

Newforge House ★

Magheralin, BT67 0QL (9261 1255, www.new forgehouse.com). Rates £120-£165 double incl breakfast.
This three-storey, ivy-clad Georgian mansion in the sleepy village of Magheralin offers luxurious accommodation less than a 15-minute drive from Lough Neagh. The six individually designed rooms are decorated in pale, relaxing tones, and seamlessly blend antique furniture with spacious, contemporary bathrooms. There are many original features, such as fireplaces and stucco plasterwork. A three-course dinner is offered on Tuesday to Saturday, with light meals availabe on Monday and Sunday evenings.

Further Reference

USEFUL ADDRESSES

www.greenbox.ie An eco-tourism initiative covering Fermanagh, Leitrim, West Cavan, North Sligo, South Donegal and North West Monaghan.
www.sustrans.org.uk Cycling routes for all abilities.

NORTHERN IRELAND

www.bbc.co.uk/northernireland Local news, weather and events.
www.belfasttelegraph.co.uk News, comment and entertainment from the capital's daily paper.
www.canoeni.com Canoe trails and hire.
www.cycleni.com Cycling trails of varying lengths.
www.discovernorthernireland.com Official website of the Northern Ireland Tourist Board.
www.doeni.gov.uk State-run heritage sites and areas of environmental interest.
www.metoffice.gov.uk Regional weather forecasts.
www.nationaltrust.org.uk National Trust properties.
www.northernireland.gov.uk Everything you need to know about the Northern Ireland Executive.
www.translink.co.uk/ni-railways Travelling by train: book tickets and check routes and timetables.
www.walkni.com Walking trails and clubs.

REPUBLIC OF IRELAND

www.cie.ie Plan your journey on public transport.
www.discoverireland.com Official website of Tourism Ireland.
www.gaelsaoire.ie Information about the Gaeltacht areas of Ireland.
www.gov.ie Information on Irish laws and public services from the official government website.
www.heritageireland.ie State-run heritage attractions.
www.independent.ie News from Ireland and around the world.
www.irishlandmark.com The Irish Landmark Trust works to preserve the country's heritage sites.
www.irishnews.com Online access to the daily newspaper.
www.irishrail.ie Plan train journeys and buy tickets online.
www.irishtimes.com News, sport and culture.
www.isasurf.ie Irish Surfing Association; schools and clubs.
www.met.ie Weather updates.

www.rte.ie News, sport and entertainment from Ireland's leading television network.
www.walkinginireland.co.uk Walking trails in County Clare.
www.walkireland.ie Walking routes across Ireland, and advice.

HOLIDAY HOME COMPANIES

Holiday Property Ireland 028 7135 6080, www.deeneyproperty.com.
Ireland Self-catering Holiday 074 910 0918, www.ireland selfcateringholiday.com.

NORTHERN IRELAND

The Holiday Cottages 01749 685153, www.theholiday cottages.co.uk.
Holiday Home Rental UK 020 7078 7523, www.holiday homerental.co.uk.
Holidaylettings.co.uk www.holidaylettings.co.uk.
Little Domain 01326 240028, www.thelittledomain.com.
National Trust Cottages 0844 800 2070, www.national trustcottages.co.uk.

REPUBLIC OF IRELAND

Dream Ireland 064 664 1170, www.dreamireland.com.
Irish Cottage Holidays 01 205 2777, www.irishcottage holidays.com.
Trident Holiday Homes 01 201 8840, www.tridentholidayhomes.ie.

TOURIST INFORMATION OFFICES

More information can be found on the websites of the Northern Ireland Tourist Board (www. discovernorthernireland.com) and Irish Tourism (www.discover ireland.com). The main tourist offices are listed below. Local tourist offices are listed in the relevant chapter in the guide.

NORTHERN IRELAND

Belfast 028 9031 2345.
Derry 028 7136 9501.

REPUBLIC OF IRELAND

Cork 021 425 5100.
Dublin 01 884 7700.
Galway 091 537700.
Mulingar 044 934 8761.
Sligo 071 916 1201.
Waterford 051 312700.

FICTION

NORTHERN IRELAND

Deirdre Madden *One by One in the Darkness* Tale about three sisters, their adolescence and the impact of the late 1960s political violence in Ulster.
Eoin McNamee *Resurrection Man* A savage and merciless Protestant killer is at large on the streets of Belfast in the 1970s in McNamee's dreamlike debut.
Sean O'Reilly *Love and Sleep* A young man, Niall, returns from years of travelling around Europe to discover a Derry where sectarian violence is rife on the streets, and the disenfranchised mope in the pubs.

REPUBLIC OF IRELAND

John Banville *The Book of Evidence* Scientist Freddie Montgomery returns to Ireland looking for money to pay off a gangster. He discovers his family has sold its painting collection and attempts to recover the works, killing a maid in the process.
JP Donleavy *The Ginger Man* Donleavy's novel about the licentious Sebastian Dangerfield, an American law student at Trinity College, Dublin.
Anne Enright *The Gathering* An alcoholic commits suicide in Brighton; his family return to Ireland for the gathering at his wake. Winner of the 2007 Booker Prize.
Henry Green *Loving* Green's novel follows the convoluted romances in an Irish country house.
James Joyce *Dubliners*, *A Portrait of the Artist as a Young Man*, *Ulysses*, *Finnegans Wake* Despite spending most of his writing life away from Ireland, Joyce's homeland remained at the heart of his fiction. The short-story collection *Dubliners* is a series of epiphanic vignettes of residents of the Irish capital, while *A Portrait* is a semi-autobiographical *Bildungsroman* of the ambitious writer-scholar Stephen Dedalus. Dedalus returns to meet Leopold Bloom on 16 June in the monumental *Ulysses*, Joyce's revolutionary modernist work about a day in Dublin. *Finnegans Wake* marks Joyce at his most experimental, as myriad languages, experiences and voices merge in this notoriously difficult novel.

Molly Keane *Good Behaviour* Booker Prize-nominated examination of the emphasis on 'good behaviour' in Irish society in the early 20th century.

Iris Murdoch *The Unicorn* Gothic novel in which Marian Taylor is employed as a companion for a lonely woman who lives in a castle on a sublime coastline. The area referred to as the Scarren is based on the Burren in County Clare, and the desolate cliffs are modelled on the Cliffs of Moher.

Flann O'Brien *The Third Policeman* Flann O'Brien was the pen-name of Irish civil servant Brian O'Nolan. In *The Third Policeman* (published after Nolan's death) all conventional laws, including physics, are undone as the unnamed narrator negotiates a comic, interminable hell of bobbies and bicycles.

Jonathan Swift *Gulliver's Travels* The great satirist's popular tale of Gulliver's fantastic adventures was written when he returned to Ireland after political disappointment in England.

Oscar Wilde *The Picture of Dorian Gray* The book in which the Irish dandy set out his theories on aesthetics and decadence. A handsome young man makes a Faustian pact to preserve his beauty and indulges in a life of pure hedonism. Extracts were later used as evidence of Wilde's 'gross indecency'.

NON-FICTION

Carmel McCaffrey *In Search of Ancient Ireland* An account of the nation's archaeology, history and legends from around 7,000 BC to the arrival of the English.

NORTHERN IRELAND
Martin McGartland *Fifty Dead Men Walking* The harrowing autobiography of Martin McGarland, in which he recounts his life as a double agent during the time of the Troubles, working as both an IRA terrorist and an informant for British Intelligence.

David McKittrick & David McVea *Making Sense of the Troubles: The Story of the Conflict in Northern Ireland* A frank and balanced look at what happened in the Northern Ireland conflict, and why.

REPUBLIC OF IRELAND
Susan Cahill (ed) *For the Love of Ireland: A Literary Companion for Readers and Travelers* A useful introduction to the nation's literature.

Pete McCarthy *A Journey of Discovery in Ireland* McCarthy (who grew up in England) returns to Cork, his mother's birthplace. The book charts his attempts to better understand the nation and find its true heritage beneath the gaudy tourist traps.

Colm Tóibín *Bad Blood: A Walk Along the Irish Border* For this work, Tóibín travelled along the Irish border, ruminating on the differences between the people and landscapes of the Republic and of Northern Ireland, particularly examining the past that haunted them in the late 1980s. With photographs by Tony O'Shea.

Christopher Winn *I Never Knew That About Ireland* A compendium of stories and facts illustrating the colourful history, heritage and monuments of the Emerald Isle.

POETRY

NORTHERN IRELAND
Seamus Heaney *Collected Poems* Nobel Prize-winner Heaney was born at his family's farmhouse in County Antrim, and the Northern Irish landscape figures heavily in his verse. One of his best-known poems, 'Digging', is based around an image of his father digging potatoes, and contains several references to the Great Famine of the 1840s.

Paul Muldoon *Meeting the British* Muldoon wrote this poem in the 1980s, before he left Northern Ireland for North America. The first meeting between native Ottawa Indians and British colonisers is at the core of the work, and can be read as an allusion to the political relationship between Britain and Ireland.

REPUBLIC OF IRELAND
Eavan Boland *The Lost Land* In this collection Boland considers what it means to be an Irish woman writing in English. In doing so, she draws on visions of the 'lost land', the rural Ireland the poet feels has been left behind.

Oliver Goldsmith *The Deserted Village* Having seen a village and its farms destroyed to make space for a wealthy man's garden, the Irish-born poet penned this polemic.

William Butler Yeats *The Tower* Anxiety regarding the transition to the modern era, and a concern about growing old, are at the centre of this collection from the Nobel Prize-winning poet. It's hard to imagine that the deeply political Yeats is not referring to Ireland when he writes

in 'Sailing to Byzantium' – 'That is no country for old men'.

THEATRE

NORTHERN IRELAND
Brian Friel *Translations* English cultural imperialism and the Great Famine of the 1840s provide the backdrop for the Northern Irish playwright's drama about reform of the school system in County Donegal.

REPUBLIC OF IRELAND
Samuel Beckett *Waiting for Godot* Beckett's bleak absurdist comedy in which two men, Estragon and Vladimir, await the arrival of someone named Godot is considered to be one of the most significant pieces of drama of the 20th century.

Brendan Behan *The Quare Fellow* A man (never seen on stage) is to face death the following day for an unnamed crime that seems to repulse the other inmates at Mountjoy Prison in Dublin in this meditation on capital punishment.

George Bernard Shaw *Pygmalion: A Romance in Five Acts* Dublin-born Shaw's witty critique of the British class system. Henry Higgins, an academic, wagers that he can teach flower girl Eliza Doolittle to lose her Cockney accent and pass as a member of the gentry at an ambassador's party.

John Millington Synge *The Playboy of the Western World* A young man stumbles into a pub in County Mayo claiming to have killed his father, and impresses the locals with his skill in recounting the story. Riots ensued at the opening of the play in 1907.

FILM

NORTHERN IRELAND
Cherrybomb *(Lisa Barros D'Sa, 2008)* Two boys become involved in a game of one-upmanship that runs from drug-taking to vandalism, in order to impress a beautiful girl. *Harry Potter* actor Rupert Grint stars in this film shot in Belfast.

The Crying Game *(Neil Jordan, 1992)* IRA member Fergus forms a bond with British prisoner Jody. After Jody's death, Fergus follows his friend's wishes and travels to London to meet Jody's girlfriend. The Irish Troubles loom large behind themes of race and sexuality in this psychological drama.

Hunger *(Steve McQueen, 2008)* Turner Prize-winning British artist

Steve McQueen made a successful move into feature films with this gruelling dramatisation of the 1981 hunger strikes at the Maze prison, focusing on IRA member Bobby Sands (a memorable portrayal by Michael Fassbender).

REPUBLIC OF IRELAND

Angela's Ashes *(Alan Parker, 1999)* Alan Parker's film version of Frank McCourt's memoir about his childhood experience of dealing with an alcoholic father in Limerick and America.

Circle of Friends *(Pat O'Connor, 1995)* Minnie Driver stars in this adaptation of Maeve Binchy's novel about the lives of three friends who grow up in 1950s rural Ireland.

The Commitments *(Alan Parker, 1991)* Humorous adaptation of Roddy Doyle's novel about a group of jobless Dubliners who decide to start a soul band.

My Left Foot *(Jim Sheridan, 1989)* Daniel Day-Lewis won an Academy Award for his role as Christy Brown, the Irishman who suffered from cerebal palsy and could only control his left foot. It was adapted from Brown's memoir of the same name, which describes his experiences growing up in a working-class family and overcoming cerebal palsy to become a writer and artist.

The Quiet Man *(John Ford, 1952)* An Irishman returns from America to reclaim his family's farm in Innisfree. John Wayne stars as Sean Thornton.

Ryan's Daughter *(David Lean, 1970)* Sarah Miles, Robert Mitchum and Trevor Howard appear in Lean's loose version of *Madame Bovary*: a married Irish woman defies her nationalist neighbours to pursue an affair with a British officer during World War I. Filmed on the Dingle peninsula, County Kerry.

Taffin *(Peter Shaw, 1988)* Irish actor Pierce Brosnan plays Mark Taffin, a debt collector willing to go to extreme lengths to get rid of the developers who intend to build a chemical plant on the outskirts of his home town. Filmed in County Wicklow.

The Wind that Shakes the Barley *(Ken Loach, 2006)* Starring Cillian Murphy, Loach's film tells the story of two brothers in Cork during the Irish War of Independence. It won the Palme d'Or at Cannes, and went on to become the highest-grossing Irish independent film ever made. It was also Ken Loach's biggest box office success.

TELEVISION

Ireland: A Television History *BBC/RTE, 1981* Robert Kee wrote and presented this comprehensive history of the nation.

The Story of Ireland *BBC2, 2011* Fergal Keane examines the history of Ireland in the context of the social and cultural development of Europe as a whole.

NORTHERN IRELAND

Murphy's Law *BBC1, 2001-2007* James Nesbitt stars as an undercover police officer in this drama shot on location in Northern Ireland. Murphy is haunted by the murder of his daughter because he refused to act as a suicide bomber.

REPUBLIC OF IRELAND

Ballykissangel *BBC1, 1996-2001* Drama serial based on the experiences of a young British priest who moves to work in a rural village in Ireland. Shot in Avoca and Enniskerry in County Wicklow.

Father Ted *Channel 4, 1995-1998* Sitcom following the exploits of three wayward priests exiled to the fictional Craggy Island, just off the west coast of Ireland. Most of the filming took place in County Clare.

MUSIC

NORTHERN IRELAND

Ash Hailing from Downpatrick, Britpoppers Ash exploded on to the pop scene in the mid 1990s with the singles 'Kung Fu' and 'Girl from Mars'.

Stiff Little Fingers Stiff Little Fingers met in Belfast in 1977, when the Troubles were at their peak. The band sought to highlight social and political issues through the lyrics of their catchy punk songs.

Them Formed when Van Morrison joined East Belfast group the Gamblers, Them made their name playing around the city. The garage-rock track 'Gloria' ranks among the greatest rock songs of all time.

Van Morrison Music legend Van Morrison grew up in Belfast, and later found fame in New York. He's best-known for the R&B-inflected singles 'Brown Eyed Girl', 'Jackie Wilson Said (I'm In Heaven When You Smile)' and 'Domino'.

REPUBLIC OF IRELAND

The Corrs Celtic folk rock group made up of three sisters and their brother who achieved international fame. They supported Celine Dion's international tour and topped charts worldwide with their album, *In Blue*.

The Dubliners Irish folk band named after James Joyce's collection of short stories. They have recorded versions of many traditional Irish songs, including 'The Irish Rover', which topped the domestic charts.

The Pogues 'Fairytale of New York' was a hit in both Ireland and the UK, and is often voted the best Christmas song ever. Named after a JP Donleavy novel, the song tells the tale of a drunk Irishman in a New York prison on Christmas Eve.

Saw Doctors *If This Is Rock And Roll, I Want My Old Job Back* The first release from the Irish rockers won them domestic stardom. It included the hits 'I Useta Lover' and 'N17', which refers to the connecting road between Galway and the band's home town, Tuam.

Thin Lizzy Notorious Irish rockers who recorded the classic tracks 'Jailbreak' and 'The Boys are Back In Town'.

U2 One of the biggest-selling bands of all time. U2's stadium-filling rock, on songs like 'With Or Without You' and 'Beautiful Day', seems to have universal appeal.

ART

NORTHERN IRELAND

Duncan Campbell Campbell's 2003 work, *Falls Burns Malone Fiddles*, is a series of photographs from the Troubles in Belfast. The artist looks past the conventional portrayals of violence and unrest to focus on the era's fashion and cultural movements.

Willie Doherty Twice nominated for the Turner Prize, Doherty has represented Northern Ireland at the Venice Biennale. Many of his works examine the Troubles (he witnessed the Bloody Sunday massacre as a child), using iconic images to depict what he considers to be a more honest version of events.

REPUBLIC OF IRELAND

Gerard Byrne Dublin resident Byrne works mainly with film, video and photography to reconstruct images from popular 1970s and '80s magazines. He represented Ireland at the 2007 Venice Biennale.

Jack Butler Yeats The Irish landscape – particularly that of Yeats's childhood home, County Sligo – people and customs feature heavily in Yeats's earlier work. His death prompted Beckett to write 'Yeats is the great of our time... he brings light as only the great dare to bring light to the issueless predicament of existence.'

Thematic Index

A-Z Index

Where to eat & drink

Where to stay

Advertisers' Index

Please refer to relevant pages for contact details